# Sir Cloudesley Shovell
## Stuart Admiral

In memory of my parents
M.H. 1914–1994
D.V.H. 1917–1990

# SIR CLOUDESLEY SHOVELL

## STUART ADMIRAL

by

Simon Harris

SPELLMOUNT
Staplehurst

British Library Cataloguing in Publication Data:
A catalogue record for this book is available
from the British Library

Copyright © Simon Harris 2001
Maps © Spellmount Limited 2001

ISBN 1–86227–099–6

First published in the UK in 2001 by
Spellmount Limited
The Old Rectory
Staplehurst
Kent TN12 0AZ

Tel: 01580 893730
Fax: 01580 893731
E–mail: enquiries@spellmount.com
Website: www.spellmount.com

1 3 5 7 9 8 6 4 2

The right of Simon Harris to be identified
as the author of this work has been asserted by him
in accordance with the Copyright, Designs
and Patents Act 1988

Typeset in Palatino by MATS, Southend-on-Sea, Essex
Printed in Great Britain by
TJ International Ltd, Padstow, Cornwall

# Contents

# List of Maps

# Glossary

| | |
|---|---|
| Admiralty | Department of state responsible for the military direction of the Navy. |
| Broach to | Force a ship into the wind. |
| Brigantine | A vessel with two masts and square sails. |
| Cathead | Timber projecting from a ship's bow to which the anchors are attached. |
| Dogger | A type of Dutch fishing vessel. |
| Fathom | A measure of the depth of water: one fathom equals six feet. |
| Flute | A type of small merchant ship. |
| Flyboat | Similar to a flute. |
| Foul | A ship whose bottom is overgrown with barnacles and weed, slowing its speed through the water. |
| Frigate | A small man-of-war whose armament normally consisted of cannons on a single deck. |
| Galley | A ship built for use in the Mediterranean, with sails and oars. |
| Heave to | Stop the movement of a ship by arranging the sails to counteract each other. |
| Hoy | A small coasting ship. |
| Ketch | A small two-masted English ship. |
| Larboard | The left hand side of a ship looking forward. |
| League | A measure of distance of about three miles. |
| Lee | The side away from the wind. |
| Luff | Keep a course closer to the wind. |
| Navy Office | The department responsible for manning, victualling and arming the fleet. |
| Pink | A small fishing vessel with a small mainsail and sometimes a foresail. |
| Privateer | An armed ship owned and officered by private persons holding a commission from the state. |
| Rate | The rate of pay of officers in the seventeenth century was based on the size of the ship. In Shovell's time, first rates had above 90 guns, second rates above 80 guns, third rates above 54 guns, fourth rates above 38 |

guns, fifth rates above 18 guns and sixth rates above six guns.

| | |
|---|---|
| Shrouds | Ropes extending from the mast to the side of the ship. |
| Skiff | A small rowing boat. |
| Starboard | The right hand side of a ship looking forward. |
| Strike | Lower a flag to signify surrender. |
| Tack | Temporary change of direction to take advantage of wind from the side. |
| Tartan | A small Mediterranean merchant vessel with a single mast. |
| Union flag | In Shovell's era the national flag combining St George's cross and St Andrew's saltire. |
| Weather gauge | On the same side as the direction of the wind. |
| Wear | Turn away from the wind. |
| Well boat | A flat bottomed boat used for landing troops on shore. |

Dates have been given principally according to the Julian calendar (old style) which was used in England until the mid-eighteenth century. Continental Europe used the Gregorian calendar (new style) which was ten days later up to 1700, and then eleven days later until 1752.

Years expressed as 1653/54 indicate that at that time the year changed in March, not in January. Consequently, dates in the first months of what we now refer to as 1654 were written 1653/54 at the time.

# Acknowledgements

During the quarter of a century I have spent researching and writing the biography of Cloudesley Shovell, a large number of individuals and institutions have given me encouragement and invaluable help.

I am grateful to the staffs of the National Maritime Museum, British Library, Public Record Office (Kew), Cambridge University Library, Bodleian Library, National Portrait Gallery, Churchill College (Cambridge), Pepysian Library (Magdalene College, Cambridge), Yale University Library, Huntington Library (San Marino), Kent Record Office, Norfolk Record Office, Guildhall Museum (Rochester) and the Castle Museum (Norwich).

With regard to the illustrations in the book, I am indebted to the National Maritime Museum, the Scottish National Portrait Gallery, Sotheby's, the incumbent of Langham (Norfolk), the Guildhall Museum (Rochester) and an anonymous descendant of Shovell, whose magnificent Michael Dahl has pride of place on the front of the jacket of the book. Peter Fox kindly provided the photograph of Shovell's entry in the Cockthorpe baptismal register. Mark French travelled to the West Country on a photographic assignment for me. Derek Stone drew the maps.

Angela Kent had the misfortune to type the first draft of the manuscript from my handwritten notes. She remains one of the few people who can read my handwriting. Debbie Bell courageously took on the second draft. The third and final draft was undertaken by Ken Hill, whose help has been invaluable. George Swann helped enormously with computerisation of the manuscript. My nephew Jack Harris undertook the translation of a number of inscriptions from the original Latin.

Nell Starley, a professional researcher, did a great deal in the investigation of Shovell's life, particularly in the Public Record Office. She found new material there concerning Shovell's career in the Mediterranean and delved into the fate of his famous emerald ring.

A number of other individuals I should particularly like to thank are John Berkeley, Geoffrey Bolt, Richard Carmichael, Elizabeth Cartwright-Hignett, Steve Ottery and the late Llewelyn Fawcett.

David Grant, the publisher's editor, has been of immense value in the preparation of this biography. His attention to detail is second to none.

Jamie Wilson of Spellmount has been a tower of strength in helping me publish my first and last book.

Finally, I would like to mention my wife, Clare, who has checked and corrected the manuscript. Both she and my children, Lucy and Charles, have had to suffer holidays in various parts of England and Europe following in Shovell's footsteps.

I am grateful to them all.

Simon Harris<br>
King's Lynn<br>
2001

# Introduction

In 1970 in Sydney, Australia, I was lying on a hotel bed during a heatwave when a letter from my mother was brought to me. Enclosed was a newspaper cutting describing a sale at Sotheby's. I had been a collector of pewter for some years, and my mother thought the report would interest me because it mentioned a pewter chamber pot retrieved from the 1707 wreck of the *Association*. That was my introduction to the name Cloudesley Shovell, and it triggered a fascination that has continued for over a quarter of a century.

In the mid-1970s I discovered that little was known about Cloudesley Shovell. In the nineteenth century, Robert Marsham Townshend, a Shovell descendant, had undertaken considerable research into the family aspects of Cloudesley's life, but had largely ignored his naval career. Since the 1960s various excellent publications have dealt with the disastrous last voyage and salvaging of sunken treasures. However, no in-depth biography has been undertaken.

Cloudesley Shovell was born of humble origins in Norfolk in 1650, soon after the execution of Charles I. He went to sea first under Christopher Myngs and then John Narbrough. He made an early impression by swimming between ships through enemy fire with his admiral's dispatches in his mouth. Shovell served in a minor capacity in the Second and Third Dutch Naval Wars, and sailed through the Strait of Magellan into the Pacific with Narbrough. He was to become a national hero in 1676 with his audacious burning of several ships in the harbour at Tripoli, right under the walls of the Dey's castle. For this service, Charles II awarded him a coveted gold medal and chain – of greater value than his lowly rank warranted. Further service followed in the Mediterranean, culminating in the infamous saluting of the King of Spain's standard, which led to calls for Shovell's court martial and execution. Fortunately he was able to justify his actions to a generous Charles II.

Shovell was to play a significant naval role in the Glorious Revolution of 1688. He was considered to be at prime risk of defecting to William of Orange's fleet under Arthur Herbert, but the elements prevented the two sides from meeting at sea. The following year Shovell was knighted for his gallant service at Bantry Bay, where the casualties on his ship were higher than on any other.

Soon afterwards he mortally offended his former sovereign, James II, by shooting up his footguards in the royal presence in Dublin Bay. The celebrated Samuel Pepys was another who disapproved of Shovell. This was partly because Pepys did not consider him to be a gentleman, and in addition, because Shovell, the plain man of principle, was not prepared to perjure himself by helping Pepys to pin the blame for abandoning Tangier on the resident naval officers. However, in the end the wily Pepys had his way.

In 1688 Shovell's great patron, John Narbrough, died while seeking sunken golden treasure off Hispaniola. Three years later Shovell married Narbrough's widow, Elizabeth, and became stepfather to his children – virtually the cabin boy marrying his late captain's wife.

As a junior admiral, under the irascible Edward Russell, Shovell had a starring role in the overwhelming defeat of the French off Cape Barfleur in 1692, but his injuries precluded him from leading the final burning and destruction of the French ships at St Vaaste La Hougue. This honour fell to Shovell's contemporary and rival, the taciturn and aristocratic George Rooke. Ex-King James watched the action from the shore, tactlessly crying out: "Who but my brave English tars could do such a thing?" in front of his French hosts.

Early in the eighteenth century, Shovell was responsible for transporting home highly valuable cargo from the successful attack on the treasure fleet at Vigo in northern Spain. Some of the silver captured in this episode was used to make coins which have the word Vigo impressed on them. This was followed by a share of the glory in the capture of Gibraltar, and command of the van at the subsequent naval battle off Malaga. Here Shovell carried out a difficult and much admired manoeuvre – getting his ships to sail backwards – to rescue the hard pressed and short of ammunition centre of the fleet under Rooke.

In 1705 Shovell was joint naval commander-in-chief with the unreliable Earl of Peterborough. The successful capitulation of Barcelona owed a great deal to the stubborn determination of Shovell to do his duty as he saw it.

Two years later Shovell was naval commander-in-chief in the unsuccessful attack on the premier French port of Toulon. This was not due to any naval failing, but rather to the irresolution of Shovell's ally, Prince Eugene of Savoy.

In October 1707, sailing home after an unusually extended summer campaign in the Mediterranean, Shovell and some 2,000 of his fellow mariners perished when several ships of his fleet ran on to the Western Rocks, off the Isles of Scilly. Legend has it that Shovell came ashore alive, and was murdered for the sake of the rings on his fingers. After initial burial in the sand of St Mary's, Shovell's corpse was dug up and laid to rest in Westminster Abbey, at Queen Anne's expense.

Today Shovell is largely forgotten. Yet he was almost as famous when he died as was that other Norfolk admiral, Horatio Nelson, at Trafalgar a century later.

The intention of this biography is to accord Cloudesley Shovell proper recognition as one of the greatest mariners in England's naval history.

# CHAPTER I
# *Origins, Birth and Early Life*
# *1650–1662*

A few miles to the east of Burnham Thorpe, the birthplace of Horatio Nelson, lies the small hamlet of Cockthorpe close to the north Norfolk coast. It was here in November 1650 that Cloudesley Shovell was born. He was to become Norfolk's second most famous native admiral.

Until the end of the nineteenth century there was doubt about Shovell's birthplace and origins. Research done at this time for Robert Marsham Townshend, a Shovell descendant, has produced sound information of his background, and laid to rest many a myth. (See Appendix 6)

The surname Shovell is most unusual and does not appear in Reitstap, the nineteenth century authority on heraldic arms. The Revd Charles Brereton, another Shovell descendant, thought that it was derived from that of Shuvaloff, the great Russian minister.[1] Another suggestion was that it was of French origin, Chauvel being a common name in Normandy. A Sir Roger de Schoville is mentioned in Blomefield's *County History of Norfolk*.[2] The most likely explanation is that Shovell is an anglicised form of a Dutch or Flemish name such as Schouvel. Indeed many natives of the low countries settled in Norfolk in the middle of the sixteenth century.[3] The earliest Shovell that Marsham Townshend could find in the Free Books of the Corporation of Norwich was one John Shovell, who was admitted as a citizen of Norwich on September 21st 1554. "Johes Shovell alien: indigena dyer apprentic: Willmi Morley jurat: et admifmis est civis die veneris in festo Sci Mathei appli anno primo et sedo Phi et Marie."[4] This John Shovell, who was Cloudesley's great-great-grandfather, was an apprentice dyer.

"Alien indigena" may mean that he was of foreign extraction but English birth, or simply that he was a foreigner settled in England.[5] In 1562–3 John Shovell was a servant to Mr Some in the Ward over the Water.[6] He was in trouble in 1568 during the mayoralty of Parker when the different traders complained about the strangers, especially the dyers. John Shovell, William Stedd and others had been summoned on May 16th 1567 for dyeing foreign goods. They agreed that "the dyers should have only one of their community to dye their commodities such as collars as they have dyed in Flanders."[7] By 1580 John Shovell had improved his

1

position, and from the Lay Subsidy Roll of that year he was of St Miles, Coslany, and was rated at 100s for goods. In the same year an Obarke Shovell, probably a relative of his, was rated at 4d. The name Obarke is foreign, adding further weight to the Shovell family's origins abroad.

Among the children of John Shovell the dyer was a son, also called John, who was to hold a number of positions in Norwich: Constable in 1568, 1571, 1589; Councillor in 1589–1606, 1608; Auditor 1596–1606; Surveyor 1597–8; Speaker 1604, and Sheriff 1606.[8] The younger John Shovell had a brother William who was a dornix weaver. Dornix was a coarse type of damask used for carpets and curtains, and was originally made in Tournai. This, too, may point to a Low Countries background. Another brother, Christopher, was also a dyer. At the end of the sixteenth and beginning of the seventeenth centuries, the parish records of the churches of Norwich show numerous entries for the baptisms, marriages and burials of the various Shovell families.[9]

On July 12th 1601 a Nathaniel Shovell, the son of Mr John Shovell, was baptised at St Saviour's, Norwich. Nathaniel appears to have spent his short life away from Norwich in north Norfolk. At Binham, near Wells-next-the-Sea, the register gives the burial of "Nathaniel Shovell gent" on April 18th 1636. In his will he bequeathed lands at Morston, which he had owned since 1623, to his son, also Nathaniel, and failing him to his son John. It seems likely that the Nathaniel Shovell who was baptised at St Saviour's, Norwich in 1601 was the son of John Shovell the former Sheriff of Norwich. Nathaniel the elder appears to have been a farmer, and was almost certainly the grandfather of Cloudesley Shovell. [10]

Marsham Townshend in the nineteenth century, and the author more recently, have failed to find any trace of Nathaniel Shovell the younger. However it seems likely that Nathaniel Shovell the elder's land at Morston passed to his other son, John, who had been baptised on June 26th 1625 in the same village. This John Shovell came to live at Cockthorpe, a small village close to both Binham and Morston, and was Cloudesley Shovell's father.[11] In summary, the Shovell family originated in the Low Countries with a Dutch or Flemish background before coming to England, probably as refugees, in the mid-sixteenth century. Initially, Cloudesley Shovell's antecedents were dyers and weavers in Norwich, before settling down to farm in north Norfolk.

The maternal side of Cloudesley Shovell's family also came from the coastal region of north Norfolk. His mother was Anne Jenkenson, the daughter of Henry Jenkenson of Cley-next-the-Sea by his wife, Lucy, daughter of Thomas Cloudesley also of Cley. Anne was baptised at Cley on July 14th 1628. Her brother, another Cloudesley, was baptised there on August 16th 1630. The Cloudesley family or one of the variants of its spelling, Clowdesly, Clowdesley or Cloudsly, first appear in the register of Little Walsingham in 1562. By 1620 Thomas Cloudesley, gentleman,

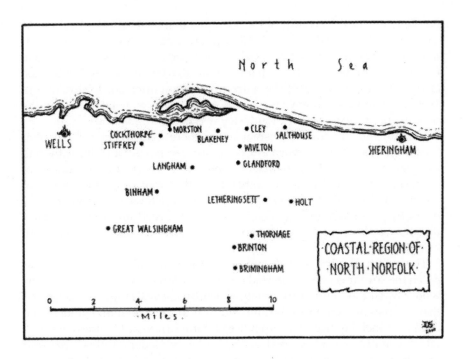

owned land at Cley. The Jenkensons were a family with armorial bearings, and came from Tunstal and Oulton in Suffolk. By 1627 Henry Jenkenson owned land at Glandford which is not far from Cley.[12]

The date and place of the marriage of Cloudesley Shovell's parents, John Shovell and Anne Jenkenson, are unknown, despite a detailed search of the parish registers in north Norfolk. Either the marriage took place outside the area or, more likely during the chaos of the Civil War, records were not properly kept. The date must have been about 1645. John and Anne Shovell had several children, of whom Cloudesley was the second or third, and the only survivor to adulthood. Crockatt* states that Cloudesley was the second son of the family that was a numerous one, but in John Shovell's will of 1654 his sons, Nathaniel and John, are mentioned before Cloudesley, indicating that he was the third son. There are no baptismal records for either Nathaniel or John, and Cloudesley's entry is odd. In the Cockthorpe register the baptism of Cloudesley Shovell is shown for November 25th 1650, indicating that he was born a few days earlier. The entry has been interpolated between two others in the register "Cloudesley Shovell batizatus vicesimo quinto Novembris 1650". The

---

* Gilbert Crockatt was Cloudesley Shovell's parish priest at Crayford.

handwriting and the colour of the ink show that the entry is an early one. Crockatt, while speaking of Sir Cloudesley's ancestors, mentions "their faithful adherence to King Charles the First", and it is possible that Cloudesley may have been baptised at that date by some Royalist clergyman in private, and the entry made soon after the Restoration in 1660. An alternative theory is that the entry was interpolated later in the seventeenth century when Cloudesley was becoming famous.[13]

Despite the unusual baptismal entry there can be little doubt that Cloudesley Shovell was born at Cockthorpe, in north Norfolk. Although Crockatt has left a little detail of Cloudesley's early life, he does not mention a specific birthplace other than that it was in the county of Norfolk. In *The Secret Memoirs of Cloudesley Shovell*, written soon after his death by an anonymous gentleman who had served under him, it states that he was born in a small town near Cley, which is compatible with Cockthorpe. [14]

The origin of Cloudesley's unusual Christian name is clear. He was given the surname of his maternal great-grandfather, Thomas Cloudesley, who was still alive in 1650, living in nearby Cley. Campbell* suggested that the parents hoped to recommend him to their relation's notice – no doubt, financial notice – by the choice of name! Thomas Cloudesley's will, which was proved in 1657, makes no mention of a legacy for his 7-year-old grandson. In all probability the choice was made to perpetuate the name Cloudesley. Anne Shovell's brother was Cloudesley Jenkenson, and Shovell was to become a common Christian name amongst the descendants of Cloudesley Shovell.[15]

Both during his lifetime and since, other places remote from north Norfolk have claimed to be the scene of Cloudesley Shovell's birth. In 1697 the diarist Abraham de la Pryne recorded that he was a poor lad born in Yorkshire, who was first an ostler at an inn at Retford in Nottinghamshire, before moving to Stockwith in Lincolnshire and becoming a sailor. There is not an iota of evidence for this.[16]

Linkinhorne in Cornwall had a Shovell family at least until late in the nineteenth century who claimed to be kinsmen of Cloudesley Shovell. In a history of the parish of Linkinhorne, written in 1727, it states that . . .

> the family of Shovell have inhabited in this parish for many generations; and they lay claim to be the only one known who bear the name. A respectable person of this family assured the writer that so far from having any doubt as to Cloudesley Shovell being a kinsman of theirs that he remembered that his ancestors were only deterred from making application for his estate by the necessary attendant expenses.

* Doctor John Campbell. See Bibliography.

This was being written at a time when Cloudesley Shovell's wife and two daughters were still alive![17]

In the parish of Linkinhorne is the Manor of Carneadon-lier that once belonged to Sir Jonathan Trelawney's family. One of Trelawney's sons was to drown with Cloudesley Shovell on the *Association* in 1707. This is likely to be a coincidence as the probable connection between the drowned Trelawney son and Shovell was through his stepsons, John and James Narbrough. The Trelawneys and the young Narbroughs were Christ Church, Oxford men.[18]

No Cloudesley Shovell appears in the parish records of Linkinhorne, but various other Shovells are recorded. The earliest is an entry for May 18th 1653 for the burial of Edward, son of William and Grace Shovell. This shows that there were Shovells in Cornwall prior to Cloudesley's birth. It is not possible to demonstrate any direct connection between the Norfolk and Linkinhorne Shovells. Possibly there was "cousinship" with an early move of a Shovell family from Norfolk in the sixteenth century. As late as 1893 Marsham Townshend received a letter from a Samuel Shovell of Linkinhorne claiming that Cloudesley was unmarried, and that there was money in chancery that he would like to claim. He was wrong on both counts![19]

Hastings on the coast of Sussex has also claimed to be the birthplace of Cloudesley Shovell. Part of a poem states that

> And 'tis Hastings – not to grovel –
> That proclaims Sir Cloudesley Shovell,
> One of many valiants who at Hastings had their birth.

In 1736 William Russell, who had been the master of a coastal vessel, was buried at All Saints Church, Hastings. Russell at an advanced age used to point out a house in All Saints Street as the one in which Cloudesley Shovell was born. According to Russell he and Cloudesley played together as boys. There is a house in All Saints Street, actually part of two medieval houses, where by tradition Cloudesley Shovell's mother or nanny lived. The house can still be seen to this day.[20]

During Shovell's lifetime, in 1697, Abraham de la Pryne recorded in his diary:

> I heard a gentleman say that was in the ship with him about six years ago that as they were sailing over against Hastings in Sussex says Sir Cloudesley Pilot put neer, I have a little business a shore here: so we put neer and him and this gentleman went a land in the boat and having walked about half a mile a shore Sir Cloudesley came to a little house. Come says he to the gentleman my business is here, I came on purpose to see the good woman of this house. Upon which they

knocked at the door and out came a poor old woman, upon Sir Cloudesley kist her and then fell down on his knees begged her blessing and called her mother (shee being his mother that had moved out of Yorkshire thither). He was mighty kind to her and shee to him and after that he had payed his visit he left her 10 guineas and departed to his ship.[21]

There is no Cloudesley Shovell recorded in either of the baptismal registers of the two Hastings parishes for the relevant period. The register of All Saints Church is imperfect for the time of his birth – there is only one entry for the period 1648–53. But this was a period of anarchy and confusion, with the Civil War and its aftermath. The name Cloudesley or Clowdesley does appear in the corporation records. In 1597 the Town Gunner, Robert Cloudesley, was buried. In the Chamberlain's accounts passed in 1657 "a watering place at Shovell field" is mentioned. However, there is no account at all of Cloudesley Shovell in the Hastings Corporation records, although the first guide book by Stell in 1794 speaks in terms of a connection.[22]

Clearly Cloudesley Shovell was not born or brought up in Hastings. The tradition of a connection with the place goes back as far as his lifetime. Possibly there was a family friend or relative living in Hastings. It is unlikely that Shovell's mother, Anne, lived there as she appeared to be firmly domiciled in north Norfolk. The Shovell family was not wealthy enough to have had a nanny.

Cloudesley Shovell's birthplace at Cockthorpe today consists of its church, St Andrews and All Saints, and a few houses scattered over an elevated plateau of land. In the seventeenth century it was a fairly flourishing place, with a record dating back to before the Norman Conquest. Cockthorpe formed part of the church lands of the See of Thetford, and in the fourteenth century its rector and "lord" was Roger Bacon, who belonged to the same family as Nicholas and Francis Bacon. From the Bacons the land passed to the family of Calthorpe, who were the owners at the time of Cloudesley Shovell's birth.[23] Cloudesley's parents, John and Anne Shovell, were in middling circumstances, renting a farm at Cockthorpe from the Calthorpes, and had land of their own at Morston. Crockatt states that the family was not inconsiderable for estate, although it had been lessened by their adherence to King Charles I. Exactly where the Shovells lived in Cockthorpe is not certain, although by tradition of a branch of the Brereton family, who were descendants, it was in the Manor House.[24]

Mrs Herbert Jones, in the nineteenth century, recorded first-hand evidence of Cockthorpe being the residence of Cloudesley's parents, and scene of his early childhood.

A gentleman born in 1688 [William Brereton] who married Sir Cloudesley Shovell's niece [Anne Shorting], and who, as a boy was well acquainted with him gave many particulars to his grandson [John Brereton] who communicated them in turn to his son [Shovell Brereton], now living in Norfolk. These relations of Sir Cloudesley Shovell lived at Brinton, a few miles from the house, an object of frequent interest, which the Shovells occupied. The grandson of Sir Cloudesley Shovell's nephew would, as his son still narrates, take him to Cockthorpe and point out the spots in the village associated with their distinguished ancestor. [See Appendix 7]

So far from being in the lowest circumstances and apprenticed through-out childhood to a shoemaker, as is usually asserted, the future admiral was the son of middle class parents, who rented a farm of the Calthorpes, and occupied the Manor House, and no shoe maker ever existed in the rural hamlet to give Sir Cloudesley Shovell so unnecessary accomplishment.[25]

Mrs Jones also records that:

Mr Shovell (John) lived in a castellated stone house, originally fortified as a defence against the incursion of the smugglers, who, in sweeping the coast, undeterred by the chain of stations which now protects it, would occasionally take forcible shelter on shore. A room in this house, entered by a doorway arched over with stone, is shown, which is still called by the villagers, Sir Cloudesley's drawing room.[26]

Information passed down through families is not always accurate, but there is a ring of truth about the Brereton tradition of Cloudesley Shovell's early home. Cockthorpe Hall has also been associated with him.[27]

When Cloudesley Shovell was a little over 3 years old, his father, John, died. There is no record of the date of death or his burial place. John Shovell signed a death bed will on March 22nd 1654 which was proved at Westminster on June 12th 1654. "John Shovell of Cockthorpe in the County of Norfolk Gent being sick of the sickness where of he dyed but perfect in mind and memory." He left his estate to his wife, Anne.

I give and bequeath unto Anne my wife, all and singular my reall and personall estate whatsoever Upon Condition that shee shall pay or give unto Nathaniel, John and Clowdsley my three sonnes one hundred pounds a peece to bee paid to them at there severall ages of one and twentie yeares. And upon this condition I make her (meaninge his said wife Anne) my Executrix.

The next few years must have been difficult ones for Anne Shovell with three young sons to bring up and no man to support her. No doubt the Cloudesley and Jenkenson families helped.[28]

Presumably Anne Shovell and her children stayed at Cockthorpe for a time, but the next known fact about her is remarriage to John Flaxman of Walcott, at Gimingham on February 8th 1658/59. By this time Cloudesley was 8 years old, and his brothers, Nathaniel and John, a little older. Walcott and Gimingham are respectively twenty-three and eighteen miles as the crow flies to the east of Cockthorpe. How and where Anne Shovell met John Flaxman is not known, but a Richard Fflaxman was living in Cley-next-the-Sea in 1661 and perhaps was a relative. It seems likely that after the marriage she took her young sons to live with her new husband at Walcott. Certainly the Walcott register records the burial of young John Shovell on February 2nd 1663/64, and his brother Nathaniel on the following February 10th. By this time Cloudesley was away at sea.[29]

The new Anne Flaxman was to have several children by her husband, John. One of them, another Anne, was baptised at Holt on January 22nd 1671/72, and married to Thomas Shorting at Morston on September 28th 1691, by whom she had eleven children. One of those eleven, yet another Anne, married William Brereton, through whose family descended the tradition of the Shovell residence at Cockthorpe. Anne and John Flaxman appear to have moved back to the region of the north Norfolk coast at some time prior to 1672, when Anne Shorting, née Flaxman was baptised at Holt.[30] In later life Cloudesley Shovell remained close to his mother, his half-sister, her husband and to their children. As will be seen later in this account, he was supportive of his brother-in-law, Thomas Shorting, in the 1690s. In his will, Cloudesley Shovell left to his mother and half-sister his lands at Morston, which he must have inherited or bought. On July 29th 1703 Shovell in his account book recorded: "To Josph Jacobs for a Calash for my Mother Fflaxman fourteen pound." A calash was a low-hooded carriage. In the same book Lady Elizabeth Shovell has written some time after Cloudesley's death, on March 1st 1708/09, "To Several Legacy's pd in Norfolke, to Mother Flaxman, Br° Shorting making together as per little book 640l." Anne Flaxman was buried at Morston on June 17th 1709, eighteen months after the death of her by now famous son, Cloudesley.

We have seen that Cloudesley Shovell's early childhood was spent in Cockthorpe until early in 1659, when the young Shovells moved with their mother on her remarriage to John Flaxman, farther around the coast to Gimingham or Walcott. There is no documentary evidence that Cloudesley set foot in either Gimingham or Walcott, but it seems likely. What education did the young Cloudesley have? In *The Secret Memoirs* it is recorded that his parents brought him up as best they could, with the implication that they were not in good circumstances. Gilbert Crockatt recorded that "his parents having carefully trained him up to such

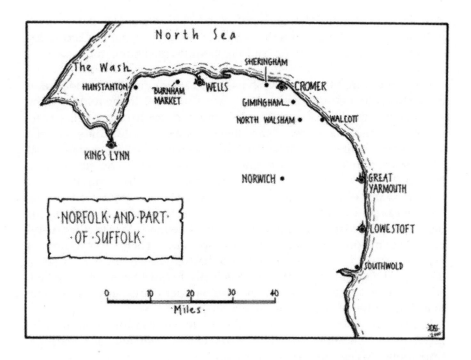

learning as their country schools afforded". Crockatt was Rector of St Paulinus Church, Crayford, between 1688 and 1708. This was Cloudesley Shovell's local church during much of his married life, and Crockatt must have got to know him well.[31]

Knowledge of education in Norfolk prior to the restoration of Charles II in 1660 is scanty. From 1581 it was a legal requirement for teachers to subscribe, which led to a record of their domiciles being kept. Although failure to subscribe should have resulted in fines and prohibition to teach, the law does not seem to have been enforced.

Matters were further complicated by the fact that much educational work in the middle of the seventeenth century was undertaken by women who did not have to subscribe, so that they were not recorded. Close to the Shovell home at Cockthorpe in 1662 were schools at Wells, Walsingham and Holt. At Cley-next-the-Sea the first teacher's subscription was not until 1717. If it is accepted that Cloudesley Shovell spent time after his mother's remarriage in the Gimingham and Walcott area, there were a number of schools in the vicinity that he might have attended. Happisburgh, Bacton, Knapton and Walcott itself all had schools in the late seventeenth century. In addition, schools were declared in South Repps and North Walsham in 1662. It is intriguing to think that Cloudesley Shovell might have attended a school in the same town, North

9

Walsham, as Horatio Nelson. Further research at this late date is very unlikely to determine exactly which school the young Cloudesley attended. In all probability he could read and write before going away to sea.[32]

It is a myth that Cloudesley Shovell was apprenticed to a shoemaker before tiring of this trade and going to sea. Campbell, in the middle of the eighteenth century, not many years after the death of Shovell's wife, Elizabeth, stated that he was "apprentice to a mean trade I think that of a shoemaker". A few years later, in 1763, *Biographia Britannica* stated that Cloudesley Shovell was "apprentice to a shoemaker or some other mechanic trade". So a legend was created: shoemaker to admiral!

In William Winks' nineteenth century book *Illustrious Shoemakers*, Shovell has pride of place with a portrait on the front page. It goes on, "his parents were glad to send him to the village shoemaker to learn the art and mystery of making and mending boots and shoes". There is not a shred of evidence that Cloudesley Shovell ever had anything to do with shoe-making. The originator of the myth is likely to have been Dr Campbell, who perhaps confused the matter with Samuel Pepys' erroneous view that Christopher Myngs' father was a shoemaker.[33]

Before leaving Cloudesley Shovell's childhood, consideration must be given to the tradition that he was related to both his early patrons, Christopher Myngs and John Narbrough.

Originally Myngs was thought to be of very humble origin, with, according to Samuel Pepys, a shoemaker for a father and a hoyman's daughter for a mother. According to Sir John Laughton this is exaggerated or false. His parents were of well-to-do families from the north of Norfolk. His father, John Myngs, though described in the register of Salthouse, where he was married on September 28th 1623, as "of the parish of St Katherine in the city of London", seems to have been a near kinsman, if not a son, of Nicholas Mynnes, the representative of a good old Norfolk family. His mother, Katherine Parr (baptised at Kelling on June 16th 1605) was the daughter of Christopher Parr, the owner of a property in the neighbourhood. Their son, Christopher, was baptised at Salthouse (close to Cockthorpe) on November 22nd 1625. Myngs, Mynge, Mine, Minn, Mynne is a foreign sounding name with a possible origin like that of Shovell in the Low Countries. Nicholas Mins or Myngs is supposed to have come to England from the dominions of the King of Spain in 1562.[34]

John Narbrough came from the same village as Cloudesley Shovell, Cockthorpe, being baptised there ten years earlier on October 14th 1640. He was the fifth child of Gregorie Narborough (John always spelt his name Narbrough) who was possibly a tenant, like John Shovell, of a Calthorpe farm in Cockthorpe. Compared with the Shovell and Myngs families, who are first recorded in England in the sixteenth century, the Narbroughs are older, beginning in approximately 1216–72.

Crockatt in his *Consolatory Letter to Lady Shovell* records that Sir Christopher Myngs was related to the Shovell family. Dyer, in her life of John Narbrough, states that he was by tradition a relation of Christopher Myngs. If these two statements are correct then there is a relationship, perhaps only by marriage, between Christopher Myngs, John Narbrough and Cloudesley Shovell.[35]

The author has commissioned research to try and demonstrate this proposed relationship. In Norwich in the sixteenth century Myngses, Narbroughs and Shovells are all represented. Henry Mynne was Town Clerk from 1553 to 1559. Robert Narbrough was a constable from 1568 to 1580. John Shovell was also a constable in 1568, and held other official posts in Norwich, as has been recorded earlier. During 1666 in Wiveton, which is close to Cockthorpe, Cloudesley Jenkenson, maternal uncle of Cloudesley Shovell, was living in the same village as a Joanne Narbrow, widow.

Despite an extensive review of the International Genealogical Index and elsewhere no definitive relationship between the three admirals has been demonstrated. It seems likely that they were related, particularly the Myngs and Shovell families, in view of Crockatt's record.

NOTES

1. Robert Marsham Townshend MSS, MAT 6.
2. Jones, Historic Memorials of the Norfolk Coast, p.333.
3. RMT MAT 25.
4. Free Books, Corporation of Norwich, Vol.II, p.64.
5. Notes and Queries January 19th 1895.
6. Rye, p.798.
7. The Descendants of the Strangers now residing at Norwich.
8. Norwich City Officer 1453–1835.
9. I.G.I. Norfolk.
10. Notes and Queries, January 19th 1895; Rye, p.798; I.G.I. Norfolk; Lay Subsidy Rolls for Norfolk, Hundred of Holt, Roll 153/579, Roll 153/605.
11. Notes and Queries, January 19th 1895; Rye, p.798.
12. Notes and Queries, January 19th 1895; Lay Subsidy Rolls for Norfolk, Roll 153/605, Roll153/613.
13. Notes and Queries, January 19th 1895; Crockatt, Consolatory Letter.
14. Crockatt, Consolatory Letter; Secret Memoirs.
15. Campbell, p.230; Admin Act Book at Somerset House of 1657 p.132.
16. RMT MAT 24.
17. RMT MAT 5; History of Parish of Linkinhorne 1727.
18. RMT MAT 5.
19. RMT MAT 5; letter to RMT August 15th 1893.
20. Brett, St. Leonards & Hastings Gazette, May 6th and 13th 1893.
21. RMT MAT 29c; Diary Abraham de la Pryne; The Hastings and St. Leonards Pictorial Advertiser and Visitors List, January 1st 1914.

22. Cousins, Hastings of Bygone Days and the Present; Stell, Guide Book of Hastings; Brett, St Leonards & Hastings Gazette, May 6th & 13th 1893; RMT MAT 29c.
23. Blomefield's County History of Norfolk, II, p.218; Dyer, p.135.
24. Crockatt, Consolatory Letter; Jones, Historic Memorials of the Norfolk Coast, p.333.
25. Jones, Historic Memorials of the Norfolk Coast pp.332–333.
26. Jones, Historic Memorials of the Norfolk Coast p.333.
27. Eastern Daily Press, October 17th 1986.
28. Notes & Queries, Jan. 19th 1895; RMT MAT 24; Principal Probate Registry, book Alcin, p.260.
29. I.G.I. Gimingham; Notes and Queries Jan. 19th 1895; Lay Subsidy Rolls for Norfolk, Roll 154/665.
30. Notes & Queries, Jan. 19th 1895.
31. Secret Memoirs; Crockatt, Consolatory Letter.
32. Carter, The Norwich Subscription Books 1637–1680.
33. Campbell, p.238; Charnock, p.16; RMT MAT 26; Winks, Illustrious Shoemakers, p.5.
34. D.N.B. Myngs; Rye, Norfolk Families.
35. Crockatt, Consolatory Letter; Dyer, p.8.

CHAPTER II
# The Early Years at Sea
# 1662–1666

Soon after the Restoration of Charles II in 1660, young Cloudesley Shovell first went to sea. There is still doubt concerning the date and ship. In Crockatt's *Consolatory Letter to Lady Shovell*, he wrote:

> when he was about thirteen years of age Sir Christopher Myngs being then an Admiral and most famous in his time coming to visit this family to which he was then related, desired to have the education of one of their sons under him in the Royal Navy, and as he was an excellent judge of persons soon observed some things extraordinary hopeful and promising in the young Cloudesley who readily and cheerfully agreed to go under him as a gentleman volunteer in the fleet, . . .[1]

In another account, written by a contemporary of Shovell's soon after his death, it is stated that friends of the young Cloudesley persuaded John Narbrough to take him on. Myngs was only mentioned in the context of Narbrough having served him as his cabin boy. There is no mention of Shovell's age on first going to sea.[2]

Shovell's grandson, Robert Marsham, 2nd Baron Romney (1712–93) in a draft letter to a Captain Locker recollected that Cloudesley Shovell had been recommended to John Narbrough very young (it is imagined about 9 years of age) who made him one of his boys.[3]

Richard Larn, in a recent account, believes that Shovell first went to sea in the *Portland* in 1664 under Myngs, perhaps following the death of Shovell's two brothers in a very short space of time in February of that year. Anne Flaxman (Shovell) had possibly agreed to let her last surviving son, Cloudesley, go to sea with Myngs for the sake of his health.[4] Larn's theory is an attractive one but is unfortunately contradicted by Shovell's own account. In a letter written by Shovell to Daniel Finch, 1st Earl of Nottingham, on August 12th 1692, Shovell stated that: "In 1663 I was in the West Indies with Sir Christopher Mings."[5] Clearly from this evidence Shovell had gone to sea in 1663 or possibly earlier. Perhaps Shovell's life was saved by being away from home in February 1664, as the fact that his brothers died within eight days of each other may indicate an infectious disease such as the plague or smallpox.

Myngs was in England on November 4th 1659, when he was one of five captains who signed a pro army and anti royalist letter to George Monck.[6] Sir John Laughton in the *Dictionary of National Biography* section on Myngs has written that he was probably in the West Indies at the time of the Restoration. In 1662 Myngs was appointed to the *Centurion* which was anchored at Jamaica in 1663.[7] Under Narbrough in the *Dictionary of National Biography*, Laughton mentioned that his early career was closely associated with Myngs. Also that Narbrough had been in the West Indies, presumably with Myngs.

If the evidence of Shovell's grandson, Robert Marsham, is correct, it is possible that he could have gone to sea with Myngs/Narbrough at about 9 years of age in 1659 or 1660.[8] It is known with certainty that the young Cloudesley Shovell was in the West Indies with Myngs in 1663.[9] Myngs was in the *Centurion* in 1662 for his assault on St Iago and in her at Jamaica the following year. It is unclear whether Myngs remained in the West Indies throughout 1662–63 or not. If he did then Shovell must have sailed with him in 1662 which would have been his 12th year. However, if Myngs returned to England at the end of 1662, and Shovell first joined him for the return voyage in 1663 he would have been in his 13th year. An age of 11 or 12 on first going to sea would fit in better with Crockatt's "about thirteen years".[10] In all probability during this period Myngs was the captain, Narbrough a lieutenant, and Shovell an officer's servant. Probably the *Centurion* was the first ship young Cloudesley Shovell sailed in.

Shovell first went to sea between the ages of 9 and 12. Many years later, in January 1706, he was summoned to the House of Commons to discuss a new Act on the Manning of the Fleet. Shovell proposed that the age of

13

boys being taken on in the fleet be altered from 10 to 12 years.[11] Perhaps he was thinking of his own early career.

At the time of Shovell's joining the navy there were two routes for becoming an officer, firstly by entry as a captain's or other officer's servant, often at 9 or 10 years, and rising through petty and warrant posts; secondly from 1661 as a volunteer 'per order' by authority of a royal letter to the captain and serving with a midshipman's pay.[12] Shovell used the former route. Most likely the officer concerned was Myngs, to whom Shovell was related, or possibly Narbrough.

The *Centurion* was a 34–50 gun ship of 531 tons in size and 104 feet in length. She had been built in 1650 at Ratcliffe and was to be wrecked in 1689.[13]

Interestingly both Shovell and an even more famous Norfolk admiral, Horatio Nelson, began their naval careers with a voyage to the West Indies.

Possibly young Shovell was with Myngs in October 1662 for the attack mounted from Jamaica on St Iago in Cuba. Myngs has left his own account of the action.

According to your Excellency's commands of the 21st of 5 bre (7 ber) we set sail from Point Cagaway (Jamaica) on the 22nd, but it was the 5th of October before we got sight of the Castle of St Iago upon Cuba. We decided to land under a platform two miles to windward of the harbour, the only place possible to land and march upon the town on all that rocky coast. We found no resistance, the enemy expecting us at the fort, and the people flying before us. Before we were all landed it was night. We were forced to advance into a wood, and the way was so narrow and difficult and the night so dark that our guides had to go with branches in their hands to beat a path. By daybreak we reached a plantation by a river's side, some six miles from our landing and three miles from the town, where being refreshed with water, daylight and a better way, we very cheerfully advanced for the town surprizing the enemy, who hearing of our late landing, did not expect us so soon. At the entrance of the town the Govenor, Don Pedro de Moralis, with two hundred men and two pieces of ordnance, stood to receive us, Don Christopher, the old Govenor of Jamaica (and a good friend to the English), with five hundred more, being his reserve. We soon beat them from their station, and with the help of Don Christopher, who fairly ran away, we routed the rest. Having mastered the town we took possession of the vessels in the harbour, and next day I dispatched parties in pursuit of the enemy and sent orders to the fleet to attack the harbour, which was successfully done, the enemy deserting the great castle after firing but two muskets. From 9th to the 14th we spent our time in pursuing the enemy, which proved not very advantageous, their riches being drawn off so far we could not reach it. The ill offices that town had done to Jamaica had so exasperated the soldiers that I had much ado to keep them from firing the churches. From the 15th to the 19th we employed ourselves in demolishing the forts. We found great stores of powder, 700 barrels of which we spent in blowing up the castle and the rest in country houses and platforms. The castle mostly lies level with the ground. It was built upon a rocky precipice, the walls on a mountainside some sixty feet high, there was in it a chapel and houses sufficient for a thousand men. We are now in safety in the harbour on our return to Cagaway.[14]

Myngs had mounted an extremely successful assault on St Iago, followed by an orgy of destruction.

In the course of the St Iago expedition Myngs took a number of Spanish ships which were considered to be good prizes by the Admiralty Court at Jamaica.[15] Probably it was the captain of one of these ships, a Spanish grandee with a long string of titles, who was so distressed to find that he had been taken by plain Kit Myngs![16]

In October 1662 Myngs was sworn in as a Member of the Council of Jamaica following his success at St Iago. Perhaps this alters the balance of probability that he remained in Jamaica a little while, as it would have been pointless to make him a Member of the Council if he was about to sail for England.[17] The voyage to England would have taken about two months.

What is certain is that both Myngs and Shovell were in the West Indies in 1663. In the letter from Shovell to Daniel Finch, written in August 1692, the presence of both Shovell and Myngs is made clear.

In 1663 I was in the West Indies with Sir Christopher Mings. We had from a thousand to two thousand bockeners and, about 200 seamen, the latter in the King's pay. When we resolved to attack any place the men that ware to land were obleaged to consert with the men that stayed a bord, sumtimes fower sumtimes more in a consert ship, and justly used to divid what they gott. But these bockeners use to find their arms, aminition and provission for the voyage, their was no publick shares, but every part keept what they gott. For a party of twenty men tooke near a brook some distance from the town twenty one chists of dollars. Their was 1,500 dollars in a chist. The odd chist they gave to Sir Christopher Mings who then was their commander both at sea and land. I can not remember any more of this affaire at present.[18]

This letter was in reply to one of August 10th from Nottingham asking

Shovell's advice on how plunder had been divided in the West Indies in former times.[19]

When Myngs returned to England in 1664 he was given command of the *Gloucester*, a 3rd rate. A few months later Myngs moved briefly to the smaller *Portland*, a 4th rate, before going to the *Royal Oak*, a 2nd rate. On the *Royal Oak*, Myngs raised his flag as Vice Admiral of the Channel Squadron under Prince Rupert. Narbrough was with Myngs as his Lieutenant in the *Portland* and the *Royal Oak*.[20] Although there is no conclusive proof of Shovell's movements at this time, it seems most likely that he was with Myngs certainly in the *Portland* and the *Royal Oak* and possibly also the *Gloucester*.

The year 1665 saw the opening of the Second Dutch War. Tension between England and Holland had been building up for some time, but the final straw was Sir Thomas Allin's attack on the Dutch Smyrna fleet off Cadiz. The Dutch declared war on January 14th and the English on February 23rd. France, the ally of the Dutch, did not actively help until 1666. Efforts were made in both England and Holland to fit fleets out. The English were ready first in April and sailed to the Texel under the command of the Duke of York, where they hoped to intercept the Dutch Admiral Michiel De Ruijter returning from counter reprisals on the west coast of Africa. It was an abortive mission and the fleet returned to Harwich. Meanwhile the Dutch fleet under Jacob van Wassenaer, Lord of Obdam, sallied forth in May and took a number of English merchantmen returning from Hamburg under the protection of a single man of war. They were carrying naval stores such as pitch, hemp, planks and copper. It was a disastrous loss both for the merchants and the government. The English fleet was hurried away and anchored at Southwold Bay on June 1st. Obdam was under instructions from his government to find the English fleet and engage it. Soon after the arrival of the Duke of York's fleet at Southwold, it was reported to him that the Dutch were in the vicinity. He weighed anchor and at 2.30 a.m. on June 3rd 1665 the two fleets, each of about 100 ships, came into contact fourteen miles N.N.E. of Lowestoft. The first major battle of the Second Dutch War was about to begin.[21]

Christopher Myngs, with John Narbrough as lieutenant, was in the 2nd rate *Triumph* for the Battle of Lowestoft. Almost certainly Cloudesley Shovell was with them as captain's servant or gentleman volunteer, although there is no conclusive documentary evidence. Myngs was Vice Admiral of the White, and was part of the English van under Prince Rupert.[22]

The English had the weather gauge with Prince Rupert leading the van, the Duke of York in the centre, and the Earl of Sandwich in the rear. At 3.30 a.m. on June 3rd the two fleets approached one another in line ahead and passed each other on opposite tacks. The Dutch altered course in succession, their van remaining their van, their centre remaining their

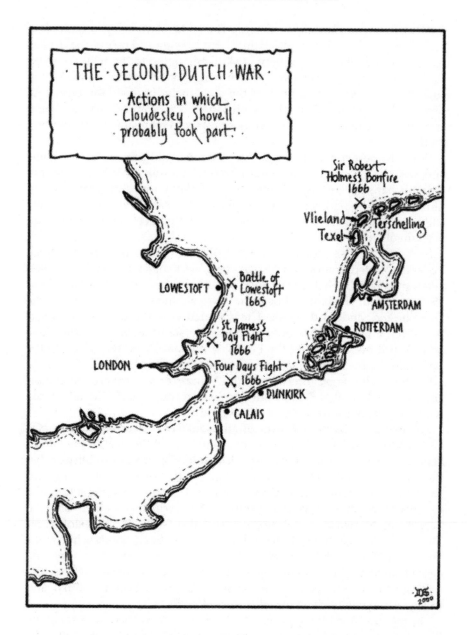

·THE·SECOND·DUTCH·WAR·

· Actions in which ·
· Cloudesley Shovell ·
· probably took part. ·

Sir Robert
Holmes's Bonfire
1666

Vlieland
Texel
Terschelling

LOWESTOFT    Battle of
Lowestoft
1665

St. James's
Day Fight
1666

LONDON    Four Days Fight
1666

DUNKIRK

CALAIS

AMSTERDAM

ROTTERDAM

centre, and their rear remaining their rear. However, the English altered course simultaneously so that when the two fleets passed again their rear became their van. About 1.00 p.m. Sandwich's squadron found itself mixed up with the Dutch centre and a general mêlée ensued. During this Obdam, the Dutch Commander-in-Chief, on the *Eendracht*, hotly engaged the Duke of York in the *Royal Charles*. The Duke of York saw a number of his courtiers killed by a single chain shot at his side and he may have been wounded in the hand by a piece of skull belonging to the fatally injured son of the Earl of Burlington. At the height of the battle the *Eendracht* suddenly blew up killing most of the crew including Obdam. His death increased the Dutch confusion with Jan Evertsen and Cornelis Tromp assuming command of the separate groups of Dutch ships surrounding them.[23]

Prince Rupert and Myngs in the van led the initial pass of the Dutch line and were involved in the general mêlée which followed. Rupert fought with his habitual courage despite the fact that he was still weak from an illness which he had contracted earlier in the year.[24] For young Shovell, still only 14 years old, it would have been the first fleet action that he had been involved in.

By 7.00 p.m. the Dutch were in full flight for their own coast. Dutch losses amounted to about thirty-two ships, 4,000 men killed and 2,000 men taken prisoner. English losses were slight with two ships lost and about 250 men killed. The Battle of Lowestoft was an unequivocal victory for the Duke of York and the English. The destruction of the Dutch fleet might have been more complete but for a misunderstanding between the Duke of York and his Captain of the Fleet, Sir William Penn, which led to the slackening of the English sails and furthered the Dutch escape.[25]

On June 27th, soon after the battle, Myngs' services were recognised and he was knighted.[26] No doubt both Narbrough and Shovell shared with their benefactor the joy of this honour.

Following the Battle of Lowestoft, the Duke of York and Prince Rupert gave up their commands, leaving the command of the fleet to the Earl of Sandwich. Early in July he took the fleet to the Texel and established that there was no likelihood of the Dutch being ready for any major action for some time. Sandwich decided to attempt the capture or destruction of a number of Dutch Smyrna and East India ships, which had taken refuge at Bergen, in Norway, in the aftermath of the Battle of Lowestoft.[27] Sir Thomas Tyddiman with fourteen ships was ordered by Sandwich to make the assault. Frederick III of Denmark, who was also sovereign of Norway, agreed not to hinder them for a share of the spoils, but a message from him to his governor at Bergen failed to arrive before the action. Tyddiman and his squadron were driven off with heavy loss.[28]

During this time Myngs served under Sandwich as Vice Admiral of the Blue. He would not have taken part in the direct assault at Bergen as he was Rear Admiral Tyddiman's senior. No doubt he and Sandwich stayed off the coast of Norway while the attempt was made. Consequently neither he nor Shovell would have witnessed the action at close hand.[29]

After their unsuccessful exploits at Bergen, Sandwich took the fleet back to Southwold Bay. At the end of August the fleet sailed again and on

September 3rd took three Dutch East Indiamen and their escort. The next day Sandwich added a further six merchantmen before returning to the buoy of the Nore.[30] On the voyage back to England, a council of flag officers decided to take their share of the booty without waiting for the king's permission which they anticipated. Sir William Penn was particularly insistent and Sandwich carelessly went along with them. Amongst the flag officers only Sir George Ayscue and stout Christopher Myngs spoke out against the unlawful division.[31] Sandwich was said to have taken £5,000 for himself and most of the other admirals a proportionately lesser amount.[32] The ordinary sailors had helped themselves, and were selling nutmegs and cloves in the taverns around the waterside. It is unlikely that Shovell was one of them in view of Myngs' attitude to the matter! The King, Charles II, and his brother, the Duke of York, were not pleased with the behaviour of their admirals, and Sandwich was packed off to Madrid as Ambassador Extraordinary.

Although Narbrough had been with Myngs in the *Triumph* at the Battle of Lowestoft, he left Myngs for a brief time in 1665 for the *Royal James*, a 1st rate, and then the *Old James*, a 2nd rate. However, in the autumn of 1665 Narbrough rejoined Myngs in the *Fairfax*. It seems likely that Shovell would have stayed with Myngs in the *Triumph* for all of the summer.[33]

The winter months of late 1665 and early 1666 were busy ones for Myngs and the crew of the *Fairfax*. Myngs was in command of a strong squadron in the Channel for a winter guard and the protection of trade. In January it was reported from Portsmouth that "by sending out ships constantly to cruise about, he [Myngs] hath kept this coast very free from all the enemy's men of war."[34] A few weeks later, "his vigilance is such that hardly anything can escape our frigates that come through the Channel".[35] March saw Myngs convoying the Hamburg trade from the Elbe to the Thames.[36]

No doubt Shovell continued his education under Myngs, and shared the discomforts of a winter in the Channel.

For the summer campaign of 1666, Myngs had moved to the *Victory*, a 2nd rate of 82 guns.[37] Narbrough was again with him[38] and no doubt Shovell as well. In April, when the fleet started to assemble under the joint command of George Monck, Duke of Albemarle, and Prince Rupert, Myngs was made Vice Admiral of the Red.[39] In Narbrough's journal for 1666, he recorded that on May 7th the *Victory* sailed from Gillingham to Blackwater and they got their guns in. On May 24th the fleet sailed for the Downs and the next day Narbrough noted how well the *Victory* sailed. The Downs was reached on May 27th, and two days later Myngs was ordered to the westward as second in command to Prince Rupert.[40]

The English fleet for the summer of 1666 under the joint command of Albemarle and Rupert consisted of eighty ships. Their Dutch opponents under De Ruijter, Jan Evertsen and Cornelis Tromp were slightly superior with eighty-five ships. In battle the superior discipline of the English should have enabled them to more than hold their own. However, a strategical blunder made by Charles II led to a division of the fleet and was to affect the outcome of the Four Days Fight, in early June. The French had entered the war on the side of the Dutch on January 14th, and Charles II was concerned that a French contingent of thirty-six ships was coming into the Channel from the Mediterranean under the Duc de Beaufort. It was for this reason that Rupert and Myngs were ordered to the westward to intercept them. Unfortunately the wind which carried Rupert to the west also brought Admiral Michiel De Ruijter and the Dutch fleet out. Poor Albemarle was left with fifty-six ships to oppose De Ruijter's eighty-five. On June 1st the bloody Four Days Fight began with the gallant Albemarle sweeping down on the Dutch off the North Foreland. He would have to fight alone until Rupert and Myngs returned on June 3rd.[41]

As the Four Days Fight opened on June 1st, Rupert and Myngs were off St Helens, but Narbrough reported that they sailed that day for the Downs. On June 3rd, he recorded, "we saw ye Dutch fleet off ye Galloper wind E".[42] That evening the two English squadrons reunited making them fifty-eight to sixty sail against De Ruijter's about seventy-eight fit for action.[43]

On the morning of June 4th the fourth and final day's action started. Myngs, still in the *Victory*, led the van and engaged the Dutch Vice Admiral, Jan De Liefde, broadside to broadside, the yardarms of the two ships almost touching. De Liefde's ship was dismasted, whereupon Myngs made an unsuccessful attempt to burn her with a fireship. The Dutch pressed in to support De Liefde, and two other admirals, Van Nes and De Ruijter himself, brought up other ships. The battle raged fiercely. The unfortunate Myngs was shot through the throat but refused to leave the deck to have the wound dressed. He stood compressing his neck injury with his fingers until another shot mortally wounded him. This final shot again penetrated his neck and lodged in his shoulder.[44] For June 4th Narbrough simply recorded in his journal: "We fought their fleet: Sir Christopher was wounded. Wind E.N.E."[45] No doubt Narbrough and Shovell witnessed their gallant chief's mortal injury.

The Four Days Fight off the North Foreland was a fine victory for De Ruijter and the Dutch. However, despite their defeat, English morale had not suffered. The battle had demonstrated that their discipline and seamanship were superior to those of the Dutch. If the two sides were to meet on equal terms they were encouraged to hope for victory. The fleet returned to the Gunfleet with the *Victory* bearing the mortally wounded Myngs. The next day, June 6th, Myngs was sent up to London, and two days later Sir Edward Spragge arrived to take over command of the *Victory*. On June 10th Narbrough recorded in his journal that he had been given a commission to command the *Assurance* and for the same date added briefly: "Sir Christopher Myngs died."[46]

Both Shovell and Narbrough were indebted to their patron, Myngs. Shovell owed his entry into the navy to Myngs, and Narbrough's career was intimately related. It is likely that Myngs died at his own house in Goodman's Fields, Whitechapel, as Pepys reported that he was buried in London on June 13th. The funeral was attended by Pepys and Sir William Coventry and afterwards they had a moving encounter. About to drive off, Pepys reported that about a dozen able, witty, proper men came to the coach side with tears in their eyes and one of them, that spoke for the rest, began and said to Coventry:

> We are here a dozen of us that have long known and loved, and served our dead commander, Sir Christopher Mings and have now done the last office of laying him in the ground. We would be glad we had any other to offer after him and in revenge of him. All we have is our lives; if you will please to get His Royal Highness to give us a fireship among us all, here is a dozen of us, out of all which choose you one to be commander, and the rest of us, whoever he is, will serve him; and, if possible, do that shall show ones memory of our dead commander, and our revenge.

Their witnesses could hardly refrain from weeping.[47]

Pepys has left us his own view of Myngs:

> Sir Christopher Myngs was a very stout man, and a man of great parts, and a most excellent tongue among ordinary men; and as Sir William Coventry says could have been the most useful man at such a pinch of time as this ... He had brought his family into a way of being great; but dying at this time his memory and name will be quite forgot in a few months as if he had never been, nor any of his name to be the better by it; he having not had time to will any estate but is dead poor rather than rich.[48]

Pepys was to have an equally favourable opinion of John Narbrough, but, as will be seen later in this account, not of Cloudesley Shovell.

On the day of Myngs' funeral Narbrough recorded in his journal, "I made way for fitting". It is unlikely that either he or Shovell attended. Narbrough had gone aboard the *Assurance* on June 11th and they sailed on the 16th.[49]

We know without doubt that Shovell had been in the West Indies with Myngs in 1663, and was with Narbrough there in 1667.[50] Narbrough was in the *Assurance* for certain in 1667, and it seems likely that Shovell rapidly followed him from the *Victory* after Myngs' death, in June 1666. This cannot be proved, as there is no documentary evidence available.

In early July 1666 the *Assurance* with Narbrough as captain and Shovell as his servant, were put under the command of Sir Thomas Allin. On July 25th the *Assurance* was part of the English van under Allin which took part in the St James's Day Fight against the Dutch.

The battle took place in the wide part of the Thames estuary between Orfordness and the North Foreland. The English fleet were under the joint command of Prince Rupert and George Monck, the 1st Duke of Albemarle. Rupert and Albemarle occupied the centre of the line, with Allin ahead commanding the van and Sir Jeremy Smyth the rear. The Dutch were commanded by the famous De Ruijter, with Jan Evertsen in the van and Cornelis Tromp in the rear. The English line, that would have been five or six miles in length, was a good one, but the Dutch line was irregular with a gap between De Ruijter and Tromp. The battle opened at 9.00 a.m. with Allin engaging Evertsen's squadron ahead, and De Ruijter setting about the English centre. Tromp, as was characteristic of him, broke through ahead of the English rear and engaged in a private battle with Symth's squadron, much to De Ruijter's displeasure.

The English van under Allin, with the *Assurance* and Narbrough, gained a rapid superiority over their Dutch opponents. In a very short period of time the Dutch van lost three flag officers, Jan Evertsen, Tjerck Hiddes de Vries and Rudolf Coenders, and they were overpowered.[51]

For the entry in his journal of July 25th, Narbrough recorded that they had

> Fair weather: little wind at N.E: smooth water this morning: we stood with ye Dutch fleet and had them to leeward of us: so we stood with their van: and our van bore downe upon ye enemy and we fought them from nine of the clocke till about three of the clock. In the afternoon then they run and we pursued them: the next morning: we fought them upon the pursuit.

In the margin he recorded that they had taken two ships.[52]

The battle was sharpest in the centre where De Ruijter's flagship, the *Zeven Provincien,* was dismasted, and there was a confused mêlée in the rear. The day ended in a brilliant English victory. The Dutch had lost about twenty ships, with 4,000 men killed and 3,000 wounded, in addition to the flag officers listed earlier. The English lost one major ship, few men, and no flag officers. The result was a very satisfactory one for them.[53]

The St James's Day Fight, or the second Battle of North Foreland, had given the English a temporary mastery of the seas. They crossed to the Dutch coast and anchored in the Schooneveld, before deciding to attack the islands of Vlieland and Terschelling, where there was a large fleet of merchantmen, magazines and stores. Following a council of war, Sir Robert Holmes was entrusted with a small squadron of nine men of war, five fireships and seven ketches plus 300 men to make the attack. Narbrough and the *Assurance* were part of Holmes' squadron.

On August 8th Holmes' squadron parted company with the rest of the fleet. The following day they sailed into Terschelling Road in order to destroy the fleet of merchantmen. The two guarding Dutch men of war were overcome and Holmes ordered Sir William Jennings to go in with all available boats to burn the merchantmen.[54]

Narbrough took part in this conflagration and recorded in his journal for that day, "went up to the Dutch fleet; and burned: 140: sail all richly laden: outward bound to all ports: this we did by one of ye clocke in ye afternoon."[55]

The next day men were landed on Terschelling and the town and its storehouses set on fire. Narbrough described the scene in his journal entry for August 10th, "this morning we landed with eight hundred men: Sir Robert Holmes general: attacked Schelling Island: and went and burned the town without loss of one man: and then marched to our boats and went aboard and set sails and went out".[56]

An enormous amount of damage was done to ships and stores. The value was at least £850,000, and for many years the incident was known in England as "Sir Robert Holmes, his bonfire".[57] The Dutch considered that the Fire of London which occurred the next month was in retribution for Holmes' "bonfire". Whether Shovell, who was probably Narbrough's servant at the time, went ashore with him or not is unknown. In any event, whether he witnessed the destruction from ship or shore, it must have been a spectacular sight for a 15-year-old boy.

The *Assurance* returned to Southwold following the devastation of Terschelling. In early September Narbrough was involved in a further skirmish with the Dutch before his journal ended on October 15th. Presumably the *Assurance* was laid up for the winter. The only other incident of note about this time, in Narbrough's journal, was that the master of his ship got drunk and he, Narbrough, hit him on the head with his hand![58]

NOTES
1. Crockatt, Consolatory Letter.
2. Secret Memoirs.
3. RMT MAT 64.
4. Larn, p.2.
5. Finch, MSS, Vol. IV, p.388.
6. Davies, Gentlemen and Tarpaulins p.129; Penn Memorials, ii, 183, 194.
7. C.S.P. America and West Indies, May 25th 1664.
8. Marsham letter to Captain Locker; RMT MAT 64.
9. Finch MSS, IV, p.388.
10. Crockatt, Consolatory Letter.
11. House of Lords MSS, Vol. VI, pp.386–387.

12. Davies, Gentlemen and Tarpaulins p.16.
13. Anderson, Lists of Men of War.
14. Heathcote MSS, pp.34–35, Myngs letter to Lord Windsor Oct 19th 1662.
15. Dyer, p.13.
16. Grainger, A Geographical Description of Norfolk.
17. Dyer, p.11.
18. Finch MSS, Vol. IV, p.388, Aug 12th 1692.
19. Finch MSS, Vol. IV, p.379.
20. D.N.B. Myngs, Narbrough; Dyer pp.13–14.
21. Laird Clowes, pp.257–259.
22. D.N.B. Myngs; Dyer, p.24.
23. Laird Clowes, pp.259–262.
24. D.N.B. Rupert; Pepys Diary, Jan 15th 1665.
25. Laird Clowes, pp.263–265.
26. D.N.B. Myngs; Le Neve, Pedigrees of Knights.
27. Laird Clowes, p.266.
28. Laird Clowes, pp.426–427.
29. D.N.B. Myngs, Sandwich.
30. D.N.B. Myngs, Sandwich.
31. Harris, Life of Edward Montagu, Vol II, pp.4–6; Pepys Diary Sept. 24th, Oct.12th 1665.
32. D.N.B. Sandwich.
33. NMM, Commissioned Sea Officers 1660–1815.
34. London Gazette, No.18.
35. London Gazette, No.39.
36. D.N.B. Myngs.
37. Marsham MSS U1515.03.
38. NMM, Commissioned Sea Officers 1660–1815.
39. C.S.P. Dom. Charles II cl iv 128.
40. Marsham MSS UI515.03; C.S.P. Dom. Charles II cl vii 40–41.
41. Laird Clowes, pp.267–278.
42. Marsham MSS U1515.03.
43. Laird Clowes, p.275.
44. Brandt, Vie Michel de Ruijter pp.359, 363; C.S.P. Dom. Charles II cl viii 48; Pepys, June 8th 1666.
45. Marsham MSS U1515.03.
46. Marsham MSS U1515.03, Journal of the *Victory*.
47. Bryant, Samuel Pepys, The Man in the Making p.295; C.S.P.Dom. 1665/6 452–4, 458, 462, 468–9; Rawlinson MSS, A195, ff 287–9; Diary 30th June and 1st, 2nd, 6th, 13th July 1666.
48. Pepys' Diary, June 13th..
49. Marsham MSS U1515.03, Journal of the *Victory*.
50. Marsham MSS U1515, letter from CS to the Earl of Nottingham; Finch MSS, Vol IV, pp.387–389.
51. Laird Clowes, pp.278–281.
52. Marsham MSS U1515.03.
53. Laird Clowes, pp.281–283.
54. Laird Clowes, pp.283–284.
55. Marsham MSS U1515.03, Journal J.N.
56. Marsham MSS U1515.03, Journal J.N.
57. Laird Clowes, p.284.
58. Marsham MSS U1515.03, Journal J.N.

CHAPTER III
# Action in the West Indies
# 1667–1668

Perhaps Narbrough and Shovell were able to visit their homes in Norfolk during the winter of 1666–7. In early April 1667 Narbrough restarted his journal and was still in command of the *Assurance*, initially in the Channel under Sir Thomas Allin and then Sir John Harman. Harman had been appointed Admiral and Commander-in-Chief in the West Indies, where the French and Dutch were causing difficulties. Narbrough, on the *Assurance*, was to be part of Harman's squadron to rectify matters. We know with certainty that Shovell was with Narbrough on this expedition to the West Indies as his servant.[1] By now 16, after a birthday the preceding November, Shovell was to pay his second and final visit to the Caribbean. Strangely, during his forty-five-year career at sea, he was not required to go there again although his advice on the area and division of plunder was asked for as late as 1692.[2]

Harman called a council of war on April 26th and two days later they sailed from Plymouth. May 11th saw Narbrough briefly anchor at Madeira before the voyage to the West Indies was continued. Barbados came into view of the *Assurance* on June 9th at about six leagues distance, and they went ashore on the following day. Narbrough visited the house of the Governor of Barbados, Lord William Willoughby, the same day.[3]

On the very day Harman and Narbrough were approaching Barbados, the Dutch under Michiel De Ruijter were starting their bold attack on Sheerness and the Medway. De Ruijter was able temporarily to capture Sheerness, destroy many of the larger English men of war in the Medway, and finally to cut out and capture the pride of the fleet, the *Royal Charles*. This perfectly executed operation by the Dutch was to speed up the ending of the Second Dutch War with the Treaty of Breda, on July 31st 1667. No doubt Narbrough and Shovell, if they had known at the time what had happened at home, would have been only too pleased not to have been associated with the nadir of English fortunes in the war.

Harman learnt that the French Admiral De La Barré was at the nearby island of Martinique with about twenty-three or twenty-four sail protected under the cannons of three forts. The English squadron consisted of seven men of war and two fireships. Despite the disparity in strength, Harman was determined to attack them and arrived off Martinique on June 19th. Over the next few days, the English approached and opened fire on the French, without being able to tempt them out. On the first day Narbrough went in at four o'clock in the morning and had about 400 guns fired at him. The next day the *Assurance* stood within pistol shot of De La Barré and fought him for an hour. Narbrough reported five men killed, eighteen wounded, and his masts and rigging damaged. He had to repair them as best he could. On the 24th the English managed to silence the French forts. The next day De La Barré's flagship was burnt by fireships and six further ships were destroyed. The English lost no ships and recorded a signal victory against the odds. Feelings must have been running high as the French would not exchange prisoners when Harman requested this. Harman himself had been lame with gout prior to the battle, but on finding the French fleet, he walked the deck and gave orders until the enemy was defeated and then he became as lame as before! After this success at Martinique, Harman called a council of war that decided that the English squadron would sail for Montserrat to take on further supplies of water. After brief stays at the islands of Dominica, Montserrat and Nevis, they returned to Barbados in early August.[4]

Next on Harman's agenda was to be a combined military and naval attempt on the island of Cayenne, which was held by the French, and then on the colony of Surinam on the mainland of South America. Lieutenant General Sir Henry Willoughby, whose father, William, was Governor of Barbados, was to command the land forces.[5] Willoughby drew up full plans for the attack. First to go ashore would be a party of soldiers under Major Richard Stevens, known as the "Forlorne Hope" who would be supported by three companies of seamen each consisting of "sixty choice and well armed mariners". Narbrough was to command the naval contingent as senior captain. Willoughby arranged to land his regiment behind the others, and would hurry to their assistance if necessary. Orders were given that, if the landing was opposed, they were to "press in upon the enemy with the club end of the muskets and swords".[6]

On September 12th the English squadron was six leagues from Cayenne (which Narbrough referred to by the old name, Cyan), and Narbrough reported in his journal, "we saw Cyan". They anchored in five fathoms of water, three leagues from the island. The following day the assault began. Narbrough stood into the Bay of Armera which was on the windward side of the island. At seven o'clock in the morning they landed with about forty men getting ashore with Narbrough. Whether Narbrough's servant, Shovell, accompanied him is uncertain. On landing, Narbrough's small party was shot at by the French, who had been tipped off that an attack was to be made on them. However, the French were charged, with about twenty of them being killed, before the remainder ran away. Narbrough did not follow as they were in unfamiliar country, but he personally took one prisoner in combat that day. Before 6.00 p.m. about 900 men had been landed, the Governor had fled, and the town was in Willoughby's hands. Unfortunately the English soldiers came across a store of strong liquor

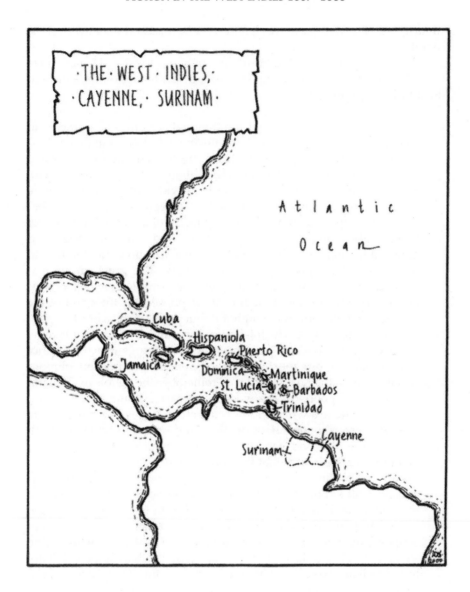

·THE· WEST· INDIES,·
·CAYENNE,· SURINAM·

Atlantic

Ocean

Cuba

Hispaniola
Puerto Rico

Jamaica

Dominica
Martinique
St. Lucia
Barbados
Trinidad

Cayenne

Surinam

from which they could not be kept. The town was burnt, and it was decided to make an attempt on the fort the next day.

The following day, September 14th, the English marched on the fort and took it. Narbrough reported, "we cruelly plundered the French". By the 15th all Cayenne was in English hands, and the guns from the fort were transported to the ships. In all about thirty-six guns and some 150 blacks were brought off, prior to the departure of the English force, on September 29th. Narbrough's final entry in his journal for the period in Cayenne sums up the state the island was left in. "We burned and destroyed all the island." [7]

Twenty-five years after the event, Shovell, in a letter to Daniel Finch, Earl of Nottingham, gave his own account of the taking of Cayenne and the division of plunder.

> As to what you writte a bout the dividents of officers, seamen and souldiers in the West Indies, I can informe your Lordship that in 1667 we tooke the island of Keyan from the French, Sir John Herman commander at sea and Lieut-General Willoby at land. I was then with Sir John Narbrough and remember the dividment was made before we left the island. The things divided ware negros, coppers and other brass or copper instruments belonging to the milles and sugger houses, also sugger, tobacco, mallasses and what else the iland afforded for marchantdise. There was but a little pow(d)er theire, and that was I think given to the buckenners. The great gunns was secured for the King, and magazeens of provision or licquer was never brought into the divident but dispoosed for the good of the men as the cheife officers thought fitt. But goods taken a bord ships in the road or harbower which fell into our hands by reason of takeing the place ware divided. There may be other things which I doe not well remember but the furniture of houses and pockett plunder remained with the takers, for I well remember the people of the iland had hid their goods in the woods and carryed sum of them sum distance from the town. We followed them in partys and sum privatte men gott great booteys both of silver and gold and remained with what they tooke, and had sum incorragement for the negros and other divideable bootey that they brought in.
>
> I know not directly every officer's shear but I think the Admirall and generall a shore had a third or halfe between them. I was one of the seven that had a good negro and Sir John Narbrough had eight negros; but he was then captain of the Assurance. He had also sum coppers but I know not whether he had them in shear or wheither he stole them. This to the best of my knowledg is what happened theire but dividents have been variously made, for their never was a settelled prop(r)tion.[8]

Shovell's comments concerning Narbrough's possible dishonesty are interesting! By the standards of the seventeenth century Narbrough was considered to be a sober and straightforward individual. A few years later a black slave was worth £20.00 or 3,287 lbs of sugar.[9] It seems likely that Shovell would have sold the slave he had been given at Cayenne.

From Cayenne Harman's squadron with Sir Henry Willoughby's troops aboard set sail for the colony of Surinam on the South American mainland.

Surinam had fallen to the Dutch in the spring of 1667, when a squadron under Admiral Crijnssen had been successful against an English garrison weakened by illness. By October 5th the English squadron had reached the Surinam River and Willoughby was landed with his regiment. The soldiers marched through a wood and a sugar plantation before reaching the fort. This proved to be a formidable strongpoint that would be difficult to take without assault ladders, as the walls were eighteen feet high. The English plan of action was to bombard the fort with the men of war at sea, and when darkness came to stop up the wells which were the sole water supply to the fort. The wells were outside the walls of the fort at about a musket shot's distance.

Harman's squadron attacked the fort from the sea on October 7th, and there were casualties on both sides. Two English captains were killed, and Narbrough himself was severely wounded. He reported that he was "wounded by a small shot through the thigh". Injuries of this sort were often fatal in the seventeenth and eighteenth centuries, as Talmash was to discover at Camaret Bay in 1694. Narbrough survived his wound, but a medical report in 1668 stated that he was still troubled by it. The report showed that a musket ball passing through the large muscle, bruising bone, tearing the tendons and causing persistent pain and numbness, caused the wound. No doubt Shovell helped look after Narbrough following his injury, and it is unlikely that Shovell would have had such a successful career if his patron had died at this time. Poor Harman was also incapacitated during the bombardment of the fort, and had to lie on a couch on his quarterdeck. This was probably due to his gout, which picked the most inconvenient times to strike him!

Eventually the fort was assaulted and taken with minimum casualties. The Dutch governor accused the English of barbarism, as they had ignored his flag of truce, while entering the fort using pieces of wood knocked off the fort during the bombardment. Of the 225 men of the Dutch garrison, fifty-six were wounded or killed.[10]

Surinam was in English hands again, but not for long. Although Harman, Willoughby and Narbrough did not know it at the time, under the Treaty of Breda, signed on the preceding July 31st, Surinam was returned to the Dutch and Cayenne to the French. It was all a wasted effort.

A short while after Surinam had fallen, Harman gave Narbrough a commission to command the *Bonaventure*, which like the *Assurance* was a 4th rate but a slightly larger one. This was as a result of the death of the *Bonaventure's* Captain, William Hammond, in the assault on Surinam. The date was October 29th, and the same day Narbrough recorded in his journal "the admiral ordered me to remove to the Bonaventure: I removed my things this day: and muster men move with me to ye Bonaventure". It amounted to a minor promotion for Narbrough. Although there is no documentary evidence that Shovell moved to the *Bonaventure* with Narbrough, it would be reasonable to suppose that he did. Almost certainly he was amongst the muster men mentioned above. There were 180 men on board.[11]

The *Bonaventure* set sail for Barbados on November 1st, and little happened on the return journey. And although Narbrough recorded, "We had a small contest about dividing the negroes", he does not mention the outcome. Before the end of the year, Narbrough had taken Willoughby back to Surinam, and in early January 1668 Sir John Harman joined them.

Between January and July 1668 the *Bonaventure* cruised all around the West Indies sometimes with Willoughby aboard. Islands visited included St Lucia, Dominica, Guadeloupe, Antigua, Montserrat, Nevis and, intermittently, back to base in Barbados. They were minor missions. In early June Narbrough and Shovell's former ship the *Assurance* returned to England in charge of eight merchant ships.

The *Bonaventure* herself was suffering structurally from the worm, and on July 23rd she was ordered home. Governor William Willoughby saw them off that day from Barbados accompanied by the *Crome* and the *Norwich*, men of war, plus some merchant ships. Narbrough had been given a packet by a Colonel Simon Lambert to give to Charles II in England.

Three days after sailing, Narbrough put the crew of the *Bonaventure* on a half allowance of water for fear of a long passage in escorting the merchant ships. Shortly afterwards Captain Poole, the senior captain, informed Narbrough that his own ship, the *Crome*, and the *Norwich* would sail with all expedition for England, leaving the *Bonaventure* with the slower merchant vessels. Narbrough handed over his packet for Charles II to Poole, and uncomplainingly got on with his job although he must have been irked by Poole's decision.

Eventually, on September 19th, Narbrough saw the Scilly Islands four miles to the north of them, and he took the *Bonaventure* into St Mary's, saluted Star Castle, and had his salute returned. By this time they had only six days' provisions left and Narbrough recorded "my men eat pease for bread".

By September 30th they were in the Downs and were soon ordered into Chatham River. Early in November Narbrough discharged his boy, Nat Marsh, and the rest of the officers' boys. Perhaps Shovell had been promoted on joining the *Bonaventure*. Narbrough visited Whitehall and kissed the Duke of York's hand.

What Narbrough and Shovell did during late 1668 and early 1669 is uncertain. Perhaps they joined Narbrough's brother-in-law, Loades, who had returned to Norfolk. The journal ends on November 27th 1668. [12]

NOTES

1. Finch MSS, Vol.IV, pp.387–388; Marsham MSS U1515, CS letter to Earl of Nottingham.
2. Finch MSS, Vol.IV, pp.387–388.
3. Marsham MSS U1515.03, Journal J.N.
4. Marsham MSS U1515.03.
5. Dyer, p.41; D.N.B. Willoughby.
6. Dyer, pp.41–43.
7. Marsham MSS U1515.03, Journal J.N.
8. Finch MSS, Vol.IV, pp.387–388.
9. Dyer, p.55.
10. Marsham MSS U1515.03; Dyer, pp.49–56.
11. Marsham MSS U1515.03, Journal J.N.
12. Marsham MSS U1515.03, Journal J.N.

CHAPTER IV
# *The Voyage of the* Sweepstakes *1669–1671*

In May 1669 Narbrough was ordered to prepare for an expedition to South America. The purpose of the expedition was one of discovery, and to see if it was possible to break the Spanish stranglehold on trade in the area. Narbrough, by a commission dated May 15th, was given command of a 4th rate, the *Sweepstakes*, to use for his voyage. The South American venture was to last for two hazardous years, and occupy Narbrough for part of the interlude between the Second and Third Dutch Wars.

Narbrough's movements between 1669 and 1671 are known with exactness, thanks to his journal, which has survived in the form of a number of copies and was published soon after his death. What of Shovell during this two-year period? Did he accompany Narbrough? Most sources believe he probably did sail in the *Sweepstakes* to South America. They include Sir John Laughton in the *Dictionary of National Biography*. It is generally accepted that, after Myngs' death in 1666, Narbrough took over the care of the young Shovell and advanced him from post to post.[1] For the next ten years or so, wherever Narbrough was, so too was Shovell. The last chapter showed with certainty that the two men were together in the West Indies in 1667, by the evidence of Shovell's own hand. It is known that Narbrough and Shovell were together on the *Prince* in January 1672, from evidence in the Public Record Office, ADM 33/103. Research done for the author has demonstrated that Narbrough left the *Sweepstakes* for the *Prince* on January 4th 1672, followed by a Claudius Shovell, on

31

January 9th. Cloudesley has been spelt in innumerable ways, even by Shovell himself, and there can be little doubt that the Claudius Shovell is one and the same as Cloudesley Shovell.[2] Later in the chapter it will be shown that after the South American voyage Narbrough discharged his men on August 1st 1671. The *Sweepstakes* was then refitted for an abortive voyage to the West Indies that autumn, and it is from this that Narbrough and Shovell were discharged the following January.

Although there is as yet no absolute documentary evidence that Shovell accompanied Narbrough on the earlier voyage, it is virtually certain that he did. The lapse of time has made records of this period sparse. In the account of Narbrough's voyage in the *Sweepstakes*, through the Strait of Magellan and up to Baldivia, it will be assumed that Shovell was there as well.

Between May and September the *Sweepstakes*, a 4th rate of 300 tons, was prepared for the voyage of exploration, firstly at Deptford and then in the Downs. On August 29th 1669 Narbrough took leave of his King, Charles II, in the presence of the Duke of York, Prince Rupert, the Earl of Sandwich and others. Charles II was interested in the voyage as a means of opening new areas of trade, and in the possibility of settlements on the south-east coast similar to those already set up in North America. The goods for trading with the natives were a private venture of Charles II. Knives, scissors, glasses, pins, bells, cloth, tobacco and pipes were supplied for bartering purposes.[3]

On September 1st Narbrough's lieutenant gave up his commission, perhaps because of his fear of a long and hazardous journey. He was replaced by Mathew Peckett who came aboard the *Sweepstakes* only a few days before they sailed. Another last minute addition to the expedition was that of a small ship of 80 tons, the *Batchelor pink*, with eighteen men under the 45-year-old Captain Humphrey Fleming.

The *Sweepstakes* and the *Batchelor pink* raised their anchors and sailed from the Downs on September 26th 1669. The first port of call was Madeira, which they reached on October 14th, staying two days before setting off again to the south-west. (Dyer records that they reached Madeira on October 17th.)[4] A few days later Narbrough and the *Sweepstakes*, accompanied by the *Batchelor pink*, crossed the Tropic of Cancer.

> Saturday October 23rd . . . this day I crossed the Tropic of Cancer, all my men in good health, I praise the Almighty God for it; many of my men that had been with me in the Indies formerly were let blood; for I take bleeding in those hot climates to be a great preserver of health, diverting Calentures*;. . .

* An old term of Spanish origin for a temporary delirium or fever occurring on board ship in hot climates.

32

No doubt Shovell, who had been in the West Indies with him, was one of those "let blood". Narbrough's views in some fields, such as treating scurvy, were sensible and advanced for his time. Blood letting for the recurrent fever of malaria, which troubled so many seventeenth century seamen, including Shovell, was not one of them.[5]

The Cape Verde Islands were reached on October 27th and Narbrough put into Port Praya to revictual. The Portuguese fleet was there and Narbrough was hard pressed to avoid an incident with them after some of their men had snatched English hats and run away! At Port Praya Narbrough gave his crew the first detailed account of the orders that he had received from Charles II and their destination. In addition, Captain Fleming of the *Batchelor pink* was given strict instructions to stay in company with the *Sweepstakes*.[6]

At the end of the first week of November the two ships left Port Praya and sailed south-westerly in the direction of South America. The voyage progressed, and in late November the *Sweepstakes* temporarily lost contact with the *Batchelor pink*. Early in the New Year of 1670, on January 2nd, Narbrough recorded in his journal "my men are all in good health: God be praised being: 87: in number the same as I came out with from England . . ." He spoke too soon as two days later John Mahon, an 18-year-old from Suffolk, died. Apart from his officers and his interpreter, little mention by name is given to the ordinary seamen and boys unless they died! This may explain why Shovell's name does not feature in the journal.[7]

On the anniversary of the execution of Charles I, January 30th, Narbrough judged the *Sweepstakes* to be off the River Plate, as a strong current was carrying them to the south. The ships were surrounded by sea fowl and whales, some of which were shot and found to be good meat. Narbrough saw that his officers ate and drank no better than the men. He wrote:

> Today the Cooper found two buts of Beer had leaked out: this day all of us drank water only, for it was ever my order that the meanest boy in the ship should have the same allowance with myself; so that in general we all drank of the same cask and eat one sort of Provision, as long as they lasted. I never permitted any Officer to have a better piece of Meat than what fell to his lot; but one blinded with a Cloth serv'd every man, as they were call'd to touch and take, by which means we never had any Difference upon that score.

No doubt this early example of care of the crew influenced the young Shovell who was fair to his men.[8]

In February, during one of the periodic losses of contact with the *Batchelor pink*, Narbrough discussed with his officers whether they should

33

wait for the *pink* or go for the Strait of Magellan by themselves, as weather conditions were favourable. The officers to a man decided that they should wait. Despite firing muskets at night to help the *Batchelor pink* keep station, on the night of February 19th at 10.00 o'clock final contact was lost. Two days later land was seen at Cape St George and Narbrough went ashore. There was evidence of old fires and there were graves on the tops of hills, some of which were opened by Narbrough and his men. Seals and penguins were killed for meat, eaten very well salted. Narbrough's greyhound killed five animals. It is interesting that not only did he take a dog with him, but that it was a greyhound. In some accounts of Shovell's drowning in 1707, it was reported that he was washed up on a hatch with his dead whippet. Perhaps Narbrough introduced him to the breed.[9]

Narbrough set sail again and on March 4th 1670 Port Desire was reached. Forty men were sent ashore, and 400 seals were killed with staffs and hand spikes, for salting. A stake and a board, with details of the direction that they were going in, was placed in the ground at Narbrough's direction, in case the crew of the *Batchelor pink* landed there. Before leaving Port Desire, the crew gave themselves strength for the journey with a meal of penguin and porridge!

In early April Port St Julian was reached. There was still no sign of the *Batchelor pink*, and Narbrough had to allay the fears of his crew of passing through the Strait of Magellan as a lone ship. He did this successfully by telling of the riches of the land they were going to, and quoting Sir Francis Drake. Drake had sailed through the Strait with a single ship, but it is doubtful that he would like to have been labelled an "ordinary navigator" which is how Narbrough described him. Narbrough's greyhound gave the crew a change of diet when it caught a young deer. On May 22nd the weather was closing in, and a decision was made to winter at Port St Julian, and to attempt the Strait in the spring. Occasional contact was made with the natives and various small trinkets were handed out. One of Narbrough's men described them as tawny-coloured, medium-sized savages, wearing a short skin. There was no evidence of gold about them, and a bracelet found in a dropped bundle was made of sea shells. Narbrough was impressed by the countryside with its plains and grassy meadows, lacking only woods to build with. He felt that European grain would grow there, and that the land could sustain cattle.[10]

The winter was bitterly cold with frost and snow. Rats were found to have badly damaged the sails of the ship, and in September the *Sweepstakes* was in danger of being driven ashore in a storm. As the weather became cold so the health of the crew declined. In August one man died of the flux, followed three days later by another with scurvy. Narbrough reported ten men ill with scurvy despite the fact that they were ashore. Further men were lame with the cold and "their legs were as black as a black Hat in spots, the cold having chilled their blood". By

September the weather was beginning to improve, and on the 16th Narbrough got the *Sweepstakes* to sea and sailed back to Port Desire to replenish his victuals with penguins and seals. There he found that the natives had made a model of the *Sweepstakes* from earth and branches. The crew tried eating penguin eggs, which were good and larger than a duck's egg. By October 12th 1670 Narbrough awaited only the Almighty's pleasure to sail with the first fair wind for the Strait of Magellan.[11]

The Almighty's pleasure came three days later, and Narbrough got out of the Bay of Port Desire. By October 25th the *Sweepstakes* was in the Strait of Magellan. During November Narbrough made a detailed exploration of both shores of the Strait and recorded it on charts. He went ashore in a number of places making contact with the natives, giving them trinkets, and all the time keeping his eyes skinned for any gold that they might have about them. Narbrough went to the length of pretending to dig gold and bright copper from the ground, but the natives did not appear to understand. Narbrough called many of the islands in the Strait after the King and members of his Court. Thus we have Charles Island, Monmouth Island, the Earl of Sandwich Island amongst others. Perhaps he ran out of names as he immodestly called one after himself![12]

On November 19th Narbrough got out of the Strait and had his first view of the South Seas or Pacific Ocean as we now know them. This was to be the only occasion on which either Narbrough or Shovell were to sail in the South Seas. By now all the ship's bread was used up, and they proceeded to the north off the coast of what is now Chile. The Bay of Baldivia was reached on December 15th. Don Carlos, a guide brought by Narbrough, was landed a mile away from the harbour, and arrangements were made to pick him up that night at the same place where he would light a fire as a signal. That night no fire was lit on the shore, and the crew of the *Sweepstakes* heard nothing further of Don Carlos.

Next day Narbrough's first lieutenant, the 40-year-old Thomas Armiger, another Norfolk man and related to Christopher Myngs, took a boat along the shore to look for Don Carlos. Inadvertently coming before the fort, Armiger was called ashore by the Spaniards. Armiger had little choice but to go and was welcomed kindly. His health was drunk and dinner provided. Armiger noted that the dishes, dinner plates, bowls for washing hands and sword hilts were all made of silver. Silver and gold were plentiful and apparently not much esteemed.

Four Spaniards accompanied Armiger back to the *Sweepstakes* and suggested to Narbrough that they pilot his ship into the harbour. Rightly suspecting that the Spaniards intended to seize the *Sweepstakes*, Narbrough declined but questioned them about their settlement and relationship with the Indians. The Spanish were perpetually at war with the Indians, although trade was still done in gold and other goods. Six ships which came each year from Lima supplied Baldivia. In turn, the

Spaniards asked Narbrough about the purpose of his voyage. Diplomatically, Narbrough replied that his ship was richly laden and bound for China, and that they had only come to Baldivia for water and wood. The Spaniards graciously agreed to provide supplies for the *Sweepstakes*.[13]

On December 17th Narbrough sent the Governor of Baldivia madeira wine and glasses as a present. In return Narbrough was given bread and local rum. The following day Lieutenant Armiger, accompanied by John Fortescue, gentlemen, Henry Cooe, trumpeter, and Thomas Highway, linguist, went ashore under a flag of truce but were detained. Armiger and Fortescue managed to get a letter off to Narbrough explaining their predicament.

> Myself and Mr Fortescue are kept here as prisoners, but for what cause I cannot tell; but they still pretend much friendship and say that if you will bring the ship into the Harbour you shall have all the accommodation that may be.

Narbrough replied:

> Lieutenant, take what notice you can of the fortifications of the fort, and what strength they have of people in it, and whether they are able to withstand a ship; and what quantities of provision they have in it; and whether Don Carlos is there; send me an account there of by John Wilkins, I will use all endeavours to have you off when I know the strength of the place.

Narbrough also sent a letter to the Spanish demanding the return of his men.[14] Narbrough himself went ashore on December 19th, near where they had landed Don Carlos but found nothing. The *Sweepstakes'* pinnace went into the harbour mouth with a flag of truce on December 28th, but was ignored by the Spanish.

The next day a canoe with a Spaniard and six Indians came out to the *Sweepstakes*, and asked for Armiger's clothing, and informed Narbrough that the Governor was resolved to keep his men. [15]

Narbrough must have agonised over whether or not he should try to reclaim his men by force. He knew that the garrison had 600 soldiers officered by the Spanish, and that in all probability he would lose his ship and remaining crew members if he tried. Narbrough has been criticised by some for sailing and leaving his men in the hands of the Spaniards.[16] The criticism is unjustified, as Narbrough had already proved his courage and resolution in the Second Dutch War and in the West Indies. He had no choice.

Shortly before Christmas 1670 Narbrough decided that it was not possible to continue his voyage and to return home. Armiger, who was left in Baldivia, married a Spanish woman and lived there for a further sixteen years before being executed by the local authorities for treason. The Spanish had acted badly in the affair, but their behaviour was understandable in the light of the English buccaneers' actions in the West Indies.[17]

The *Sweepstakes* sailed down the coast of what is now Chile towards the Strait of Magellan. On December 30th Narbrough was troubled by damage to the main mast, and two days later by one of his men falling overboard and being drowned. The Strait was entered on January 6th 1671, and by mid February Narbrough had anchored in Port Desire. They found that turnips and carrots had grown from the seed that they had planted the previous October. Soon the *Sweepstakes* sailed on again, this time for England and home. The Azores were reached in May, and Narbrough sent ashore for oranges and lemons as some of his men were suffering from scurvy, and even the best seamen were drooping. He was pleased to hear that there was peace between Christian nations, and that Charles II and the Duke of York were in good health.[18]

From the Azores the *Sweepstakes* sailed for England, and on June 10th they were off Scilly. Narbrough could see the sea breaking over the Bishop and Clerks rocks, the Bishop standing to the west of his Clerks. Three days later they were in the Downs and Lieutenant Peckett was sent ashore. Orders were received for Narbrough to report to Whitehall, and taking his draughts and journal, he discussed the voyage with the King and the Duke of York. In July the *Sweepstakes* was moved to Deptford, where she had started her momentous voyage nearly two years before. On August 1st 1671 the crew was paid off. Narbrough's journal records:

> I never saw better payment in my days: this night we parted and went every man his way with his money in his pocket. All seamen mightily satisfied.[19]

The *Batchelor pink*, having lost contact with the *Sweepstakes* all that time before, had not sunk but had returned to England claiming that Narbrough was lost at sea. Grenville Collins, author of *Great Britain's Coasting Pilot*, who was with Narbrough on his voyage to the South Seas, accused the *Batchelor pink*'s crew of cowardice and desertion. [20]

Overall Narbrough's voyage had achieved two of its main objectives. Firstly, he had demonstrated that the Spaniards would not permit trade on the west coast of South America. Secondly, he was able to report on the climate and natural resources of the east coast, so that the government could decide upon the feasibility of setting up colonies there.[21]

In October 1671 Charles II required urgent business to be dealt with in the West Indies, and two ships under Narbrough were to be fitted out.

Narbrough found that the vessels selected for this purpose were unsuitable, and suggested that the *Sweepstakes* and the *Francis* be sent out instead, as they were of a shallower draft. Consequently the *Sweepstakes* was prepared for sea, but by the time that she was ready, the need was over.[22] As was shown earlier, Shovell was definitely part of the *Sweepstakes'* crew for this proposed voyage to the West Indies.[23]

NOTES

1. Crockatt, Consolatory Letter.
2. ADM 33/121, *Sweepstakes* Pay Book.
3. Dyer, pp.58–60; Marsham MSS U1515.03.
4. Dyer, p.60.
5. Dyer, pp. 60–61.
6. Dyer, pp. 61–68.
7. Marsham MSS U1515.03, Journal J.N.
8. Dyer, pp.66–67.
9. Marsham MSS U1515.03, Journal J.N.
10. Marsham MSS U1515.03, Journal J.N.; Dyer, pp.70–73.
11. Marsham MSS U1515.03, Journal J.N.; Dyer, pp.74–75.
12. Dyer, pp.76–77; Marsham MSS U1515.03, Journal J.N.
13. Dyer, pp.79–82.
14. Marsham MSS U1515.03, Journal J.N.; Dyer, pp.85–86; Coventry MSS 599, f91.
15. Marsham MSS U1515.03.
16. Burney J., Voyage to the South Seas p.374.
17. Marsham MSS U1515.03, Journal J.N.; Dyer p.87.
18. Marsham MSS U1515.03, Journal J.N.
19. Marsham MSS U1515.03, Journal J.N.
20. Dyer, p.89.
21. Dyer, p.91.
22. Dyer, p.91; C.S.P. Dom. 1671 p.514.
23. ADM 33/121, *Sweepstakes*.

# CHAPTER V
# *The Third Dutch War*
# *1672–1674*

The third and final Dutch War began in 1672. In 1668 a triple alliance of England, Sweden and Holland had been set up to check the power of Louis XIV's France. The French had designs on the Netherlands which were frustrated by the new alliance, and Louis set out to detach Charles II from his partners. Louis was well aware of the king's chronic shortage of money and jealousy of the Dutch. In 1670 Charles II was persuaded to sign the secret Treaty of Dover, the object of which was to divide the Netherlands between France and England. Charles was to be given a pension of £120,000, and the islands of Walcheren, Cadzand and Sluys, which would allow him to control Dutch shipping in the Scheldt and the Maas. In return Louis would have the support of fifty men of war to add to his own thirty and an army of 5,000 men. Pressure was exerted on the Dutch who tried to avoid a conflict. In mid March 1672 Sir Robert Holmes attacked the homecoming Dutch convoy from Smyrna and Lisbon, and on the 19th Charles II declared war. Louis XIV followed him on March 27th. The war was to be fought on both land and at sea. Only the naval genius of the great Admiral Michiel De Ruijter was to save his country from collapse.[1]

Both Narbrough and Shovell had fought in the Second Dutch War, and they were destined for action in the two principal naval battles of the Third War, at Sole Bay and the Texel. Narbrough was discharged from the *Sweepstakes* as commander on January 4th 1672, and Shovell followed him on the 9th.[2] A commission signed by the Duke of York, on January 5th, made Narbrough first lieutenant of the *Prince* or *Royal Prince* under Captain John Cox. Cox was to be knighted the following April and had been Commissioner at Chatham since 1669. The commission did not reach Narbrough until January 7th. Shovell officially joined Narbrough in the *Prince* as a midshipman on January 22nd, seventeen days after Narbrough became lieutenant.[3] It is possible that Shovell actually joined the *Prince* on January 15th, as Narbrough recorded in his journal, "this forenoon I was entered on board the Prince and eight seamen came with me".[4]

Narbrough as first lieutenant, and Shovell as a midshipman, were to serve together in the *Prince* for the next nine months. During this time Narbrough kept a detailed journal on a day-to-day basis that still exists, and can be seen in the Pepysian Library in Cambridge. Unfortunately Shovell is not mentioned by name in the journal. Rarely in any of his journals does Narbrough mention seamen below the rank of lieutenant, unless to report their deaths. However, the journal does show us the kind of life Shovell was exposed to, and the major action at Sole Bay in May 1672.

Earlier in this account, the close connection between Myngs, Narbrough and Shovell has been discussed. During February 1672 Narbrough regularly stayed with a Mr John Myngs on his visits to London. John Myngs is thought to have been the brother of Sir Christopher, with whom Narbrough certainly, and Shovell probably, had been, when he was mortally wounded during the Four Days Fight in 1666. John Myngs had been the surgeon in the *Gloucester* in 1664.[5]

Much of February and March 1672 was spent in getting the *Prince*, a 100 gun 1st rate, ready for sea firstly at Chatham and then at Blackstakes. March 20th saw Charles II with his brother the Duke of York and Prince

Rupert visit the *Prince*. By the beginning of April the *Prince* had all her stores aboard and was ready for sea. On April 2nd the Duke of York took up residence in the *Prince*, which he intended to use as his flagship for the summer's naval campaign. The *Prince* sailed past Sheerness and anchored at the buoy of the Nore, while the remainder of the fleet prepared for sea. The Duke of Monmouth was a visitor and Charles II slept on board the *Prince* for a night, in late April. Shovell, the 21-year-old new midshipman, must have been impressed by the presence of his King and his brother, the Lord High Admiral (the Duke of York). He was beginning the long climb up the naval hierarchical ladder, and it was a far cry from his relatively humble beginnings in Norfolk.[6]

De Ruijter and the Dutch fleet sailed from the Texel on April 30th, with the intention of surprising the English fleet or shutting them up in the Thames before they could join with their new allies, the French. Unfortunately for the Dutch, De Ruijter was delayed by the late arrival of the Zeeland fleet. By the time the two sections of the Dutch fleet had combined, giving them over forty ships, the English had vanished. Word had got back to the Duke of York of the intentions of the Dutch, and he set off with the English fleet for Portsmouth on May 2nd. The Duke sailed with his victualling still incomplete, hoping to find the French squadron which had left Brest to join him on April 30th.[7]

The Duke of York with Narbrough and Shovell, in the *Prince*, reached the Isle of Wight and anchored there on May 5th. The French under Jean D'Estrées joined them on May 7th. The plan was to attempt the annihilation of the Dutch fleet well away from their ports to which, previous experience had shown, they were wont to slink away if worsted, and thus avoid pursuit. Accordingly the Anglo/French fleet sailed towards the Gunfleet which was the supposed position of the Dutch. On May 19th the Dutch fleet were seen heading for their own coast and were followed by the Duke of York and D'Estrées. De Ruijter cunningly tried to trap his Anglo/French enemy on the shoals around his native coast. By this time the English were short of water and they sailed for Southwold.[8]

Narbrough wrote in his journal on May 21st, "We anchored in 16 fathom [of] water; the town of Southwold bore N.W. of us distance about three leagues." The next day the long boat was sent ashore for water. Perhaps Shovell went with her. If he did he would have known the town from previous visits during the Second Dutch War. On the 23rd Narbrough reported:

> We weighed with all the fleet and stores into Sole Bay and anchored in 8½ fathom water, the better to ride smooth, to take in our provisions. We rode about two miles from the shore side; the church of Southwold bore W.N.W. of us. This day many gentlemen of the fleet went ashore and many people of the shore came aboard our fleet.

40

The Duke of York's flagship, the *Prince*, and the rest of the red squadron were in the centre off Southwold. The Earl of Sandwich with the blue squadron was to the north off Covehithe, and D'Estrées' French squadron to the south off Dunwich and Aldeburgh. The Anglo/French ships continued with their revictualling having sent out frigates as scouts. Initially, the English were very much on guard against a sudden Dutch attack while they were close to their own coast, making movement difficult. Narbrough reported on May 26th, "We rode fast unmoored keeping a good watch for I expect the enemy will be with us in the morning if the wind hang easterly." The same day Captain Christopher Gunman, who was with Narbrough in the *Prince*, reported that "we received intelligence that the Dutch were gone off our coast over to their own". At a council of war in the *Prince*, on the 27th, the Duke of York ignored the Earl of Sandwich's opinion of the dangers of lying on a lee shore. Perhaps it was the intelligence of the previous day that made him relax his guard.[9]

Narbrough and his crew were up early on the morning of May 28th. At 2.00 a.m. Narbrough noted that the weather was fair and that the water was very smooth. Orders were given for the ship to be heeled and washed. At 3.30 a.m. guns were heard to the east and the wind was at the E.S.E. One of the English scouts was standing towards the *Prince* firing his guns, and astern of him about three leagues away was the Dutch fleet. Narbrough gave rapid orders for the *Prince* to be righted, and made ready to sail. He informed Sir John Cox and the Duke of York. The Duke presently came to the quarterdeck, and gave orders to sail which was done at 5.30 a.m.[10] The Battle of Sole Bay was about to begin.

De Ruijter's fleet bore down on the combined Anglo/French fleet from the E.N.E. They were divided into two divisions of line abreast. The leading division consisted of frigates and fireships, and the rear division of the main ships of war. De Ruijter himself commanded the centre, with Lieutenant Admiral Adriaen Bankers commanding on the left, and Lieutenant Admiral W.J.Van Ghent on the right. The Dutch fleet consisted of some seventy-five men of war and frigates, 4,484 guns and 20,738 men. The Anglo/French fleet was its superior with ninety-eight men of war and frigates, 6,018 guns and 34,496 men. The number of fireships on either side was roughly equal.[11]

The oncoming Dutch fleet must have been an awesome sight to Narbrough, Shovell and the crew of the *Prince*. The Earl of Sandwich's worst fears had been realised with an easterly wind, and the Dutch fleet catching them unprepared on the English coast. Sandwich with his blue squadron to the north off Covehithe were quick to react, cutting their cables and getting away to meet the Dutch right under Van Ghent. De Ruijter made for the red squadron off Southwold in the centre, where the Duke of York commanded in the *Prince*. Bankers isolated the French under

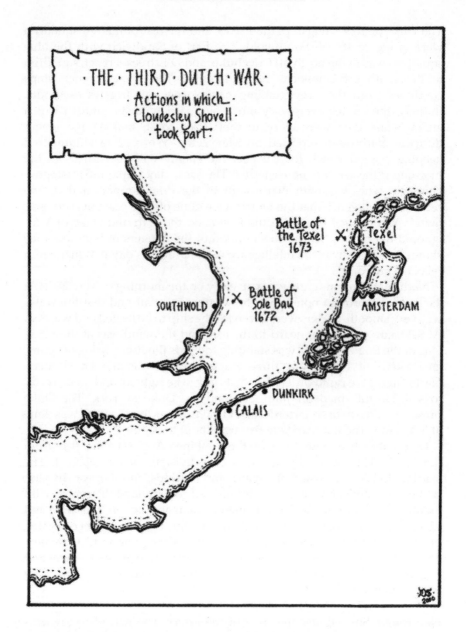

·THE·THIRD·DUTCH·WAR·
· Actions in which ·
· Cloudesley Shovell ·
· took part ·

Battle of
the Texel
1673     ✗     Texel

SOUTHWOLD •  ✗  Battle of
Sole Bay
1672

AMSTERDAM

• DUNKIRK
• CALAIS

D'Estrées to the south off Dunwich and Aldeburgh, keeping them at long cannon shot, and preventing them from joining the English. In fact doubt remains as to whether D'Estrées had secret orders from Louis XIV not to involve himself too much. In any event he was feuding with his second in command, Abraham Duquesne, which did not help matters. Duquesne, at

42

a later date, was to be responsible for the mortal wounding of the great De Ruijter, in a naval battle off Sicily.[12]

The Earl of Sandwich was in action in the *Royal James* at 7.00 a.m. An hour later the *Prince*, with the Duke of York, Narbrough and Shovell, was warmly engaged by De Ruijter himself in his favourite flagship, the *Zeven Provincien*. De Ruijter was supported by his seconds and others, making seven ships against the solitary *Prince*. The remainder of the red squadron was becalmed and unable to help their commander-in-chief. Despite their overwhelming local superiority, the Dutch were unable to board the *Prince* because of the speed at which the English were able to fire their guns. The Duke of York, showing no fear, went fore and aft in the *Prince* encouraging the men. He constantly ordered his ship to be luffed nearer the enemy. To quote Narbrough on the subject of the Duke:

> I do absolutely believe no Prince upon the whole earth can compare with his Royal Highness in gallant resolution in fighting his enemy, and with so great conduct and knowledge in navigation as never any General understood before him. He is better acquainted in these seas than many Masters which are now in his fleet; he is General, Soldier, Pilot, Master, Seaman; to say all, he is everything that man can be, and most pleasant when the great shots are thundering about his ears.[13]

Allowing for the fact that Narbrough guessed that the Duke would read his journal at a later date, he was too much of a professional to give undue praise.[14] No doubt the Duke's courage and skill would have impressed the lowly midshipman, Shovell, whose views about him were to change radically at the time of the Glorious Revolution, some sixteen years later.

Between 9.00 a.m. and 10.00 a.m. the Captain of the *Prince*, the newly knighted Sir John Cox, was killed by a great shot while standing close by the Duke of York on the poop deck. Several other gentlemen were slain on either side of the Duke on the poop and quarterdecks. After Cox's death Narbrough found himself in command of the *Prince*, and endeavoured to get the ship by the Duke's instructions to the windward of the enemy. During the next hour or two the masts and rigging of the *Prince* became progressively more damaged. The main top mast was shot off, falling on the deck, and stopping the use of the main sail. The damaged rigging prevented the upper gun deck from being used and the shot flew so thick that men were unable to repair the rigging and sails. To quote Narbrough's journal again:

> . . . our great guns plying all this time as fast as our seamen could load and fire at the enemy's men of war and fireships; the enemy shooting as fast at us, killing and wounding our men very briskly and slapping the ship's sides and rigging.

The *Prince* was all alone facing this ferocious Dutch onslaught. To make matters worse the Dutch towed two fireships towards them. Narbrough ordered his two boats to tow the *Prince* away from the Dutch towards the north, and their own ships. About this time the Duke of York, realising that his ship was so disabled, took his standard in a boat to the *St Michael* where Sir Robert Holmes was in command.

Soon after the Duke of York had left the *Prince*, the Dutch ceased firing at them. Between 12.00 noon and 1.00 p.m. Narbrough got the *Prince* onto the other tack, and they sailed southwards having got up as far as Lowestoft. The wind had changed to the E.N.E., and Narbrough fired intermittently at the Dutch. There was great confusion, and this was added to by smoke that made visualisation of land and ships difficult. Between 3.00 and 4.00 p.m. the *Prince* passed the burnt out flagship of the Earl of Sandwich, the *Royal James*. The *Royal James* was anchored with her head to the S.b.E. and was still lightly on fire with the burnt yards and booms dropped from her. Sandwich was drowned trying to escape the fire in his boat that had become overloaded.[15]

Narbrough tried to join the Duke of York who had had to change ships yet again. As the *St Michael* became disabled, he boarded the *London*. The battle continued into the evening, and at about 8.00 p.m. Narbrough was joined by Sir John Harman and Sir John Kempthorne with about thirty ships of their squadrons. In the late evening the Dutch set their sails and stood to the south-east and their own coast.[16]

Further contact was made with the Dutch fleet on May 29th, but fog prevented any action. By the 31st the Dutch were back on their own coast, and the Anglo/French fleet returned to Sole Bay on June 1st.[17]

The losses on both sides were heavy in men. Although each side claimed a victory, the Battle of Sole Bay was in reality a draw. The Anglo/French fleet held the field and made a prize. The Dutch had achieved their objective of stopping allied co-operation in the Netherlands.[18]

The Anglo/French fleet made for the Gunfleet, which was reached on June 3rd. Much of June was taken up with repairs to the men of war. The sails of the *Prince* were repaired at Sheerness. On June 18th the Duke of York, who had by now returned to the *Prince,* entertained his brother, Charles II, and the Queen. Narborough wrote:

> At seven o'clock the King and Queen came aboard the Prince and several of the nobility. His Royal Highness received them with a bountiful entertainment having all the colours and pendants flying at the yard arms, the Standard at the main top mast head, the Anchor-standard at the fore-topmast head, and the Union flag at the mizzen top mast head.[19]

The *Prince* must have been a spectacular sight. That night the Queen slept alone on the *Prince* and the King on his own yacht!

By the end of June 1672 the Anglo/French fleet was ready for further action against the Dutch. The Battle of Sole Bay had delayed but not stopped the Allied fleets from crossing to co-operate with the French in the Netherlands. Troops were actually transported across the North Sea (the North Channel of the time) in late June, but De Ruijter cunningly watched from amongst the shoals around the Dutch coast, and could not be tempted out. The Anglo/French fleet first blockaded the coast, and then made preparations for a landing on the Island of Texel on July 4th. A storm put an end to this and the project was dropped.[20]

During July and August, when the events described in the preceding paragraph were taking place, the Duke of York commanded the fleet from the *Prince* with Narbrough as captain and Shovell remaining as the lowly midshipman. The entries in Narbrough's journal for July and August 1672 in the main concern the bad weather, provisions and the sickness of the men. On August 1st the sailors were selling haddock, whitings, codlings and gurnets to the Duke's gentlemen for 5d the piece. For August 23rd Narbrough wrote, "This afternoon I put ashore out of the Prince 101 men sick on the Kings account, most of them having the scurvy. This day went out of our fleet above a thousand men sick, the major part having the scurvy." By this time they had returned to the buoy of the Nore. Even for a voyage of a month or two scurvy was an enormous problem in the seventeenth century navy. On August 31st the fleet were supplied with 3,950 cabbages, 21½ buckets of carrots, 15 dozen and nine bunches of turnips, and fresh meat to refresh the men.[21]

By mid September it was time to lay up the great ships (1st and 2nd rates) for the winter. On September 11th Narbrough was ordered to put 230 men out of the *Prince* into the smaller *Fairfax*. Narbrough went aboard the *Fairfax* for the first time on the 15th, taking some men with him. Further men were turned over from the *Prince* to the *Fairfax* on the 16th, and 210 men mostly as volunteers on the 17th. In the Public Record Office there are records to show that Narbrough and Shovell went as volunteers from the *Prince* to the *Fairfax* on September 17th 1672. This time Shovell was a master's mate.[22] On September 18th Narbrough received his commission to command the *Fairfax*, a 52–80 gun ship. The same day D'Estrées weighed and sailed for France with his French squadron.[23]

Narbrough's commission from the Duke of York to command the *Fairfax* enabled him to take part in Sir Edward Spragge's expedition into the North Sea. Little seems to have happened except their interference with the Dutch herring fleet. The *Fairfax* took a dogger, the *Maasland Sluis*, from Holland, fourteen leagues east of Southwold on September 22nd. The dogger had the correct pass and was freed by Spragge. Further small Dutch ships, the *Katharine* and the *Young Tobias*, were chased and taken by

Narbrough in late September. In mid October the *Fairfax* became separated from the *Resolution*, which was Spragge's flagship, and Narbrough returned to the buoy of the Nore, anchoring there on October 13th. Spragge was already there, and he gave Narbrough the post of commander-in-chief at the buoy.

In mid November 1672 Narbrough, still in the *Fairfax* with Shovell as master's mate, was ordered to the Downs by the Duke of York, to take a convoy of merchantmen to the Mediterranean. The Duke's orders were signed on November 15th, and reached Narbrough on the 25th. Narbrough left the Downs on November 30th, having collected about 100 sail and sailed down the English Channel, then known as the West Channel. The weather was bad and they overshot Plymouth, where there were more merchant ships to be collected, but sent word to them overland from Falmouth. Leaving Falmouth they were forced back into Plymouth, and it was not until the New Year that they were able to get away.[24]

Narbrough sailed from Plymouth on January 15th 1673 for the Mediterranean. By this time his convoy had been reduced in number to eighty-five sail. Various ships left for Oporto, and on January 26th Narbrough saw the *Sandadoes* and six merchant ships into Lisbon without actually anchoring there. By the 29th they were off Lagos, and a tartan brought out a letter from Sir Martin Westcombe, Consul at Cadiz, informing Narbrough of the presence of seven Dutch men of war on the coast. This was the same Consul Westcombe whose advice Shovell was to seek nearly ten years later (1683), in his difficulties with Matthew Aylmer in being made to salute the Spanish flag. On February 1st Narbrough took merchant ships into Cadiz. A further twenty-five ships ignored Narbrough, and headed directly for the Straits of Gibraltar. He had intended to sail for Tangier, but the wind prevented him from getting there, and he was forced to anchor before Cadiz. A council of war decided to send the Smyrna and Scanderoon ships onto their destinations. To this end Narbrough escorted his fleet to the mouth of the Straits before getting into Tangier Roads on February 6th. This was to be Shovell's first view of the mole that he would use for the next ten years, and involve him in controversy over its final destruction.[25]

The stay in Tangier Roads seems to have been a pleasant one. On the 7th the sea officers dined at the Earl of Middleton's, and were entertained in the evening with a ball. All the ladies in the city and persons of quality were there. This sounded to be a much more refined affair than the bawdy house that Arthur Herbert was to keep there, when in command in the Mediterranean between 1679 and 1683. One may be certain that Shovell, the lowly master's mate, did not attend the Earl of Middleton's Ball.

Leaving Tangier Narbrough returned to Cadiz. When he arrived on February 10th 1673, Consul Westcombe informed him that the seven Dutch men of war had gone out wearing Dutch colours (they were in

Spanish service) two days before. The *Tiger*, an English ship accompanying the *Fairfax*, had a damaged bowsprit. Consul Westcombe managed to buy a new one, costing 446 pieces of eight, from the Dutch consul of all people. On March 4th Narbrough left Cadiz and sailed to the westward with twenty sail of English ships, two French and two Spanish merchant ships. However, on the 12th they were forced back to Cadiz.[26]

On his return to Cadiz, Narbrough was persuaded by the Consul and merchants that he should join his ships to those of a Captain Robinson at Malaga, for fear that the Dutch would destroy the latter's vessels. A message was sent to Robinson, whose small fleet arrived at Cadiz, on March 29th. Robinson and Narbrough agreed to sail together, and they left Cadiz between April 3rd and 5th. By April 17th they were off Lagos with the Governor allowing them ashore for water. A little later, on April 21st, Robinson was becoming difficult and threatening to sail straight for England without going to Lisbon. Narbrough was able to placate his fit of pique by suggesting that they took it in turns, twenty-four hours about, in leading the convoy. It all seems a little petty. The voyage to Lisbon continued uneventfully with about eighty-six sail in all. About this time Narbrough had the gunner and carpenter of the *Thomas and Edward* fireship ducked at the *Fairfax*'s yardarm for bringing a black from the shore.[27]

From Lisbon the convoy proceeded in the direction of the Soundings where a near disaster was to take place. On May 21st four small ships left the convoy bound for Bristol, Ireland and Glasgow. Narbrough in his journal wrote:

> I feared the wind to be northerly and that it would blow so I could not fetch Plymouth (and this) caused me to keep so northerly a course tonight, reckoning we were shot to the eastward of Scilly Islands.

It has been suggested that this sentence may have been written after the difficulties of the next night.[28] The following day, May 22nd 1673, Narbrough recorded in his journal:

> Hazy cloudy weather this morning at 1 o'clock and rain; the wind at S.W., a fine small gale. We steered E. by N. Between one and two this morning it blew a fresh gale and rained.

Later he continued:

> At 2 o'clock this morning we saw false fires to the eastward of me; we answered them again with false fires and a musket. At a quarter of an hour past 2 o'clock this morning we saw a breach of rocks by us on

our larboard side; several vessels ahead of us and on our larboard side did not see it. I caused the ship to be put a-stay, setting our after sails, and 2 guns to be fired, and to show as many lights as we could, that the fleet might take notice of it and look out. I saw the ship did stay, and it fell little wind, and the tide set the ship within the breach to the northward; we also saw the breach of several other rocks ahead. I immediately let go the best bower anchor and brought the ship up and rode fast until daylight, that we might see about us where we rode.

The ships that were ahead of Narbrough plied around him until daylight, and then stood out N.W. into the sea. The ships astern of the *Fairfax* tacked when they heard the guns and stood off. To his horror Narbrough found that:

after it was daylight, that I could see round about me, I saw that we were entangled with rocks called the Bishop and Clerks. The windmills on St Mary's Island I saw plain; they bore N.E.b.E. from me. I was right before Broad Sound. I saw several breaches of rocks about a quarter of a mile within me, and but one rock without me, about 2 cables length from me S.W. I saw it was clear of rocks to N.W. and the open sea, and the ships that were got within the breach, as I was, stood out that way. I caused a hauser to be passed out at the gun-room port and forward and bent to the cable and roused it taut and veered out the cable, to cast the ship the right way. When the ship was cast and the sails full, we cut the cable and stood out N.W. into the sea until I was got off the rocks out of danger.[29]

Narbrough attributed this near catastrophe to a number of factors. Firstly, a great indraught of a current set into the River Severn and St George's Channel. Secondly, when they neared the Scilly Islands a flood tide set them to the northward. Thirdly, the constant changing of course to bring in lagging ships made it difficult to give a good account of the actual course followed. Fourthly, they reckoned that they were clear of the Scilly Islands. Fifthly, "the current that do set northerly". Sixthly, variable soundings. Jennifer of the *Sandadoes*, which had accompanied Narbrough and the *Fairfax*, described him as an ingenious navigator who in a great measure could be excused for his compasses were found afterwards to be half pointed. In addition, others who stated that they were to the east of Scilly had overruled him the day before. He went on, that in his experience one always got further north than one's reckoning, in coming into the Channel from the south.[30]

Although no ships were lost on May 22nd 1673, it was by luck rather than good judgement. This near disaster has been looked at in detail because Shovell was the master's mate of the *Fairfax*, and thirty-four years later he was to be Commander-in-Chief of the English fleet returning from the Mediterranean, which made a similar mistake. On this second occasion, on October 22nd 1707, three major men of war plus several other lesser ships went down, and Shovell himself lost his life. He had not learnt from this early lesson.

The fortunate fleet got into Plymouth on May 27th. On the 30th Narbrough anchored in the Downs. No doubt, the most relieved of all to see him safely returned were the English merchants, as the men of war were carrying nearly two million pieces of eight and some silver.[31] Early in June 1673 Narbrough travelled to Whitehall, and kissed the hands of Charles II and the Duke of York.[32]

The four months Narbrough had been away on convoy duties had been eventful ones at home. In March 1673 the Test Act had been passed which deprived the Duke of York of the post of Lord High Admiral.[33] No new Lord High Admiral was appointed, but Prince Rupert was put in charge of the fleet. The Anglo/French strategy, in the summer of 1673, was to bring the Dutch fleet to action and destroy it, before landing troops on the coast of Holland. If the Dutch fleet refused action then they were to be blockaded, prior to a descent on their coast.[34]

The Dutch were in a vulnerable position, and with Michiel De Ruijter again in command of their fleet, proposed to stop the junction of the English and French contingents. This had been his aim in 1672. In 1673 De Ruijter planned to block the exit channels of the Thames by sinking ships full of rocks. Rupert may have got wind of his plans, for on May 2nd he sailed with all his available ships from the Thames.[35] When De Ruijter arrived at the channels on the 4th, he found Rupert in place and withdrew. In mid May Rupert's ships joined the French under D'Estrées and English vessels from Portsmouth off Rye. On May 28th the combined Anglo/French fleet under Rupert moved in to attack De Ruijter's fleet, at anchor at Schooneveld. De Ruijter came out and fell upon Rupert with remarkable speed. After an inconclusive battle the two fleets parted. This was the first Battle of the Schooneveld. The second Battle of the Schooneveld took place on June 4th, when De Ruijter, taking advantage of a favourable wind, came out and inflicted considerable damage on the Allied fleet, before returning with consummate timing to his anchorage. Despite the damage done to the Anglo/French fleet, the result was again inconclusive.[36]

Both Narbrough and Shovell missed the two battles of the Schooneveld because of their late return from Tangier. It has been suggested that Narbrough's fortunate escape, on the Bishop and Clerk rocks, had happened because he was pressing to get home for the summer's campaign.[37] Following the first Battle of the Schooneveld, Prince Rupert wrote home asking for Narbrough's ships to join him.[38]

On June 29th Thomas Butler, Earl of Ossory, the eldest son of the Duke of Ormonde, brought Narbrough an order from Prince Rupert, to be his senior captain in the *St Michael*. The commission had been signed by Rupert on the 28th.[39] It must have been galling to Narbrough not to have an independent command, despite the fact that Ossory, who was Rear Admiral of the Blue, was an indulgent superior. According to a pamphlet printed in 1673 Narbrough was unlucky not to be Rear Admiral of the Blue himself.

> The appointment of Rear Admiral of the Blue was Captain Narbrough who being absent in the Straits, came not in till after the two first engagements; which otherwise might have occasioned some competition among the officers of the fleet for that place: For, though he was a good seaman, yet there were many others in the fleet that were of better merit, and longer service; and the offence that must have been given to others, had he enjoyed it, was taken off by putting a person of so great quality as my Lord Ossory into the place.[40]

Narbrough took up his new command on July 1st.

> This day I took command of eldest captain on board his Majesty's ship St. Michael, the Earl of Ossory on board her, Rear Admiral of the Blue Squadron. I carried with me out of the Fairfax 176 men and boys volunteers into the St. Michael, the St. Michael being badly manned having 520 seamen, soldiers, and trounsers*.

Among the 176 men joining the *St Michael* that day was the master's mate of the *Fairfax*, one Cloudesley Shovell by name. At this time, wherever John Narbrough went, Shovell was not far behind.[41]

Narbrough spent early July getting the *St Michael* provisioned and ready for sea. On the 7th Narbrough sent his Lieutenant, James Watts, in the ketch to Chatham to get water and men. The next day he gave the Admiral of the Blue, Sir Edward Spragge, an account of his squadron.[42]

July 17th saw the fleet, under Prince Rupert, plus the French contingent weigh anchor and make for the Gunfleet. Narbrough reported at this time that there were 105 English/French ships of above 40 cannon a ship, thirty-eight fireships, and sixty odd ketches, hoys, tenders, in all about 200 sail and 28,000 men. The next day the *Greyhound* frigate came in with M. Schomberg, the General of the land forces. Unfortunately the *Greyhound* failed to salute Prince Rupert, and he fired at it for their trouble! The Captain was then put in irons for flying the St George flag at the main top mast head.

The fleet sailed soon after and on the 19th were off Southwold, where Narbrough reported that he was very sick. Possibly this was sea sickness,

Trounser is a useless member of the crew.[43]

and is the only mention of Narbrough's own health in any of his journals. Prince Rupert took them over to the Dutch coast, where De Ruijter's fleet were spotted on the 21st, off Walchen. The following day Spragge and his blue squadron became separated from the main fleet by a league. The Dutch bore down on them. Ossory sent his Lieutenant, Henry Carveth, over to Spragge to find out if he should keep his wind or bear away to the English fleet. Sir Edward told him to bear away towards the English fleet before him, but would not put it in writing. The St Michael bore away towards the protection of Rupert's main fleet.[44]

During late July and early August the fleet sailed off the Dutch coast. They came within two leagues of the shore before Scheveningen and the steeples of Delft and The Hague could clearly be seen. Later, they were off Texel Island and then Vlie Island, before on August 7th it was reported that the Dutch fleet were only seven leagues away off Camperdown. On the 9th the Dutch were seen about four leagues south of Prince Rupert, and the next day they were plainly visible from the St Michael's main top, near Texel Island. The line of battle was drawn up with the French in the van, Rupert in the centre with the red squadron, and the rear brought up by the blue squadron. The St Michael with Narbrough and Shovell was of course with the blue squadron under Spragge. The Anglo/French contingent bore down on the Dutch, who shot ahead avoiding battle for that day.[45]

At daybreak on August 11th 1673 the final major encounter of the Third Dutch War, the Battle of Texel or Kijkduin, began. During the night the wind had shifted to the E.S.E., giving the Dutch the weather gauge. Narbrough thought the Dutch fleet consisted of about eighty-eight major ships, and his own fleet of about ninety. Laird Clowes shows a much greater disparity in favour of the Allies of ninety-two to seventy-five. The mouth of the Texel was about three leagues away.

As on the previous day, Rupert was in the centre, with the French in the van, and Spragge's squadron in the rear. De Ruijter had also organised his fleet into three squadrons, but unlike the Allies not into equal numbers. Bankers, in the Dutch van, was sent to bottle up the French under D'Estrées with only ten to twelve ships, a move that he had carried out with such success the previous year at Sole Bay. De Ruijter in the centre with thirty-two to thirty-three ships would take on Rupert, and Cornelis Tromp with the same number of ships the rear under Spragge. By isolating the French, De Ruijter would have a local superiority over the English by about sixty-five ships to sixty-two.

Early in the morning, at first light, the Dutch with the advantage of the wind bore down on the Allies with both fleets pointing into the shore. Rupert, while engaging De Ruijter, tried to draw the Dutch away from their coast, which led to a gap developing with his own van and rear squadrons. D'Estrées with his French force made no attempt to join his

Commander-in-Chief, Prince Rupert, and Spragge was settling into a private battle with Tromp, by heaving to and waiting for him.

Spragge had his blue squadron subdivided into three divisions. Ahead of him was Lord Ossory, Rear Admiral of the Blue, in the *St Michael*. Behind him was Sir John Kempthorne, Vice Admiral of the Blue, in the *St Andrew*. Spragge himself occupied the centre in the *Prince*.

At about 7.30 a.m. Kempthorne was the first of the blue squadron to go into action against Vice Admiral Sweers on the *Olifant*. A little later Spragge fired on Tromp in the *Gouden Leeuw*. Narbrough reported that the *St Michael* came within fair gun shot at 8.00 a.m. He saluted the Dutch with trumpets and three hollows before firing began. Their immediate opponent was Rear Admiral N.A. De Haen, in the *Hollandia*. It was battle according to strict etiquette.[46]

In the extreme rear Sweers got the better of Kempthorne, forcing his division to leeward. However Ossory more than held his own against De Haen. Narbrough noted that the Dutch shooting was both faster and more accurate than the English. Spragge and Tromp fought fiercely for more than three hours with the *Prince* suffering the greater damage.[47] Sir Edward Spragge and Cornelis Tromp were men of a kindred spirit, brave, rash and insubordinate. They had fought each other before, and it had been reported that Spragge had vowed to sink Tromp or be killed in the attempt. Both men appeared to revel in personal conflict.[48]

Between 12.00 noon and 1.00 p.m. the wind swung to the S.W., a fine fresh gale. The Dutch were now to the leeward, and Narbrough was unable to see either Prince Rupert in the centre or D'Estrées in the van. About 1.00 p.m. Spragge sent his lieutenant across from the *Prince* to the *St Michael* to find out what Lord Ossory intended to do. Ossory confirmed that the *St Michael* would stay with Spragge. Shortly afterwards, Spragge was forced to remove his flag to the *St George*, as the *Prince* had become disabled by the battering she had taken from eight or nine Dutch ships.[49]

Later, Narbrough was sent by Ossory across to the *St George* to suggest to Spragge that they board the enemy. It was agreed that the *St Michael* should attempt to board Tromp in the *Gouden Leeuw*, and that the *St George* would second the attempt. However, the plan came to nothing as Tromp bore away, and Spragge failed to give support. Between 1.00 and 2.00 p.m. the *St George* also became disabled, and Spragge attempted to remove to a third ship, the *Royal Charles*. The boat he was using had got no farther than ten boat lengths, when a round shot went through the *St George* and hit the boat. They rowed frantically back to the *St George*, but the boat sank before they came within the throw of a rope, and Spragge was drowned. He was taken up dead, his head and shoulders above the water, having taken such a firm hold to the side of the boat in death, that they could hardly disengage him from it. Two others died with him but his lieutenant survived. Spragge probably died of hypothermia rather than drowning.[50]

The crew of the *St Michael* witnessed the sinking of Spragge's boat astern of the *St George*, although they were unaware at the time that he was on it. Later the fact that the blue flag was not put up again on another ship must have made them realise that Spragge was dead.

The private battle of the blue squadron raged during the afternoon with the Dutch set on taking or destroying Spragge's former flagship, the *Prince*. A stout defence was put up by Kempthorne and in particular Ossory. Tromp was forced to leave the *Gouden Leeuw*, as she was in danger of losing her masts and unfit to continue the fighting. The *Komeetster* was Tromp's choice as a new flagship, and he continued his attempts on the *Prince* from her.

Rupert in the centre had had a difficult day with De Ruijter, and particularly so when Bankers was able to leave the reluctant French in the van and support his Commander-in-Chief. At about 5.00 p.m. Narbrough, in the *St Michael,* saw a large body of ships approaching alone, which he first thought to be the main English fleet. As they came closer he realised that it was indeed the main English fleet, but that they were accompanied by a large Dutch contingent, although they were not firing at each other.[51]

By the time Rupert arrived, at 5.00 p.m., Narbrough felt that the blue squadron had got the better of Tromp's squadron. Tromp did not agree with this view, feeling that the English would have been overwhelmed if Rupert had not made a timely entrance. The *Prince* was taken in tow by two frigates and Ossory supported them. Rupert gave the signal for all the allied ships to follow in his wake, which was ignored or not understood by the French. Narbrough reported that it was between 7.00 and 8.00 p.m. before the *St Michael* was able to join the main fleet. A little later, the two sides separated, much to Narbrough's chagrin, as the Allies held the weather gauge. At midnight the Anglo/French fleet were nine leagues from the Texel.

The Battle of Texel was over. Yet again the result was inconclusive. However, the Allies had failed to destroy the Dutch fleet which was necessary before a landing could be effected on the Dutch coast. The Dutch had succeeded in holding their own and still had a fleet in being. Their objective of preventing an invasion of their coast had been achieved.

Although, on August 13th, a resolution was made to sail to Scheveningen, nothing came of it and the Anglo/French fleet returned to Southwold, on the 22nd, and by the 24th were anchored in the Gunfleet. The *St Michael* was taken into Chatham by Narbrough, on Prince Rupert's orders, on September 9th. The same day Narbrough witnessed Rupert's prickly attitude to correct protocol. "This day a Dane's ship came up with a black flag at his main top mast head; he had our Duke of Richmond's corpse in. When he came near our General shot at him; he struck his flag and plied up."[52] Charles Stuart, Duke of Richmond had been sent to Denmark in 1671, and had died there in 1672. Not even the dead were excused the correct salute!

The Earl of Ossory was promoted to be Vice Admiral of the Red over Sir John Kempthorne, and on September 19th John Narbrough at last reached flag rank as Rear Admiral of the Red.[53] He was knighted on September 30th 1673.

Although the Third Dutch War was to officially drag on into 1674, until the Treaty of Westminster was signed, in practice it ended at the Texel. Cloudesley Shovell had spent the war in lowly ranks, but he had served a tough apprenticeship in naval battle against the likes of De Ruijter and Tromp. The experience would stand him in good stead for over thirty years.

Narbrough received a commission on September 12th 1673 to command the 50–62 gun *Henrietta*.[54] The commission had been signed by Prince Rupert. Narbrough went aboard the *Henrietta* on September 29th and prepared her for sea. One of his first actions as Commander was to persuade the Admiralty that Shovell should be made a lieutenant under him. Samuel Pepys wrote to Narbrough, on September 23rd, promising to speak for Shovell as Lieutenant of the *Henrietta*.[55] He must have been successful for on that very day Shovell was made the *Henrietta*'s Second-Lieutenant.[56] It is interesting to note that Shovell owed his first commission as an officer, at least in part, to Samuel Pepys. Pepys looked on Narbrough as one of the most able naval men of his day, but he did not have the same high opinion of Shovell as will be seen later in this account.

Narbrough and Shovell were to spend the autumn of 1673 protecting shipping in the Channel. Pepys wrote to Narbrough on November 11th, informing him of the King's satisfaction that the coast had been cleared of privateers, and that Narbrough could bring in his four ships as soon as the merchant ships from Smyrna had arrived. Two days later they arrived at Plymouth and were escorted by Narbrough safely to the Downs. Narbrough's squadron was then brought in for refitting.[57]

The year 1674 opened with Narbrough and Shovell still in the *Henrietta* in the River Thames with the other ships of the squadron. By January 17th they had moved to the Downs, and on March 3rd Narbrough reported to Pepys of his retaking an English ship from the people of Terceras (Azores). The signing of the Treaty of Westminster, on February 9th 1674, brought formally to an end the Third Dutch War, and led to a lower level of naval activity. Narbrough and Shovell spent the summer of 1674 in the Channel and its ports.[58] In June Charles II and Pepys came on board the *Henrietta* at Spithead.[59]

NOTES

1. Richmond, pp.168–171; Laird Clowes, pp.298–299.
2. ADM 33/121, *Sweepstakes*.
3. ADM 33/103 ticket No 55; Le Fevre, M.M. 1984.
4. Pepysian MSS 2555, Journal J.N., *Prince*.
5. Journal J.N., *Prince*; C.S.P. Dom. 1663–4 p.595.
6. Journal J.N., *Prince*.
7. Richmond, pp.172–173.
8. Journal J.N., *Prince*; Richmond pp.173–174.
9. Pepysian MSS 2555, Journal J.N., *Prince*, Journal Gunman, *Prince*; Laird Clowes, p.302.
10. Journal J.N., *Prince*.
11. Laird Clowes, pp.301–303.
12. Laird Clowes, p.303.
13. Journal J.N., *Prince*.
14. Dyer, p.115.
15. Laird Clowes, p.306.
16. Journal J.N., *Prince*.
17. Journal J.N., *Prince*.
18. Laird Clowes, p.307.
19. Journal J.N., *Prince*.
20. Laird Clowes, p.309.
21. Journal J.N., *Prince*.
22. ADM 33/91, Ticket 1076; Le Fevre, M.M.1984.
23. Journal J.N., *Prince*.
24. Pepysian MSS 2556, Journal J.N., *Fairfax*.
25. Journal J.N., *Fairfax*.
26. Journal J.N., *Fairfax*.
27. Journal J.N., *Fairfax*.
28. Journals and Narratives of the Third Dutch War p.285.
29. Journal J.N., *Fairfax*.
30. Journals and Narratives of the Third Dutch War p.287.
31. C.S.P. Dom. 1673 p.297.
32. Journal J.N., *Fairfax*.
33. C.S.P. Dom. 1673 p.175.
34. Laird Clowes, pp.309–310.
35. Corbett, A note of the drawings . . . of the battle of Sole Bay and the Texel p.30.
36. Richmond, pp.181–183.
37. Dyer, p.119.
38. C.S.P. Dom., Car II, No 261.
39. Journal J.N., *Fairfax*.
40. An Exact Relation of Several Engagements. Anno 1673.
41. ADM 33/104, Ticket No. 1398; Le Fevre, M.M. 1984.
42. Journal J.N., *St. Michael*.
43. Pepysian MSS 2556, Journal J.N., *St. Michael*.
44. Journal J.N., *St. Michael*.
45. Journal J.N., *St. Michael*.
46. Journals and Narratives of the Third Dutch War pp.50–51, pp.392–394.
47. Journals and Narratives of the Third Dutch War pp.50–51.
48. Dyer, p.128; Laird Clowes, p.310.
49. Journal J.N., *St. Michael*.
50. Journal J.N., *St. Michael*; Journals and Narratives of the Third Dutch War.

51.  Journal J.N., *St. Michael.*
52.  Journal J.N., *St. Michael.*
53.  Journal J.N., *St. Michael.*
54.  Journal J.N., *St. Michael*; Anderson, Lists of Men of War.
55.  Tanner, Pepysian MSS, Vol. II, p.66.
56.  ADM 33/98, Ticket No. 680.
57.  Tanner, Pepysian MSS, Vol. II, pp.120–154.
58.  Tanner, Pepysian MSS, Vol. II, pp. 221–299.
59.  Bryant, The Years of Peril p.137.

# CHAPTER VI
# The Burning of the Tripoli Ships
# 1674–1676

On September 21st 1674 Samuel Pepys wrote to Narbrough asking him about the condition of his ship, as there was trouble brewing with Algiers. Sir Edward Spragge had signed a peace treaty with the Algerians in 1671, and it was the custom to have a general redemption of slaves when a peace was proclaimed. This had not happened and the Algerians had become impatient, insisting that money and ships must be provided by the following November 30th. Narbrough must have known about the problem, as he had received a packet containing a letter for Charles II from an Algerian man of war. Four days later, on the 25th, Pepys ordered Narbrough to Portsmouth to refit for a four-month voyage to the Straits. Initially it was envisaged that he would go alone, and pick up the money for the redemption of slaves at Cadiz. Later the *Cambridge, Mary Rose, Bristol* and *Roebuck* joined the *Henrietta* to make up a small squadron under Narbrough's command.[1]

On October 18th Narbrough received his sailing orders and final instructions from Charles II. He was appointed Commander-in-Chief for the expedition with the rank of Commodore, although he had already served as a rear admiral. On reaching Algiers, he was to redeem the slaves before going on to Tunis and Tripoli to ratify peace treaties. As was necessary in dealing with the Barbary states, Narbrough had £400 to divide equally between the people of Tunis and Tripoli. The £400 was officially described as presents, but in fact was to be used as a bribe to the various advisers of the Dey, in order that any business could take place at all.[2]

Narbrough's squadron with Shovell, the new Second Lieutenant in the *Henrietta*, reached Algiers on December 8th, a little later than the deadline of November 30th, having put into Cadiz to collect the money needed for the redemption of slaves. In case Narbrough was delayed, Pepys had sent an express overland to Marseilles for the *Deptford ketch* that was stationed there, to take a message across the Mediterranean to Algiers to the effect that Narbrough was on the way. Unfortunately, when the express reached Marseilles, the *Deptford ketch* had gone on a private trip to Livorno, and had been wrecked. The captain who had disobeyed orders was not employed again. On arrival in Algiers, the beauty of the place would have impressed Shovell and Narbrough, with its country houses as white as chalk on either side of the town, and vineyards abounding in all kinds of fruit and vegetables. Oranges and lemons had only recently been planted, but they grew so abundantly that sixty could be bought for a royal. Although it was near Christmas, apples, cauliflowers, roses and carnations were available. No doubt the fruit kept the scurvy at bay after the voyage out to the Mediterranean.[3]

Narbrough was assisted in his negotiations with the Dey at Algiers by the Consul, Samuel Martin, and by Judge Advocate General Brisbane. Martin lived in Algiers and Brisbane had come out to the Mediterranean with Narbrough from England. By January 1675 some 189 English captives had been redeemed at a cost of $56,248 or pieces of eight. Other captives taken on foreign vessels were liberated with money collected by the crews of the English squadron. The Algerian government sent a letter to Charles II concluding a peace, which, as was customary with them, was perpetual and inviolable, or at least until the next richly laden merchant ship should fall into their hands![4]

Shovell played a part in the redemption of the English slaves by assisting the joint commissioners, Narbrough, Brisbane and Martin. For his services he was awarded $100 or pieces of eight. No doubt it was a welcome bounty for him.[5]

Having successfully completed his business at Algiers, Narbrough took his squadron on to Tunis where the peace treaty was ratified. Narbrough wrote to Charles II on March 16th 1675, stating that he had confirmed the late treaty and was leaving for Tripoli.[6]

While Narbrough's squadron was sailing to Algiers, Pepys had written to him to the effect that the Turkey merchants had complained of two of their ships being forced into Tripoli. The two ships, the *Martin* and the *Hunter*, had on board a valuable cargo worth £30,000. The Dey of Tripoli argued that, since their change of government, no letter had been received from Charles II, and that they were uncertain whether the treaty with England was in force or not. Pepys instructed Narbrough to insist on the return of the ships and that they ratify the treaty. It was feared that if the Dey of Tripoli was allowed to get away with this hostile act, it would give ideas to Tunis and Algiers.[7]

In early April Narbrough reached Tripoli and put before the Dey the demands of the English government. They were the restitution of all

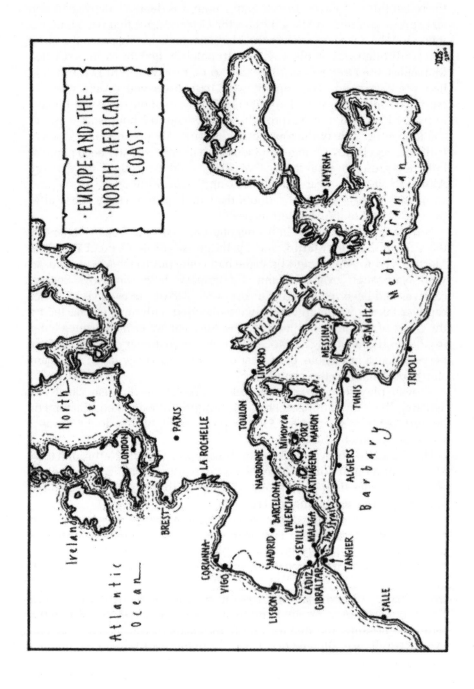

goods, release of all prisoners, and the return of the *Hunter* and the *Martin*. Narbrough was rebuffed and proceeded to blockade Tripoli, and destroy any of the Dey's shipping that he came into contact with. Even before Narbrough reached Tripoli, all English ships in the Mediterranean were ordered to join him, as it was thought that the Dey would prove obstinate. The blockade would go on for almost a year and Narbrough required a base for his ships. In the first instance he chose Livorno and the squadron attempted to revictual there. The local inhabitants were not helpful, and Narbrough then selected Malta for his base, with the approval of Charles II. Finding a new base was not the only problem Narbrough had at this time. The ironwork of his ship, the *Henrietta*, was noted to be rusty, which he thought was due to the new sheathing of her. In mid April 1675 Pepys ordered the *Harwich* out to the Mediterranean to replace the *Henrietta*. The *Harwich* was to be the ship on which Narbrough's young Second Lieutenant, Cloudesley Shovell, was to find fame.[8]

Early in May the Dey of Tripoli died and the English government thought it a suitable moment to soften its demands. Narbrough was told that the return of the cargoes from the *Hunter* and the *Martin* was no longer essential, but that all slaves, whether English or foreign, were to be released. Additionally a few heads should roll! Unfortunately for Narbrough, the new Dey had commanded the corsair ships that had brought in the *Hunter* and the *Martin*. Naturally he was not enthusiastic about the new English conditions.[9]

The blockade of Tripoli went on throughout the summer of 1675 with Narbrough's ships revictualling at their new base at Malta. Charles II suggested blocking the channel into Tripoli harbour by sinking a ship or two in it, to make it impassable. Another suggestion was to use fireships. Narbrough thought neither suggestion practicable. During the summer the English squadron took various ships from Tripoli. Narbrough sold ninety-eight blacks (men, women and children) from them at Malta. Twenty-four of the crew, who were Greek Christians, were sent as slaves to the galley at Tangier. Charles II approved his actions.[10]

As autumn came Narbrough's squadron was further strengthened. He now had on station, or would shortly have, the *Henrietta, Dragon, Newcastle, Roebuck, Swallow, Dartmouth, Diamond, Assistance, Portsmouth, Harwich, Anne, Christopher, Holmes* and *Yarmouth*. If peace was made Narbrough was ordered to send them home, and not allow them to loiter around ports in the hope of lining their own pockets with a good voyage. The new Dey of Tripoli was still not prepared to submit to the English demands, although he did offer salt in the place of money. Narbrough did not think this worth taking on behalf of Charles II, but suggested that the releasing of foreign slaves would make the King popular with foreign states.[11]

Sent out as part of Narbrough's reinforcements was the *Assistance*, with the celebrated Henry Teonge as chaplain. Teonge has left a personal account of his experiences. The *Assistance* was off Tripoli in August/September of 1675, and Teonge records that Narbrough took several pinnaces on a jaunt to the shore near Tripoli. The English colours were displayed before they all came aboard again.[12]

During an autumnal fog, four of the largest corsair galleys slipped out of Tripoli harbour into the open Mediterranean. Narbrough, reducing his blockading ships to a minimum, followed them, but without coming up with them. However, they were able to convoy back the Levant fleet in safety. The King ordered Narbrough to court martial the captain of the *Success*, who was thought to be responsible.[13]

Little is known of Shovell during 1675, other than that he was Second Lieutenant on board the *Henrietta*, with Narbrough. No doubt he played a full part in running the ship and maintaining the blockade of Tripoli. During 1675 he would have come into contact with Charles Mordaunt, third Earl of Peterborough, who had joined the *Henrietta*. Thirty years later he and Shovell would be the joint commanders of a much larger expedition to the Mediterranean, which led to the capture of Barcelona. Mordaunt was not an easy man to deal with, as Henry Teonge was to discover a few years later, when he clashed with him over working on the Sabbath, and who was to preach. Another man whose affairs were to be later intimately involved with those of Shovell was Edward Russell, the future Earl of Orford, who joined Narbrough's blockade in 1676, on the *Reserve*.[14]

As late as November 22nd 1675 it is recorded in Samuel Pepys' *Admiralty Journal* that Charles II was intent on continuing the war with Tripoli, unless all foreign passengers from the detained ships were released. There was stalemate. However, in mid January 1676 Narbrough struck the decisive blow of the war.[15]

During January 1676 Narbrough sent Shovell ashore to further negotiate with the Dey of Tripoli. Shovell delivered his instructions with great spirit, but the Dey, despising his youth, treated him with disrespect, and sent him away with an inconclusive answer. Narbrough ordered Shovell back to the Dey for a second time, but his behaviour was even worse. Although angry, Shovell bore it with patience, and used the verbal assault as an excuse to stay on shore longer. He made the most of his time to study the disposition of the corsair ships in Tripoli harbour. Returning to the *Harwich*, he reported to Narbrough that it was possible to attack the Dey's ships in their harbour. On the preceding December 20th Narbrough had exchanged the *Henrietta* for the *Harwich* with Henry Killigrew, and had taken Shovell with him. Killigrew, another man who would have much to do with Shovell in the 1690s, had been delayed in coming out from England for rather doubtful reasons (it being likely that he was conducting business of his own).[16]

On the night of January 14th 1676 Cloudesley Shovell was to lead the boat action against the shipping in Tripoli harbour, and bring his name to national prominence. Narbrough wrote an account of the action that was issued as a special supplement to the *London Gazette*.

> Friday, the 14th January 1675/76. I being before Tripoli in Barbery with his Majesties Ships under my command, namely these, Harwich, Henrietta, Portsmouth, the Anne and Christopher and Holmes Fireships, and two Merchant ships, Guiney and Martin, attending on me for convoy to Scanderoone.
>
> I hoped to have made an honourable and lasting peace, but the Dey and Government of Tripoli refusing to make restitution for the injuries done to his Majesty and his subjects, I, seeing four of the Tripoli ships of war of considerable force in the Port of Tripoli, preparing to go out to cruise, I then having the fireships with me with fireworks, I fitted a fire-boat accordingly out of them; commanding that all the boats of my Squadron being 12 in number should be mann'd, arm'd and fitted with fireworks: Also I ordered a considerable Officer to be commander in every boat and my Lieutenant Cloudesley Shovell to be commander in chief of them all, I, being resolved by God's permission that night to attack the Enemies ships in their Port, gave directions requisite for such a design.
>
> About 12 of the clock in the night, my boats resolvedly entered the Port, seized the guard-boat, boarded the ships, fired them and utterly destroyed them all; some Turks and Moors slain, the rest fled to save themselves. These four ships lay under the deep castle walls, which were all that were in the Port, excepting a Tunis merchant ship, which I ordered should not be meddled with, so escaped firing. This action was performed in less than an hours time without sustaining the least damage on our part, more than the expense of some ammunition, fire-works and fire-boat which effectually were bestowed as designed, to the great astonishment of the Turks, that endeavoured to impede our design by plying several great and innumerable small shot at our boats and men, which were within pistol shot of the Dey's own castle and palace. Such was the wonderful mercy of Almighty God towards us, that not one man of ours was killed, wounded or touched, nor a boat in any ways disabled, but all returned in safety, bringing the guard boat, two Moors and the Turkish colours of the two ships in triumph along with them, to my ship. Our men employed in the boats in this particulr action were 157, they all behaving themselves as becometh Englishmen. And for a present reward of their good service I caused the next day 1956 Pieces of eight to be distributed among them.

Narbrough then gave a list of the various boats involved in the action, the number of men in them, and their reward.

Names of the Tripoly Ships of War that were burnt with their Guns.

|                      | Guns |
|----------------------|------|
| White Crown'd Eagle  | 50   |
| Looking-glass        | 34   |
| Sancta Chiaro        | 24   |
| French Petach        | 20   |

Guard-boat brought off with one
    Pedreroe and two Moors in her.

John Narbrough
From on Board His Majesties
Ship Harwich at Maltla
Feb 18th 1675/76

The boats involved were

| | |
|---|---|
| *Harwich* pinnace | 16 men |
| *Harwich* long boat | 20 men |
| *Harwich* yawl | 4 men |
| *Guiny's Merchant* pinnace moved out of the *Harwich* | 10 men |
| *Anne and Christopher fireship* long boat | 14 men |
| *Martin* merchant | 8 men |
| *Henrietta's* pinnace | 15 men |
| *Henrietta's* long boat | 20 men |
| *Portsmouth* pinnace | 14 men |
| *Portsmouth* long boat | 15 men |
| *Anne and Christopher fireship* pinnace | 10 men |
| *Holms fireship* pinnace | 11 men |

In all 157 men and twelve boats were involved in the destruction of the corsair ships. Shovell, whose number was 438 in the sea book of the *Harwich*, led the attack from the pinnace of his own ship. The master's mate of the *Harwich*, James Greeve(also known as Greeves), who travelled with Shovell, assisted him. The guard boat was taken first, followed by the assault on the four corsair ships drawn up close under the walls of the Dey's castle. The success of the attack was principally due to surprise, and to the resolution of Shovell and his English sailors at the dead of night. A contemporary print by Hollar shows the layout of Tripoli harbour, and the position of the ships during the various stages of the action. Of the 1,956 pieces of eight distributed amongst the victorious English sailors by Narbrough, Shovell received eighty and his assistant James Greeve thirty-two. The money actually came from Narbrough's own pocket, and he had a certain amount of difficulty reclaiming it from the Treasury on his return to England.[17]

James Greeve, who assisted Shovell in the boat action, was another Norfolk man, and his grave can still be seen in the churchyard of St Margaret's Church, Cley-next-the-Sea, beneath the window of the south transept. Part of the inscription which is on the family's table tomb reads:

> Here lyeth the Body of James Greeve who was an assistant of S[r] Cloudisly Shovel in burning ye Ships in ye Port of Tripoly in Barbary Jan[ry] 14th 1676 and for his good service was made Cap[t] of the Ship called the Orange Tree of Algier in 1677 presented w[th] A Medal of gold by King Charles y 2 he died April 14th 1686 Aged 48 years.

The inscription could still be read in 1984, but is gradually deteriorating. Cley, of course, is very close to the birthplace of Shovell, but there is no evidence that he and Greeve were related.

A painting by Willem van de Velde the younger, showing Shovell's boat action at Tripoli, is in the possession of Her Majesty the Queen. The British Library has a preparatory sketch for the painting, and the National Maritime Museum a finished drawing of the scene tentatively attributed to his father, Willem van de Velde the elder.

Despite the success of Shovell on January 14th, the Dey of Tripoli did not immediately seek peace. Narbrough recorded:

> The 26th of January I fired about One hundred shot into the City of Tripoli amongst the inhabitants; the first and third of February I took and destroyed five corn-boats on the coast to the eastward of Tripoli twenty leagues, and landed and burnt a stack of wood and timber which was for building their new ships, and some small masts and yards and some bags of bread brought off and two guns spiked up which could not be got off it, begining to blow and likely to be bad weather, so I was constrained to leave them, and repair on board and leave the Coast. The 10th the Portsmouth took a Samberkeene in her ballast 30 leagues to the eastward of Tripoli, she belonging to that Government: the Moors got all on shore, the Samberkeene she brought into Maltha.
> John Narbrough.[18]

About two months later Narbrough fought with four Tripoline ships, killing 600 of their men, and chasing them into their harbour. This was the final blow for the Dey who sent out asking for terms of peace. Narbrough was keen to settle the matter rapidly as the plague had broken out in his base at Malta. The terms agreed were not dissimilar to those offered in the autumn of 1674. All English slaves residing in Tripoli were to be freed without charge. In addition, Narbrough received on behalf of Charles II $80,000 worth of goods including brimstone, with the balance being made up of redeemed foreign slaves. The foreign Christians, who received their freedom by courtesy of the generosity of Charles II, included Knights of Malta in recognition of the hospitality that Narbrough's fleet had received.

The treaty was signed on March 5th 1676. However, as Narbrough was preparing to sail for home, a revolution broke out in Tripoli, and the Dey, who was the principal cause of the war, fled. Narbrough, knowing how unreliable the people of Tripoli were, insisted on the articles of peace being ratified again by the new Dey. Under threat of a further bombardment this was done and Narbrough spent several weeks off Tripoli collecting up slaves and goods.[19]

One who witnessed these events was the chaplain of the *Assistance*, Henry Teonge. He reported the return of Narbrough's contingent without casualties to Malta on February 11th, and was off Tripoli during the period February 23rd to March 3rd when a peace was concluded.[20]

By April 1676 news of Narbrough's success at Tripoli had reached England. On April 3rd Samuel Pepys wrote to Narbrough:

> The King and Lords have commanded me to signify to you the extraordinary content they take in the effects of that action of yours, and what they observe to your utmost advantage in reference to your conduct therein, perfected with all the acceptable circumstances that can attend any attempt of that kind – namely, the being effectual, speedy, and not chargeable to his Majesty in his treasure nor to his subjects in their lives – his Majesty's esteem of which service to your particular benefit I doubt not but you will live to understand by better proofs than my bare telling it you, as also will Lieutenant Shovell (with whose management his Majesty and my Lords are most particularly satisfied) and the rest of the officers and boats companies when they shall return home.[21]

Rarely would Pepys make complimentary remarks about Shovell in the future.

On the way home to England Narbrough stopped off at Algiers. The day before, June 26th 1676, corsairs had brought in an English merchant ship, the *Leopard*, worth £150,000. Friends of Narbrough, the Houblons, in fact owned the cargo. The reason that the *Leopard* was brought in was the lack of a new pass that would have given her free movement in the Mediterranean. The Algerians agreed to release the crew and ship plus another one, the *Diligence* of London, which had suffered the same fate, but adamantly refused to part with the cargoes. As was their custom, they agreed not to interfere with English shipping in the future. Narbrough appears to have been satisfied with this, and sailed away. Perhaps his exertions at Tripoli had weakened his resolve.[22]

News of the Algerians breaking the peace treaty reached England, and frantic instructions were sent out by Pepys ordering Narbrough to remain at Cadiz, and then to return to Algiers to demand restitution. Although Narbrough received these orders at Cadiz, he decided to ignore them, and to return to England for direct consultations with Charles II and his advisers. Narbrough's squadron reached Plymouth on September 16th 1676, and the next day it was recorded in the *Admiralty Journal* that the King and their Lordships approved of his not complying with the orders sent to Cadiz, so that he might speak directly with them. They recognised that at a distance they did not have a full picture of the current state of Algerian affairs. Narbrough reported that the mole at Algiers could not be attacked.[23]

Charles II was delighted with the success against Tripoli and had promised to reward those involved. The first ships which had taken part in the blockade of Tripoli appear to have returned to England before Narbrough. In the *Admiralty Journal* for July 22nd 1676, it is recorded that the King would pay £10 extra per man to those who had already received ten pieces of eight from Narbrough. If they had received more than ten pieces of eight, this would be paid on a pro rata basis. Shovell, who was still in the *Harwich* on the return voyage from the Mediterranean, was to receive a medal. In November the various officers used in the action by Narbrough had requested a medal from the King. The *Admiralty Journal* of the 9th stated that this was to be granted. The commanders of the men of war should have one of £60 value, and those of the lesser vessels cheaper medals. Unfortunately Shovell, the lowly Second Lieutenant of the *Harwich*, had persuaded the King to give him a gold medal worth £100!

Early in the new year of 1677 the *Admiralty Journal* for January 27th stated that:

It being observed to his Majesty that whereas his Majesty had been pleased to promise a medal in reward to each of the commanders of the boats employed in the late action under Sir John Narbrough against Tripoli, and his Majesty's direction was become necessary to be expressly delivered touching the value of the said medals, for that Lieutenant Shovell had obtained a medal from his Majesty upon account of that service above the value of any hitherto given by his Majesty for any other service, and it being upon inquiry found that the same did arise by the said Lieutenant Shovell's applying himself to his Majesty for the same by hands unacquainted with the practice of the Navy in like cases; His Majesty was pleased to declare his being surprised in that matter and to signify his being disatisfied therewith, and to order that from henceforth no medals nor rewards of this kind be granted but at the public Board of the Admiralty, This having passed through the hand of my Lord Chamberlain without their knowledge, and that the value of the medal granted by this surprise to Lieutenant Shovell amounting to about £100, be not brought into precedent, but that those (to) be given to the residue of the officers concerning that action be proportioned according to the values of the medals heretofore given by his Majesty in other cases.

Nearly six months later the saga of the medals continued. On June 2nd the *Admiralty Journal* recorded that Charles II had decided finally to give Narbrough a £100 medal, the frigate commanders, such as Henry Killigrew, one worth £60, the fireship commanders one worth £50, and the boat commanders, such as James Greeve, one worth £30. A week later instructions were given to the mint to provide the medals. In this letter of instruction there is no mention of Cloudesley Shovell. Charles II was too generous a man to ask for the return of the medal or to hold a grudge. As a postscript to the action it is worth recording that the First Lieutenant of the *Harwich*, one William Long, asked that he might be given a share of the gratuity, as he had offered his services for the boat action, but had been ordered to remain behind. He received nothing, and it is difficult not to have some sympathy for him. It must have been galling to see his junior, Shovell, given command of the boats over him and then receive all the glory.[24]

During the period 1686–9, Shovell recorded that, amongst other things that he had left in a strong box with his future father-in-law, John Hill, was a chain, and medal of gold worth in all seventy pounds. The chain had 440 links. It is likely that this was his Tripoli medal, although he valued it at only £70.00.[25]

NOTES

1. Tanner, Pepysian MSS, Vol. II, pp.357–359; Playfair, pp.114–116; Dyer pp.138–143.
2. Tanner, Pepysian MSS, Vol IV, p.68; Laird Clowes, pp.446–460; Dyer, p.143.
3. Playfair, p.117; Tanner, Pepysian MSS, Vol II, pp.362 & 366.
4. Playfair, p.117; Rawlinson MSS, A.215, fol.117; Rawlinson MSS, C.353, fol.27.
5. Rawlinson MSS, A.215, fol.117.
6. Tanner, Pepysian MSS, Vol. IV, p.164; Dyer, p.144.
7. Tanner, Pepysian MSS, Vol. II, p.403.
8. Tanner, Pepysian MSS, Vol IV, pp.173,181,185; Vol. III, p.37; Dyer, pp.143–146.
9. Tanner, Pepysian MSS, Vol. III, p.63; Dyer, pp.146–147.
10. Tanner, Pepysian MSS, Vol. III, p.38, p.114; Vol. IV, p.218.
11. Tanner, Pepysian MSS, Vol. III, p.109; Vol. IV, p.225.
12. Diary of Henry Teonge, p.66.
13. Dyer, pp.150–151; Tanner, Pepysian MSS, Vol. III, p.129.
14. D.N.B. Mordaunt, Russell; Diary of Henry Teonge, p.226.

15. Tanner, Pepysian MSS, Vol. IV, p.246; Dyer, p.151.
16. Campbell, Vol. IV, p.239; Log book *Harwich* 1675, P.R.O. 216.
17. London Gazette, No. A1080 July 21st 1676; Dyer, pp.151–153; RMT MAT 40; Rawlinson MSS, A.214, f.21b; Tanner, Pepysian MSS, Vol. IV, p.295.
18. London Gazette, No. A1080 July 21st 1676; Dyer, p.154; RMT MAT 40.
19. C.S.P. Dom., Car II, 380, 157; Rawlinson MSS, A.215, ff.117 & 123; Sloan MSS, 2755, f.48; Dyer, pp.154–157.
20. Diary of Henry Teonge, pp.127–132.
21. Tanner, Pepysian MSS, Vol. IV, p.179.
22. Playfair, pp.121–122.
23. Tanner, Pepysian MSS, Vol. IV, pp.352, 356.
24. Tanner, Pepysian MSS, Vol. IV, pp.333, 373, 396, 398, 437; Rawlinson MSS, A.214. 21b, ib, 27b, 28.
25. Marsham MSS U1515.011.

# CHAPTER VII
# *Return to the Mediterranean 1677–1682*

Narbrough and Shovell remained in England during the winter of 1676 and into the early summer of 1677, before further trouble with Algiers required their return to the Mediterranean.

Narbrough took the opportunity of a break in England to marry. His wife was Elizabeth Calmady, daughter of Josias Calmady, who had an estate at Wembury, Devonshire. Josias was the son of an Elizabethan lawyer, Vincent Calmady, who had bought a number of estates in Devonshire. The marriage took place on April 9th 1677.[1]

Shortly after the wedding Samuel Pepys wrote to Narbrough asking, "how soon the state of his new affairs would allow him to be looking after the carrying out of his old". In fact, on April 16th Charles II gave Narbrough a commission to command the *Plymouth*, with a view to taking a squadron to the Mediterranean, in order to put the Algerians in their place. The *Plymouth* was a 54–60 gun ship, which had been built at Wapping in 1653. After his triumph at Tripoli in the preceding year there was little doubt about who would be the *Plymouth*'s Lieutenant. Cloudesley Shovell was made First Lieutenant on April 16th. In *The Secret Memoirs of Cloudesley Shovell* it is stated that Narbrough procured a 6th rate for Shovell on their return from the Mediterranean. This is not correct. Shovell was indeed to receive his first command of a ship from Narbrough, but not until the autumn of 1677.[2]

Time was spent in putting together a squadron to go to the

Mediterranean. On June 15th instructions for Narbrough were recorded in the *Admiralty Journal*. He was to demand satisfaction from the Algerians, and to insist that they did not come into the King's seas to the north of Cape Finisterre. In addition, Narbrough was to renew any treaty on the Barbary Coast where the government had changed. During the same month the Consul in Algiers, Samuel Martin, reported that further ships had been carried in, in defiance of the treaty, and that the Algerians intended to break with England.[3]

Narbrough eventually left England on August 9th 1677 with his squadron of nine ships. At the end of the month, Narbrough in the *Plymouth*, with Shovell as his First Lieutenant, sailed into Tangier Bay. For this expedition Narbrough had been given the rank of Admiral, as during the previous voyage the Grand Master of Malta had not received him, because he was only styled Commander-in-Chief. On September 2nd Narbrough wrote to Pepys outlining his plan of action against Algiers. He proposed to annoy and weaken them by keeping his squadron in the mouth of the Straits, and to attack any Algerian ship that attempted to slip home from the Atlantic. Within the first few days of their arrival in the Straits, Narbrough's squadron had already taken two Algerian ships, the 18 gun *Date Tree* and the 22 gun *Orange Tree*, commanded by the romantic sounding Buffllo Ball. The *Orange Tree* had recently been in the English Channel, and had taken two small vessels there.[4]

Soon after Narbrough had written to Pepys, the unfortunate Captain Thomas Harman of the *Sapphire* was mortally wounded, in an action against two Algerian ships on September 10th. Harman had been outgunned by the two Algerian ships, one of which carried 46 guns. The *Sapphire*'s main mast was shot away with the first broadside, and she would surely have been taken but for the timely arrival of the *Pearl*, which towed her into Tangier. The *Orange Tree* was forced to seek shelter at Sallee with 100 men killed or wounded. Thomas Harman was shortly to die of his wounds, and there were sixteen further casualties amongst his ship's company. He was no relation to the famous Sir John, with whom both Narbrough and Shovell had been in the West Indies ten years before. Ironically, Sir John's own son, James, was to be killed in 1678 fighting another Algerian ship, the *White Horse*.[5]

Little is known of Shovell's time in the *Plymouth* although the journal of George Orton, probably another lieutenant in the *Plymouth* at the time, exists. According to Robert Marsham Townshend there is nothing of interest in it.[6]

Harman's death led to Narbrough giving his young protégé, Shovell, a commission on September 11th 1677 to command the *Sapphire*. The 32 gun 5th rate had been built in Harwich in 1675 and was eighty-nine feet long. It was Shovell's first command and he was to serve in her for the best part of two years. A record of this period kept by Shovell exists in the Public

Record Office. In this journal of the *Sapphire*, Shovell recorded that he took over the ship in Tangier Road, on September 18th, a week after Narbrough had signed his commission.

> Tuesday 18th. This day I received my Commission from Sir Jno Narbrough to be Commander of HMs ship Saphire. Also received my signals and an order to entertain Mr Robert Taylor my Chaplin with his servant. I also received sayling instructions and went aboard ye Saphire.[7]

The *Sapphire* had been damaged in her encounter with the *Orange Tree*. Narbrough was forced to write to Henry Sheeres, the engineer in charge of the Mole at Tangier, asking for wood with which to repair the *Sapphire* and his other ships.[8]

The Algerians were intrepid fighters and difficult to overcome. Grenville Collins described an action against their ship, the *Rose of Algier*, on September 28th 1677. Despite overwhelming odds, the Algerians below continued to fire small shot out of their lower gun ports, long after those on the upper decks had been beaten. Captain George Canning of the *James galley* was killed in laying the *Rose of Algier* on board, with a small shot in the breast. The mortality amongst the officers was high. Shovell witnessed this action from the *Sapphire* which he described as a "notable scuffle", but was called away to investigate another ship. This he found to be an Englishman from Newfoundland.[9]

In mid October 1677 Shovell chased a French ship, and the next day, the 12th, the *Sapphire* was in action against an Algerian ship with a golden marigold painted on her stern. The Algerian first showed English colours, and then changed them to French ensigns with a view to making her escape. Shovell came up with her, and shot down her topsails and rigging with little damage in return. The Algerian ship, Shovell learned from a Turk he had on board, was commanded by a Captain Bustangh and had thirty-six guns, manned by 400 men. Shovell thought "it was not convenient to board him", which was unusual behaviour for a man usually so forward in action.[10]

Having taken as many Algerian ships as he could, Narbrough sailed with his squadron on November 19th from Altea Bay for Algiers. In *The Journal of Grenville Collins*, the captain of the eighth frigate was "Cloudes Shovall" and Narbrough was still in the *Plymouth*. They reached Algiers on November 23rd, with the intention of having the Peace Treaty confirmed. Narbrough sent a boat under a flag of truce with letters for the Algerians. It was not surprising that the boat was shot at, as Narbrough had been attacking their shipping, and had brought three of their vessels with him. The Algerian economy was largely dependent on piracy, and they now had a fleet of thirty-eight ships, the loss of any one of which was

69

a serious matter. The Algerians were refused terms, and after four days the weather forced Narbrough to sail away, and cruise in the mouth of the Straits.[11]

During the next few months, Narbrough's small squadron attempted to police the Mediterranean from the Straits to Scanderoon. Not only did he lack ships, but also the corsair vessels specifically built for service in the Mediterranean out-performed them. Matters were made more difficult for Narbrough and his men by English merchant captains, who exposed themselves to capture by refusing to be taken in convoy to their destinations. Narbrough was told to warn these men that if they were captured, the English government would not redeem them.[12]

Surprisingly, many of the merchant ships' captains were prepared to run the risk of becoming slaves for the sake of a quick profit. In 1890 Stanley Lane-Poole quoted a French writer of 1649, who described the fate of a slave.

When they were landed they were driven to the Besistan or slave market, where they were put up for auction like the cattle which were also sold there; walked up and down by the auctioneer to show off their paces; and beaten if they were lazy or weary or seemed to "sham". The purchasers were often speculators who intended to sell again, bought for the rise, in fact; and Christians are cheap today was though they had been stocks and shares! The prettiest women were generally shipped to Constantinople for the Sultan's choice; the rest were heavily chained and cast into vile dungeons in private houses till their work was allotted to them or into large prisons or bagnios, of which there were then six in Algiers, each containing a number of cells into which 15 or 16 slaves were confined. Every rank and quality of both sexes might be seen in these wretched dens, gentle and simple, priest and laity merchant and artisan, lady and peasant girl, some hopeful of ransom, others despairing ever to be free again. The old and the feeble were sent to sell water; laden with chains, they led a donkey about the streets and doled out water from the skin upon his back, and an evil day it was when the poor captive did not bring home to his master the stipulated sum. Others took the bread to the bake house and fetched it back in haste, for the Moors love hot loaves. Some cleaned the house (since Mohammedans detest dirt) whitened the walls, washed the clothes, and minded the children; others took the fruit to market, tended the cattle or laboured in the fields, sometimes sharing the yoke for the plough with a beast of burden. A grim fate was the sore labour of quarrying stone for building and carrying it down from the mountains to the shore.[13]

By far the most unpleasant fate of all to befall a slave was to be sent to the galleys. Lane-Poole quotes a French account of a galley slave of 1701.

> Think of six men chained to a bench, naked as when they were born, one foot on the stretcher, the other on the bench in front, holding an immensely heavy oar (fifteen feet long), bending forward to the stern with arms at full reach to clear the backs of the rowers in front, who bend likewise; and then having got forward, shoving up the oar's end to let the blade catch the water, then throwing their bodies back on the groaning bench. A galley oar sometimes pulls thus for ten, 12, or even 20 hours without a moment's rest. The boatswain, or other sailor, in such a stress, puts a piece of bread steeped in wine in the wretched rower's mouth to stop fainting, and then the captain shouts the order to redouble the lash. If a slave falls exhausted upon his oar (which often chances) he is flogged till he is taken for dead, and then pitched unceremoniously into the sea.[14]

In December 1677 the Admiralty Board authorised Narbrough to sell non-Christian slaves taken from the Algerians. It was left to Narbrough's discretion how to deal with captured renegades. He might hang them, keep them for exchange, or return them to their own countries.[15]

In his journal on the *Sapphire*, Shovell's entry for December 31st 1677 stated, "God send us a happy and successful Yeare ensuing".[16]

The summer base for Narbrough's squadron in 1678 was to be Tangier. From there he continued his attacks on Algerian shipping and attempted to protect merchantmen in convoys. A further worry for the English contingent in the Mediterranean was the French, who were suspected by the government of preparing for war. In October a French ship with Moors on board was stopped. One of the Moors leapt into the sea, despite the fact that he was several miles from land. In the past he had escaped as a slave at Gibraltar by swimming over the Straits mouth to Apes Hill! Narbrough removed the remaining Moors from the French ship.[17]

On November 26th 1678 Narbrough appeared before Algiers in force, and attempted to stop their ships returning to port. Five ships got past the blockade into the shelter of the Mole. Shovell in the *Sapphire*, aided by the *Hampshire*, got close to three of them, but could not capture them. Narbrough finding that his presence off Algiers had no effect, sailed away to Port Mahon in Minorca.[18]

At Port Mahon, Narbrough received an account of the Titus Oates papist plot against Charles II. There were suggestions in England that Narbrough's squadron should be used to mount an attack to steal the Vatican Library as a reprisal! Needless to say nothing came of the idea. It is amusing to imagine Narbrough and Shovell returning to their ships with arms full of looted manuscripts.[19]

71

Early in 1679 fear of war with France became more acute, and a decision was taken by the Admiralty Board to bring most of Narbrough's squadron home. It was feared that if they were left in the Mediterranean superior French forces would overwhelm them. Arthur Herbert or Roger Strickland was to be left behind with one 3rd rate, four 4th/5th rates, and two fireships to attend Tangier and the mouth of the Straits. The stores at Port Mahon were to be returned to England. In the event war with France did not materialise.[20]

Before returning to England, Narbrough wrote to Henry Sheeres at Tangier from Port Mahon, on February 22nd 1679. "His grace the Duke is in good health, continually coming in boats to and fro this harbour, in a short time will make a tarpauling sailor, fiting for a voyage of discovery, Cloudisly is one of his graces great favourites."[21] The name of the Duke was not given. It was most likely to have been Henry Fitzroy, first Duke of Grafton, the second son of Charles II and Barbara Villiers, later Duchess of Cleveland. Grafton, who would have been in his 16th year, had been sent to sea as a volunteer under Sir John Berry. Berry was reported to have been intermittently in the Mediterranean between 1675 and 1680. If there is some doubt concerning the Duke, there is no doubt about Cloudisly. Without question this was the captain of the *Sapphire* at the time, Cloudesley Shovell. Grafton and Shovell were to sail again together, in 1687, to the Mediterranean.[22] On March 4th 1679 Shovell in the *Sapphire* and George Rooke in the *Nonsuch* forced the ship of Treguee, son of the Dey of Algiers, ashore where it was burnt. Rooke described this action in a letter to Samuel Pepys.

> Nonsuch, in the bay of Cadiz April ye 26 79. Hon[d] Sr This is the first oportunity has presented to advise you that on ye 4th March last past, cruising w[h] the Saphire off Cape-Faulcon wee mett w[th] an Algier man of wa[r], w[ch] at three a clocke afternoone we chast ashore about 3[l] to ye W[t] W[d] of Cape Fegalo. The Turks immediately sett her a fire and left her. I am informed by some . . . w[ch] Cap[tn] Shovells boate tooke up, that she was the King of Algiers Shyppe built on a Portugues Carvell. She had the sunne in her sterne and was mounted w[th] 22 gunns and 10 Pettreroes, the same shyppe w[ch] took the Quaker K[ch]. I have beene since the 28th of the last month w[th] y[e] Vice Admir[ll] by whose order I am now heere excepting the l'res shall come by this port either for him or Tangier, we looke dayly for Sir John Narborough who I do imagine this Levant w[ch] now blows may putt through. I have nought else at p[r]sent but the Tender of my most humble service w[ch] ends from,
>
> Hon[d] S[r]
> Yo[r] most obedient and most humble Serv[t]
> G. Rooke[23]

In a letter from Alicante in early March, Narbrough informed Henry Sheeres that he had received orders from Charles II to leave the Mediterranean, and that Vice Admiral Arthur Herbert was being left with six frigates at Tangier. The *Sapphire* with Shovell was to be one of the frigates.[24]

Before returning to England, Narbrough made one final attempt to bring the Algerians to heel. At the end of March 1679 he went once more before Algiers. Several times Narbrough sent officers ashore to make a peace treaty without success. Later, it was said that if he had waited just one more day, the Algerians would have agreed to one.[25]

Shovell was not with Narbrough during the final negotiations with Algiers. On April 12th 1679 Vice Admiral Herbert moved Shovell from the *Sapphire* to the *Phoenix*. The move appears to have followed the death of Captain Anthony Langston of the *Royal Oak*, twelve days earlier. Captain Coyle of the *Phoenix* went into the *Royal Oak*, Shovell into the *Phoenix* and William Blagge into the *Sapphire*. The *Phoenix* was a 5th rate with 40–42 guns and was eighty-nine feet in length. In many ways she was very similar to the *Sapphire*. Shovell's command of her was to be brief, as on May 3rd at Tangier Narbrough signed his commission to return to the *Sapphire*. A council of war was held in the *Plymouth* on April 29th, and it may well be that this was when Narbrough decided on the move. The reason is unknown, but possibly Shovell felt happier in the *Sapphire* and his Admiral returned him to his former ship as a parting gesture. In any case, Shovell recorded in his journal for May 4th, "This day I removed from ye Phoenix to command ye Saphire and received the sacrament and tooke ye oath." [26]

Finally on May 12th 1679 Narbrough sailed from Tangier for England. He believed that he had so weakened the Algerians that Herbert's small squadron, which was to remain in the Mediterranean, could cope with them. The Consul at Algiers, Samuel Martin, wrote home in 1680 that of the thirty-two ships that the Algerians had in their fleet, before Narbrough's campaign, only nineteen remained. Narbrough reached Plymouth Sound on June 9th, and was told of the death of his wife, Dame Elizabeth, on January 1st 1677/78, over eighteen months before. It was a great shock to him, and in 1681 he was to commission a drawing on vellum of her memorial in Wembury Church, Devon. The drawing is still in existence. Even by the standards of communication of the seventeenth century, it is surprising that the news had not reached Narbrough in the Mediterranean.[27]

Narbrough's return to England brought to an end the close connection between Shovell and himself. They had served together, almost without break, since Shovell first went to sea with Myngs. Shovell, by now in his 29th year, was to see little of Narbrough until the late 1680s, although they remained in contact as will be seen later.

Arthur Herbert, later the Earl of Torrington, was left in command in the

Mediterranean, initially with the local rank of Vice Admiral and later in 1680 as Commander-in-Chief. He was to remain in the Mediterranean until 1683, and used Tangier as his base.[28]

Herbert kept Shovell in the *Sapphire*. On October 29th 1679 the *Sapphire* met an Algerian ship of thirty-four guns and chased him from Apes Hill to Cape Tresforcas. Although his ship was inferior in firepower, Shovell would have taken him had not the *Sapphire* suffered damage to her masts and rigging. Captain Richard Carter was sent out by Herbert to escort the *Sapphire* into Malta, and then on to Cadiz for a new mast. Herbert wrote to Samuel Pepys at the Admiralty on the following November 2nd in praise of Shovell.

> Captain Shovell has on many occasions and particularly in his last behaved himself with so much courage and conduct that I think it my duty warmly to recommend him to their [? honours] as a man as well qualified as any man in England to serve the King in his station wherefore I humbly desire if their honours design any 5th rate to be employed in this war it may be the Saphire and Captain Shovell in her or rather a good sailing fourth rate for I am sure he will do service if it to be done; I should think that James Galley or the Dragon very fit ships for this war which I am sure would be good service with Captain Shovell in her.[29]

Shovell was to command the *James galley*, but not until 1681. He had made a smooth transition from Narbrough's patronage to Herbert's. Actions such as that of October 29th are made more personal by a letter signed by both Shovell and his Lieutenant, John Neville, of March 17th 1679/80, reporting that one Nicholas Halls, an able seaman, unhappily had been slain in the action against the Algerians.[30]

During 1679 and 1680 Tangier was under siege by the Moors. Herbert and the fleet supported the Deputy Governor, Sir Palmas Fairborne. At the beginning of November 1679 Shovell was sent ashore by Herbert to assist in the defence of Tangier. On November 8th the Moors were repulsed but Shovell was wounded. The nature of his wound is not known but it only caused a temporary loss of his services.[31]

While based at Tangier, Herbert had a house on shore. His captains, such as Shovell, George Byng, Richard Carter, Thomas Hopsonn, Anthony Hastings, John Neville, Matt Aylmer, Francis Wheeler and George Rooke would meet him there. Samuel Pepys, during his visit in 1683 to Tangier, took a very dim view of the behaviour of Herbert and his relationship with his captains.

> W. Hewer tells me of captains submitting to the meanest servility to Herbert when at Tangier, waiting his rising and going to bed,

combing his periwig, putting on his coat, as the King is served. He living and keeping a house on shore, and his mistresses visited and attended one after another, as the King's are. For commanders that value themselves above tarpaulins, to attend to these mean things, as Wheeler particularly is said to do.

Pepys had also heard of a drunken surgeon being stripped on Herbert's orders. The thought of Shovell combing Herbert's periwig is too ridiculous to be taken seriously! Julian Corbett believed that it was acceptable to have a house on shore, and that Pepys' dislike of Herbert had coloured his views. John Narbrough insisted on his captains remaining on their ships while in harbour.[32]

When not in Tangier, Shovell spent his time patrolling against the Algerians about the Straits or in the Mediterranean. On April 4th 1680 his appointment to command the *Sapphire*, made by Narbrough the preceding year, was confirmed by the Commissioners of the Admiralty. However, three months later Herbert moved Shovell to the *Nonsuch*. The *Nonsuch* had been built in 1668 at Portsmouth as a 5th rate, but had been converted into a 42 gun 4th rate, the following year. Shovell was to remain in the *Nonsuch* only for a short time, for on September 9th 1680 Herbert moved him back to his old ship, the *Sapphire*. The reasons for this change round are not known. In the Public Record Office is a logbook of the *Nonsuch*. It is headed "A journal of our proceedings by his Majesties Ship the Nonsuch keep by me Cloudesley Shovell commander of the ship begining ye 14th of July 1680". This heading and the whole of the journal itself are in a clerk's handwriting. The journal begins "14th Wednesday. This day we had faire weather and calme I removed out of the Sapphire into ye Nonsuch." This was in Tangier Road and for the next two months the *Nonsuch* was either there or cruising about in the Straits. There is little of interest in the log, except that it was the only Shovell log that Marsham Townshend could find in the Public Record Office, although others have come to light since. It ends on September 11th 1680 in Tangier Road, "Today I received a commission to command ye Sapphire and Lieut Wheeler command of ye Nonsuch." Shovell has signed the log himself at the end. There is a two-day difference between the date given by Tanner (September 9th), and the one given in the log (September 11th). Perhaps Herbert signed the commission on the 9th, but that the move was not effected until two days later.[33]

Early in April 1681 Shovell, in the *Sapphire*, took a 22 gun Algerian ship, the *Golden Rose of Algiers*. In Arthur Herbert's letter book for the period there is a brief account of the action.

A letter from Captain Shovell bearing the date 12th of April I find he hath brought into Cadiz the Golden Rose of Algier a ship of 22 guns.

75

I do not yet know how many men; it seems that he met her the day after I sent him out of Tangier road as you will find by his letter to me of which I send you his inclosed copy by which you will find that Capt Shovell's discretion in not charging when it was little wind and the Turk so considerable a distance from him was the occasion of drawing him nearer and consequently of Captain Shovell performing this service which he hath done with great prudence and valour; He is a man that I never knew slip any occasion of advancing the king's service and his own reputation.

In a letter to Sir Lionel Jenkins, the principal Secretary of State at Whitehall, Herbert wrote on April 15th:

I have notice of the Saphire taking the Golden Rose a ship of 22 guns but do not yet know how many men, I judge about 30 Christians, Captain Shovell in the chase showed all the prudence and in the fight all the valour that becomes an experienced and brave Commander and indeed is a man to be admired for his behaviour on all occasions.

An account of the action appeared in the *London Gazette*, on May 18th.[34]

Soon after his success against the *Golden Rose of Algiers*, Shovell was given command of the *James galley*. Herbert signed the commission on April 22nd 1681. The *James galley* was a 4th rate of 32 guns, 104 feet in length, 436 tons, and had been built in 1676 at Blackwall. The *James* and her sister ship, the *Charles galley*, had been constructed to replace the foreign *Margaret galley*, on the grounds of expense. They had been built to a French design that had been obtained by a resident of Toulon. Both ships could be used as a genuine galley or as a frigate in other circumstances. Shovell was to serve with distinction on the *James* for the next five years.[35]

Six months later, Shovell in the *James galley* was out cruising with his former ship, the *Sapphire*, commanded by Anthony Hastings. About forty leagues off Cape St Vincent, they came across the 32 gun ship the *Half Moon of Algiers* with forty English slaves and a woman aboard. After a hard battle the Algerian was taken. She was said to be very little inferior to another well known corsair vessel, the *Golden Horse*. Henry Sheeres sent a detailed account of the action, written by Shovell, to Daniel Finch, the Earl of Nottingham. The account still exists.

'A narrative of Captain Shovell's command of his Majesties frigate the James Galley touching the taking the Half Moone of Algier . . . September ye 9th about 10 in ye morning the Saphire and we cruising in company we saw a ship which we immediately chased ye wind being then at E n E or N.E. where it continued all day he hailed us in several languages we answered him we were French men; he told us they were ye halfe Moon of Algeirs and had been from thence about 10 weeks we asked for Sally men and told him we suspected he was of Sally commanded his boat aboard which he refused to do in such like discourse we held him till we were alongst his larboard side which was the weather side. I was resolved to board him athwart ye hawse by Reason there went such a sea that I was confident by that means of bringing his bowsprit and foremast by the board but he suspecting my design put his helm a[? port] and made his starboard side the weather side whereupon I fired all my guns into him the Saphire being a quarter of a mile astern of us soon took this advantage and before the Turk could trim his sail run him aboard on the starboard side abaff the Foxshrouds. It was then half an hourer past 8 upon which as before I endeavoured to be thwart his hause and twice missed the third time I had him aboard so that his bowsprit was amongst ye main shrouds but which the fresh way we had we brought his ship a little about ye foxebraces being shott we could not back ye head sailes so that we were cleare of him again in little more than a quarter of an hour. Soon after ye Saphire was likewise cleare of him and fell astern occasioned by the loss of her bowsprit and foremast. This was about 10 a clock. I now having the algeir to deal with all alone with all his masts standing steering away before the wind was resolved to be once more thwart his hause. Considering that my guns being but 6 pounders it was not likely I could do much good in shooting their masts by the board accordingly with all his sailes full I steerd thwart his hause in which attempt we broke two of ye main shrowds also ye main chains and two mizzen shrouds and ye mizzen chains and shrouds ye [? gunnell] down to the deck but we broke his bowsprit, head and catswater, knee and cheeks of his head so that he had a smooth stern quite below the waters edge. we lay thus thwart his hause about half an hour and then being intangled with his rigging fell alongst his side – with our head to his stern where we lay about half an hour. When ye rigging broke we swung clear again. I then layed him abord on ye starboard bow where we lay to keep him from securing his masts which I expected to fall any moment for the knee of his head being gone ye collar of his main stay came on ye deck so that both main and foremast were equally in danger and at a quarter after one his foremast came by the board. Soon after his main mast and mizzen mast. I then laid my sailes aback and called to them. They told me they yielded the ship whereupon we immediately fell to work to secure ye masts and mend ye boat that she might swim which was not done before day light at which time we went on board and took possession. She is ye halfe moon of algier carrying 32 guns and come out of Port with 246 men where of 39 were xptians of which 20 English they had taken a small English vessel bound to Bermoodus with 7 English men and a woman which they took on board and sank ye vessel. The captains name is Jonas Raife a Turk his lieutenant an English renegado which I caused to be hanged at my yard arm. The damage we have received is 18 men killed and 32 wounded and both main and foremast spoiled – we took her 45 leagues SWN ½ N from Cape Spartel. There was killed aboard the Turke 93 Turkes and Moores and most of the living were wounded. They assure me that there is but two better ships in Algier which ye Canary and the White Horse.'[36]

The next month, December, Shovell commanding the *James galley* with the assistance of the *Adventure* under William Booth, took another Algerian ship, the *Flower Pot*. The year 1681 had proved fruitful for Shovell, with the capture of three well known corsair ships – the *Golden Rose*, the *Half Moon* and finally the *Flower Pot*.[37]

The war with Algeria had dragged on throughout 1681. Herbert had suggested that if the war was becoming too expensive for Charles II it would be better to go over to the defensive. Strong convoys could be used to protect the merchant ships, rather than pursue the corsairs with the fleet. The Admiralty considered the matter, but decided against the idea on the grounds that it could be ruinous to trade, and shameful to England to admit to the fact that she was unable to cope with the "seventeen little pirate ships". In February 1681, following instructions, Herbert once more anchored before Algiers.[38]

In his negotiations with the Algerians in the spring of 1681, Herbert was to use Shovell as his principal envoy. The Algerians were difficult people to deal with, and capable of great violence if they did not get their own way. On one occasion the Vicar Apostolic and twenty other Frenchmen were blown away at the mouth of a cannon, after a breach with France! Shovell has left an account of events in Algiers at this time. It is not in his own handwriting, but was probably dictated to a clerk and is endorsed "Capt Shovell's account of severl passages at ye treaty of a peace with the Algereens".

About y[e] middle of february last (168½) Adm:[ll] Herbert parted from y[e] Spanish coast with 5 ships bound for Argeir to demand a peace and twas supposed by all people in those parts that it would easily be granted to his satisfaction, at our coming before Argeir y[e] Adm:[ll] writs to ye Government to know if they were inclinable to peace but y[e] Adm:[ll] was answered by M[r]: Cole an English m cht [ie merchant] (sent off by Boba Hafsan y[e] Generall of their army who having marryed y[e] Dij's daughter had all publicke matters at his disposing) told y[e] Adm:[ll] y[t] Boba Hafsan would not consent to peace without being presented with 10000 Barrills of powder and as many hundred weight of lead and 1000 Turks y[e] Adm:[ll] told Cole that Boba Hafsan had not dealt like a soldier by him in not answering his letter that he could not believe that they expected any amunition from him more than from the mouth of his cannon; Imediately M[r] Cole was set ashore and soon after the Adm:[ll's] boat was ordered to come abord and returne no more, Adm:[ll] Herbert after having given Barbarosa their old Adm:<sup>ll</sup> his liberty by setting him ashore immediately apply'd himself to cruising on ye coast of Argeir and took and destroy'd severall of their small trading vessels but meeting with bad weather and short of water he put of y<sup>e</sup> coast of Argeir till about y<sup>e</sup> latter end of march then all our squadron being either ordered or by foul weather separated from y<sup>e</sup> Adm:<sup>ll</sup> onely my selfe and he haveing often tryed to treat with y<sup>e</sup> Governours of Argeir haveing sent them several letters but never could receive an answer The Adm:<sup>ll</sup> thought that going before Argeir himselfe any more too much looked like begging a peace therefore sent me into y<sup>e</sup> bay with orders to send ashore to y<sup>e</sup> English m^chts there and try if I could find how y<sup>e</sup> people were inclinable or if possible to speak with Barbarosa or get a letter from him. I anchored before argeir and sent my boat ashore with a flag of truce and letters for y<sup>e</sup> English m^chts letting them know I had things for them abord and desired they would come abord to receive them but not being answered y<sup>e</sup> third day I wrote againe then got a letter from Mr Cole that he could not be permitted to come abord that Boba Hafsan was in y<sup>e</sup> camp y<sup>t</sup> y<sup>e</sup> people were inclinable to peace, he had heard some of y<sup>e</sup> great ones say now was y<sup>e</sup> time and wished y<sup>e</sup> Adm:<sup>ll</sup> were here upon y<sup>e</sup> receipt of this letter y<sup>e</sup> Adm:<sup>ll</sup> being then in sight I made a signe which he perceived and anchored in Argeir bay this night.

In y<sup>e</sup> morning being y<sup>e</sup> 3<sup>d</sup> of april (1682) ye Adm:<sup>ll</sup> wrote ashore to y<sup>e</sup> Dij that he once more came to try if they were inclinable to peace y<sup>e</sup> Adm:<sup>ll</sup> had an answer frô the Dij y<sup>t</sup> they were willing to make peace and if y<sup>e</sup> Adm:<sup>ll</sup> would send an officer ashore to treat with them he gave his word y<sup>e</sup> Officer should be safe and have liberty to returne w:<sup>n</sup> he pleased to command him of.

The 4<sup>th</sup> Ditto I was sent a shore and had instructions from Adm:<sup>ll</sup> Herbert to demand satisfaction for two ships which they tooke y<sup>t</sup> had passes (in y<sup>e</sup> time of y<sup>e</sup> late peace) also for y<sup>e</sup> ships they tooke without passes in y<sup>e</sup> seas appertaining to y<sup>e</sup> King my Masters dominions and for y<sup>e</sup> Quaker Ketch also y<sup>e</sup> reasons why they ought to make satisfaction I went ashore waited on y<sup>e</sup> Dij he told me I was welcome and should stay ashore that night and on y<sup>e</sup> morrow he would call a full Divan to hear what I had to say.

The 5:<sup>th</sup> Ditto in ye forenoon I was sent for by y<sup>e</sup> Dij and in publick Divan I made demands according to my instructions laying before them their unjust proceedings in y<sup>e</sup> late peace and giveing them y<sup>e</sup> reasons why they ought to make satisfaction. When I had ended y<sup>e</sup> Dij answered 'twas true his people had committed some disorders by bringing in English ships and making prize of their goods. he acknowledged they had done contrary to y<sup>e</sup> articles but said he 'tis also written in our articles that it should not be lawfull to break y<sup>e</sup>

peace before satisfaction be demanded for such like disorders therefore you broke y^e peace in taking our ships and killing our men before you demanded satisfaction and he thought they were the people injured and expected to receive satisfaction from us; I urged that satisfaction was demanded by our Consull and upon their denying y^e King fitted out a squadron he answered y^e Consull was a false man and was y^e occasion of all y^e Disorders and finding I still insisted on y^e demands he told me 'twas folly to talk of satisfaction because 'twas unreasonable I must let fall those pretensions or breake of the treaty urging we broke y^e peace and he expected a large present from us I let him know that since satisfaction was denyed my orders from my Adm:^ll were to treat no further he told me he would write and send off some officers to wait on y^e Adm:^ll he sent Adm:^ll Canary and another Capt^n: their business was to complement y^e Adm:^ll and tell him if a peace was made he expected a present of three thousand barr:^ls of powder and many 100:^t of lead & 100 Turks Our Adm:^ll gave them good reasons that their demands were unjust & did sufficiently satisfie them they must never expect to exact presents from our King when y^e Dij understood our Adm:^ll's answer he sent me word he would have me go abord y^t night and let y^e Adm:^ll know he would abate of y^e present proposasl but something must be given or y^e treaty must end he desired I might bring y^e Adm:^ll's answer on y^e morrow this night I went abord.

The 6:^th of aprill I went ashore with introductions from y^e Adm:^ll to tell y^e Dij I had acquainted y^e Adm:^ll with all that passed yesterday in y^e Divan and y^e Adm:^ll to show how ready he was to make peace would let fall his pretensions to the satisfaction demanded but as y^e Adm:^ll had layd by his they must lay theirs made by Adm:^ll Canary for y^e King my Master never ever would buy peace of the powerfullest Monarch in y^e world much less of an Enymy whom we have had y^e advantage of: y^e Dij told me I might go abord for without somewhat was given him he would treat no more this night I went abord. The 7th y^e Adm:^ll writ y^e Dij that he had given him an opportunity of making a good peace and contrary to his pretensions he is y^e occasion of y^e continuing y^e war and y^e blood. y^t is hereafter shed be on him and his country; y^e Dij writ y^e Adm:^ll he would lay by y^e pretensions of oblidging y^e King to make a present but where as many Turks were in o^r ffleet if y^e Adm:^ll would make him a present of 50 Turks (let their Quality and condition be never so mean) he would make peace y^t this present would oblidge him and y^e souldiers who have a great share in y^e government & y^t it would be y^e occasion of a lasting peace and he would make a present to y^e Adm:^ll if he did condiscend to this way of treating he might send y^e articles ashore to be perused if not he might follow his occasions Adm:^ll Herbert considered yᵉ Dij a peevish old man and apt enough to break of (knowing 'twould please his son in law Boba Hafsam whom he deerly loved) also if their ships should meet with any good prizes 'twould be yᵉ occasion of a long war and had to get them to such a conclusion resolved to condiscend and accordingly.

On yᵉ 8ᵗʰ: of Aprill sent me ashore with yᵉ articles of peace, yᵉ Dij sent for me had them read and interpreted verbatim he stopped at yᵉ third article & disputed yᵗ 'twas unreasonable we should carry forreigners and their goods & protect them in oʳ: m cht ships, by which means 'twould be hard for them to find prizes without which they could not subsist , I told him yᵉ cheife reason of our making peace was yᵗ our m cht ships might have free trade yᵉ world over and yᵗ forreigners and their goods might be safe abord them or yᵉ peace would be of no use to us he yeilded to yᵉ article but said he hoped that oʳ: m chtmen would be cautious of taking too many forreigners abord them I answered it must be left to themselves and our ships must be sufficient protection to any forreigners abord them, yᵉ 4th article he much wondred to hear which was yᵗ mayors or magistrates of any sea ports of England Scotland or Ireland their passes might be sufficient to know they yᵗ had them were yᵉ King of England Subjects yᵉ Dij told me yᵗ by this means there would be near 40 severall passes I told him their formes would be all one he answered it was yᵉ form of writing they so much minded about yᵉ hand and seale yᵗ 'twas impossible to keep all those severall hands and seales in memory abord every ship of theirs and that it was impossible to know yᵉ seale of yᵉ mayor of Dunkirke Callis Diepe or any other foreign place from our English Scotish or Irish mayors by which means there would be Loondrogers which would occasion yᵉ breach of yᵉ peace for in yᵉ last peace when yᵉ passes went through but one man's hand there was corruption and now will be much more when it lyeth in yᵉ power of 30 or 40 severall men to make passes he ordered me to read no further till that article was mended.

I desired to read yᵉ articles through I would take notice of his objections with which I would acquaint my Adm:ˡˡ so we read on till we came to yᵉ 11th article which was if any Christian slave should get abord any of yᵉ Kings ships they should be free he gave many reasons why this was no good article.

ffist said he when your ships come here we shall not receive you kindly because we fear your doing us an injury and some disafected people will say you come for no other intent than to steal our Christians then to chaine up oːʳ Christians is both a loss and a great trouble to us a loss because it cannot be expected a man yᵗ lyeth in chaines can work like a man yᵗ lyes free. A great trouble because some must repair to yᵉ Citty others to yᵉ Country for the security of their slaves y$^t$ y$^e$ trouble of watches and guards must be y$^e$ same as if an Enimy were in y$^e$ bay and this must be every time an English man of war appear here which will breed ill blood and give my people occasion to affront you which is impossible to be prevented if you come ashore, Next if any English man of war should have occasion to come into our mole 'twas impossible to prevent 100 Christians getting abord in a day these are injuries cannot be endured then I have near 10000 of my subjects. The 12th article he would not meddle with all which is to redeeme English Christians at y$^e$ price of y$^e$ market unless y$^e$ Adm:$^{ll}$ would engage y$^e$ King should redeem them all in two years we read on to y$^e$ 22$^d$ which was an additional article y$^t$ they should be oblidged to salute ye King of Englands flagg wheresoever it appeared before their City with 21 cannon he disputed this saying that it had never been in former articles and 'twas unreasonable their City and Castles should be oblidged to salute a ship. I answered y$^e$ salute was not to y$^e$ ships but to y$^e$ King my Masters flagg which is never carried at our maintop mast head but by a person of honour and quality who represents y$^e$ Lord High Adm:$^{ll}$ of England and is saluted by all y$^e$ Italian Dukes and Princes as also y$^e$ kingdoms of Tunis and Tripoly then he replied he was willing to salute but would not be oblidged to it by articles I told him that y$^e$ way to make a firm and everlasting peace which he declared was his desire was to write in articles all things y$^t$ was agreed and since he was willing to salute y$^e$ way to prevent disputes (which seldom end in love) was to suffer y$^e$ salute to be written in y$^e$ articles of peace to which he yeilded after haveing ended reading y$^e$ articles of peace I came abord told y$^e$ Adm:$^{ll}$ their objections who altered y$^e$ 4th article allowing no other passes to be good but what came from y$^e$ Adm:$^{ll}$ty of England & Scotland and for y$^e$ 11th article it should not be but care should be taken that they should be no loosers by any Christians that should swim of from Argeir but if any got from their ships abord ours or ashore to any of our Garrisons or other places belonging to y$^e$ Dominions of y$^e$ King of England they should not be required, for y$^e$ 12th article y$^e$ Adm:$^{ll}$ would not engage y$^e$ King in a debt of 6 or 800000 Dollars to be paid in two years but rather left y$^e$ Christians to get off as cheap as they could with their patteroons but if any publick redemption came from England they are to abate ye Custome of ten p cent upon every slave redeem'd.

The 9th of aprill I went ashore with those articles which were well liked by y$^e$ Dij and he promised to sign them whensoever y$^e$ Adm:$^{ll}$ sent them ashore too night I lay abord y$^e$ Adm.$^{ll}$

The 10th by Adm:$^{ll}$ Herberts order I went ashore with y$^e$ Articles haveing 4 or 5 gentleman of y$^e$ ffleet with me to see them signed I carryed them to y$^e$ Dij who immediately signed and sent for y$^e$

Bashaw and had his seale to y$^e$ articles then came y$^e$ Aga with y$^e$ seale of y$^e$ Divan and signed after y$^e$ signing y$^e$ articles y$^e$ Dij told me 'twas customary and reasonable at y$^e$ signing of articles of peace y$^t$ guns should be fired by both parties as a testimony of peace and friendship I agreed in his opinion and desired to know when he would begin to fire and what number that y$^e$ Adm:$^{ll}$ might know it and be ready to answer him gun for gun but he disputed fireing first saying we came to them for a peace and 'twas granted us we ought to give y$^e$ first testimony of joy I told him I wondred he could imagine our Adm:$^{ll}$ would first fire when one of the articles was that they were to salute y$^e$ flagg y$^t$ y$^e$ dispute delayed time and I was confident to no purpose for y$^e$ Adm:$^{ll}$ would not fire first he ordered 20 guns which were answered with 20 by y$^e$ Adm:$^{ll}$ then all y$^e$ ships and small vessels in y$^e$ mould [ie mole] fired which was by y$^e$ Adm:$^{lls}$ order answered with 15 guns a piece from my selfe and Capt: Elmore.[39]

Herbert and Shovell had done well, in April 1682, to get the Algerians to agree to a peace treaty that proved to be more stable than many earlier ones. Passes given to merchant ships to enable them to have safe conduct were a constant source of friction between the corsairs and the English government. The redemption of slaves, and the niceties of saluting, particularly who saluted first, were also a recurring problem in the last quarter of the seventeenth century.

During the remainder of 1682 Shovell continued to be based at Tangier, cruising around the Straits and into the Mediterranean. In mid October Herbert was concerned that the *James galley* had lost a mast in a storm, and sent the *Crown* out to look for her. It appears that Shovell had got into Cadiz, as four days after Herbert's report of the storm, Shovell wrote to him from there on October 21st. In this letter Shovell appeared to be thanking Herbert for allowing him to have a "good voyage" to Italy. "Good voyages" were ones where goods or money were transported for merchants, to the financial benefit of the captain of the ship concerned. Some captains were inclined to put profit before the King's business. On one voyage Francis Wheeler made £10,000 and on another occasion Henry Killigrew tried to persuade Samuel Pepys to get him one. No doubt "good voyages" supplemented the captain's pay.[40]

NOTES

1. Dyer, p.164; Lysons, Magna Britannia, Vol. 1, p.CXXXVII.
2. Dyer, p.165; Tanner, Pepysian MSS, Vol. III, p.404; Tanner, Catalogue of Sea Officers; Anderson, Lists of Men of War.
3. Tanner, Pepysian MSS, Vol. IV, pp.450 & 454.
4. Dyer, p.169; Journal Grenville Collins pp.204–205.
5. Dyer, pp.170–172; Journal Grenville Collins p.206; Laird Clowes, pp.446–460.

6. RMT MAT 13; Marsham MSS U1515.06.
7. Tanner, Catalogue of Sea Officers; Anderson, Lists of Men of War; ADM 51/857, Part I, Journal of the *Sapphire*.
8. ADD MSS 19872, f.29.
9. Journal Grenville Collins p.207; Laird Clowes, pp.446–460; ADM 51/857, Part I, Journal of the *Sapphire*.
10. ADM 51/857, Part I, Journal of the *Sapphire*.
11. Dyer pp.176–178; Journal Grenville Collins p.208.
12. Dyer pp.178–179.
13. Lane-Poole, The Barbary Corsairs; Dan, Histoire de Barbarie et ses Corsaires.
14. Lane-Poole, The Barbary Corsairs; Adm Jurien de la Gravière, Dernier Jours de la Marine à Rames.
15. Tanner, Pepysian MSS, Vol. IV, p.538.
16. ADM 51/857, Part I, Journal of the *Sapphire*.
17. Dyer, pp.180–182.
18. Dyer, p.182.
19. Dyer, pp.184–185.
20. Tanner, Pepysian MSS, Vol. IV, p.630.
21. ADD MSS 19872, f.40.
22. D.N.B. Grafton, Berry.
23. Duckett, pp.112–113; Diary of Henry Teonge, p.243; Rawlinson MSS, A.181,90.
24. ADD MSS 19872, f.43.
25. Dyer, pp.186–187.
26. Tanner, Catalogue of Sea Officers; Log book *James galley* 1679, P.R.O. no 238; Diary of Henry Teonge, p.250; Anderson, Lists of Men of War; ADM 51/857, Part 1, Journal of the *Sapphire*; ADM 51/4140, Book 2, Journal of the *Centurion*.
27. Dyer, pp.187–88,192; ADM 51/4140, Book 2, Journal of the *Centurion*.
28. Laird Clowes, pp.446–460.
29. Letter book of Herbert, Yale.
30. ADD MSS 18986, f.429.
31. Charnock, p.17; Laird Clowes, pp.446–460; Corbett, pp.114–115.
32. Tangier Papers of Pepys pp.52 & 59; Corbett, pp.114–115.
33. Tanner, Catalogue of Sea Officers; RMT MAT 29; P.R.O. Log No.344; Anderson, Lists of Men of War.
34. Letter book of Herbert, Yale; RMT MAT 26; London Gazette, May 18th 1681.
35. Anderson, Lists of Men of War; Journal Grenville Collins pp.198–199.
36. Finch MSS, Vol.II, pp.120–121; Dartmouth MSS, Vol.I, p.68.
37. Charnock, p.17; Laird Clowes, pp.446–460.
38. Playfair, p.138.
39. ADD MSS 28093, f.190; RMT MAT 26 (32).
40. Herbert Letterbook, Yale, Herbert to Lionel Jenkins Oct. 17th 1682; RMT MAT 27, Shovell to Herbert Oct. 21st. 1682; Tangier Papers of Pepys, pp.59 & 89.

# CHAPTER VIII
## *Iberian Challenges*
## *1683–1688*

Early in 1683 Shovell and the *James galley* were at Cadiz, before going into the Mediterranean to Majorca. On January 14th, the seventh anniversary of his ship-burning exploit at Tripoli, Shovell took an Algerian saitea.* [1]

The following June Shovell found himself in great difficulty with the Spanish fleet on his return to Cadiz. The Spanish Admiral Conde de Acquila demanded that Shovell's ship, the *James galley*, fire its guns in salute. Shovell refused on the grounds that his orders forbade him, and the Spaniards issued an ultimatum that if he did not, they would sink him. [2]

A great deal of the correspondence and statements concerning the affair are still in existence. Shovell wrote to Sir Martin Westcombe on June 23rd 1683.

> Hon Sir,
> Papachin with three other ships of 70 guns apiece came this morning by day-light to anchor round me. Their chief sent me a message to salute their flag, or that they would compell me to it; and upon my denial Papachin fired a great gun at me shot and all, with near 100 small shott; and upon sending my boat aboard him to know his reason, he could give me no other than that he complyd with his General's commands. I do not think myselfe able to fight ye Spanish Armada and therefore must be obliged to comply with their demands. I desire you would capitulate with their General yet he would give me Gun for Gun or give leave to some of his other ships to answer me Gun for Gun or I firing 5 guns he answering me with ye same now I return 3 again. If none of these propositions take and you think fitt capitulate with him yet he give 5 guns for 7. They have fired again into an English ship near me which was hit her under water and made her very leaky. Not else to trouble your honour.
> I remain etc.
> Cloudesley Shovell.

Sir Martin Westcombe, the English Consul and Agent at Cadiz, advised Shovell that he had seen Conde de Acquila, who was insisting on the

* Small Algerian merchant ship

salute being made by eight o'clock the following morning. Westcombe suggested that Shovell should sail the *James galley* out of Cadiz Bay that same night, and pretend that he was following his own Admiral's orders. Additionally, Shovell should not divulge Westcombe's private intelligence to him to the Spanish authorities. Privately, the Consul protested "if hee and all had bin lost by Maintaineinge our Kings honor, hee had don his Deutye and left a famous Name behynde him".[3]

There is little doubt that Shovell intended to escape from Cadiz without saluting, but was unable to do so as the Spaniards had hemmed him in. He wished to sail to the Bay of Bulls. In Shovell's statement on oath to Judge Advocate Will Morgan he said:

> Each of themselves (Spanish ships) that we could not cast our ship without being aboard of one of them and ye Guns in ye Towne made ready to fire at us. I finding his majesty's ships and subjects in such unavoidable danger of being destroyed without saluting, I thought 'twas better to redeem ship and lives with a salute that [than] to ruine ye whole.[4]

Shovell was supported by his officers, who signed a statement for the Judge Advocate similar to his own. They included the First Lieutenant, Alexander Lawson, who had done most of the negotiating with the Vice Admiral; the General of the Flanders squadron, Honorato Boneficio Papachino, and one Christopher Myngs, son and namesake of Shovell's original patron. The final officer to write on the document was Edward Taylor, who clearly was illiterate, having to leave his mark rather than a signature.[5]

Shovell had little choice but to salute the Spanish Admiral's ship or face destruction. The *James galley* fired nine guns, but was only answered with an insulting three guns by the Spanish. They were allowed to leave.

Shovell was not the only English captain to have difficulty with the Spanish fleet, and the wish of their Admiral to have his flag saluted. Another of Shovell's contemporaries, Matthew Aylmer, fell foul of them shortly after the events of Cadiz Bay. In early July Aylmer, who was in command of the *Tiger* prize, fell in with the Spanish fleet in open seas near the Straits. In his letter written on July 8th 1683 from Tangier Road, Aylmer gave an account of the accidental meeting. He made clear that he had been forewarned by Shovell of his difficulties with the Spanish over saluting, so that the *James galley* and *Tiger* prize must have been in contact shortly after Shovell's exit from Cadiz Bay. Aylmer was summoned to the Spanish Admiral's ship and ordered to salute. While making his approach, Aylmer had secretly sent his men aloft and prepared to make a dash for it. He took the Spanish by surprise, and the *Tiger* prize initially shot away from them. Unfortunately for Aylmer, his ship was foul, and some of the Spanish ones extraordinarily clean, so that he was overtaken and called upon to salute. Lieutenant E. Stagings was sent by Aylmer across by boat to the Spanish Admiral where he put up a spirited defence of his commander's action. Stagings pointed out that there was "no need to salute unless assured that it will be returned gun for gun. If my captain salute you it might be his ruin. Do not take an advantage of a young gentleman's fortune." Eventually Stagings was told by the Spanish admiral: "If it were not for the respect for his Majesty of Great Britain he would have sent for the Commander and hanged him for doing what he did. Salute or be sunk." Aylmer, like Shovell, had little choice but to comply. He did so with thirteen guns, and the Spanish reply was an insulting three guns, two more than the Admiral thought necessary. It is not surprising that Aylmer made enquiries of his superiors as to what he should do in future.[6]

Both Shovell and Aylmer were potentially in great difficulty in having saluted the Spanish flag, in violation of their standing instructions. Word of their humiliation had soon reached England, and matters were further complicated by George Legge, 1st Baron Dartmouth's mission to Tangier which had set out for that place in the middle of the summer of 1683. Dartmouth was under orders from Charles II to extricate him from his expensive colony there, which he had received as part of his wife's dowry, on his marriage to Catherine of Braganza in 1662. Accompanying Dartmouth was the redoubtable Samuel Pepys. The Dartmouth expedition was to remain in Tangier from September 17th until December 1st 1683.

According to Pepys, Dartmouth was intending to try Shovell and Aylmer for their behaviour, once they had reached Tangier.

> My Lord of Dartmouth, when we first came out of England, was so full of a resolution to try Shovel and Matt Elmer, for taking affronts from the Spaniards that I have several times bethought myself, now he is here, that I hear nothing from him, and have once spoken to him. He answered that the Lords of the Admiralty have already determined something, which I have not yet seen but will inquire after. Memorandum Mr Elmer when he struck to the Spanish flag, had the same money on board that Shovel had when forced to strike to the same flag. So that the merchants at Cadiz concerned there is said, they believed their money was bewitched.
>
> I find by Sir W. Booth that George Elmer, the other Elmer's brother, gives out, that my Lord declared to him he hath foreborne to try his brother out of kindness to him. Likely enough, it being like all the rest a pure instance of the force of favour above zeal for the King's Service.[7]

Pepys described the two young captains as poltroons, and compared them unfavourably with a French commander who had refused to salute in similar circumstances, and had gone to the bottom with all hands. Pepys also brought Shovell's humble origins into it.

> And it is plain here that led him to it in another nation's port, and may be a good argument of the use of having gentlemen employed who can better judge of what is fitting in that kind, he being in everything else spoken of as a man of valour and knowledge in his trade and a good man.[8]

Pepys' argument was fallacious as Aylmer was an Irish aristocrat, and he had behaved in an identical manner to Shovell. There was also a suspicion that both young captains were hanging around Cadiz for their own benefit. This may be partially true, but Shovell had actually received orders from his Commander-in-Chief, Arthur Herbert, to go to Cadiz to await the arrival of a Lieutenant Nicholson.[9] Pepys was always grudging in his praise of Shovell; perhaps he had not got over the expensive medal that Charles II had given him after the ship-burning sequence of 1676!

Herbert had been recalled from the Mediterranean at the end of June 1683, and he was fortunately back in England in time to defend Shovell and Aylmer against their detractors. The suspense that Shovell must have felt ended on his receiving a letter from J. Brisbane, dated August 27th.

> What I have to say in answer to yours of the 13th of July is, that upon Admiral Herbert's arrival in England he did acquaint the Lords of the Admiralty with what happened between you and the Spanish ships at Cadiz, and they laid it before his Majesty, who I doubt not will come to some resolutions thereon in few days. In the meantime all I can advise you is his Majesty thinks there is wrong done him, and is not dissatisfied with you.[10]

By the time Shovell received this letter, with Pepys and others breathing down his neck at Tangier, he must have sighed with relief.

An enquiry was held by the Lords of the Admiralty into the whole question of saluting Spanish ships, with the Spanish Ambassador, Don Pedro Ronquillo, giving the other side of the story. The Spanish Admiral de Acquila appears to have been piqued that Shovell's ship was the only one in the Bay of Cadiz not to salute him, and also that he was expected to reply with an equal number of guns. The final report of December 1st 1683 spoke in terms of violence recently done to the *James galley* and *Tiger* prize. The final opinion of the Lords of the Admiralty was:

> That at sea to ye southward of Cape Finisterre your Majesty's ships be ordered not to give any salutes by firing of guns to any of ye King of

Spaine's ships whether flag ships or others of any rank or quality whatsoever and that they are not to require any such salutes from any of ye King's ships.

That in ports of Spaine ye same orders be observed or else that your Majesty's ships may be ordered in ye ports to salute ye ships of ye King – being of equal or superior quality as they salute ye forts and castles of Spaine that is to say on assurance first given that equal returns shall be made and not otherwise.

Among the signatories to this document are Daniel Finch, the Earl of Nottingham and Arthur Herbert. Perhaps for Shovell's sake, it was as well that Pepys was well away from all this, in Tangier.[11]

Nowadays it seems extraordinary that so much time and energy could be expended on such an issue. However, saluting was a very serious matter in the seventeenth century!

Within a week of Shovell's difficulties in Cadiz Bay, Arthur Herbert was leaving orders for Shovell to remain based on Tangier in command of the few remaining ships in the Mediterranean. From his ship, the *Tiger*, in Tangier Road, on June 29th 1683, he ordered Shovell to continue cruising in his station off Tangier with command of the *Crown*, *Tiger* prize, *Centurion* and his old ship, the *Sapphire*. Shovell was to endeavour to take, burn or destroy ships belonging to Sallee, Mamora, Tetuan or any other territory under the control of the Emperor of Fez and Morocco. Additionally, any prizes they took were to go to Tangier, and they should liaise with Governor Kirke there.[12]

Shovell was to act as Commodore to a small squadron of frigates. Among the captains placed under him was Matthew Aylmer. Having sent orders to his successor, Shovell, Arthur Herbert sailed for England. There were two main reasons for his recall. Firstly, the peace that he had concluded with Algiers in 1682 had allowed a lesser naval presence in the Mediterranean. Secondly, the experienced and outspoken Herbert, it was feared, might obstruct the outward-bound Dartmouth expedition, whose aim was to discreetly abandon the costly port at Tangier.

Captain David Lloyd of the *Crown* complained to Shovell, on July 20th, that his ship was leaking. Shovell in the *James galley* accompanied Lloyd to Gibraltar where she was careened. Personally inspected by Shovell, the *Crown* was found to have a defective stern post, and leaky planks suffering from worm. Cleaning was effected as far as possible, and the two ships then set out for the coast of Sallee. However, on August 22nd Shovell ordered Lloyd and the *Crown* home to England, because of her lack of sea worthiness.[13] Early in September Lloyd was unlucky enough to come across one of the frigates attached to Lord Dartmouth's expedition, and was pressed to speak to the Admiral. This Lloyd declined to do, and crowded on sail and did not alter his course for England. When Samuel

Pepys heard of this altercation, he made sarcastic remarks about the King's business being placed second to the private benefit of Lloyd, who was supposed to be carrying money that he had picked up in Cadiz. Also Pepys said that "... a commander can easily get certificates of his ships being foul and out of order, unfit and unable to keep the sea, as Lloyd now pretends, and so is sent home by Shovell."[14] Possibly Lloyd had agreed to carry money home from Cadiz, but the charge that his ship did not need to go to England because of leakiness is a false one. We have seen that Shovell personally inspected the *Crown* during careening at Gibraltar.

While cruising in the Bay of Bulls in August, Shovell and the *James galley* took a fly boat. On August 13th he wrote to the Consul at Cadiz, Sir Martin Westcombe.

> On Friday last being a cruising on the coast of Sally, I took a fly boat of about three hundred tunns which the Moors of Sally had taken from a Dutch man off Cape Finisterre. She is ladden with timber, if the post has not gone pray doe me the favour to give notice of it home. I hope the post have brought news of the taking of the principle traitors that would have murdered his Majesty.[15]

No doubt with the furore over his saluting in Cadiz Bay at its height, Shovell was keen for his successes to be known at home as soon as possible. The final sentence in the letter refers to the Titus Oates plot.

Despite his difficulties in Cadiz during June, Shovell went back again in August and there is a record that the *James galley* picked up stores there on August 16th.[16] By August 24th the *James galley* was back at Tangier unloading guns and ballast off the Mole, with a view to careening. However, a levant (wind from the east) delayed careening until September 2nd when Shovell reported that it had gone well.[17] Events in Shovell's journal during this period, from Herbert's departure on July 1st until September 9th, are recorded amongst the Dartmouth Manuscripts.[18]

Shovell's brief period of command in the Mediterranean was to end on September 16th 1683 with the arrival of Dartmouth's expedition at Tangier. Dartmouth had instructions that Shovell's small squadron could be called to his flag, provided that it did not interfere with their operations against the Barbary corsairs about the Straits. Dartmouth's remit was to evacuate Tangier because of its expense, and to find plausible reasons for doing so. Despite going out of his way to show his goodwill towards them, Dartmouth soon fell foul of Shovell and other naval officers over the Mole at Tangier.

The Mole that was being built to protect shipping at Tangier was an enormous structure nearly 500 yards long, and containing three million cubic feet of concrete. Prior to the evacuation the Mole would have to be destroyed, and the naval captains were expected to provide a legitimate reason for this, by declaring that Tangier was unsuitable as a base. Sir John Berry and Sir William Booth were charged with getting the captains to sign a report effectively damning the Mole and Tangier as a naval base.

Berry and Booth immediately had difficulty with Shovell, Aylmer, Francis Wheeler and others who had worked closely with Arthur Herbert, and resented his recall to England. They knew that Tangier was a suitable base for the higher rates to deal with the Barbary corsairs, to gain intelligence, and for harbouring small merchantmen.

Samuel Pepys who witnessed these events recorded:

> It is pretty also to see that no kindness obliges these rogues. I have shown my Lord, to his surprise, instances in Shovel, Wheeler, and Matt Elmer (to all of whom, especially the last, as being Herbert's creatures, he hath thought fit to be very kind since his being here,) their making a difficulty to sign the paper prepared by my Lord's orders for the sea captains to sign, about the condition of the harbour of Tangier, and the impractableness of making it a good one. Though they have been prevailed with by Booth to sign this, yet they did declare to Booth their satisfaction in the harbour when they signed it, and will be ready to do the like when they come to England. This is your men of honour and gentlemen! at least the two latter.[19]

Shovell, whose relatively humble origins precluded him from being described by Pepys as a gentleman, was initially not prepared to perjure himself to help Dartmouth and Berry. The most obstinate of the captains was said to be Shovell and perhaps the atmosphere was not helped by Berry, who had been one of those calling for Shovell to be court martialed over the saluting affair. One man who was compliant was George Rooke. However, Shovell and his colleagues were no match for the wily Pepys, who framed a series of cunning questions for them. Shovell and Rooke had to admit that careening under the Mole was difficult with the swell, and that Herbert had taken the hulk used for repairing ships across to Gibraltar as being an easier place to work.

Finally, on October 13th 1683 Dartmouth received the signed report damning the Tangier Mole. Among the signatories were Berry, John Ashby, Henry Killigrew, William Booth, the Aylmer brothers, Shovell, Rooke, Wheeler and Anthony Hastings. Pepys had done his work well. The report took the form of eight questions and answers.

1.Q: What is the length of the Mole and the depth of water within it?
  A: The Mole is 479 yards long. [The various depths of water at twenty-yard intervals were then given.]

2.Q: How have the depths changed in the last three to four years and if they have changed what is the cause?

A: The depth had been reduced by silting up with sand.

3.Q: What type of ground is there for ships riding within the Mole?

A: The ground is full of rocks and foul which cut cables.

4.Q: How many ships and of what quality may ride within the Mole?

A: Four or five 6th rates, drawing not more than eight feet of water, carefully moored head and stern, with setteas and small vessels between.

5.Q: What security is there against an enemy from the sea or Moors from the land?

A: It is not possible to render security against a bold enemy from the sea. The Moors overlook the port from the land.

6.Q: Whether a counter mole could be built?

A: No security for ships in the port unless the high ground overlooking it is taken and fortified. Levants [winds from the east] would stop ships getting out into Tangier Road.

7.Q: Whether ships had been careened within the Mole and any difficulties?

A: Rooke in 1678 careened the *Nonsuch* outside the Mole with difficulty. Captain Shovell had careened the *James galley* and *Sapphire* but with some difficulty, long expense of time and hazard of the King's ships.

8.Q: Those captains who served under Herbert. Why did he not make use of the port to keep the hulk, lodge the stores, careen ships rather than move them to a foreign port?

A: Shallowness of the water, danger from the weather, inability of the Mole to contain other than small ships and other things which do not now occur to them.

As an addendum the signatories added that the proximity of the Atlantic Ocean with its great waves would damage the Mole, that it would silt up, and that the water supply was meagre and bad.[20]

The Mole was doomed and poor Henry Sheeres, who had built it, was forced to use drills and explosive charges to destroy it.[21]

By early December 1683 Dartmouth was ready to take his contingent back to England, having accomplished an orderly withdrawal from Tangier. Shovell and the lighter frigates sailed with him, although the intention was to leave them to patrol off the Straits mouth, Sallee and South Cape.[22]

On February 27th 1684 Shovell recorded in his journal on the *James galley*, "We saluted Lord Dartmouth and so took our leave of him and this evening anchored in Cadiz by whom we found ye Bonaventure and Tyger Prize."[23] Shovell was to start a prolonged period of independent command as commodore of a small light frigate squadron, which was to last until the end of 1686 when he returned to England.

The period 1684–6 is a part of Shovell's life about which little is known. Laughton in the *Dictionary of National Biography* states that he appears to have continued in the *James galley* until his return to England in November 1686, the implication being that he was in the Mediterranean during this time. Shovell's own journal in the *James galley* is available in the Public Record Office for the period in question, and his account book also gives valuable clues to his activities. In fact, Shovell was indeed in command of the *James galley* throughout 1684–6, and he did spend part of this period in the Mediterranean. However, he was based at Lisbon and most of his time was spent in the Atlantic Ocean, off the mouth of the Straits and Sallee. [24]

With Tangier no longer available to Shovell, Lisbon was to be a suitable port for patrols to the Straits and Sallee. The first entry in Shovell's account book mentioning Lisbon is for March 27th 1684 and they continue intermittently until August 1686. Many are for pilotage fees, but others include money for pitch, powder, ironwork and careening for the *James galley* and the other frigates.[25]

Among the ships serving under Shovell was his old command, the *Sapphire* (Captain Anthony Hastings), the *Pearl* (Captain William Botham), the *Lark* (Captain Thomas Leighton) and the *Drake* (Captain Will Barron). The ships did not always serve together as a squadron, but went off at times in ones or twos on patrol. Merchant ships were escorted to the Straits and the ships of Sallee harried. Sometimes they were reinforced from England. But Shovell's squadron can hardly be described as the strong naval force that was considered important to keep near the Straits to protect commerce, after the withdrawal from Tangier.[26]

In August 1684 Shovell was off Sallee and exchanged letters with the Emperor of Morocco. The Emperor acknowledged that Shovell had taken several of their ships with mainly Mohammedan crew members, and could do what he liked with them including throwing them into the sea! The Emperor continued that he was pleased that the English had left Tangier, threatened to make ships go as far as England, and considered Shovell's behaviour a poor way to make peace.

Shovell replied, "Your Majesty tells us that we may threw them overboard if we please: All this we very well know: but we are Christians and they bear the form of men which is reason enough for us not to do it." Shovell pointed out that England had left Tangier of its own volition, was prepared to exchange his slaves for English captives, and played down the possibility of Sallee building ships big enough to get to England. He was prepared to take peace proposals to his master Charles II and was soon to sail.[27]

Shovell's compassionate attitude to the captured Sallee crews was in sharp contrast to the usual behaviour of the seventeenth century, when life was treated cheaply. A few years later, following a bombing assault on Algiers, the French Consul was fired away at the mouth of a big gun with four other Frenchmen. The French retaliated by shooting four captured Turks and sending them ashore dead on a raft. The Algerians in turn replied by cutting off the ears and nose of the Father Vicaire and then firing him from a gun. The French then strangled four Turkish captains in the Turkish manner and sent them ashore on a raft. Still the cruelties continued. No wonder the North African coast was called Barbary.[28]

The following February 1685 Shovell was back again off Sallee. He destroyed one of their richest merchant vessels, and also forced a 28 gun corsair to seek refuge under the walls of their fort.[29] The next month Shovell took his ships into the Mediterranean, and was at Messina and Livorno in March, and Malta in April.[30] Much of Shovell's journal in the *James galley* concerns revictualling, the weather and minor skirmishes. But on April 23rd 1685 he recorded, "Today ye King's Coronation Day we fired all our guns twice also all our small arms." Of course the new King was James II, who had earlier helped Shovell's career. Before long James' behaviour and religion would lead to a permanent rift between the two men.[31]

Life for Shovell at this time seems to have been a prosperous one, and included a trade in slaves. In August 1685 Shovell left various goods in the care of a merchant at Tenerife. The goods, consisting of gold, silver, silk and seven Moors, were to be sold for him, and the money sent to Cadiz or to Sir John Narbrough in London.[32]

Narbrough, who had done more than anyone to establish Shovell in the Navy during the 1680s, appears to have been acting in the capacity of banker in London for him. At times Shovell lent money to his officers and men, for it to be returned to Narbrough in London. Debts Narbrough held for Shovell included Lord Mordaunt for 50 guineas in 1680, George Rooke for £200 in 1681, and John Ashby for £390. In all, these debts amounted to more than a massive £2,000. Shovell also used Narbrough to pay off his own accounts. For example, about 1685 he wrote asking Narbrough to pay the balance of his account to Francis Wheeler, another naval officer. Throughout the 1680s young Christopher Myngs (son of Shovell's original benefactor, also Christopher) was lent money by Shovell. In 1684 he received a loan of £140 and repaid part of it in 1688, leaving a residual debt of £90. Young Christopher Myngs served in the *James galley* with Shovell. Not only officers were lent money by Shovell, but also his men. There are a number of references to men who had served in the *Sapphire* or *James galley* using their tickets as collateral. As was mentioned in the account of

1676, Shovell in the later 1680s used Captain John Hill (his future father-in-law) to look after a strongbox for him which contained gold chains, silver medals and bonds.[33]

In the late autumn of 1686 Shovell, still in the *James galley*, returned to England. On December 4th they reached Deptford and two days later began to pay off the crew. So 1686 came to an end.[34]

Most accounts of Shovell's career make little mention of 1687, possibly because of the momentous upheavals of the Glorious Revolution the following year. In addition, raw material for this period is scarce. Unless stated to the contrary, this account of 1687 is taken from the Marsham Papers[35] that contain much of Shovell's correspondence with the Admiralty, Navy Office and various ships at this time.

Shovell was to spend the greater part of 1687 and early 1688 aboard the *Anne* on a voyage to Portugal, to take the betrothed Queen to her new home, and then on to the Mediterranean. The *Anne* was a 70 gun 3rd rate, built at Chatham in 1678.[36]

On May 6th 1687 Shovell joined the *Anne* at Chatham, and spent the next two and a half months getting her ready for the voyage. Samuel Pepys sent books with details of the peace treaties with the Barbary States for Shovell to study. Algiers, Tunis and Tripoli were to be reminded of their obligations. The Navy Office wrote to Shovell on May 12th, advising him to be careful in the type of officer he selected for the *Anne*. The signatories included his old chief and friend Sir John Narbrough, and the letter is signed familiarly "your affectionate friends".

A daughter of the Prince of Orange was to marry Pedro II, the King of Portugal. The Duke of Grafton, the Vice Admiral of England, was to accompany the future Queen and her retinue from Rotterdam to Lisbon in the *Anne*, with Shovell as his Flag Captain. Various alterations were needed on the ship to accommodate the Royal party. Grafton required his cabin to be varnished and a lock supplied for it. In addition, extra space would have to be found for his servants and staff, as he was a flag officer of quality. The Earl of Sunderland had told Grafton that a convenient apartment should be made for the Portuguese Ambassador. Poor Shovell must have been hard pressed to prepare his ship for sea, as well as please his Royal charges.

Why had Shovell been chosen as the commander to accompany Grafton and the new Queen of Portugal to Lisbon? It may have been chance or it may have resulted from Grafton's time in the Mediterranean eight years before. In February 1679 Sir John Narbrough had written to Consul Sheeres at Tangier. "Cloudesley was one of his graces great favourites", while they were together at Port Mahon, in Minorca. Shovell also had very considerable experience of both diplomacy and battle against the Barbary States, which were to be visited. Henry Fitzroy, first Duke of Grafton, was the second son of Charles II by Barbara Villiers, the Duchess of Cleveland.

He was a handsome man and a formidable fighting sailor, who was to die in 1690 after the siege of Cork, as a result of fractured ribs caused by a musket shot.

By the end of May 1687 the *Anne* had taken on supplies, and had left Chatham for the Downs. During June Shovell was in correspondence with Pepys and the Navy Office concerning Sir Robert Gourdon's new pump. Shovell reported that he had no spare tackle and that the pump would not work. Gourdon was told of Shovell's complaint and asked that his workmen be allowed to repair it. Concern was also expressed by Gourdon that the French had designs on his pump, and in this he was supported by the Navy Office, in a letter of June 9th 1687 to Shovell and signed by Falkland, Narbrough and others. Shovell replied that he would try and keep the pump a secret. Whether it functioned properly or not during the subsequent voyage is not known.

The excitement over Gourdon's pump paled into insignificance compared with the furore over the return of the *James and Mary* merchant ship from the West Indies. The *James and Mary*, with a Mr William Phips as master, had been on a successful treasure hunting voyage to a Spanish wreck on the shoals off Hispaniola (Haiti/ Dominican Republic), where a large quantity of plate had been recovered. On June 9th Shovell reported to the Navy Office that he had received orders from James II for securing the *James and Mary*. That same day, Shovell ordered his lieutenant on the *Anne* to go aboard the *James and Mary* to see that no gold or silver was removed. Shovell reported to Samuel Pepys that he had put Second Lieutenant Francis Wivell and seventeen men aboard her. By the next day Shovell had further thoughts on the matter. Not only must no plate be removed from the ship, but the ship must not be moved from her moorings. The *James and Mary* was taken up the River Thames with her precious cargo intact. Off Grays, the Duke of Albemarle with Sir John Narbrough and others aboard a yacht, came to inspect the ship. As Shovell reported to Pepys, "they came up but did not offer to meddle in anything. I have strictly commanded Phips that nothing is to be carried from her". The same day Sir Roger Strickland had been sent to secure the plate, and Shovell had the *James and Mary* anchor a little above the port at Tilbury for better security.

The successful retrieval of the plate from Hispaniola was indirectly to change Shovell's life. The total value of the treasure was between £250,000 and £300,000. For each shareholder who had invested £100 in the expedition, the return was £8,000 to £10,000. No wonder that the Duke of Albemarle, son of the famous admiral of the First and Second Dutch Wars, and Sir John Narbrough were out in a yacht to watch the arrival of the *James and Mary*. Albemarle, the principal backer, is thought to have made £80,000, and Narbrough, who had invested nearly half as much, about £32,000. One naval man who certainly did not come to watch the return of

96

the treasure was Sir Richard Haddock who had bought a £100 share, but had sold it before Phips' return! [37]

Phips, by now Sir William, having been knighted by James II, reported that there was further treasure to be salvaged. On September 3rd 1687 Narbrough set sail in the *Foresight* to convoy Phips back to the West Indies to bring up the rest of the plate from off north-east Hispaniola. The *Foresight* reached the wreck on December 15th and commenced work. Little treasure was brought up, not enough in fact to cover expenses, and on the following May 27th (1688) Narbrough fell ill, and died of a fever.[38] Shovell had lost his longstanding friend and patron. Three years later Shovell was to marry Narbrough's widow, Elizabeth, and become stepfather to his three living children, Elizabeth, John and James. Narbrough's final voyage and a subsequent one were unsuccessful. As late as 1704 Narbrough's widow, by now Lady Elizabeth Shovell, and her second husband were endeavouring in an appeal to the House of Lords, to make the estate of the Duke of Albemarle pay its share of the expenses for Narbrough's final voyage. They were successful.[39] Probably it was during June and July 1687 that Shovell saw the last of Narbrough, who had done so much to promote his early career. They had seen little of each other since Narbrough returned to England from the Mediterranean in 1679.

On July 6th 1687 Sir Roger Strickland joined Shovell at the Gunfleet with four frigates. Shovell, in the *Anne*, sailed on the 9th for the Maes, which he reached on the 12th. The new Queen of Portugal came on board and her retinue and baggage were distributed throughout the ships. Shovell left the Maes on July 19th and passed through the Downs in order to put the pilots ashore. Foul weather forced them into Plymouth on July 24th, where they took the opportunity to rewater.

After a brief stay at Plymouth the contingent set sail for Portugal. Fair, windy weather allowed them to reach the Lisbon River after a journey of nine days. On August 2nd Shovell reported in a letter to Samuel Pepys that, "yesterday at about three in the afternoon we got up the river, and anchored before the King's palace and at about six this evening the King came on board and after staying about half an hour he returned with his Queen to his palace, we are now discharging ourselves of the Queen's retinue of baggage". As the *Anne* and escorts passed up the Lisbon River all the castles on the way saluted them. Shovell had been justified in asking for extra powder as the Queen's presence meant constant saluting!

The Duke of Grafton had an audience of King Pedro II, his Queen and family on August 1st. Shovell does not appear to have been invited to the palace. He wrote to Pepys on August 10th 1687 from Lisbon, stating that the Duke of Grafton had taken his leave of their Majesties, and that they intended to sail the next day, though they much desired to stay till the King's marriage was celebrated. This was to be done the next week with great solemnity. While at Lisbon, Shovell charged Grafton's account with twelve guineas for a gold watch. Later in the voyage Shovell advanced the Duke £15 to buy a black.[40]

From Lisbon the *Anne* set sail for Gibraltar, which was reached in early September. Little time was spent at Gibraltar except to make alterations to rigging and sails before leaving for Algiers. The Bay at Algiers was reached in mid September 1687.

As was customary in the second half of the seventeenth century, the people of Algiers were behaving in an uncivilised manner. Shovell was used by Grafton to deliver the English demands to the government. On October 6th 1687 Shovell reported to Pepys that they had been before Algiers for three weeks. He listed the forces available at Algiers, complained that Sallee men of war were able to sell prizes there, contrary to the peace articles, and said that they had demanded the return of various captives. All Englishmen discharged by the Sallee men of war bar one were returned, a Dutch woman and her child who had lived in England for nearly four years, and four blacks were successfully freed. Eventually the government of Algiers promised to keep all the articles of the peace treaty. Grafton and Shovell must have secretly smiled at this, as the Barbary states were inclined to forget peace treaties as soon as the English men of war were out of the vicinity.

From Algiers the English squadron set sail for Tunis. On the way they watered at Callery. The water was found to be poor as the sea was breaking into the river. Tunis was reached on October 27th, and Shovell found the people for once observing the articles of peace, and behaving in a civilised manner. He informed Samuel Pepys that there were five men of war of 40 to 50 guns and three galleys at Tunis.

Next port of call was Tripoli, where they remained for nine days. True to form Shovell found all manner of complaint against that government.

> I find the Government very fickle for they generally have two to three King's every year, but they all pretend great friendship with the English and say they resolve to keep the peace with us, they are mightily fallen off from their pirating for from ten ships they had when we made peace with them, they have but four, one of twenty four guns and another of upwards of forty.

Perhaps the government of Tripoli remembered what Shovell had done to their ships in 1676 and had hidden them. Shovell does not record whether or not they promised to behave themselves in future. He would not have believed them anyway.

From Tripoli the English squadron sailed for Malta, where they stayed for nine days. The *Anne*'s main mast was shortened by fourteen inches and forty tons of ballast and water were taken on. After leaving Malta they made their way briefly to Messina in Sicily, before going on to Livorno. The journey from Messina to Livorno took nine days and was unremarkable. At Livorno, Grafton dispatched the *Crown*, and Shovell hoped that they would soon follow. By January 10th 1688 the *Anne* was still taking on provisions at Livorno for the journey back to England.

Shovell gives little detail of the return journey to England. From Livorno, the English squadron sailed for Gibraltar where they arrived on January 31st 1688. After a stay of three days, there was just enough of a levant (easterly wind) to get them out of the Straits. By March 12th 1688 the *Anne* was off Falmouth, and on the 19th Shovell reported to Pepys at the Admiralty that they had reached the Downs.

Grafton's small squadron had accomplished everything that they had set out to do. The new Queen of Portugal had been safely carried to Lisbon, and the various Barbary states had been reminded of their Peace Treaty obligations.

NOTES

1. Marsham MSS U1515.01; Charnock, p.18.
2. ADM 51/489, Journal *James galley*.
3. Pepys Library MSS 2877, ff.199–234; Rawlinson A190, 248–50–7; Davies, Gentlemen and Tarpaulins p.64; All Souls Oxford MSS 240, f.417.
4. Pepys Library MSS 2877, ff.199–234.
5. Pepys Library MSS 2877, f.205.
6. Pepys Library MSS 2877, ff.213–234.
7. Pepys, Tangier Papers pp.77–78.
8. Pepys, Tangier Papers p.167.
9. Marsham MSS U1515.011.
10. Dartmouth MSS, Vol. I, p.89.
11. Pepys Library MSS 2877, ff. 199–234.
12. Marsham MSS U1515.011; ADM 51/3817, Log *Crown*; ADM 51/489, Journal *James galley*.
13. Marsham MSS U1515.011; ADM 51/3817, Log *Crown*.
14. Pepys, Tangier Papers pp.17–18.
15. Rawlinson A190, 248–50–7.
16. Marsham MSS U1515.011.
17. Marsham MSS U1515.011.
18. Dartmouth MSS, Vol. I, p.83.
19. Pepys, Tangier Papers p.59.
20. Printed in full Dartmouth MSS, Vol. III, pp.40–43.
21. Corbett, pp.132–137.
22. Dartmouth MSS, HMC 11th Report, Appendix Part V, Vol. I, p.105, Dartmouth to Charles II (draft).
23. ADM 51/489, Journal *James galley*.
24. ADM 51/489, Journal *James galley*; Marsham MSS U1515.011.
25. Marsham MSS U1515.011.
26. Marsham MSS U1515.011; Playfair, p.144.
27. Ockley, Account of South West Barbary.
28. Playfair, p.156.

29. Charnock, p.18.
30. Marsham MSS U1515.011.
31. ADM 51/489, Journal *James galley*.
32. Marsham MSS U1515.011.
33. Marsham MSS U1515.011.
34. ADM 51/489, Journal *James galley*.
35. Marsham MSS U1515.012.
36. Anderson, Lists of Men of War.
37. Dyer, pp.216–218; Marsham MSS U1515.012.
38. Notes and Queries, Dec. 29th 1888.
39. House of Lords MSS 1704–1706.
40. Marsham MSS U1515.011.

CHAPTER IX

# The Glorious Revolution

# 1688

In April 1688 Shovell joined a new ship, the *Dover*, a 48 gun 4th rate at Woolwich.[1] The reason for Shovell being given command of an inferior ship to the 70 gun *Anne* is not clear. The *Anne* would have been foul and in need of repairs after the nine-month cruise to the Mediterranean. Probably no ship of an equivalent size was available.

Shovell was to spend the next year on the *Dover*, which at the end of 1688 included the momentous events of the fall of the monarch, James II, in the Glorious Revolution.

April was quiet enough with the revictualling of the *Dover* and the checking of her rigging. By April 29th the *Dover* was fully rigged and she sailed from Woolwich on May 1st. On May 9th Shovell reported to Samuel Pepys that he had waited on James II at Tilbury, and had been ordered to Sheerness to await further instructions. In addition, he was told to take on board a Master Levstone and his servant as supernumeraries.[2] The *Dover* was still at Sheerness on May 21st, taking on further stores. At the end of May Shovell took the opportunity to go up to London to deal with his own affairs. However, on arrival in London, he got wind that Sir Roger Strickland was about to sail, and hurried back to the *Dover* without accomplishing anything. The nature of his business is unknown. Was it really personal or did it possibly relate to the Orange cause? Shovell was back in the *Dover* in the Downs on June 1st.[3]

A few days later, on June 3rd, Shovell was in communication with Pepys again. He sought clarification concerning the forwarding of orders to the Commissioners of the Admiralty. Pepys replied in a terse letter of

June 8th, that it was all orders, and not just those from foreign ports. Shovell's relationship with Pepys remained an uneasy one.[4]

While in the Downs, on June 11th 1688, Shovell and the crew of the *Dover* were informed of the birth of a son to James II. The Lieutenant of the *Dover*, Francis Wivell, wrote, "we hereing the Joyfull news of A Prince being Borne & Joy was demonstrated by firreing gunns & Spread y Coulors". The newborn Prince was the Prince of Wales, afterwards Chevalier St George or the Old Pretender.[5]

A few days later, on June 20th, Sir Roger Strickland sent the *Dover* to cruise off Orfordness to gain what intelligence they could of Dutch movements. The voyage took eight days and Shovell was back in the Downs by July 2nd. He did not stay for long, as on July 5th the *Dover* was off again to Sole Bay, and from there to the Nore. During this voyage Shovell gave an account (July 14th) of the state of the *Dover*. She had 150 men on board, provisions for nearly two months, and the crew had not been ashore for three months and four days. This was a long period of time, and not conducive to good health and morale. Shovell wanted the *Dover*'s main mast to be shifted two or three feet aft, as "she does not keep a good wind". In addition he wanted her girdled as "she lies along mightily in a gale".[6]

While at the Nore, on July 18th 1688, Wivell in his journal recorded that, "this day the King Came Downe to see the fleet we all fired gunns". On the following day he continued, "the King Came on board O$^r$ Shipp & at night y$^e$ King went to London".[7] What did James II and Shovell say to each other? It is reasonable to assume that the King asked for Shovell's loyalty. No doubt Shovell found it expedient to be non-committal. He was a straightforward man and not one to lie. From the Nore the *Dover* sailed to the Downs, arriving on July 31st.

Shovell appears to have spent the month of August quietly in the Downs, as there are no entries in his letter book for the period. At the beginning of September the *Dover* made a further trip to Orfordness, and back to the Downs. On September 17th Shovell asked for James Cleghorne, who had served as master's mate under him in the *James galley*, to join him in the *Dover*. Ex-men of the *James galley* were again in his mind when on September 22nd he asked for payment of the cook of his former ship, who had supplied tallow for the boatswain and the carpenter. Shovell pointed out that it was nearly two years since the end of the *James'* last voyage under his command.[8]

By October 2nd Shovell in the *Dover* had accompanied Sir Roger Strickland to the Nore, before going on to the Gunfleet and then back to the South Foreland on October 4th.[9] Shovell was still in the Downs on October 15th, the day George Legge, Baron Dartmouth, took most of his ships to the Gunfleet from the Nore.[10] Samuel Pepys wrote to Dartmouth on October 14th, stating that, "his majesty approves your sending Shovell to the Gunfleet, and the cautions that you have given him".[11] Exactly when Shovell joined Dartmouth at the Gunfleet is uncertain, but he was there by October 23rd. On this date he wrote to Dartmouth from the *Dover* (at the Gunfleet) stating that he had received his Lordship's orders of the 20th, and thanking him for the ships put under his command. Shovell went on to describe how he would place two ships to gain intelligence of the Dutch, with the remainder of the ships staying put at the Gunfleet. "If they have seen or heard any news of ye Dutch fleet and to give me notice of all creditable intelligence which I will immediately transmit to your lordship." Shovell had found a ketch at the Gunfleet that had removed the buoy according to the crew's orders. He sent the ketch into Harwich for supplies and water. Shovell had taken care that the removal of the buoy did not mislead any vessel.[12] Presumably the buoy had been removed to hinder Dutch invasion attempts.

Shovell's frequent movements during September and early October were almost certainly on scouting trips, to gain intelligence of the Dutch. Matters must have been made more difficult for him as he had a change of lieutenant about this time. On October 11th Sir Anthony Deane wrote to Dartmouth stating that the son of Sir John Dawes wished to be Shovell's lieutenant, as the post was now void.[13] On October 29th Shovell reported to Pepys that his Lieutenant Hay had joined the *Mary* and Lieutenant Dawes had replaced him.[14]

Before continuing with events directly concerning Shovell, it is necessary at this stage to take a wider view of naval events of the time. James II's reckless pursuit of Catholicism had undermined his standing in the Kingdom. In March 1687 Arthur Herbert, later Earl of Torrington, refused on principle to support James II's plan to repeal the Test Act. Herbert was Master of the Robes and Rear Admiral of England, being paid £4,000 a year, and with little other means of supporting himself. There was considerable surprise that Herbert not only sacrificed his income, but that he did so on grounds of conscience. We have seen earlier, in his behaviour in Tangier in the period 1679–83, his immorality and lack of principle.[15]

As one poet put it, "Murders and rapes his honor can digest – Boggles at nought but taking off the Test." [16] At this point Herbert was approached by Edward Russell on behalf of the Prince of Orange, and he eventually commanded William's fleet which carried the future King to Torbay.

James II had attempted to bring Catholicism to the services. The army was Protestant and the navy partially so. The majority of officers in the navy rejected Catholicism.[17] Catholic priests were introduced by James II into the navy, and the seamen threatened to throw them overboard. It was said at the time that, "all the great seamen are averse to Popery and lovers of liberty".[18]

James II's lack of sensibility to the feelings of the fleet made him appoint a Roman Catholic officer, Sir Roger Strickland, to be Commander-in-Chief.

This was a mistake and caused a great deal of resentment. Not until September did James II realise his error, and Dartmouth was appointed in his place. Strickland was downgraded to second in command, before a few days later being superseded by Sir John Berry.[19] Dartmouth took command on October 3rd 1688[20], and had the main responsibility for stopping the landing of William of Orange.

For James II to remain King of England, he depended on Dartmouth's fleet defeating William of Orange's invasion force under Herbert, before they could establish themselves ashore. The key to the whole matter was the site of the invasion, and which anchorage Dartmouth's fleet should wait at to counter it. James II anticipated a landing in the north of England, but his fleet had to be in a position to sail either to the north or south-west. No anchorage was ideal for a flexible response. On October 15th Dartmouth took his fleet from the Nore to the Gunfleet.[21] James II wished his fleet to lie off the Dutch coast, but at councils of war on October 26th and 28th the captains of the fleet decided that this would be risky, because of the possibility of inclement November weather. They decided to remain at the Gunfleet.[22] A council of war consisted of two parts. Firstly, a meeting of the elite council made up of the flags, and senior captains such as Dartmouth, Strickland, Berry and Berkeley. Secondly, a full council consisting of the above plus the other captains of the fleet. Usually the elite council made up its mind, and the full council endorsed their view.[23]

During the second half of October, with the fleet based on the Gunfleet, there was much informal discussion amongst the captains of Dartmouth's ships. Dartmouth wrote to James II on October 17th:

> I would be glad to have more sea room and keep my commanders now they are in good order as much as may be aboard their own ships and not liable to be caballing one with another, which, lieing idle together they may be apt as Englishmen naturally do to fall into, especially being in the way of dayley pamphlets and newes letters.[24]

On October 22nd Dartmouth was again writing to James II.

> I must acquaint your Majestie that on Friday last I had some hints of dissatisfaction in some young men in the fleet, and hearing Mr Russell is gone for Holland (if it be so) makes me more jealous then of any interest Herbert can have here . . . The Duke of Grafton was down here a little after my comeing tho' he would not let me know it. My Lord Berkeley. [John, 3rd Baron of Stratton]. I am told is very pert but I have taken him in next shipp to me and shall know more of their tempers in a little time.[25]

Herbert's pamphlet was almost certainly read in the fleet as a supplement to a circular letter from the Prince of Orange. "I as a true Englishman and your friend exhort you to join arms to the Prince for the common cause."[26] Another declaration by Herbert suggested that the English fleet was being used as an instrument of "Popish Slavery".[27] Herbert hated Dartmouth personally, and had considerable supporters in the form of men who had served with him in Tangier during the period 1679–83. Captain Matthew Aylmer and Lieutenant George Byng were active in the Orange cause, having been recruited by the senior army officers, Percy Kirke and the Duke of Ormonde. Aylmer had served with Herbert during his days in Tangier, and Kirke had been Deputy Governor, and a boon companion of Herbert's.[28] The anti-Catholic view of the army was disseminated in the fleet by officers such as Kirke and Ormonde, and in addition by some serving naval captains, who also held positions in the army.

What of Shovell himself at this critical period? His exact movements from late October to the beginning of the New Year are difficult to follow, as the log of the *Dover* for the period is not in the Public Record Office, and his letter book has no entries between October 23rd and December 26th 1688.[29] Shovell is known with certainty to have been in the Gunfleet on October 23rd when he ordered, on Dartmouth's instructions, two ships to go out on scouting missions, and it is likely that he attended the critical councils of war at the Gunfleet on October 26th and 28th. It was at these meetings that the fateful decision was made to remain at the Gunfleet with the English fleet, and only the eccentric Sir William Jennens wished to sail for the Dutch coast.[30] Shovell undoubtedly took part in the caballing that took place in the fleet during late October. Samuel Pepys had singled out Shovell along with Aylmer, a principal conspirator, and Wheeler as being "Herbert's creatures".[31] They had all served under Herbert, based on Tangier, in the period 1679–83.

Shovell was a friend of Aylmer's, and indeed when the *Association* sank in 1707 and Shovell drowned, one of Aylmer's sons died with him.

Shovell had spent a large part of the previous year in the *Anne* with the Duke of Grafton, who we have seen earlier was well disposed towards him. Grafton had been upset by James II, his uncle, not giving him command of the fleet in 1688, and had made contact with William of Orange. In addition, Grafton had visited the fleet during the autumn, in what was seen as an attempt to subvert the loyalties of the captains.[32] Another conspirator, Sir John Berry, who was later involved in a plot to kidnap Dartmouth on board ship, was also well known to Shovell. Berry had taken part in the decision to destroy the Mole at Tangier in 1684, which Shovell and others had opposed.

What was Shovell's attitude towards his King, James II? Both his early patrons, Myngs and Narbrough, had been favourites. James had helped his own early career, and had been the Lord High Admiral of England between 1660 and 1673 when Shovell had begun his career in the navy.

At the Battles of Lowestoft in 1665 and Sole Bay in 1672, in both of which Shovell had fought, James had been the Commander-in-Chief. Shovell must have felt some loyalty towards him. As late as October 5th 1688 James II had asked Dartmouth to "let Shovell and Skelton know if this war continues they will soon be better mounted after the first brush shall be over".[33] Clearly this meant promotion to a bigger and better ship than the *Dover*. James II came to loathe Shovell after the events in Dublin Bay in 1690, when the Royal Guards were shot by Shovell's men in front of the by then ex-King. Shovell was a Protestant and had no time for Catholicism. He had with others resisted James II's attempts to bring it to the navy.[34]

Shovell's sympathies lay with William of Orange. Arthur Herbert, later Earl of Torrington, had been chosen by William to command the Dutch fleet. We have seen already that Shovell had been closely connected with Herbert at Tangier in the period 1679–83. Herbert thought highly of Shovell[35] and the feeling was reciprocated. Herbert was a hard living, immoral and foul-mouthed man. Shovell was the opposite, being faithful to his wife and not inclined to swear.[36] It is strange that the two of them should hit it off so well. The fact that his old chief, Herbert, was commanding the Protestant William of Orange's fleet, must have helped Shovell decide to desert James II.

According to some sources, the Protestant commanders at the Gunfleet, who would have included Shovell, had decided amongst themselves that it was better to avoid meeting the Dutch fleet, than having to desert to them if they met. This view was carried to the councils of war on October 26th and 28th, and may have been a factor in the decision to remain at the Gunfleet rather than go to the Dutch coast as James II and Jennens wished.[37] James thought that two thirds of his captains would not fight.[38] Edward Russell, later Earl of Orford, thought the number to be eight. In a letter to Herbert dated November 13th from Exeter, Russell stated that the "captains were resolved to salute my Lord Dartmouth and come over to us the names Berry, Deane, Hastings, Delavall, Churchill, Aylmer, Shovell, Berkeley".[39] Assuming that Russell was correct, and there is no reason to think that he was not, this puts Shovell at the heart of the conspiracy.

On October 30th Dartmouth received intelligence that William of Orange's fleet was about to sail, and tried to get out of the Gunfleet. William's fleet under Herbert, consisting of fifty-nine sail of which thirty-two were ships of the line, were indeed about to sail.[40] On November 1st 1688 a brisk north-easterly gale allowed the Dutch fleet out into the open sea. Dartmouth's fleet, which was roughly the same size as that of the Dutch, was prevented from getting round the Gunfleet shoal by this same north-easterly wind. Dartmouth was not able to leave the Gunfleet until November 3rd, by which time William's fleet was in the Channel off

Dover. On November 5th William came ashore at Brixham with Dartmouth's fleet still off Beachy Head. Dartmouth held a council of war that same day which resolved not to attack what was thought to be a superior force. Storms on November 7th forced Dartmouth and his ships back to the Downs, where they remained until November 16th. On the 16th they sailed west again, and on the 17th actually saw the Dutch fleet in Torbay, before storms drove them back to Spithead. The fleet remained at Spithead until it surrendered to William on December 13th.[41] It was indeed a Protestant wind that kept Dartmouth's fleet in the Gunfleet, and drove William's down the Channel to Brixham. James II's worst fears had been realised.

Shovell, in the *Dover*, was in Dartmouth's own red squadron, and he was part of the fleet which attempted to follow the Dutch down the Channel in early November. During part of the first week of the month, the *Dover* was out cruising and away from the main fleet, but by November 9th she had returned to Dartmouth's side.[42] Shovell may not have attended the council of war, on November 5th, which resolved not to fight a supposedly superior fleet. However, he took part in the move up the Channel to Torbay, back to the Downs, and finally to Spithead.

Between November 20th and 22nd Lieutenant George Byng, of the *Defiance*, a leading conspirator against James II, was sent ashore at Gosport to make contact with William of Orange. After an adventurous horse ride, Byng made contact with Edward Russell and then William at Sherborne. Byng had returned to the fleet by December 3rd, with a letter for Dartmouth from William making it clear that he should desert James II. On the 3rd Byng and Wolfran Cornewall watched a house in Portsmouth where the baby son of James II was supposed to be, prior to being taken by Sir Roger Strickland to France. Shovell, Aylmer and Hastings were ordered by Dartmouth to stop the unauthorised egress from the harbour. Despite the fact that the baby Prince's baggage was already on board the *Mary yacht*, he was returned to London on the Duke of Powis' coach. Shovell never had to make an effort to stop him leaving by sea.[43]

On December 23rd James II finally left England via Rochester, where in later years Shovell was to be the Member of Parliament, and on Christmas Day he heard mass in France. William of Orange's gamble of invasion had succeeded.

The end of the momentous year of 1688 found Shovell still on the *Dover* at Spithead, soon to serve a new Protestant King who was more to his liking.

NOTES

1. D.N.B. Shovell; Anderson, Lists of Men of War.
2. Marsham MSS U1515.012.
3. Marsham MSS U1515.012.
4. Marsham MSS U1515.012.
5. RMT MAT 26; Journals of the *Dover* 1679–1694, Francis Wivell.
6. Marsham MSS U1515.012.
7. RMT MAT 26; Journals of the *Dover* 1679–1694, Francis Wivell.
8. Marsham MSS U1515.012.
9. Marsham MSS U1515.012.
10. Davies, James II etc. p.83.
11. Dartmouth MSS, HMC. 11th Report, Appendix V, p.161.
12. Marsham MSS U1515.012.
13. Dartmouth MSS, HMC. 11th Report, Appendix V, p.157.
14. Marsham MSS U1515.012.
15. Powley, p.13; Davies, James II etc pp.89,90.
16. G.M. Crump ed., Poems on Affairs of State, iv, 1968.
17. Secret Memoirs.
18. Leake, pp.17–19.
19. Laird Clowes, pp.323–324.
20. Davies, James II etc. p.83.
21. Davies, James II etc. p.83.
22. Davies, James II etc. p.84.
23. Davies, James II etc. p.94.
24. Powley, p.67.
25. Powley, pp.67–68.
26. Powley, p.69.
27. Japikse Correspondentie; Davies, James II etc. p.85.
28. Davies, James II etc pp.85–87; Le Fevre, Tangier, the Navy and its Connection with the Glorious Revolution of 1688.
29. Marsham MSS U1515.012.
30. Davies, James II etc. p.93.
31. Le Fevre, Tangier etc.
32. Davies, James II etc p.88.
33. Dartmouth MSS, HMC 16th Report, App V, p.144.
34. Secret Memoirs.
35. Le Fevre, Tangier etc.
36. Secret Memoirs.
37. Leake, pp.17–19.
38. Davies, James II etc. p.86.
39. Egerton, MSS 2621, f.47.
40. Richmond, p.196.
41. Davies, James II etc p.84.
42. Powley, pp.67–69, 84–86, 100.
43. Powley, pp.137–138; Torrington, pp.31–34.

# CHAPTER X
## *The Battle of Bantry Bay*
## *1689*

In the first three months of 1689 Shovell, in the *Dover*, was frequently on the move in the service of William of Orange. Dartmouth had surrendered his fleet to William in the preceding December, and Shovell had been put under the command of Sir John Berry at Spithead.[1] On January 15th 1689 Berry split his squadron with Captain John Ashby becoming Commodore.[2] Shovell was sent to the Channel Isles to make certain that the French had not occupied them. On January 24th he was victualling in Guernsey Road, and by February 9th he was back at Spithead being ordered by Ashby to Plymouth.[3] Shovell returned to the Downs with the flyboat from New England on February 13th, and was still there on March 14th.[4]

Phineas Bowles had been Dartmouth's secretary, as Admiral of the Fleet, and he had been inherited by Arthur Herbert in February 1689. On March 9th Bowles replaced Samuel Pepys as Secretary of the Admiralty. At about this time Shovell had been offered a new command, the *Kent*. On March 14th he wrote to Bowles at the Admiralty stating that he had never refused a commission to a bigger ship before. Shovell wanted to carry 100–150 men, some of whom had been under his command for seven to ten years, plus his surgeon, to the *Kent*. "I humbly beg their honours pardon that I do not remove till I hear further and rather they give me leave to continue where I am than remove into the best ship in England without my men."[5] Although it was usual for commanders changing ships to take some of their men with them, this large number of 100–150, plus the fact that some of them had served with Shovell for ten years, gives an indication of his popularity with the common sailor. Bowles had been a victualler's agent at Lisbon and Tangier during Shovell's time in the Mediterranean, and the two were said to be particularly friendly.[6]

Shovell escaped going to the *Kent* for the present, although he was to serve on her briefly, in 1692, after the Battle of Barfleur. However, he did join a new ship on March 27th 1689, when he went on board the 64–72 gun, 3rd rate, *Edgar*. Shovell was able to take some of his men with him from the *Dover*. They included John Flaxman, Midshipman, Thomas Shovell, Able Seaman and John Jenkenson, another Able Seaman. It is likely that they were all related to him at least by marriage. Shovell's commission as Captain of the *Edgar* was dated March 30th 1689.[7]

A month after joining the *Edgar*, Shovell was to come to the attention of the new King, William III, after the first naval engagement of the war with France at Bantry Bay.

James II had deserted his Kingdom. A convention of the House of Lords and Commons, on February 13th 1689, declared William of Orange and his wife Mary, King and Queen. Louis XIV of France supported the cause of James on the grounds of religion, and the common cause of Kings.[8] Louis ordered the fitting out at Brest of about thirty ships of the line and seven frigates. This fleet carried James and 5,000 men to Kinsale in southern Ireland where they landed on March 12th.[9] Catholic Ireland (with the exception of Ulster) was anti William III and pro James II. James hoped that he might use Ireland as a stepping stone to regain his throne. At this particular juncture things looked favourable for him.

News of the expeditionary force from France reached William III, who ordered Arthur Herbert to get a fleet to sea at once. This took time as ships needed collecting from eastern and western ports, as well as the usual difficulty with supplies. Herbert was unable to sail until mid April and then with only twelve ships. The remainder of the fleet was ordered to follow. Herbert's orders were to stop ships from leaving Brest, but the situation was complicated by the fact that war had not yet been formally declared.[10]

Herbert with his fleet of twelve ships, including Shovell in the *Edgar*, reached Cork on the Irish coast on April 17th. As there was no sign of the French, Herbert took his ships to Brest and also into the Soundings, without meeting the enemy. He returned to the Irish coast, and on April 29th he sighted a considerable French fleet which he lost again. On April 30th Herbert looked into Baltimore without success, and believing the French to be to the west of him, bore away towards Cape Clear with an easterly wind. Later that same day he sighted the enemy standing into Bantry Bay.[11]

The French fleet that Herbert and Shovell saw entering Bantry Bay, on the evening of April 30th, consisted of twenty-four ships of the line, ten fireships and two frigates, which had carried ammunition and stores from Brest for James II's army. The French were under the command of Louis François de Rousselet, Compte de Châteaurenault in the *Ardent*, 66 guns, with Chefs d'Escadre Jean Gabaret in the *Saint Michel*, 56 guns, and Forant in the *Courageux*, 56 guns, as second and third in command respectively. In addition to the fleet from Brest were three frigates under Captain Duquesne-Mosnier, who had stayed behind after the previous expedition to help James II on the coast of Ireland.[12]

Poised outside Bantry Bay, Herbert now had nineteen ships of the line (a further seven ships had reinforced him) to Châteaurenault's twenty-four, a considerable disparity.

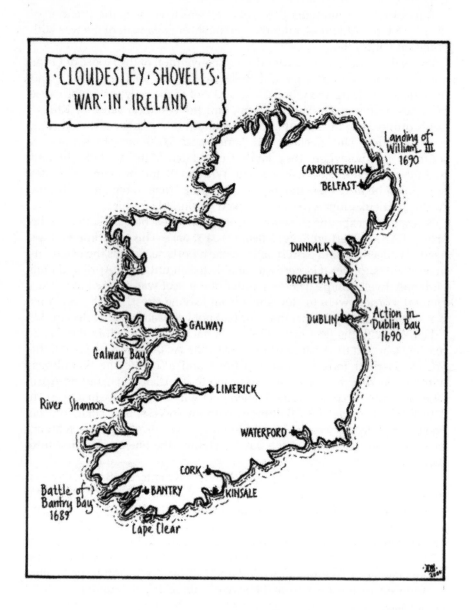

·CLOUDESLEY·SHOVELL'S·
·WAR·IN·IRELAND·

Landing of
William III
1690

CARRICKFERGUS
BELFAST

DUNDALK

DROGHEDA

DUBLIN
Action in
Dublin Bay
1690

GALWAY

Galway Bay

LIMERICK

River Shannon

WATERFORD

CORK

Battle of
Bantry Bay
1689
BANTRY
KINSALE

Cape Clear

Order of battle of the English fleet at Bantry Bay:

| Rate | Ship | Guns | Men | Commanders |
|------|------|------|-----|------------|
| 3 | *Defiance* | 64 | 400 | Captain John Ashby |
| 4 | *Portsmouth* | 46 | 220 | Captain George St Loe |
| 3 | *Plymouth* | 60 | 340 | Captain Richard Carter |
| 4 | *Ruby* | 48 | 230 | Captain Frederick Froud |
| 4 | *Diamond* | 48 | 230 | Captain Benjamin Walters |
| 4 | *Advice* | 48 | 230 | Captain Hon. John Granville |
| 3 | *Mary* | 62 | 365 | Captain Matthew Aylmer |
| 4 | *St Albans* | 50 | 280 | Captain John Layton |
| 3 | *Edgar* | 64 | 445 | Captain Clowdisley Shovell |
| 3 | *Elizabeth* | 70 | 460 | Captain David Mitchell |

(Flag of Admiral Arthur Herbert)

| | | | | |
|------|------|------|-----|------------|
| 3 | *Pendennis* | 70 | 460 | Captain George Churchill |
| 4 | *Portland* | 50 | 230 | Captain George Aylmer |
| 4 | *Deptford* | 54 | 280 | Captain George Rooke |
| 4 | *Woolwich* | 54 | 280 | Captain Ralph Sanderson |
| 5 | *Dartmouth* | 36 | 150 | Captain Thomas Ley |
| 4 | *Greenwich* | 54 | 280 | Captain Christopher Billop |
| 3 | *Cambridge* | 70 | 400 | Captain John Clements |
| 4 | *Antelope* | 48 | 230 | Captain Henry Wickham |
| 3 | *York* | 60 | 340 | Captain Ralph Delavall |

Fireships

| | | | | |
|------|------|------|-----|------------|
| 5 | *Firedrake* | 12 | 65 | Commander John Leake |
| 5 | *Soldadoes* | 16 | 75 | Captain Francis Wyvill |
| – | *Salamander* | 10 | 35 | Commander Thomas Crawley |

On the morning of May 1st 1689 Herbert took the English fleet into Bantry Bay. Among his captains were a number of men who had already featured or would feature in Shovell's life. Rooke, Leake, Delavall, Churchill, Mitchell and the Irish Aylmer brothers were all present at the first naval battle of the War of the League of Augsberg. When Châteaurenault saw the English fleet come into the bay, he stopped unloading soldiers and stores and weighed to meet them. Herbert, who was to the leeward, had difficulty working up to the French. Once the English fleet was within two miles, the French bore down upon them in a very orderly line, and the battle started at 10.30 a.m. John Ashby on the *Defiance* led the English van, with Shovell in the *Edgar* next to his admiral in the centre.

Herbert realised that he had taken on a superior enemy force, and steered out of Bantry Bay with a gentle sail. He intended to get his fleet into a regular line, come close to the French and if possible to try to gain the wind. The line was improved, but Herbert could not gain the wind.[13]

The action was a brisk one with the French using tactics which were to become characteristic of them, firing at long range to dismast, and then retiring before the wind. They avoided any opportunity for the English to bring them to close quarters.[14]

The *Edgar* with Shovell in command was heavily engaged. Indeed the casualties at the end of the battle on her equalled the number on all the other English ships put together.[15] One of them was Shovell's midshipman, Stephen Martin, who was to become brother-in-law and biographer of Sir John Leake. Martin had his left thigh broken by a cannon ball which had passed through the side of the *Edgar*, and had taken a man's legs off before reaching him. This happened late in the afternoon, and Martin was carried below almost insensible from pain and loss of blood. Confusion reigned below because of the number of casualties, and the surgeon decided to amputate his leg. At this news Martin revived himself, and refused to have his leg cut off, saying that he would live or die with his leg on. The surgeon changed his mind, and set the leg, albeit badly so that it had to be done again, otherwise the leg would have been useless. Martin had saved his limb but it was to be shorter than the other one, which left him with a limp for the rest of his life. It can be readily imagined the awful suffering Martin must have undergone with the injury, and setting of his fractured thigh, without an anaesthetic or pain relief. Another midshipman in the *Edgar* was John (later Sir John) Norris, and an admiral of the fleet whose career was to be intimately connected with Shovell's from this time on.[16]

Martin's future brother-in-law, John (later Sir John) Leake, like Shovell, was another to enhance his reputation in the battle. Although he was only in the *Firedrake*, classified as a fireship but in fact used as a bomb ketch, he managed to cause considerable damage to the French ship of Chevalier Coëtlogen. This ship, the *Diamant*, was set on fire with Leake's father's invention the "cushee piece" or mortar. Coëtlogen came close to losing his ship through the fire, and indeed part of her blew up. From this time on bomb ketches became a feature in every English fleet. Leake himself did not seem to be keen on the new weapon, perhaps because his brother had lost his life in an accident with it. Leake's performance at Bantry Bay was brought to Herbert's attention and led to his promotion.[17]

The battle continued until 5.00 p.m. with the English fleet in the afternoon getting the worst of it. Châteaurenault had the advantage of the superior force and the wind, and he might have comprehensively defeated the English at this point. Two factors were against him. Firstly, his fireships were not available to him as they were still unloading at Bantry, and secondly, the difficulty he had with his leading subordinates Gabaret and Forant. Both men were senior in service to Châteaurenault, and it was said that they tacitly avoided pressing home the advantage. In any event, the French broke off the action and stood in towards the shore. Having completed the discharge of troops and stores, they set sail for Brest and arrived there on May 8th.[18]

Herbert's fleet had been considerably mauled. He led them first to the Scillies looking for possible reinforcements, and having failed to find them he made for Portsmouth, arriving there on May 12th.[19]

The English losses at Bantry Bay were ninety-four killed (including George Aylmer, brother of Matthew) and 270 wounded. The French had forty killed and ninety-four wounded.[20] Clearly the French had had the best of the action, and although Châteaurenault had done what he set out to do in landing his troops, he had missed a golden opportunity to convert a tactical victory into overall superiority at sea. His conduct was severely criticised in France. Herbert's performance, with a weaker fleet, was generally approved.[21]

William III went in person to Portsmouth to meet those who had distinguished themselves in his cause at Bantry Bay. The *London Gazette* of the day recorded the scene.

Portsmouth, May 15th. The King came hither this morning from Colonel Norton's House, where His Majesty lay last night: The Principal Inhabitants, to the number of above 100, went out on Horseback to meet him on the way, and drawing up in a Line, exprefs'd their Dutiful Affection to His Majesty with repeated Acclamations. Mr Mayor and the Corporation received His Majesty at the Gate of the Town, where Mr Recorder having made a speech, they walk'd by the King's Coach, Mr Mayor carrying the Mace, to the Water-side; the Regiments in Garison here being drawn out, and lining the Streets; Admiral Herbert, with the Chief Officers of the fleet, met His Majesty near the main Guard, and attended Him on Board the Elizabeth, where he splendidly entertained His Majesty at Dinner. The King was pleased, as a Mark of his great Satisfaction in the Conduct and good Services of Admiral Herbert, to declare His Royal Intention of Conferring upon him the Title and Dignity of an Earl of this Kingdom. And was likewise pleased to confer the Honor of Knighthood upon Capt. John Ashby Commander of the Defiance and Capt. Clowdesley Shovell of the Edgar. And farther, to encourage the Seamen, His Majesty was Graciously pleased to bestow upon such of them as were in the late Engagement with the French, a Donative of 10s. a Man, which was distributed accordingly, amounting to about 2600l. The Officers, and all the Seamen of the fleet, exprefs'd on this Occasion the greatest joy and loyalty that can be imagined, accompanied with loud Shouts and Huzza's, and with all the Demonstrations of a brave Resolution to employ their lives in

113

their Majesties Service. The King being come ashore again, rid round the Town to view the Fortifications and afterwards took Coach and returned to Colonel Norton's, the Mayor and Aldermen attending His Majesty out of the Gates.[22]

Thus Cloudesley Shovell became a knight on May 15th 1689, in his 39th year. Arthur Herbert was made Earl of Torrington at the same ceremony, in his flagship, the *Elizabeth*. Sir John Laughton in the section on Herbert in the *Dictionary of National Biography* gives the date erroneously as June 15th. As well as the *London Gazette* report quoted above, a contemporary journal written on Ashby's ship, the *Defiance*, clearly stated that the date in question was May 15th. Laughton took the view that there was no apparent reason for the general satisfaction expressed, and that the rewards handed out by William after the engagement at Bantry Bay were in reality for services rendered during the Glorious Revolution. [23]

The unfortunate Stephen Martin was put on shore with the wounded at Portsmouth. The newly knighted Shovell was very kind to him, gave him a certificate of good behaviour and told him that if he would return to him as soon as he was able, he would prefer him to be a lieutenant. Martin, through affection, decided to follow John Leake, despite the fact that he was a new captain. Shovell as an older officer, and with the expectation of a flag, would have been in a better position to help his career.[24]

As late as December 27th 1701 Shovell was still writing testimonials for men who had served with him at Bantry Bay.

> These are to certify that Mr Edward Mann served as pilot extra-ordinary on board his Majesty's ship the Edgar under my command in the year 1689, where he acquited himself very soberly and carefully in all points of his duty and was very forward and active in line of service in that years engagement in Bantry Bay, and is I think well affected to ye Government as by law established. Dated this December 27th 1701. Clow. Shovell.[25]

Following Bantry Bay, war was officially declared between France and England. James II and his troops swept from the south to the north of Ireland. The Protestants of Ulster had retreated into Londonderry and Enniskillen. In April 1689 James began the siege of Londonderry, and by the middle of the year he had reached Dublin with French officers and money. By late July the Protestants besieged in Londonderry were starving and on the verge of giving up, when John Leake and George Rooke got relieving ships down the river to them. In August the Duke of Schomberg landed William III's army in Antrim. There was to be no decision on land in 1689.

At sea the French had missed a golden opportunity by failing to follow up their advantage at Bantry Bay. They had but twenty-six ships at Brest and six more at Rochefort. The Compte de Tourville, with the Toulon squadron of twenty sail, had passed the Straits on July 2nd, with the intention of concentrating French forces at Brest. Herbert, by mid June, had put together a force of forty-three sail and twelve fireships. He had sailed from Portsmouth, and had positioned himself off Brest to stop the junction of the Toulon and Brest fleets. It is likely that Shovell, still on the *Edgar*, accompanied Herbert's fleet. William III was in a difficult position, in that General Kirke was trying unsuccessfully to free Londonderry from its siege, and 12,000 men under the Duke of Schomberg were embarking for Ireland. These forces would be put in jeopardy if a superior French fleet reached the Irish Sea. Herbert maintained his position off Brest, but on July 19th Tourville and the Toulon squadron slipped into Brest, under cover of fog. The English and French fleets were roughly equal. In August the French came out of Brest, but by then Herbert had had to withdraw into Torbay to revictual. By now it was too late in the year for a major naval engagement.[26]

In October 1689, by command of Arthur Herbert, newly created Earl of Torrington, Shovell had removed from the *Edgar* to a new ship for him, the *Monk*. She was a 52–60 gun ship, built at Portsmouth in 1659.[27] Soon after changing ships Shovell found time to write to the Earl of Torrington seeking patronage for one of his friends, John Maine, Captain of the *Sampor fireship* in 1678 and "who hath declined serving King James his wicked reign".[28] On November 5th he was still at Spithead revictualling the *Monk*. The day before Shovell had ordered the captain of the *York*, on Torrington's instructions, to take on board three companies of Colonel Talmash's regiment with their baggage and drums, and to accompany the *Monk*. Similar orders were given to the captain of the *Advice*.[29] On November 11th the *Monk, Kent, Henrietta, Advice* and *York* set sail from Spithead with the troops for Ireland.[30]

Early in December Lord Berkeley of Stratton sailed with twenty-six English and Dutch men of war to look for the French. Among the ships accompanying Berkeley was the *Monk*, with Shovell on board. Berkeley detached Shovell with a squadron to go to the Irish Coast to gain intelligence of French shipping movements.[31] After leaving Berkeley on December 21st, Shovell recorded that he had met several French privateers and two small men of war, but that as they were all clean, they had outsailed him. The *Kingfisher*, which was part of Shovell's squadron, managed to get up to one privateer, and fired about 100 guns into him, but he escaped by tossing his boats and spare mast overboard. In addition, Shovell reported that about ten French men of war had been out on a number of occasions around the Scillies, and over to Ireland. Shovell had been forced to leave his station, because of a sprung main mast and wished to return to port to clean his ship, as he had no hope of catching the French.[32]

So 1689 came to an end. If it had been an inconclusive year for the war in Ireland, it had been a successful one for Shovell personally, with the recognition by a knighthood of his valour at Bantry Bay and his services to the Glorious Revolution.

NOTES

1. Powley, p.152.
2. Powley, p.158.
3. Marsham MSS U1515.012.
4. Marsham MSS U1515.012.
5. Marsham MSS U1515.012.
6. Ehrmann, pp.289–293.
7. ADM 51/4215, Captain's Log *Edgar*; RMT MAT 26; Ticket book *Dover* April/May 1689; Anderson, Lists of Men of War.
8. Leake, p.20.
9. Laird Clowes, p.327.
10. Richmond, p.203; Laird Clowes, p.327.
11. Laird Clowes, p.327; Richmond, p.203; Torrington, pp.36–37; Martin, p.8.
12. Laird Clowes, p.327.
13. Torrington, p.38; Laird Clowes, pp.328–329.
14. Leake, p.22.
15. Secret Memoirs.
16. Martin, pp.8,9.
17. Leake, pp.22–23.
18. Torrington, p.38; Laird Clowes, p.329.
19. Torrington, p.38; Richmond, p.204.
20. London Gazette No.2451.
21. Richmond, p.304.
22. London Gazette No.2454, May 16th–20th 1689.
23. D.N.B. Herbert; Journal of the *Defiance* 1689, Log Book No.13.
24. Martin, p.9.
25. Document in author's collection.
26. Richmond, pp. 204–205.
27. Marsham MSS U1515.012; Anderson, Lists of Men of War.
28. Le Fevre, Tangier, the Navy etc.
29. Marsham MSS U1515.012.
30. Master's Log *Kent*.
31. Torrington, p.41.
32. Marsham MSS U1515.012.

# CHAPTER XI
# *Action in Dublin Bay*
# *1690*

Late in 1689 Shovell, in the *Monk*, had been forced to return to harbour because of a sprung main mast. On February 9th 1690 the Commissioners of the Admiralty ordered Shovell to take his eight or nine ship squadron into the Irish Sea again, to protect the transport services of the army in Ireland.[1] In his letter book at about this time (February 7th), Shovell mentioned that the doctor had got his "things" on board. These consisted of white sugar, brown sugar, currants, tamarins, fresh barley, maize and nutmeg, presumably for use in attempting to keep the crews healthy, which was one of the great problems of the seventeenth century navy. In addition, the doctor took on board two large table cloths and saucepans! [2]

February 1690 was spent in getting Shovell's squadron ready for sea, with the various ships revictualling, firstly at Spithead where they had been based at the beginning of the year, and then later at Plymouth. Shovell's letter book at this time is full of sailing instructions, his line of battle, signals, and the usual difficulty of poor supplies. In Plymouth Sound, on February 28th, Shovell complained about the "damnified and stinking beer" in the *Dartmouth*.[3]

Early in March Shovell took his squadron over to the Irish coast. On March 14th the *Monk* returned to Milford Haven. Shovell reported that:

> . . . since we parted from Plymouth the wind has been from the east. Stretched over to the coast of Ireland where off Waterford we took two vessels. One full of salt for Dublin. The other a small vessel of Lord Clincarty's came from Dublin bound for Cork. Letter to the Governor of Cork on ye Dublin man of war stating that the Duke of Berwick was returned to Dublin and had his horse killed under him.

Shovell complained about the high cost of provisions, in particular mutton, brandy and salt. No doubt he liberally helped himself to James II's salt from the captured vessels.[4] In addition, Shovell pointed out that he was expected to protect the shipping of the English forces in the Irish Sea with fifteen men of war, as opposed to France's forty.[5]

Shovell spent the remainder of March 1690 on intermittent cruising between the coasts of Ireland and Wales. He wrote to James Southerne, the Secretary of the Admiralty, stating that he intended to cruise between Dublin and Holyhead, with ships off Waterford and St David's Head. Each week he would either come in to port himself or send vessels to Hoylake (Highlake) and Holyhead, for the Admiralty's instructions. On March 28th Shovell sent a letter from the *Monk*, at sea, to His Grace the Duke of Scarburgh who was General of Her Majesty's Forces in Ireland, with important information of French troop movements. "One of our frigates cruising on the coast of Ireland took a French man of war that came out of Brest in company with 35 men of war. This French man saith that they brought seven to eight thousand men and landed them at Corke."[6]

The French were ready at Brest before the English, and had been allowed to carry 6,000 French troops across to Cork without any real hindrance.[7] The frigate that had provided Shovell with the news of the French squadron and troops at Cork was commanded by George Byng, another naval man whose career was to be interwoven with that of Shovell, from their Tangier days to the fateful October 22nd 1707. The French squadron was commanded by Vice Admiral D'Amfreville. According to Byng's biographer, Shovell went immediately to Hoylake to forward the transport of soldiers to Carrickfergus. Hoylake was the assembly point for English troops.[8]

Certainly, by April 2nd 1690 Shovell was at Hoylake. His letter book, at this time, contains orders for the men of war and convoys to go to Milford Haven, Cork or Carrickfergus, with attendant instructions for signalling and revictualling. In early April Shovell wrote to Southerne stating that he was still at Hoylake with the *James, Charles, Mary galleys* and the *Swift*, two hoys and a ketch. They were ready to sail with the transport ships with Colonel Cutts's Regiment, and also 400 carriage horses with their carriages. Mention was made of some of the ships that they had come across as having King James' pass. In another letter to Southerne at this time, Shovell reported that "the Irish are mightily high and transported with the news they hear that Scotland have declared for King James and that our Parliament disagree with King William". Later in another report which is unheaded, but probably also for Southerne, Shovell mentioned that King James intended to make a French regiment his "Royal Regiment", and that this had displeased the Irish. "People had been killed over it." [9]

In mid April Shovell took his squadron (seven men of war, a fireship, and four tenders) from Hoylake across to the Irish coast.[10] On April 19th 1690 he went into Dublin Bay, and a vigorous action took place in full view of James II himself. In his letter book, Shovell gives a graphic account of this encounter with the enemy. The letter from Shovell is addressed to Major General Kirke and is undated. However, the letter before and the one after it are dated the 26th of April 1690, which is the likely date.

I make bold to trouble your honour with an account of my going into Dublin and what happened there —. On ye 19th in the morning we stood into Dublin bay and saw a ship about a mile within ye Barr at a place called Polebege after we anchored in the bay I went aboard ye Monmouth yaucth [yacht] and at a little more than half flood ye wind which was northerley which made a smooth barr and having water enough I with ye yaucth, two hoys, a ketch and ye pinnaces went over ye barr upon which ye ship run higher up about a mile and a half to a place called Salmon Pool: and there run aground within shot of a Frenchman of 12 guns, and also an English ship or two filled with soldiers of ye Kings guards and kept firing at us: we followed him and gave him battle but he defended himself for above an hour and a halfe, then I made a sign for ye fireship to come in which when they saw coming in they foresook their ship and gott ashore in their boats. We went aboard and gott out an anchor and by heaving some of her things overboard we got her off; they filled this Frenchman of 12 guns full of men and also five or six other small ships and made a show of sayleing therefore I expected they would have attacked us but they never offered at us: the wind weared out of ye sea and in turning out one of our hoys about a mile and a half within ye barr: run aground so that we could not get her off before ye water fell away, therefore we lay by her and took her guns and other things out ready to heave off next high water, at low water ye Hoy was dry round and many thousand people came upon ye sand also King James was there as were his guards, we lay in our boats armed to keep ye enemy from attempting the Hoy and two Protestants among many others that were running about ye sand at length came running to us and we took them in, likewise ye Guards to show their briskness came rideing near us, Among the rest a Frenchman came rideing to ye water and called us in English as well as he could speak a great many hard names and fired his pistols at us, we shott down his horse and rowed ashore ye Frenchman slipped his leggs out of his boots and run away, but ye saylors went ashor and unrigged his horse. Ye ship we took was ye Pelican ye biggest of ye scotch men of warr taken last summer by ye French and she lay there in order to take in some of King James ill gotton goods which he forced from poor Protestants for his damned brass money. In this ship was twenty guns and she had upward of forty men, two or three we found dead upon deck and one mortally wounded we also found a Spaniard and an Englishman which were forced aboard her – they inform us that twelve men were killed and several others wounded that went ashoar –

The Protestants that came to us are people of no intelligence and can tell us no more than what your Honour already know: they think there is two regiments besides ye Royall Regiment in Dublin: and two or three companies of French white coats are come to town: tis talked that King James will make one of his regiments his Royal Regiment which have so much displeased ye Irish: that they are ready to go together by ye ears and some have already been killed about it: nothing else but my humble service to your honour.

Honourable Sir your honours humble servant.

Shovell wrote a similar letter to James Southerne at the Admiralty, with the additional comments that the French ship taken, the *Pelican*, was one of King James' best men of war, and that Captain Writtle had done well in the action. Writtle was the man who had carried them into Dublin Bay.[11] The *Pelican*, commanded by Captain Bennet, was bound for France laden with hides and tallow.[12]

Shovell had been directly responsible for the taking of the *Pelican* and the saving of the hoy. His comments about "King James' ill gotten goods which he forced from poor Protestants" made quite clear Shovell's feelings for his former sovereign. The contempt Shovell had for James II was reciprocated, as James was said to have conceived a mortal aversion to Shovell. Shovell, in turn, was said to have no more valued his threats than formerly he did James' promises.[13] In some quarters Shovell was criticised for shooting the ex-King's guards in the royal presence – a charge that had been trumped up by James II's friends.[14] Others saw the action in a different light. "Cloudesley Shovell bravely fell upon the French ships in the sight of James II and he has retaken a scotch man of war taken last summer."[15]

In the action in Dublin Bay Shovell had shown great dash, courage and resolution. The question that has to be asked is why a senior captain, soon to reach flag rank, had charged around with small boats in a bay with the tide about to go out, let alone staying with the stranded hoy, and shooting up his former sovereign's guards on the sands around him. Surely Shovell would have been better directing operations from the *Monk*, at a safe distance, with his lieutenant taking the risks in the bay. We have seen how Sir John Narbrough sent the young Shovell to burn the ships of Tripoli, while he stayed put in the *Harwich*. However, Shovell was not that kind of man, preferring to be where the action was hottest and the risk greatest. Another Norfolk sailor, Horatio Nelson, was to behave in a similar fashion a century later. No doubt Shovell would have countered any criticism with the simple reply that he had been successful.

By April 27th Shovell's squadron had returned to Hoylake with the exception of the *James galley*. Shovell appears as early as late April to have been put on stand-by to take William III across to Ireland. At this time he wrote a letter to the Admiralty asking if he had to stay with the ships until His Majesty came, as he would "rather be seeing our forces safe across" (to Ireland). As there was no news of William, Shovell intended to send two ships over to Waterford for intelligence. Sick and wounded sailors, as was the custom in the seventeenth century, were put ashore in sea ports for the local inhabitants to take into their homes to look after until they had recovered. In his April 27th letter to the Admiralty, Shovell requested that the people of Liverpool and Pembroke be paid for taking the sick in. The sailors were disheartened by the reception they were receiving, because of lack of payment for their hosts. There is no record that Shovell was successful in this. Shovell reported that navigation was difficult in the seas off Hoylake, and asked that stores might be delivered at Milford which had an easier access to it. He had further complaints about the dilatoriness of the Office of Ordinance. The Admiralty must have found this a welcome change from the constant criticism of victualling! [16]

Shovell spent the month of May either at Hoylake, or in the later part of the month cruising off the coast of Wales and then over to Ireland. Following his cruise off the coast of Wales, Shovell wrote a long report, dated May 23rd, to the Commissioners of the Admiralty. The report opened with Shovell informing them that he had been so ill that he had been unable to write to them for a day or so because of his indisposition but was now "something better". The nature of this illness is unknown but he was subject to gout, malaria and quinsies. It is unlikely that gout would have stopped him being able to write at all. While cruising off Wales looking for enemy vessels, Shovell found Colonel Trelany's own company on "ye backside of Wales", from a vessel that was unable to proceed. Shovell ordered the *Ruby* to take them across to Carrickfergus, before going himself to Dublin and the Isle of Man. Two of his ships, the *Dover* and *Experiment*, had attacked and driven ashore five or six Irish vessels, near Waterford. Other ships had been met, without being in a convoy, and by good fortune had escaped. [17]

Shovell experienced difficulties with his ships in chasing enemy vessels in St George's Channel. He had intelligence that one Anthony Thompson, in the employ of James II, was sailing from Dublin in a clean sloop of 18 guns. Thompson was transporting men either to Wales or some part of Lancashire. Shovell intended to prevent him, but believed "you had as good set a cow after a hare as put any ship in the station after a vessel that is clean tallowed". This was not a new problem, and could only be prevented by the constant cleaning of ships. [18]

In his report to the Commissioners of the Admiralty of May 23rd 1690, Shovell mentioned the perennial problem of manning. Some of his ships had little more than half their complement of crew, because of illness and desertion. Shovell requested that if he had to stay much longer at Hoylake, that he be given powers to hold courts martial, and thus be able to punish deserters. On a happier note, Shovell had appointed Mr Edmund Loades to act as the *Dover*'s Lieutenant, until their honours' pleasure was known. Mr Loades "is a pretty seaman and has gone to sea from his childhood and about two years last has served as a midshipman and masters mate", wrote Shovell.[19] Loades was the bachelor son of Sir John Narbrough's favourite sister, and Shovell had offered him a helping hand in his career, as Narbrough had done for Shovell himself. Loades was to drown as Shovell's Flag Captain, on the fateful October 22nd 1707.

While going into Hoylake in late May, Shovell's barge from the *Monk* had met with an accident.

> My barge was yesterday sailing ashore and either through careless-ness or foolishness she overset on their heads, and my first lieutenant Mr Dawes and all my boats crew except one man drowned. I have appointed Mr Robert Hancock who has served under my command nine years and is at present my chief mate, and is able bodied and brave to act.

Dawes had been with Shovell for nearly two years, and had been recommended by Sir Anthony Deane.[20] Robert Hancock was yet another man to drown with Shovell, as Captain of the *Eagle*, which sank the same evening as the *Association*.

In Ireland, the land campaign had gone badly for the Duke of Schomberg who commanded William III's troops. Many had died of disease at Dundalk. William decided that the time had come for him to lead his troops in person.[21] Victory for William in Ireland was essential before his main front in Flanders could be pressed. His Cabinet were wary of supporting the movement of large numbers of troops to Ireland, as the French controlled St George's Channel. William was intent on making 1690 a decisive year for the campaign in Ireland.[22] An English army of 27,000 men was collected at Hoylake by mid June, to be taken in transport ships across to Carrickfergus. A squadron of six to eight ships under Shovell, in the *Monk*, was to cover their passage, and William III would lead them in person.[23]

On June 8th 1690 William III travelled to Chester Cathedral where he heard divine service and a sermon preached by the Bishop. From Chester, William went to Hoylake where he was met by Shovell and the rest of the sea commanders. After inspecting the ships William moved on to Gayton and to the house of a Mr Glegs to await a fair wind for Ireland.[24] During this period, William made Shovell Rear Admiral of the Blue, and gave him the commission with his own hands.[25] The date on the commission is June 3rd 1690, so William III must have signed the document before starting his journey.[26] In a little over a year, Shovell had been knighted and had reached flag rank, all before his 40th birthday – no mean feat for a relatively poor boy from Norfolk. No wonder Shovell recorded "humble and hearty thanks" for the commission in his letter book.[27]

At noon on June 10th William III came on board the *Mary yacht* which was commanded by Grenville Collins, famous for his sea charts.[28] On June 11th 1690 William, his army in 250 transports, escorted by Shovell and his squadron, left Hoylake at about noon. The journey was not an easy one as there was thick fog which Shovell reported as keeping visibility down to two ships' lengths. The north of the Isle of Man was not reached until the 13th, but on the 14th the wind blew fresh, and they reached the Bay of Carrickfergus. That afternoon William went ashore and then travelled by land to Belfast where he was met by his land commanders.[29]

Shovell spent the next four days at Carrickfergus revictualling his ships. He waited on William III at Belfast, and was ordered to return to England to join Torrington and the main fleet. Shovell sailed on June 18th, but did not reach Milford Haven until June 23rd because of a calm sea and lack of wind.[30]

In this chapter, Shovell's movements in the first six months of 1690, and the transport of William III's troops to Ireland have been dealt with. What had happened to the main English fleet under the Earl of Torrington, and its French counterpart? The English fleet had had its numbers reduced in late 1689 and early 1690, because Edward Russell was sent with a squadron of thirty ships, plus 400 merchant vessels and a Dutch princess to Spain. Russell reached Corunna in March and returned to England on April 28th. Of more importance was the loss of Henry Killigrew's squadron of thirteen ships, which had been sent to the Mediterranean on March 7th to defend trade there and to shadow the French Toulon squadron. Neither Killigrew's squadron nor Shovell's, which had been used to cover the transport of troops and William III to Ireland, would be available to Torrington for the major naval battle of 1690 at Beachy Head. In May the French Toulon squadron of five ships slipped past Killigrew and out of the Mediterranean. They joined Compte de Tourville with the principal French fleet at Brest in time for the Battle of Beachy Head on June 30th. Killigrew's squadron had followed in a rather dilatory fashion, but did not reach Plymouth until well after the battle, on July 14th. At about the same time as William III was landing at Carrickfergus, Tourville with the main French fleet, strengthened by the Toulon squadron, was sailing out of Brest. Tourville's plan was to meet and destroy the inferior English fleet of Torrington, before it could be reinforced by the squadrons of Killigrew and Shovell.

The first news reached England that Tourville was off Falmouth on June 21st, and Torrington was ordered to put to sea and engage the enemy. Torrington held a council of war at which it was decided to try to get to windward of the superior French fleet. He hoped to link up with a few ships under Ralph Sanderson at Plymouth, and the missing Killigrew and Shovell squadrons. Failing this, Torrington would lead the English fleet back up the Channel, if necessary, as far as the River Thames, in order to keep the fleet in being. With the addition of his missing squadrons,

Torrington would have had something approaching parity with the French, and his "fleet in being" he felt would preclude an invasion attempt. Queen Mary, who was temporarily in charge in London in the absence of her husband William, and her advisers were not happy with Torrington's attitude, and he was given positive orders to attack the superior French fleet. One of the reasons behind the decision may have been concern about the vulnerability of Shovell's and Killigrew's squadrons, and especially a fleet of merchantmen worth £700,000 who were to the west of the French.

On June 30th 1690, off Beachy Head, the combined fleet of fifty-six Anglo/Dutch ships under Arthur Herbert, Earl of Torrington, swept down on Compte Anne Hilarion de Tourville's sixty-eight French ships. Torrington's fleet was damaged, losing fifteen ships and the Dutch suffered particularly severely. A comprehensive victory followed for the French with Torrington retiring into the Downs. Unfortunately for the French, Tourville did not follow up his victory with the total destruction of the English fleet. It was there for the taking, but Tourville contented himself with a threatening passage back down the Channel and an attack on Teignmouth, before returning to Brest in August. Torrington was blamed for the defeat and clapped in the Tower of London. Killigrew, on reaching Plymouth on July 14th, withdrew into the Hamoaze and set up batteries to protect his ships from a possible French attack.[31]

Among the English ships lost after Beachy Head was the *Anne*, on which Shovell had served in 1687. Her captain was John Tyrrel, the same Tyrrel who had sought the advice of Samuel Pepys in a disagreement with Shovell over the wearing of distinction pendants in 1689.[32]

Where was Shovell at the time of the Battle of Beachy Head on June 30th? In *The Life and Glorious Actions of Cloudesley Shovell* it is stated that he acted as Rear Admiral of the Blue Squadron at the battle and was deeply engaged. This is incorrect. We have seen that Shovell, still on the *Monk*, and his squadron had reached Milford Haven on June 23rd. From Milford Haven, Shovell took his squadron to Plymouth, arriving on about June 26th. In his letter book, there is a report to Southerne at the Admiralty to the effect that Shovell, on the orders of Torrington, must find the first secure harbour. The report continued, "this morning we went into Plymouth Sound which was not secure enough". Although the report itself is not dated, the letters before and after it bear the dates of June 25th and June 26th respectively. This makes it likely that Shovell reached Plymouth on either the 25th or 26th, and was still there on June 30th, the day of the Battle of Beachy Head.[33] Clearly, Shovell was not in a position to sail down the Channel to help Torrington and the main Anglo/Dutch fleet, because Tourville was blocking the way.

During the little over two weeks that he was at Plymouth, Shovell secured the post of Commander of the *Pelican*, the ship he had taken in front of James II in Dublin Bay, for another protégé of his, John (later Sir John) Norris. Shovell described Norris as a "very fit man for such a command for he is a diligent, sober and good officer". We have already seen that Norris was in the *Edgar* as a midshipman with Shovell at Bantry Bay, and had later become his lieutenant. In early July Shovell sent the *Hopewell ketch* to the Soundings to look for Killigrew, the *Advice* to Scilly, and the *Crown* to Brest to gain intelligence of French movements. Shovell's letter book for this period also deals with signals, further difficulties of manning, and the complaints of the merchant ships who were having crew members removed from them by the navy. Shovell assured Southerne at the Admiralty that he would leave sufficient crew on the merchant ships to do the necessary work. A report dated July 10th shows the line of battle drawn up by Shovell for his squadron. *Pembroke, Swiftsure, Nonsuch, Crowne, Archangel, St Albans, Monk, Advice, Dover, Mordaunt, Sweepstakes, Essex, Mary galley* with the *Experiment, Half Moon, Greyhound* and *Pearle* in the second line.[34]

William III had intelligence that French frigates were to be sent to St George's Channel to burn the English transport vessels on which his army depended. On July 10th Shovell was ordered by William to take his squadron to the west of Scilly, and then to the coast of Ireland off Waterford, to counter this possibility. If Shovell met Killigrew, he was to apprise him of the situation. On July 13th Shovell sailed from Plymouth.[35]

Sir John Laughton in the *Dictionary of National Biography* section on Shovell, states that Shovell and Killigrew, with their squadrons at Plymouth, to an extent controlled the movements of the French. It is unlikely that Shovell and Killigrew were there together, as Shovell is reported to have left Plymouth on July 13th, and Killigrew did not arrive until the next day.[36] This means that Shovell would not have taken part with Killigrew in the withdrawal into the Hamoaze, and the setting up of batteries in fear of an attack from the sea by Tourville.

The Battle of Beachy Head had been disastrous for the naval interests of England, and more particularly for those of the Earl of Torrington, who was largely blamed for the defeat. It was fortunate that the very next day after Beachy Head, July 1st, William III had won a major land victory, at the Battle of the Boyne. This spelt defeat for James II in Ireland, with Dublin soon falling, and James himself fleeing from Kinsale. William III marched on Limerick but was checked by Patrick Sarsfield, and in early September 1690 left for England with most of the Irish coast in his hands, apart from the ports of the south-west.

From July 13th to July 21st Shovell cruised off Scilly. On the 21st the *Dover* and *Experiment* joined him from the coast of Ireland. They had taken a ketch from Kinsale with a number of James II's retainers endeavouring to follow him to France. Among them were Captain Hacket, Captain John Hamilton, Archibald Cockburne, Anthony Thompson, Captain Thomas

Power, William Sutton and six servants. The retainers told Shovell that earlier in the month, on July 3rd, James II had arrived at Duncannon and had taken some shipping before sailing on to Kinsale. Here he stayed for only two hours before sailing for France with two frigates which had long been ready for such an eventuality. James had taken with him Lord Powis, Sir Roger Strickland and Captain Richard Trevanion. Further orders reached Shovell on July 21st, to sail for Kinsale and to intercept several French frigates reported to be there. [37]

In the execution of his fresh orders Shovell found himself off Waterford on July 27th. Although Waterford had surrendered on July 25th, nearby Duncannon Castle had refused to give up. Shovell wrote to the commander of the King's forces near Waterford, Major General Piercey Kirke, on July 27th, stating that he was off Waterford with sixteen men of war. He had sent frigates for Duncannon and was in the river with his boats a sounding.* In addition Shovell mentioned that he was to secure William III's safe passage to England. The letter was written from the *Experiment,* a smaller vessel than the *Monk,* which would have been easier to use in Waterford River.[38] Kirke was well known to Shovell from earlier days in Tangier, and Shovell offered the assistance of his frigates in the assault on Duncannon Castle. Shovell in the *Experiment,* with another frigate the *Greyhound* and all the boats of the squadron, went in. The castle's defenders fired on them, but then said that they would surrender on terms. The terms allowed them to march out with their own arms, as had been permitted at Waterford on July 25th and earlier at Drogheda. The next day the Governor of the castle, Bourk, marched out with about 250 men with their arms and baggage, leaving forty-two guns mounted in the castle. The sudden surrender of the castle was a direct result of the presence of Shovell and his squadron.[39]

Following the success of the reduction of Duncannon Castle, Shovell and part of his squadron returned to Plymouth. This may have been in response to William III's orders to Shovell on July 28th. Shovell was to leave the frigates and take his bigger ships as previously ordered.[40] Information was received by Shovell and the Admiralty that French ships were being collected at Limerick, with a view to evacuating the remains of the French army if another battle should be lost. Later reports indicated that the French ships had gone from Limerick to Galway, and had been reinforced by a squadron under Vice Admiral D'Amfreville. Shovell's movements during this period are confused. On August 14th William III sent orders to Shovell. William understood from Nottingham that Shovell and his squadron were heading for Limerick, to destroy such French ships that might be in the river. Shovell was to sail for the River Shannon at

* Testing the depth.

126

once, and go up it as far as possible to near the city of Limerick. He was to leave defences below to resist any French squadron that might be about. The French fleet was reported to be at Brest. As soon as Shovell reached the Shannon, he was to notify William III by any means he could.[41]

On August 20th William wrote to Shovell through Sir Robert Southwell, from his camp near Limerick, hoping that Shovell would not be long from the Shannon. "You may safely send up your long boat to Castle Town about 9 miles below Limerick where Richard Waller will be directed to convey thither what you send."[42] By September 2nd Southwell was informing Shovell "that having long battered the walls of Limerick, and made an assault on August 27th, we were repulsed with 1000 men killed". William III had left camp on August 30th, and was embarking on a ship for Bristol or Milford Haven. The rains made the continuation of the siege of Limerick impossible, and it was left to Shovell to find success at Galway, to make a glorious end to the campaign.[43] Shovell had been ordered by William III the same day, September 2nd, to go straight away to Galway and fight Vice Admiral D'Amfreville, who was reported to have a squadron of eighteen men of war there.[44] William repeated his orders on September 8th, from Badminton House where he was staying on his journey back to London, for Shovell to go to Galway.[45]

Although the exact date is uncertain, Shovell and his squadron left Plymouth in late August bound for Galway. His squadron, consisting of five 3rd rates, ten 4th, eight 5th and six fireships, did not get far, as early in September they were driven back into Plymouth by the poor weather. Shovell took the opportunity to write to Sir Robert Southwell, asking for a stronger squadron in view of the latest intelligence of the French reinforcements for the Irish Sea.

> I will take all opertunitys to putt his Majestie's commands in execution, but we can hope for small success if our enemy be stronger, for at sea, if the fleets be near equall, there must be great success to gaine a great victory; for by that time the one is beaten the other generally is wearey. Sir, we ought to make use of this opertunity, for since we have ships enough at sea, why not a squadron that will leave no doubt of a victory; for I believe nothing but necessity will obleage the French to give you such an opertunity as this may prove.[46]

Shovell frequently repeated his view concerning the necessity of a superior force to gain a significant victory at sea.

Nothing came of this plea, and eventually on reaching Galway, Shovell heard that D'Amfreville and his French fleet had left about a week before, but that five sail remained there. Sending two frigates into the bay rather than risk his whole squadron, Shovell waited for their report. The frigates returned to him on September 26th, with the news that D'Amfreville had sailed from Galway on September 13th, with about sixty ships, of which eighteen were men of war. On these ships were the Earl of Tyrconnel and Mr Fitzjames, the natural son of James II. On September 15th 1690 D'Amfreville was joined by further French ships from the Shannon, and sailed away from the coast of Ireland on hearing of Shovell's presence, despite the fact that he had superior numbers.

Recall orders for Shovell had been sent out on September 18th, and he reached the Downs on October 10th with the remainder of his squadron.[47]

In the British Library there is a pamphlet "An account of the late bloody sea fight between part of their majesties fleet commanded by Sir Cloudesley Shovell and that of the French fleet commanded by the Sieurs Turville and Amphibille." It was printed on September 27th 1690[48] and is reproduced in its entirety.

Sir In a letter from Plymouth.

On Monday was seven night, Sir Cloudesley Shovell sailed out of this harbour with the squadron under his command consisting of 22 capital ships with six fireships and several tenders, the wind at east north east, and by seven o'clock in the evening the whole fleet was out of sight. Steering their coast westward for the ports of either Cork and Kinsale, upon which coast have been cruising by some ships put into this port near 40 sail of the French under Sieur Turville, the next morning by 3 o'clock, came in here 6 Dutch men of war, in order to join Sir Cloudesley Shovell, but understanding Sir Cloudesley Shovell was sailed before, they immediately sailed after him without casting anchor.

And

And this morning came in here a small Pink from the coast of Ireland, the Master where of gives an Account, that being the 20th Instant, early in the morning one of Sir Cloudesley's Advice ships brought him an account, that they espied at the head of them, from their top mast about 27 sail of ships which they supposed to be the French, upon which Sir Cloudesley made all the sail he possibly could after them, and about nine in the morning, both fleets came in sight of each other, upon which Sir Cloudesley caused his fleet to be drawn up in a line in order to engage, the exact form of a half moon, but while this was doing, they espied several sail of ships at their stern which at first put them in some amazement, thinking that they must be more French, but coming nearer, they plainly described them to be the 6 Dutch that should have joined them at Plimouth; upon the arrival of whom Sir Cloudesley changed his order of Battle, dividing his fleet into two squadrons, one of which consisted of 15 sail, all English led the van. The other consisting of 13 Dutch and English: And by this time they could perceive 4 more joyn the squadron of the English, under the French.

Command of Sir Cloudesley as aforesaid with the English (himself being in the Monk) attacked the French Monsieur Turville and his squadron with great resolution, standing himself on the quarter deck, with his hanger drawn all the engagement, encouraging the seamen, and giving necessary orders. The other 13 Dutch and English behaved themselves to admiration and the whole engagement lasted from one in the afternoon till six, during which time, scarce anything else was heard but the loud mouthed engines of destruction, and nothing seen but the dreadful appearance of smoke and fire: Sir Cloudesley in the Monk, being engaged with Turville (who was on board the ship called the Terrible of 80 brass guns) with a chained shot brought Monsieur's Main Mast on Board and killed her a vast number of men and was sending in two fire ships to her and had she not been towed off immediately by 4 French ships that came to her assistance. The Magnificent commanded by the French vice admiral Ampheville of 72 guns, with the Agreeable a ship of 54 guns, and the Sea Horse of 42 guns were sunk and 7 or 8 more disabled: About half past 6 the French drew off and made all the sail they could with a great deal of precipitation; and the night coming on favoured their flight; so that our fleet could not pursue the engagement. In this whole action our fleet have not lost one ship and but very few men, but several ships are disabled, chiefly in their rigging. This is all at present that occur from

Your friend and servant

Nick Jackson.

Is this account accurate? The author has been unable to confirm the incident from other sources. The size of Shovell's squadron in the Jackson letter is approximately the size given in Josiah Burchett's record, twenty-three to twenty-two ships respectively. If Amfreville was sunk in 1690, he was certainly back in action at Barfleur in 1692. Burchett makes no mention of a battle at this time, and gives the strong impression that Amfreville had steered away from the coast of Ireland, thus avoiding Shovell, and had sailed for France and home.

By October 10th 1690 Shovell had arrived in the Downs, where he was met with orders to proceed to Plymouth with all his ships that were fit for sea. From Plymouth, Shovell was to cruise in the Soundings for the security of trade. Shovell left Plymouth on December 3rd and chased a number of ships in the Soundings, but was unable to come up with them because of the foulness of his own ships. At length, two of his ships, the *Deptford* and the *Crown*, took a small French man of war of 18 guns called the *Frippon*. Shovell ended his cruise, sending some of his ships to the coast of Ireland and leaving others in the Soundings. He arrived back in the Downs in the middle of January 1691.

After Beachy Head, Torrington was removed from command of the English fleet. His place was taken by the joint commission of Sir Richard Haddock, Sir John Ashby and Henry Killigrew. The Admiralty Commissioners had wanted a single commander-in-chief, and for Edward Russell to be that man. However, Queen Mary resolved that the command should be put into commission, and she had her way. At least this three-man commission was not to be responsible for a disaster, as was a similar commission in 1693. The main English fleet did little in the latter part of the summer except during September, when it supported Marlborough in his successful efforts to take Kinsale and Cork, in the south-west of Ireland. The year ended with William III in control of most of Ireland, and James II back where he had started in 1689, in France.

The final naval event of 1690 was the trial of Arthur Herbert, Earl of Torrington, on a charge of "keeping back and not engaging and coming into the fight and not relieving and assisting a known friend in need". This was a capital offence. Early in December Torrington was taken from the River Thames to the *Kent* frigate at Sheerness, where his court martial was to be held. The president of the court was Sir Ralph Delavall, who had been at Beachy Head, and a number of other captains including John Leake were members. The Dutch contingent, who had borne the brunt of the battle, were vitriolic about Torrington's behaviour. Rumour had it that William III had given orders that Torrington was to be executed immediately if he was found guilty. Leake's biographer has written that Leake himself was principally responsible for persuading the court to find in Torrington's favour. In London, for three days, from the Exchange to coffee houses, nothing else was heard but the trial. Torrington was unanimously acquitted by his peers, and on December 11th returned to London in his barge, with his flag flying, only to be superseded, and never again employed at sea. William III was livid and refused to see him. It seems an odd way to treat the man who had come over early to his side, and had commanded his invasion fleet.[49]

Shovell himself did not take part in the court martial, perhaps because he was considered to be one of "Torrington's creatures" as Samuel Pepys put it. However, there is in existence a letter from Shovell to Herbert which makes his views on the matter clear. Extracts from the letter state that, "Tis not unknown to your Lordship that both your loyalty and your courage are questioned". "Your retreat was absolutely necessary." "Nothing more rejoiced me than your Lordship declined fighting them." "It was my opinion that nothing more to your Lordships honour nor to our country's safety than keeping out of reach of them."[50]

Let Shovell have the last word on the matter.

NOTES

1. Richmond, p.211; Marsham MSS U1515.012.
2. Marsham MSS U1515.012.
3. Marsham MSS U1515.012.
4. Marsham MSS U1515.012.
5. Finch MSS, Vol.II, p.273.
6. Marsham MSS U1515.012.
7. Richmond, p.211.
8. Torrington, p.42.
9. Marsham MSS U1515.012.
10. Luttrell, Vol.II, pp.34, 35.
11. Marsham MSS U1515.012.
12. Luttrell, Vol.II, pp.34, 35.
13. Secret Memoirs.
14. Secret Memoirs.
15. Portland MSS, E.Harley to Sir Edward Harley April 26th 1690.
16. Marsham MSS U1515.012.
17. Marsham MSS U1515.012.
18. Marsham MSS U1515.012.
19. Marsham MSS U1515.012.
20. Dartmouth MSS, 11th Report, Appendix V p.157.
21. Secret Memoirs.
22. Feiling, pp.583–585.
23. Richmond, pp.212, 213.
24. Luttrell, Vol.II, p.55; Finch MSS, Vol. II, p.291.
25. Campbell, pp.240–243.
26. RMT MAT 25. Section 2.
27. Marsham MSS U1515.012 June 14th 1690.
28. Marsham MSS U1515.012; Journal Grenville Collins.
29. Marsham MSS U1515.012; Richmond, p.213; Luttrell, Vol.11, p.59.
30. Marsham MSS U1515.012; Finch MSS, Vol.II, pp.293–298.
31. Richmond, pp.214–221; Laird Clowes, pp.322–346; Leake, pp.32–43; Aiken, p70; Finch MSS, Vol.II, p.318.
32. Laird Clowes, p.343; Bryant, Samuel Pepys, The Saviour of the Navy, p.387.
33. Marsham MSS U1515.012.
34. Marsham MSS U1515.012.
35. Campbell, pp.240–243; Luttrell, Vol.II, p.77; Burchett, pp.431–434; Marsham MSS U1515.012.
36. Marsham MSS U1515.012; Leake, pp.32–43.
37. Burchett, pp.431–432.
38. ADD MSS 12102.
39. Burchett, p.432; Luttrell, Vol.II, p.86; Finch MSS, Vol.II, p.387.
40. ADD MSS 38146, f.169b.
41. ADD MSS 38146, f.60; Finch MSS, Vol.II, p.414.
42. ADD MSS 38146, f.173b.
43. ADD MSS 38146, f.175.
44. ADD MSS 38146, f.376.
45. ADD MSS 38146, f.446.
46. Finch MSS, Vol.II, p.453.
47. Burchett, pp.432–433; Finch MSS, Vol.II, pp.450–457.
48. BL 816 m23 (94).

49.  Macaulay, pp.956–957; Leake, pp.38–42; Richmond, pp.220–221; Laird Clowes, p.344; Finch MSS, Vol.II, pp.382–383.
50.  Document in the Huntington Library.

# CHAPTER XII
# *Hide and Seek at Sea*
# *1691*

Shovell had been appointed Rear Admiral of the Blue, under Edward Russell, on December 23rd 1690. It was in this capacity that he was to serve at sea in 1691.[1]

Shovell's first duty of the New Year was to help escort William III to Holland as part of George Rooke's squadron. The King went on board one of the four yachts that had been prepared for his retinue, at Gravesend, on January 18th. The journey was not to be a pleasant one. To start with the yachts and the escorting men of war were becalmed for many hours off the Goodwin Sands, and it was not until the fifth day that the coast of Holland was reached. Thick sea fog obscured the land, and it was not thought safe to make for the shore that night. William was impatient to reach his native country and insisted on trying to land in an open boat, despite the pleas of his accompanying nobles. Off William set in a skiff, but floating ice barred his way and ice cold water broke over him, his courtiers and the crew. The crew were becoming anxious, but William remained calm and said to the sailors, "Are you afraid to die in my company?" A Dutch seaman jumped out of the skiff and with difficulty swam through the ice to the shore, where he fired a musket and lit a fire to show that he was safe. Not surprisingly, no one followed his example and the King spent the night in the open but in sight of the flames of the fire on the shore. In the first light of day, they discovered that they were close to the island of Goree. William and his nobles struggled ashore, stiff with cold and covered with icicles. No doubt Shovell was only too happy to be sitting out this little escapade in the relative warmth of his man of war![2]

Having escorted William III to Holland, Shovell returned to England. On February 17th 1691 he received a commission from William and Mary to be Major of the First Marine Regiment. The vacancy occurred when Lt Colonel Sir Richard Onslow left the First Marines and was replaced by Major Henry Davies. Shovell in turn replaced Davies. Seven months later Shovell transferred to the Second Marine Regiment with promotion to Lieutenant Colonel, in place of an officer who had drowned in the *Coronation* disaster, and was to become its full Colonel in 1697. Shovell, in his own hand, has added this fact to the commission signed by William III on September 4 1691. All these posts were said to be lucrative, undemanding sinecures. It is true that Shovell was paid while in post. For example, between February 17th 1692/93 and February 22nd 1693/94, a period of 370 days, he received as Lieutenant Colonel seven shillings per day, as a Captain eight shillings per day and three servants at eight pence a piece. In all seventeen shillings a day giving £314:10:0 for the period in question. However, Shovell did work for his money, as his correspondence shows. He was involved with the question of marines taking their arms to sea, suitable numbers of sergeants/corporals, clothing, tickets, and supported his officers against the Treasury in getting them back pay.[3]

The First and Second Marine Regiments had been formed in 1690 following the disbandment of Prince George of Denmark's Maritime Regiment of Foot, the year before. Both regiments had a full colonel, lieutenant colonel, major and several captains. Each officer, including the full colonel, had his own company. Shovell's company served sometimes on land and sometimes at sea. The marine posts that Shovell held between 1691 and 1698, although strictly speaking naval, were to be his first and only military connection. We have seen how a number of the leading naval men of the day had commissions in the army as well, and the possible effect it had on the Glorious Revolution.[4]

Luttrell, in his diary, reported that in February 1691 a squadron of English and Dutch ships was to be sent to the Straits under Prince George of Denmark, the husband of the then Princess Anne, to relieve Nice. Shovell was to serve under him and would in practice have had the command, because of Prince George's lack of direct naval experience. However, nothing appears to have come of this proposal.[5]

During the same month Luttrell also recorded that, "Sir Cloudesley Shovell, the famous seaman, hath lately married the widdow of Sir John Narbrough."[6] Luttrell was a month early. In fact Shovell married Elizabeth Narbrough, née Hill, on March 10th 1691 at Allhallows, Staining, London. Elizabeth Hill was the daughter of Captain John Hill of Shadwell, Middlesex, and was born on December 12th 1659. Hill was a rich man and was to be a Commissioner of the Navy from 1691 until his death in 1706. The actual date of his appointment is given as January 27th 1691. Among the commissions once belonging to Shovell is a patent appointing John Hill Esquire "Our Commissioner in quality of a principal officer of our Navy for and during our pleasure. January 27th 1691."[7] Luttrell, in his account, gives the date as December 1691.[8] In the early 1700s, in his role as Commissioner of Victualling, Shovell was to sign documents, many still in existence, which also have the signature of John Hill. Hill was to leave Shovell £100,000 on his death in 1706. This was an enormous sum in the early eighteenth century.[9] Much of this money was

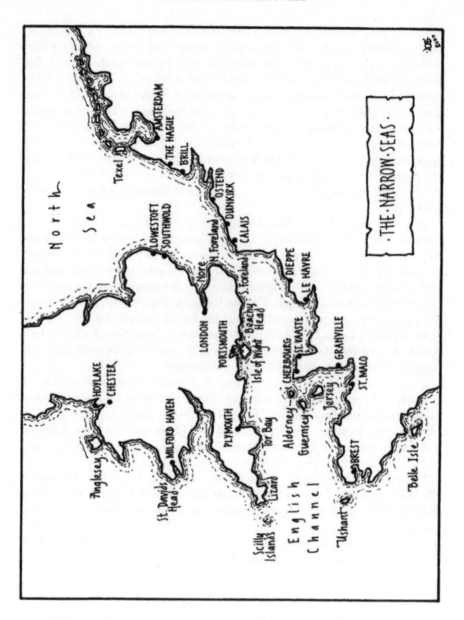

made in trading with countries in the Mediterranean. Account books for John Hill going back to 1675–6 for trade with Smyrna and Cadiz can still be seen to this day.[10]

Elizabeth Hill, aged 21 years, had married the 41-year-old Sir John

134

Narbrough in 1681. She was his second wife. As was recounted earlier, his first wife, Elizabeth Calmady, had died nine months after their marriage in 1677, while Sir John and Shovell were serving in the Mediterranean. Elizabeth Calmady probably died of tuberculosis and was also pregnant. There is a memorial to her in Wembury Church near Exeter. A drawing of the memorial on vellum has come down through the centuries amongst the heirlooms of Shovell's family. Originally it was the property of Narbrough.[11]

Sir John Narbrough had died in the West Indies in 1688 leaving Elizabeth (née Hill) a widow. Shovell was the protégé of John Narbrough and was known to Elizabeth. On their marriage in March 1691, Shovell took on Narbrough's young children, Elizabeth, John and James. He is reported to have treated them as his own. John and James were to drown with their stepfather on the *Association*. Narbrough's daughter, Elizabeth, was to marry Thomas D'Aeth, and inherit the Narbrough family home at Knowlton, Kent on the death of her brothers.[12]

A portrait of the now Lady Elizabeth Shovell, which belongs to one of her descendants, shows a rather masculine woman. In *The Secret Memoirs of Sir Cloudesley Shovell*, it is recorded that he had married the widow of Narbrough who was both his master and friend.

> She [Elizabeth Shovell] prooved as kind a wife as she had shewed herself an indulgent mistress carrying herself without either pride in general or contempt to that Gentleman in particular tho formerly in her Service merited as much her embraces as he who was honoured with her early kindness or any person whatsoever, tho' he drew his extraction from a long and successive train of glorious ancestors.

For his part Shovell was faithful and tender to his wife.[13]

Although Elizabeth Shovell had married her former husband's lowly protégé, she had not really married beneath herself. By 1691 Shovell was a rear admiral, had been knighted, and was very much the highly respected coming man of the navy. He was 40 years old and she 31 years. There were to be two daughters of the marriage, but no son.[14]

Shovell was not the only senior naval officer to marry that March. Captain George Byng, later Viscount Torrington, married Margaret Master.[15]

Having conducted the King to Holland and found time to marry, Shovell joined the main English fleet under Edward Russell as Rear Admiral of the Blue.[16] There is some confusion about which ship Shovell was on in the summer of 1691. The *Monk*, under the command of Shovell, was listed amongst the ships on the Irish station.[17] In fact, Shovell had been given command of the *London*, a 96 gun 1st rate, on December 23rd 1690.[18] Shovell spent most of 1691 in the *London* with two other Shovells,

James and Thomas, who were both able seamen and no doubt related to him.[19] However, Shovell briefly moved into the *Montagu* and the *Kent* during the summer, before returning to the *London* again.[20]

Unlike in 1690, there was to be no major naval engagement in 1691. Edward Russell had succeeded Richard Haddock, Henry Killigrew and John Ashby in command of the fleet the preceding December. By the spring of 1691 the English fleet had been restored to full strength and was to be superior in size to its French counterpart, although the latter would still be a formidable force. Eventually the combined Anglo/Dutch fleet would have seventy-four men of war (fifty-seven English/seventeen Dutch) to France's sixty-nine.

Russell received instructions, firstly to send a squadron to keep an eye on Dunkirk, and so cover the transport going to Holland and also the northern trade; secondly, to send a detachment to Ireland to stop French aid getting there, and to prevent Irish troops being transported to Scotland; thirdly, to keep his main body of ships in the Soundings to deal with the French fleet, and thus protect the returning Smyrna trade, which was valued at one and a half million pounds. Naturally, Russell was loathe to send a large contingent to Ireland for fear of being caught by the French with a divided fleet. Undoubtedly, he remembered only too well Torrington's fate of the year before.[21]

Russell, Shovell and the English fleet sailed on May 23rd from the Downs, but were soon forced back there by a gale. Shortly afterwards, information was received that the French were in the River Shannon with a great number of transports. Russell was given further orders, by Queen Mary, to go to Brest and to send to Ireland for intelligence. In addition, Matthew Aylmer and the Smyrna trade were to be protected.[22]

The French had managed to get to sea first in 1691, because of their better administration. The fact that their fleet was concentrated at Brest, and not scattered throughout a number of different ports, helped. Compte de Tourville, who commanded the French fleet, was given instructions to get to sea, and attack the English trade in general and the Smyrna convoy in particular. He was ordered to avoid a superior English fleet. Perhaps this was as a result of the lesson learnt by Torrington at Beachy Head in 1690. If so it was soon forgotten, with disastrous results for the French at Barfleur in 1692.

During the following June, July and August, a gigantic game of hide and seek was played by Russell's and Tourville's fleets. The setting for this game was off Brest, in the Soundings and off the coast of Ireland. The fleets did not meet, although on one occasion the French scouts were seen, but Tourville was able to slip away without action. In June 1691 Russell came before Kinsale, and found Aylmer and the valuable Smyrna fleet in safety there.[23]

Shovell took part in the search for the French fleet and was in command of one 1st rate, one 2nd rate, six 3rd rates, one 4th rate, and three fireships of the blue squadron. On June 17th Shovell was sent by Russell to look into Brest.[24]

A short time later, on July 20th, Shovell was in the *Montagu* and sent an account of his experiences at Brest to Russell.

> About 8 this morning we were within a league of St. Mathews Point, when we espyed a fleet of about fourty sayle comeing out of Brest, which to our great comfort proved to be Brittons all, except three men of warr of about 36 to 40 guns each, one of which men of warr stood to leeward of me, and I wared my shipp and missed him but half a shipp's length, fireing at him, shott downe his maine yard. He putt before the wind and got from us all by putting his shipp amongst the rocks called the Chickens, and notwithstanding I had three pilots on board I could not persuade them to follow him, but they carried me through amongst the island neare the point of Comorett, but 'twas too late , for he gott up his maine yard and out sayled me much. By all I can learne from the pilots 'twas well I did not follow my inclination in pursueing him through those rocks; the breach was all over him and hardly water for a shipp of that draught to passe. In the scuffle we have got five or six Brittons. The fleet was bound to Bourdeaux and have nothing but stores; they all stood into Brest water. Some of our shipps were neare the castle, which is not such a bugbear as reported. What I have hitherto learned concerning their fleete is that they have beene at sea near forty days, and about a week since a shipp of about 80 guns sailed from hence to joine them, and about two or three days agoe a water shipp came from them, and one man sayes he left them about forty leagues to the westward of Ushant, where, 'tis said here, they have beene, and in the Soundings ever since they have been out. What made those shipps soe bold was that the news here is that theire fleet has taken severall English men of warr and marchant men, and some of our shipps that stood in with French colours they tooke to be French men of warr, and the shipps that had noe colours abroad they tooke to be prizes.[25]

Russell sent Shovell's account, quoted above, to the Earl of Nottingham on July 21st with some comments of his own.

> I here send your lordship a copy of his letter to mee, which sufficiently shews how prudently hee has executed his orders, and I am very sure hee will doe the like in any service he is employed on. I doe not flatter him [Shovell] when I say in all respects I doe not know a better man.[26]

Like Torrington, Russell had come to appreciate Shovell's capabilities.

Similar accounts of Shovell's voyage to Brest are given by Burchett[27] and by John Charnock.[28] Charnock states that Shovell was in the *Plymouth* rather than the *Montagu*, but this is unlikely to be correct.

In a final letter to Nottingham concerning these events, Russell on July 31st stated that when Shovell's squadron had gone into Brest the "drumm was beat and the burghters took arms", as they thought the ships had soldiers on board. They were mistaken.[29]

By mid August, the Anglo/Dutch fleet had found it necessary to go into Torbay to obtain further provisions. On August 19th a council of war was called by Russell to decide how long the great ships should be kept at sea that year. Shovell attended the council, and a decision was made not to stay out later than September 10th.[30] When this view was communicated to Queen Mary, she suggested rather than ordered that an attack on the French fleet, who were by now back in Brest, should be considered. A further council of war decided that it was too late in the year for an attempt to be made.[31]

Early in September 1691 a south-easterly gale forced Russell to look for shelter at Plymouth. Part of the fleet just missed running onto the Eddystone Reef and others had difficulty weathering Penlee Point. Some ships ran foul of each other off Mount Edgcumbe while trying to get into the Hamoaze. The *Harwich*, a former ship of Shovell's, became a wreck under Mount Edgcumbe. The *Royal Oak* and the *Northumberland* both grounded, but were got off again. Shovell in the *London*, with two other 2nd rates, the *Duchess* and the *Coronation* plus some other ships, anchored off Rame Head while attempting to weather the storm. On September 3rd Shovell witnessed from his poop deck, at a distance of three cables length, the dismasting and foundering of the *Coronation*. Her Captain, Charles Skelton, with over 600 crew and marines, drowned before Shovell's eyes. Russell supposed that the disaster was caused by some of the guns breaking loose or the lower gun deck ports breaking open. It must have been a harrowing spectacle even for a battle-hardened man.[32]

Russell was censured in some quarters for attempting to get into Plymouth in a storm rather than trying to ride it out at sea.[33] Russell was not an easy man to advise. John Leake described him at this time as "excessively proud and haughty; difficult to be pleased unless flattered; and implacable if offended".[34] Shovell's views on Russell are not known, although he was to serve loyally under him.

On September 8th 1691 Russell sailed from Plymouth for Spithead, leaving orders for Shovell to wait for the repair of the damaged ships. When they were ready, Shovell was to send ten sail to the Soundings, and then go to Spithead himself with the remainder of the fleet.[35]

Following the *Coronation* disaster, Shovell uncharacteristically took the opportunity to press his claim to be Lieutenant Colonel of the Second Marine Regiment, in the place of a drowned man. On September 8th 1691 he wrote from the *Kent* in Plymouth Sound to the Earl of Nottingham.

> I am humbley to thanke your Lordship for the unexpected favour of
> being made Major of the first mareen regiment and give your
> lordship this truble to begg, if I be not too impertinent, to be Leiut
> Collonell of the second mareen regiment in the room of leiut collonell
> Paston who is drowned in the Crownation. I hear, my Lord, that tis
> designed that Rear Admiral Rooke shall have the leiut collonellshipe;
> he is a gentleman I have no objection against but humbley wish he
> had been a major before me or I may be a leiut collonell before him.
> 'Tis argued he is an older flagg. I confess it but doe not see that should
> have any influence on the officers of them regiments, and further, my
> Lord, if my friends had been so good as my pretentions I beleave I
> might have had the prehemence; for in King Charles'[s] time I
> commanded a squadron against Salley by comission and had power
> to hould court martialls and execute condemned men by my order,
> which power exceed the power of the admirall in these seas, and trust
> farr greatter the[n] that of a private flagg. Another thing I must begg
> your Lordship's leave: that my humble opinion is that a major of
> these regiments ought to be an officer who very well understand the
> discipling, managing and fighting a regiment ashore, which at
> present I do not understand. I will at present give your lordship no
> further truble.[36]

Shovell's plea for Nottingham's support was successful and on September
11th Nottingham wrote to Viscount Sydney. "Sir Cloudsly Shovell is a
humble suitor for Mr Paston's place, and I must be so too for him, if his
Majesty dos not think fitt to gratify my Lord Pembroke, who is mightily
concerned for Major Webberly, and with great reason." In fact William III
had already signed Shovell's commission by the time of Nottingham's
letter.[37] Shovell was not normally one to push himself forward quite so
blatantly. Perhaps the additional expense of having married in the spring
of that year was uppermost in his mind.

By the end of September Shovell had reached Spithead. On September
29th he sat as president of the court martial of the gunner of the *Exeter*
frigate. The man was condemned to death, and was said to have been
executed at Execution Dock.[38] Shovell often sat in judgement at courts
martial and had the reputation of being merciful to the vanquished. He
pardoned crimes in others which he was never guilty of himself.[39]

Following this court martial, Shovell took a squadron across to Holland
to bring William III back to England. Luttrell reported that:

> on October 19th, about nine in the morning the King came in the Mary
> yatch, attended by several others and a squadron of men of war

under Sir Cloudesley Shovell and landed at Margate in Kent, and came in his coach through the city to Whitehall about 11 that night, where the Queen was, and immediately they went to Kensington; the whole town was filled with bonfires and illuminations in the windows, ringing of bells and the guns at the Tower were discharged. His majesty had the misfortune to be overturned in his coach near Gravesend but got no hurt.[40]

William's journeys seemed to be fated. If it was not ice in the sea it was an overturned coach!

On September 29th 1691 Shovell's half-sister, Anne Flaxman, was married to Thomas Shorting at Morston in Norfolk. Almost certainly Shovell's mother, another Anne, attended the wedding in her home village. Shovell himself could not be there in person, as he was sitting as president of a court martial before sailing to Holland to fetch the King. Thomas Shorting was the Collector of Customs at Cley in Norfolk. Judging by some of his letters to his half-sister and brother-in-law, Shovell was fond of them and went out of his way to help them.[41]

Shovell's protective role in his King's return from Holland was to be his last official duty of 1691. This had been an undistinguished naval year for both France and England, but at least Ireland had finally fallen to William, with the taking of Limerick and Athlone.

The following year was to be much more eventful for the English navy, and particularly so for Shovell himself.

NOTES

1. RMT MAT 25, Section 2.
2. Macaulay, IV, pp.1968–69; Relation de la Voyage de Sa Majesté Britannique en Hollande, errichie de planches tres curieuses 1692; London Gazette Jan 29th 16 90/91; Burnet, ii.71.
3. RMT MAT 25; Finch MSS, Vol.III, p.2; Edye, Vol.I, pp.361, 376, 405, 483, 495, 500, 502, 592–3; H.O. Mil. Entry book, Vol.ii, f.188 and Vol. iii, ff.93 & 282.
4. Edye, Vol.I.
5. Luttrell, Vol.II, p.182.
6. Luttrell, Vol.II, p.179.
7. RMT MAT 25, Section 2.
8. Luttrell, Vol.II, p.327.
9. Dyer, p.207.
10. Marsham MSS, p.171 01.
11. RMT MAT 23.
12. RMT MSS; Secret Memoirs.
13. Secret Memoirs.
14. RMT MSS.
15. Torrington, p.52.

16. Charnock, pp.18–19.
17. C.S.P. Dom. 1691–92.
18. RMT MAT 25.
19. ADM 33/134.
20. Finch MSS,Vol.III, pp.170–171; Anderson, Lists of Men of War.
21. Richmond, pp.222–226.
22. Torrington, p.57.
23. Torrington, pp.57–62; Richmond, pp.224–226.
24. Torrington, p.59.
25. Finch MSS, Vol.III, pp.170–171.
26. Finch MSS, Vol.III, p.170.
27. Burchett, p.442.
28. Charnock, p.19.
29. Finch MSS, Vol.III, p.190.
30. Finch MSS, Vol.III, p.219.
31. Torrington, pp.56–60.
32. Torrington, p.62; Larn, p.8; Laird Clowes, pp.345–346; Finch MSS, Vol.III, p.251.
33. Leake, p.44.
34. Leake, p.43.
35. Torrington, p.62.
36. Finch MSS, Vol.III, pp.255–56.
37. Finch MSS, Vol.III, p.260.
38. Luttrell, Vol.II, p.289.
39. Secret Memoirs.
40. Luttrell, Vol.II, p.296.
41. RMT MAT 19.

CHAPTER XIII

# The Battle of Barfleur
# 1692

On New Year's Day 1692 it was said that Shovell was to be Rear Admiral of the Blue again for the summer's campaign. This was changed on January 20th to the position of Rear Admiral of the Red under Edward Russell. In this position, under Russell's overall command, Shovell was to come to national prominence as one of the heroes of the Battle of Barfleur, the following May.[1] On January 26th Shovell, accompanied by Russell and John Ashby, viewed the great ships at Chatham.[2]

Earlier in January, on the 6th, Shovell had been granted a coat of arms in commemoration of his victories over the Turks and French (Gu. a chev. erm. betw. two crescents in chief ar. and a fleur de lis in base or. Crest –

141

Out of a naval coronet or, a demi lion gu. holding a sail ar. charged with an anchor or.*).[3]

Late in 1691 William III had decided that the principal effort in 1692 was to be on land in Flanders, and at sea the fleet would cover the military expedition and stop supplies from reaching the enemy. Russell, Lord Galway and the Duke of Leinster were ordered to prepare plans for offensive action against Brest and St Malo, which were the most dangerous ports to English designs.[4] Fourteen thousand soldiers were to be encamped near Portsmouth ready for the expedition.[5]

The English were not alone in planning offensive action. By February 1692 there were strong rumours of an impending French invasion,[6] but it was to be another month before they were confirmed.[7] By March a large French force and transports had been collected at St Vaast La Hougue in readiness for an invasion of England. James II was there in person to inspect them.[8]

During the early part of March Shovell, with a squadron of ten men of war, took William III to Holland. William was landed at the Brill on March 6th.[9]

On March 14th Shovell had time to write to the Commissioners of the Admiralty concerning bounty money for volunteers. Shovell pointed out that, by a proclamation of December 21st 1691, their Majesties (William III and Queen Mary) had stated that all seamen voluntarily entering themselves on 1st, 2nd or 3rd rate ships before January 20th were to have six weeks' pay as a bounty. Many sailors listed themselves accordingly, but were unable to get to their ships before March, because of the hard winter. The clerks of the cheque at Sheerness and Chatham refused to enter men until they appeared. Shovell considered this unfair. On March 21st Shovell received a reply from the Navy Board on the subject, pointing out the increased cost involved but agreeing to partially rectify the matter.[10] Actions of this type, showing Shovell's concern for the welfare of his men, help to explain his popularity with the ordinary seaman.

The French troop concentrations at La Hougue were at first thought to be of a defensive nature against an English descent. [11] By April William III and his government suspected an attack on the Channel Isles. Richard Carter, with a small squadron, was sent to cruise off Guernsey.[12] English concern grew and Ralph Delavall, with an advance squadron of the main fleet, was sent to reinforce Carter's small force.

On April 19th 1692 came the stunning news that the French design was not limited to the Channel Isles, but that the real objective was England itself. The day before a small French vessel had run ashore on the

---

* The arms incorporate a lion, a sail, a naval coronet, a fleur de lys and two crescents. The fleur de lys and crescents commemorate Shovell's victories over the French and Barbary corsairs respectively.

Goodwin Sands, and letters had been found addressed to Jacobites in England making clear what Louis XIV really intended.[13]

Troop movements and the collection of stores for the attack on France were suspended and Russell, with the main fleet, was ordered to move at once to the Flats of the Foreland to await further orders. [14]

Throughout the latter part of March and April Shovell had been a member of the council of flag officers considering such matters as when to leave the Nore, where the fleet should water, and what to do if the French came to sea. On April 11th Russell wrote to the Earl of Nottingham giving his own, Shovell's and other flag officers' views on a list of potential ship commanders. Most of the commanders were unknown to Russell and the view was expressed that they should be accepted as they had excellent references. If they did not come up to expectations they would be dispensed with. [15] At the end of April Shovell took command at Chatham of the newly launched 100 gun ship, a 1st rate, the *Royal Prince*.[16] In fact the *Prince*, which had been first built in 1670, was reconstructed in 1692 and renamed the *Royal William*.[17] On April 26th it was reported that Russell and his flag officers would be going on board their ships within two to three days. Shovell was, of course, amongst them.[18]

Louis XIV signed orders for the Compte de Tourville, commander of the principal French fleet, on March 16th, giving him strict instructions that he must sail from Brest on April 15th 1692, even if he had intelligence of the enemy being at sea with a superior force. The orders continued that, if on the way to La Hougue he actually met the enemy, he must engage them, however numerous they might be. If he defeated the enemy (the English), he must follow them to their ports, after detaching part of his fleet to escort the transport ships and troops for the invasion of England. If he was defeated he was to save the remnants of his fleet as best he could.[19] These insulting orders were the foundation of the French defeat at the Battle of Barfleur, and the subsequent destruction of a large part of their fleet at St Vaaste La Hougue a few days later.

What Louis XIV and his Secretary of State for the Navy, Pontchairtrain, intended was that Tourville and the Brest fleet should rush the transports and troops to Torbay before the English were ready. They would return to Brest and there join with the ships from Rochefort and more importantly with D'Estrées' ships coming from Toulon. The combined French fleets would then protect the communications between their invasion forces and France.[20] Louis XIV's orders were based on the false premise that the French would be ready before the union of the English and Dutch fleets. This was a gamble, in that the Brest fleet would be too small to take on a combined Anglo/Dutch fleet with any hope of success. In addition, Louis XIV may have been influenced by Jacobite reports that morale was poor in the English fleet, and that some of them did not wish to fight. Russell's, Ashby's, Delavall's and Carter's names were all mentioned in this report without foundation. Poor Richard Carter, who was considered to be most sympathetic to the Jacobite cause, proved his loyalty to William III with the loss of his life at the Battle of Barfleur, a short time later.[21]

Before sailing Shovell had time, on April 29th, to write to the Earl of Nottingham sending him a Shovell cousin and recommending him for a command.[22]

Russell rightly judged that it was important to join the English and Dutch fleets as soon as possible. He took the English ships from the Nore, plied over the flats and through the sands with a scanty wind. This was against the advice of his pilots and many of the captains, but fortunately they got safely through. On May 9th Russell, with Shovell and the flag officers, reached Rye where they met the Dutch. The combined fleets set sail for St Helens which was reached on May 15th.[23]

A council of English and Dutch flag officers met on the day of their arrival at St Helens aboard the *Britannia*. Shovell was among the flags who recommended that the fleet should not proceed west of St Helens until it was known for certain that "the French were on our coast and then fight them". In addition, with the first fair weather, they would go over to the French coast for one day and anchor, before returning to St Helens.[24]

At the council of flag officers on May 15th, an address was signed and sent to Queen Mary reaffirming the loyalty of the fleet. Shovell was among the signatories. Rumours had reached Mary that the fleet might defect to her father, James II. It is unlikely that she believed this, but she passed the information on to Russell.[25] Shovell's lack of sympathy towards the Jacobites was well known. "He was not a man to be spoken to", reported a Jacobite emissary.[26]

Even at this moment of great anxiety, Shovell wrote from the *Royal William* on May 15th to the Earl of Nottingham on the thorny question of the listing of volunteers. He explained that the Navy Board was acting in an unjust manner, against the wishes of the Queen and her Council. In addition, Shovell had a further complaint, which was that Sir Richard Haddock had paid bounty money to the other ships, but Shovell and his ships had gone to sea before they could receive their due reward. Shovell pointed out that, "this fell very untoward towards our men", who had had the trouble of fitting out the *London*, *Vanguard* and *Royal William* at great speed. He went on:

> . . . my Lord, if it was possible, in fitting that ship [*Royal William*] the men did more than their common duty, but since this could not be helped, I have thought how it may be salved, which is if six hundred pound were imprested to any of the commissioners of the navy here in the fleet or, if they think it to much trouble, to myself, and the money to be paid as bounty by one of these commissioners who allways pay the bounty. This will wholly satisfie the men. I humbly

beg your lordship will not think of deferring the bounty till pay day; for be assured, my Lord, that twenty shillings is better accepted by the saylor when he may justly aske for it, then five pounds at pay table.[27]

What of the French? Tourville, with forty-four ships, the bulk of the fleet, had firm orders from Louis XIV to leave Brest by April 15th. However, the weather conditions precluded him from sailing until May 2nd, when he managed to get out to sea. D'Estrées, with the Toulon squadron of eighteen ships, had sailed on March 29th, but had been held up by contrary winds and eventually reached Brest on May 19th, the very day of the Battle of Barfleur. The winds that held up D'Estrées enabled the Dutch contingent to join Russell and the English fleet at Rye. At the Battle of Barfleur, Tourville was sorely to miss D'Estrées' ships, but in addition in the western ports of France were a further twenty-six unmanned ships. These ships would have been ready for sea by June.[28]

Meanwhile in Paris, Pontchairtrain, the Secretary of State for the Navy, had received intelligence from Holland and England showing what a mess he had got himself into. On May 9th he wrote to Marshal Bellefonds, who commanded the troops at St Vaaste La Hougue, stating that Louis XIV had left it to him and James II to direct the movements of Tourville. Bellefonds, James and M. de Bonrepaus, the Intendant General, did nothing until May 18th, when they sent two boats with letters warning Tourville to draw back, if he had no greater force with him than when he left Brest. One of these boats got alongside the *Soleil Royal*, Tourville's flagship, on May 19th, just before the start of the Battle of Barfleur. It was too late.[29]

Louis XIV had put Tourville's fleet of forty-four ships into a position where they were to meet Russell's much superior force of ninety-nine ships. Louis XIV laid great store by the fact that his ships were larger and carried more armament than the English and Dutch. The English considered that numbers of ships were more important than size. If numbers were not greater than the enemy's, then victory rarely occurred. In 1702 Shovell wrote the following to the Earl of Nottingham.

The misfortune and vice of our country is to believe ourselves better than other men, which I take to be the reason that generally we send too small a force to execute our designs. But experience has taught me that where men are equally inured and disciplined in war, 'tis without a miracle, number that gains the victory; for both in fleets, squadrons and single ships, of near equal force, by that time one is beaten and ready to retreat, the other is also beaten and glad the enemy has left him. To fight, beat and chase an enemy, I have sometimes seen, but have rarely seen at sea any victory worth boasting where strength has been nearly equal.[30]

Although Shovell's words were written ten years later, it was a view that he had held for some time and they are relevant to Barfleur.

By May 18th Richard Carter and Ralph Delavall had joined Edward Russell and the fleet at St Helens. Information that Tourville and the French fleet were out was received by Russell and he sailed with his combined Anglo/Dutch fleet.[31] After twenty-four hours at sea, and twenty-one miles S.W.b.S. of Cape Barfleur, the two fleets came into sight of one another.[32]

The Anglo/Dutch fleet was organised with the Dutch in the van under Philip Almonde, the red squadron under Russell in the centre and the blue squadron under John Ashby in the rear. The French fleet had the white and blue squadron under Vice Admiral d'Amfreville in the van, the white squadron under Tourville in the centre and the blue squadron under Jean Gabaret in the rear.

| ALLIES (DUTCH/ENGLISH) | | FRENCH | |
|---|---|---|---|
| Flag Officers | Ships | Flag Officers | Ships |
| V.Adm. G. Van Callenburgh | | M. de Nesmond | |
| R.Adm. P. Van der Goes | | Lt. Gen. d'Amfreville | 14 |
| V.Adm. G. Scheij | | M. de Relingues | |
| Lt.Adm P. Van Almonde | 36 | | |
| R.Adm. J. Muijs | DUTCH | | |
| V.Adm. C. Van de Putte | Van | | |
| R.Adm. G. Evertsen | | | |
| R. Adm Sir C. Shovel | 31 | M. de Villette-Murcai | |
| Ad. E. Russel | ENGLISH | Compte de Tourville | 16 |
| V.Adm. Sir R. Delavall | Centre | M. de Langeron | |
| V.Adm. G. Rook | 32 | M. de Coëtogon | |
| Adm. Sir J. Ashby | ENGLISH | V.Adm. Gabaret | 14 |
| R.Adm. R. Carter | Rear | M. Pannetier | |
| | | | |
| Total Ships of the line | 99 | Total Ships of the line | 44 |
| "Frigates" & Fireships | 38 | "Frigates" & Fireships | 13 |
| Guns | 6,756 | Guns | 3,240[33] |

THE ENGLISH FLEET AT BARFLEUR
Flags

CENTRE OR RED SQUADRON
Admiral of the fleet Edward Russell
Captain of the fleet David Mitchell      } *Britannia*

146

# THE BATTLE OF BARFLEUR 1692

Vice Admiral Sir Ralph Delavall          *Royal Sovereign*
Rear Admiral Sir Cloudesley Shovell      *Royal William*

| Ships | Guns | Captains |
|---|---|---|
| *Plymouth* | 60 | John Maine |
| *Ruby* | 50 | George Mees |
| *Cambridge* | 70 | Richard Lestock |
| *Oxford* | 54 | James Wishart |
| *Sandwich* | 90 | Anthony Hastings |
| *Royal William* | 100 | Thomas Jennings |
| *Breda* | 70 | David Lambert |
| *Kent* | 70 | John Neville |
| *St Albans* | 50 | Richard Fitzpatrick |
| *Swiftsure* | 70 | Richard Clarke |
| *Hampton Court* | 70 | John Graydon |
| *Phaeton* | 8 | Robert Hancock |
| *Fox* | 8 | Thomas Killingworth |
| *Strombolo* F.S. | 8 | Thomas Urry |
| *Hopewell* | 8 | William Jumper |
| *Grafton* | 70 | William Bokenham |
| *Restoration* | 70 | James Gother |
| *Greenwich* | 54 | Richard Edwards |
| *London* | 96 | Matthew Aylmer |
| *Britannia* | 100 | John Fletcher |
| *St Andrew* | 96 | George Churchill |
| *Chester* | 48 | Thomas Gillam |
| *Eagle* | 70 | John Leake |
| *Rupert* | 66 | Basil Beaumont |
| *Elizabeth* | 70 | Stafford Fairborne |
| *Flame* | 8 | James Stewart |
| *Roebuck* | 8 | Francis Manly |
| *Vulture* F.S. | 8 | Hovenden Walker |
| *Spy* | 8 | John Norris |
| *Burford* | 70 | Thomas Harlow |
| *Centurion* | 48 | Francis Wyvill |
| *Captain* | 70 | Daniel Jones |
| *Devonshire* | 80 | Henry Haughton |
| *Royal Sovereign* | 100 | Humphry Sanders |
| *Royal Katherine* | 82 | Wolfran Cornewall |
| *Bonaventure* | 48 | John Hubbard |
| *York* | 60 | Robert Deane |
| *Lenox* | 70 | John Munden |
| *St Michael* | 90 | Thomas Hopsonn |

| Extravagant | | 10 | Fleetwood Emes |
| Wolf | | 8 | James Greenaway |
| Vulcan | F.S. | 8 | Joseph Soanes |
| Hound | | 8 | Thomas Foulis |

Flags

BLUE OR REAR SQUADRON

| Admiral Sir John Ashby | *Victory* |
| Vice Admiral George Rooke | *Neptune* |
| Rear Admiral Richard Carter | *Duke* |

| Ships | Guns | Captains |
| --- | --- | --- |
| *Albemarle* | 90 | Sir Francis Wheeler |
| *Resolution* | 70 | Edward Good |
| *Monck* | 60 | Benjamin Hoskins |
| *Expedition* | 70 | Edward Dover |
| *Chatham* | 50 | John Leader |
| *Windsor Castle* | 90 | Earl of Danby |
| *Neptune* | 96 | Thomas Gardner |
| *Royal Oak* | 74 | George Byng |
| *Advice* | 50 | Charles Hawkins |
| *Northumberland* | 70 | Andrew Cotten |
| *Lion* | 60 | Robert Wiseman |
| *Half Moon* | 8 | John Knapp |
| *Owner's Love* | 10 | John Perry |
| *Cadiz Merchant)* F.S. | 12 | Robert Wynn |
| *Lightning* | 8 | Lawrence Keek |
| *Berwick* | 70 | Henry Martin |
| *Defiance* | 61 | Edward Gurney |
| *Montagu* | 52 | Simon Foulks |
| *Warspite* | 70 | Caleb Grantham |
| *Adventure* | 44 | Thomas Dilkes |
| *Vanguard* | 90 | Christopher Mason |
| *Victory* | 100 | Edward Stanley |
| *Duchess* | 90 | John Clements |
| *Monmonth* | 66 | Robert Robinson |
| *Edgar* | 72 | John Torpley |
| *Speedwell* | 8 | Thomas Simonds |
| *Griffin* | 8 | Robert Partridge |
| *Etna* F.S. | 8 | Richard Carveth |
| *Blaze* | 8 | Thomas Heath |
| *Stirling Castle* | 70 | Benjamin Walters |

| Dreadnought | | 64 | Thomas Coall |
|---|---|---|---|
| Crown | | 50 | Thomas Warren |
| Suffolk | | 70 | Christopher Billop |
| Woolwich | | 54 | Christopher Myngs |
| Ossory | | 90 | John Tyrrel |
| Duke | | 90 | William Wright |
| Cornwall | | 80 | Edward Boys |
| Essex | | 70 | John Bridges |
| Deptford | | 50 | William Kerr |
| Hope | | 70 | Henry Robinson |
| Thomas & Elizabeth | | 10 | Edward Littleton |
| Vesuvius | F.S. | 8 | John Guy |
| Hunter | | 8 | Thomas Rooke |
| Charles galley | | 32 | Joseph Waters |
| | | | One joined after action.[34] |

The Captain of Sir Cloudesley Shovell's ship, the *Royal William*, was Thomas Jennings.

The description of the Battle of Barfleur will be largely based on the account of it given by Richard Allyn, who was the Chaplain of the *Centurion* and was in the action. Part of Allyn's account was drawn up at Shovell's direction and indeed he wrote some of it.

At 3.00 a.m. on Thursday May 19th 1692 the *Chester* and the *Charles galley*, which had been scouting to the westward, fired guns and made their way to Russell in the *Britannia*. They reported the approach of the French who were to the S.W. of the Anglo/Dutch fleet.[35] The wind was a fine gale from the S.W.b.W. and the visibility hazy.[36]

Tourville, with the weather gauge, was in a position to fight or discreetly withdraw. Probably he was unaware of the junction of the Dutch and English fleets and he had his sovereign's direct orders to fight whatever the superiority in numbers of the enemy. In addition, he held the view that in open sea during the summer, with its short nights, an inferior fleet would have to fight unless it abandoned its duller sailors.[37] Tourville for all these reasons bore down on the Anglo/Dutch fleet.

As day broke the French were seen approaching from the S.S.W. and Russell's fleet responded by forming their own line of battle. The Dutch under Almonde were in the van, the red squadron under Russell himself in the centre, and the blue squadron under Ashby in the rear. Russell's initial concern was that Tourville might move northward, and he ordered the blue squadron to tack to cover this. However, before this could be done, at 4.00 a.m. the French were seen to be on the same tack as the Anglo/Dutch fleet and the order was cancelled.[38]

The two lines of battle now extended from the N.N.E. towards the S.S.W. The wind was still from the S.W. but decreasing in strength, and the

149

French continued to have the weather gauge. It took until 8.00 a.m. for Russell's line of battle to form fully, and it was an indifferent one. Tourville's line was also described as being ragged. Russell's last instruction, before the battle began, was to order Almonde to try to weather the French.[39]

The wind had decreased to such an extent that it was 11.00 a.m. before the battle started in earnest. Tourville, in the 106 gun *Soleil Royal*, stood directly for Russell in the 100 gun *Britannia*. Russell ordered three cheers from his men in the *Britannia* for Tourville, who inhospitably replied at close range with a volley of musket shot. Russell's counter was to give the *Soleil Royal* a broadside and the first casualties of the battle occurred. Strictly speaking, the first casualty of the campaign was the unfortunate surgeon's mate of the *Deptford*, who had been killed while easing himself in the head during a birthday salute for the Queen on April 30th. Shot from a chase gun hit him![40]

In Shovell's account of the battle, in Allyn's book, he recorded that he had never seen anyone come as close before opening fire. The red squadron was soon in action, carrying the brunt of the battle with Tourville's white squadron in the centre. It was as hot an engagement as the experienced Shovell had ever been involved with.[41]

In the van, thirty-six Dutch ships were attacked by Amfreville's fourteen ships of the French white and blue squadrons. Although Amfreville had five or six three deck ships and none under 60 guns, he rightly felt that he was overmatched and tried to keep the exchanges at long gunshot.[42] Some heavy fighting did take place in the van with the *Zeven Provincien*, De Ruijter's former flagship, losing nineteen men killed with fourteen more badly wounded, and the Admiraal Generaal losing nine killed with thirty wounded. Rear Admiral van der Goes was among the wounded.[43]

The French blue squadron, under Gabaret, tried to stretch the English rear under Ashby, but having failed to do so, some of them closed to support Tourville. Seven of these ships were heavily involved with Shovell and his division in the centre.[44]

For about two hours the battle continued with an ever decreasing wind from the S.W. The heaviest fighting, without question, was in the centre and Russell aided by Shovell was in the thick of it. By 1.00 p.m. the *Britannia* had so beaten the *Soleil Royal* with shot that the French let down the main sail and tacked away. The *Soleil Royal*'s main topsail could not be used as it had been shot away. The wind shifted from S.W.b.W. to W.N.W., which took Tourville farther away from Russell. Shovell judged this to be the point where the French began to run, taking every opportunity to get away from the English. He took his chance to make one of the critical moves of the battle.[45]

When the encounter began, the blue squadron under Ashby was

somewhat to the leeward of the rest of the Anglo/Dutch line of battle. Seven or eight ships of the French rear, under Gabaret, had no ships to fight unless they could bear to leeward of their line. These vessels reached astern of Shovell and his division. When the wind shifted to the W.N.W., Shovell made his move. Accompanied by six of his division plus fireships, he kept his luft (turned towards the wind) and weathered Tourville and all his squadron. This broke the French line, separating their white and blue squadrons. Part of the English blue squadron under Ashby followed Shovell, and the vice admiral of the French blue squadron, with five or six other ships that were near him and had not fired a gun all day, set their sails and ran.[46]

While this was happening, Carter's division (Rear Admiral of the Blue) was in action against Gabaret and further French ships of their blue squadron, allowing them to cross Shovell and join Tourville's squadron.[47]

By this time it was 4.00 p.m. on a misty afternoon and the wind fell away. The battle had produced a general mêlée, with confusion on both sides made worse by the mist that intermittently turned into a thick fog. Shovell and part of his division chased Tourville and his division through the haze. Tourville was forced to anchor because of a strong north-easterly tide. Shovell followed suit and anchored half a shot ahead of him. Unfortunately the *Sandwich*, a 90 gun ship under Anthony Hastings, was not held by her anchors and drove through the French attracting a hail of shot. Hastings was killed.[48] It was the same Hastings who had shared with Shovell the taking of the *Half Moon* in the Mediterranean in 1681.[49]

Shovell realised that Tourville was vulnerable and ordered his fireship to attack. The captain of the fireship did his duty, but the tide was running very strongly and Tourville was able to escape by cutting his cable and towing away. He soon anchored again. The intermittent fog made fighting very difficult, as at times Shovell was forced to stop firing while at point blank range.[50]

At 8.00 p.m., with the fog at its thickest, some of the English blue squadron, together with Shovell's division, drove through part of the French fleet.[51] Richard Carter, the Rear Admiral of the Blue, the officer whose Jacobite sympathies were most suspected, was hit by shot. As he realised that he was dying on the deck of the *Duke*, Carter told his flag captain, "Fight the ship as long as she will swim." Forever he silenced his critics.[52]

As night came the battle of Thursday May 19th 1692 came to an end. Much damage had been done to the ships and men of both sides. Neither the French nor the English or Dutch had lost a single significant ship, although Shovell had the impression that a French three decker had been set on fire by fireships. In this he was mistaken.[53] The injuries to the men were mainly due to shot or splinters. In the *Centurion*, which had been in Delavall's division in the centre, seven men had been killed and eighteen wounded, most of them having their legs shattered or shot off above the knee. The unfortunate Webber, a member of the crew, had half his face shot away, but lived for two days and sang for most of this time.[54] Among the injured was Shovell himself. The exact details of his injury are unknown. One report stated that he had been slightly wounded in the thigh by a splinter[55] and another from Russell himself that "he is a little hurt in a fall, but will do very well again".[56] Robert Marsham Townshend has also recorded that Shovell's injury occurred on May 19th.[57] Whatever the nature of Shovell's injury, it is likely that this was the reason that he did not have an even greater share of the credit for the subsequent destruction of the French ships at St Vaaste La Hougue. More will be related about this later.

If the battle had ended at nightfall on May 19th, Tourville could have counted himself successful. He had attacked a greatly superior Anglo/Dutch fleet, and had extracted his ships without loss. Unfortunately, the events of the next few days were not to be to his or indeed to Louis XIV's liking at all.

At daybreak on Friday May 20th Shovell found the weather "mighty thick and foggy".[58] By 8.00 a.m. the weather had improved a little with the wind from E.N.E. The Dutch, who were south of Russell and the English contingent, sighted the French and a general chase was ordered. The French sailed towards the west. By evening the wind had changed to the S.W. and had lightened. Neither the French nor Dutch/English ships could make headway against the flood tide and were forced to anchor between Cape Barfleur and Cherbourg. Shovell had found that the *Royal William* had suffered considerable damage during Thursday's battle and decided that, unless he changed ship, he would be unable to take a further part in the chase of the French. That evening he moved his flag from the *Royal William* to the 70 gun *Kent,* under John Neville. The *Kent* was a good sailing ship, and with that night's tide moved towards Russell in the *Britannia*.[59] At 10.00 p.m., with a favourable tide and freshening breeze, the English and Dutch weighed anchor.

At midnight the *Britannia* lost her foretop mast that had been damaged the previous day. Shovell, with the red squadron, waited with her while the blue squadron, under Ashby, and the Dutch continued the chase of the French.[60]

On Saturday morning May 21st Shovell clearly saw the French at anchor in the Race of Alderney, and there was a fine fresh gale from the S.W. When the flood tide came, fifteen of the French ships found that their anchors would not hold them, and they were forced to cut their cables before being driven along their shoreline to the east. The Dutch with Ashby and some of the other English ships remained fast, in order to be in a position to continue the chase of the French who had not driven, once conditions improved. Russell, Shovell and some others cut their cables and followed the fifteen French ships that were being driven along the shore to the east.[61] Tourville, in the *Soleil Royal*, was among them. He realised that, unless the wind changed, he would be driven ashore, and during the morning moved his flag to the *Ambitieux*, 92 guns, which already carried the flag of De Villette-Murcai. [62] Tourville was correct and at about 11.00 a.m. the *Soleil Royal*, *Admirable* and *Triomphant* were driven ashore in Cherbourg Bay. Russell ordered Delavall with sufficient ships to see to their destruction, which he successfully accomplished the next day.[63]

The twelve remaining French ships being driven to the east outsailed the entire English contingent except for Shovell in the *Kent*, and two or three others. Shovell kept close to them, that is sometimes within shot, but did not fire, in case it slowed him down. That Saturday night the French ships anchored near the shore not far from St Vaaste La Hougue. Shovell too anchored in sight of them, and rode fast all night with his boats out watching them.[64]

On Sunday May 22nd Russell and the bulk of the fleet came up to St Vaaste La Hougue. The twelve French ships had got as close to the shore as possible, and appeared to be preparing to defend themselves. It was decided to make an attack on the French the next day with boats, and Shovell was appointed to take command of this action by Russell.[65] Normally the junior admiral would be selected to lead an action of this sort. The junior admiral had been poor Richard Carter, the Rear Admiral of the Blue, but he had been killed during the evening of May 19th.[66] Therefore Shovell, who had already played a prominent role during the last four days and who was the next most junior admiral, was the logical choice.

While Russell and Shovell were drawing up their plans for a boat action in the Bay of La Hougue the next day, Ashby with the Dutch was chasing twenty other French ships, that had escaped through the dangerous Race of Alderney to safety in St Malo. Five more French ships escaped to the east and four were said to have rounded Scotland before reaching sanctuary in a French port.[67]

As described earlier, Delavall had been detached, on the Saturday, to organise the destruction of the three French ships that had gone aground in Cherbourg Bay. On this day Delavall had reconnoitred in the *St Albans*, and the next day, Sunday, he sent in three fireships plus boats covered by the guns of his larger vessels. Thomas Heath, in the *Blaze* fireship, succeeded in burning the *Soleil Royal* of 106 guns, but largely by chance. The *Soleil Royal* fired her guns at the *Blaze* without great effect, but it proved impossible to lay the fireship alongside, as the French used their boats and cut masts to protect themselves. Heath left the *Blaze* floating on the tide, and by chance the wind and sea drove her onto the one unprotected part of the *Soleil Royal*, the stern. Thus she was successfully burnt. The *Wolf* fireship burned the *Triomphant* of 74 guns, and boats destroyed the *Admirable* of 90 guns. All three ships were stoutly defended by the French, both on board the ships and by a fort from the shore.[68] This was in sharp contrast to the behaviour of their compatriots at St Vaaste La Hougue the following day.

Monday morning May 23rd came in the Bay of La Hougue with Shovell expecting to lead the action. However, he had fallen very ill, and Russell was forced to replace him with Vice Admiral George Rooke. Charnock described this as "a grievous and sudden indisposition".[69] Larn, in his account of the loss of Shovell, has suggested that his sudden incapacity may have been caused by gout, as he was subject to this ailment, as was Rooke.[70] Acute gout, particularly in a big toe, could certainly come on quickly and would preclude jumping about in boats. Shovell was subject to quinsies that can also produce sudden incapacity.[71] On balance, it seems most likely that his inability to lead the boat action was in fact due to the injury that he had sustained on May 19th, the day of the Battle of Barfleur. Whether this was due to a splinter[72] or a fall[73], as described previously, is debatable. After three and a half days, either stiffening in the injured limb or infection could have set in. In any event, Shovell was unable to lead the Monday's boat action.

Rooke, with several men of war and fireships, went into the Bay on Monday May 23rd and tried to attack the French ships. The French had hauled their vessels so close to the shore, under cover of the forts, that only small craft could approach them. That night the ships' boats and fireships went in and the six outermost French ships in La Hougue Bay and off Tatihou Island were destroyed. The soldiers who were part of the invasion force against England helped in their defence, and the sea was so shallow in places that cavalry were able to ride into the water. English sailors with boat hooks pulled some cavalrymen off their horses.[74] The soldiers behind the parapets of La Hougue and Tatihou were demoralised and fought poorly.[75] In fact, there were sufficient small French boats in La Hougue Bay to have beaten off the English attack and to have stopped the ship burnings, if they had had more courage.[76]

On Tuesday May 24th the English boats went in again, and a further six French men of war were burnt. In addition, about twenty transport ships which had taken shelter deep in the Bay, up a creek, were also destroyed.[77] The ships burnt at St Vaaste La Hougue were:

| St Louis | 56 guns | Tonnant | 70 guns |
|---|---|---|---|
| Fort | 52 | Terrible | 74 |
| Gaillard | | Fier | 68 |
| Ambitieux | 92 | Bourbon | 66 |
| Magnifique | 76 | Merveilleux | 92 |
| St Philippe | 80 | Foudroyant | 90 |

In addition fireships, transport and storeships were also destroyed.[78]

Until well into the nineteenth century, the remnants of the twelve destroyed French men of war could be seen at low spring tides. In March 1883 relics were taken from the wreckage and placed in the Maritime Museum in Paris.[79]

James II witnessed with Tourville and French ministers the destruction of part of the French fleet in La Hougue Bay. With it went his hopes of an invasion of England and the regaining of his crown. James did not endear himself to his hosts by declaring "who but my brave English tars could do such a thing?"[80] Later James II was to write plaintively to Louis XIV about the lack of success.[81]

Russell had achieved a great victory over Tourville. He had had the advantage of an overwhelming force and had relied on his Captain, David Mitchell, and his Master of the Fleet, John Benbow, for advice. Laughton has written: "Tourville was the superior of Russell as a seaman, officer, and honest man." Fortune does not always reward the worthy. Barfleur marked the end of French bids for command at sea. For the rest of the war, they were content to limit their attacks to English trade.[82]

Shovell had come out of the battle with nothing but credit. He had been one of the leading figures, if not the leading figure, on May 19th when his ship had broken the French line. In the subsequent chase, he had been among the first to reach St Vaaste La Hougue. Only illness prevented him gaining even greater fame in leading the ensuing boat action in La Hougue Bay.

Russell recognised the value of Shovell. In a letter to the Earl of Nottingham on May 23rd 1692, Russell wrote:

> As to the behaviour of the officers in the red squadron (whom I mention because the stress of the battle fell upon them) they did extremely well. Cloudesley Shovell lay upon my weather quarter, by which means he is pretty well mauled, but he will always be shewing the young gallant. He is a little hurt with a fall, but will do very well again; a better man the King has not in his service.[83]

Later, on June 22nd, Russell wrote again to Nottingham suggesting that Delavall be sent to command in the West Indies. "I do not know any one so proper as Sir Ralph Delavall, for he is diligent, except Shovell, who in my opinion ought not to be spared. The rest are not fit for that service." In fact, Russell was only too keen to rid himself of Ralph Delavall, but he was quite specific in not wishing to lose Shovell to distant parts.[84]

On June 20th David Butts wrote to William Blathwayt, the Secretary at War:

> Sir William Jennings is hear and gives the English all the glory of the

late action at sea in general; but in particular to Sir Cloudesley Shovell and Sir John Ashby who were on the two ships that disabled the Soleil Royal; the Dutch Squadron never came into doe anything for want of wind he say.[85]

Russell had won a notable sea victory over the French, and he had been given a wonderful opportunity to follow it up with a combined attack by land and sea on either St Malo or Brest. His fleet was intact and 14,000 men were at his disposal in England to act as a land force. The French fleet had been partially destroyed and the remainder had had the stuffing knocked out of them.

May 23rd saw Russell returning with most of his fleet to St Helens, although he felt the Downs would have been a more proper place. Ashby and the Dutch Vice Admiral Gerrit Callenburgh were left by Russell on the coast of France, to stop or preferably destroy the twenty odd ships which had escaped after Barfleur into St Malo, from coming out and sailing for Brest. They were not successful.[86]

Queen Mary, on receiving the information that Russell and the fleet were on their way to St Helens, commanded Nottingham, the Secretary of State, to signify her pleasure that they were to remain there. Thus, they would be in a better position to attack St Malo or Brest, as the King had determined before leaving the country. Mary correctly suspected that Russell would do nothing, and sent Lords Rochester, Romney and Portland to Portsmouth to discuss the matter with him.[87]

By the time this meeting and the subsequent council of war had been arranged, Russell was already feeling ill used and depressed. In La Hougue Bay on May 23rd, having overseen the destruction of part of the French fleet, Russell's justifiable pleasure was ruined by receiving the Queen's orders written prior to the battle, which were critical of his proposals. In his letter to Nottingham written that day, he stated that he would not be used in this manner again.[88]

Nottingham replied on May 26th, chiding Russell as a friend for having melancholic thoughts after so glorious a victory.[89] By May 27th Russell's reply to Nottingham spoke in terms of his friendship and stated that he would serve out this campaign, but he would then go and hunt.[90] It can be seen that Russell was not in a frame of mind to seriously contemplate an attack on St Malo or Brest, or indeed anywhere.

Russell and his flag officers met Rochester, Romney and Portland on May 28th 1692 at Portsmouth, and it was agreed that sixty men of war, without troops, would be sent to attack the French shipping at Brest. Nothing was done.[91] The Queen then ordered Russell to attempt St Malo, which he pretended to do.[92]

Throughout the months of June, July and early August 1692, earnest debate took place between the Queen, her council, the land officers and

Russell plus his flag officers, about the most appropriate action to follow up the successes of the early summer. In June and July Russell did take part of his fleet to sea with St Malo as his goal, or at least to stop ships sailing for Brest from there. A combination of the weather and the reluctance of his pilots ended the attempt.[93] During July a further council of war decided that:

> St Malo: The flag officers were resolved that nothing can be done by ships against the ships at St Malo, till the town be so reduced by land forces as that our ships may not be much annoyed by the enemy's guns. The land officers say that troops can do nothing without the assistance of the fleet.
> Brest: The flag officers say that though Brest might be attempted with hopes of success, if the summer were not so far spent, yet now it would not be fit to attempt anything against the enemy's ships there. And the land officers say the troops can do nothing without the protection of the fleet.[94]

The end result was that neither the fleet nor the waiting 14,000 troops were used with effect against either St Malo or Brest that summer.

What of Shovell in this wasted two-month period at the height of summer, the ideal time for naval action? He appears to have made a rapid recovery from his sudden indisposition in La Hougue Bay. Russell, in a letter of May 27th, mentioned that the masts of the *Royal William*, the ship that Shovell had been in at the beginning of the Battle of Barfleur, might have to come out. Shovell's men and guns would be better transferred to a new ship.[95] Presumably, Shovell had transferred back to the *Royal William* from the *Kent*. Indeed, on June 2nd Russell sent the *Royal William* to Chatham for new masts and girdling. On June 7th Shovell removed into the *Duke*, a 90 gun 2nd rate, built at Woolwich in 1682.[96]

As a flag officer, Shovell had taken part in the various debates concerning the feasibility of attempts on Brest, St Malo and other French ports. He was bound by the collective view of these councils. Nottingham has suggested that it was rare for a council of war to go against the view of its commander-in-chief, and that Russell either called the council after action had already been taken or he had expressed his view beforehand.[97] Nottingham reported that both the Dutch Admiral Almonde and Sir Cloudesley Shovell would gladly have been employed in this enterprise (on Brest) if the council of war had allowed. He described them both as brave men.[98]

In mid June 1692 Russell had taken the main part of the fleet on the abortive mission towards St Malo. Shovell was temporarily left at Spithead to bring the remaining ships to join the fleet. Shovell in the *Duke*, with the *Eagle*, *Captain*, *Swiftsure*, *Restoration* and *Bonaventure*, sailed after

Russell on June 17th.[99] At about this time there was mention of a privateer called the *Cloudesley galley*. Whether it was named in Shovell's honour is unknown.[100]

By early August it was clear that it was too late in the year for any major undertaking against St Malo or Brest involving the great ships of the English fleet. Shovell, who had returned to the *Kent*, was ordered by Russell on August 6th to take the Duke of Leinster, his army in their transport ships and a number of men of war to the Downs or Margate Roads, if he thought that was more secure. The ships to sail with Shovell were the *Bredah, Monck, Greenwich, Woolwich, Chatham, Charles galley, Delft, Medenblick* (Dutch), *Greyhound, Strombolo, Griffin, Roebuck, Owner's Cove, Charles, Signet* (all fireships), *Shark* (brigantine), and *Salamander* (bomb vessel). In addition, if Shovell met William Meesters, a controversial Dutch artillery officer, or any of his bomb vessels, he was to take them with him.[101] Leinster's troops were to be transported to Holland to reinforce the King. Namur had fallen in June, a fortnight after La Hougue. However, at the end of July the allied victory at Steenkirk forced the French army back across the Scheldt.[102] The vessels of Meesters were to be used against the forts of Dunkirk.

Russell's choice of Shovell to take Leinster to the Downs did not meet with the approval of Ralph Delavall. Delavall moaned to Nottingham on August 7th, "Shovell out of all course is appointed to go with the Duke of Leinster and you may be confident he will see the King as soon as possible and to tell a story as he did last year."[103] These carping comments referring to Shovell's junior position were part of a letter pointing out how ill used Delavall felt he was. It is ironic that the next year, 1693, both Shovell and Delavall were to be cooped up together in the *Britannia*, as joint Commanders-in-Chief with Henry Killigrew!

By 8.00 p.m. on August 8th Shovell was able to report that he was safely in the Downs with his charges. He mentioned that Russell had ordered his removal back into the *Kent*, the 2nd rate, in which he had spent the latter part of the Battle of Barfleur and subsequent chase.[104] On August 19th the King wrote to Shovell ordering him, as it was not possible to attack St Malo/Brest at this time of year, to escort the transports and troops to Neuport or Ostend, by August 22nd or 23rd. In addition, he was to bring pilots from Zealand to the Downs. Shovell sailed on August 20th from the Downs with a S.S.W. wind. He wrote to Nottingham the same day to the effect that he had received information that twenty-eight privateers from Dunkirk were at sea, with designs on the East Coast fleet, and with good intelligence of his own convoy. In addition, the Dutch were not blockading Dunkirk properly and ships were going in and out at will. By August 22nd Shovell had arrived off Ostend. Leinster and his men disembarked and by September 7th were encamped near Fearne.[105]

Shovell was not impressed by William Meesters' plan to bomb the forts at Dunkirk. He informed Nottingham on August 26th that, "I wish the project may take its designed effect though I much doubt it." Shovell had promised to assist with fireships and anything else that he could. Admiral Geleijn Evertsen had arrived at Ostend at this time to command the Dutch squadron before Dunkirk.[106] On September 7th Shovell reported to Nottingham that a Captain Jean Bart, leader of the privateers, was intending to come out of Dunkirk with four ships. Shovell was sending two frigates and two fireships to stop this. He was hoping to join them soon.[107]

Shovell took part in the bombing of Dunkirk between September 10th and 13th. By the 15th of the month there was a general view that it was too late in the year for a siege of Dunkirk.[108]

September 28th saw Shovell back at Deale because of lack of provisions. He had kept four shallow bottomed well boats to use at Dunkirk. On the return journey, one had sunk close to Shovell's ship, and with difficulty they had saved the men out of her. Another was lost on Zealand and the remaining two had got to "our coast" but were badly damaged. Shovell asked Nottingham if the weather had altered the King's intentions against Dunkirk. He reported that he had been sick with a fever and ague. Ague is a malarial fever with hot, cold and sweating stages. It is possible that Shovell had picked up malaria during his time in the Mediterranean, or more likely still on one of his earlier trips to the West Indies. In any event, he had recovered from it.[109]

In October 1692 Shovell went to Flanders to bring the King home. He had a certain amount of difficulty getting there because of bad weather. However, on October 18th an express reported that a tender of the *Kent* had got into Yarmouth reporting that the King on board the *Mary yacht*, escorted by Shovell and his squadron of five ships, were twelve leagues E.S.E. off Yarmouth. It was believed that the King would land at Yarmouth, Southwold, or Orford.[110] By October 22nd Shovell, having safely delivered the King, was out chasing six French men of war.[111]

In the late summer Shovell advised Nottingham on the division of booty in the West Indies. Shovell had been in the West Indies in 1663 with Sir Christopher Myngs and again with Sir John Harman in 1667. He was able to give an account of how the booty had been divided up.[112] In November Shovell advised Sir Francis Wheeler on the best way to attack Cayenne, as he had been with Harman at its taking in 1668. Shovell said that it was a sickly place in the rainy season and that it had a strong fort. In addition, as it was a long way to windward of Barbados, it could not be taken from there without a long and sickly passage.[113]

November was a happy month for Shovell and his wife, Elizabeth, as the birth of their first child occurred, on November 2nd 1692, at their home in Prescot Street, Goodman's Fields, London. She was a daughter called Elizabeth like her mother, and was christened on November 22nd at St Mary's, Whitechapel.[114]

Towards the end of the year Shovell addressed two important letters to the Admiralty on the subject of the embarkation of detachments of marines. He was, of course, at the time Lt Colonel of the Second Regiment of Marines. In the first, written on December 19th, he suggested and the proposal was afterwards approved "that orders be given for putting the ticketts of the marine soldiers that are to be turned over, into the hands of the commander of the ships they are turned over to and by them delivered unto the soldiers when they come into the Downs or where they cannot run away". This order evidently referred to those ships which did not carry an officer of marines and was no doubt necessary as the "ticketts" which each man was entitled to possess recorded the amount of wages due to him, and were therefore commodities of marketable value, and an incentive to desertion.[115]

Shovell's second letter, written two days later, discloses two details concerning the embarkation of marines. In future "Marine soldiers ... carry their arms with them to sea" and "Sargeants and Corporals be appointed to each ship according to their numbers on board the ships they are." It seems likely that, when embarking previously, marines had not carried their arms with them and that there were too few non-commissioned officers.[116]

The autumn of 1692 saw a parliamentary enquiry into the alleged mismanagement of naval affairs that summer. Russell defended himself, and the House of Commons decided that he had acted with courage, good conduct and fidelity. Disappointments had been occasioned by want of timely and proper orders. The finger was pointed at Nottingham, but he too justified himself in the House of Lords. The King approved his service for that summer with thanks for his great labour and diligence in it.[117] The Queen gave £30,000 and medals to be distributed amongst the Barfleur victors.[118] Greenwich Hospital, in its final form, sprang partly from the fate of the casualties suffered in the Battle of Barfleur.[119] Russell looked upon Barfleur as the climax of his career at sea. In later years he gave the home farm on his estate at Chippenham the name "La Hougue" and planted a grove of trees, some of which were still alive in the 1950s, to represent his tactical formation that day.[120]

Despite the plaudits all round, it is hard to escape the conclusion that naval affairs during the summer of 1692 were mismanaged. It is difficult to apportion blame for this, but the Queen, her council, Nottingham and Russell must take a share of it. Barfleur was a fine victory but it was not followed up effectively.

Shovell had had a year of unqualified success as a junior admiral. On the last day of the year, William III sent for him from Chatham to come to Kensington Palace. Rapid promotion was in store for him, but not success, as the next chapter will tell.[121]

NOTES

1. RMT MAT 25.
2. Luttrell, Vol.II, p.345.
3. The General Armorg; RMT MAT 25.
4. Richmond, pp.226–227.
5. Aiken, p.92.
6. C.S.P.Dom 1691–92 p.197.
7. Ehrmann, p.392.
8. Laird Clowes, p.346.
9. Luttrell, Vol.II, pp.375, 383.
10. Finch MSS, Vol.IV, pp.28–29 & pp.38–39.
11. C.S.P. Dom 1691–2 pp.207, 217.
12. Ehrmann, p.393.
13. Ehrmann, p.392.
14. ADM 1/4080 f.123.
15. Finch MSS, Vol.IV, pp.46, 47, 65, 76.
16. Luttrell, Vol.II, pp.383, 422.
17. Anderson, Lists of Men of War.
18. Luttrell, Vol.II, p.432.
19. Quarterly Review, Vol.CLXXVI, p.476.
20. Richmond, p.228.
21. Quarterly Review, Vol.CLXXVI, p.470.
22. Finch MSS, Vol.IV, pp.105–106.
23. Torrington, p.63.
24. Finch MSS, Vol.IV, p.158.
25. Secret Memoirs; Laird Clowes, p.347.
26. RMT MAT 26, 85.
27. Finch MSS, Vol.IV, pp.158–159.
28. Quarterly Review, Vol.CLXXVI, p.482.
29. Quarterly Review, Vol.CLXXVI, p.482.
30. Quarterly Review, Vol.CLXXVI, p.483; Shovell to Earl of Nottingham July 18th 1702.
31. Ehrmann, p.395.
32. Laird Clowes, p.349.
33. Laird Clowes, p.348.
34. Laird Clowes, p.349.
35. Laird Clowes, pp.349–350.
36. Allyn.
37. Quarterly Review, Vol.CLXXVI, p.475.
38. Laird Clowes, p.350.
39. Laird Clowes, p.351.
40. Allyn.
41. Allyn.
42. Allyn.
43. Laird Clowes, p.351.
44. Allyn.
45. Allyn.
46. Allyn.
47. Allyn.
48. Allyn.
49. Dartmonth MSS, Vol.I, p.68.
50. Allyn.

51. Allyn.
52. Laird Clowes, pp.352–353.
53. Quarterly Review, Vol.CLXXVI p.471; Allyn.
54. Allyn.
55. Luttrell, Vol.II, p.465.
56. Finch MSS, Vol.IV, pp.176–178.
57. RMT MSS.
58. Allyn.
59. Allyn.
60. Laird Clowes, p.253.
61. Allyn.
62. Laird Clowes, p.353.
63. Allyn; Laird Clowes, p.353.
64. Allyn.
65. Allyn.
66. D.N.B. Shovell, Carter.
67. Laird Clowes, p.354.
68. Allyn; Laird Clowes, p.354.
69. Charnock, p.19.
70. Larn p.8; HMC 12th report, Part VII, p.320.
71. Luttrell, Vol.III, p.451.
72. Luttrell, Vol.II, p.465.
73. Finch MSS, Vol.IV, pp.176–178.
74. Laird Clowes, p.355.
75. Quarterly Review, Vol.CLXXVI, p.467.
76. Quarterly Review, Vol.CLXXVI, p.468.
77. Allyn; Laird Clowes, p.355.
78. Laird Clowes, p.356.
79. Laird Clowes, p.355.
80. Laird Clowes, p.355; Atlas of Maritime History p.67.
81. Secret Memoirs.
82. Richmond, p.234.
83. Finch MSS, Vol.IV, pp.176–178.
84. Finch MSS, Vol.IV, p.256.
85. Finch MSS, Vol.IV, p.220.
86. Laird Clowes, p.357.
87. Aiken, p.97.
88. Finch MSS, Vol.IV, p.178.
89. Finch MSS, Vol.IV, p.185.
90. Finch MSS, Vol.IV, p.191.
91. Aiken, p.98.
92. Aiken, p.98.
93. Finch MSS, Vol.IV, p.356.
94. Aiken, p.99.
95. Finch MSS, Vol.IV, p.189.
96. Finch MSS, Vol.IV, pp.200 & 212; Anderson, Lists of Men of War.
97. Aiken, p.102.
98. Aiken, p.104.
99. Finch MSS, Vol.IV, p.244.
100. Burchett, p.470.
101. Finch MSS, Vol.IV, p.330.
102. Richmond, p.235.

103. Finch MSS, Vol.IV, p.372.
104. Finch MSS, Vol.IV, p.374.
105. Finch MSS, Vol.IV, pp.394, 408,448.
106. Finch MSS, Vol.IV, p.420.
107. Finch MSS, Vol.IV, p.448.
108. Luttrell, Vol.II, pp.563, 566.
109. Finch MSS, Vol.IV, p.474.
110. C.S.P. Dom. 1691–92 p.484.
111. Luttrell, Vol.II, p.598.
112. Finch MSS, Vol.IV, pp.387, 388.
113. Finch MSS, Vol.IV, p.502.
114. RMT MAT 76.
115. Edye, Vol.I, p.376; Minutes of the Admiralty Library, Vol.IV, Dec.19th 1692.
116. Edye, Vol.I, p.376; Minutes of the Admiralty Library, Vol.IV, Dec.22nd 1692.
117. Aiken, p.107–109.
118. Campbell, p.244.
119. Ehrmann, p.399.
120. Ehrmann, p.399.
121. Luttrell, Vol.II, p.653.

CHAPTER XIV

# The Smyrna Convoy Disaster
# 1693

The year 1692 had been an excellent one for Shovell. His brave conduct at the Battle of Barfleur had been recognised by the Commander-in-Chief, Edward Russell, and he was popular with the navy and public alike. If 1692 had been one of the high points of Shovell's career, then 1693 was to be amongst the low ones.

Shovell's anonymous biographer, a man who had served with him, made little reference to 1693 apart from stating that, "Shovell was upset that in his eminent station he was unable to humble the French with a remarkable engagement."[1] No mention was made of the Smyrna Convoy.

Since September 1691 the Turkey Company, which specialised in trade with the eastern Mediterranean, had been collecting together merchant ships from England, Holland, Germany, Denmark and Sweden to be convoyed in safety from the French into the Mediterranean.[2] The Admiralty had been petitioned several times to provide an escort for the convoy, and by the spring of 1693 the merchants were becoming restive at the continuing delays. By this time, about 400 merchant ships containing principally woollen goods had collected in England's southern ports. The name that has become associated with this convoy is that of Smyrna, the principal Levant port, where woollen goods were traded for oriental silks, yarn and grogram (coarse fabric of silk stiffened with gum). Hence the Smyrna Convoy Disaster.[3]

Early in 1693 Sir George Rooke had received a commission to command the Mediterranean squadron. The Admiralty instructed Rooke on February 20th to accompany the assembled merchant ships to their destinations throughout the Mediterranean.[4] Twice Rooke was told to proceed, and on both occasions his orders were cancelled.[5] It would be May before Rooke and the merchant ships left with the Grand Fleet.

Edward Russell had commanded the fleet in 1692 and had rightly been given credit for the defeat of the French at Barfleur. However, he had not followed up his victory as successfully as he might have done, later in the summer. At least this was the prevailing view at the time. Suggestions had been made that a joint commission in 1693 should command the fleet, as it had in 1691 under Richard Haddock, Henry Killigrew and John Ashby. Russell did not wish to share the command with others and in addition refused to go to sea in 1693 if he had to take orders from the Earl of Nottingham.[6] Once Russell had told William III that he would go to sea no more, various names were put forward for the commission including that of the Earl of Pembroke.[7] Eventually the King chose Henry Killigrew, Ralph Delavall and Shovell. The suggestion that the command of the fleet should be a commission of several men came from Nottingham. The choice of Killigrew, Delavall and Shovell was the King's. Nottingham had no objections and the Council supported them.[8] The choice was not popular with the Whigs who denounced Killigrew and Delavall as Jacobites.[9]

Who were the men who shared the commission with Shovell in 1693? Henry Killigrew was a gentleman captain, whose father had been chaplain to Charles I and later to the Duke of York, after the Restoration. In addition, his mistress, the Duchess of Cleveland, had been a paramour of Charles II. Shovell must have known him well as they had served together in the Mediterranean in the 1670s and 80s. Killigrew's background lent itself to suspicions of covert Jacobitism, although he had impressed Samuel Pepys with his neatness and gentlemanly living.[10]

Sir Ralph Delavall was another gentleman captain who had served in the Dutch Wars, and was to die in the same year as Shovell, 1707. He had come to national prominence at Beachy Head in 1690, where in Russell's absence he had led the blue squadron with considerable distinction. Delavall had also been President of the Earl of Torrington's court martial at which he was scrupulously fair.[11] Shovell cannot have known him as well as he knew Killigrew.

In the early 1690s it was possible to discern three factions in the navy. The first consisted of men such as Shovell, Francis Wheeler and John Benbow, who were primarily sailors and were not interested in politics.

They were keen to serve their country under any commander as best they could. The second faction consisted of a group of restless, ambitious politicians such as Russell whose power was exerted through the Admiralty. Opposed to Russell and his friends was a third faction which operated through the Cabinet against the Admiralty. Nottingham himself, Delavall, Killigrew and possibly Rooke belonged to this faction. Charges of Jacobitism were later laid against some members of this group such as Delavall and Killigrew.[12]

Although the names of Killigrew, Delavall and Shovell had first been put forward by the King in January 1693, it was not until March 18th that the command of the fleet was officially put into a joint commission.[13] The joint admirals chose the *Britannia*, a 100 gun 1st rate, as their flagship, and offered the position of First Captain to George Byng, with the pay and rank of a rear admiral. Byng was attached to Russell and declined the post, preferring to retire to his country seat.[14] On January 26th Captain John Neville was given the post.[15]

On March 18th the joint admirals received orders from the Admiralty to put to sea with the eighty-one ships allocated for the main fleet plus a Dutch contingent, and to proceed westwards to annoy the French and to secure the trade in the Channel. These orders could not be obeyed as the fleet had not been collected together and victualled.[16] On April 4th Sir John Trenchard, the Second Secretary of State, who had taken over correspondence with the fleet from Nottingham, told the joint admirals to consider means of attacking the French in Brest. In addition, they must find ways to stop the junction of the Brest fleet with the Toulon squadron.[17]

On April 6th Shovell had been made a Commissioner of the Navy with a salary of 1,000 pounds, that must have improved his already secure financial position.[18] Shovell had some light relief from the difficulties of assembling and revictualling the fleet, as on April 21st he and the other two joint admirals had been ordered to open a court martial on a Captain Henry Boteler of the *Mary*. The *Mary* had opened fire on a privateer without warning, damaging her and killing one of the crew. On going on board the *Mary* the privateer's crew found most of her men drunk![19]

Throughout April ships had been coming out of the Thames and sailing to the Downs. On April 29th the joint admirals went on board the *Britannia* at Deale, sailed for St Helens on May 4th and arrived there the following day. Difficulties had been experienced in collecting the fleet because of the inclement weather. In addition, revictualling had proceeded slowly and was in its usual chaotic state.[20]

As late as early May Trenchard was still informing the joint admirals that Queen Mary required further consideration to be given to an attack on Brest. His letter of May 3rd made clear that an attack must be launched before the Toulon squadron arrived.[21] Indeed, on April 28, the day before leaving London, the admirals discussed the proposed attack on Brest with the Cabinet Council. A force of sixty-five ships would be required to overwhelm the Brest batteries and fleet. Concern was expressed that the Dutch would not help in the attempt unless directly ordered to. At the end of the meeting, Shovell returned to the room to talk privately with the Marquis of Carmarthen. He was worried about the Dutch attitude, and felt that if the English were allowed to consider the matter at a council of war, they would find an excuse for not going ahead with the attack. Carmarthen wrote a letter to William III informing him of Shovell's view.[22] The ever-thrustful Shovell was keen for action!

Queen Mary's and Trenchard's interest in an attempt on Brest had lessened by mid May. On May 13th Trenchard wrote to the joint admirals stating that the Queen wished some Lords of the Council to go on board the *Britannia* and be present for the discussions on what was best to be done with Rooke and the Straits squadron.[23] A number of Lords, including Carmarthen, Rochester, Pembroke and Secretary Trenchard, arrived in Portsmouth on May 14th and attended a council of war in the *Britannia* that evening.[24] The meeting produced no firm conclusions and it was agreed to meet again the following day.

On May 15th a further council of war considered the Straits squadron. This turned out to be a vital meeting and, as well as the three joint admirals, the other flag officers, George Rooke, John Berkeley, Matthew Aylmer, David Mitchell and John Neville, were present. The Dutch contingent led by Admiral Philip Almonde also attended. Apparently the Lords of the Council were not at this meeting, although they were made aware of its conclusions immediately afterwards.

The conclusions of the May 15th council of war will be quoted in full, as they became important in the joint admirals' defence of their actions, in the aftermath of the loss of the Smyrna Convoy.

> It is our opinion that if the Toulon squadron be come out of the Straits and joined those of Brest, that 10 men of war, a small frigate and a fireship may be a sufficient convoy for the Turkey fleet, and the separate convoy for Spain proceed with them, as by the Admiralty designed; and that the Turkey fleet sail with the Main fleet; and if the French fleet be joined and at Brest, that the Turkey fleet proceed with their convoy. But if the French fleet be not in Brest and joined, that then the Main fleet proceed with the Turkey fleet as far into the sea, as it shall be adjudged at sea convenient by a Council of Flag Officers. But if there be no certain intelligence of the Toulon Squadron being come out of the Straits, or where they are, before the fleet sail from St. Helens, that then the Turkey fleet remain here with the convoy we have here proposed, till further intelligence be had of the Toulon Squadron.[25]

The underlying findings of this meeting were sound. If the whereabouts of the Brest fleet and Toulon squadron were not known, then the rich merchant Smyrna ships were to stay at St Helens until they were. The Lords of the Council and Trenchard had been made aware of the admirals' conclusions, but there appears to have been a failure of communication, in that Queen Mary and the Admiralty Commissioners either did not receive this information or took no notice of it.

Following the May 15th deliberations, the joint admirals remained in expectation of orders. They came on May 20th, having been written on the 19th by the Commissioners of the Admiralty. The signatories were Lord Falkland, J. Lowther, H. Preistman and R. Austen. The orders stated that:

> with the first opportunity of wind and weather, to sail with their Majesties fleet under your command, together with the squadron of their Majesties' ships under the command of Sir George Rooke and the merchant ships under his convoy, bound to the Mediterranean and to keep company with the said squadron and merchant ships, so far as you shall think it requisite; and you are to order Sir George Rooke, after your parting with them, to steer such course for their passage to Cadiz as shall be thought most safe by a Council of War, with relation as well to the Brest fleet, if gone out to sea, as to the Toulon Squadron.[26]

These latest Admiralty orders were considered at a further council of war in the *Britannia* at St Helens on May 22nd. All the English and Dutch flag officers who had attended the May 15th deliberations attended again with the addition of Sir John Ashby. Ashby was soon to die, apparently from the effects of alcohol, and it is likely that he had been too ill to attend the May 15th council of war. Admiralty Commissioners in the name of Queen Mary had given the joint admirals direct orders. These had to be obeyed, whatever their misgivings and despite the fact that their views of May 15th had been ignored. The May 22nd council of war merely decided the various rendezvous in relation to different wind directions and the signal for Rooke and his convoy to leave. If the wind was fair, the rendezvous would be thirty leagues W.S.W. of Ushant. The parting signal was to be a blue flag on the foretop masthead and the firing of five guns. The actual wording of the conclusions was ambiguous, in that it was not absolutely clear whether the thirty leagues W.S.W. of Ushant was merely a rendezvous or the point of departure for Rooke. Lord Falkland seized on this ambiguity at the subsequent enquiry.[27]

The joint admirals intended to sail, but were held up firstly by the weather and secondly by more trouble with victualling, particularly of Rooke's squadron. Rooke had already complained to the joint admirals that the main fleet was being victualled at the expense of his Straits squadron.

Eventually, on May 30th 1693 the main fleet, Rooke's squadron and the merchant convoy got away from St Helens and reached the point of rendezvous thirty leagues W.S.W. of Ushant on June 4th. According to Rooke's account, early in the morning the joint admirals in the *Britannia* made the signal for him to depart with the merchant ships, in accordance with the resolutions of the council of war of May 22nd. As there was little wind, Rooke decided to go to the *Britannia* and enquire what intelligence the admirals had received from Brest about the French fleet. Rooke was perturbed that no ship had been sent into Brest for intelligence and the admirals called a further council of war.[28] Rooke's record has a ring of truth about it, despite the fact that he was trying to protect himself, in that the joint admirals' account is consistent with it. The admirals stated that on the morning of June 4th the signal for Rooke's departure was given and thereupon they called a council of war which was to consider an extension to the main fleet's cover for Rooke. They were not specific in giving reasons for calling the council of war.

The hastily convened council of war of June 4th, in the *Britannia*, decided to accompany Rooke and the merchant ships a further twenty leagues and then to proceed to ten leagues N.W. of Ushant.[29] This bland statement hid the earnest debate that took place in the *Britannia*. In a letter written by Sir Ralph Delavall to his friend, a Mr G. Clarke, less than one month later, he gave an account of the council of war on June 4th.

> As for leaving Sir George Rooke it was not without the approbation of a council of war and the Dutch showing a particular aversion for going above ten leagues to the westward of Ushant and it was not without some difficulty that we prevailed with them to go 30 leagues and after that at my particular instigation we called another council of war to propose going 50 leagues further with George Rooke or until we had some intelligence of the French fleet and which proposal all the Dutch and some English differed with me that I in some passion declared at the council of war that I see no proposal of our doing the nation so much good service this summer as our proceeding with and securing the Streights fleet as far as our provisions would give us leave, upon which Sir Cloudesley Shovell and Mister Killigrew joined with me and so did the rest but all we could bring the Dutch to was to sail 20 leagues further and indeed before they had well done that they kept astern so far they were quite out of sight.[30]

June 6th saw the separation of the main fleet from Rooke and his merchant convoy. Rooke stated that, "we lost sight of them at night".[31] The joint admirals reported that, "this evening we parted with the Mediterranean fleet". In any case, whether the departure was intended or accidental, Rooke's squadron and the merchant ships under their care were sailing directly into the arms of the Brest fleet.

Where were the French? The French had been more efficient than the English in getting their ships repaired, manned and victualled for the campaign of 1693. Intelligence had reached Paris of English designs on Brest. In late April Compte de Tourville had led the Brest fleet out and down the coast of Portugal to Lagos Bay. Tourville hoped to join the Brest fleet with the Toulon squadron off Cape St Vincent, to make a force capable of challenging the combined Anglo/Dutch fleet in the Channel.[32]

Rooke had under his command thirteen ships of 40–60 guns, six smaller vessels and eight ships under the Dutch Admiral Van der Goes. His squadron was to protect the 400 odd merchant ships and was a match for the Toulon squadron but certainly not for the Brest fleet.[33] Unfortunately for Rooke, he ran slap into the Brest fleet under Tourville in Lagos Bay on June 27th. Wisely he retreated with his squadron and the merchant ships scattered in all directions.[34] The Anglo/Dutch squadron lost four men of war (three Dutch, one English), forty merchant ships were taken (including four rich Smyrna ships) and fifty more were destroyed. Just under a quarter of the merchant convoy had been lost.[35] Rooke, in the *Royal Oak*, returned to England via Kinsale in southern Ireland, arriving at Torbay on August 17th. He brought with him the *Monmouth, Lyon, Woolwich, Stirling Castle, Speedwell* and *Dispatch*.[36]

Let us return to the main fleet which proceeded to move to its allotted position ten leagues N.W. of Ushant, apparently without a backward glance. On June 8th Shovell wrote to Captain John Hill (his father-in-law), concerning the departure of Rooke and stated that the Straits' ships would sail close to the coast of Portugal sending a frigate ahead to Lisbon to see if the French were off Cadiz. Shovell wrote in terms of arriving at the place of rendezvous, on June 4th, thirty leagues W.S.W. of Ushant and that Rooke had steered with the Straits ships to the south-west. No mention was made of the extra twenty leagues or final departure on June 6th. The letter is difficult to understand. Did Shovell not take too seriously the extra twenty leagues accompanying Rooke or is this a simple factual error? One cannot be certain.[37]

In addition to Shovell's letter to Captain Hill quoted above, the joint admirals also wrote to Trenchard on June 8th.

> The wind having blown hard from S. and S.S.E. we doubt not that in all probability he [Rooke] is out of the way of danger which might happen to him in these parts. We have not yet been able to gain any intelligence of the French fleet, but shall use all possible endeavours to that purpose.[38]

The admirals were wrong about Rooke being out of danger and were soon to receive firm intelligence that the French were out of Brest.

Various ships had been trying to obtain intelligence of the whereabouts of the French for some weeks. In May the *Montagu* with the *Rochester* had been cruising between Scilly and Ushant without success.[39] On June 14th the joint admirals ordered the *Warspite* and two brigantines to stand in, to see if the French fleet was in the Bay of Brest or Camaret, with the main fleet lying within two or three leagues of Ushant. Consideration was to be given to the possibility of attacking the French fleet if it was in Brest. The *Warspite* returned on June 17th, and informed the joint admirals that Brest was virtually empty apart from some fishing boats. This was vital and reliable information, as the pilot was a French Protestant who knew the area well. What should the admirals do? They decided to look for the enemy off Scilly, and if they failed to find them there, to return to Torbay as they were short of provisions.[40] It may well be asked why the joint admirals did not send the *Warspite* or some other ship to look into Brest before Rooke was sent on his way. The matter will be returned to in due course.

On June 12th Sir John Ashby had died, apparently as a result of a surfeit of alcohol. Until his death, he had attended most of the councils of war. There was a vacancy to fill, but the joint admirals referred the matter to Her Majesty's pleasure.[41] The main fleet did not find the French off the Scilly Isles and returned to Torbay on June 21st. They were greeted by a letter from Trenchard stating that the Lords of the Council were concerned that the French had plans to interrupt the passage of the Mediterranean squadron and convoy in its passage to Cadiz. The joint admirals were to consider what position to occupy to support Rooke. No limits were to be placed on them as to the distance from England that the main fleet might go. Trenchard ended this letter of June 21st with the instruction that everything possible must be done to repossess the Mediterranean squadron and merchant ships should they have been taken.[42]

The letter quoted above from Trenchard must have alarmed the joint admirals. Their first reaction, on June 25th, was to proceed at once to Lisbon hoping to join Sir George Rooke. However, they had insufficient provisions to undertake a voyage of this distance.[43]

Revictualling was carried out and several letters were exchanged between Trenchard on the one hand and the admirals on the other. Trenchard and the Admiralty wanted the fleet to go back to sea as soon as possible and the admirals replied that they would put to sea as soon as they had revictualled.[44] In the event the main fleet sailed again on July 11th, but was forced back to Torbay by bad weather and damaged ships. They had intended to move to a position forty leagues S.W. of Ushant and to reconsider the situation.[45]

On July 14th the *Lark* arrived at Torbay carrying Rooke's secretary,

Captain Martin. Rooke had not sent the admirals a written account of the disaster and the admirals sent Martin directly to the Admiralty to report. From this time onwards the admirals were under continual attack concerning their conduct.[46]

The main fleet sailed again from Torbay on July 17th, heading for a station forty leagues S.W. of Ushant with a view to intercepting the French on their return to Brest. They failed to find them, and on August 16th retired yet again to Torbay. The weather was poor, with gales making it difficult for the flag officers to meet and draw up plans for a final redeeming attack on the coast of France. It was not to be, the weather was too stormy, and on August 25th the Admiralty sent orders that the fleet remove itself to St Helens. They left Torbay on August 28th and reached St Helens on the 29th.[47]

The season was now far advanced, and on September 9th the joint admirals recommended to the Admiralty that it was time for the fleet to be laid up for the winter.[48] Their advice was followed. Between September 9th and 27th the joint admirals, Killigrew, Delavall and Shovell, were stuck at Portsmouth and not allowed to go to London despite frequent requests to the Admiralty and Queen Mary. The admirals were only too well aware of the attacks being made on their management of the fleet during the summer and they were naturally keen to defend themselves. In addition, the *Britannia* was being laid up and there was no proper accommodation for the three of them together. Finally, on September 27th Queen Mary relented, although the admirals were told to report directly to the Admiralty and Trenchard.[49]

The onslaught on the joint admirals over their actions or rather lack of them began in earnest in September and continued into 1694. In September, while they were cooped up in Portsmouth, the Admiralty continued with detailed questioning and this was taken up by the Privy Council on October 9th and 19th.[50] In November the House of Commons started its own enquiry, and the House of Lords did the same.[51] These investigations became the fullest of naval affairs of the whole war.[52]

The questioning at the enquiries was repetitive, and the various interested parties were concerned to steer any blame for the Smyrna Convoy Disaster away from themselves and firmly into the laps of the hapless Killigrew, Delavall and Shovell.

The nub of the matter was Tourville's Brest fleet. If the Brest fleet was in harbour it posed no threat to the Smyrna convoy, provided they had been accompanied past Brest by the main fleet. Rooke's squadron was capable of dealing with D'Estrées' Toulon squadron or other small groups of French ships that might be met. If the Brest fleet was out of harbour, they posed a potential threat to the Smyrna convoy, unless its position was known and it could be avoided. It seems inconceivable that the Cabinet Council, Admiralty Commissioners and the joint admirals could overlook this most basic of facts. They did not.

The Earl of Nottingham had received reports of French preparations at Brest, and in the light of this, Trenchard was supposed to give clear orders to the joint admirals prior to sailing, concerning the Brest fleet.

> The Earl of Nottingham, having an account of the French prepara-tions at Brest (inasmuch as this account was) so particular as to mention (the number of their ships and) the disposition in which they lay at anchor in Brest water, which was such as if they had apprehensions of being attacked there by their enemy's fleet, he laid this before the Cabinet Council; and a copy of it was ordered to be given, and was given, to Secretary Trenchard, and he was directed to transmit it to the admirals of the fleet; and (he was at this time likewise informed) that they should be ordered to take Sir George Rooke's squadron and the fleet of merchants with them to Camaret Bay and look into Brest water. And if the French fleet were there, (it was commanded that) they should send away Sir George Rooke with the merchants; but if the French fleet were (on the other hand) come out to sea (their instructions were that) Sir George should not proceed on his voyage till they had got some account of the French fleet. But neither these orders in their full extent, nor the list of the French fleet, were transmitted to the three admirals; so they sailed down the Channel and in the Soundings dismissed Sir George Rooke, who when he came to turn the point of (Cape St. Vincent) saw the whole French fleet in Lagos Bay.[53]

In addition to this damning evidence against Trenchard, on January 15th 1694 Nottingham produced in the House of Lords a letter dated the previous May 30th (the date of sailing of the main fleet and Rooke) which said that the French fleet was out.[54] Clearly, the man most responsible for the Smyrna Convoy Disaster was the Second Secretary of State, Sir John Trenchard. This fact does not appear to be widely known.

Killigrew, Delavall and Shovell all had had experience in the command of squadrons in the past. Can they be excused for not attempting to gain intelligence of the Brest fleet of their own volition? The joint admirals felt that they had considered the whereabouts of the French fleet and advised accordingly, but that their advice had been ignored. Their principal argument was that the conclusions of their council of war of May 15th had stated that, if the whereabouts of the Toulon squadron were not known, then the merchant ships should stay at St Helens. When they received the Admiralty's instructions of May 19th, they viewed them as a direct order to sail which overruled their own advice of May 15th. Much play was made of whether at their council of war on May 22nd they had discussed the question of looking into Brest or not. The joint admirals, supported by the senior Dutch Admiral Philip Almonde, stated that they had not, because this matter had been fully aired on May 15th. Only Rooke thought that they had discussed looking into Brest on May 22nd. Herbert Cran, secretary of the fleet of the States General, made a statement on October 10th confirming the joint admirals' and Almonde's view.[55]

The admirals' explanation of their not looking into Brest is still questionable, in that they had only spoken in terms of the whereabouts of the Toulon squadron on May 15th and had made no mention of the Brest fleet. The matter was further complicated in that Rochester, Trenchard and others had not passed on the conclusions of the May 15th council of war to the Cabinet Council. The admirals cannot be considered entirely blameless, as they made no direct attempt to look into Brest until after Rooke's departure. Common sense dictated that they should have done so.

If the admirals had failed to gain intelligence of the Brest fleet before the departure of Rooke, what efforts had they made? They had repeatedly sent out ships to search for the French fleet between Scilly and Ushant. The *Deptford, James galley* (Shovell's old command), *Portsmouth, Montagu, Winchester* and others had all failed to provide firm intelligence of the French.[56] In addition, there was a shortage of cruisers. When the admirals were asked why they had not sent a scout directly into Brest, they explained that, as the harbour was some way inland, only by sending a squadron could the information be obtained. This was a view held by Torrington and Russell who were considered good judges, they said. To send a squadron into Brest Water would require close support from the fleet. It was for this reason that their council of war on May 15th wanted the Smyrna ships to remain at St Helens while Rooke and his squadron came with the main fleet to provide that intelligence.[57] Their view had not been passed on or had been ignored. The admirals' argument, concerning the merits of using a squadron rather than a single ship, is disproved by the fact that between June 14th and 16th the *Warspite* was able to declare Brest Water empty. Unfortunately, by this time Rooke and his merchant ships were on their way to disaster.[58]

Before leaving the question of obtaining intelligence of the French fleet and its whereabouts, mention must be made of the evidence of one John Rutter. Rutter was the captain of a pink, who had been brought before the joint admirals by Captain William Kerr of the *Lenox* on May 11th. Rutter's pink was laden with French goods. The admirals interviewed Rutter, and according to his account he told them that he had seen nineteen ships coming out of Brest Water on May 7th. Killigrew was supposed to have threatened him with hanging if Parliament sat, and winked at Shovell to come across and listen to him. Shovell was said to be the only admiral to be interested in the fact that the French fleet was coming out of Brest. Unfortunately, Rutter had only his mate as a witness, as the rest of his crew were below decks at the time. Killigrew and the other admirals stated that Rutter's account of the Brest fleet coming out was a complete fabrication, and that the only mention of French ships he had made at the time was of a few small Bretons. Although Rutter's testimony was clearly false, he was frequently produced at the House of Commons enquiry. On November 21st the admirals were actually confronted by him.[59]

A further point of criticism, made by the admirals' accusers, was that they had not taken Rooke and the merchant ships far enough to be out of danger. The admirals replied that they had taken Rooke firstly thirty leagues W.S.W. of Ushant, in line with the findings of the council of war of May 22nd, and following a further council of war on June 4th, another twenty leagues. The main fleet was unable to accompany Rooke farther for fear of leaving England's coasts unguarded and for lack of victuals. Against this must be set the fact that it was purely chance that a council of war was held on June 4th, as the signal for Rooke to depart had already been given, when lack of a suitable wind prevented him from doing so, and thus gave the admirals an opportunity to go on another twenty leagues. As Richmond points out, in 1691 Tourville had not gone farther than fifty leagues in search of trade, i.e. more than fifty leagues was outside usual French cruising distance.[60]

On October 19th, on the question of Rooke's departure, Lord Falkland castigated the admirals for failing to notify the Admiralty of how far they intended to accompany Rooke. The admirals contended that the resolutions of their May 22nd council of war had been sent to the Admiralty. Killigrew, in particular, insisted that a clerk read aloud Falkland's papers on the subject. It was apparent to the Council that Falkland had withheld information from them. Falkland countered that the admirals had only spoken in terms of a rendezvous rather than a departure point. There was some truth in this, but afterwards the admirals lost no time in telling their friends of Falkland's deception and this may have been a factor in his eventual fall from power.[61] Others noted the vehemence of Falkland's attack on the admirals. *L'Hermitage*\* gave an account of it.[62] Falkland was also quoted as saying "Those that sit at the helm how can they serve the kingdom and King James too?" [63] More will be said about Jacobitism later.

The Admiralty, again led by the vocal Falkland, wanted to know why the admirals had not instructed Rooke in the course he was to steer, following Admiralty instructions of May 19th. The admirals replied that this order was unreasonable and impractical, as they had no prior knowledge of the wind direction or movements of the French. Their view was a logical one, but the Admiralty were not satisfied, wanting to know why, if the admirals had not thought their orders reasonable or practical,

\* French newspaper.

they had not notified the Admiralty of this fact. The admirals had no answer to this.[64]

When asked to explain their delay in getting out of St Helens in May and again from Torbay in June/July, a major reason that the joint admirals gave was lack of victuals. Both the admirals and Rooke had had difficulty in getting sufficient supplies for their respective ships in May. Rooke had written to the admirals on May 14th complaining that the main fleet was getting preferential treatment over his own ships.[65] Once Rooke had come under the admirals' direct command on May 19th, the situation was rectified. There was a disagreement between the Victualling Office and the admirals over what supplies they had actually received. On June 16th the admirals had had to come in with their ships because of a shortage of beer, cheese and butter. On June 22nd, at Torbay, the fleet had used supplies as quickly as they were brought aboard.[66] Early in July there had been trouble getting beer and what they got was bad. However, on August 17th the admirals allowed the sale of wine and brandy for health reasons! [67]

Here is a list of supplies calculated by the Victualling Office for June 6th, which were supposed to be present in the ships of the main fleet.

Beer for 48 days
Bread for 110 days at short allowance
Beef for 119 days
Pork for 121 days
Peas for 122 days
Oatmeal for 29 days
Butter for 85 days
Cheese for 83 days.[68]

The joint admirals did not agree with this assessment, as lack of victuals was a reason given by them for coming into Torbay in late June. The Victualling Office were a law unto themselves, for no one could understand their accounting system or practices. It was for this reason that the victuallers escaped censure in the House of Commons.[69]

As a final plea to the Admiralty, the joint admirals contended that, "they had answered questions not with art but with the truth and plainness of seamen". They had acted by calling councils of war in response to express orders and had followed the unanimous advice of the flag officers. In addition, the admirals pointed out that the Dutch had approved the actions of Philip Almonde and it was very hard that their self same actions were considered a crime.[70] It is difficult to disagree with the logic of their view.

The House of Commons enquiry and debates followed a speech made by William III on November 7th concerning the miscarriages of affairs at sea. "For what relates to the latter (which has brought so great a disgrace upon the Nation) I have resented it extremely; and as I will take care that those who have not done their duty shall be punished, so I am resolved to use my utmost endeavours, that our power at sea may be rightly managed for the future."[71] On November 13th a member of the Commons, Colonel Titus, said that, "the fleet should have convoyed the Turkey fleet out of danger. They fiddled and danced at Torbay and we must pay the music."

A number of motions were debated and voted on in the House of Commons.

1. On November 17th. That there has been a notorious and treacherous mismanagement in that affair (i.e. the Smyrna Convoy).
140–103 Passed.

2. On November 27th. Resolved that there was sufficient beer on board the main fleet when Rooke separated to have convoyed Rooke's squadron and the merchant ships out of danger of the Brest fleet.
188–152 Passed.
The words and the Toulon squadron. 191–165 Rejected.

3. On November 29th. That it does appear to this House that the Admirals that commanded the fleet the last summer had on May 11th last information that part of the Brest fleet was going out to sea.
170–161 Rejected.
(This was after the obviously untruthful evidence of John Rutter)

4. On December 6th. That the admirals that commanded the fleet the last Summer, by not gaining such intelligence before they left the Streights Squadron are guilty of a high breach of Trust that was put in them to the great loss and dishonour of the Nation.
185–175 Rejected.[72]

The House of Lords on January 10th 1694 had been a little kinder to the admirals. "The Lords had resolved that the Admirals who had commanded the fleet last summer had done well in the execution of the orders they received." However some Lords entered their protest.[73]

William Blathwayt, who was the Secretary of State at War, Member of Parliament for Bath from November 20th, and a great favourite of William III, aptly summed up the position of the admirals: "they had been cut down after hanging."[74]

The admirals were not the only ones to suffer in the aftermath of the Smyrna Convoy Disaster. The Earl of Nottingham, who in an age of political corruption was a man of unimpeachable integrity, was made to resign as Secretary of State on November 6th, largely because of Whig pressure. William Aiken sums up the position of Nottingham.

> This unfortunate episode might easily have been avoided. After clerical carelessness and inefficiency had done their worst, therefore it was inevitable that a scapegoat should be found. Nottingham's political enemies were quick to discover in this fact an ideal opportunity to effect his ruin. Although none of the charges against

him could be sustained, yet they were pressed so bitterly in Parliament that as a result he was forced out of office.[75]

It is ironic that the Turkey Company had indirectly led to Nottingham's downfall. The Finches had had associations with the Company for forty years.[76] The Wharton brothers, Thomas and Goodwin, with Edward Russell, were largely responsible for Nottingham's downfall. They may well have circulated the scandalous couplet in city taverns: "That the Turkey fleet was sold is true and not a sham; You may find it out by searching as far as Nottingham."[77]

Nottingham has left a record of his views on Shovell.

> Then some attempted to blame the admirals (or rather two of them, Killigrew and Delavall), and great endeavors were used to separate Sir Cloudesley Shovel from joining with them in defense of their conduct, for he was in great esteem, and very deservedly, with every faction in the fleet and with all seamen. But he could not be persuaded to do so dishonorable a proceeding but frankly owned to the committee that he had heartily concurred in every resolution which had been taken by them and declared further that, if he had had sole command of the fleet, everything which had been done he would and must have done and should have thought it his duty.[78]

Sir George Rooke came off remarkably lightly from the scandal. As regards his departure with the merchant vessels, he could justifiably claim to have been following the orders of Killigrew, Delavall and Shovell. However, the management of his squadron and convoy afterwards was casual, in that little attempt had been made to scout ahead for the French. During the various enquiries, he was severely inconvenienced by gout.[79] On one occasion Rooke had to be carried in in a chair. Gout had an unhappy knack of causing incapacity at the most inconvenient moments for seventeenth century naval officers. Sir John Harman in the West Indies in 1667, Rooke at Vigo in 1702 and possibly Shovell himself at Barfleur in 1692 had all suffered from gout at inappropriate moments.

Killigrew and Delavall were both Tories and were thought to be sympathetic towards James II.[80] Shovell was a Whig and by now not at all sympathetic towards James II. There is no firm evidence that either Killigrew or Delavall in any way aided James II and they certainly did not betray the Smyrna fleet. Abraham Anselme, who had been Torrington's secretary and had acted in the same capacity to the joint admirals, was active in support of James II. A Captain Peter Wall warned both Killigrew and Delavall of this in May 1693. Shovell was not. Anselme was confronted by Wall's letter and was eventually replaced by Phineas Bowles in July. There is no evidence that Anselme betrayed the Smyrna convoy.[81] Little evidence is available that Jacobitism was prominent in the fleet in 1693. On June 25th it was reported that Jacobites were sending circulars to members of the fleet in support of James II, particularly boatswains. This did not amount to much, as the boatswains in the main handed the documents to their captains.[82]

William III treated Killigrew and Delavall harshly. On November 11th Trenchard informed the two admirals that they should no longer come to the Admiralty Board, nor act as Commissioners of the Admiralty, until further orders from the King.[83] By December 12th the King, in order to show his resentment and dissatisfaction at the conduct of the three commanding admirals the previous summer, declared them discharged from all military and civil employment. Killigrew lost his Marine Regiment to Lord Berkeley of Stratton on December 1st, and Delavall was to lose his Company of Foot Guards. Shovell had not been removed from the Navy Board and it was said that he would be employed again at sea. The clear inference is that Killigrew and Delavall were being separated from Shovell in the magnitude of their punishment.[84]

Neither Killigrew nor Delavall was to have command at sea again. Their naval careers were over. Shovell's was not, although it had suffered a temporary setback. He made no attempt to distance himself from Killigrew and Delavall. According to Campbell, at the bar of the House of Commons he defended his colleagues as well as himself, "giving so clear and plain account of the matter, that it satisfied all people who were capable of being satisfied of the innocence of the commanders, I mean in a point of treachery".[85] Shovell would not have accepted a piece of contemporary Dutch wit, of a picture where the taking of the Smyrna fleet was represented at a distance with Shovell on board his own ship, with his hands tied behind him, one end of the cord being held by each of his colleagues. This was to insinuate that he would have prevented this misfortune if Killigrew and Delavall had not hindered him.[86]

In November Killigrew, Delavall and Shovell had been refused permission to come and kiss the King's hand.[87] On March 8th 1694 Edward Russell took Shovell to meet the King and kiss his hand. "Tis said he will be employed at sea this Summer." He had been forgiven.[88]

NOTES

1. Secret Memoirs.
2. Laird Clowes, pp.357–359.
3. D.N.B. Rooke; House of Lords MSS 1693–95, N.S., Vol.I, pp.104–106, 193.
4. House of Lords MSS 1693–95, N.S., Vol.I, p.107.
5. Richmond, pp.238–245.
6. Luttrell, Vol.III, p.18; Horwitz, Parliament, etc., p.109; Horwitz, Revolution Politics, p.139; Bodleian Carte MSS 79, f.473; Grey, Debates, X, p.293.
7. Luttrell, Vol.III, p.17.

8. Aiken, p.131.
9. Horwitz, Parliament etc. p.109.
10. Aiken, pp.67–68; Pepys, Tangier Papers p.46.
11. Aiken, p.90.
12. Aiken, pp.90–91.
13. Laird Clowes, pp.357–359.
14. Torrington, p.65.
15. House of Lords MSS 1693–95, N.S., Vol.I, p.178.
16. House of Lords MSS 1693–95, N.S., Vol.I, p.128.
17. ADD MSS 35855 f.1.
18. Luttrell, Vol.III, p.71.
19. House of Lords MSS 1693–95, N.S., Vol.I, p.167.
20. House of Lords MSS 1693–95, N.S., Vol.I, p.128.
21. ADD MSS 35855 f.3.
22. C.S.P.Dom., Vol.4, 1693 pp.111–112.
23. House of Lords MSS 1693–95, N.S., Vol.I, p.230.
24. Luttrell, May 13th 1693.
25. House of Lords MSS 1693–95, N.S., Vol.I, p.231; ADD MSS 35898 f.2.
26. House of Lords MSS 1693–95, N.S., Vol.I, p.231; ADD MSS 35898 f.3.
27. House of Lords MSS 1693–95, N.S., Vol.I, p.232; ADD MSS 35898 ff.4,5.
28. House of Lords MSS 1693–95, N.S., Vol.I, pp.215–216.
29. House of Lords MSS 1693–95, N.S., Vol.I, p.233.
30. Egerton, MSS 2618 f.178. Letter June 29th.
31. House of Lords MSS 1693–95, N.S., Vol.I, p.216.
32. Richmond, pp.238–245.
33. D.N.B. Rooke.
34. Richmond, pp.238–245.
35. Leake, pp.60–61.
36. ADD MSS, 35855 f.23.
37. House of Lords MSS 1693–95, N.S., Vol.I, p.237.
38. House of Lords MSS 1693–95, N.S., Vol.I, p.130.
39. House of Lords MSS 1693–95, N.S., Vol.I, p.242.
40. House of Lords MSS 1693–95, N.S., Vol.I, pp.130–131, 212–213.
41. House of Lords MSS 1693–95, N.S., Vol.I, p.170.
42. ADD MSS 35855 f.11.
43. House of Lords MSS 1693–95, N.S., Vol.I, p.212.
44. ADD MSS 35855 ff.12–16.
45. House of Lords MSS 1693–95, N.S., Vol.I, p.212.
46. House of Lords MSS 1693–95, N.S., Vol.I, p.177.
47. House of Lords MSS 1693–95, N.S., Vol.I, pp.133–135.
48. House of Lords MSS 1693–95, N.S., Vol.I, p.136.
49. House of Lords MSS 1693–95, N.S., Vol.I, pp.179–180.
50. House of Lords MSS 1693–95, N.S., Vol.I, pp.174–177, 240–242, 251–255; Horwitz, Parliament etc. p.118.
51. Grey, pp.311–375.
52. Ehrmann, p.505.
53. Aiken, p.117; Nottingham's notes on MSS Hist. f.12 line 45 – f.14 line 39.
54. House of Lords MSS 1693–95, N.S., Vol.I, p.101.
55. ADD MSS 35898 f.31.
56. ADD MSS 35898 f.10.
57. ADD MSS 35898 f.10.
58. House of Lords MSS 1693–95, N.S., Vol.I, p.241.

59. House of Lords MSS 1693–95, N.S., Vol.I, pp.98–99; Grey, pp.311–375. Nov 21st and 29th.
60. Richmond, pp.238–245.
61. ADD MSS 9764 ff.78–80.
62. ADD MSS 17677 ff.377 & 378.
63. Grey, pp.311–375, Nov. 20th.
64. House of Lords MSS 1693–95, N.S., Vol.I, p.174.
65. House of Lords MSS 1693–95, N.S., Vol.I, p.255.
66. House of Lords MSS 1693–95, N.S., Vol.I, p.158.
67. House of Lords MSS 1693–95, N.S., Vol.I, pp.156, 164, 165.
68. House of Lords MSS 1693–95, N.S., Vol.I, pp.270–271.
69. Ehrmann, p.506.
70. ADD MSS 35898 f.39.
71. Grey, pp.311–375.
72. Grey, pp.311–375; Horwitz, Parliament etc. p.125.
73. Grey, p.375.
74. Jacobsen, William Blathwaite p.290.
75. Aiken, pp.5, 20, 24.
76. Aiken, p.55.
77. Aiken, p.106.
78. Aiken, p.120–121.
79. House of Lords MSS 1693–95, N.S., Vol.I, p.243.
80. Campbell; Buccleuch MSS, Vol.II, Part I, p.396.
81. House of Lords MSS 1693–95, N.S., Vol.I, p.294.
82. House of Lords MSS 1693–95, N.S., Vol.I, p.187.
83. C.S.P. Dom. 1693 p.395.
84. C.S.P. Dom. 1693 pp.426–427; Edye.
85. Campbell, p.245.
86. The Complete History of Europe for 1707 p.507.
87. ADD MSS 35855 f.28.
88. Luttrell, Vol.III, p.280.

CHAPTER XV

# Camaret Bay

# 1694

The early years of the war at sea against France had not gone well. Defeats at Bantry Bay and Beachy Head had been followed by success at Barfleur. However, the French losses at Barfleur/La Hougue were no greater than the Anglo/Dutch losses at Beachy Head. Then came the Smyrna Convoy Disaster. In the final years of the war the French commissioned fewer ships, and there were to be no further fleet actions. They concentrated on supporting their army in Catalonia and harrying English and Dutch trade with their formidable force of privateers. During 1693 the French fleet was divided between Toulon and Brest. In 1694 the English and Dutch navies endeavoured to counteract the French both in the Channel and Mediterranean. In addition, the final years of the war saw the bombardment of French sea ports from Dunkirk to Brest.[1]

In the last chapter, Shovell's involvement with the Smyrna convoy debacle and his temporary fall from grace has been described. Possibly, this setback to his career at sea saved his life. In the winter of 1693/94 a squadron under the command of Sir Francis Wheeler was sent to escort trade to the Mediterranean. The unfortunate Wheeler was drowned on the night of February 18th/19th 1694 when his ship, the *Sussex*, and the vast majority of its crew, were lost in a storm while attempting to enter the Mediterranean. Initially, Shovell had been chosen to command the squadron before being replaced by Wheeler in the aftermath of the Smyrna convoy investigation.[2]

In mid March 1694 there were reports that Shovell was to join Wheeler in the Mediterranean with between twenty-five and thirty-six English and Dutch ships. William III appeared to have forgiven him earlier that month and decided to re-employ him at sea. At this time, news of Wheeler's death had not reached England. In the event Shovell did not go to the Mediterranean and neither did the squadron.[3]

On April 12th Luttrell recorded that Shovell had lately fought a duel with the Commander of the *Hampton Court* and was slightly wounded. There is no confirmatory evidence that the duel took place nor, if it did, the reason for it. The Captain of the *Hampton Court* at the time was John Graydon, and his journal for late March and early April shows that his ship was at the Nore. Graydon had fought at Bantry Bay with Shovell and in 1702 the two men were to work together again in bringing the treasure home from Vigo. In 1703 Graydon's career at sea came to an abrupt end following his alleged mismanagement of a convoy to Newfoundland. Possibly the cause of the duel related in some way to the controversy over the Smyrna convoy. The *Hampton Court* had been with the fleet in 1693. But this is pure conjecture.[4]

In the autumn of 1693, on his return from Flanders, one of the first steps William III took on hearing of the Smyrna Convoy Disaster was to appoint Edward Russell, Admiral and Commander-in-Chief, for the following spring's campaign. On April 16th 1694 Shovell was appointed Vice Admiral of the Red in Russell's fleet. Technically this was promotion as he had been Rear Admiral of the Red between January 20th 1692 and January 23rd 1693. For most of 1693 he had held the position of joint Commander-in-Chief of the fleet with Killigrew and Delavall, without a definitive rank. No doubt Russell, who had been impressed by Shovell's courage and leadership at Barfleur in 1692, was instrumental in his rapid rehabilitation. On the same day that he received his commission as Vice Admiral of the Red, Shovell was given command of the *Neptune*, in which he was to serve in 1694. The *Neptune* was a 90 gun 2nd rate, which had been built at Deptford in 1683.[5]

Early in 1694 plans had been drawn up to make an attempt on Brest and to send a strong fleet into the Mediterranean, to succour the King of Spain and to prevent the French ships at Toulon from joining those at Brest. Efforts were made to prepare the English fleet so that it would be ready for sea early in the season and before the French.[6]

At the beginning of May Russell took most of the Anglo/Dutch fleet to sea, leaving Shovell with a strong squadron at Portsmouth to embark troops for the attempt on Brest. On May 11th 1694 Queen Mary signed the official orders for Shovell to take the soldiers on board. "To receive on board our men of war at Spithead our trusty and well beloved Lieutenant General Talmash and as many of the forces under his command as the ships can receive without putting them to great inconvenience." When the troops were embarked, Shovell was to sail and join the main fleet under Russell.[7]

Lieutenant General Thomas Talmash or Tollemache, who was to command the troops in the assault on Brest, was a rough, dissolute and hot headed soldier. Lord Dartmouth described him as "lewd", but he was brave and popular with his men. No doubt Shovell knew him well, as they had both been in Tangier in 1680 and in the Irish campaign of 1690–91.[8]

While Russell and the main fleet were cruising off the Lizard, he received intelligence from an agent disguised as a sailor on a Swedish ship that a French merchant convoy was ready to sail from Camaret or Bertheaume Bay. A small number of ships were detached to destroy the convoy, which they did successfully. On May 17th Russell was informed that most of the French fleet had sailed from Brest for Toulon, and he put into Torbay briefly before joining Shovell at St Helens on the 22nd.[9] Confirmation that the French had left Brest was received by Russell in a letter from the Earl of Shrewsbury on May 23rd, quoting William III's instructions to speed up Russell's departure.[10] Russell himself was not happy about the proposed attack on Brest, and on May 26th he wrote to the Second Secretary of State, Sir John Trenchard, pointing out that the delays would have allowed the enemy time to have made defensive preparations. He felt that Talmash should not be too tied to his orders and that they should be allowed to attack Port Louis instead, if their prospects there were thought to be better. In any event, something should be attempted.[11]

At St Helens, Russell found that Shovell had successfully embarked the troops, some 6,000 in number. On May 29th the whole fleet sailed. In a final letter to Trenchard on the 29th, Russell restated his reservations about the proposed action.

> I apprehend by the delay the alarm in France will occasion a great resistance at Brest, but I hope it may have no other effect than their

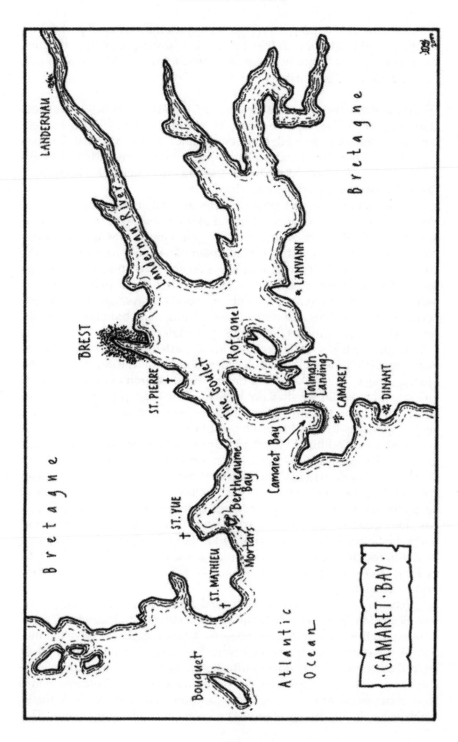

· CAMARET · BAY ·

not being able to perform service so considerably as in all probability they might have done if they had gone in any degree within the time proposed, but 'tis now five weeks later. I am sure Mr Talmash will perform what is possible to be done.[12]

Two days after sailing from St Helens, on May 31st, a council of war was held in Russell's flagship, the *Britannia*. Those present included Russell, Lord John Berkeley, Shovell, Matthew Aylmer, David Mitchell, Thomas Talmash and the Commander of the Dutch contingent, Admiral Philip Almonde. It was resolved to detach the squadron under Berkeley with Talmash's troops immediately for Brest.[13]

Shovell, who had been responsible for the embarkation of Talmash's troops at St Helens, was to go as second in command to John, third Baron Berkeley of Stratton. Berkeley, from a noble family, was thirteen years younger than Shovell and had served under him in 1693 as Admiral of the Blue, after the death of Sir John Ashby. Berkeley was still Admiral of the Blue to Shovell's lesser position of Vice Admiral of the Red, and it was quite proper for him to have overall command of the squadron for Brest. Berkeley was a jealous and domineering young man, but Shovell loyally served under him until his death three years later.[14]

Berkeley, with his contingent for Brest, parted from Russell and the main fleet on June 5th. Russell sailed south for the Straits and the Mediterranean. His final words on the Brest operation show his misgivings. "I am afraid we shall not have much to brag of for the year is so far advanced and the enemy prepared for both our designs. I am not a very desponding man but I am a little out of hope." [15]

Russell's foreboding of French preparations at Brest proved to be well founded. During early 1694 information concerning the English design on Brest had got back to Louis XIV in Paris. When ex-King James II, who also knew of the plan, went to Louis to pass on this choice piece of intelligence, he got the reply: "Sure you are ill served by your friends in England, for I have long ago had account of it, as the English will find by their reception when they come here."[16] Tradition had it that John Churchill, later Duke of Marlborough, had leaked information to the French and particularly to ex-King James II. This has been refuted convincingly by his biographer, Winston Churchill.[17]

In February, when news of the intended attack reached Paris, Louis XIV sent Sébastian le Prestre de Vauban, the celebrated designer of fortifications, to Brest to improve its defences. Vauban had over three months in which to carry out his work before Berkeley, Shovell and Talmash arrived on the scene. The town of Brest was surrounded by strong walls and good ramparts; deep ditches were cut in the rock and bastions made. New batteries of cannons were set up and the vaults of the castle made bomb proof. In all, there were ninety mortars and 300 large cannon. The ships remaining at Brest were placed out of reach of even bombs. In respect of men, there were 4,000 foot soldiers, 3,000 gentleman volunteers, 1,400 bombardiers and a regiment of dragoons. Thanks to Vauban the chances of Talmash being able to take Brest were remote.[18]

On June 6th, the day after the departure of the main fleet under Russell, a council of war was held at which it was agreed that Lieutenant General Talmash and Lord Cutts should go ashore in person. The next day, the squadron anchored between Camaret Bay and Bertheaume Bay. They were now within range of the French batteries which began playing bombs on them. At a further council of war on the 8th, Talmash was advised not to expose his men in an attempt on Brest, as the enemy was so well prepared to resist them. Bravely but unrealistically, he replied:

> This advice comes too late: the honour of the English nation is at stake, and therefore I must and will land. I know that I sacrifice myself and the men; but it is necessary, and must be done, that both our enemies and allies may know, that even desperate undertakings cannot daunt English courage.[19]

The die was cast and on that day, the assault began.

Shovell had taken part in the various councils of war as the second most senior naval officer present at the action. He has almost certainly left a personal record of his affairs, which is to be found amongst the Portland manuscripts. The document is titled "Engagement in Camarett Bay" and is dated 1694 June *Neptune*. The *Neptune* was the ship in which Shovell was serving as Vice Admiral of the Red. It seems inconceivable that it could have been written by anyone other than Shovell himself, as he was the senior officer aboard, although it is not signed. In 1912 Laughton published this account, stating that there was no clue to the writer or addressee of the letter.[20]

> Engagement in Camarett Bay. After our departure from St. Helens which was on the 29th past, we met with little winds, veerable to the northward and to the southward of the west, and often-times calm. We used all immaginable diligence to get out of the Channel, which we did not accomplish till the 6th instant, at which time the wind being northerly Admiral Russell kept on to the south westward with 32 English and 15 Dutch ships of the line of battle, and of both nations there were 11 fireships and six frigates, a list of which I enclose, compared with the French in and gone to the Mediterranean.
>
> My Lord Berkeley was left here with 18 English and 11 Dutch ships of the line of battle, and of both nations there were twelve fireships, six frigates, and five bomb vessels, and we had on board the fleet about 6,000 land soldiers. We directed our course to Ushant, in order

to go to Brest, and on the 7th inst we anchored in the evening with our fleet from St Matthews Point towards the narrow going into Brest Sound, keeping out of shot of the shore, but were entertained with bombs from the land on Camarett side, also from both sides going into Brest Sound, and along the north shore almost as far as St. Matthew's Point, and although we were out of gun shot, yet to my wonder the bombs reached where we rid, which I am confident was two miles and a half, rather more than less: I am also convinced by reasonable argument (contrary to my former opinion) that if one of the great shells fall into one of our ships and burst, it will quite disable if not destroy her. Here we rid all night taking care with our boats and brigantines that the enemy made no insult on our storeships and small vessels.

The 8th instant in the morning, the weather was foggy; but about 7 in the forenoon it cleared up, and the signal being made, we embarked all our land forces in our boats and tendors in order to land them in Camarett Bay; but discovering there were forts and batteries of guns and lines and trenches all near where we intended to land, we sent seven frigates (three were English and four were Dutch) to batter the aforesaid fortifications, the better to facilitate the landing of the soldiers. The ships that went on this service were commanded by my Lord Carmarthen, who placed them with a great deal of skill, and performed his duty with much bravery and hazard.

Between 3 and 4 this afternoon four or five hundred of our soldiers landed (most of them grenadiers), and Lieutenant General Talmash landed with them; but they were so warmly received by the enemy that Talmash was shot through the thigh, and with difficulty was brought off; and the rest not being able to advance by reason of entrenchments and fortifications and number of horse and foot upon the shore, in so much that most of our men that landed were either killed or taken prisoner, the rest of our soldiers were returned on board, we having lost five of our well boats which were grounded and left on shore, which the enemy burnt upon the retreat of the soldiers. My Lord Carmarthen came off with the ships, all but one of the Dutch frigates of 32 guns. I am pretty well satisfied the French knew of our coming, and may easily be persuaded they knew where we intended to land, they being more particularly fortified at that place, though at other places they had industriously provided to oppose our landing. I suppose about 300 English and Dutch seamen suffered in this skirmish, that is, were killed, wounded or taken prisoners, for several men suffered in our well boats, and other boats, and few men escaped from the Dutchman that was sunk.

This evening at a council of war it was considered whether we could attempt any other place with the land forces; but General

Talmash declared he had not power to carry the forces anywhere else. It was also considered if the fleet could not go into Brest Sound, and bomb the town. It was thought too great a hazard to go in with the fleet, unless we could be certain we could ride without reach of their bombs; for 'tis most of our opinions that if a shell break in any ship it will disable if not destroy her. Then 'twas considered if the frigates and bomb vessels might go in and bomb the town: that was also thought unreasonable and impracticable, first, because our number of frigates are few and those much disabled by this day's action; secondly, we knew not the enemy's strength, which might probably be sufficient to take both frigates and bombs; and thirdly, our number of bomb vessels, being but five, is very insufficient to perform so great an undertaking. In all this you see we make no difficulty of passing their castles, there being no other danger than the hazard of their shot and bombs, which they can ply at you all the way through the narrow land, the rock in the middle of the narrow: therefore 'twas concluded we should return to Spithead and there expect further orders. So that on the 9th, in the morning, we weighed and stood to sea. About noon I saw four galley; they came down the Channel and went into Brest. This evening the Dreadnought sailed for England with General Talmash. 10th – To day, about 11 leagues to the northward of Brest, the Elizabeth came to us with eight bomb vessel. 11th – To day a Dutch Rear Admiral with four great ships from Holland joined us.
    Endorsed Mr Dumner

The object of the assault on Camaret Bay appears to have been a preliminary move, prior to taking the Quelern peninsula, which forms the south shore of the Goulet. Once this was in English hands, it would be safer for vessels to pass through the Goulet into Brest Roads, so that the town and French shipping could be attacked. Of course, none of this came to fruition.[21]
    Rear Admiral Lord Carmarthen, a temporary flag appointment who made a reconnaissance of Camaret Bay on June 7th and led the covering force of ships on the 8th, was fortunate to escape. His ship, the *Monck* was severely damaged by a bomb and had to be towed out of the Bay. Carmarthen was of the opinion that even if the English force had been double its number they would have found the attempt impracticable.[22]
    General Talmash had behaved with his customary great courage and had led the assault in person. The flat-bottomed well boats laden with troops came ashore under heavy battery fire. The landing at the south end of the Bay was chaotic, as the first boats to discharge their troops grounded and blocked the way for the next wave. Talmash ordered his troops to land as quickly as possible and is said to have offered a guinea a head for volunteers, as some were not eager to land. An attempt was made

against the entrenchments, but Talmash rapidly realised that the situation was hopeless and ordered a retreat to the boats. Many of the boats were unable to get off as the tide had gone out, leaving the troops in them to be captured. At this stage Talmash was wounded in the thigh and, as Shovell recorded in his account, was taken off with difficulty.[23]

The attempted landing by the Anglo/Dutch force at Camaret Bay had been a fiasco, and Berkeley, Shovell and their damaged ships returned to their own coast, reaching St Helens on June 15th. The unfortunate Talmash was landed at Plymouth on June 11th, and at first was thought to be doing well. However, his wounded thigh had become infected and he died the next day, almost certainly of septicaemia.[24]

The assault on Camaret Bay has rightly gone down in history as a disaster. What had gone wrong? The proposal to destroy the French fleet in Brest, using Camaret Bay as a stepping stone, was a sound one. However, in late 1693 and early 1694 details of the plan had reached the French King's ears, allowing him plenty of time to improve the defences there and to bring in additional troops. Clearly there was poor security, but this was not surprising considering the confused loyalties of many Englishmen with ex-King James domiciled in France. Many members of the English Parliament and in the military thought it sensible to stay in touch with their ex-King, in case he should regain his throne.

The putting together of ships to take the troops into Camaret Bay was delayed and they did not sail from St Helens until late in May, by which time the bulk of the French fleet had left Brest. Every late spring and early summer there was difficulty in manning, refitting and revictualling the fleet, due to lack of resources and poor organisation. The French were usually ready for the summer's campaign before the English – 1694 was no exception.

Once it was clear that the French defences were fully prepared, Talmash should have abandoned the attack on Camaret Bay and looked for a less heavily defended part of the coast to attack as his orders allowed. His obstinacy, in the face of the obvious, was the prime cause of the failure at Camaret Bay. Talmash and many of his troops as well as Berkeley's and Shovell's sailors, to a lesser extent, paid for his foolhardiness with their lives.

What of the principal naval officers in this disaster? Russell, Berkeley, Shovell and Carmarthen had all been present at the council of war on May 31st when the decision to go to Camaret Bay and land Talmash's troops, as they had been instructed to, was confirmed. All bar Russell, who had by then departed for the Mediterranean, were present at the council of war on June 6th when the final details were worked out, and on June 8th when Talmash was advised not to land.[25] Some reports state that no pressure was brought to bear on Talmash until after the operation started to go badly.[26] In any event, if the main responsibility must lie with the land forces commander, Talmash, then the principal sea commanders must bear a measure of it. Either they did not oppose Talmash firmly enough in the first instance or early enough, depending on which report is correct.

The decision not to send frigates and bomb vessels into Brest Roads to bombard the town was sensible, in that in addition to having only five bomb vessels, the wind that took them in would preclude their coming out. The senior naval officers must also accept responsibility for launching the assault on an ebb tide, so that many of the boats could not be got off.

At Camaret Bay, Shovell had played a subordinate role as second in command to Berkeley. His embarkation of the troops at Portsmouth had been efficient, but he did not play a direct part in the landings. Shovell did not enhance his reputation in this action, but no one among the senior naval officers did, with the possible exception of Carmarthen.

On their return to St Helens, on June 15th, Berkeley and Shovell found instructions from Queen Mary to call a council of war to decide what was best done with the troops and ships after their misfortune at Camaret Bay. Initially, it was intended to make an attempt on the coast of Normandy and this view was transmitted to the court. An answer was received on June 27th and, following a further council of war, a decision was made to attack the port of Dieppe and then proceed along the French coast. The English plan was to do as much damage as possible to the coastal towns of France and to generally alarm its inhabitants.[27]

On the expedition to Dieppe and along the coast of Normandy, Shovell was again to be second in command, under Berkeley. At Camaret Bay, Shovell had been in the *Neptune* with Thomas Jennings as Commander. According to the pay book of the *Neptune,* Shovell was discharged to the *Cambridge* on June 15th, the day of the expedition's return to St Helens. This cannot be correct. The *Cambridge*, a 70 gun ship, had been lost with Francis Wheeler earlier in the year in February, attempting to get into the Mediterranean. Her replacement, also called the *Cambridge*, was not completed until 1695. Shovell was to serve on her during part of 1695. For the campaign season of 1694 it is likely that Shovell remained in the *Neptune*.[28]

In late June/early July, the Berkeley/Shovell squadron sailed and met in the Channel a fleet of Swedish and Danish ships carrying corn and contraband goods to Havre de Grace, now Le Havre. Although they were under Swedish convoy and had passes, Berkeley took them into harbour. English and Swedish interpretation of contraband goods differed. This action was to cause a potential problem later in the summer as will be seen.[29]

Two attempts were made to take the squadron to Dieppe Road, but on each occasion Berkeley and Shovell were driven away by inclement weather. It was not until July 12th that the bombardment of Dieppe began at nine in the morning and continued unabated for twelve hours, with about 1,100 bombs thrown. The bomb ketches discharged a mixture of granado shells and carcasses. The granado shells were explosive in nature and the carcasses incendiary shells. A carcass was an iron cylinder pierced with holes and filled with combustibles to set buildings on fire. A particular variety of bomb or sea mortar had been designed by Richard Leake, the father of Sir John Leake, and was known as the cushee piece. The town of Dieppe burnt during the whole of the following day.[30]

At about 11.00 a.m. on July 12th Berkeley sent in a machine vessel with the intention of destroying the pier. The machine vessel or infernal was effectively a ship crammed with explosive which was ignited close to its target. They had possibly been developed from fireships, which themselves had originated at the siege of Tyre in 332 B.C. The first machine vessel had been used at the much later date of 1585 by Gianibelli, in the destruction of a bridge over the Schelde. In the early 1690s the Dutch artillery officer, William Meesters, had updated them, and with John Benbow had used them against St Malo for the first time in the autumn of 1693. In the *Secret Memoirs of Cloudesley Shovell* it is stated that he was present at this bombardment. There is no confirmatory evidence of this, and at the time he was very much preoccupied with the enquiry into the Smyrna Convoy Disaster, which makes his presence unlikely. Meesters will feature again in this account.[31]

In the hold of a machine vessel or infernal were placed 100 barrels of gunpowder covered with pitch, sulphur, rosin, tow, straw and faggots. Above beams were laid with holes bored through to vent the fire. On top were 300 carcasses filled with grenades, chain shot, iron bullets, loaded pistols and broken glass. When ignited the machine vessel blew up. Although an enormous explosion ensued, it was mainly downwards into the sea bed, so that the damage done was not nearly so great as might have been expected from the noise. During 1694–95 thirty machine vessels were in service, but the last one was paid off in 1695 because of its lack of effectiveness.[32]

The attempt on the morning of July 12th to burn the pier at Dieppe was unsuccessful. The French had sunk several ships filled with stones in front of it and when the machine vessel, the *Nicholas*, exploded it was not close enough to cause significant damage. No doubt the noise terrified and deafened the citizens of Dieppe who had not already fled. With great courage, the captain of the *Nicholas*, Robert Dunbar, returned to the ship to reignite the fuse after it had gone out.[33]

By July 14th nearly the whole of Dieppe was in ashes. The houses were old, made of timber and crammed together in narrow streets. Once ignited the fires spread rapidly. The French court in Paris did all it could to suppress reports of the destruction. However it was not successful and, if militia had not been sent to restrain the inhabitants, the coastal towns would have been deserted.[34]

English casualties at Dieppe had been light, with only four or five men killed or wounded by the 1,500 shot and shells fired by the French. Many of the inhabitants of Dieppe had been able to escape the bombing, but returned to find their houses in ashes. It is difficult to justify the wholesale destruction of a town in this way, but English opinion of the time was that the French had been the first to use this barbaric form of warfare at Genoa.[35]

After their destruction of Dieppe, Berkeley and Shovell took their squadron along the coast to Havre de Grace. The French, fearing a landing, moved their forces around the coast to cover this eventuality. Berkeley had no intention of doing this, and on July 15th arrived before Havre de Grace. Shortly afterwards a bombardment was begun and continued on the 16th, 17th and 18th. The French moved troops into the town to help the inhabitants fight the fires started by the rain of bombs. Berkeley had soundings made of the harbour and engineers inspected the fortifications of Havre. During the bombardment, the *Granado* bomb vessel was blown to pieces by a shell that fell into her from one of the shore batteries. The English squadron was hindered by a constant wind from the shore until the 21st, when a further bombardment was unleashed. By this time the French in the area were greatly alarmed, with a third of their homes burnt down and a great part of the town wall destroyed. John Benbow who commanded the bomb vessels and machines was beginning to make a reputation for himself in this form of warfare.[36]

Less damage was done at Havre de Grace than at Dieppe, but a medal was struck in England in honour of the former action. On one side, the medal had the King's head in profile with the words *Gulielmus magnus invictissimus* [William the great and invincible]. The reverse had Perillus' bull with the inscription *Suis perit ignibus auctor* [He first perished with his flames], alluding to the fact that the French King had begun this barbarous form of warfare, by burning the Palatinate and bombarding Genoa. Medals of this type were to become the fashion and another one was to be struck the following year.[37]

From Havre de Grace, Berkeley and Shovell drew the French forces to La Hougue and Cherbourg, but were in no fit state to undertake anything further and returned to St Helens on July 26th, in order to refit. On the following day Berkeley left for London, leaving Shovell with the task of getting the squadron ready to sail to the Downs.[38]

The Privy Council sent instructions to Shovell on August 1st to take the regiment of Cutts, Rada and Collier on board empty horse ships, hospital ships and victualling ships. If they were unable to accommodate them all, the remainder were to be put on board the men of war.[39] Discussions concerning the next part of the French coast to be attacked must have taken place during the first week of August, as the Privy Council minutes for August 6th show that Dunkirk had been selected for bombardment, and that Shovell had asked for either Captain Benbow or Captain Warren to be sent to him for the enterprise.[40] Whether Shovell was making arrangements of this sort because Berkeley was away in London, or whether even at this early stage he had been chosen to command the squadron in Berkeley's place, is uncertain.

Shovell had collected the revictualled squadron together and sailed to the Downs, arriving on August 13th. Immediately he was involved in controversy. Shovell communicated with a Danish man of war, convoy to a number of prizes brought in, and ordered him to strike his flag. The Dane refused to do so, stating that he had orders not to. Shovell was affronted by this behaviour and ordered the *Stirling Castle* of 70 guns to lie by him, thinking that the captain was drunk. The next morning the Danish commander still declined to strike his flag and the *Stirling Castle* fired a broadside into him that was answered. A sharp engagement took place between the two ships, in which the Danish flag was taken down and then put up again. Fighting continued until the Dane was boarded and taken. Forty Danes were killed, including the captain, and the *Stirling Castle* lost eight men in reply. A Cabinet Council was held, in which it was agreed that the ships and their officers be secured and satisfaction demanded of King Christian V of Denmark for the affront. There was a view that this had been done intentionally by Denmark to cause a breach. The Danish agent retorted in a haughty and, from the English viewpoint, un-reasonable manner, blaming Shovell's men of war. The Earl of Shrewsbury in a letter to the Secretary at War, Blathwayt, felt that the Danish agent deserved worse usage than the frigate received! A year later the matter grumbled on with the Danes maintaining that not long before some of their ships had passed through Russell's fleet and saluted them with guns, but were not required to take in their pennants. Perhaps Shovell's hard line on the matter was due to the particular consideration the officers of the English fleet had to the Royal Chamber of the Downs, where the original incident had occurred. Shovell himself had called the Downs a sacred place. Saluting was taken very seriously in the seventeenth century.[41]

Early in August Dunkirk had been selected by Queen Mary and her Council as the next French coastal town to be attacked. Besides the town, Jean Bart had a squadron of eight men of war and there were also forty to fifty privateers based there. Thomas Hopsonn, with a squadron of sixteen sail, was stationed off the port to cover Bart. However, while Bart was securely tucked up in a safe harbour, Hopsonn was at the mercy of the sea and the changeable weather. Bart could afford to bide his time before slipping out past the protective English screen and attacking English merchant ships. It was imperative that Bart be destroyed or made to stay in harbour, because a large fleet with naval stores, such as pitch and hemp, was shortly expected at Elsinore. If Bart succeeded in taking this fleet,

English naval operations in 1695 would at the very least be severely curtailed. The matter was further complicated in that Denmark might hold up the supply fleet, in retaliation for their own and Swedish merchant ships being taken by Shovell near Dieppe, in late June/early July. It was for these reasons that an attack on Dunkirk was necessary.[42]

The court was keen for an attempt to be made on Dunkirk. The sea officers, and in particular Berkeley and Shovell, were not. Having sought the opinion of pilots and engineers, they felt that the season was too far advanced for anything to be undertaken that year. The English and Dutch pilots did not have any experience of Dunkirk and its approaches and would not be held responsible for taking ships there. William Meesters, the Dutch artillery officer, whose machine vessels had been used against Dieppe earlier in the summer, had gone to Ostend and Neuport to find Flemish pilots with experience of Dunkirk Harbour and its Flemish Roads. On August 27th Berkeley gave up command of the squadron, leaving Shovell in his place. He returned to London. At the same time, the 1st and 2nd rate ships were taken up the Thames for the winter. Shovell was left with the 3rd and 4th rates, with instructions to try something against Dunkirk at all events.[43]

Although loyally prepared to lead an attack on Dunkirk, Shovell was unhappy about the whole business. In a letter to the Secretary at War, Blathwayt, on September 11th, Shrewsbury quoted Shovell as "having no great opinion of the design, desired a positive order, and the Admiralty sent the enclosed . . .".[44] In another letter to Blathwayt in person, written during September 1694, Shovell again showed his reservations, particularly about the use of machine vessels, "which some people think absurd".[45]

Despite the fact that Berkeley did not leave his command until August 27th, Shovell had been sent formal orders on the 24th to take Berkeley's and Hopsonn's ships to attack the ships, pier, harbour and town of Dunkirk. The destruction was to take place with machines, bomb vessels and fireships. Meesters' pilots from Ostend and Neuport were to be used and the squadron was to return to the Downs afterwards.[46] In the event, only two bomb ketches and no fireships were taken along. Late August and early September were spent in the Downs getting the squadron ready for sea and waiting for Meesters and his pilots. Thomas Hopsonn had been recalled to the Downs in late August, because he had complained of the condition of his ships and the danger they were in. Hopsonn left a clean ship to watch Bart who was in Dunkirk and returned to the Downs. On August 30th Shovell himself was ordered to send a further ship to Dunkirk to observe Bart.[47]

Stormy weather prevented Shovell from getting away from the Downs, and on September 7th Meesters joined him with twenty-six Flemish pilots. Eventually they sailed and appeared before Dunkirk on September 12th.

The squadron consisted of thirteen English and six Dutch men of war, two bomb vessels, seventeen machines and other small craft. In the evening John Benbow, who was in command of the small ships, went in to sound the western channel. He received a prodigious fire from the ships and the citadel. Meesters' pilots proved to be ignorant, cowardly and insubordinate.[48]

The next day Shovell sent in the small vessels, two bomb ketches and the *Charles galley*. In the afternoon two machine vessels, the *William and Mary* and *Abram's Offering* followed them to attack the piers. Shovell had encouraged the seamen of the machines by saying that he would distribute £500 among the crew of any vessel doing an exploit before Dunkirk. He was not to lose his money! One of the machines was hit by French fire or fired by her own crew when they realised that they were unable to approach the pier. She was allowed to burn and exploded innocuously. The other machine vessel went in boldly and nearly reached the mole head, but at the last moment was drawn away by the tide and set on her side. She blew up without doing damage. In any case, the French had early intelligence of the operation and had sunk ships and driven in piles to protect the piers. It is unlikely that these defences would have been breached even if the tide had not taken the second machine vessel off course.[49]

When Shovell was told that the two machine vessels had been expended without damage to the French, he called the attack off and sailed away to Calais. Jean Bart, his small squadron, the piers and the town of Dunkirk were all untouched. The fears of both Berkeley and Shovell had proved to be well founded. The Earl of Shrewsbury reported to Secretary Blathwayt on September 14th.

> An express is just now come from Cloudesley Shovell and gives an account that between the insufficiency of the pilots and machine vessels, and the preparations they had made at Dunkirk to receive them, nothing had been done in that attempt but blowing up two machines to no purpose. He has sent for the bomb ships and intends to proceed to destroy Calais.[50]

Shovell reached Calais on September 17th and sent the bomb vessels in. Many shells were thrown into the town and forty houses were destroyed. That night the wind got up and the sea became rough, forcing Shovell to bear away with his squadron. The storm continued for two days, precluding a further bombardment of Calais and Shovell prudently took his ships back to the Downs. The bomb vessels and the machines were sent up the River Thames to winter.[51]

By September 21st Shovell was considering a further attack on Calais, but it was not to be. He went to London and reported to Queen Mary.

Shovell said that the charts and maps of the French coast were inaccurate and that he had made an exact record of all the sands, depths and soundings about Calais and Dunkirk for future use.[52]

The attempt on Dunkirk and Calais had been a failure. No blame was attached to Shovell. Dr John Campbell has recorded:

> Sir Cloudesley Shovell, however, took care to demonstrate from his conduct, that there was no fault lay in him; for he went with a boat within the enemy's works and so became an eye witness of the impossibility of doing what his orders directed to be done; and therefore, on his coming home, he was perfectly well received and continued to be employed as a man who would command success, where it was possible; and omit nothing in his power, where it was not.[53]

Shovell's final duty of 1694 was to take five men of war and two fireships to Gottenburgh, to escort home the Eastland fleet with naval stores. They left England in mid October and arrived at Gottenburgh in November. From Gottenburgh the English squadron and merchant ships sailed to Elsinore, to pick up a Dutch merchant convoy to be escorted home. The homeward journey was made difficult by storms and two of Shovell's men of war were separated from him and went into Yarmouth.[54]

William, despite being King of England, spent a lot of time in his native Holland. Usually he returned to England in the autumn. Shovell – a reliable and a good sailor – was often the commander of the squadron which accompanied and protected William III. On this occasion Shovell was on his way to Gottenburgh, and was replaced by the Marquis of Carmarthen.[55]

So 1694 came to an end. If it had not been a successful year for the English at sea, with their failure at Camaret Bay, at least Shovell had rehabilitated himself after his difficulties of the preceding year.

NOTES

1. Richmond, pp.247–248; Laird Clowes, p.360–365.
2. Ehrmann, p.504; Burchett, p.204.
3. Luttrell, Vol.III, p.283.
4. Luttrell, Vol.III, p.293; RMT MAT 30; Log of the *Hampton Court* 1694, P.R.O. No.227; D.N.B. Graydon.
5. Campbell, Vol.III, pp.139,146; Ehrmann, Appendix X, p.648; RMT MAT 25; Anderson, Lists of Men of War.
6. Campbell, Vol.III, p.146.
7. Campbell, Vol.III, p.147; HMC 3rd Report London 1872 p.282.
8. D.N.B. Talmash; Aiken pp.82–83.
9. Torrington, pp.66–67.

10. Buccleuch MSS, Vol.II, Part I, pp.69–70.
11. Buccleuch MSS, Vol.II, Part I, pp.70–71.
12. Buccleuch MSS, Vol.II, Part I, pp.73–74.
13. Campbell, Vol.III, p.148.
14. D.N.B. Berkeley; Aiken, p.101.
15. Richmond, p.252.
16. Aiken, p.134.
17. Churchill, pp.368–394.
18. Richmond, p.249; Campbell, Vol.III, p.152; Hist. Militaire, iii, pp.77–79.
19. Campbell, Vol.III, pp.149–150.
20. Portland MSS, Vol.VIII, p.41; Laughton, N.R.S. Vol.40, 1912.
21. D.N.B. Tollemache; Burchett, Russell's instructions to Berkeley.
22. Campbell, Vol.III, pp.149–151; Journal of the Brest expedition by Carmarthen 1694.
23. D.N.B. Tollemache; Luttrell, Vol.III, p.327.
24. D.N.B. Tollemache; Campbell, Vol.III, p.153.
25. Campbell, Vol.III, pp.149–150.
26. D.N.B. Tollemache.
27. Campbell, Vol.III, p.153; Laird Clowes, p.476; Richmond, p.253.
28. Marsham MSS U1515, 17; ADM 33/169; ADM 33/187; Anderson, Lists of Men of War.
29. Laird Clowes, p.476; Richmond, p.253; House of Lords MSS 1693–95, N.S., p.495.
30. Campbell, Vol.III, pp.153–154, Vol.VI, p.185; Laird Clowes, p.476; Fyers, Machine Vessels p.50; Leake, p.10; Secret Memoirs.
31. Campbell, Vol.III, p.154; Laird Clowes, p.476; Fyers, Machine Vessels pp.51–53; Secret Memoirs.
32. Campbell, Vol.VI, p.186; Laird Clowes, p.476.
33. Campbell, Vol.III, p.154; Laird Clowes, p.477; Burchett, p.501.
34. Campbell, Vol.III, pp.154–155.
35. Laird Clowes, p.476.
36. Campbell, Vol.III, p.155; Laird Clowes, p.477; Secret Memoirs.
37. Campbell, Vol.III, pp.155–156; Portus Gratiae, exustus et eversus bombardis Anglo Batavis, 1694. I.B.F.Gerard Van Loon Histoire Metallique des Pays Bas, Tom iv, p.165.
38. Campbell, Vol.VI, p.186; Marsham MSS U1515.17.
39. Buccleuch MSS, Vol.II, Part I, p.109.
40. Buccleuch MSS, Vol.II, Part I, p.111.
41. Luttrell, Vol.III, p.156; Buccleuch MSS, Vol.II, Part I, p.116, Shrewsbury to Secretary Blathwayt August 14th 1694; Buccleuch MSS, Vol.II, Part I, pp.240–241, H.Grey to Secretary Trumbull.
42. Richmond, p.253; House of Lords MSS, N.S., 1693–95 p.495.
43. Campbell, Vol.III, p.156; Luttrell, Vol.III, pp.363–369; Buccleuch MSS, Vol.II, Part I, p.122.
44. Buccleuch MSS, Vol.II, Part I, p.132.
45. Bodleian MSS, Autogr.C.19, f.118.
46. Marsham MSS U1515.17, Lords of the Admiralty to C.S. Aug.24th 1694.
47. Buccleuch MSS, Vol.II, Part I, p.124; Marsham MSS U1515.17.
48. Campbell, Vol.III, p.157; Laird Clowes, p.477.
49. Campbell, Vol.III, pp.151–158; Laird Clowes, pp.477–78; Luttrell, Vol.III, pp.363–369; Secret Memoirs.
50. Buccleuch MSS, Vol.II, Part 1, p.135.

51. Campbell, Vol.III, p.158; Laird Clowes, p.478.
52. Luttrell, Vol.III, p.375.
53. Charnock, p.20.
54. Luttrell, Vol.III, pp.382, 398, 403; Marsham MSS U1515.17.
55. Marsham MSS U1515.17.

CHAPTER XVI

# Bombardment of
# French Coastal Towns
# 1695

Prior to the assault on Camaret Bay in 1694, Edward Russell had taken the main English fleet into the Mediterranean. His presence there led to the withdrawal of the French fleet into Toulon and gave a measure of support to the Spanish army, who were hard pressed in holding the French in Catalonia. Russell had been ordered to spend the winter of 1694/95 in Cadiz, which he was reluctant to do. However, he loyally obeyed William III.[1]

At the beginning of 1695 the strategy for the year was drawn up by William. There were to be three major land campaigns – in Flanders, Spain and Savoy. The Mediterranean was to be the main centre of naval activity in 1695. Consideration was given to the bombing of the French fleet at Toulon, but Russell thought that the defences there were too sound. He hoped to force the French to sea and then to destroy them in battle. The Compte de Tourville, who commanded the French fleet, wisely refused to come out of harbour and effectively contained a greater force. Russell had to make do with transporting Spanish troops from Genoa to Catalonia. In September 1695 he returned to England and George Rooke came out to replace him.[2]

Action in home waters was to be subsidiary to that in the Mediterranean. Lord John Berkeley, with Shovell under him, was again to be in command. They were to stop supplies getting through from the Baltic to France, stop Jean Bart and alarm the coasts. Alarming the coasts meant a continuation of the destruction of French coastal towns, which had begun in 1692 and continued the following year. How effective were these coastal bombardments? The strategy behind them was to force the withdrawal of French troops and ships from other theatres of war, such as Flanders and the Mediterranean. There is no evidence that in this they were in any way successful. The local defence and militia proved capable of dealing with the attacks. The only people to suffer were the civilian inhabitants of the coastal towns, such as Dieppe and St Malo, whose homes were destroyed. Berkeley was unhappy about this form of warfare, but Shovell's personal views are not known. The justification for these barbaric and largely pointless attacks was that the French themselves had initiated this form of warfare.[3]

In the early months of 1695 Shovell was based at Chatham as Vice Admiral of the Red and under the command of John Berkeley. Berkeley, at this time, does not appear to have had direct contact with the ships of the Home Waters squadron, as most of his letters and orders to Shovell came from the Cockpit, Whitehall. Shovell was left to see to the ships. The months of January, February and March were to be busy ones for him. Shovell had to organise a number of courts martial, including that of Captain William Bridges, Commander of the *Montagu*, that had been ordered by the Secretary of the Admiralty, Josiah Burchett. Bridges was alleged to have removed a coronet from a French ship that he had taken. Shovell then had to escort a convoy to Flanders, and no sooner had he returned to England than he had to enquire at another court martial into the loss of the *James galley* that had been wrecked. Perhaps Shovell felt sentimental about his old ship, for he had been captain of her for six years in the Mediterranean during the 1680s. Another problem was that of ships' captains claiming wages and victuals for men who had died on their ships or moved on, for their own benefit. The Lords of the Admiralty ordered Shovell to enquire into the complaint that the surgeon of the *Roe ketch* had been threatened by his captain for reporting that there were fictitious names on his book. Shovell was also informed by the Admiralty that John Benbow, the bombing expert, was to be given an allowance for his exploits the previous summer.[4]

Shovell's winter life at Chatham continued until the death of Queen Mary. In a letter from Berkeley to Shovell on February 27th 1695, permission was given for Shovell to come to London for the funeral, on March 5th. He was to leave the senior captain in charge of the ships until the Marquis of Carmarthen came down. Berkeley wrote that a chamber had been taken for Shovell and his lady and that a place had been reserved, presumably for the funeral service. The day before the funeral, Shovell was ordered to see that all the ships at Blackstakes fired their guns between 2.00 p.m. and sunset on the 5th. In the event, it is uncertain whether Shovell and his lady were able to attend Mary's funeral, for on March 6th Berkeley informed Shovell that it was not possible for Shovell himself to come to town for the present, but that it would be arranged before he had to leave. This refers to the fact that Shovell had been ordered to take a squadron to Cadiz with troops and supplies for Russell. Shovell wanted to sail in his ship, the *Neptune*, a 2nd rate, but William III had ordered that nothing larger than a 3rd rate should go. In a letter of March 6th Berkeley promised to speak to the King about it.[5]

Shovell did not go to the Mediterranean at this juncture. In fact, he nearly did not go anywhere. On March 14th 1695 Luttrell reported that Shovell had fallen ill of a quinsy and that he had been let blood four times, as was the custom in the seventeenth century. Two days later Shovell was reported to be out of danger. A quinsy is an abscess surrounding the tonsil in the throat, which can cause asphyxia and death. Rarely seen in the era of antibiotics, in Shovell's time it was a very serious matter. By the standards of the twentieth century blood letting is pointless. Shovell was not fit enough to take the squadron to Cadiz and Carmarthen went in his place.[6]

On April 25th Shovell wrote a letter to his brother-in-law, Thomas Shorting, who was the Collector of Customs at Cley, Norfolk. In this he gave support to Shorting for not living at Wells, prayed for his sister's safe delivery and was pleased that his mother got "well home". Had she been to visit him when he was seriously ill? He ends the letter, "I bless god I am pretty well on my recovery." Clearly, this is a reference to the quinsy.[7]

During the early summer the squadron, consisting of bomb vessels, fire-ships, machines, smoke ships with some smaller ships of the line and frigates for support, was prepared for the start of coastal actions against the French. On June 3rd 1695 Shovell, still as Vice Admiral of the Red, took over command of the *Cambridge*, a new 3rd rate of 80 guns, which had been built at Deptford. Shovell does not appear to have arrived at Portsmouth until mid June, for he wrote to the Commissioners of the Admiralty on June 16th praising Captain Crawley, who had got the *Cambridge* into good sailing order, and requesting that he be given command of the *Neptune* until his return. The smaller 3rd rates were more suitable for bombing expeditions than the larger 2nd rates such as the *Neptune*, in which Shovell had been serving. Berkeley, who was in overall command, hoisted his flag on the *Shrewsbury* at Portsmouth in the middle of June and was soon joined by a Dutch contingent under Philip Almonde. Further delay was caused by disagreement between the English and the Dutch about whether St Malo or Dunkirk should be the first town to be attacked. The Dutch, with the support of William III, favoured Dunkirk, but Berkeley and the English felt that there was a greater chance of success at St Malo. After threats of independent English action, Berkeley had his way.[8]

Having settled on St Malo, a base for privateers, the combined squadrons sailed on June 23rd under Berkeley and Shovell, reaching St Malo on July 4th. John Benbow, who led the bombing, has left an account of the action in a report written for the Earl of Shrewsbury a few days later.

The 4th at 10 in the forenoone, our whole fleet anchored about 4 miles without the Quinch Channell which leads into St. Malo, the Tide

being done, and little wind, soone after I received Lord Berkeley's orders to command all Men of Warre, Bomb vessels etc: which was ordered to attack the Towne. About 4 this afternoon I weighed anchor in the Northumberland and stood in and battered ye Quinch rock with 4 bomb vessels Dutch and English, and continuted till Dark, One shell fell upon the top of their workes. There was 2 Galleys and 8 or 10 great Boats with each a Gun, which came out and fired at us; the 5th at 4 in the morning the Wind at N.E. and fine weather, my Lord Berkeley hoisted an English Ensign at his Fore top mast head on board the Shrewsbury, which was the signal to prepare to go in with our small frigates and bombs; by his Lordship's order I went on board the Charles Galley, and there hoisted a broad Pendant, about 6. We were all under sayle, and before 7. Our bombships and Men of Warre were laid to pass and played on the Towne, without any visible success till 10 and then sett fire neare the Eastend, but made no great hast to increase but continued; About 2 in the afternoon another Fire was blown up about the Middle of the Towne, which blazed above the Tops of the Houses, but by their blowing up of Houses in the Towne, and great help, it was putt out before it was dark; Having received my Lords orders about 7 this evening we came out, leaving one of our Bombs behind, she being so much disabled by the Enemy, could not bring her off, burnt her, We have been very warmly recd by the Enemy both with Canon and Mortars. There was that went in, six English and Four Dutch Men of Warre, and Nine Bomb vessels English, 14 Wellboats, 2 Brigantines and one Spy boat. I can not tell certainly what men we have left, There was four Well Boats Sunk and 5 or 6 other Boates, My Lord Berkeley will give your Grace the particulars more at large. I am ordered with Seven or Eight light fregatts and Eight Bomb Ships to go to Granville and bombard that and to joyne My Lord Berkeley at Guernsey.
I remaine
Your Graces
Most obedient Servant
Benbow
Northumberland
6th July 95 before St Malo's[9]

Other English accounts, such as Berkeley's and that in Burchett, are similar, but the French in theirs have magnified the number of ships used against them and minimised the damage done to the town. The assault on July 4th was concentrated either side of the Channel leading into St Malo. An Anglo/Dutch force of bomb vessels took on the Quince Fort to the westward, leaving the remaining Dutch vessels to attack a battery at Danbour to the east. On the 5th Benbow, by now in the *Charles galley*, raised a suitably coloured flame flag and the bomb vessels and support frigates followed him in, to within a mile and a half of St Malo. Between six and seven o'clock in the morning the bombardment of the town began. This was answered by French batteries ashore and by boats coming close enough to the bomb vessels to fire small shot into them. During the late evening a great fire broke out in the east part of the town with vast clouds of smoke. Berkeley, Shovell and the Dutch Commander, Almonde, rowed about in their boats encouraging the sailors and expressing satisfaction with the way the assault was going. A fireship set the wooden fort on Quince rock alight. By seven in the evening the bomb vessels had run out of ammunition, having thrown 9,000 bombs and carcasses into St Malo. Sixty-six English and Dutch men were killed in the action, and the bomb vessel *Dreadful* had been so damaged that she had to be set on fire to stop her falling into the enemy's hands. A number of small boats had been sunk in the action that day, which had lasted more than eleven hours. A considerable part of St Malo had been destroyed before the withdrawal. French reports, which seem unrealistic, gave ten to twelve houses burnt, thirty-five to forty damaged and eighteen or twenty people killed or wounded.[10]

Following the attack on St Malo, Benbow was detached with eight frigates and eight bomb vessels to move down the coast to burn Granville. This he accomplished on July 8th, while Berkeley and the remainder of the ships sailed for Guernsey Roads. Shovell did not take part in the destruction of Granville, and on July 10th he left Guernsey Roads with Berkeley, arriving at Spithead two days later. [11]

Soon after the action at St Malo, Shovell felt the need to strengthen the crew of the *Cambridge*. On July 8th he ordered the commander of the *Yarmouth* to discharge about 100 men who had been with him in the *Neptune*, and to send them to the *Cambridge*.[12]

Shovell had been in the *Cambridge* for most of the action off St Malo, except for a period when he went in his boat to encourage the sailors and bomb vessels close to the shore. His part in the destruction of the town had been a small one. In the *Secret Memoirs of Cloudesley Shovell*, written soon after his death, it is recorded for 1695:

> All the Saints of France were invoked to no purpose and the priests said as many masses as there are minutes in the year: but Sir Cloudesley's cannons were deaf to all intreaties; a bomb from a mortar piece of his no more thought of a praying priest than it would have done an ignorant unsanctified lay man.[13]

Berkeley and Shovell soon left St Helens with their squadron for the Downs, which was reached on July 19th. Here final preparations were made for an attack on Dunkirk. Both William III and the Dutch were keen that an attempt on the town be made, as it was a base for privateers and, unlike St Malo, had a military significance in that it might take pressure off the land forces in Flanders.[14]

The attack on Dunkirk was not to go well. The defences had been strengthened with boats, chains, piles and floating pontoons with guns. William Meesters, who had been with Shovell the previous year, was to command the machine vessels. Wherever Meesters went things never seemed to run smoothly. Meesters, whose name was really Meester, was a Dutch artillery officer who probably came over to England with William of Orange in 1688. He served with William in his campaign in Ireland and narrowly escaped death in 1690, when he had to hide in a bed of nettles! That year he filled a vacancy as Storekeeper of the Ordnance with a salary of £400 a year and a good house in the Tower. Meesters proceeded to develop his variant of the machine vessel. When he died at the Hague in 1701, his son mentioned that he had always received orders verbally, direct from William III and had had no written instructions. The secrecy was perhaps necessary, as there were numerous Jacobite agents happy to delve into his activities. Sir John Laughton has aptly described Meesters as at least as much a charlatan as an inventor![15]

Shovell has left his own account of the attack on Dunkirk in a letter to Berkeley on August 22nd 1695, and in a very similar one written to the Commissioners of the Admiralty on the following September 14th. The letter is worth quoting in full. Sir Cloudesley Shovell to Lord Berkeley dated *Northumberland*, in the Downs, August 22nd 1695.

> My Lord,
>     I have received from Mr Hibart a copy of Mr Meesters his narrative, on which I cannot help making the following remarks. First, he cunningly begins his Narrative the 30th of July, by which he let slip his tedious preparations of two months, which he promised should be ready in a fortnight: also he buries in oblivion his repeated assurances of his being ready, and his great assurance in asking convoy for some machine, or sink ships, he pretends to have at Ostend; when, as far as I can learn from thence, there have been none there, neither are there any expected. I verily believe, and am not singular in my opinion, that these sink ships and machines, were only an invention to swell his accounts, which, I suppose, if they were well looked into by some understanding man, would appear monstrous, for it is said he had some materials on board his smoke ships, or machines, as barrels of guns etc which were of no more use than if he had put so many stones there.
>     An account of what has occurred to my observation and memory, in relation to the attempt against Dunkirk. Friday 19th July 1695. We came to the Downs in order to put the aforesaid attempt in execution,

where we expected to have found Mr Meesters in readiness to proceed, but he arrived not till next day.

Monday 22nd. A council of war was called, at which Mr Meesters was present. The admiralty's order being positive for attempting of Dunkirk, it was considered in what manner to make the attempt.

Upon conference with my Lord Berkeley before that, I found it was his lordships intention to make the attack against the pier heads and risbank with seventy and eighty gun ships; but at that council of war, upon examination of the pilots which Mr Meesters had provided for carrying on the ships to the attack, finding they all in general absolutely refused to take charge of any ship of so great a draught of water, we were obliged to come to a resolution of employing frigates of about fifty guns; and even these frigates (when the resolution came to be put in practice) these same pilots refused to to carry in, as the sequel will show.

Tuesday 23rd. Sailed with the whole fleet, English and Dutch, under command of my Lord Berkeley, and stood over to the coast of France.

Saturday 27th. Being at anchor off Gravelin, a council of war was called, and Mr Meesters who had left the fleet (it blowing pretty fresh) and was returned to the Downs with great part of the machines and having now positive orders from my lord to come away; and being expected on the morrow, it was thought advisable to sail nearer into Dunkirk, and to send in eight frigates pretty close towards the brake, to observe what provision was made by the enemy, at the risbank and wooden forts, for their defence, which accordingly was put in execution.

Monday 29th. Mr Meesters arrived with the machines.

Tuesday 30th. All the small frigates and vessels sailed in nearer Dunkirk and anchored a little to the westward of the brake. Preparations were made for attacking the pier-heads and risbank; and a council of war was called, at which it was resolved (if the weather proved fine) to begin the attack on the morrow morning.

Wednesday 31st. This morning the weather not promising fair we did not begin.

Thursday 1st August. This morning the weather being fair, the frigates, and bomb vessels appointed to go with them, went in and began to bombard about seven in the morning. About the same time I went with my lord in a boat, and we rowed about to observe in what readiness each vessel was to begin the attack. We met Mr Meesters, he told my lord he would be ready between ten and eleven o'clock: but I very well remember, after eleven, some of the captains of the machines, and with whom my lord spoke, said they had no other orders but to keep near Mr Meesters.

As I have before observed, the pilots which Mr Meesters had provided, and had undertaken to conduct the ships appointed for battery, now would not take charge of them, though they draw but sixteen or seventeen feet Flemish. This, admiral Allemonde acquainted my lord Berkeley with, who sent captain Wassenaer to Mr Meesters, to inform him of the same. As I understood captain Wassenaer, upon his return from Mr Meesters, he brought word Mr Meesters said he could do his business without the battering ships; and most certain it is, when we met Mr Meesters in his boat afterwards, he made no complaint for want of them, nor did he lay any thing to my lord about altering this disposition of his attack.

Tis further observable that the pilots, notwithstanding the assurance given that they would take charge of the frigates to carry them in to the attack, and out at the east channel, yet when they were to the eastward of the forts, they rather chose to turn the ships back to the westward, though they again passed the enemy's shot, than trust to their judgement to sail through the east channel, which makes me of the opinion none of the pilots knew the east channel; for I generally find pilots had rather trust their judgement, where they have knowledge, than encounter the enemies shot.

Indeed as I understood admiral Allemonde, these pilots of Mr Meesters were men of no account, or reputation, for their skill in pilotage, all their pretentions to their knowledge of this place being only grounded upon their having been there once or twice in ships as sailors, never as masters, or having charge of any ships, and therefore could not reasonably be thought sufficiently skilled, or fitly qualified to undertake such a difficult and hazardous enterprize.

I am pretty positive, that when my lord met Mr Meesters in his boat the first time, it was near eleven o'clock; and upon his lordships doubting whether his smoke ships were ready (having observed his men in a hurry) Mr Meesters replyed, then tomorrow will be as well: and my lord said, he would not lose that opportunity for ten thousand pounds, therefore would have it done, if possible, alledging, the weather being good and the bombardment having been begun; Mr Meesters then assured his lordship all was ready. After this I went with my lord to the machines and smoke ships which lay about a mile without Mr Meesters, some of their captains said they had no other orders than, when they had fitted their vessels (which they were in hand with) they were to anchor near Mr Meesters. After my lord had hastened them all towards Mr Meesters, his lordship met Mr Meesters in his boat again; it was then one o'clock, and we judged upon the pitch of high water, or rather falling water which my lord told Mr Meesters, and said he thought it was too late; but he pertly replied that there was nothing, that he knew of, to hinder the attack. He spake this with so much boldness and confidence, that I must needs say, I was then, as I am now, of opinion, that if my lord had not immediately ordered the attack, he would have thrown the miscarriage upon his lordship.

Upon the signal being made, the other frigates weighed and did their duty, as far as their knowledge of the place and the skill of the pilots would permit: but no machine, or smoke ship went with the frigates, neither did they begin the attack, though contrary to the method prescribed, lord Berkeley ordered the Lime to cut and support them in their disorderly attack.

I remember capt. Carleton, who commanded one of the machines, did cut, but did not sail in, having anchored amongst other bomb vessels, or frigates, that supported them: and Carleton has since told me himself, that he rid near them out of danger of any but random shot from the enemy.

I further remember Mr Meesters was very fond of a ship he said he would make shot proof, and said he would lye with her within a cable's length of the pier-head and take care to order the attacks aright; but I saw no such vessel in that dangerous post.[16]

Although this letter to Lord Berkeley was written from the *Northumberland* on August 22nd, Shovell was in the *Cambridge* for the assault on Dunkirk. The attack had been a failure, with slight damage done to the town and three French half gallies sunk. The Dutch ship, the *Batavier*, grounded under the batteries and was burnt by the French, with her captain taken prisoner. Meesters slipped away with his machine vessels under the cover of darkness. This infuriated Berkeley, who sent orders after him to have him brought back a close prisoner. "He is afraid," he wrote on August 4th, "to stand the trial of his machines, and now his business is done, with what money he has got, he is for packing off, but I hope to stop him. All his actions and words have been every day nothing but contraiety, and his design to cheat his Majesty and the nation." Berkeley took his squadron, including Shovell, back to the Downs.[17]

Meesters, on arrival back in England, wasted no time in going to London and laying the blame for the failure of the enterprise firmly at the door of the senior naval officers.

Mr Meesters is come to town, and endeavours to lay fault upon his not being protected by the frigates, brigantines, and well boats, as was agreed at the council of war; for which reason, he says, the masters of the smoke ships were obliged to set their vessels on fire before they could be laid to do any execution, to prevent their own ships being taken prisoners. For the same reason, he says, he ordered the machines off, because, there being no strength ready to sustain them, they must have unavoidably fallen into enemies hands.[18]

Berkeley was not slow to respond, with a letter to the Earl of Shrewsbury.

As for Mr Meesters, it has been my ill fortune to have to do with him; I foresee [foresaw] it, and did all I could to avoid it, but it was inevitable. My Lord, he is certainly near akin to the father of falsehood; but to lay down such matters for truth, as in some cases I can bring a hundred witnesses, and in others his own hand to vouch the contrary, I protest, though I pretty well know the man, I wonder at his confidence or forgetfulness; sure he takes no notes. The frigates of which he complains stood the enemy's fire above half an hour, staying for Mr Meesters; some of the captains spoke to him and told him that if he would bring one of his ships to them, they would convoy them as near as they pleased; others of the frigates were within pistol shot of the smoke ships and no enemy's boat near them when they set on fire. As for the brigantines and well boats, it was agreed at the last council of war on board the Charles Galley, which good Mr Meesters has forgot, that they were not to go on till after the machine vessels, which Mr Meesters took care we should not see the trial of. As for his denying his taking the machine ships with him when he came away, besides that the whole fleet are witnesses of it, I have an order by me, signed by him, to 5 of them (to follow him immediately as they would answer it at their perils), in case they had not, as they all did, sailed with him. This shows his sincere way of dealing, and I suppose he has carried up three captains of smoke ships, who, two of them, set their ships on fire much nearer to us than the enemy, to be his vouchers.

I send a short account to Mr Vernon of the whole transaction with Mr Meesters, taken from a little higher, to show your Grace when you are at leisure. Since I frighted Mr Meesters, I am glad the ship I sent after him missed him, for he would have been a trouble to me, though I should be very glad some way were found to have this business tried, to prove where the fault lies. He was so little himself when before Dunkirque that he had ordered all the provisions and spare things from the machines on board the Ephraim, and next day having, I suppose, forgot it, clapped a bag or two of tow in her, and burnt her for a smoke ship. He said, since he came away, that he would not have gone on the attack of Calais for a thousand pound; there I give him credit; nor on that of Dunkirkque for three.

I beg your Grace's pardon for troubling you with his follies, but if one did not contradict a prating fellow, some there are, who would

206

believe him. All our bomb vessels are, thank God, got in safe, but several of them miserably shattered.[19]

Berkeley's invective against Meesters came pouring out. Perhaps Shovell's measured letter to Lord Berkeley carried more weight. The defences at Dunkirk were strong enough to stop any but the most overwhelming assault. Meesters arrived late in the Downs, failed to provide experienced pilots, failed to organise or use his machine vessels and ran away at the first opportunity. Despite this, an enquiry was held to determine where the blame for the failure lay! There was a view that there had been a misunderstanding between Meesters and the sea officers. From current knowledge no blame could be attached to Berkeley, Shovell and Almonde, who had done their best. Meesters' behaviour was deplorable and it is hard to disagree with Laughton in calling him a charlatan. Even if the machine vessels had been used in a determined fashion against Dunkirk, it is still doubtful whether they would have had any success, in view of the strength of the defences. In strategic terms, the attempt on Dunkirk did not lead to a reduction in pressure on the troops in Flanders, as it had been on too small a scale to be a real threat. In all it was a costly failure.[20]

In the Downs, Berkeley prepared his squadron and bomb vessels for a further attack on the French coast at Calais. Meesters had declined to go, which was no doubt a relief to Shovell and Berkeley, who by this time had no faith in him. John Benbow, the bombing expert, had not been at Dunkirk and was not to be involved at Calais. He had left his ship in July, feigning illness, after some sort of disagreement with Berkeley. Shovell was to remain in his 3rd rate, the *Cambridge*, for the assault on Calais.[21]

Coming before Calais, Berkeley called a council of war at which it was resolved to burn a wooden fort erected at the entrance of the pier heads. The fort had fourteen cannons and several other batteries, making an assault impossible until they were neutralised. On the morning of August 17th 1695 this was accomplished, and the bombardment began. The French sent out half gallies to break up the line of bomb vessels, but the frigates and brigantines forced them away. The bombardment continued all through the afternoon, by which time some 600 bombs had been thrown into Calais. The magazine and the risbank were burnt and considerable damage done to the houses of the town. Despite a prodigious fire from the French batteries, English losses and damage were slight. Captain Robert Osborne of the *Aldborough ketch* was killed by a cannon ball from the French half gallies.[22]

While still before Calais, Berkeley had decided to give up his command to Shovell. Shovell wrote to the Admiralty on August 19th, from the *Cambridge,* stating that Berkeley was coming away for London and that he would like to as well. Probably both men wanted to put their side of the

Dunkirk fiasco and refute Meesters' allegations of failure to support him. It is also clear from this letter that Shovell intended to have the *Duchess* as his next ship, as he requested the command of her to be given to Captain James Stewart and that Captain Crawley should be restored to the *Cambridge*. The real reason for Berkeley giving up command of the squadron at this juncture may have been that his ships on return to the Downs were to go to Spithead, where George Rooke was getting ready to go out to the Mediterranean to relieve Russell. Berkeley had already written on the subject, "since it has been thought fit to appoint Sir George Rooke to command in the Straits, I suppose care will be taken that he and I may not meet at sea without he will obey, for I can own no superior at sea but admiral Russell." This was odd to say the least, as Rooke and Shovell were both senior to him and the latter had acted under him throughout the summer. It says much for Shovell's equable temperament that he could serve under such a self-seeking commander without rancour.[23]

Calais was the last coastal town to be attacked that year and, according to English reports, the damage was said to be considerable. Both sides had medals struck to commemorate the coastal actions of 1695. The English medal had on one side a Jupiter with a fenestrum in his hand with these words, *Jovi Tonati* [Jupiter the thunderer] below *Gulielmo Tertio, D.G. Magnae Britanniae Regi* [William III King of Great Britain by the grace of God], and round about the circumference,*Vangionum Nemetumq; ignes ulcifcitur Anglus, Difce timere gravem nunc Ludovice vicem.* [Now then the Vangiones; the Englishman avenges the flames, now O Ludwig learn to fear this pain in turn]. On the other side were to be seen several sea towns, fired by bombs thrown from a fleet riding at sea, with a sun overhead representing Louis XIV with this motto, *Afpicit accenfas, nec tantos fultinet aeftus.* [He sees them burnt, nor does the heat sustain so many]. Underneath these words, *Librata in maritimas Galliae urber fulmina.* [Thunderbolts were hurled on the coastal towns of France].[24]

On August 20th Shovell, with the squadron, was back in the Downs. That same day Shovell raised his flag on the *Northumberland*, as the *Cambridge*, with two other ships, had been ordered to Portsmouth. The *Northumberland* was a 70 gun 3rd rate built in Bristol in 1679, and Shovell was to spend the autumn in her. In late August Shovell received reports of the considerable damage done to Calais, and appealed to the Admiralty for benevolence for the widow of Robert Osborne, the Captain of the *Aldborough ketch*, killed before Calais.[25]

On September 1st Shovell spent the night ashore at Knowlton, near Deal, close to the Downs. Knowlton was the country home of Shovell's great patron, Sir John Narbrough, until his death in 1688. Under the terms of his will of August 26th 1687, Sir John left Knowlton to his eldest son, another John, a boy rising 11 years at this time. Of course, Shovell had

**1.** Young Cloudesley Shovell. Unsigned miniature. (Guildhall Museum, Rochester)

**2.** Cloudesley Shovell by Michael
Dahl. (Private Collection).

**3.** A naval action of the Barbary Wars by Peter Monamy. (Author's collection).

**4.** Drawing of Shovell's action against the ships of Tripoli, 1676. Attributed to Willem van de Velde the elder. (National Maritime Museum).

**5.** Cloudesley Shovell.
Attributed to Michael Dahl.
(Guildhall Museum, Rochester).

**6.** Pewter chamber pot salvaged from the *Association* and possibly owned by Shovell.
(Isles of Scilly Museum Association).

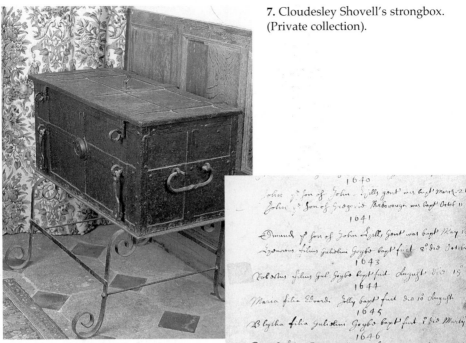

**7.** Cloudesley Shovell's strongbox. (Private collection).

**8.** Cloudesley Shovell's baptismal entry in the Cockthorpe, Norfolk register. (The incumbent of Langham, Norfolk).

**9.** May Place, Crayford, Kent. Shovell's country estate. (Engraved by J. Greig for *The Excursions through Kent*).

**10.** Lady Elizabeth Shovell by an unknown artist. Cloudesley Shovell was her second husband. The first was John Narbrough. (Scottish Private collection).

**11.** Christopher Myngs by Peter Lely. Shovell's first patron who was to die from a throat wound following the Four Day's Fight in 1666. (National Maritime Museum).

**12.** Arthur Herbert, Earl of Torrington by the studio of John Closterman. Immoral, foul-mouthed intriguer, under whom Shovell was to serve loyally in the Mediterranean and at the Battle of Bantry Bay in 1689. (Author's collection).

**13.** Edward Russell, Earl of Orford by Godfrey Kneller. The irascible commander-in-chief under whom Shovell was to shine at the Battle of Barfleur in 1692. (National Maritime Museum).

**14.** John Leake by Godfrey Kneller. He never forgave Shovell for ignoring his advice to follow the French van out of the line at the Battle of Malaga in 1704. (National Maritime Museum).

**15.** John Norris by Godfrey Kneller. A Shovell protégé and personal friend. Their naval careers were to be intimately related. (National Maritime Museum).

**16.** George Rook by Michael Dahl. A reserved member of the gentry. Shovell's contemporary and great rival. (National Maritime Museum).

**17.** Matt Aylmer by Jonathan Richardson. A flamboyant Irish aristocrat and contemporary of Shovell. His son was to die with Shovell in 1707. (National Maritime Museum).

become young John's stepfather on his marriage to Elizabeth Narbrough in 1691. It is not clear whether the Shovells were regularly using Knowlton at this time, as they had a house in London and had purchased a country home, May Place at Crayford, in 1694. In any event, Shovell wrote a letter from Knowlton to George Rooke, who was preparing to go out to the Mediterranean, asking him to pay particular attention to a merchant ship owned by friends of his. The ship was going out to the eastern Mediterranean and Shovell wrote further letters to Cadiz and to the commodore of the escort ships inside the Mediterranean. Judging by the care taken, it is difficult not to believe that Shovell had some financial interest in the venture, or perhaps that of his father-in-law, John Hill, who had traded with Smyrna since 1675.[26]

By September 4th Shovell was back in the *Northumberland* in the Downs. He lobbied the Secretary at War, William Blathwayt, over the appointment of a replacement for Lieutenant Colonel Davies, killed at the siege of Namur, in the First Regiment of Marines. Shovell was looking for advancement for the Rear Admirals David Mitchell and John Neville, who were both absent in the Mediterranean. He himself had been made Lieutenant Colonel of the First Marine Regiment in 1692. Shovell wasted no time in pushing his friends for lucrative positions.[27]

It is clear Shovell never forgot the debt that he owed his first patron, Sir Christopher Myngs. In mid September Shovell wrote to Josiah Burchett at the Admiralty, trying to further the career of Sir Christopher's son, also Christopher. "I own myself under manyfold obligation to Capt. Myngs his friend and therefore think my selfe bound in confidence as well as gratitude." Shovell pressed for Myngs to be given a larger ship, rather than be moved sideways into one of a similar rate. It is not clear whether Shovell was successful or not, but young Christopher did go on to serve as a captain with Shovell at the Battle of Malaga in 1704.[28]

Shovell was just as interested in the humble sailor as in his fellow officers. While in London on September 12th, collecting orders to go to Holland to transport the King, William III, back to England, Shovell took the opportunity to recommend one Robert Jerome for the post of cook. Jerome had served under him in the *Neptune* and had lost a leg in the firing of a gun. It was customary for disabled men to be supported by being made cooks. Many were severely handicapped, either being without hands or blind. A mate would have to do the work for them. Shovell also felt that it was sensible to pay off crews on returning home, to make it more likely that they would re-enlist. This was not always the case and led to much resentment. "A little liberty of enjoying their silver as they terme it in spending their money before they are forced to sea again." [29]

On September 20th Shovell arrived in Margate Roads in the *Berwick*, a 3rd rate. By October 10th he had returned there, having escorted William III's yacht back from Holland. Shovell used the *Northumberland* for the crossing. He also appeared to have been briefly in the 90 gun 2nd rate, the *Duke*, as orders were sent by him from this ship on October 19th.[30]

In early October William III reached Kensington and immediately dissolved Parliament and called for a new one to meet on November 22nd. This was to be the start of Shovell's political career, although it cannot be described as a very active one, as his sea duties took priority. In September 1695 the town of Rochester agreed to elect Shovell "a burgess of that place" in case Parliament was dissolved. Between 1295 and the nineteenth century, two persons were elected to Parliament for Rochester. In the seventeenth century one member was normally a senior naval officer and the other a local dignitary. The electors until 1832 were the freemen of the city, who in the early days met under a large tree on Boley Hill, Rochester, for the election. The site is marked by a stone in the road engraved "Boley Hill 1831", the date the tree was cut down. Shovell was elected a Member of Parliament for Rochester in October 1695 and remained in post until 1701. Some authorities state that he was in Parliament continuously between 1695 and his death in 1707. This is incorrect, as there was a gap between 1701 and 1705. For the first three Parliaments that Shovell represented Rochester, his companion Member of Parliament was Sir Joseph Williamson. Williamson was a very experienced man who had been an Under Secretary of State as early as 1665.[31]

Perhaps to mark his election as a Member of Parliament for Rochester, Shovell paid for the magnificent decorative plaster ceilings in the Guildhall of the city. The ceilings are over the Court Hall and the main staircase. The identity of the master plasterer was probably John Grove II. The ceiling of the Court Hall is enriched with trophies of war, fruit, flowers and the arms of the city and those of Shovell. Work began in 1695 and was completed the following year. The Guildhall, its ceiling and portraits of Shovell and Williamson can be seen to this day.[32]

During the summer and autumn of 1695 Shovell had used the 3rd rates, the *Cambridge* and the *Northumberland*, for his various activities. He looked upon them as temporary appointments, and on December 8th he was made Commander of the *Duchess*, a 90 gun 2nd rate, which had been built at Deptford in 1679. During the autumn he had been trying to get his former chaplain in the *Neptune* for the *Duchess*. Shovell succeeded in getting a Lieutenant Hughes to be first lieutenant, and in November had ordered a Frenchman to come down to be his cook.[33]

Towards the end of the year came the first rumblings of a possible French invasion from Dunkirk and Calais. They would provide a further challenge for Shovell in the New Year.

NOTES

1. Richmond, pp.255–57.
2. Richmond, pp.258–259.
3. Richmond, pp.254–255, 260–261.
4. Marsham MSS U1515.17.
5. Marsham MSS U1515.17; Luttrell, Vol.III, p.450.
6. Luttrell, Vol.III, p.451.
7. RMT MAT25, Shovell to Thomas Shorting.
8. ADM 6/3 f.59; NMM, SMF 221 (PHB/17); Anderson, Lists of Men of War; Burchett, p.293; Campbell, Vol.III, p.173.
9. ADD MSS 21494 f.33.
10. Campbell, Vol.III, pp.173–176; London Gazette No.3096; Burchett; Histoire Militaire, tom. iii, p.323; Secret Memoirs.
11. Campbell, Vol.VI, pp.187–188; NMM, SMF221 (PHB/17).
12. NMM, SMF221 (PHB/17).
13. Secret Memoirs.
14. Richmond, pp.261–262; NMM, SMF221 (PHB/17).
15. Campbell, Vol.III, p.177; Fyers, Machine Vessels pp.58–59; D.N.B. Berkeley of Stratton.
16. Charnock, pp.21–23; NMM, SMF221 (PHB/17).
17. Campbell, Vol.III, p.177; Laird Clowes, p.482; D.N.B. Berkeley.
18. Buccleuch MSS, Vol.II, Part I, p.211, Shrewsbury to Berkeley.
19. Buccleuch MSS, Vol.II, Part I, p.212, Berkeley to Shrewsbury Aug. 8th.
20. Campbell, Vol.III, pp.177–180; Burchett p.298; London Gazette No.3102.
21. NMM, SMF 221 (PHB/17); D.N.B. Benbow.
22. Campbell, Vol.III, pp.178–179; Burchett, p.303; London Gazette No.3107; Laird Clowes, p.482.
23. NMM, SMF221 (PHB/17); D.N.B. Berkeley.
24. Secret Memoirs.
25. NMM, SMF221 (PHB/17); Anderson , Lists of Men of War.
26. NMM, SMF221 (PHB/17); RMT MAT 24, will of Sir John Narbrough; RMT MAT 33, Chart Pedigree of Cloudesley Shovell; Marsham MSS U1515.01, Account Book of John Hill.
27. NMM, SMF 221 (PHB/17); D.N.B. Shovell.
28. NMM, SMF221 (PHB/17).
29. NMM, SMF221 (PHB/17); Davies, Gentlemen and Tarpaulins p.21; Tanner Catalogue, Vol.IV, pp.118, 351.
30. NMM, SMF 221 (PHB/17); Luttrell, Vol.III, p.526.
31. Campbell, Vol III, p.183; Burnet, Vol. ii, p.160; Folger Lib, Newdigate newsletter l.c.2523 September 19th 1695; Smith, Rochester in Parliament; Smith, History of Rochester; Return of Members of Parliament.
32. Smith, History of Rochester; The Guildhall Rochester, a Brief History.
33. ADM 6/3 f.109; NMM, SMF221 (PHB/17); Anderson, Lists of Men of War.

# CHAPTER XVII
## *The End of the War*
## *1696–1697*

Louis XIV had decided to attempt a rapid invasion of England in 1696, before the Anglo/Dutch fleet was ready for sea. Twenty thousand soldiers were quietly collected at Calais and Dunkirk. Transports and squadrons of men of war, under the Marquis de Nesmond and Jean Bart, were prepared to carry them. Ex-King James would lead them in person and he had high hopes of regaining his throne. William III, his son-in-law, was to be assassinated and the Duke of Berwick with other supporters of the ex-King were sent to England to foment internal unrest. Although rumours had abounded since late the previous year, the first signs of greater than normal activity in the eastern French Channel ports confirmed William's suspicions. On February 24th he went to the House of Lords, sent for the Commons and informed them of the affair. Edward Russell, who had returned from the Mediterranean, was to go to sea with all available ships to put a stop to the proposed invasion. Shovell, as Vice Admiral of the Red, was to go with him.[1]

Much of Shovell's time between September 1695 and mid January 1696 was spent at Crotchott Fryare, which the author has not been able to trace, but suspects was a house close to the Downs. In early January Shovell was ordered by Russell, via John Berkeley, to get ready the ships of his division at Chatham. He sailed from Gravesend on January 17th, reaching Chatham two days later. Shovell's letter book during this period does not show any great urgency to be ready for sea.

James Stewart, his captain in the *Duchess*, was permitted six days' leave, although a week later Berkeley was complaining at the number of Shovell's officers being ashore and putting a stop to it. Many of Shovell's letters at this time are endeavouring to help former members of his crews or their families. There was support for a disabled man who had served with him in both the *James galley* and the *Anne* for the position of cook, and assistance for the son of the late boatswain of the *Dover*, whose mother was a distressed widow. It is not surprising that Shovell had little difficulty in manning his ships, in view of the care he gave to his men.[2]

It was not until February 24th that Shovell was ordered to go to the Downs with as many ships as he could get ready. At this stage he was at the Nore in the *Duchess*, and Russell was still in London. Shovell took men from the *Duchess*, which was too large a vessel to take to sea in February, and redistributed them amongst the ships of his division. The next day Russell hoisted the union flag on board the *Victory* as Commander-in-Chief, and went to sea with about fifty ships to stop the French invasion. On February 27th he was joined by Shovell with a further thirteen ships and a Dutch contingent. Shovell had sailed in the old *Montagu*, a 52–62 gun 3rd rate, which had been built as long ago as 1654. Soon they were off the coast of France and consideration was given to attacking the French shipping in Dunkirk.[3]

On March 1st 1696 Russell sent Shovell, with some of the senior captains, to see if it was possible to attack the French men of war at Dunkirk. They wrote the following report on March 3rd.

> We have viewed the ships in Flemish Road and observe[d] nine sail had their yards and topmasts struck, some with their shrouds lashed to the mast; of which number we judge five carry from fifty to sixty guns or upwards. Two of the biggest of the five are Dutch built, the rest French. The other four are of forty guns or upward[s], one of them a fly boat. They are placed to the eastward of Dunkirke pier head. They have also in Flemish Road four frigates of about twenty guns, which lie near the pier head, and get [got?] under sail upon the approach of our ships; with whom lie about ten half galleys and other boats.
>
> Upon examining the Dutch pilots sent by Mr Meesters, they declare that three days hence, when the tides are mended, if the wind be from the S. to the W.S.W., a fresh gale, they will venture to pilot our ships of fifteen to sixteen foot water (Flemish) through the Flemish Road, and out at the East Channel by Neuport, provided we do not anchor; and they say they must not be contradicted by the captains or any officers in conducting the ship[s]; and if accidents happen to any ships masts, so as to bring them by the board, it will endanger losing the ship.
>
> We also examined the pilots that came from Neuport; they declare themselves ignorant of the sands or channels about Dunkirke, and came only to take charge of such ships as shall sail to Ostend or Neuport, in order to convoy the forces from thence.
>
> This being what we have observed and heard from the pilots, [we] do think it proper to acquaint General [Russell] with the whole matter, in order to receive his further directions.
>
> Signed by Clowd Shovell and nineteen captains.[4]

After further consultation between Russell, Shovell, the captains, Mr Meesters and the engineers, an attack on Dunkirk was deemed impractical.[5] The decision was not surprising, but it is amazing after his failures of the previous year that Meesters was involved at all. While at sea off Dunkirk on March 3rd Shovell found time to write to his brother-in-law, Thomas Shorting, who was at home in north Norfolk.

> Brother,
> On French coast with 50 men of war and have happily prevented an invasion from France for James II ready to embark 20,000 french in order to make a bloody war in our country. I hope ye gentlemen about you will not handle the Jacobites so tenderly since they take part with him who was bringing a foreign army of papists to lay our country in blood and ashes and all ye plagues and misfortunes that attend war. Pray deliver the inclosed to Cap. Brittife and let me know from you how he behave himself as to this present government. This with my duty to my mother, humbly craving her blessing also my love to my sister and your self and all friends.
> I remain,
> Your loving brother,
> C.S.[6]

Two days after writing to his brother-in-law, Shovell received orders from Russell to remain on station with thirty-one ships. He was to stop men of war and transports from getting out of Calais and Dunkirk. If the opportunity arose to use his fireships or bomb vessels, he was to do so. Parting with these instructions, Russell returned to the Downs.[7]

Shovell did his best to blockade Dunkirk and Calais, but his task was not made easy by the blustery weather that even delayed his reports. Virtually the only ships able to get out of the French ports at this time were fishing vessels being used for intelligence purposes, and privateers. In mid March Shovell took a pink, which had sailed a week before, with a number of privateers under Chas Jacobin. The master of one of the privateers was in the captured pink and explained to Shovell the difficulties of using the channel to the east of Dunkirk, and that Jean Bart usually went to sea in the 56 gun *Blackamoor*. Later in the month Shovell made the point to the Admiralty that, even if he had the whole Navy of England at his disposal, he would be unable to stop privateers coming out of Dunkirk, as they ran in and out over the sands. Captain William Kerr of the *Burlington* was to fall foul of this, when privateers escaped into Dunkirk by sailing over the sand bar. Shovell in a letter to the Admiralty defended him. "I can not but observe to your Lordships how great a misfortune a commander must needlessly be under if his reputation must depend upon the knowledge or will of a pilot." He was not successful and at a later date was ordered to court martial poor Kerr.[8]

On March 23rd, while still off Calais Roads, Shovell received orders from the Admiralty to leave some ships to cover the French coast and to return to the Downs. As he was about to depart from his station, some bomb vessels appeared in sight and Shovell called his captains together to discuss the possible bombing of Calais. The bombing specialists, John Benbow and Colonel Richards, were also present, but it was decided not to attack.[9]

By March 26th Shovell had anchored in the Downs in the *Montagu*. He returned to the *Duchess*, his usual flagship, from which his letters were written for the next few days. Shovell complained to the Admiralty about lack of payment for his sailors. "The seamen of the fleet begining to be mightily down in the mouth for want of their pay and bounty money there being no manner of appearance of either of them." Shovell's rest in the Downs was to be brief. The King, William III, was dissatisfied that better use had not been made of the bomb vessels, in an attempt to destroy the transports and town of Calais. He was ordered back to Calais.[10]

Transferring back to the *Montagu*, Shovell sailed for Calais on April 2nd 1696. Three days later he was back, anchored off the North Foreland and writing a report for the Commissioners of the Admiralty.

Pursuiant to your lordship's orders of 31st of March, we, the 3rd instant, having very fair weather, got before Calais with our bomb vessels; and the wind being southerly, which made a smooth sea, we laid our bomb vessels in a line and about noon began to heave shells at the town, and continued so doing till evening; in all which time we expended upwards of 300 bombs and carcasses, many of which were seen to fall and break both in the town and among their embarkations at the pier. I suppose they have done considerable damage to the enemy, though nothing appeared to us more than a vessel being on fire in the harbour, and the town in two or three several places, which were immediately extinguished.

The enemy were very active with their row-boats and half galleys; but to prevent them from hindering or injuring our bomb vessels, the frigates and brigantines kept very near them as indeed they were obliged to do.

The damage we received is, the bomb vessels have their rigging much shattered, and two of them are very leaky by reason of shot received under water; the mortars all spoiled but two; the brigantines have their rigging much shattered too, and two of them have lost their top masts; the Jersey has both main mast and fore mast shot through and spoiled, as also a shot under water which makes her leaky; a bomb fell into her, broke in her hold, and set her on fire; it was soon extinguished; but it is requisite they should go into some port to refit. The Norwich has her mizen mast shot through and spoiled; her foremast is also spoiled. She has been a ground near Calais, and has

215

knocked away a part of her halfe keel, and her rudder, since which she makes more water than usual.

The Captain's fore-yard was broke by a bomb from the enemy. Captain Benbow had the flesh torn from his leg, by an accident on board one of the bomb-vessels in the action, and, I doubt, will hardly be able to stir within a fortnight.

I have an account of fifteen men killed and wounded.[11]

John Benbow's legs seem to have been particularly vulnerable, as he was to die of complications following his right leg being shattered in the West Indies, in 1702.

Shovell spent the month of April in the Downs. He still had overall command of the blockade of Calais and Dunkirk. Francis Wyvill had been left as Commodore of the ships guarding the west channel leading into Dunkirk. Wyvill wrote a letter to the Earl of Shrewsbury complaining that he had insufficient ships for the purpose. The Admiralty told Shovell bluntly to either reinforce or replace him. Shovell appears to have been quite relaxed about the situation, replying to the Admiralty that Wyvill had sufficient ships to hinder a squadron or fleet of transports, such as might reasonably be expected to go from Dunkirk to Calais. He did send a squadron to guard the eastern channel into Dunkirk. Only clean 4th, 5th, or 6th rates could hope to catch the privateers.[12]

While aboard his flagship, the *Duchess*, in the Downs, Shovell had to deal with various courts martial. Robert Ball, Boatswain of the *Southampton*, had disobeyed a superior officer. For April 9th 1696 Shovell's order book has the following entry.

Where as at a Court Martial held on board his majesty's shipp Dutchess in the Downs on the 9th day of April instant a sentence was passed that Robert Ball, boatswain of the Southampton shall be carried in a boat with a halter about his neck and yet he shall receive 11 lashes on the bare back by ye side of each of those English flagg ship in the Downes and the like by ye side of ye Southampton whereon he belonged and his crime to be then declared with beat of drum.

The *Southampton* must have had problems of discipline at the time, as Shovell had had to court martial the stewards in her, for buggery, before sailing to bombard Calais.[13]

On April 11th Shovell was ordered with forty-nine ships to leave the Downs for Spithead. He prepared to sail, but five days later, just as he had raised his ship's anchor, orders came from the Admiralty to stay where he was. Probably the reason for this was the news that George Rooke would soon be back in England having wintered abroad with the Mediterranean fleet. Rooke had been sent out as a replacement for Edward Russell in the autumn of 1695, but had been able to achieve little as he considered that he had too few ships. He had been recalled with his ships that spring, to reinforce the Anglo/Dutch force in the Channel who were countering French invasion plans. In reality, the French had rapidly seen that an invasion was out of the question, once Russell and Shovell had placed their fleet off Calais and Dunkirk. Ex-King James had left Calais as early as March 10th 1696.[14]

While awaiting Rooke in the Downs, Shovell had been investigating the bizarre behaviour of Captain Smith of the *Hind pink*. Smith had been seized with a violent calenture and at two o'clock in the morning had gone ashore followed by his officers, who brought him back to the ship again. At eleven o'clock the next morning he had gone ashore again and had spent the day wandering in the fields, until that evening he was detained near Deal Church. The following morning he was taken to Canterbury jail where he recovered his senses and was released. Shovell in his report for the Admiralty does not give an explanation, although it is difficult not to think Smith was suffering from an excess of alcohol![15]

From mid April Shovell was clearly dissatisfied with his ship, the *Duchess*, and sought permission to move to the *Victory*. The *Victory* was a 100 gun 1st rate, originally built at Portsmouth in 1675 as the *Royal James*. She had been renamed the *Victory* in 1691 for no obvious reason. The Admiralty gave permission for the move on April 19th. A few days later it was agreed that Shovell could take his captain, two lieutenants, chaplain and surgeon with him from the *Duchess*. He actually received a commission to be Captain of the *Victory* dated April 22nd 1696, but the change of ship did not take place. The reason for the alteration of his plan is not clear, although it may have been associated with Rooke's arrival back in England.[16]

At the end of April 1696 Rooke, with his squadron from the Mediterranean, arrived in the Downs. His departure from this station opened the way for the French to move their Toulon fleet to Brest and so change the main sphere of naval activity for the year from the Mediterranean to the Channel. On arrival back in England, Rooke was immediately ordered to prepare his own ships and those of Shovell for sea. He was to block the path of the forty-seven ships of the Toulon fleet, under Louis Châteaurenault, from getting into Brest. For this expedition, Rooke was to go as Admiral and Commander-in-Chief and Shovell was promoted to be Admiral of the Blue. Shovell's commission as Admiral of the Blue is dated April 28th 1696, although according to Rooke's journal the commissions were not received until May 2nd, by which time they had reached St Helens.[17]

While at St Helens, Shovell did take the opportunity to change ships. Until May 6th Shovell was writing letters and signing orders from the

*Duchess*, but from the 9th onwards they were dictated from the *Queen*. The *Queen* was a 100 gun 1st rate, originally built as the *Royal Charles* at Portsmouth in 1673. The change over was effected at St Helens and Shovell was able to retain his captain from the *Duchess*, James Stewart, and several of his lieutenants.[18]

Early in May Rooke and Shovell, with a considerable number of ships, actually got underway to stop Châteaurenault's Toulon ships from getting into Brest. By May 10th they were off Ushant and four days later Rooke had firm intelligence that the Toulon fleet were already safely at Brest. Rooke and Shovell decided that, as the combined Brest and Toulon fleets outnumbered them and that their ships were foul, they would return to Torbay. This they did, and their fleet was reinforced there to 115 sail, of which eighty-five were larger vessels of the line of battle.[19]

Matters were made worse when Jean Bart escaped from John Benbow's blockade at Dunkirk during the same month, to attack two convoys in the North Sea before Benbow eventually caught up with him.[20]

At the end of May 1696, while at Torbay, it is possible that Shovell was told the news of the death of his uncle, Cloudesley Jenkenson, earlier that month. He had been buried at St Mary's, Whitechapel, on May 21st, in his 66th year. Cloudesley Jenkenson had also had a career in the navy as a midshipman, captain's clerk and probably Deputy Judge Advocate in 1690. It is likely that he and Shovell were close, in that Jenkenson's three children, William, Anne and Abigail, were all mentioned in Shovell's will. Shovell's daughter, Elizabeth, had been baptised in 1692, in the same church as Jenkenson's funeral had taken place. Elizabeth had been born in nearby Prescot Street, and probably uncle and nephew had houses in close proximity at the time. It was common for poorer tarpaulin officers to have houses in the eastern suburbs of London. Shovell himself, in the mid 1690s, had taken a much grander house in Soho Square.[21]

Rooke was recalled to London on May 27th to serve as one of the Lords of the Admiralty. Before leaving the fleet, he received reports that seventy French men of war were lying in Camaret Bay. On his arrival in London, Rooke suggested to the Secretary of State, the Earl of Shrewsbury, that they be attacked. The Privy Council asked for its consideration by a council of war, where it was promptly turned down.

John Berkeley of Stratton came down to the fleet as Commander-in-Chief on June 3rd, the same day as Rooke actually left for London. He too proposed the attacking of Brest, that had the support of the Privy Council, but was turned down in the same way as Rooke, in that the plan was deemed impracticable. Shovell's views on the matter are not recorded, but it seems likely that he was against the proposed assault on Camaret Bay. It is inconceivable that the other captains would have gone against the combined views of the two most senior naval officers without Shovell's support.[22]

218

Berkeley was not one to remain inactive for long, and he sailed on June 24th for the French coast. Shovell as second in command, in the *Queen*, went with him. They proposed to attack several islands in the Bay of Biscay. While passing Camaret Bay, the English fleet came across the Marquis de Nesmond who, with his squadron, was convoying some merchantmen. The French scuttled back to their anchorage to await a more favourable opportunity to sail. On July 3rd Berkeley detached the *Burford, Newcastle* and a fireship to the island of Groix. Numerous villages in Groix were destroyed and about 1,300 head of cattle taken. The main body of ships under Berkeley himself arrived off Belle Île on July 5th and anchored there for two days. Landings were made on the smaller islands of Hoat and Hoedic and more cattle brought off. Berkeley sent a further contingent to the Island of Rhé. Here the town of St Martin was bombarded before the local commander, George Mees, in the *Sandwich*, took his squadron to Olonne on the French mainland and threw a great number of bombs and carcasses into the town.[23]

What part did Shovell play in these attacks? Between July 5th and 9th his ship, the *Queen*, was anchored off Belleisle with the main contingent. There is no evidence of him being involved in the attack on the island of Rhé as is implied in his *Secret Memoirs*. His letter book for the period is full of minor matters, such as the distribution of bounty money that he and Matthew Aylmer had started in Torbay before sailing. Shovell gave Berkeley information about which ships in the blue squadron under his command had French colours. Presumably they were considering sailing under French colours as a means of confusing the enemy. On arrival at Belle Île, on July 5th, he did give orders to Vice Admiral David Mitchell to send two longboats with their crews to the *Kent*, to help with the landings. Shovell did not go ashore himself. Young Christopher Myngs, Captain of the *St Michael*, and Shovell's former ship, the *Duchess*, were both in his division for this action.[24]

Leaving Belle Île, Berkeley and Shovell spent the remainder of the month with their ships alarming the coast of France. By July 25th they were back in Torbay as they were running short of supplies.[25]

Shovell spent most of the month of August at Torbay in the *Queen*. His letter book is full of mundane matters such as new masts, stinking beer and rotten cheese. Berkeley wanted to come to London to deal with his private affairs, but Shrewsbury refused his request. On August 31st Berkeley and Shovell took the fleet to Spithead. It was decided that the larger ships be laid up for the winter as autumn was upon them and it was customary to use the higher rates during the winter.[26]

In the life of Captain Stephen Martin, it is stated that Shovell hoisted his flag as Admiral of the Blue on board the *London*, a 96 gun 1st rate, on August 20th, but struck the next day. The *London* was at the Nore. This does not fit in with known facts. Certainly Shovell was at Torbay aboard the *Queen* on August 17th, and it is likely that he was still there on the day in question, the 20th.[27]

In mid August a decision was made to send a squadron to the Mediterranean. The Duke of Savoy had abandoned his allies in June 1696 and had made a separate peace with France. Since Rooke had returned in the spring, the Mediterranean had been largely abandoned to the French. It was hoped that the squadron would help defend Spain and discourage others from throwing in their lot with the French. The expedition was of a size to be led by a vice admiral and the only two in pay at the time were David Mitchell and John Neville. Both asked to be excused, as they had served in the Mediterranean for a prolonged period and were not inclined to return so soon. The ever loyal Shovell agreed to take the squadron despite the fact he was a full Admiral of the Blue. He might well have claimed that he had had more than enough of the Mediterranean, having served there almost continuously between 1674 and 1686. Shovell received a commission to be Admiral and Commander-in-Chief of His Majesty's ships in the Mediterranean, dated August 25th 1696. In the event, neither he nor a large squadron sailed for the Mediterranean because of lack of money and provisions. Between August and the following November Luttrell recorded some details of the planned expedition. Shovell was to have confirmed peace treaties with Algiers, Tripoli and Tunis. Twenty thousand pounds had been sent to pay off the squadron at Portsmouth. Neville was to have gone with Shovell after all. On November 5th Neville did take some ships to the Straits, but Shovell was retained for the winter guard.[28]

On September 18th 1696 Shovell received a certificate to register him as a seaman. The responsible office had been set up earlier in the year to help make seamen available for manning the fleet. John Hill, Shovell's father-in-law, and George Byng were to serve in this office as Commissioners, until it was abandoned in 1699. Shovell's certificate stated:

> These are to certify that Cloudesley Shovell aged forty five years being a tall and well set man of a fair complexion is registered for the service of his Majesty in the Royall Navy according to an act of Parliament made in ye seventh year of his Majesties reign. Instituted an act for the increase and encouragement of seamen and the said Cloudesley Shovell is accordingly registered in the books of this office on the 18th day of September 1696.

Among the Commissioners' signatures are those of both Hill and Byng. The document is interesting in that it tells us about Shovell's physical appearance at the time. He was tall, well set and of a fair complexion. In later life he was to run to fat.[29]

During the period from October to December 1696 the House of Commons considered the alleged miscarriages of the fleet during the summer and in particular the allowing of the French Toulon fleet into Brest. Both Rooke and Shovell were subjected to several strict examinations. Shovell gave a good account and nothing could be found against the naval officers in the way of an omission or breach of duty. They had simply followed the orders they had been given. This must have been a worrying period for Shovell, as earlier in the autumn the conduct of Henry Killigrew, Ralph Delavall and himself with the Smyrna Convoy, in 1693, had been raised again. Sir John Fenwick, in a letter passed on by the Duke of Devonshire to William III, alleged that Delavall and Killigrew intended to keep the fleet out of the way of a proposed landing in England by ex-King James II. Shovell was not directly implicated as he was considered not a man "to be spoken to", but Killigrew and Delavall were said to be able to master him as they pleased. There was no evidence for any of this, and Fenwick's testimony does not seem to have been taken seriously. Shovell by this time loathed James II and his religion, and was a man of principle who would not be manipulated in this way by anyone.[30]

During his difficulties with the House of Commons, a happier event took place in the Shovell household. On November 18th 1696 his second child, another daughter Anne, was baptised at St Olave, Hart Street, having been born earlier in the month. This was the church of the parish of her maternal grandfather, John Hill, and where her mother, Elizabeth, had been married firstly to John Narbrough.[31]

Shovell's final naval activity of the year was to take a combined Anglo/Dutch contingent of forty-two ships to sea in December, to stop the French Admiral, Jean de Pointis, from leaving Brest with a squadron. There had been speculation in England that de Pointis was intent on invading England, but in fact his destination was the West Indies. Unfortunately, Shovell arrived on the French coast six days after de Pointis had left Brest. Shovell's voyage continued until the middle of January 1697 when he returned to Spithead.[32]

After his unsuccessful attempt to stop the French leaving Brest, Shovell went to London, leaving the fleet under the command of Matthew Aylmer. The next month, on February 27th, John Berkeley of Stratton died of a violent and obstinate pleurisy. In modern terms, it seems likely that he died from pneumonia. In the last three years he had worked closely with Shovell as his immediate superior. His death enabled Shovell to succeed him as Colonel of the Second Marine Regiment on March 1st, with Aylmer becoming Lieutenant Colonel in Shovell's place.[33]

On April 9th 1697 Shovell wrote to the Mayor of Rochester, the city he represented in Parliament, one J. Conney. The Mayor appeared to have been pushing a man for the post of surgeon.

Tower Hill 9th April '97

I have yours of the 26th instant and desire you be pleased to do me the justice to believe it is that I have been diverted by the business of some more than ordinary importance that it is so long unanswered especially in the matter that might naturally cause an expectation as to which I must acquaint you that I had before been engaged by several friends to continue the surgeon that did belong to my Regiment. But give me leave withall to assure you that nothing need have been added to your recommendation to engage me to the choice of a person for that employment were I not under a preengagement as after that I am.

Clearly, Shovell was keen not to offend a civic dignitary of the city he represented. The author has found few letters concerning his representation of Rochester in Parliament.[34]

Perhaps Shovell's preoccupation with some "business of more than ordinary importance" was the preparation for escorting William III to Holland, which he carried out later that April.[35]

At about this time a Captain John Shovell of Ratcliff died. His will was proved on May 11th 1697. The exact relationship between him and Cloudesley Shovell is uncertain. However, he may have been a son of Cloudesley's Uncle Nathaniel, making him a first cousin. John Shovell is mentioned in Cloudesley's account book as a cousin and appears to have served in the same squadron, as Captain of the *Expedition*, in 1696. The son of John Shovell, another John and again mentioned in Cloudesley's account book, is thought to have died early in 1699. According to the account book, he was starting a voyage to New England in October 1697 and was lent ten pounds by his kinsman. Cloudesley appears to have been generous to his various relatives in supporting them financially if need be. The death of John Shovell senior left a vacancy as captain of the *Expedition* and Cloudesley appears to have given the command to his flag captain in the *Duchess* and *Queen*, James Stewart. Certainly Stewart was involved in a celebrated fight in her with two French ships on the following August 22nd.[36]

The summer campaign season of 1697 in home waters, where Shovell served in the fleet under George Rooke, was not an auspicious one. The main centre of naval activity that year was in the West Indies, where Jean de Pointis sacked Carthagena in New Spain (now Colombia), before returning to France. John Neville had chased him with a squadron, but was just too late in arriving at Carthagena to catch him.[37]

Rooke's and Shovell's fleet in the Channel and the Western Approaches during the summer, met with little success. A French squadron under Louis Châteaurenault was allowed to get out of Brest, and beyond the convoying of trade, little was done. The ships were usually foul, poorly manned and never properly provisioned. Rooke's and Shovell's views on this subject have been recorded in a letter from James Vernon to the Earl of Shrewsbury.

> June 24th 1697
> Sir G. Rooke sailed to St. Helens two days ago. He writes very melancholy accounts to the Admiralty and Cloudesley Shovell speaks yet plainer not only of the small quantity of their provisions but the quality too is not very good especially of the bread and the want of pease and oatmeal is so visible that already the scurvy exceedingly increases in the fleet to a high degree.[38]

There is some doubt about exactly which ships Shovell served in in 1697. He appears to have been in the *Queen* at the beginning of the year, and may have had young Christopher Myngs as his flag captain from June 20th. Presumably James Stewart moved into the *Expedition* at this time. However, Luttrell reported that in early June Shovell was in the *London*, a 96 gun 1st rate that had been built at Deptford in 1670.[39]

The situation in the summer of 1697 was one of stalemate. Barcelona had fallen, and Catalonia without the support of the English fleet was at the mercy of France. In September Louis XIV offered reasonable terms of peace, and the eight-year-war was brought to an end by the Treaty of Ryswick.[40]

The English Navy had not added much to the reputation that it had gained under Cromwell and Charles II. Shovell and Rooke were the only successful flag officers of the war. Both had achieved fame as subordinates and mostly under Edward Russell.[41]

Soon after the Treaty of Ryswick was signed, Shovell as the new Colonel of the Second Marine Regiment wrote to the Navy Board complaining about the payment of marines and the clothing deduction.

> I observe there is great clamour about the officers receiving the marine pay. I therefore take the opportunity to acquaint your lordships that it has always been my opinion that the marines should receive their own pay due for their services as the seamen do at the pay of the ships and I dread such an innovation as that the man that serves his Ma[ty] at sea should be denied what he serves for. I know not where that mischief will end. But [at] the same time the money due for Regimental clothes, or for recruits of shoes, stockings, shirts, or tobacco (which are all the recruits that I think absolutely necessary) should be stopped at pay table out of wages of the Dead and Runn; and in case it should happen that their wages shall not suffice, that the King should stand to the loss, as it is in the seaman's case, which I am confident, will seldom happen and be very inconsiderable. And that

if a marine happens to be turned over out of a ship into another before he has wages enough due to pay for his cloathes, that the debt for his cloathes shall be transfered to any ship he serves in, as is likewise in the case of seamen. And that the man's receipts, witnessed by an officer etc or any other instrument in writing such as their lordships shall think fitt, shall be an authentick voucher with, and a sufficient direction to the Commissioners of the Navy to stop money due for such regimental cloathes etc as well from the Dead and Runn as from the living.[42]

Shovell received an unsatisfactory reply from the Navy Board. However, in due course the Lord Commissioners of the Admiralty decreed that marines would be paid in the same manner as seamen at the pay of their ship, rather than through their colonel. In the end, Shovell had had his own way with at least part of his request for the marines.[43]

Shovell's final duty of 1697 was to convoy the King back to England in October.[44]

## NOTES

1. Campbell, Vol.III, pp.186–188; London Gazette No. 3161; Laird Clowes, p.487; Richmond, p.262.
2. Marsham MSS U1515.011; NMM, SMF21 (PHB/17).
3. NMM, SMF21 (PHB/17); Campbell, Vol.III, pp.188–189; Anderson, Lists of Men of War; Torrington, p.78.
4. Buccleuch MSS, Vol.II, Part 1, p.309.
5. Campbell, Vol.III, p.189.
6. RMT MAT 25; *Montagu* log by Lt. R. Coleman 25/12/95–29/8/96 P.R.O. No. 315.
7. Marsham MSS U1515.17; Buccleuch MSS, Vol.II, Part I, pp.310–311.
8. NMM, SMF21 (PHB/17).
9. NMM, SMF21 (PHB/17).
10. NMM, SMF21 (PHB/17); House of Lords MSS 1693–95, N.S.
11. Charnock, p.24; NMM, SMF21 (PHB/17).
12. Marsham MSS U1515.17; NMM, SMF21 (PHB/17).
13. Marsham MSS U1515.17; NMM, SMF21 (PHB/17).
14. NMM, SMF21 (PHB/17); Marsham MSS U1515.17; Torrington, p.79; Richmond, pp.262–263.
15. NMM, SMF 21 (PHB/17).
16. Marsham MSS U1515.17; NMM, SMF21 (PHB/17); Anderson, Lists of Men of War; RMT MAT 25, CS Commissions.
17. NMM, SMF 21 (PHB/17); Marsham MSS U1515.17; Richmond, p.263; RMT MAT 25, CS Commissions; Portland MSS, Vol.X, p.13.
18. NMM, SMF 21 (PHB/17); Anderson, Lists of Men of War.
19. NMM, SMF 21(PHB/17); Marsham MSS U1515.17; Campbell, Vol.III, pp.190–191.
20. Laird Clowes, pp.487–488.
21. Notes and Queries, 8th S., VII, Jan 19th 1895; Davies, Gentlemen and Tarpaulins p.56.

22. Campbell, Vol.III, pp.191–192; NMM, SMF 21 (PHB/17).
23. Campbell, Vol.III, pp.192–193; Laird Clowes, pp.488–489; Secret Memoirs; London Gazette No. 4204.
24. NMM, SMF 21 (PHB/17); Secret Memoirs.
25. Campbell, Vol.III, p.193; Burchett, pp.547, 548.
26. NMM, SMF 21 (PHB/17); Buccleuch MSS, Vol.II, Part i, p.382; Campbell, Vol.VI, pp.192–193.
27. Life of Stephen Martin, p.26; NMM, SMF 21 (PHB/17).
28. Richmond, p.264; Buccleuch MSS, Vol.II, Part I, p.385; Luttrell, Vol.IV, pp.102, 105, 112, 118, 124, 125, 134, 136; RMT MAT 25; ADM 6/4 f.19.
29. RMT MAT 25.
30. Campbell, Vol.III, p.196; Luttrell, Vol.IV, p.152; Buccleuch MSS, Vol.II, Part 1, p.396.
31. Notes and Queries, 8th S, VII, Jan 19th 1895; RMT MAT 33.
32. Richmond, p.273; Luttrell, Vol.IV, pp.156–159, 161; Campbell, Vol.III, pp.223–224.
33. Luttrell, Vol.IV, pp.170, 191; Campbell, Vol.VI, p.195; Edye, p.495; H.O. Milt. Entry book, Vol.III, p.282.
34. Bodleian Library, Rawlinson MSS A.289.144.
35. Luttrell, Vol.IV, p.211.
36. RMT MAT 3, 24; NMM, SMF 221 (PHB/17); Laird Clowes, p.496.
37. Laird Clowes, pp.487–496; Richmond, pp.273–274.
38. Illustrative letters of the reign of William III, edited by G. James 1841; Laird Clowes, p.365.
39. ADM 33/186; Lutterell, Vol.IV, p.235; Anderson, Lists of Men of War.
40. Richmond, p.274.
41. Laird Clowes, p.365; Ehrmann, p.605.
42. Sergisson MSS Sept. 18th 1697.
43. Edye, Vol.I, pp.500–502.
44. Luttrell, Vol.IV, p.289.

# CHAPTER XVIII

# Vigo and the Spanish Succession
# 1698–1702

The War with France had ended the previous autumn with the signing of the Treaty of Ryswick, on September 11th 1697. Under its terms France withdrew support for James II and acknowledged William III to be King of England, with his sister-in-law, Anne, as his successor. In addition, France surrendered all conquests since the Treaty of Nijmegen, and the main fortresses of the Netherlands were placed in the hands of the Dutch. Peace of a sort reigned in Europe.[1]

From the naval viewpoint, the years 1698 until the beginning of the War of the Spanish Succession in 1702 were relatively quiet ones. During this time Shovell was able to find a certain amount of time for his own affairs and those of a non-naval nature.

Early in 1698, on February 5th, Shovell's account book shows that he paid Tom Shorting £2.00 for the christening of his child. Shorting was married to Shovell's half-sister, Anne Flaxman, and they were to have eleven children.[2] On March 10th Shovell witnessed a document paying interest to Edward Russell for money that he had loaned in the recent war.[3]

Shovell and Sir Joseph Williamson had been the Members of Parliament for Rochester since 1695. That Parliament came to an end on July 7th 1698, and the two of them were returned to the House of Commons on July 22nd, and were to continue until further elections in December 1700.[4] Shovell had been Colonel of the Second Marine Regiment since the previous year. On July 18th 1698 William III gave orders that the two marine regiments under the Earl of Carmarthen and Shovell were to be reformed into a single regiment under Colonel Thomas Brudenall. The cause of the amalgamation and the removal from command of their two colonels is unclear. Carmarthen was said to be dilatory and inclined towards the War Office rather than the Admiralty. Indeed, he was said to be indifferent to Admiralty orders! On the other hand, Shovell, who at first had declined the command of one of the regiments of marines, had since his appointment taken a most practical and useful share in the higher development of the service, having regard to its efficiency and well being. Perhaps William III brought the disbandment about because of the unpopularity of the marine regiments in the country.[5]

The disbandment of the marine regiments would drag on into 1699 and later. On April 1st 1699 the House of Commons ordered the Commissioners of the Admiralty to lay before the House an account of what was due to the officers of the two marine regiments commanded by Carmarthen and Shovell. The next month Shovell was told to discharge all marine officers from his ships. On October 23rd Shovell was ordered to London to do all in his power to adjust the accounts of his former marine regiment. As late as 1700 Shovell was writing to the Treasury in support of the ex-subalterns of his regiment who had received only half pay since early 1697.[6]

In July 1698 Shovell commanded the squadron convoying William III to Holland and the following October escorted him back to England. For the return journey Shovell was in the *Swiftsure* and a copy of his signals drawn up on October 2nd is in existence. The *Swiftsure* was a 3rd rate of 70 guns.[7]

In August Shovell was made Admiral of the Blue and Commander-in-Chief in the Thames and Medway.[8]

During the spring of 1699 Shovell received further commissions to continue as Commander-in-Chief in the Thames and Medway. By May there was concern in England at the possible hostile intentions of the French court, and preparations were made for a squadron to cruise in the Channel. Command of this squadron of fourteen ships was given to Shovell and its presence probably led to the continuation of the peace.[9]

Shovell had been an extra Commissioner of the Navy since April 20th 1693. On March 26th 1699 he was made Comptroller of the Accounts of the Victualling Office and was to continue in this capacity until Christmas Day 1704. Soon after this appointment, in May, there were suggestions that Shovell should move to the Admiralty Board. Nothing came of it, but Shovell's concern about the proposal can be seen from the following letters. Extract from a letter to Mr James Vernon:

> Swiftsure, in the Downs, 17th May 1699.
> Right honourable,
> Before I came to the fleet it was talked that I should be removed to the admiralty board; I then solicited my Lord Orford [Edward Russell], that he would be so far my friend as to let me continue at the navy board, from whence, if I fell, my fall would be easy.
> I hear my Lord Orford is out of all his employment; and still the report holds that I shall remove from the navy to the admiralty board. If such a thing be designed (as I hope not) I humbly and heartily beg you will excuse me to his majesty. I am now easy and quiet in an unenvied employment; but to put me into the admiralty is to set me up where I am pretty sure to be tumbled down – for if my Lord Orford cannot stand, whose services have been so eminent, what can poor I expect?
> I know your goodness will excuse my impertinence; and I hope you will ever give me leave to subscribe myself,
> Right honourable, your most obedient and humble servant
> C.S.

In a further letter on the matter, this time to the Earl of Orford himself, Shovell went on:

> I do hear, from several hands, that I shall be removed to the admiralty. I have written to secretary Vernon, to desire he will excuse me to his Majesty; and do beg of your lordship, if you meet the secretary in your walks, that you will engage him to excuse me. I know your lordship can do anything with him, he having expressed much honour and friendship for your lordship.[10]

Shovell shows a curious lack of ambition and confidence at this juncture. Perhaps he had still not got over the Smyrna convoy problems of 1693.[11]

Also in May Shovell escorted William III to Holland, and on the following September 21st he sailed again with ten men of war to protect the King's return to England. There is in existence an original document signed by Shovell, on September 29th 1699, from the *Swiftsure* to William Blathwayt, at the Hague, stating that he is off the coast of Holland waiting to escort His Majesty to England.[12]

During the summer of 1700 Shovell again commanded a squadron in the Channel, keeping a watchful eye on the French as Admiral of the Blue. In April there were suggestions that, if George Rooke were indisposed, Shovell would take his place as Commander of the squadron for the Baltic. In the event, Rooke took the squadron in June 1700, plus a Dutch contingent, to support Charles XII of Sweden against the Danes. A peace was signed in August.[13]

Shovell did not accompany Rooke to the Baltic, but did his customary escort duty of William III to and from Holland, in the late summer and early autumn. In May he took part in the trial of a Mr Fitch, a master builder of His Majesty's docks, in an action for defamation brought by Edward Dummer, who had been displaced as Surveyor and Commissioner of the Navy, the previous year. Fitch claimed that Dummer had been taking bribes and as a result of these accusations, which he was unable to prove, Dummer had lost his job. In the action heard before Lord Chief Justice Holt, Shovell with the other Commissioners of the Navy gave evidence for the plaintiff who was awarded damages of £500.[14]

In the 1690s, after his marriage to Elizabeth Narbrough, Shovell had bought a country house, May Place, at Crayford in Kent, not far from his Parliamentary seat at Rochester. On July 1st 1700 Shovell was made a Deputy Lieutenant of Kent, with his commission signed by Henry, Earl of Romney.[15]

In December 1700 Parliament was dissolved, and in new elections on January 4th 1701 Shovell and Sir Joseph Williamson were again returned for Rochester. Later that month, on January 23rd, Shovell's stepdaughter Elizabeth Narbrough (daughter of Sir John) married Thomas D'Aeth, who was to be made a baronet in 1716.[16]

Late in 1700 Charles II, last Spanish King of the Hapsburg dynasty, died. Louis XIV claimed the Spanish crown on behalf of his grandson Philip, Duke of Anjou. Some time later, the Holy Roman Emperor Leopold I made a counter claim for his son Charles. Ultimately, England and Holland were to side with the Emperor against Louis XIV, and this question of inheritance led to the War of the Spanish Succession, which was to start in 1702 and in which Shovell was to play a leading role. Louis XIV compounded the problem in 1701, after the death of James II at St Germains, by proclaiming Prince James Edward King of England, Ireland and Scotland. Naturally this caused great offence in England and to William III in particular.

Yet again, during the summer of 1701 Shovell was to serve in the

Channel as Admiral of the Blue, on this occasion under the overall command of George Rooke. His ship in 1701 was the *Barfleur*, a 90 gun 2nd rate. If anything, the atmosphere with France was even more tense than in the previous year, in what was to be a gradual build up to the War. Early in April Shovell was reported to have gone down the river to Greenwich to take command of ships drawing together in the Downs. He must have got ashore again later in the month for on April 29th he was signing his will! Why his final will, which was to be proved after his death some six and a half years later, was drawn up at this particular juncture is unknown. Later in the summer Shovell took part in discussions with Rooke on the question of gunnery and the date by which the great ships should be brought in for the winter. Finally, he carried out his customary autumnal duty of escorting William III back from Holland.[17]

In September 1701 Shovell found time to pay a rare visit to Rochester, the city that he had represented in Parliament since 1695. No doubt his naval duties kept him fully occupied. The Mayor of Rochester entertained him to dinner and the city records give an account of the fare and its cost.

| | |
|---|---:|
| Bread and Beir | 15 4 |
| Wine | 9 11 8 |
| 6 Fowls with beacon and sproats | 13 0 |
| A rump of beef | 7 6 |
| 2 geese with apple sauce | 8 0 |
| 2 piggs | 8 0 |
| A Pedgione pye | 8 0 |
| A legg of Mutton and Turnipps | 4 0 |
| A dish of wild fowle | 10 0 |
| A shoulder of mutton & pickells | 3 6 |
| A large apple pye and cheese | 4 0 |
| 2 dishes of mince pyes | 10 0 |
| Fire | 10 0 |
| Tobacco | 9 0 |
| | £15 2 0 |

The Mayor could afford to provide a sumptuous banquet for Shovell, after his generosity in paying for the elaborate ceiling in the Guildhall, on first being elected to Parliament for Rochester in 1695.[18]

On November 11th 1701 Parliament was dissolved, and in the new one of December 30th neither Shovell nor Williamson had seats. Francis Barrell, a Tory, Oxford-educated barrister, and Captain William Bokenham replaced them. Bokenham had been Captain of the *Grafton* at Barfleur and the following year was to command the *Association* at Vigo. He also had had a company in Shovell's Second Marine Regiment.[19]

Early in the New Year of 1702, on January 28th, Shovell was given a commission to continue as Admiral of the Blue.[20] On March 8th William III died and Anne, his sister-in-law, came to the throne. William's death did not stop the outbreak of the War of the Spanish Succession which began on May 4th, with English support for Charles, the son of Leopold I.

In March 1702 Shovell commanded a squadron in the Downs and Rooke one at Spithead. Possibly during this period, Michael Dahl painted one of his portraits of Shovell that is now in the National Maritime Museum. The portrait shows a ship in the background with a blue flag at the main mast indicating an admiral of the blue. Shortly after the opening of the War of the Spanish Succession, Shovell was to be promoted and was no longer entitled to fly this particular flag.[21]

Contrary to Campbell's view, that Shovell was not much in favour at the beginning of Anne's reign, he was made Admiral of the White, two days after the outbreak of war on May 6th.

In June both Shovell and Rooke were at Spithead with their respective squadrons. Rooke had been given orders to take a fleet of ships plus the troops of the Duke of Ormonde (14,000 men) to Cadiz with a view to capturing the port. Cadiz was looked upon in England as a stepping stone to an attempt on the important French naval base at Toulon and control of the Mediterranean. If Cadiz were to prove too strong, Rooke and Ormonde would attack Vigo, Corunna or Gibraltar. A council of war, in the *Royal Sovereign*, was held on June 15th with Rooke, Shovell, Ormonde and the Dutch admirals present. A decision was made to attempt Corunna if French ships were present, and if not to proceed south and to think again. Rooke ordered Shovell, the same day, to take command of the ships remaining at Spithead and to try the unfortunate Sir John Munden.[22] Munden, at the end of May 1702, had commanded a squadron attempting to stop the Spanish West Indian fleet under convoy of Admiral de Casse, which had sailed from Rochelle, from getting into Corunna. The combined French/Spanish fleet had slipped past him at night and there was little he could do to rectify the matter. Munden was suspended on June 28th and he was tried by court martial and acquitted. Queen Anne insisted upon a revision of the sentence so that he was declared guilty and dismissed the service. He never commanded a ship, let alone a squadron again. What Shovell, who had been forced to carry out the court martial, thought about the affair, is unknown. It is likely that the government acting in the Queen's name had yielded to public pressure.[23]

In early July 1702 Shovell received what he considered to be humiliating orders to take three clean ships under his command at Spithead and search for a French squadron of which the Admiralty had intelligence. A mission of this sort, he felt, did not warrant an Admiral of the White and he was even more displeased when he discovered that Admiral George Churchill was trying to displace various people from their posts, in order to advance others. Shovell discussed the matter with one of his captains, George Byng, and then wrote a stiff letter of complaint to the Admiralty. In the letter he said that the order was particularly meant to treat him with indignity and that this command was very improper for his flag. Shovell wanted to go ashore and suggested that the orders be given to his senior captain, as they were more proper for him. When Churchill and the Admiralty found him so angry and not knowing how much he might expose them, they got Queen Anne to write him a placatory letter. It was unlike Shovell to show his anger in this way, but in the event when he sailed he had only two ships beside his own and a fireship! He was soon back in Spithead.[24]

On July 20th Rooke, Ormonde and the army sailed from Torbay for Corunna, leaving Shovell to command in the Channel. By now Shovell had eleven ships to stop French vessels from Brest following Rooke to the south or making mischief in the Channel proper. Matters had been further complicated, on July 14th, with news from John Benbow, in the West Indies, that the French Admiral Châteaurenault had sailed for Europe with the Spanish Plate fleet. Three days later the Admiralty ordered Shovell to look out for Châteaurenault and to intercept him in his passage back to France, with liberty to cruise in any station this side of Cape Finisterre. Shovell's slender resources would have to be stretched even further.[25]

Well might Shovell write on July 19th to Daniel Finch, the Earl of Nottingham:

> ... the misfortune and vice of our country is to believe ourselves better than other men, which I take to be the reason that generally we send too small a force to execute our designs; but experience has taught me that, when men are equally inured and disciplined in war, 'tis without a miracle, numbers that gain the victory. For both in fleets, squadrons and single ships of nearly equal force, by the time one is beaten and ready to retreat, the other is also beaten and glad his enemy has left him. To fight, beat and chase an enemy of the same strength I have sometimes seen, but rarely seen at sea any victory worth the boasting when the strength has been near equal.[26]

Clearly Shovell was concerned by the impracticability of his orders, for the next day he wrote to the Admiralty:

> This order directs me to take all possible care to prevent the French from proceeding to the southward after that part of the fleet that's gone with Sir George Rooke, as also to obstruct their coming into and committing insults in the Channel; and it further directs me to look out for and endeavour to intercept Mons. Château Rénault, who

[probably] will be in these seas very shortly. To do either of which three services, modestly speaking, will require three times as many ships of the line of battle as are in that list [of his squadron].

If I had a squadron that was able to cope with or exceeded the enemy in these seas, then my opinion would be to lie a station from 20 to 40 leagues W.S.W. and S.W. from Ushant; for there I might probably meet any ships going from Brest to follow Sir George Rooke; and there chance might bring Château Rénault, if he comes for Brest or Rochefort; and there, if we are superior to the French, 'tis highly probable they would never venture to insult our Channel and leave a squadron that is able to attack them without them.

(From a prize taken about a month ago, he [Shovell] learns that they might have in these western ports of France thirty ships of the line of battle.) And as for Château Rénault's squadron, I have seen a list of twenty eight sail, which I suppose to have been just upon his sailing from Martinique, twenty six of which have upwards of fifty guns. I am apt to believe the bulk of it, for such a treasure will pay for a very extraordinary convoy.

And I having but ten men of war with me of the line of battle, which as soon as they are ready I shall put to sea with, as my orders direct, but in this condition it will be impossible for me to perform any of those services my orders seem to require; and I think of taking my station in the Chops of the Channel, between the Lizard and the Forne Head, to endeavour as much as I can to interrupt their insulting the Channel. In which case the two other services will lie wholly neglected, and the third not well secured; for if the enemy come with great superiority I cannot prevent them from insulting the Channel, for they will either drive me before them or take me along with them.

You will see by what I have writ that I am in a great dilemma how to perform my orders. And as I esteem Admiral Churchill and it as a great favour and service to me and to the country that they will send me word that they approve my design, or direct me where they think I made a misjudgement.[27]

Twice Shovell was to inform the Admiralty that the orders given to him could not be successfully followed without an increase in the number of available ships. He was to spend the latter part of July, August and September in the approaches of the Channel and the Bay of Biscay with his inadequate force. By August Shovell's contingent was further reduced by sickness amongst the seamen, although in mid September efforts were made to reinforce him with six men of war which had convoyed home the East Indian ships.[28]

A number of ships were taken by Shovell during this period, who spent 1702 in the 100 gun 1st rate, the *Queen*. One of them was said to be worth

£60,000 and was sent to Portsmouth. Possibly this was the *Saint Josepf* of Brest. Amongst a bundle of Shovell's commissions is a French commission or letter of marque, signed by Louis Alexandre de Bourbon to Jacques Latouche, to equip and arm the *Saint Josepf* and signed on August 25th.[29]

While Shovell and his squadron occupied themselves in the Channel, Rooke with sixty men of war plus transport ships, making about 200 sail in all, was carrying Ormonde's troops to Corunna. Finding no French ships there, they sailed on to Cadiz. Rooke and Ormonde received information that Cadiz was too strongly held to be taken by a coup de main. Ormonde decided, on August 15th, to land his troops on the other side of the bay at Rota and to take Cadiz by degrees. Almost immediately disagreement broke out amongst the English sailors, soldiers and the Dutch contingent about what course of action to follow. Rooke yet again was incapacitated by gout and was confined to bed in his cabin, unable even to sign documents which were left to his second in command, Vice Admiral Thomas Hopsonn. For three weeks aimless and undisciplined operations were conducted around the suburbs of Cadiz, with a great deal of plundering and drunkenness. Prince George of Hesse Darmstadt, who was representing the Emperor Joseph, vetoed the idea of a bombardment or anything that would put the Spanish people against the Hapsburg cause. He suggested proceeding to a port near Alicante while he promised to raise Valencia, Aragon and Catalonia to the allies' cause. Possibly, because of his ill health, Rooke, who by now was suffering from a fever as well as gout, would have none of it, pointing out his orders to go no farther than Cadiz. Rooke decided to return home despite the protests of Ormonde and others.[30]

Meanwhile, Shovell in the Channel and on the French coast had been forced back to Spithead with a sprung main mast. The Admiralty ordered him to range down towards Corunna as they considered all possible options for the destination of Châteaurenault and the Spanish Plate fleet. In fact, on reaching the Azores, Châteaurenault received intelligence of the whereabouts of Rooke's fleet. His original destination had been Cadiz, but he now tried to persuade his Spanish colleagues that they should make for Brest and safety. Perhaps not surprisingly, the Spanish would not accept this, suspecting that would be the last they saw of their treasure. Eventually Vigo was selected as their final destination. On September 11th they slipped in there unopposed, with Shovell to the north and Rooke to the south.[31]

During mid September Rooke's fleet, set on returning to England, sailed up the coast of Portugal. On the 18th Paul Methuen, the Ambassador at Lisbon, was given intelligence that the Plate fleet was in Vigo harbour. He sent off messenger after messenger to the coast, to make contact with Rooke. Eventually Rooke received the information from the captain of one of his frigates, the *Pembroke*, which had been late in starting the return journey and had battled her way through bad weather and heavy seas to catch him. By this time, Rooke was off the extreme north of Portugal and was said to be reluctant to make any attack on Vigo, as were many of the other officers. However, the Dutch contingent under Philip Almonde prevailed and a course was set for Vigo. The government in London had also received intelligence that the Plate fleet was in Vigo and letters were sent to both Rooke and Shovell, but did not reach them until later.[32]

On October 10th 1702, as Rooke and his fleet approached Vigo, they came across a small English division of ships commanded by George Byng, who had been sent out to reinforce Shovell's squadron. Byng told Rooke that Shovell's squadron was on its new station not far away off Cape Finisterre. Rooke ordered Byng away to fetch Shovell and his squadron as reinforcement for the attack on Vigo. Byng was most unhappy at being sent away just as an attack was to be launched on Vigo, and found all kinds of reasons for not going. However, Rooke was adamant and he went off in search of the Shovell squadron. Byng was lucky, for on the morning of October 11th he came upon several ships belonging to Shovell's squadron, who unfortunately had not seen their admiral for several days, having been separated by bad weather. Byng left three ships on station to pass on Rooke's orders for Shovell, and immediately set sail for a rapid return to Vigo. Having been lucky to find members of Shovell's squadron so quickly, Byng was even more fortunate to be able to sail back to Vigo before the day's action, on October 11th, was over. Byng had not followed Rooke's orders to the letter, so keen was he not to miss the action.[33]

Shovell had, on October 5th, been sent orders from England to join Rooke and to discuss the possibility of taking or destroying the Plate fleet at Vigo. It is likely that this information did not reach him until after he received Rooke's direct orders, via Byng, to go to Vigo. In the event, Shovell and his squadron were not to reach Vigo until five days after the action, on October 16th.[34]

Rooke reached Vigo on October 11th. He found the Plate fleet in the innermost recesses of the Gulf, protected by a strong boom and a fort. The ships had been arranged in a pattern for a concentrated fire. Rooke made no attempt to wait for the arrival of Shovell's reinforcements. Vice Admiral Thomas Hopsonn, Rooke's second in command, was selected to lead the assault, and Rooke returned to his sick bed. With great courage, Hopsonn charged the boom and broke it. Once into the harbour, the breeze dropped and Hopsonn's ship was isolated between two French men of war. Eventually the breeze returned and reinforcements came to Hopsonn's aid. Troops took the surrounding batteries and the scene became one of carnage. Stephen Martin, who was present at the action, recorded that "for some time there was nothing to be heard or seen but cannonading, burning, men and guns flying in the air, and altogether the most lively scene of horror and confusion that can be imagined". By the

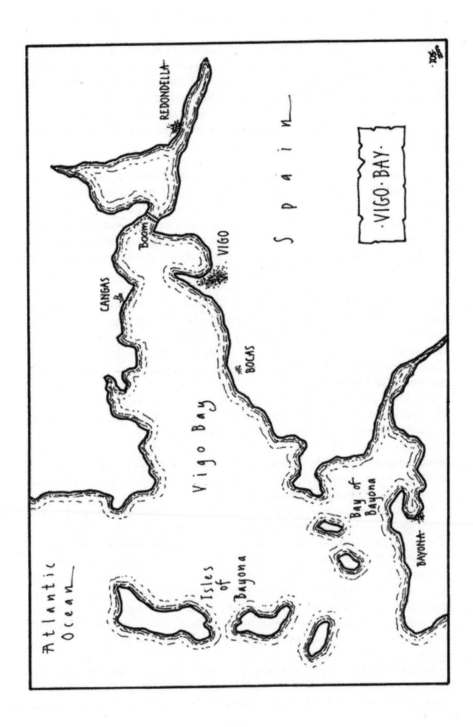

end of the day, Châteaurenault's ships and the Plate fleet had ceased to exist.[35]

Much of the treasure had been unloaded from the Plate fleet and carried up country before Rooke's men could lay hands on it. Some had been lost in Vigo harbour during the destruction of the ships. However, about £1,000,000 – £1,750,000 worth of goods fell into English hands.[36]

Poor Shovell came sailing into Vigo five days after the action, on October 16th. Two days later Rooke recorded in his journal his orders for Shovell.

> To remain at Vigo till he should get the prizes rigged and in a condition to sail, and unlade those galleons that were ashore, and such of them afloat as cannot be brought away, with a strict order against embezzlement and a power to suspend immediately any officer he should find so doing and to lose no time on that service, but to burn and destroy all the ships he could not bring with him and make the best of his way to Spithead.

Rooke was determined to go home to England. Ormonde and Hesse Darmstadt begged him to leave a strong squadron at Vigo, so that they might establish themselves for the winter. Rooke was unmoved and could not wait to get home to England. On October 19th, the day after he had given Shovell his orders to bring the treasure home, he sailed from Vigo without a backward glance.[37]

No doubt disappointed to have missed the action, Shovell set about the removal of the treasure into the English ships. In one week he organised the collection of sixty iron cannons from the forts at Vigo, plus an additional sixty bronze guns which weighed between fifty and sixty hundredweight from the beached French ships. Later, a petition would be made to Queen Anne on his behalf for a reward, recognising his diligence and citing the retrieval of these brass guns.

His task done, Shovell got away from Vigo on October 26th and sailed for home. The fleet was scattered by bad weather in the last few days of the month and Shovell was forced to collect them up. Despite further bad weather in the Soundings, Shovell and part of his fleet got into Spithead on November 11th. Rooke had sent out cruisers to look for Shovell and to give him the distance and bearing of the land. Perhaps if this had been done five years later in 1707, when Shovell was returning from Toulon, his life and that of many others need not have been lost. It was no mean feat to bring home the treasure intact in appalling weather conditions, so late in the season.[38]

Rooke had been very lucky indeed to meet the Plate fleet, and despite his initial reluctance to get involved, to take it at Vigo, after the debacle at Cadiz. Ormonde and others complained bitterly about Rooke's conduct and the House of Lords held an enquiry. Rooke calmly defended himself by claiming that the plan of campaign was contradictory, and that the expedition had been badly prepared. He got away with it and was made a Privy Councillor! Ormonde was silenced with the Lord Lieutenancy of Ireland. Thomas Hopsonn received a pension of £500 a year for life from Queen Anne, in recognition of his exceptional service at Vigo.[39]

Shovell had done everything that could have been expected of him. He had not been involved with the unfortunate assault on Cadiz and he was very unlucky that the Plate fleet had not fallen into his hands, but into those of Rooke. If Châteaurenault had had his way and sailed for Brest, the Plate fleet would have run straight into Shovell's squadron. As Campbell recorded, bringing the treasure home under difficult circumstances was considered a remarkable service, and it was resolved to employ him in affairs of the greatest consequence for the future. This was indeed to be proved correct, as will be seen.[40]

Some of the silver taken at Vigo was used in the production of coins which bear Queen Anne's head and below it the date 1702 and Vigo. In 1969 a bronze cannon was raised from the *Association*, the ship on which Shovell drowned in 1707. The cannon shows the original French markings, with the addition of the English broad arrow and Vigo. Clearly the cannon had been taken as part of the booty.[41]

NOTES

1. Laird Clowes, pp.365–387.
2. RMT MAT 3.
3. RMT MAT 27.
4. RMT MAT 25; Smith, Rochester in Parliament; Return of Members of Parliament.
5. Edye, Vol.I, pp.536,544.
6. Edye, Vol.I, pp. 579, 588, 592–93; Admiralty Orders and Instructions, Vol. XXIV, f.277; Admiralty Minute Book, Vol. XV, 2nd June; Treasury Papers, Vol. XXII, f.153.
7. Luttrell, Vol.IV, pp.441, 446, 449; RMT MAT 25; Anderson, Lists of Men of War.
8. RMT MAT 25.
9. RMT MAT 25; Charnock, p.25; Luttrell, Vol.IV, pp.510–532.
10. Charnock, p.30.
11. Duckett, pp.10–11; Luttrell, Vol.IV, p.555.
12. Luttrell, Vol.IV, p.517; Charnock, p.25; RMT MAT 27.
13. Luttrell, Vol.IV, p.639; Charnock, p.25.
14. Luttrell, Vol.IV, pp.645, 657, 663, 682; Duckett, pp.10–11.
15. RMT MAT 25.
16. RMT MAT 16C & 25; Smith, Rochester in Parliament; Return of Members of Parliament.
17. Charnock, p.25; Luttrell, Vol. V, pp.36, 95; Rooke Journal, p.60; Burchett, p.587; RMT MAT 24, will of C.S.
18. Smith, History of Rochester.

19. Smith, Rochester in Parliament; RMT MAT 25; Return of Members of Parliament; Edye, p.483.
20. RMT MAT 25; Rooke Journal, p.145.
21. Luttrell, Vol.V, p.151; Collins Baker.
22. Rooke Journal, pp.157, 165; Richmond, pp.286–287; Owen, p.72.
23. Rooke Journal, p.165; D.N.B Munden.
24. Torrington, p.87.
25. Corbett, pp.210–13; House of Lords MSS, N.S., Vol.V., p.111, July 17th.
26. Home Office, Admiralty XI, July 19th 1702.
27. Owen, pp.74–5; ADD MSS 29591; Board Minutes.
28. Luttrell, Vol.V, pp.186, 214, 216; Richmond, pp.288–9.
29. Anderson, Lists of Men of War; RMT MAT 25; ADM 33/216; Huntington MSS, San Marino.
30. Corbett, pp.212–217; Richmond, pp.287–290; House of Lords MSS, N.S., Vol.IV, p.115.
31. Richmond, p.90; Corbett, p.221; Owen, p.82.
32. Corbett, pp.222–223.
33. Corbett, pp.223–224; Torrington, pp.90–91.
34. House of Lords MSS, N.S., Vol.V, p.113; Burchett, pp.628–631.
35. Corbett, pp.224–225; Richmond, pp.290–291; Torrington, pp.93–94; Burchett, pp.628–631.
36. Richmond, p.225; D.N.B Rooke; Larn, p.9.
37. Rooke Journal, pp.235–236; Corbett, p.225.
38. Torrington, pp. 96–97; Rooke Journal, p.237; Larn, p.9; C.S.P. Treasury 1702/7, Vol. LXXXIX, Entry 87.
39. Corbett, pp.225–226; Luttrell, Vol.V, p.234.
40. Campbell, p.247.
41. Larn, p.9; Owen, p.82.

# CHAPTER XIX
## Voyage to the Mediterranean and the Great Storm
## 1703

The early months of 1703 found Shovell conducting Navy Office business in London. There are still in existence instructions from Shovell appointing Henry Lewis cook on board the *Pendennis* dated January 3rd, and other letters concerning stores to respective officers at Woolwich dated February 14th and 21st 1703.[1]

In early March 1703 Shovell was ordered to take a strong squadron of ships into the Mediterranean.[2] Sir George Rooke had been offered the command by Queen Anne, but had declined it on the grounds that it was a command "too small for his character" and that he would rather remain with the main fleet.[3] No doubt his ego had been inflated by his success at Vigo!

Shovell's squadron was to consist of twenty ships of the line plus a Dutch contingent, and was to carry a year's stores. Wine and oil were to be obtained at Leghorn (Livorno) or Genoa.[4] On March 17th Shovell wrote to Josiah Burchett, the joint Secretary of the Admiralty, requesting mortars, great guns, provisions and a prize officer.[5] C. Hedges at the Office of Ordinance sent Shovell a warrant from Queen Anne on March 30th for mortars, shells, powder and carcasses. Bomb vessels were to be fitted with mortars for service with the fleet in the Mediterranean.[6]

Prizes were clearly on Shovell's mind at this time. On May 3rd he wrote to the Prize Office claiming that he should receive one eighth of the prizes taken under his flag. He said that he had already written on February 23rd about the matter. A reply from the Commissioner for Prizes stated that the money would not be paid, as there was doubt about whether the ships were under his orders at the time.[7] No doubt this referred to the 1702 campaign.

The actual instructions issued to Shovell in the spring of 1703 were complicated and constantly modified. In essence, they were to bring increased pressure to bear on the French in the Mediterranean, principally by assisting the Emperor Joseph and Prince Eugene. Shovell's Anglo/Dutch squadron was to proceed to Naples and Sicily, to co-operate with any imperial troops that they might find there. Authority was given for him to attack Cadiz, Toulon or any other place in Spain or France that was suitable. Venice was to be visited and imperial seaborne communications in the upper Adriatic, which were being disrupted by the French, were to be secured. The Grand Duke of Tuscany, who had been leaning towards the French, was to be persuaded to practise more strict neutrality. The peace and commerce treaties with Algiers, Tunis and Tripoli were to be reviewed and these states were to be persuaded to declare war on France. Malta was mentioned, but on the final drafting of his orders, left out.[8]

On May 4th further orders were issued to Shovell concerning assistance that he was required to give to the Cevennois.[9] In 1702 the Protestants living in the Cevennes Mountains, in southern France, had rebelled against Louis XIV. The area involved lay about forty miles north of the Port of Cette, where the Languedoc canal reached the sea and close to Savoy. The Duke of Savoy had been wavering about whether he would join the allies or not. Joint action by Savoy and the Cevennois on the one hand, and from the sea on the other, would disrupt French communications with their naval base at Toulon and with Italy. Shovell was charged, as a first priority, with making contact with the Cevennois in the Gulf of Narbonne and supplying them with arms.[10]

Further orders sent to Shovell on May 7th instructed him to accompany

239

the merchant ships bound for Lisbon, Genoa and Leghorn. In addition, he was to organise convoys for Smyrna, Constantinople and Scanderoon.[11]

On May 12th the Secretary of State, Daniel Finch, Earl of Nottingham, wrote to Shovell to say that thirty to forty French ships were in Cadiz and asked whether Shovell with sixty ships could make an attempt on them. Shovell was told to keep this matter to himself. His reply is unknown.[12]

At the end of June 1703, while Shovell and his squadron were still lying at Spithead, matters were further complicated in that Portugal formally joined the Grand Alliance. Shovell was now told that his primary objective was to prevent the French Toulon squadron from passing through the Straits and to bring it to action if it did so. Eight further ships of the line would reinforce him.[13]

Shovell had raised his flag in the *Triumph* in the middle of May.[14] On July 1st 1703 Shovell and the combined Anglo/Dutch squadron set sail from Spithead for the Tagus.[15] The many delays had been caused by the late arrival of the Dutch squadron and inclement weather. Even on July 1st the full squadron was not ready for sea and Shovell recommended to Prince George of Denmark, the Lord High Admiral, that Vice Admiral John Leake should follow with eight further ships. Shovell well knew Leake's zeal and his advice was followed. Leake discovered that there were more than a thousand sick men on board the eight ships. He managed to man five ships fully, set sail and caught up with Shovell before he reached Lisbon. The five ships taken by Leake were the *Prince George* and *Association*, 2nd rates, and the *Shrewsbury, Russell* and *Lancaster*, 3rd rates.[16]

Shovell had with him Stafford Fairborne and George Byng as his flag officers and the Dutch contingent were led by Admiral Philip Almonde. The combined squadron consisted of twenty-eight English and twelve Dutch ships, making forty ships of the line in all. In addition, there were fireships and bomb vessels, plus 160 merchantmen.[17] The Turkey merchants may have influenced the strengthening of the squadron, as on June 10th they informed the Admiralty that unless there were re-inforcements their ships would not sail. This was on advice that the French were fitting out most of the ships of France and Spain, "to disrupt our passage into the Straits".[18]

Once in the Channel, Shovell directed Byng to guard the rear of the fleet and sent further ships into Plymouth to bring out the trade. As the wind was blowing hard, Shovell took the fleet into Torbay. On July 5th the weather had improved and the fleet set off again, being joined by the Plymouth ships off the Lizard. The fleet now consisted of 215 sail, which passed through the Bay of Biscay with fresh gales, and down the coast of Portugal. Shovell directed men of war to conduct the trade into Port St Ubes and several other places.[19]

On July 24th the fleet reached Cascaes, the entrance into the Tagus, and anchored.[20] Shovell sent Stafford Fairborne to Lisbon to see the King of Portugal (Pedro II) and the Dowager Queen of England (Catherine of Braganza) and he was received with great respect. The Portuguese were reassured by the presence of the fleet, as they felt threatened by a French squadron which had been sent against them.[21] The King of Portugal viewed the fleet drawn up in a half moon from the fort of St Anthony and sent Shovell a present, which he did not receive, as the boat carrying it arrived after he had left.[22] Members of the nobility inspected the fleet, and some reports stated that the King had visited the fleet incognito.[23]

On July 25th a council of war was held at Cascaes which was attended by Shovell, Byng, Fairborne and the three Dutch admirals, Almonde, Van der Goes and Wassenaer. It was proposed that they would water at Cascaes until July 29th and then proceed through the Straits to Altea Bay. If the wind was from the east they would go to Almeria in Granada.[24]

The fleet set off again on July 31st and by August 4th was off Cape Spartel, where they were met with a fresh easterly wind. Captain John Norris, who had been detached earlier to look into Cadiz, joined them. Norris reported that there were twelve galleys in Cadiz, but no French men of war on the coast of Spain. In addition, further information from Sir Thomas Hardy, who had been detached to inspect Lagos, suggested that twenty-two ships of the line had passed through the Straits and that the consul there reported forty ships at Toulon.[25]

By August 9th Shovell and his fleet were off Tangier Bay. A fresh easterly wind got up forcing Shovell to anchor. The Alicaid at Tangier was welcoming and offered them fresh provisions. However, he also pointed out that the Queen of England owed his master eighty-six barrels of powder, locks and other goods for the earlier redemption of English captives. Shovell, discovering that the Alicaid wished a firm peace and after due discussion with his flag officers, ordered the powder to be sent ashore.[26] The Alicaid was most hospitable to Shovell and his men. The fleet remained for three days and the officers and men went ashore to view the country and watch a demonstration skirmish put on by the Alicaid with 400 horses.[27]

On August 12th the fleet sailed again, and with a westerly wind got through the Straits that night.[28] Soon after passing through the Straits the wind shifted to the east, making progress difficult. The fleet became stretched out along the coast of Barbary, and by August 19th had become short of water in the intense heat.

Shovell sent Byng into a bay between Cape Tresforcas and Cape de Hone to find somewhere to water. Byng discovered that the local Alicaid had recently been beheaded and that the people were in revolt. One of the boat's crew was killed outright and the lieutenant mortally wounded. On August 20th Byng reported to Shovell and the fleet moved across to the coast of Spain, as there was no further hope of watering in Barbary. Many men were now dying of thirst and Shovell called a council of war for August 29th.[29]

The council of war took place aboard Shovell's flagship, the *Triumph*. Queen Anne's instructions to Shovell, of May 4th, were reviewed. Shovell and his flag officers did not consider it wise to take the fleet or even a squadron into the Bay of Narbonne, to make contact with the Cevennois. The reasons they gave were that it was too late in the year and the Gulf was shallow and subject to appalling weather. Instead two ships would be sent to succour the Cevennois. In addition, it was agreed to take the fleet to Altea Bay for watering, unless there was a strong south-westerly wind, in which case they would sail for Cagliari in Sardinia. The final rendezvous would be at Leghorn.[30]

Shovell sent the *Eagle*, under Lord Archibald Hamilton, and the *Hampton Court* into Altea Bay. Both ships came under fire from a small castle there, which they returned and silenced. On August 31st the fleet arrived at Altea Bay and Shovell ordered Brigadier Seymour to prepare his marines to go ashore. Reports of the number of marines sent ashore varied between 2,500[31] and 1,400,[32] because of sickness. Prior to the landing of the marines, Shovell sent a message to the Governor under a flag of truce, stating that he meant no harm to the place and would pay for any food and water that was available. The marines landed and took up their appointed posts. The Spaniards provided victuals for the fleet once they realised that they would not be harmed, and many declared a hatred for the French and support for Archduke Charles. On the afternoon of September 3rd the marines embarked again and that evening the fleet set sail for Leghorn.[33]

On September 2nd Shovell sent orders to Captain Robert Airis of the *Pembroke*, instructing him to take the *Tartar* (Captain John Cooper) under his command, to make contact with the Cevennois in the Bay of Narbonne.[34] Airis was given a list of ships in the fleet from which to take swords, barrels of shot, powder and money. For example, Shovell's flagship, the *Triumph*, supplied sixty barrels of shot. The *Pembroke* and the *Tartar* set sail for the Bay of Narbonne, and were told to go as close to the shore, as the French pilots and three French gentlemen (Charles Portalis, Paul L'Abbillier and S. Tempie) would allow. Shovell instructed Airis to make signals if they saw any persons on the shore. The Cevennois signals for knowing friends were to make three smokes during the day and three fires at night, a rod apart. If the ships or their boats made the first signal, they were to light fuses at the bow, middle and stern of the ships. This was to be answered by smokes or fires as previously described.[35] If the signals were not answered, but the people on the shore were judged to be friends, Shovell instructed that boats should be sent in with the French gentlemen, to make contact.

The password for friends was "Londres". The Cevennois, or Camisards

as they were known, were to be taken on board to discuss their circumstances and the possibility of destroying the salt works at Peccais. When
nothing further could be done, the *Pembroke* and *Tartar* were to join
Shovell at Leghorn.[36]

The signalling system and password seem uninspired. Shovell had been
given an identical signalling system for use at Naples and in Sicily. The
use of the word "Londres" might cause all kinds of confusion, when the
French met the English and asked where they came from.

Although it is out of the time sequence, this is a suitable point to
consider what happened to the *Pembroke* and *Tartar* in the Bay of
Narbonne. On September 17th Captain Robert Airis wrote a report for
Shovell. Airis stated that they arrived in the Bay of Narbonne four leagues
from Agde and that he went on board the *Tartar* with the French
gentlemen and pilots. They resolved to anchor between Porte Cette and
Peccais. If they could not get near enough to make signals from the ships,
they would do so from their boats, to give the Cevennois notice of their
arrival. The wind was variable, making it difficult to go into the bay. Airis
ordered the *Tartar* to go ahead to make signals and he did the same from
the *Pembroke*. The *Tartar* stood in ten fathoms of water about two miles
from the shore. There was no reply to the signals. Airis called Captain
Cooper and the French gentlemen on board the *Pembroke*, and at four
leagues from Porte Cette they decided not to venture close to the shore
again for fear of the many alterations of the wind. In view of the fact that
there would be strong winds at this time of year, they left the French coast
bound for Leghorn.[37]

Shovell was certainly correct in not taking the fleet with its large
number of merchant ships into the Bay of Narbonne. One cannot help
thinking that Airis and Cooper did not go to any great lengths to set foot
ashore. No attack was mounted on the salt works at Peccais, which would
have hindered the main French fleet at Toulon indirectly, by a reduction
in the amount of salt available for salting meat ready for sea. The whole
operation appears to have been conducted in a half-hearted fashion.

Shovell, less the *Pembroke* and *Tartar*, set sail from Altea Bay on
September 3rd with the rest of the fleet, with Leghorn as his destination.
Off the island of Formentosa, Shovell allowed the merchant vessels to go
independently for Smyrna, Constantinople and Scanderoon. He judged
that there were no French ships around to interfere with them, but his
mind must have gone back to 1693 and an earlier Smyrna Convoy
Disaster. Soon afterwards* the Dutch senior Admiral, Philip Almonde,
requested a council of war.

Almonde explained that his orders were to cooperate with the English

* John Leake gives the date as September 5th and George Byng thought it was
September 11th.

fleet, but that he and his ships must be back in their home ports in Holland by November 20th at the latest. He stated that Queen Anne knew his orders and that he intended to leave the Mediterranean by September 20th, his fleet being victualled for no longer time. What were Shovell's intentions? Shovell said that he had orders to proceed to Leghorn and pointed out the dangers of dividing the fleet, with the uncertainty surrounding the whereabouts of the French. Almonde's compromise was to stay with Shovell if the winds were easterly until September 15th, but if they turned westerly he would extend the time until the 20th before setting sail for Holland. Shovell appears to have made no comment, leaving it to Almonde to make his own decision. Later Shovell wrote to Almonde formally pointing out the dangers of separating the fleet. Almonde sent his rear admiral to Shovell and agreed to continue, if there was a likelihood of his achieving his aims in a reasonable time. Shovell had had his own way.

On September 17th Shovell had a private consultation with the English flag officers, Stafford Fairborne and George Byng. He told them again that he had been directed to go to Leghorn and that it was necessary to revictual and allow the men to recover for the return journey to England. As it was getting late in the year, the flag officers decided that if they had not reached Leghorn by the end of September, they would return to England, having sent the remaining merchant vessels on independently.[38]

On the night of September 19th Shovell and his combined fleet reached Leghorn Road. They were greeted with a five-gun salute that Shovell did not answer, as he thought that it was insufficient. The Governor of Leghorn stated that the same salute had been given to Shovell's great patron, John Narbrough, amongst others. Much toing and froing by couriers took place between Leghorn and Florence to diffuse the matter. A compromise was made in that Leghorn fired eleven guns, as a salute to the Queen's flag and a further twenty-three guns for Shovell's person. Shovell replied in kind and similar arrangements were made for the Dutch. Honour was satisfied after three days of negotiation.[39]

While anchored in Leghorn Road, Shovell attempted some forceful negotiations with the Duke of Tuscany. Providore General Teriesi was one of the main lines of communication used, in addition to the Governor of Leghorn. Shovell demanded that the injustices done to a Mr Plowman and other English subjects must be rectified. The Governor of Leghorn must be removed, in view of his misdemeanours and partiality for the French. Her Majesty's subjects must have free embarkation on Her Majesty's ships. Some of them had starved or had been forced into the employ of the French, because they had been unable to join English ships. With twenty-four hours' notice, Her Majesty's ships must be able to leave Leghorn or any of the Duke's ports without hindrance, and the French must not be allowed to follow for at least twenty-four hours.[40]

Shovell threatened to use the fleet if his demands were not met.[41] In a letter to General Teriesi, on October 2nd, Shovell stated bluntly that satisfaction of his demands must be confirmed directly to himself or to Sir Lambert Blackwood, English envoy at the Duke of Tuscany's court.[42]

Shovell appears to have been largely successful with his forceful tactics. In a letter written after the English fleet had left Leghorn, General Teriesi agreed to the main requests. However, there was no mention of the removal of the Governor of Leghorn.[43]

On September 28th Shovell received a message from Count Lamberg, the Imperial Ambassador at the Court of Rome, on board the *Triumph*, to the effect that the Emperor had declared his younger brother, Charles, Duke of Austria, King of Spain. Shovell sent George Byng to the Dutch Admiral Philip Almonde, stating that he intended to fire a celebratory salute which he would like the Dutch to join him in. Almonde was clearly piqued at not being informed personally by Count Lamberg and, although professing suitable respect for Shovell, declined. The English then fired. Poor, obese Count Lamberg, who was sea sick, went to the side of Almonde's ship to smooth his ruffled feathers! This was done and the Dutch fired their salute.[44] The thundering of Shovell's guns that could be heard far inland, in salute of the Hapsburg King of Spain, had shown the Duke of Tuscany how he lay between the devil and the deep blue sea. Had Shovell been bombarding Leghorn, his guns could not have spoken with a louder voice.[45]

The combined Anglo/Dutch fleet left Leghorn on October 2nd. The Dutch soon separated from Shovell and the English ships. By October 12th only the Dutch Admiral Van der Goes remained with Shovell, and he finally departed on October 18th, sailing for Holland.[46]

Shovell had hoped to take his fleet to Tripoli, Tunis, Algiers and Tangier to renew the peace and commerce treaties with those places. In addition, he hoped to persuade them to declare war on France. As it was late in the season, Shovell ordered Captain Thomas Swanton and Robert Airis to Tripoli and Tunis. George Byng was sent to Algiers, and instructions to Tertius Spencer at Tangier were forwarded with Captain Thomas Hardy, to conclude this business. Shovell himself would return with the main part of the fleet to England, after watering at Altea Bay.[47]

The fleet had difficulty in getting to the westward of Corsica and once there, Byng, with a small number of ships, left in the direction of Algiers. In the vicinity of Minorca, Byng's ships were battered by a storm, but on October 23rd they reached Algiers and came to anchor. A suitable twenty-one gun salute was received and returned. Shovell had ordered Byng, on October 2nd, to renew the treaties with the Kingdom and City of Algiers.[48] On October 27th Byng went ashore and was received by the Dey in the King's house. The treaties to be renewed were particularly those concluded between the Dey and Arthur Herbert on April 10th 1682, and Sir William Soams on April 15th 1686. In addition, the articles agreed with Captain John Munden in August 1700 were to be included.[49]

Detailed bargaining began between Byng and the Dey, following Shovell's instructions. Shovell had told Byng in a letter of October 2nd of the details of the agreement made by Munden and Cole in 1700.[50] Robert Cole, Her Majesty's agent and consul, had renewed the agreement in general terms. Firstly, Byng was told that under the Munden agreement, if an English ship had no pass, then the goods were confiscated and the master, men and ship were to be freed. Byng was to call for the ship and master to be held. The crew, passengers and goods were to be restored.

Secondly, Byng was to request that in future prizes taken by Her Majesty's ships and ships built in Her Majesty's plantations, should not be molested if they did not carry a pass. Clearly passes that had been signed in England would not be available to them.

Thirdly, Byng was to insist on the additional article concluded by Matthew Aylmer with Tunis, on May 16th 1699, preventing Her Majesty's subjects from being seduced to become Turks. If any of Her Majesty's subjects turned Turk, he should be sent to the consul's house for three days. If he did not recant in this time nothing further should be done for him. Some British subjects had been persuaded to turn Turk under the influence of alcohol. Presumably, three days was considered long enough to recover from even the longest bout of inebriation!

If Byng was unable to prevail with detention of the master, rather than the confiscation of goods and hindering the seduction of Her Majesty's subjects from turning Turk, he was to renew Herbert's treaty of 1682. Once this had been agreed, Byng was to give the Dey presents that Consul Cole had in his charge.

Finally, Byng was to persuade the Algerian government to go to war with France. If he was successful, he could promise them further presents to the value of 8,000–10,000 thousand dollars.

Byng was successful with the question of passes for prizes and ships built abroad, but he failed to persuade the Dey on the subject of Englishmen being seduced to become Turks. Nor could Byng persuade the Dey to declare war on France. Although not in Shovell's original instructions, Byng managed to get the custom duty on English goods reduced from 10% to 5%. Both sides finally signed the treaty on October 28th 1703.[51]

The Dey received his presents. They were:

> A large handsome cabinet japanned in a case.
> A case containing a large table clock.
> Two gold watches.

A box with doubled barrelled pistols.
A case with six perspective glasses.
An easy chair in a case.
Another containing three small ones.
Two silver watches.
A case with four eight square gun barrels.
A bail of cloth.[52]

Such was diplomacy in the early eighteenth century!

On October 30th Byng and his small squadron sailed for home, arriving in the English Channel just in time for the Great Storm.

Captains Thomas Swanton and Robert Airis left Shovell's fleet on its return journey through the Mediterranean. Airis had already been in charge of the unsuccessful operation to supply arms and encouragement to the Cevennois. The fact that Shovell again selected him for an independent enterprise indicated that it was thought that he had done all that was possible in the Bay of Narbonne. In his orders, dated September 28th 1703, Shovell instructed Swanton and Airis to proceed to Tunis and Tripoli. In Tunis, with the Consul, John Goddard, they were to renew the peace treaties, in particular those of Sir John Lawson of 1662 and Matthew Aylmer of 1699. While in Tripoli with Consul Benjamin Loddington, they were also to confirm the peace treaties, particularly of Sir John Narbrough of 1676 and Matthew Aylmer of 1699.[53] Perhaps Shovell had further thoughts on the matter, as on October 2nd he again wrote to Swanton. Swanton, in Tunis, was to insist that the English were not to pay more than 3% customs duty, as was due under Aylmer's agreement. In Tripoli, Swanton was to renew Consul Baker's additional articles.[54]

Shovell himself wrote to Consul Goddard, at Tunis, on October 2nd, and in addition to the renewal of the peace treaties, instructed him to persuade the government in Tunis to declare war on the French.

You must instill in the people that the French king, having got the kingdom of Spain into his hands is setting up for the Emperor of the whole world and therefore every nation that have friendship with France nourish a viper that in the end will destroy those that favour it.[55]

On the outward journey, Shovell had promised the Alicaid at Tangier that he would prepare articles of peace with the Emperor of Morocco.[56] On October 25th Captain Thomas Hardy, in the *Orford*, left Shovell and the main fleet in the Straits mouth with instructions for Tertius Spencer, the Consul at Tangier, to conclude a peace with Morocco.[57] In a letter to Spencer himself, on October 25th, Shovell stated that as the season was so late he did not have time to negotiate a treaty with the Moroccans personally, and instructed Spencer to do so.[58] Shovell sent Spencer nineteen articles for the proposed treaty, and stated that if there was any charge, then the Secretary of State, the Earl of Nottingham, must be notified.[59] The articles of peace were similar in most respects to the peace treaties concluded with the other Barbary states.

Shovell and the remainder of his fleet sailed through the Straits and headed north towards England. On the return journey, the *Orford* (Captain John Norris), *Warspite* (Captain Edmund Loades) and *Lichfield* (Captain James, Lord Dursley), took the 52 gun French ship the *Hasard*, which resisted in a determined fashion for six hours.[60] Loades was to drown on the *Association* four years later with Shovell, and Dursley was to have a narrow escape the same night.

The first members of Shovell's fleet reached England on November 16th. They reported that the fleet had been very sickly and that several officers of note and seamen were dead. Their provisions had not been properly salted, and a great deal of it was spoiled before they reached the Straits.[61] Over 500 men had died on the voyage and three quarters of the survivors were in poor health.[62]

Shovell struck the union flag on November 15th on sighting land and hoisted the correct flag as Admiral of the White.[63] On the 17th Shovell reached the Downs and wrote a long account of the voyage for the Earl of Nottingham.[64] On Saturday November 20th there were reports that Shovell was expected in town.[65] It was a great pity that he did not go, for he would have escaped being at sea during the Great Storm a few days later.

The Mediterranean campaign of 1703 cannot be described as an overwhelming success. On the positive side, the Toulon fleet had been kept in port by Shovell's presence. The Duke of Tuscany had been pressured into being less partial to the French. Treaties had been confirmed with the Barbary states. Merchant vessels had been safely convoyed to their destinations. On the negative side, no attack had been possible on the coast of Spain or France and no contact made with the Cevennois.

That little was accomplished by Shovell is not surprising. His orders were constantly changed before sailing; he did not get away until the beginning of July and was expected to return through the Straits by the end of September! Although questions were asked in the House of Commons, all parties agreed that Shovell had done his duty in every respect.[66]

The campaign can be summarised as too much expected in too short a time.

On November 24th Shovell, in the *Triumph*, sailed with the *Association*, *St George, Cambridge, Russell, Dorsetshire, Royal Oak* and *Revenge* from the Downs. That evening, in the Gunfleet, they anchored in twelve fathoms of water with the North Foreland about six leagues away to the south-west.[67]

On the evening of November 26th, which was a Friday, a great storm arose with the wind blowing fiercely from the south-west.[68] The storm reached a peak in the early hours of the morning of Saturday November 27th, wreaking havoc over the south and west of England in particular.[69] The centre of the storm was in the Downs and caused catastrophic damage to Shovell and his fleet, as well as to shipping in general, in the English Channel.[70]

No one could recall a storm of this force in living memory and it became known as the Great Storm. A vast number of the tops of houses and chimneys were blown off. Trees were uprooted in St James's Park, the Temple and Gray's Inn. A great many people were killed by falling debris, including the Bishop of Bath and Wells and his Lady who were struck down by a falling chimney stack.[71]

Shovell and his fleet were not the only ones to suffer at sea. An East India ship and several merchant vessels were cast away near Blackwall. Over 100 ships from Yarmouth Broad, mainly colliers, were missing.[72] The coast of the south of England became a mass of wreckage and bodies.

There is in existence a letter from Shovell to John Leake, who was on the *St George*, describing his experiences in the Great Storm. The letter is worth quoting in full.

> Triumph near the Gunfleete
> Dec 3rd 1703
> Gen[m]
> The 24th ultimo the day wee sayled out of the Downes
> with the ships in the Margine about the Long Sands
> head, we anchored in the evening in twelve fathome
> water, the North Foreland South West, distant about
> six leagues, On Saturday last soone in the morning
> wee had a most miserable Storme of Wind, which
> drove us to some streights, for after wee had veered
> out more than three cables of our best bower that
> Anchor Broke, soon after our Tillar broke, and before
> wee could secure our Rudder, it broke from our sterne,
> and has shaken our Stern Post that we prove very
> leakey, and had our four Chaine Pumps and a hand
> Pump going to keep us free, Wee lett go our Sheete
> Anchor and Veeredout all the Cables to it, butt that did
> not ride us, butt wee drove neare a Sand called the
> Galloper of which wee saw the breach, I directed the
> Maine Mast to be Cutt by the Board, after which we ridd
> fast of Eight Ships that came out of the Downes four are
> mifsing, the Association, Rufsell, Revenge and

Triumph
Association
St George
Cambridge
Rufsell
Dorsetshire
Royal Oake
Revenge

Dorsetshire, pray God they drove clear of the Sands,
Wee have now fitted a Jury Maine Mast & Rudder, and
the Ship works very well with them, and the Carpenter
has stopt some of our Leakes, We are gott in nearethe
Gunfleete, and if the Weather proves faire I hope we
shall gett neare in, the Cambridge is now with us and I
have ordered her to stay by us till we gett up,
I am
Gen:m
Yr &C
Clo Shovell
PS I doubt it has fared worse with the four ships
that have drove away than it has done with us. I
have some hopes that some of them have drove to Sea,
but if so they are without Anchors or Cables and may
be without Masts, I judge it will be of service if
some Frigg[ts]: were sent out to look for them.
C:S:[73]

Shovell had been forced to cut down his main mast in order to save the *Triumph* and he must have realised how fortunate he had been.

Shovell was correct in thinking that other ships that had been with him had survived, although they had been driven out to sea. Stafford Fairborne, Vice Admiral of the Red, with his flag on the *Association*, had an equally eventful time. The *Association*'s cable parted at four in the morning of November 27th and, although the pilot let out the sheet anchor, this did not hold her. At about 7.00 a.m. the *Association* drove over the north end of the Galloper sandbank, in eight fathoms of water, but a great sea forced her to lie along without any hope of righting again. Eventually, she drove into deeper water and the crew wore her and brought her head to the northward. Later, on the night of November 27th, Fairborne thought that he was on the coast of Holland, and with yards and topmast down made the best of the way he could. On December 11th Fairborne and the *Association* arrived in Gottenburgh. After proceeding to Copenhagen, to be furnished with anchors and cables, he arrived back in the Gunfleet on January 15th 1704. Poor Fairborne had no sooner come to anchor than he was greeted by another storm, but fortunately for him the *Association* rode fast. It is worth noting that the *Association* was the ship that sank with Shovell on board less than four years later, off the Scilly Isles.[74]

Vice Admiral John Leake, in the *Prince George*, having returned with Shovell's fleet, was in the Downs on the night of November 26th/27th. The Downs, that the evening before had been a forest of ship's masts, were within two hours reduced to a desert. Leake had been managing to ride the storm out, but at 3 a.m. the *Restoration*, a 3rd rate ship, drove down upon them. The anchor of the drifting *Restoration* caught on the hause of the *Prince George* and she stopped riding fast by them. It seemed impossible for the anchor of the *Prince George* to hold both ships and Leake thought that the end had come. The crew of the *Prince George* endeavoured to cut the *Restoration* away, but they failed to do so. For half an hour the two ships rode together until either the cable of the *Restoration* broke or her anchor slipped and she shifted away shortly afterwards, to break up with the loss of all hands. Leake and his Captain, Stephen Martin, had taken special precautions with leather and hempen bindings for their cables, which may partially explain why the *Prince George* was able to hold fast for so long. Leake had done extraordinarily well to save the *Prince George* and her 700 crew, without having to cut down his masts. In fact, the damage done to the *Prince George* was no more than could be expected in any gale.[75]

When day broke, Leake had the melancholy sight of twelve ships ashore upon the Goodwin, Burnt Head and Brake Sands. Among them was Admiral Basil Beaumont in the *Mary*, the *Stirling Castle*, the *Northumberland* and the *Restoration* that had so nearly been Leake's undoing during the night. By ten in the morning all these ships had been dashed to pieces and most of the crews drowned to a man. In all between 2,000 and 3,000 men were said to have been lost in this way. The crew of the *Nassau* had been forced to cut away her masts, and the *Lichfield* and *Dunwich* had lost all theirs involuntarily. The remainder of the shipping in the Downs was either driven out or foundered at anchor.[76]

During November 27th Leake ordered all available boats to the *Stirling Castle*'s wreck to save the lieutenant, chaplain, cook and seventy frozen men, who were clinging to the remains of the poop. Perhaps the most remarkable escape of all was that of the coxswain of the yawl of the *Mary*, who had managed to swim in gigantic seas from his own ship to the poop of the *Stirling Castle*. The coxswain was the only survivor from the *Mary* and he was able to report on the death of Admiral Basil Beaumont. Beaumont, his lieutenant and clerk had lashed themselves to a piece of the ship which had been driven out to sea.[77]

On November 28th Leake wrote to the Lord High Admiral, Prince George of Denmark, giving him an account of what had happened and asking him for a variety of stores such as anchors, cables and jury masts. Leake, on December 1st, ordered a search to be made between North Sand Head and South Sand, to assist distressed merchant shipping. The search was extended on December 5th to the North Sea between England and Holland for the *Association, Dorsetshire, Revenge* and *Russell* that had been driven out of the Gunfleet. The extension of the search may have followed Shovell's letter to Leake of December 3rd, which was quoted in full earlier and certainly explains why the *Triumph* was not included on the list of ships. Leake had done all that he could, and on December 10th he struck his flag and went to London.[78]

251

George Byng, having completed his negotiations with the Algerians on Shovell's orders, reached the Lizard on November 26th. The wind began to blow very hard from the south-west, and at midnight Byng also found himself caught in the Great Storm. Byng's ship, the *Ranelagh*, had her few sails blown down and soon after was broached to, to the southward. Unable to wear her, Byng was forced to cut down her main and mizzenmasts. The *Ranelagh* had started to leak, partly because a gun had broken free and made a hole in the ship's side. With six foot of water in the hold, their chain pump broke and a member of the crew went down through the water to mend it. He was later rewarded with a gunner's warrant. Despite pumping and bailing, the water in the hold increased and Byng retired to his cabin to consider how best their lives could be saved. His Lieutenant, Davenport, reported that the men were all in and asked Byng if he had any brandy to give them. Byng instructed that every man should be given some and the bailing/pumping went on apace. The storm reached a peak at 2.00 a.m. and by daybreak, on the 27th, had quietened considerably. At this stage, the tiller broke in the head of the rudder and it took several hours to fit another. By noon they had made the Isle of Wight and that afternoon came to anchor in St Helens' Road. The *Ranelagh* was in a poor state, the bowsprit sprung, the tiller broken, the rudder loose, the main yard broke in the slings and most of her sails split. The other ships in Byng's squadron had survived, but were in a similar state. On November 28th Byng ordered all available vessels to give assistance to the distressed shipping and then he sailed for Spithead, which he reached on November 29th. At Spithead, Byng, who was unwell, applied to Prince George of Denmark to go ashore, but was refused because of the chaotic situation. Byng was made Commander-in-Chief at Spithead. During this time two sailors were condemned to death for desertion, but in view of the enormous loss of life in the Great Storm, Byng asked for them to be pardoned. The pardons were granted and this must have been one of the few happy events at this difficult time.[79]

The fortunes of the flag officers, Shovell, Fairborne, Leake and Byng in the Great Storm of 1703 have been described in detail. The other ships that survived had similar stories to tell.

The Great Storm was one of the worst disasters in the annals of the Royal Navy. Over 1,500 lives were certainly lost, although some sources put it as high as 2,000–3,000. This does not include merchant shipping. The details of the ships lost, and the men, are recorded by Laird Clowes.[80]

NOTES

1. RMT MAT 27.
2. Torrington, p.97.
3. Corbett, p.230; ADD MSS 29591, March 3rd 1703, f.193.
4. Corbett, p.230; ADD MSS 29591, March 10th 1703, f.195.

5. ADD MSS 29591 f.203.
6. ADD MSS 5795 f.223.
7. ADD MSS 5439 f.97.
8. Corbett, pp.230–231; Torrington, pp.98–100.
9. Torrington, p.98.
10. Corbett, pp.234–235.
11. Torrington, p.100.
12. Hatton Finch MSS 29595 (228).
13. Corbett, p.236; Despatches, i, 117, Marlborough to Nottingham June 14th; Shovell's orders are in H.O. Admiralty, XIII, June 29th; Torrington, p.100.
14. Torrington, p.100.
15. Torrington, p.100; Leake, p.118.
16. Leake, p.119.
17. Torrington, pp.100–101.
18. Luttrell, Vol.V, p.307.
19. Torrington, p.101.
20. Leake, p.120.
21. Torrington, p.101; Leake, p.120; Secret Memoirs.
22. Secret Memoirs.
23. Torrington, p.101.
24. Leake, p.100.
25. Leake, pp.120–121.
26. Torrington, pp.102–103.
27. Secret Memoirs.
28. Leake, p.121.
29. Torrington, pp.103–104; Leake, pp.121–122.
30. Torrington, p.104; Leake, p.122.
31. Leake, p.123.
32. Torrington, p.105.
33. Torrington, p.105; Leake, p.123.
34. ADD MSS 29591 f.238.
35. ADD MSS 29591 f.238.
36. ADD MSS 29591 f.239.
37. ADD MSS 29591 f.240.
38. Leake, p.123; Torrington, pp.106–107.
39. Leake, p.124; Torrington, p.107.
40. ADD MSS 29591 ff.213, 217, 225. Shovell to Nottingham. Shovell to Duke of Tuscany.
41. ADD MSS 29591 f.225, Shovell to Duke of Tuscany.
42. ADD MSS 29591 f.226, Shovell to Teriesi.
43. ADD MSS 29591 f.233, Teriesi to Shovell.
44. Torrington, pp.108–109; Leake, p.125.
45. Corbett, pp.238–239.
46. ADD MSS 29591 f.213.
47. ADD MSS 29591 ff.227, 228, 230, 237.
48. ADD MSS 29591 f.229.
49. ADD MSS 29591 f.229; Torrington, p.110.
50. ADD MSS 29591 f.230.
51. ADD MSS 29591 f.230; Torrington, pp.110–115.
52. Torrington, p.117.
53. ADD MSS 29591 f.227.
54. ADD MSS 29591 f.228.
55. ADD MSS 29591 f.229.

56.  ADD MSS 29591 f.213.
57.  ADD MSS 29591 f.213.
58.  ADD MSS 29591 f.237.
59.  ADD MSS 29591 f.237.
60.  Laird Clowes, p.505.
61.  Luttrell, Vol. V, p.359.
62.  Leake, p.126.
63.  Leake, p.126.
64.  ADD MSS 29591 f.213.
65.  Luttrell, Vol. V, p.361.
66.  Campbell, p.248.
67.  ADD MSS 5440 f.3.
68.  Luttrell, Vol. V, p.363.
69.  Burchett, p.656.
70.  Leake, p.127.
71.  Luttrell, Vol. V, p.363.
72.  Luttrell, Vol. V, p.363.
73.  RMT 25 Section 11; ADD MSS 5440 f.3.
74.  Burchett, p.657.
75.  Leake, pp.126–128.
76.  Leake, p.129.
77.  Leake, p.129.
78.  Leake, pp.129–130.
79.  Torrington, pp.116–118.
80.  Laird Clowes, p.389.

# CHAPTER XX
## The Siege of Gibraltar
## 1704

In 1704 Shovell spent the campaign season in the Mediterranean, where he was closely involved with, and for much of the time under the command of, Sir George Rooke.

To appreciate Shovell's movements in the summer campaign, something of the background to the War of the Spanish Succession must be understood, and in particular the instructions given to Rooke by the authorities in England.

In the latter part of the winter of 1703 Rooke had taken a small squadron to Holland to escort Archduke Charles, the second son of Emperor Joseph and the candidate of the Allies for the Spanish throne, to England. Rooke returned to Spithead in December, and the newly proclaimed Charles III landed at Portsmouth on December 26th.[1] The first naval business of 1704 was to carry Charles III to Portugal and this was undertaken once again by Rooke. They sailed on January 6th 1704, but were forced back by bad weather. Eventually they reached Lisbon on February 25th.

By mid March the broad plan for the continuation of the war was drawn up. In essence, the Duke of Marlborough would carry the Allied army into Bavaria and the fleet would provide a powerful diversion for the French in the Mediterranean. In two letters of March 14th and 28th, Sir Charles Hedges, the Secretary of State, clarified a list of instructions to Rooke regarding the manner in which he was to conduct his fleet. As number one priority, Rooke was to give support to the Duke of Savoy, particularly if Nice and Villefranche were besieged. Secondly, Rooke was to keep a close eye on the French fleet at Toulon and prevent any junction between it and the fleet at Brest. Ideally, Toulon should be taken, but this was impossible without support from Savoy. Thirdly, Rooke should "alarm" the coast of Spain and in particular Catalonia, where it was considered that the population would be for King Charles III.[2]

Rooke left Lisbon at the end of April, with seventeen English ships of the line plus fourteen Dutch ones, and in May bombarded Barcelona with a view to persuading them to declare for Charles III. The Catalonians, although sympathetic, were not prepared to do so, as Rooke lacked sufficient troops. Rooke weighed anchor and set sail for Nice. However, on May 27th his cruisers reported the presence of a French fleet of about forty sail. This was the Brest fleet under the Compte de Toulouse. Following a council of war, chase was given, but the French could not be overtaken before they had reached Toulon, and Rooke returned to the Straits.[3]

Shovell had had a narrow escape in the Great Storm of November 1703 and he had spent the early part of 1704 in England. On February 13th he was made an Elder Brother of Trinity House.[4] On March 16th it was rumoured that Shovell was to command a squadron in the Baltic, to bring the King of Sweden to order. Nothing had come of this.[5]

The first intimation that Shovell was to command a squadron in the Channel came on April 4th,[6] and on April 15th the Lord High Admiral (Prince George of Denmark) gave instructions for the squadron to be fitted out, in response to French naval activity.[7]

Prince George gave formal instructions to Shovell on April 25th. Shovell was to proceed to Brest to prevent the junction of shipping from Rochefort and Port Louis with those already at Brest. He was to sink or burn these ships if a council of war thought that it was practicable. If the French were too strong, he had permission to withdraw back up the Channel as far as the Gunfleet, where he might find security amongst the sands. Here ships from the River Thames and Holland could join. In the event of a retreat up the Channel, he was to bring with him the victuallers, storeships and trade bound for Lisbon, unless he had an opportunity to get them into Portsmouth harbour.

If Shovell found that the French fleet had left Brest and had good reason for thinking that they had sailed for the Straits, he was to detach a force after them, sufficient to give Rooke a superiority over a combined West France (Brest, Rochefort, Port Louis)/Toulon fleet. Shovell was instructed that a maximum of twenty-two ships should be sent to aid Rooke and that, depending on the number of ships detached, who was to command them. If eighteen or the majority of the ships were to sail for Lisbon, Shovell himself should continue in charge, leaving a flag officer to be nominated by Shovell to command the remainder in the Channel. If it were considered that Rooke needed a minority of the ships, Shovell's nominated flag officer would command them and Shovell himself would remain in the Channel. Once the squadron had reached Rooke, either Shovell or the flag officer was to subordinate himself to Rooke as Commander-in-Chief.[8]

In 1690, after the Battle of Beachy Head, Arthur Herbert, Earl of Torrington, had been censured for withdrawing his fleet back towards the Gunfleet. Shovell must have seen the irony of being allowed to withdraw there, if he thought that he was outnumbered.

After receiving Prince George's instructions, Shovell left for Portsmouth and arrived there on April 27th.[9] After approximately twelve days, Shovell sailed with the ships that were ready for St Helens, where the transports and storeships for convoy to Portugal lay. Here Shovell called a council of war and explained his orders from Prince George. In addition, he informed the council of the information he had received by an express, that the Scanderoon fleet was on this side of Lisbon and that the ships bound for the West Indies had put back into Plymouth, in view of the reports that a French fleet from Brest, under the Compte de Toulouse, was at sea.[10]

After due deliberation, Shovell's council of war decided that the squadron should proceed to Plymouth, to reinforce itself with further men of war and the ships going to the West Indies. Following this Plymouth rendezvous, they would join their cruisers on a station between the Lizard and Forne Head (the N.W. point of Bretagne) and ascertain whether Toulouse had really left Brest. If he had and they had no intelligence of his recent movements, they would take the whole squadron, plus merchant ships, into the Soundings to look for the French fleet.

Toulouse was thought to be most likely to position himself, with the Channel open, either to come in with the first westerly winds, or to intercept the outward bound fleet or the homeward bound Scanderoon fleet. Failure to find the French in the Soundings would lead to Shovell taking his squadron to a position 140–150 leagues W. or W.S.W. of the Scilly Isles. If the French were still not found, the West Indies ships would be sent on their way and a squadron detached, under a flag officer, to take the storeships and victuallers to Lisbon, to replenish Sir George Rooke's fleet.[11]

After the council of war at St Helens, George Byng was sent ahead to Plymouth to get further men of war ready to sail, and Shovell followed with the fleet. Shovell reached Plymouth on May 12th, and by the 15th had taken up his proposed position between the Lizard and Forne Head.[12] Burchett gives the line of battle at this stage of the campaign.[13]

### The Line of Battle

The *St George* to lead with the starboard and the larboard tacks on board.

| Frigates & fireships | Rate | Ships | Men | Guns | Division |
|---|---|---|---|---|---|
| | 2 | St George | 680 | 96 | |
| | 4 | Moderate | 365 | 60 | |
| Bridgwater | 3 | Torbay | 500 | 80 | |
| Lightning | | Shrewsbury | 540 | 80 | Vice Admiral |
| Fireship | | Essex | 440 | 70 | of the Red |
| | 4 | Gloucester | 365 | 60 | Sir Stafford |
| Terror | 3 | Royal Oak | 500 | 76 | Fairborne |
| Bomb | 4 | Monk | 365 | 60 | |
| Roebuck, Vulcan | 3 | Boyne | 500 | 80 | |
| Fireship | | Warspight | 540 | 70 | |
| | | | | | |
| William & Mary | 4 | Triton | 280 | 50 | |
| Yacht | 3 | Orford | 440 | 70 | Admiral of |
| | 2 | Barfleur | 710 | 96 | the White |
| | | Namur | 680 | 96 | Sir Cloudesley |
| | 4 | Medway | 365 | 60 | Shovell |
| Princess Anne | 3 | Swiftsure | 440 | 70 | |
| Hospital | | Lenox | 440 | 70 | |
| | | | | | |
| Vulture | | Nassau | 440 | 70 | |
| Fireship | | Rupert | 440 | 70 | |
| | | Norfolk | 500 | 80 | Rear Admiral |
| Star | | Ranelagh | 535 | 80 | of the Red |
| Bomb | | Dorsetshire | 500 | 80 | George Byng |
| | 4 | Kingston | 365 | 60 | |
| | | Assurance | 365 | 60 | |
| | | Revenge | 440 | 70 | |
| | | | 11,635 | 1,514 | |

On reaching his allotted position between the Lizard and Forne Head, Shovell called a further council of war to consider the latest intelligence reports that he had received, concerning the whereabouts of Toulouse's fleet. The Admiralty Office advised that Toulouse would be ready to sail at the beginning of the month (May), and a frigate had reported that there was only one ship in the Roads at Brest. The council of war concluded that Toulouse was at sea with his fleet and decided to move to their second rendezvous in the Soundings, about twenty leagues from the Scilly Isles. There they would leave a single ship for forty-eight hours, to inform any following English vessels of Shovell's intentions. The remainder of Shovell's fleet would sail to a station 150 leagues from Scilly, in a westerly or W.S.W. direction. There the West Indies fleet would leave under Captain William Kerr and Sir Stafford Fairborne, with eight men of war plus four prizes. The rest would sail first to Kinsale to collect the home-ward bound trade, and then to Plymouth. Shovell himself would take the bulk of his fleet to join Rooke at Lisbon. Some officers at the council of war believed that the whole of Shovell's fleet should make for Lisbon to support Rooke. However, Shovell pointed out that he might take no more than twenty-two ships, under his orders from Prince George.[14]

By May 28th 1704 Shovell's fleet was to the westward of the Scilly Isles and there was still no trace of the French. The fleet split up and Shovell with the major part sailed for Lisbon.[15]

Early in June Shovell reached Lisbon and found that Rooke was not there before him. In addition, Toulouse was thought to be in the Mediterranean, which would put Rooke's inferior fleet at risk. Shovell sailed again and on June 16th came across Rooke and his ships off Lagos. Rooke and Shovell decided to follow Toulouse into the Mediterranean and perhaps make an attempt on Cadiz or Barcelona, if sufficient forces were available. About July 17th a council of war called by Rooke considered instructions sent out by Queen Anne that the fleet should do nothing, unless it had the prior agreement of the Kings of Portugal and Spain. The council of war decided that there were insufficient troops to make a successful attack on Cadiz, but that an attempt on Gibraltar was feasible.[16]

Present at the council of war on July 17th were Rooke, Shovell, John Leake, George Byng, James Wishart and the Dutch flag officers.[17] Gibraltar was an attractive target to Rooke and his fleet. Cromwell had considered taking it, and in Charles II's reign careening hulks had been stationed there, in preference to Tangier. William III had coveted the place and, ever since his death in 1702, every admiral passing through the Straits had been instructed to capture it if he could.[18]

Exactly who first proposed that an attempt on Gibraltar should be made is difficult to determine. Leake is said to have suggested it to Rooke sometime before. Prince George of Hesse Darmstadt felt that its conquest would be of benefit to trade and the fleet during the war with France and Spain. Both Rooke and Hesse Darmstadt were reported to have approved in principle, but acting in accord with the wishes of the Kings of Portugal and Spain, were concentrating on Cadiz or Barcelona. Once they were deemed impracticable, Rooke could concentrate on Gibraltar.[19] In *The Life of Captain Stephen Martin* (Leake's friend, brother-in-law and ship's captain at the time), the only comment made is "... the admirals having determined to attack Gibraltar ...". There is no specific mention of Leake.[20] As Martin normally saw Leake's action in a favourable light, this must count against him.

Shovell's anonymous biographer tells a different story.[21]

> The two admirals returned forthwith into the Mediterraneane and whereupon a council of war being called, it was argued by Cloudesley Shovell that since the French had got into Toulon and secured themselves from any attempt to be made upon them in that impregnable city it was expedient for the good of this Catholick Majesty and the honour of our arms to make some sudden attempt upon the Spanish Coast, that if the town of Gibraltar could be taken, it would easily be made tenable, that it would be a sure retreat for such Spaniards as were in the interest of King Charles III would give him a strong place of arms and be an inlet into the Conquest of Spain, from which Town if it fell into our hands, we might easily penetrate into the heart of Andalusia and without ennumerating all the advantages which seemed infinitely material, such a harbour would be a refuge for our merchant ships too frequently exposed to the insults of the French and Spaniards in those foreign seas.
>
> These arguments being very solid, had so strong an influence over the officers that composed this Council of War, that they without hesitation sailed for Gibraltar in order to attempt the reduction of that place.[22]

Here rests the case for Shovell.

Corbett, in his account of the decision to take Gibraltar, states that the original idea was generally attributed to Prince George of Hesse Darmstadt who was with the fleet, still in hope of effecting something in Catalonia. It is known that a memorandum from Hesse Darmstadt was laid before the council of war.[23]

However, Rooke was in overall command and success would be to his credit and failure to his detriment. In fact, he was taking a minimal risk, as he knew that Gibraltar had been the secret aim of successive governments and was weakly defended. Additionally, he had Queen Anne's instructions and the support of the Kings of Spain and Portugal.[24]

One man who made no claim to be suggesting the Siege of Gibraltar was George Byng, who has been quoted as believing that he and the others thought lightly of the attack.[25] Perhaps it does not matter where the idea came from. All that is important is that a firm decision to attack Gibraltar was made and a plan drawn up for a combined naval and marine assault on the town.

The honour of leading the naval forces was given to Byng who was said to have been a vocal critic of the enterprise! The land forces, consisting of 1,800 marines, commanded by Hesse Darmstadt, were landed on the neck of land to the north of the town on July 21st. In effect this would have cut off Gibraltar from the mainland. Hesse Darmstadt sent a summons to the Governor to surrender the town to the service of Charles III. The Governor refused. On July 22nd Rooke ordered Byng, with a combined Anglo/Dutch squadron, into the Bay of Gibraltar, to bombard the town from the sea. A contrary wind delayed the bombardment until the following day, July 23rd. For six hours Byng's squadron blasted the town until the enemy were beaten from their guns, particularly at the south mole in front of the English. Boats were ordered in under Captain Edward Whitaker, and despite a considerable loss of life following the detonation of a mine at the south mole, the enemy were driven from their cannons. A small bastion situated halfway between the south mole and town was also captured. At this, Hesse Darmstadt called upon the Governor to surrender yet again. This time he did and was no doubt helped to make up his mind by the fact that many of the womenfolk were trapped away from the town in the Church of Our Lady of Europa, at the southernmost tip of the peninsula. Hesse Darmstadt, with his 1,800 marines plus naval reinforcements from the small boats, discovered that the defending garrison consisted of no more than 150 men, although 100 guns were mounted.[26]

What of Shovell's role at the taking of Gibraltar? We know that he was a participant at the council of war, which made the decision to attempt the siege, and was possibly instrumental in getting Rooke to agree to its undertaking. During the siege, the admirals, including Shovell, gave instructions to Byng to take his squadron into the bay. Here he was to cannonade the town, send his boats in and dispatch a final letter to the Governor, calling on him to surrender.[27]

In addition, during the siege Shovell had left his own ship to go on board Byng's ship, the *Ranelagh*, to get a better view of the action. At the stage when the boats had been sent in, priests, women and children attempted to run back from the vicinity of the Europa Church in the direction of the town, to escape from the English seamen. Shovell, from the *Ranelagh*'s deck, suggested cannons be fired in their direction, not with a view to injuring them, but to drive them back into the church and away from the town. The knowledge that English sailors separated their womenfolk from them may have helped the Governor to make up his mind to surrender Gibraltar.[28]

Shovell had played a relatively minor role in the taking of Gibraltar, but he was to play a major one in the subsequent Battle of Malaga, a few days later.

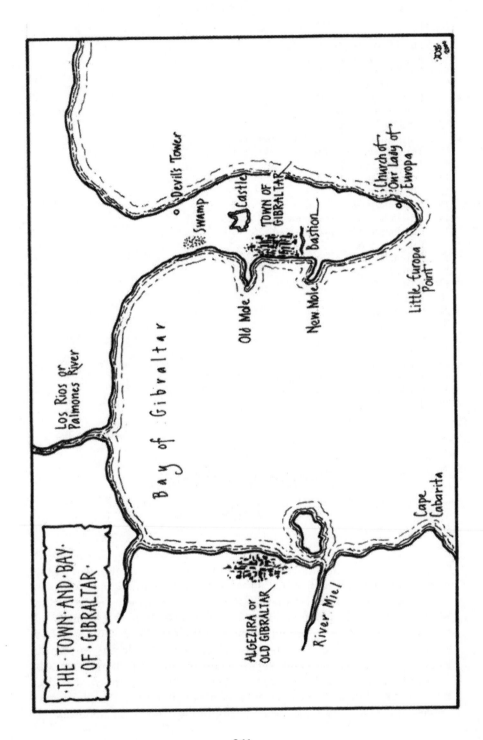

THE·TOWN·AND·BAY· ·OF·GIBRALTAR·

Los Rios or Palmones River

Bay of Gibraltar

Devil's Tower

Swamp

Castle

TOWN OF GIBRALTAR

Church of Our Lady of Europa

Bastion

Old Mole

New Mole

Little Europa Point

ALGEZIRA or OLD GIBRALTAR

River Miel

Cape Cabarita

NOTES

1. Laird Clowes, pp. 389–390.
2. Richmond, pp.301–302.
3. Laird Clowes, pp.390–391.
4. Court Minutes of 1704.
5. Luttrell, Vol.V, p.403.
6. Luttrell, Vol.V, p.410.
7. Luttrell, Vol.V, p.413.
8. Torrington, pp.122–123; Burchett, p.673.
9. Torrington, p.123; Luttrell, Vol.V, p.418.
10. Torrington, p.123.
11. Torrington, pp.123, 124.
12. Burchett, p.674.
13. Burchett, p.674.
14. Burchett, p.675; Torrington, pp.124–125.
15. Burchett, p.675; Torrington, p.125.
16. Burchett, p.677.
17. Burchett, p.677.
18. Corbett, p.255.
19. Leake, p.153.
20. Martin, p.75.
21. Secret Memoirs.
22. Secret Memoirs.
23. Corbett, p.255.
24. Corbett, p.256.
25. Torrington, p.137.
26. Leake, pp.154–155; Torrington, pp.138–145.
27. Secret Memoirs.
28. Torrington, p.142.

# CHAPTER XXI
# The Battle of Malaga
# 1704

On July 25th 1704 Sir George Rooke held a council of war attended by the flag officers of the fleet, to discuss their plans for the immediate future in the aftermath of their success at Gibraltar.[1] Letters had been received from Secretary of State Hedges and from the Ambassador at Lisbon, Paul Methuen.[2] The letters informed Rooke that the Compte de Toulouse had safely reached Toulon with the Brest fleet (this was already known to Rooke), but Toulouse was unlikely to venture out again as his force was inferior to the combined Rooke/Shovell fleet.[3] The council of war decided that it was too late in the year to make a further attempt on Barcelona, and indeed the Dutch had inadequate supplies for such an undertaking.

However, Rooke and his admirals, including Shovell, were prepared to make an attempt on Cadiz provided that the Kings of Spain and Portugal supplied troops and a garrison for Gibraltar. In the meantime, while the Kings deliberated, the fleet would water on the Barbary Coast.[4]

The news of the fall of Gibraltar reached Madrid, and the Marquis de Villadarias was detached with 8,000 men either to retake the place or at least to stop the progress of the Allies.[5] The information sent to Rooke that Toulouse had an inferior fleet and was unlikely to put to sea from Toulon was incorrect. Toulouse was already at sea, and when he reached Barcelona, which Louis XIV believed was Rooke's real objective, he received the shattering news that Gibraltar had fallen.[6] Toulouse was ordered to seek out and fight Rooke's fleet and to do all in his power to assist Villadarias in the recapture of Gibraltar. He sailed south.[7]

Rooke sent the Dutch Admiral Paulus Van der Dussen to Lisbon and then on to Plymouth to bring Dutch troops to Portugal. Prince George of Hesse Darmstadt was left with 1,800 marines and seamen to garrison Gibraltar while the fleet went in squadrons to water on the Barbary Coast.[8] John Leake and Shovell, with their respective divisions, had set off for the Barbary Coast on July 26th, but on the 28th were forced back to Gibraltar without watering. On August 1st the whole fleet sailed again to water in Barbary. Rooke and the bulk of the fleet moved into Ceuta Bay, while Shovell and his division plied up with his squadron to a watering place several miles to the eastward, called Reifi (eight to ten miles east of Tetuan) where a river runs into the sea. The coast of Barbary must have been well known to Shovell from the 1670s and 80s, when he served there under John Narbrough and then Arthur Herbert. Difficulty was encountered in filling the wood casks as a great sea was running, and Shovell was unable to water satisfactorily at Reifi, being forced to join Rooke in Ceuta Bay. On August 3rd watering had been largely completed and the fleet moved over to Gibraltar.[9]

On August 9th, early in the morning, one of Rooke's scouts, the *Centurion*, signalled that the French fleet had been spotted. Byng was the first to see the signal and went aboard Rooke's ship to tell him. Doubt was expressed, but some officers climbed to the masthead enabling sixteen sail to be counted, confirming the close proximity of Toulouse's fleet.[10] A council of war was called consisting of the English and Dutch admirals. The English representatives were Rooke, Shovell, John Leake, George Byng, Thomas Dilkes and James Wishart. The Dutch were Lieutenant Admiral Garrit Callenburgh and Vice Admiral Jan Wassenaer. The commander of the *Centurion* was present and stated that he had seen sixty-six sail of the enemy's fleet about ten leagues to windward of them. The plan that was agreed upon was to get half the marine force back from Gibraltar and, while the wind was easterly, to lie to and receive the French. If the wind became westerly, Rooke and his fleet would attempt to fight the French, but if battle was declined they would sail no farther than Cape Malaga, as it was thought likely that the French would not stop until they had reached Toulon.[11] James Wishart, Rooke's First Captain, had expressed the view that the English fleet should return to Gibraltar. Rooke was against this, as it would put him at a disadvantage to receive the French while at anchor, and he still had twelve ships watering in Barbary.[12] Shovell's views at this stage are not known.

The wind was easterly, but the French made no attempt to bear down. The opportunity was taken to return 1,000 marines to the fleet from Gibraltar. This was carried out on August 10th. The next two days were spent plying to windward and following Toulouse's French fleet by the sound of their signal guns. On August 11th a French ship, which had been watching Rooke's fleet, was chased on shore by cruisers and burnt. A further council of war was called on August 12th, at which it was decided that if the enemy did not appear before nightfall, Rooke's fleet would sail for the Straits' mouth and remain there for forty-eight hours. If the French still did not appear, they would go into Gibraltar and try to secure the place. Soon after the council of war broke up, at about 11.00 a.m. on August 12th, the French fleet was seen to the north-west of Rooke's fleet, off Cape Malaga and going away with the wind. The English were surprised to see the French in that position, having missed them in a sweep to the south-east. Rooke and his admirals were concerned that the French intended to place themselves between Gibraltar and the English fleet. Immediately, the signal was given by Rooke to form a line of battle, but as they bore down on the French, the wind failed and battle was delayed until the next day.

Toulouse had first been spotted on August 9th and he had used the time since then to collect his galleys from Malaga. During the night of August 12th the English and French fleets lay about three leagues apart. The next day the Battle of Malaga, the only major sea battle of the War of the Spanish Succession, was fought.[13] At daybreak on August 13th the two fleets lay eight to ten leagues south of Cape Malaga and about three leagues apart. The French line of battle faced south towards the Barbary Coast and was shaped in half moon fashion, with their van and rear closer to the English than their centre. Byng was of the opinion that the semi circular battle line had been drawn up so that the van and rear of the French line might, with the help of their gallies, gain the wind of the English, if the wind was slight.[14]

The French line consisted of fifty ships of the line. Their van was commanded by the Marquis de Villette of the white and blue squadron, with the Duke of Tursis in his second line with seven French and five Spanish galleys, two frigates and four fireships. In the centre was the white squadron under the command of the Compte de Toulouse himself, with the Marquis de Roye with four galleys, four frigates, two fireships and two round sterned ships or flutes in his second line. The rear was made up of the blue squadron under the Marquis Langeron, having in his second line eight French galleys, three frigates and three fireships. The Marquis de Fenville commanded this second line.[15]

The combined Anglo/Dutch fleet, consisting of fifty-three ships, had the white squadron in the van commanded by Cloudesley Shovell, Admiral of the White and John Leake, Vice Admiral of the Blue. Leake's division led the van, but Shovell was in overall command of it. In their second line were two frigates, three fireships and one hospital ship. The centre had the Commander-in-Chief, George Rooke, with the red squadron assisted by Rear Admirals George Byng and Thomas Dilkes. In the second line of the centre were two frigates, four fireships, two bombs, one yacht and one hospital ship. There was also a third line in the centre consisting of two 50 gun ships, two frigates and two fireships. They had orders to lie to windward, in case the galleys and fireships should push through Rooke's line. The rear was made up of the Dutch squadron of twelve vessels under Lieutenant Admiral Callenburgh assisted by Rear Admiral Van der Dussen.[16]

Lines of battle of the respective fleets

## English Line

| Ships | Men | Guns | |
|-------|-----|------|---|
| Yarmouth | 440 | 70 | |
| Norfolk | 500 | 80 | |
| Berwick | 440 | 70 | John Leake |
| Prince George | 700 | 90 | |
| Boyne | 500 | 80 | |
| Newark | 500 | 80 | |
| Lenox | 440 | 70 | |
| Tilbury | 280 | 50 | |
| Swiftsure | 440 | 70 | |
| Barfleur | 710 | 90 | |
| Namur | 680 | 90 | Cloudesley Shovell |
| Orford | 440 | 70 | |
| Assurance | 440 | 66 | |
| Nottingham | 365 | 60 | |
| Warspight | 440 | 70 | |

| | | | |
|---|---|---|---|
| Burford | 440 | 70 | |
| Monk | 365 | 60 | |
| Cambridge | 500 | 80 | |
| Kent | 460 | 70 | Thomas Dilkes |
| Royal Oak | 500 | 80 | |
| Suffolk | 440 | 70 | |
| Bedford | 440 | 70 | |
| | | | |
| Shrewsbury | 500 | 80 | |
| Monmouth | 440 | 70 | |
| Eagle | 440 | 70 | |
| Royal Katherine | 730 | 90 | |
| St George | 680 | 90 | George Rooke |
| Montagu | 365 | 60 | |
| Nassau | 440 | 70 | |
| Grafton | 440 | 70 | |
| | | | |
| Le Firme | 440 | 70 | |
| Kingston | 365 | 60 | |
| Centurion | 280 | 50 | |
| Torbay | 500 | 80 | |
| Ranelagh | 535 | 80 | George Byng |
| Dorsetshire | 500 | 80 | |
| Triton | 230 | 50 | |
| Essex | 440 | 70 | |
| Somerset | 500 | 80 | |
| | | | |
| Dort | 375 | 72 | |
| Ann of Friesland | 325 | 64 | |
| Lion | 325 | 64 | |
| Bavaria | 325 | 64 | Callenburgh |
| Albemarle | 375 | 64 | |
| Ann of Utrect | 375 | 64 | |
| Flushing | 238 | 50 | |
| | | | |
| Nymwegen | 440 | 74 | |
| Gelderland | 320 | 60 | |
| Union | 500 | 90 | Wassenaer |
| Damiuta | 220 | 50 | |
| Catwyk | 440 | 72 | |
| | 22,543 | 3,614 | |

## French Line

| Ships | Men | Guns | |
|---|---|---|---|
| Eclatant | 750 | 96 | |
| Oeolus | 380 | 62 | |
| St Philippe | 700 | 90 | D'Infreville |
| Heureux | 450 | 70 | |
| Rubis | 330 | 56 | |
| Arrogant | 350 | 62 | |
| | | | |
| Marquis | 350 | 60 | |
| Constant | 450 | 70 | |
| Fier | 800 | 88 | de Villette |
| Intrépide | 600 | 84 | |
| Excellent | 350 | 62 | |
| | | | |
| Sage | 330 | 54 | |
| Ecueil | 380 | 62 | |
| Magnifique | 600 | 86 | de Belle Isle |
| Monarque | 600 | 84 | |
| Perle | 300 | 54 | |
| | | | |
| Furieux | 350 | 60 | |
| Vermandois | 350 | 63 | |
| Lys | 60 | 88 | |
| Tonnant | 700 | 90 | Cöetlogon |
| Orgueilleux | 600 | 88 | |
| Espérance | 350 | 50 | |
| Sérieux | 380 | 58 | |
| | | | |
| Fleuron | 450 | 70 | |
| Terrible | 900 | 104 | |
| Foudroyant | 950 | 104 | |
| Entreprenant | 350 | 60 | Toulouse |
| Fortune | 350 | 58 | |
| Parfait | 470 | 74 | |
| | | | |
| Magnanime | 600 | 84 | |
| Sceptre | 600 | 88 | de Pointis |
| Fendant | 350 | 58 | |

| | | | |
|---|---|---|---|
| *Zelande* | 350 | 60 | |
| *St Louis* | 380 | 60 | |
| *Couronne* | 500 | 88 | |
| *Admirable* | 675 | 92 | de Sepville |
| *Cheval Marin* | 260 | 44 | |
| *Vainquer* | 600 | 88 | |
| *Diamant* | 350 | 58 | |
| | | | |
| *Gaillard* | 330 | 54 | |
| *Invincible* | 450 | 70 | |
| *Soleil Royal* | 850 | 102 | de Langeron |
| *Ardent* | 400 | 66 | |
| *Trident* | 350 | 56 | |
| | | | |
| *Content* | 380 | 60 | |
| *Maure* | 330 | 52 | |
| *Toulouse* | 380 | 60 | |
| *Triomphant* | 750 | 92 | de Harteloire |
| *St Esprit* | 490 | 72 | |
| *Henri* | 400 | 66 | |
| | 24,275 | 3,577 [17] | |

## Flag Officers

| Van | Van |
|---|---|
| Sir John Leake | D'Infreville |
| (Vice Admiral of Blue) | (Vice Admiral of White & Blue) |
| *Prince George* | *St Philippe* |
| Sir Cloudesley Shovell | DeVillette |
| (Admiral of White) | (Admiral of White & Blue) |
| *Barfleur* | *Fier* |
| | De Belle Isle |
| | (Rear Admiral of White & Blue) |
| | *Monarque* |
| | |
| Centre | Centre |
| Thomas Dilkes | Cöetlogon |
| (Rear Admiral of White) | (Vice Admiral of White) |
| *Kent* | *Tonnant* |
| Sir George Rooke | Compte de Toulouse |
| (Admiral) | (Admiral) |
| *Royal Katherine* | *Foudroyant* |
| George Byng | de Pointis |

(Rear Admiral of Red)
*Ranelagh*

(Rear Admiral of White)
*Sceptre*
de Sepville
(Rear Admiral of Blue)
*Admirable*

Rear
Callenburgh
(Admiral)
*Albemarle*
Wassenaer
(Vice Admiral)
*Union*

Rear
de Langeron
(Admiral of Blue)
*Soleil Royal*
de Harteloire
(Vice Admiral of Blue)
*Triomphant*

(The chart above shows the flag officers at the Battle of Malaga and their opponents. There was some overlapping of squadrons.)

The Anglo/Dutch fleet had fifty-one ships in the line of battle, 22,543 men and 3,614 guns. Against them the French had fifty ships in the line of battle, 24,275 men and 3,577 guns. From these figures it can be seen that the two fleets were well matched, the Anglo/Dutch having slightly more guns and the French slightly more men. However, there was a disparity in available ammunition, as a great deal of shot had been fired by Rooke's ships into Gibraltar during the siege and had not been replaced. This was to be a significant factor in the coming battle. In addition, the French Fleet's ships were clean, which allowed them to sail faster through the water than their Anglo/Dutch counterparts.

Early on the morning of Sunday August 13th, with the wind from the east, Rooke's Anglo/Dutch fleet bore down on Toulouse's French fleet. The French still faced south, in a semicircular line of battle, concave to the east. Tourville had used a similar curved line of battle at Beachy Head in 1690, but the full significance of this formation has not been explained. Presumably, Toulouse or at least his principal advisor, D'Estrées, felt that this was the best configuration to counter Rooke's fleet, which held the weather gauge.

At ten o'clock in the morning the van, with John Leake leading and Shovell in command, came up with the French van commanded by de Villette. The Anglo/Dutch line had approached the French in an oblique fashion, and as often happened, the various divisions had become separated, leaving gaps between them. Shovell, seeing this potential danger, hove to within half a gunshot of de Villette in the *Fier*, and waited for Rooke with the English centre to catch up. Shovell, in the *Barfleur*, was fourth in his line, whereas his opponent, de Villette, was third in his, which meant that the English van overlapped the French by one ship. De Villette's leading captain realised that there was a possibility of the

269

English doubling the French van. He informed de Villette, who ordered that the whole van must make sail to come up level with the head of the English line.[18] This movement ahead by the French van made Shovell fear being doubled himself, particularly as he had only fifteen ships to de Villette's seventeen, and he ordered a similar movement forward of the English van. The effect of this movement was that the English van became even more separated from Rooke and the centre.

D'Estrées, in name Toulouse's chief adviser, but in effect the originator of the tactics of the French fleet, saw his opportunity. The French centre was strong in comparison with that of the English and had gallies in support if things started to go wrong. D'Estrées, with Toulouse's assent, ordered part of the French centre through the gap with the intention of doubling on and crushing Shovell and the English van with superior force. The French hoped that this could be achieved before the Dutch under Callenburgh, in the rear, could get into the action. Rooke saw the danger, although he took the movement of the French centre to be an attempt to weather him and he made the signal to engage. Dilkes, in the *Kent*, in the leading part of the English centre, moved up on the rear ships in the French van and this produced an equality of strength in the two vans. Battle commenced all down the line, with the exception of the Dutch in the rear who were still too distant.

Leake and Shovell fought a fierce battle of attrition against the French van. Leake was engaged against D'Infreville in the *St Philippe*, and Shovell against de Villette in the *Fier*. At 2.00 p.m., after four hours hard pounding, Shovell had made the rear of the *Fier* blow up and de Villette was forced out of the line to extinguish the fire. Inexplicably, the rest of the division followed de Villette's example. Leake sent his Captain, Stephen Martin, to suggest to Shovell that they close upon de Villette's ships and force them back farther, until the French line was completely broken. This would ensure that Toulouse and the French centre would have to fall back, to avoid being doubled and destroyed. This was sensible advice and under normal circumstances Shovell would probably have followed it, as it would have given him a good chance of a favourable decision over the French. However, Shovell was aware that Rooke's centre was under the most intense pressure, as a number of his ships had had to pull out of the line. Subsequently, it was shown that they had run out of shot, as a consequence of the profligate bombardment of Gibraltar a few weeks before. Shovell ignored Leake's advice and ordered part of his van to back astern and come to Rooke's assistance. This was a difficult sailing manoeuvre, but was carried out with panache and had the effect of stabilising Rooke and the English centre. Leake fumed at the head of the van with little to do and never forgave Shovell.

Prior to all this, at about 10.30 a.m., Rooke and the English centre had engaged. Rooke, in the *Royal Katherine*, a 90 gun ship, took on the Compte de Toulouse in the 104 gun *Foudroyant*. The battle went on for most of the day and Rooke suffered greatly. Not only was he on a less well gunned ship than Toulouse, but both his seconds were weaker than Toulouse's two supporters, who had almost 100 guns each. Matters were made worse when various ships in the divisions of Dilkes and Byng pulled out of the line from lack of shot. John Jennings, in the *St George*, fought a heroic battle against Toulouse and one of his supporters. At one stage, he had twenty-five guns dismounted on one side and was forced to transfer guns across his deck to make up the deficit. Captain Josiah Crowe, on the *Shrewsbury*, was also heavily involved. In the afternoon, having broken the French van, Shovell and some of his ships came to the assistance of Rooke and the English centre. A few of Shovell's ships gave De Belle Isle in the *Monarque*, and Cöetlogon in the *Tonnant* such a hard time that they declined to face a single Shovell broadside and sailed away from him, being clean and faster through the water. At 7.00 p.m. Toulouse himself towed out of the line and the battle for the day was over in the centre.

The Dutch in the rear, under Callenburgh, were not involved in the battle until the afternoon and required some persuasion from Byng to close. However, they then fought a fierce battle with the French rear under De Langeron until after dusk. The French then towed out of the line.[19]

During the day casualties on both sides had been heavy. Later the *Paris Gazette* gave the French killed and wounded as 1,500. The Anglo/Dutch killed and wounded were given at over 2,700. Doubt has been expressed about the lower French figure. The French style of cannonade was to destroy rigging and that of the English to aim for the hull. Cannon balls through the hull of a ship would be more likely to kill and maim larger numbers of men, than balls through the rigging.

### Anglo/Dutch Casualties

| Division | Officers | | Men | |
| | Slain | Wounded | Slain | Wounded |
| --- | --- | --- | --- | --- |
| Rooke | 6 | 2 | 219 | 508 |
| Shovell | 1 | 7 | 105 | 303 |
| Leake | 0 | 7 | 86 | 211 |
| Byng | 1 | 5 | 155 | 361 |
| Dilkes | 0 | 10 | 119 | 249 |
| | 8 | 31 | 687* | 1,632 |

Total English killed/wounded = 2,368

| | | | | |
| --- | --- | --- | --- | --- |
| Dutch | 1 | ? | 91 | 268 |

Total Anglo/Dutch Casualties = 2,728

(* Incorrect addition)

The division with the greatest number of casualties was Rooke's with 735. Shovell had 416 in his division. The Dutch in the rear had 360. The figures merely show where the battle was fiercest, which was in the centre.

If the French had fewer casualties than the English and Dutch, then they lost more persons of a "higher quality". Although John Leake "spilt blood" for the first time in his career, as the result of a splinter, of the English captains only Sir Andrew Lake of the *Grafton* and John Lowe of the *Ranelagh* (Byng's flag captain) were killed. The Dutch lost one. In this respect the French came off much worse. De Belle Isle (Rear Admiral of the White and Blue), the Bailli de Lorraine (Captain of the *Mercure*), Chevalier de Lanneon (Captain of the *Vainquer*), Chevalier de Phelypeaux (Captain of the *Content*) and thirty-two other persons of distinction died. The Compte de Toulouse was slightly wounded and had four pages killed around him. There were no reports that Sir Cloudesley Shovell suffered any injury.

On neither side was any ship taken. The Anglo/Dutch fleet had no ship sunk or destroyed in the battle. The loss of the Dutch ship, the *Albemarle*, was not associated with French action. The French were thought to have lost the *Cheval Marin* and two galleys during the engagement and a further four ships as a result of it.[20]

August 13th closed inconclusively, with both the Anglo/Dutch and the French fleets still in being. During the early hours of the morning of August 14th the wind switched to the north-west, giving the French the weather gauge. Daybreak came, and through the haze the Anglo/Dutch fleet saw the French about three leagues away forming a battle line with their heads to the north. Rooke immediately gave instructions to his fleet to prepare to receive the French, and placed his disabled ships to the leeward. It soon became apparent that the French were not going to continue the fight. Some of their ships were seen to be towed by galleys, as they were unable to make way themselves. At length, it became clear that the French had no intention of using the wind to come down on Rooke and his fleet. Rooke held a council of war and a decision was made to share out the little remaining shot. Leake reported that a number of his ships had no shot and had been firing powder only on the previous day, to hide their weakness. Having made arrangements for the distribution of the remaining shot, Rooke, Shovell and the other admirals decided that they must fight their way through to Gibraltar, once they had the opportunity. Night came on August 14th with no further battle, and during the hours of darkness Toulouse took his fleet to the northward with the aid of his galleys. He had made no attempt at all to seek an outcome to the engagement that day. Rooke, Shovell and the Anglo/Dutch fleet were not in a position to renew hostilities, even if they had been capable, as they lacked a suitable wind.

Sunrise on August 15th showed the French to be about four to five leagues to windward. At noon a slight breeze sprang up from the east, giving the opportunity for Rooke to attack the French and make his way to Gibraltar, if he was able. By 4.00 p.m. Rooke and his fleet had come close to the French, but it was considered too late in the day for battle. The Anglo/Dutch fleet lay to with their heads to the northward for the night. The sweep of Rooke's ships towards Toulouse's fleet had been an act of bravado, as they were really in no condition to fight and most of them had very little ammunition left. Some captains were prepared to burn their ships, rather than fail to reach Gibraltar.

On August 16th the wind continued from the east giving the initiative to Rooke. The French were nowhere to be seen and the inference was that they had made for Cadiz. Intelligence from the Barbary Coast and Gibraltar showed that they had not gone through the Straits and were most likely to be sailing as quickly as possible for Toulon. This surmise was correct. A further Anglo/Dutch council of war decided to take the fleet to Gibraltar. Gibraltar was reached on August 19th, but not before Callenburgh's flagship, the *Albemarle*, had blown up with the loss of all hands except nine. Fortunately, Callenburgh was absent at the time and the catastrophe was put down to the accidental ignition of gunpowder.

A council of flag officers took place on the day after arrival at Gibraltar, August 20th. A decision was made to reinforce the garrison at Gibraltar, to leave John Leake with a small squadron as a winter guard and then to return to England. Two thousand marines, further provisions and forty-eight cannons were unloaded. By August 25th repairs had been made to the fleet and it sailed for England. Subsequently, Leake with twelve frigates and one fireship separated from the main fleet, on September 1st, bound for Lisbon, and from there to act as the winter guard on the coast of Portugal and Spain.[21]

Reports and letters from the fleet were sent to England. Some of them, including one from Shovell, have been published in a "Review of the late engagement at sea being a collection of private letters never before printed" and will be quoted.[22] Shovell wrote on August 28th from the *Barfleur*.

> This brings news of my health and that we are on our way homeward: That which sends us home so soon is a very sharp engagement we have had with the French; our number of ships that fought in the line of battle were pretty equal, I think they were 49 and ours 53 but George Rooke reserved 2 or 3 of the 50 gun ships to observe if they attempted anything with their gallies, of which they had 24. Their ships did far exceed in bigness, I judge they had seventeen three deck ships and we had but seven. The battle began on Sunday 13th instant, soon after ten in the morning, and in the centre and rear of the fleet it continued until night parted; but in the

van of the fleet where I commanded, and lead by Sir John Leake we having the weather gauge, gave me an opportunity of coming as near as I pleased which was within a pistol shot, before I fired a gun, through which means, and Gods assistance, the enemy declined us and were upon the run in less than four hours by which time we had but little wind and their Gallies towed off their line ships and others, as they pleased for the Admiral of the White and Blue [Villette], with whom we fought, had seven gallies tended on him. As soon as the enemy got out of reach of our guns, and the battle continuing pretty hot astern, and some of our ships in the Admiral's squadron towed out of the line, which I understood afterwards was for want of shot, I ordered all the ships of my Division to slack all their sails to close the line in the centre, this working had that good effect that several of the enemy's ships astern which had kept their line having their top sails and fore sails set, shot up abreast of us, as the Rear Admiral of the White and Blue and some of his Division; and the Vice Admiral of the White and some of his division; but they were so warmly received before they got a broadside that with their boats a head, and their sprit-sails set, they towed from us, without giving us the opportunity of firing at them.

The ships that suffered most in my division were the Lenox, Wa(r)spight, Tilbury, Swiftsure, the rest escaped pretty well and I the best of all; tho' I never took greater pains in all my life to have been soundly beaten; for I set all my sails and towed with three boats ahead to get a long side with the Admiral of the White and Blue; but he out sailing me, shunned fighting, and lay a long side of the little ships. Not withstanding the Engagement was very sharp and I think the like between two fleets never has been in any time. There is hardly a ship that must not shift one mast and some must shift all, a great many have suffered much, but none more than Sir George Rooke and Captain Jennings in the Monk. God send us well home, I believe we have not three spare top masts, nor three fishes in the fleet, and I judge there is ten jury top masts now up. After the fight we lay two days in front of the enemy, preparing for a second engagement but the enemy declined and stood from us in the night. I am of the opinion the enemy would have given in in the centre before night had not several of our ships towed out of the Line of Battle for want of shot and the Dutch in the rear with little ships (the Admiral carrying but 64 guns) they fought very well, but had not weight enough to make the enemy give way. We did not lose one ship, nor can I say the enemy lost any: Of our Captains Sir Andrew Lake and Low were killed and Mings, Kirton, Jumper and Baker were wounded but are like to do well: Of the Lieutenants Captain Jennings son and Lestocks youngest son and some others killed. Among the wounded are Edibury, my 3rd & 5th Lieutenants, but like to do well. Mr Cary tells me there is about 3000 killed and wounded, 300 which are Dutch. Two days after the engagement, the Dutch admirals ship by an unknown accident blew up, only nine men saved. They lost more in the Fight. Tis reported in Spain that the enemy had four ships and gallies sunk.

From one of Shovell's crew in the *Barfleur* to his parents, August 23rd:

Bloody engagement with the French fleet in the Streights and several old men in our ship say that none was ever so sharp. We had about thirty killed and wounded. I was in the boat the greatest part of the time to tow our ship up to the French Admiral who out sailed us.

From a member of the crew of the *Swiftsure* to his brother, August 22nd. (The *Swiftsure* was in the van with Cloudesley Shovell.):

Most bloody engagement with the French fleet off Malaga which lasted from morning to night but not so long in the van where we were for Cloudesley Shovell who commanded it, broke the French line by two o'clock, one or two were fired by the bombs; no ship suffered more than we have being three great ships on us at once bigger than our selves and have suffered worse had not Cloudesley Shovell come to our assistance. We had two captains killed and three or four wounded. The two Admirals fought one another all day but the Admiral that commanded the French van did not engage Cloudesley Shovell.

From a member of the crew of the *Tilbury* to a friend, August 24th. (The *Tilbury* under Captain George Delavall was in the van with Shovell.):

Loving friend
You remember the fight at Beachy Head but that was nothing to that which we have lately had with the French off Malaga. We have some on board who have been in all engagements since Bantry Bay who say that none of them were so sharp.

Shovell himself had figured prominently at Bantry Bay in 1689.
From a man on the *Assurance* to his wife, August 25th. (The *Assurance* under Captain Robert Hancock was also in the van with Shovell.):

I received no hurt at all more than that a shot went through my breeches and broke a knife that was in my pocket.

From a wounded man on the *Shrewsbury*, from Gibraltar Road. (The *Shrewsbury* was in the centre with Rooke.):

> Though I am unwilling to let you know I am wounded being in hopes I shall recover again. I was wounded by a splinter in my thigh at the begining of the engagement and carried down to be dressed, don't be disheartened the surgeon gives me great hopes I shall soon be well again.

Rooke and the remainder of the fleet reached St Helens on September 24th. On September 28th Shovell left with the great ships bound for Chatham.[23]

So ended the naval campaign of 1704. The Battle of Malaga was the only major naval encounter of the War of the Spanish Succession. Both sides claimed it was a victory. Toulouse, with his battered fleet, returned to Toulon and a Te Deum was sung at the command of Louis XIV at Notre Dame in Paris. The Duke of Marlborough on the Danube heard accounts of a French naval victory that dampened the satisfaction of his recent success at Blenheim.[24] Reports had been sent to England claiming an Anglo/Dutch victory. However, the *Observator* and *Mercury* stated that the French reports were more accurate. Early in the New Year (1705) Queen Anne gave a cold reply when Malaga was described with Blenheim as a double success.[25]

The deeds of some of the naval officers at Malaga were recognised. George Byng, Thomas Dilkes and John Jennings were knighted. Shovell was presented to Queen Anne on his return to England and, by family tradition, received from her a gold snuffbox. It was adorned with a portrait of the Queen, surrounded with diamonds, set in the lid. In the nineteenth century the box was still in existence, in the hands of the Romney family and with some of Shovell's snuff still in it.[26]

The Battle of Malaga is generally considered to have had no victor. The advantage should have been with the French, who roughly matched the Anglo/Dutch fleet in numbers of ships, men and guns. However, the French were close to their own ports, their ships were quicker through the water, as they were clean and their crews were fresh. The Anglo/Dutch fleet had been away from home for many months and, as with all long voyages, many of their crews were not in good health. The most crucial advantage that the French had was in ammunition, although they were unaware of it. The Siege of Gibraltar had used up more shot than had been necessary and Rooke may be criticised for not ensuring an equal distribution of the remaining shot prior to the battle, rather than after it. Shovell was certainly of the opinion that the day could have been carried, if ships of Byng's and Dilkes' squadrons in the centre had not had to pull out of the line through lack of ammunition.

What of Shovell's role at the Battle of Malaga? He commanded the van with Leake leading it and had forced De Villette's French van to give way. In a skilful demonstration of seamanship, he had been able to back some of his division, in the early afternoon, to come to Rooke's assistance in the hard pressed centre. The manoeuvre was much admired at the time. Leake and his biographer, Stephen Martin, have been very critical of Shovell's failure to follow Leake's advice to drive the French van right out of the line, rather than playing safe by backing to the assistance of Rooke. Shovell's actions have been more than justified, and the only real criticism of his action at this time is that of Leake. Laird Clowes stated that Shovell throughout the engagement greatly distinguished himself both as an able and as a brave officer.[27] This was abundantly true. Perhaps the inconclusive result of the Battle of Malaga was not unexpected. Shovell is on record as repeatedly stating that, where two fleets are equal in size, then no result could be expected.

Toulouse and his French fleet had come to help Villadarias in the retaking of Gibraltar. While Rooke's fleet was in being, this could not be done. Following the battle, Toulouse slunk back to Toulon, never to come out again with large numbers of ships. Gibraltar is still in British hands. Rooke was the real victor.

On 25th October 1704 the Lord Mayor of London entertained Shovell, Rooke and some of the other leading sea officers to dinner.[28] On November 16th Shovell was made one of the Council of the Lord High Admiral, Prince George of Denmark, and the following Boxing Day, Rear Admiral of England.[29]

In the three remaining years of his life, Shovell was to be at the height of his powers as Rear Admiral of England and Commander-in-Chief of the naval forces in the main theatre of war, the Mediterranean.

NOTES

1. Leake, p.157.
2. Torrington, p.146.
3. Corbett, p.262.
4. Leake, p.157.
5. Secret Memoirs.
6. Corbett, p.263.
7. Secret Memoirs.
8. Torrington, p.147.
9. Leake, p.158; Torrington, p.147.
10. Torrington, pp.147–148.
11. Leake, pp.158–159.
12. Torrington, p.148.
13. Leake, pp.159–160; Torrington, pp.149–151; Secret Memoirs.
14. Leake, p.160; Torrington, p.151.
15. Leake, pp.160–161; Secret Memoirs.
16. Leake, p.161; Secret Memoirs.

17. Leake, pp.162–163.
18. Memoires du Marquis de Villette, p.350.
19. Leake, pp.158–165; Torrington, pp.151–160; Corbett, pp.268–273; Secret Memoirs; Burchett, pp.678–680; Owen, pp.86–96.
20. Laird Clowes, pp.402–403; Torrington, pp.163–164; Leake, pp.168–169.
21. Torrington, p.165.
22. London MDCC IV, BL 1093.c.83.
23. Torrington, p.165.
24. Corbett, p.276.
25. Leake, p.171 note 2.
26. Laird Clowes, p.404: RMT MAT 63; Jones, Historic Memorials of the Norfolk Coast, p.335.
27. Laird Clowes, p.402.
28. Luttrell, Vol.V, p.480.
29. Luttrell, Vol.V, p.487; RMT MAT 25.

CHAPTER XXII

# The Capture of Barcelona
# 1705

Early in the New Year of 1705 Shovell was made President of the Council of War "for the trying of several sea captains who went out of the line in the last battle [Malaga] against the French when they did not lack powder". All the captains of the fleet were to congregate at Deptford, on January 8th 1705, to assist at the trials.[1]

Captain William Cleveland of the *Montagu*, who had been in the centre with Rooke, pulled out of the line of battle still having ten rounds of ammunition in his lower tier. His defence was that the lieutenant commanding the deck had wrongly informed him of the situation and could not be questioned, as he was dead. In addition he had had Rooke's permission to do so. Captain Edward Acton of the *Kingston* could not find any shot in the hold as water had come in over the ballast. The gunner, now dead, had said there was none and Byng had given his permission for them to draw out of the line. Once the *Kingston* had been pumped free of water, the ten rounds were found. Both Cleveland and Acton were rightly cleared.[2] Shovell had the reputation of being merciful at courts martial at which he presided.

The autumn and winter of 1704 saw the eclipse of Rooke as Naval Commander-in-Chief. In England there was a feeling of disappointment that, as the two fleets at Malaga had been well matched, there had not been an overwhelming English victory. The English were too accustomed to winning sea battles. The fact that Rooke had taken Gibraltar was overlooked.

On February 22nd 1705 Rooke wrote that "some of my services of the last year have been so ill received by some and so ill rewarded by others that I could no longer forbear gratifying my inclinations to quit command of the fleet". The Duke of Bolton, chairing a House of Lords committee which had looked into possible miscarriages in the fleet in 1704 and, finding none, remaining silent particularly stung Rooke. He had had enough.

If Rooke's star was in eclipse, Cloudesley Shovell's was to shine brightly in 1705. Prince George of Denmark, as Lord High Admiral, had made him Rear Admiral of England on December 26th 1704. On the following February 7th Shovell was given a patent by Queen Anne for this office, which is still in existence with part of her great seal in place. Rooke was a Tory and Shovell a Whig. Shovell had played no part in the attempt to reduce Rooke's reputation. It was not in his straightforward nature to behave in such a dishonourable manner.[3]

Shovell was made Admiral and Commander-in-Chief of the fleet on January 13th 1705. That same day John Norris joined the *Britannia* from the *Oxford*, as First Captain. The *Britannia*, a 100 gun 1st rate ship built at Chatham in 1682, was to be Shovell's flagship throughout 1705. He had joined her himself on December 18th 1704. Norris and Shovell were, of course, well known to each other. When Shovell was captain of the *Edgar* at the Battle of Bantry Bay in 1689, Norris had been one of his midshipmen. More recently, at the Battle of Malaga, Norris had been one of Shovell's seconds.[4]

During the period January to February 1705 George Byng, newly knighted after the Battle of Malaga, wrote to his Commander-in-Chief, Shovell. Byng appears to have been commanding the winter guard. Before sailing, Byng suggested that privateer catching was to be their main business and that he was pleased to have been thought of for that service. He asked Shovell for "his thoughts and advice in the service he was employed". There is no record of Shovell's response.[5]

During the spring of 1705 it was clear that there would soon be Parliamentary elections. Between 1695 and 1702 Shovell had been a Member of Parliament for Rochester City as an Admiralty nominee, with Sir Joseph Williamson as the second member. Neither had been in Parliament during the intervening period. On March 15th Sir Stafford Fairborne, another distinguished naval officer, wrote to the Duke of Ormonde from his ship, the *Royal Sovereign*, in the Medway, concerning his candidature for Rochester. At this time Rochester's two Members of Parliament would consist of one "sea officer" and one "country gentleman". In the past Shovell had been the sea officer and Williamson the local man. However, Fairborne hoped to argue that Shovell with his nearby estate could be considered the local man and he, Fairborne, the sea officer.

The punctiliously correct Shovell had refused to support Fairborne in his endeavours, as he had declined to help others with similar aspirations. In addition, Fairborne asked Ormonde to stop his friend Sir Edward Gregory from opposing him.[6] Shovell's country estate referred to in the letter was May Place, Crayford, which he had owned since 1695.

Some fine hairs had to be split to have Shovell in the second seat as a local landowner. However, on May 8th 1705 both Shovell and Fairborne were returned for Rochester, with the first Parliamentary session on June 14th. Shovell was to remain as a member for Rochester until his death in 1707. On January 3rd 1708 yet another naval officer, John Leake, filled his position, again without local difficulty.[7]

During early 1705 the general strategy for the coming year was considered. The principal naval activity was to be in the Mediterranean, with the aim of drawing enemy forces away from the main military campaign in Flanders. The Earl of Galway, who had been sent to support the Portuguese, was in need of reinforcements. The Duke of Savoy might be persuaded to make a combined attempt with the English fleet on Toulon, the principal French naval port in the Mediterranean and the gateway through which an invasion might take place into southern France. The Emperor was independently and rather selfishly endeavouring to seize Naples and Sicily. Finally in Catalonia, it was reported that the local inhabitants were in favour of Charles III for the throne of Spain, and might be stimulated into military activity. Command of the sea was vital, in that it would give freedom of movement for military forces.[8]

A major error in the strategy for 1705 was the failure to consider a serious attempt on Port Mahon, in Minorca, where there was a large harbour which could be used as a base the whole year round. In 1704 thoughts had been turned in the direction of Port Mahon, but it was by then too late in the year for an assault. Although later in the campaign of 1705 the possibility of taking the port was raised, nothing was done about it and it was to be another three years before it was eventually taken. But by this time the Mediterranean was no longer a centre of major military activity.[9]

On March 31st 1705 Charles Mordaunt, 3rd Earl of Peterborough, was given a warrant by Queen Anne to be the General and Commander-in-Chief of the troops which the fleet were to transport to the Mediterranean. Under Peterborough, Major General Henry Conyngham and Generaal Majoor Schratenbach were to have subordinate commands. A month later, on May 1st, Peterborough was made a joint Admiral of the Fleet with Shovell, to command the combined Anglo/Dutch ships bound for the Mediterranean. Under Peterborough and Shovell were to be Vice Admirals Stafford Fairborne and John Leake, and Rear Admiral Thomas Dilkes. The Dutch contingent was to be led by Lieutenant Admiral Philip Almonde.[10]

Peterborough was an odd choice to command both the army and fleet, as he was not a soldier and his experience at sea was limited. The Duke of Marlborough, possibly influenced by his wife Sarah, was behind the appointment. A contemporary of Peterborough's, Johann Hoffmann, an Imperial envoy in London, reported back to his government. "He is of such a temperament that he can not brook an equal. He is a thoroughly restless and quarrelsome character, incapable of dealing with anybody, . . . and on top of that he has no war experience on land or sea."[11]

So this was the man with whom Shovell would have to share command of the fleet! The two would have known each other for more than twenty years, as they had been in the Mediterranean with Narbrough and Herbert between 1674 and 1680. Both, in 1680, had helped defend Tangier against the Moors. Arthur Herbert was Peterborough's mother's stepbrother and a staunch supporter of Shovell, as has been seen already in this account. No doubt Shovell was well aware of Peterborough's temperament. The only advantage Peterborough could claim was that as a peer he might command respect at foreign courts. However, that "plain gallant man", Sir Cloudesley Shovell did well enough with Prince Eugene and the Duke of Savoy two years later.[12]

Joint commissions to command the fleet were not unknown and had been used twice during William and Mary's reign. Shovell had held a joint commission with Killigrew and Delavall in 1693. What was unusual about Peterborough's appointment was his complete lack of naval experience other than in a very junior position. Since the Restoration in 1660, only James, Duke of York, had been given supreme command with so little experience.[13]

During the first week of May 1705 Peterborough and Shovell received a number of orders from Queen Anne concerning the forthcoming Mediterranean enterprise. They were to join John Leake at Lisbon.

Leake had spent the winter there and had relieved the hard pressed garrison at Gibraltar during the previous autumn. The principal objectives given to Peterborough and Shovell were the taking of Barcelona and Cadiz. If possible, the Duke of Savoy was to be assisted. A treaty was to be made with Morocco and presents given to the Governors of the Barbary states in exchange for water and provisions. Gibraltar was to be supported. If a French naval force should come out of the Straits, a squadron was to be sent after them. Neutral states were not to be molested. Additionally, Peterborough and Shovell were given liberty to agree on any other enterprise that might promote the common cause, provided that other orders were not countered.[14]

Further secret orders were sent to Peterborough and Shovell on May 7th. They were told that cooperation with the Duke of Savoy, in attacking Toulon, came before all other operations. Savoy had said that he was ready to make an assault from the land. No one, and in particular the King of Portugal, was to be told of this plan, until a council of war was held, and it was to be carried out under the disguise of attempting Barcelona.[15]

Queen Anne gave instructions about the way Peterborough and Shovell should conduct their business. Peterborough might stay on board or go ashore, was to preside at councils of war ashore, and was to be governed by the results of these councils. Shovell was to command the fleet when Peterborough was ashore. Both Peterborough and Shovell were told that they had only a single joint vote at councils of war and must subscribe to a single opinion there. If they differed they must send home their reasons.[16] With these odd arrangements, a multitude of conflicting orders, some secret, plus Peterborough's quixotic character, it is not surprising that events in the Mediterranean were to be dogged by endless debate and mind changing.

Shovell had gone aboard his flagship, the *Britannia,* at the Nore on April 9th, and arrived at Spithead on May 13th. He set about getting the ships in readiness and the 5,000 English soldiers embarked. Queen Anne was not happy at the delay in sailing and sent instructions, on May 22nd, to hurry matters along. Peterborough arrived on May 23rd, and the fleet got away the next day.[17]

The fleet made its way down the Channel and cruised for some days off Ushant, while George Byng investigated Brest with John Jennings. They reported that there were eighteen French ships under the Marquis de Cöetlogon at Brest. It was known that the French Mediterranean naval force, under the Compte de Toulouse and based at Toulon, consisted of about forty ships. The English fleet under Peterborough and Shovell consisted of about twenty-three vessels which would be reinforced by Leake's squadron at Lisbon. The admirals were uneasy about dividing their force, which would make Cöetlogon's eighteen ships a superior force to either of the two English squadrons, but felt they had no alternative. Byng and Jennings were left to shadow the Brest squadron, and on May 31st the remaining English vessels sailed with Peterborough and Shovell for Lisbon. No doubt Shovell remembered all too well his experiences with the Smyrna convoy in 1693. An additional worry was that the Toulon squadron might join that of Brest, while the bulk of the English fleet was still in the Mediterranean. If the Dutch contingent had been in company, the problem would not have been so acute.[18]

In the event, neither the Brest nor the Toulon squadron came out of its harbour in any force, and played no real part in events during the summer of 1705. The first to arrive in Lisbon, on June 3rd, was the Dutch contingent under Philip Almonde. Peterborough arrived in the *Swallow* on June 9th, soon followed by Shovell in the *Britannia*, with the rest of the English fleet. Leake's squadron had arrived at Lisbon about a week earlier. The Anglo/Dutch contingents were now united.[19]

Soon after their arrival at Lisbon on June 15th, Peterborough, Shovell and the other commanders conferred with the courts of Spain and Portugal, the English Ambassador, John Methuen, and Lord Galway, who commanded the Anglo/Dutch troops serving in Portugal. The expedition could not go forward into the Mediterranean because a third of the army that was coming from Ireland still had not arrived. Also Galway had offered two regiments of dragoons who had to collect their transport and forage. It was agreed at the council on June 15th to send Shovell with most of the fleet to cruise between Cadiz and Cape Spartel, to prevent the possible junction of the Brest and Toulon squadrons. Two days later the English flag officers decided at a private council that it was not advisable to detach ships, because of a probable junction of the two French squadrons. Shovell got away from the Tagus on June 22nd, and the same day William Jumper arrived with the troops from Ireland.[20]

While Shovell and the fleet were cruising between Cadiz and Cape Spartel, earnest debate was taking place in Lisbon about how best to employ the expeditionary force. The Duke of Savoy was by this time so hard pressed that he could not support an assault on Toulon. Over the next few months he would write plaintively to Queen Anne asking for assistance and reporting that the enemy was at the gates of Turin. Peterborough played with the idea of attacking Toulon with his own resources or trying to secure Naples for Charles III. The Portuguese court refused to join in any design on Cadiz or anywhere else. Charles III, his ministers and the Earl of Galway had concluded that an assault on Catalonia was the most sensible course of action. The Queen (Anne) had sent Colonel Mitford Crowe to Italy to make contact with the Catalans. Quoting Crowe, Peterborough in a letter to Shovell stated that there were 6,000 men, 12,000 horse and a favourably disposed population in Catalonia. Prince George of Hesse Darmstadt had arrived to join the expedition from defending Gibraltar. He argued against this plan and proposed a landing in Valencia and a march on Madrid. The advantage of this proposal was that Valencia was only half as far from Madrid as was Catalonia, and there would be no French interference across the Pyrenees. Peterborough agreed with Hesse Darmstadt's military reasoning, but Charles III and his court were adamant that an attempt should be made on the main city of Catalonia, Barcelona. The die was cast.[21]

For much of the time that Barcelona was being chosen for assault, Shovell was at sea and unable to influence the debate. One opportunity that was again missed was the possibility of taking the fine all-year-round harbour at Port Mahon, Minorca. Later, while at Barcelona, consideration was given to Port Mahon, but by that time it was too late in the campaign season to be feasible. Perhaps if Shovell had been present at all the councils at Lisbon, he would as an experienced naval officer have brought the matter up. It was a fine chance missed.

On July 20th the ships from Lisbon joined Shovell. Charles III went straight on to Gibraltar, where raw battalions from home were exchanged for experienced ones and marines left behind by Rooke the previous year rejoined. Shovell with the English and Dutch admirals met at a council of war the next day, and formally agreed to cooperate and assist with the fleet in the assault on Barcelona. It was agreed that the forces from Gibraltar would rejoin the main fleet at sea and then the combined force would sail for Altea Bay, on the east coast of Spain, to rewater. It is clear from the council of war of July 21st that Shovell and the admirals had played no part in the selection of Barcelona for attack.[22]

Shovell's fleet and the forces from Gibraltar united in the Straits on July 25th, and sailed for Altea Bay which was reached on the 30th. The fleet spent a week watering there. On August 2nd Peterborough attended a council of war with Shovell and the admirals. At this meeting, Charles III's great assurances of a favourable reception by the people of Catalonia were recorded, and it was agreed that with the first fine wind they would sail for Barcelona.[23]

They sailed from Altea Bay on August 4th. Hesse Darmstadt, in the *Devonshire*, whose Captain was James, Lord Dursley, a Shovell protégé, was sent ahead with the small frigates to find out if the people of Catalonia were truly well disposed towards Charles III. Shovell sent another protégé, John Narbrough's nephew Edmund Loades, in the *Orford*, with a small squadron to Denia, a small town near Altea Bay with a castle on a hill. After Loades had threatened the town with his ships and bomb ketches, the inhabitants threw out the governor. They agreed to admit a governor sent by Charles III and took an oath of loyalty to him. It was an excellent beginning to the venture. The main fleet continued on course for Barcelona hindered by the slow sailing transport ships. However, on August 11th Shovell anchored in front of Barcelona. Hesse Darmstadt was not there, but a landing point was selected and Peterborough gave instructions for the marines to go aboard the smaller frigates and boats with a view to an immediate landing. By the time this had been carried out, it was too late in the day to go ashore.[24]

Dursley carried Hesse Darmstadt about fifty miles to the north of Barcelona to San Feliu, sending on shore intermittently to gauge the feelings of the inhabitants. They arrived back in Barcelona on the morning of August 12th, in time to take part in the landings.

The night of August 11th was unpleasant for the ships anchored off Barcelona, with a high sea and thunder and lightning. However, the next morning, Sunday 12th, the weather had improved and half the foot soldiers were carried ashore, four miles north-east of the city. Shovell has left his own description of the landings.

> Sunday 12th, the army landed, and the Prince of Hesse [Darmstadt] came time enough to get ashore with them. There was no manner of

opposition, not so much as a musket fired to interrupt our landing, and the people in the neighbouring towns and little villages keep in their habitations, and esteem us their friends, and the garrison their enemies. We landed from the fleet of our ships' complements about 1150 who were all marines.[25]

The landing had been unopposed, and over the next three to four days the remaining foot soldiers, dragoons and baggage were brought ashore by working parties of seaman. Peterborough's troops set up camp to the north-east of Barcelona, at St Martin.[26]

What of the city that the combined Anglo/Dutch troops faced? Barcelona, the capital of Catalonia, was the largest and most prosperous city in Spain. It had an extended sea front of about one mile and rather less than that distance inland. The fortifications, though not so formidable as those designed by Vauban in Flanders, were sufficient to demand siege operations on a considerable scale: a strong wall with eight large bastions, numerous small towers and a ditch of moderate depth. On the south-west a hill called Montjuic rose 700 feet above sea level. It was crowned by a small detached fort; a precipitous cliff dropped down to the shore; from the inland the ascent was rugged and steep, but possible. Obviously no landing could be attempted on this side of the town. On the north-east the ground was reported to be level but marshy, and the engineers declared it to be quite unfit for sapping the siege approaches; there was no cover to conceal the advance of the troops. Ships could bring massed fire on the sea front, but troops could only approach it in boats, an attempt which must be attended with heavy loss in the face of a strong garrison.[27]

Don Francisco Velasco, who was Viceroy of Catalonia, commanded the city of Barcelona. Velasco, a Spaniard, was dedicated to the Bourbon cause with forces amounting to 3,200 foot soldiers and 800 horse. Orders had been given to destroy all the straw and forage in the surrounding countryside. A large store of provisions had been collected in Barcelona. Velasco's position was helped by the fact that Peterborough could neither starve nor generally bombard the city into submission, for fear of alienating the inhabitants. They in turn were reluctant to show where their sympathies lay for fear of reprisals.[28]

If Peterborough received no active help from the inhabitants of Barcelona, then he did get support from an irregular force of 1,500 Miquelets* in the surrounding countryside. They had little discipline, but hovered around the area denying Velasco the opportunity of making sallies outside the city of Barcelona.[29]

While the troops were being carried ashore, Shovell and his fellow

* Undisciplined local irregulars loyal to Hesse Darmstadt.

admirals felt little threat from French men of war based at Toulon or from Cöetlogon bringing the Brest squadron into the Mediterranean. Intelligence from Genoa, Turin and sometimes from England indicated that Cöetlogon was unlikely to leave Brest, and that there were few ships at Toulon fit for sea. Shovell did not feel the need to keep cruisers off Brest, and made do with a few frigates to cover his anchorage.[30]

A week after the first landings, on August 19th, Peterborough called a council of land officers, who stated bluntly that they were of the unanimous opinion that no attempt should be made on Barcelona, and that the fleet should carry them to Italy instead. The reason for this decision was that they had hoped to find an open city, which Hesse Darmstadt had indicated would be the case. Instead, they found a committed garrison only a little smaller in number than their own forces. In the previous war, the French had needed a force of 26,000 men, of whom they lost 10,000, to wrest the city from Hesse Darmstadt himself, who had been the governor at the time. That same day, August 19th, Shovell and his admirals considered the matter at their own council of war. Having re-examined their instructions, they felt that the attempt on Barcelona should continue and that, if it really was not feasible to take the city, something else on the Spanish coast should be attempted. Only if troops could be spared from Spain should they be sent to help the Duke of Savoy.[31]

Shovell and the admirals had no intention of deviating at all from their orders as they saw them. It is little wonder that Peterborough gave this description of Shovell to the Earl of Godolphin at about this time.

> Sir Cloudesley Shovell is a man possessed of many good qualities. . . . He is brave if I may say to a fault, and in matters he does not understand thinks that whatever is directed first must be begun, and when begun must be carried on what accidents soever occur, or whatsoever improbabilities come in the way. He sticks close to what he calls orders, and will conceive no latitude in such instructions that I think were calculated for the greatest.[32]

On August 24th Peterborough came aboard the *Britannia* to discuss with the admirals a letter that he had received from Charles III, who was by now ashore with his staff. Charles wanted the attempt on Barcelona to continue for a further eighteen days, after which he supposed that there would be time for other duties. Peterborough reiterated the view of the land officers that it was not possible to take Barcelona, although he personally was prepared to accede to the King's wish, and there was further pressure from the Lord Treasurer, at home, to assist the Duke of Savoy. Could the fleet accompany the army, if the siege was allowed to continue for the eighteen days, and was it possible to help Savoy if the troops were embarked again in one week? The admirals under Shovell collected together in the *Britannia* to consider their position. They concluded that the fleet would provide all reasonable assistance to the army in continuing the assault on Barcelona, and that they would help if the army decided to march to Tarragona and Valencia. If there was nothing further to be done on the coast of Spain and the troops were embarked in a week, they could be carried to Nice or thereabouts.[33]

Three days later, on August 27th, Brigadier James Stanhope came to Shovell in the *Britannia* with further resolutions from the combined Anglo/Dutch land officers. At this stage, they appeared to have reluctantly come to accept Charles III's wish to continue the attempt on Barcelona, while at the same time covering themselves by pointing out that it went against their professional judgement. Charles had personally persuaded Stanhope and the Dutch Brigadier St Amant, and the others were prepared to follow Peterborough's orders. The land officers took up Shovell's offer of support from the fleet. They required 5,000 men to work and guard the assault trenches. The whole army consisted of only 7,000 men (including 1,100 marines) and could realistically only supply 2,500 men on a daily basis to work on the trenches. Shovell was asked for 1,500 men daily from the fleet, to work in the trenches, plus fifty-two battering guns and their gunners. The 1,000 shortfall in men would be made up of Miquelets. The admirals were called together by Shovell, who sent Edmund Loades to ask Peterborough to attend the meeting. He did not come, and his absence was officially noted. "The Earl of Peterborough not thinking fit to afford us his company at this great council." Shovell agreed to the 1,500 men to serve in the trenches and to the landing of the fifty-two battering guns, which would be carried out with the first favourable weather. He reported that the Dutch would send a contingent and requested tents or houses for his men ashore, as the fleet could not spare canvas to provide shelter for them. Shovell's only stipulation was that his sailors be returned immediately to their ships if the French approached by sea. Peterborough added a memorandum to Shovell's report for Prince George, agreeing that he had been asked to attend the admirals' discussions, but adding lamely that he did not want to stop the flags from showing their zeal for King Charles! Peterborough still hankered after going to Italy.[34]

Shovell's help did not satisfy Peterborough and the land officers. At further councils of war ashore, on August 28th and 30th, they reverted to their original view of the impracticability of taking Barcelona with its garrison almost as strong as their besieging forces. The land officers complained that the fleet was only supplying 900 of the promised 1,500 men daily, for service in the trenches. The discrepancy had arisen because the navy considered the marines to be part of the ship's complement who were on shore and the army considered them to be land forces. Once again the army's view was to re-embark the troops and go to the support of the Duke of Savoy.[35]

Charles III was well aware of Peterborough's and the army's attitude in wishing to leave Barcelona. Using Hesse Darmstadt, he enlisted Shovell's and the admirals' support to maintain the siege. Between August 28th and September 2nd Hesse Darmstadt wrote no fewer than eight letters seeking Shovell's help. On August 28th Hesse Darmstadt, on Charles III's behalf, expressed the King's gratitude for the great zeal Shovell had shown in the expedition and asked that all the guns be landed to hinder any attempt to leave. In a further letter to Shovell, on August 30th, Hesse Darmstadt wrote:

> His Catholic Majesty [Charles III] relies in every part on your good zeal and particular love you have showed in all occasions to his person, shall always owe to you the good success of this present undertaking, which, if well supported, will lead him to the possession of this Monarchy.[36]

By August 29th Charles was beginning to accept the reality of the situation, and although reluctant to desert his supporters in Catalonia, was looking for a way out. He played with the idea of marching to Tarragona, to extend his winter quarters to Tortosa and even into Valencia. Peterborough was prepared to accept this and Shovell with the flag officers discussed the situation at a council of war on August 31st. With the change of plan, they agreed to support the army from the sea in its march to Tarragona. However, they changed their earlier view in stating that it was now too late in the year, with storms in the Gulf of Lyons, to consider sailing to Nice to help the Duke of Savoy, and that they intended to sail for home no later than September 20th. No doubt this concentrated the generals' minds.[37]

At this stage Charles III, via Hesse Darmstadt, asked Shovell to consider taking Majorca, Minorca and Ibiza. Of course Minorca had Port Mahon, with a harbour large enough to be used by a fleet the whole year round. Once again the opportunity was lost, but through no fault of Shovell's. As events unfurled before Barcelona it became impossible for him to leave, and by the time he was free it was so late in the year that he had to sail for home.[38]

During late August and early September 1705 there was an air of confusion in both the army to the north-east of Barcelona and to a lesser extent in the supporting fleet. The main reason for this was the inability of the leading participants to make up their minds about what was the best course of action to follow. Charles III, Hesse Darmstadt and the Prince of Lichtenstein, aided and abetted by Shovell, were keen to attempt

Barcelona come what may. Peterborough for part of the time, Scratenbach, Conyngham and most of the land officers were against it. To make matters worse their orders from England were open to interpretation.

Personality also came into it. Peterborough, although he got on well with Charles, loathed his German advisers and treated them with open contempt. Shovell was considered by Peterborough to be too much under the influence of Hesse Darmstadt and Lichtenstein. John Norris, the First Captain of the *Britannia*, was used by Shovell as an emissary ashore and fell foul of Peterborough. Peterborough credited Norris with having persuaded Shovell that Barcelona must be dealt with before any other scheme. Peterborough rudely described him as "a governing coxcomb"! Shovell must have found the temperamental and inconsistent Peterborough difficult to cope with, although he has left no record of direct criticism. According to one account, Shovell was not happy with Peterborough's treatment of Charles III. For this reason, his executors freely allowed his papers to be used, after his death, in the preparation of "An Impartial Enquiry into the Management of the War in Spain" as a counterbalance to Peterborough's apologist in "An Account of the Earl of Peterborough's Conduct in Spain".[39] Hesse Darmstadt also had his difficulties with Peterborough. In a letter to Shovell on September 1st he wrote: "I ask your pardon that I have not answered yet your last letter, having been so tormented by our good Lord [Peterborough] that I had no moment for myself left to satisfy all his demands, but shall not fail to do it today."[40]

At this stage, the attempted assault on Barcelona appeared to be drawing to an unsatisfactory conclusion for Charles III, Peterborough and Shovell. Failure stared the commanders in the face, but the surprise attack and taking of the outworks of the castle of Montjuic, on September 3rd, was to change all that.

Peterborough has been generally credited with making the plan to take Montjuic castle, 1,300 yards from the city of Barcelona. Although not the key to the city, its capture would allow more suitable trenches to be dug than in the marshy north-east, and better artillery positions. Other authorities have emphasised the part played by Hesse Darmstadt who was to lose his life in the action. Both men were present at the assault, but it is difficult to believe that the original idea had not originated in Hesse Darmstadt's fertile mind, with his long-standing experience of military matters and several years as Governor of Barcelona. Peterborough by contrast had little military experience and no knowledge of the city. As an Englishman, he could give orders to the troops where Hesse Darmstadt could not. However, dead men cannot sing their own praises, and at this distance of time it is unlikely that we shall ever know for certain where the plan originated. Perhaps it came from a number of minds. Shovell and the admirals had no part in the decision.[41]

Early on September 2nd the fleet and the army were preparing for the withdrawal to Tarragona. That night Peterborough was determined to march round and attack Montjuic early the next morning. He intended to use rock paths among the foothills to the west of Barcelona. Secrecy was to be maintained until the last moment by letting the soldiers believe that they were part of an advance guard to seize a pass on the road to Tarragona. A thousand Anglo/Dutch soldiers formed the storming party under Brigadier Lord William Charlemont, and Lieutenant Colonels Southwell and Allen. A second column of 1,000 foot and Royal Dragoons under Brigadier James Stanhope was to be in support.

Peterborough was reluctant to let Charles III know of the plan, but Hesse Darmstadt was to inform Shovell and the fleet. This was done via John Norris, Shovell's Captain of the *Britannia*, who went off to prepare scaling ladders and to give new orders to Captain Philip Cavendish of the *Antelope*. Cavendish was to have taken troops to Tarragona, but his orders were now changed to carrying them to help with the attack on Montjuic from the sea. In the event he was able to do little to help the assault because of bad weather.

The columns moved off at dusk on September 2nd under Charlemont, followed soon afterwards by Peterborough and Hesse Darmstadt. Charles III was told of the plan at the last moment. The troops did not reach Montjuic until daylight, having lost their way during the night. Southwell led his men into action from the west side of the castle and Allen from the east. Almost at once they came under small arms fire which alerted the castle and city. The poorly guarded outworks of Montjuic castle were taken and the defenders driven back into the citadel. The scaling ladders prepared by the fleet proved too short to get into the castle proper. At this stage, Peterborough and Hesse Darmstadt came up and the latter proposed the cutting of communications between the castle of Montjuic and the city of Barcelona. While pushing forward, Hesse Darmstadt was shot in the right thigh just below a wound he had received at the siege of Bonn. He continued walking for a further fifty paces, collapsed and died before the wound could even be looked at. The musket ball had torn the femoral artery and poor Hesse Darmstadt had bled to death. Peterborough was temporarily absent and the command had fallen on the inexperienced Lord Charlemont. He feared a sally from the city to cut them off, and ordered a retreat. At this stage, some of the defenders of the castle came out crying "Viva Carlos Tercero" and pretending to lay down their arms. No sooner had the Anglo/Dutch soldiers shown themselves, than the Spaniards opened fire, causing casualties and further confusion. This trick was played several times, and Colonel Allen and 200 of his soldiers were taken prisoner. Reinforcements from the city reached Montjuic at about this time, bringing the numbers of defenders up to about 500 men.

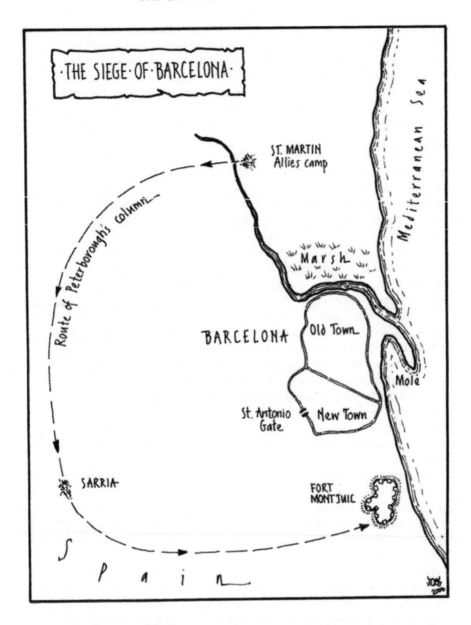

At this juncture Peterborough re-appeared on the scene and, falling into a great rage, led the soldiers back to the posts they had captured earlier. Whatever his faults may have been, Peterborough at this critical point showed enormous courage and resolution that saved the day. Further reinforcements of 3,000 men started to come out of Barcelona, that would have swung the advantage in favour of the defenders. Miraculously they turned back. The reason for this was that the prisoners had told them that Peterborough was there in person and that Hesse Darmstadt had been killed in the action. The Spaniards could not believe that such distinguished persons could be present without substantial forces. Soon afterwards, Stanhope's 1,000 reserves came up in support. Peterborough had taken most of the castle at Montjuic and was keen to complete the work. He sent messages to Charles III and Shovell, to let them know what had gone on.[42]

The body of the gallant Prince George of Hesse Darmstadt was laid out in state in a convent which had been hired by Peterborough for the purpose. He was dressed with his wig, hat, naval clothes, boots, a sword in one hand and a cane in the other. A priest was constantly with the corpse praying, and the place was crowded with Spaniards wanting to see him.[43]

The day after Peterborough took the outworks of Montjuic, September 4th, he wrote to Shovell requesting the active support of the fleet. He was already getting it in the form of Cavendish, who had anchored abreast of Montjuic on the evening of the 3rd. Although neither he nor the troops he had transported played a role in the initial attack, he had stayed to help unload guns for the batteries that would be set up once Montjuic fell.

Shovell and the admirals discussed Peterborough's letter on the day that it was written. Attitudes both in the fleet and ashore had changed with Peterborough's success. The possibility of taking Barcelona was now a very real one. Peterborough would get everything that he had asked for. Forty guns from the fleet, 24 and 18 pounders, would be sent for the batteries and the fleet would start a bombardment of the city. Vice Admiral Stafford Fairborne was to command eight men of war, bomb vessels and boats for this undertaking.

On September 6th a lucky bomb from a mortar hit a powder magazine in the isolated citadel of Montjuic. The ensuing explosion killed the governor and his officers who were at dinner. Vigilant Miquelets rushed in and took the citadel through a rent in the wall. All Montjuic was in Peterborough's hands. It was a clever piece of work. Now he could concentrate on his real goal, Barcelona.[44]

While the fleet was getting its guns ashore, to set up batteries so that a breach could be made in the walls of Barcelona, Fairborne was overseeing the bombardment from the sea. Consideration was given to filling a fireship with powder and running her ashore near the arsenal and west bastion of the town. In the event this came to nothing. The eight men of war under Fairborne took up station off the city but did not open fire. However, the bomb ketches threw a large number of shells and carcasses into the city between the 4th and 22nd of September. Among the captains supervising the bombing was the young Christopher Myngs, who had long been associated with Shovell.[45]

After the capture of the castle of Montjuic, the siege of Barcelona continued in earnest from the land. The camp to the north-east of Barcelona was maintained, perhaps because of better communications with the fleet. Montjuic was garrisoned to stop any sortie by Velasco on that side of the city. Shovell's main consideration was to get sufficient guns from the fleet ashore for the batteries, so that a breach could be made in the walls of Barcelona. The guns were landed from the beach to the south of Montjuic. It was difficult work and the shore so steep in parts that horses could not be used. One enterprising captain made special harnesses for 200 men at a time, to drag the guns right up to the battery positions over the most difficult ground. The chief gunner of the expedition, Colonel John Richards, was less than happy with Peterborough's decision to keep the camp at St Martin, which meant that he had to rely on the local country people to carry stores. Worse still the seamen ashore disappointed Richards with their casual ways. "I must confess that in my life I never saw so much disorder, ignorance and confusion; and what is still more shameful, not one half of the men designed came to the work, or slipped away in the dark." Perhaps this was unfair, as by the end of the siege the sailors had had no victuals or money for seven days, and they had been forced to forage in gardens for food.[46]

On September 11th Shovell sent on shore three of the youngest captains without posts and six lieutenants, to command the guns of the naval batteries which had been set up to the south-west of the city. The following day, the 12th, the first batteries opened fire on Barcelona. Considerable damage was done to the enemy by dismounting their cannon. Peterborough requested some smaller 9 pounder guns to be sent ashore, as they were more manageable for use against the defenceless batteries. September 17th saw the largest of the naval batteries begin to fire. Fourteen of them concentrated on a single spot where the breach was designed.

Peterborough came aboard the *Britannia* on September 17th, to discuss with Shovell the shortage of money for the subsistence of the army and the carrying on of the siege. At once, Shovell called his admirals to a council of war and a decision was made to let Peterborough have all the money the fleet had available. The short allowance money for the seamen, amounting to 35,000 dollars, was made over for Peterborough's order. In addition, 5,000 dollars from the fleet's contingency money was made over to him, making a total of 40,000 dollars.

On September 19th Shovell and the admirals met again in the *Britannia*. It was agreed to send more guns from the fleet ashore. A further fourteen were landed making a total of seventy-two guns, of which thirty were 24 pounders. Gun crews were sent with them. A previous decision that the fleet was to start its return to England by September 20th was rescinded, as the attack on Barcelona was now in full swing.

The next day the admirals received a request for further shot for the shore batteries. The need was for 18 and 24 pound shot and the fleet were reduced to forty rounds per cannon and the remainder sent ashore. By September 22nd the batteries were again low on ammunition. Shovell agreed to reduce the fleet to thirty rounds per cannon. He calculated that in all the fleet had provided 20,872 of 18 pound shot, 12,146 of 24 pound shot and 1,423 barrels of powder. Shovell had reduced the English reserves of shot and powder as low as he dared. They could not reasonably supply any more, although the better supplied Dutch contingent still had a little in reserve. At the request of Charles III and Peterborough, on the 22nd, fifty barrels of powder were sent to the town of Lerida.

On September 23rd, three weeks after the decision to take Montjuic, a breach was made in the city wall between the bastions of St Antonio and St Paul. Velasco, the governor, gave orders that an earthwork was to be made to fill the breach and mines placed in it. Under the direction of Peterborough, the sailors pitched shells so accurately that the mines were blown up. The way was clear, but Peterborough, wanting to avoid casualties and unnecessary destruction, wrote a letter to the governor requesting his surrender. Velasco agreed provided he received honourable terms. The gate of St Antonio would be handed over at once and if no relief came within four days, the garrison would march out. Hostages were to be exchanged as a guarantee of the terms. On the English side Brigadier James Stanhope and on the Spanish the Marquis of Rivera were chosen.

Negotiations dragged on for a while, as Velasco had made several extravagant demands, including being transported to Tortosa or Tarragona. Tortosa had already declared for Charles III and Tarragona was under siege. On September 26th Shovell had sent the redoubtable Captain Philip Cavendish there in the *Antelope*, with a few small ships, after secret intelligence from Charles that the town would surrender before a suitable show of force. Cavendish went before the town and fired some guns and bombs into it. A flag of truce was put out. The magistrates came aboard and said that they had imprisoned the governor and secured the place for Charles. It was not until October 5th that Cavendish was able to return and give his report to Shovell.

The terms of the capitulation of Barcelona were signed in the evening of September 28th, and stated that the garrison would march out in four days. That day and the next a storm blew up making the ships ride hard and for their security veer away three cables.

On October 3rd the garrison was preparing to march out of Barcelona. Stephen Martin was in the city at the time and has recorded the event that precipitated the general disorder. A prisoner being brought out with the garrison, towards the mole, seeing some supporters of Charles III, called out "Viva Carlos Tercero". The French officer in charge of him drew a pistol and shot him dead on the spot. The supporters of Charles III, to whom the prisoner had spoken, then killed the French officer and announced that Velasco, before leaving Barcelona, intended to cut their throats and plunder the city. General disorder followed. Velasco, in fear of his life, asked Peterborough to restore order. Peterborough marched into Barcelona with his troops and took Velasco to his quarters outside the city. He could not stop the pillaging and rifling of many of the houses of the Bourbon sympathisers. That night Peterborough took Velasco and several other persons of quality on board the *Britannia*, to put them under Shovell's protection. Peterborough, ever gallant, is reputed to have saved the life of the Duchess of Popoli in the city and to have received a shot through his wig for his trouble! The defeated garrison of Barcelona, not thinking themselves safe anywhere in Catalonia, would now be transported to Malaga or Almeria.

Now that the siege was effectively over, Shovell and the admirals considered at two councils of war, on October 1st and 8th, what to do with the fleet. They correctly decided that it could not be kept out all winter, for lack of provisions and a suitable port. A winter squadron under John Leake, consisting of fifteen English and ten Dutch ships, was to make a brief attempt on Majorca and then winter at Lisbon. Peterborough, who was remaining in Catalonia, might have use of the whole or part of the squadron, provided that it had no other commands from Queen Anne, and confirmation was given at a council of war. The suggestion has been made that, "if it shall be thought advisable by a council of war", had been inserted by Shovell to stop Peterborough interfering with Leake. This is unlikely, as all decisions at the time were made jointly at councils of war, although they could be manipulated. This was to become relevant the following year, when Leake saved Barcelona by disobeying Peterborough.[47]

Shovell left all the available shot and powder at Barcelona. In a letter to Prince George of Denmark, on October 12th, Shovell was very critical of the amount of shot supplied to the English fleet in comparison with that of the Dutch. "And here I cannot but observe to you, if this garrison had held out longer we had been at a very great loss for want of shot." The Dutch had furnished almost as much shot as the English, with half the number of ships and still left themselves with fifty to sixty rounds, in comparison with the English's thirty and under. Shovell would take the bulk of the fleet home himself with the first fair wind after October 11th.

In the event, Shovell sailed on October 12th, reached the Straits on the 16th and was back at Spithead on November 26th.[48]

Charles III made his formal entry into Barcelona on October 12th and was officially proclaimed King of Spain. By the end of October all Catalonia was in his hands. The more important fortresses, including

Gerona to the north facing the French frontier, Lerida inland facing the neighbouring Aragon, Tarragona on the coast and Tortosa, with its bridge near the mouth of the Ebno, were in his hands. Hesse Darmstadt had been essentially correct in believing that the Catalans would rise against Bourbon rule. Only fear of Velasco had held them back. The unfortunate Hesse Darmstadt was not to live to see it. Charles III, with boyish enthusiasm, had spent the siege of Barcelona sometimes on land and sometimes with the fleet. This October was to be a high point for him in Spain.

In a letter to Queen Anne after the campaign was over, Charles sang Peterborough's praises.

> I must do justice to all the officers and common soldiers and particularly to my Lord of Peterborough that he has shewn in this whole expedition a constancy, bravery and conduct worthy of the choice that your Majesty has made of him, and that we could no ways give me better satisfaction than he has by the great zeal and application which he has equally testified to my interest, and the service of my person.[49]

The taking of Barcelona was a great success and the day after Shovell's arrival at Spithead on November 27th 1705, Queen Anne gave Parliament the news in person. If Peterborough was rightly given the lion's share of the credit, the part played by Shovell and the fleet was crucial. While Peterborough was ashore for the siege, Shovell had sole command of the fleet. When the land officers were all for leaving Barcelona for Italy, Shovell was constant in his support for Charles III and Hesse Darmstadt in continuing the siege. Whether it be shot, powder, gunners, money or general bombardment from the sea, the army were never let down by Shovell and the fleet. Without their support, Barcelona could not have been taken and, as will be seen later, held. Shovell had done his country proud.

The year 1705 ended quietly for Shovell, with his family at home in England. On December 4th his appointment as a Deputy Lieutenant of his adopted county, Kent, was renewed. Also that month Shovell's mother-in-law, Elizabeth Hill (née Kingsman from Maldon, Essex) died. Her will was proved on January 1st 1706, and the administration of it granted to her daughter, Elizabeth Shovell.

This was to be the last Christmas of his life that Shovell would spend with his family at home in England.[50]

NOTES

1. Luttrell, Vol.V, p.507.
2. Torrington, p.161; Minutes of Court Martial (Court Martial Vol.13); House of Lords MSS 1704–1706, N.S., Vol.VI.
3. RMT MAT 25; Campbell, Vol.IV, p.250; The Complete History of Europe for 1705; Secret Memoirs.
4. RMT Introduction; ADM 33.235; Anderson, Lists of Men of War.
5. Torrington, p.175.
6. Ormonde MSS, N.S., Vol.VIII, p.147.
7. Holmes, British Politics in the age of Queen Anne; RMT MAT 25; Return of Members of Parliament 1213–1874, Part II.
8. Richmond, p.314.
9. Owen, p.130.
10. Owen, pp.130–131; House of Lords MSS 1706–08, N.S., Vol.VII, p.361.
11. Hoffmann's despatch April 7th; Kunzel (German Life of Hesse Darmstadt), p.555, quoted in Klopp, Der Fall des Hauses Stuart, XI, 489; Churchill, p.57.
12. D.N.B. Mordaunt; Owen, p.131.
13. D.N.B. Mordaunt.
14. House of Lords MSS 1706–8, N.S., Vol.VII, pp.361–363.
15. House of Lords MSS 1706–8, N.S., Vol.VII, p.363.
16. House of Lords MSS 1706–8, N.S., Vol.VII, pp.361–363.
17. Burchett, p.684; Owen, p.130; Campbell, p.251; D.N.B.Mordaunt.
18. Burchett, p.685; Owen, p.132; ADD MSS 28056, Peterborough to Godolphin May 30th.
19. Leake, pp.277–278; Owen, p.132.
20. Leake, pp.278–279; Owen, pp.132–133; House of Lords MSS 1706–8, N.S., Vol.VII, p.409.
21. Owen, pp.135–136; House of Lords MSS 1706–8, N.S., Vol.VII, Duke of Savoy to Queen Anne, August 16th, p.365; Peterborough, Shovell to Prince George, August 3rd, p.409; ADD MSS 5441, Peterborough to Shovell, July 20th.
22. House of Lords MSS 1706–8, N.S., Vol.VII, Peterborough, Shovell to Prince George, August 3rd, pp.409–10.
23. Owen, pp.136–37; House of Lords MSS 1706–8, N.S., Vol.VII, Peterborough, Shovell to Prince George, August 3rd, pp.409–10.
24. House of Lords MSS 1706–8, N.S., Vol.VII, Shovell to Prince George, September 10th, pp.410–411.
25. Shovell to Prince George September 10th.
26. Owen, pp.138–139; House of Lords MSS 1706–8, N.S., Vol.VII, Shovell to Prince George, September 10th, p.411.
27. Ballard, p.138.
28. Ballard, pp.139–141; Leake, p.281.
29. Ballard, p.151.
30. Owen, p.139.
31. House of Lords MSS 1706–8, N.S., Vol.VII, Shovell to Prince George, September 10th, p.411.
32. Churchill, pp.244–245; ADD MSS 39757, Peterborough to Godolphin, September 9th 1705.
33. House of Lords MSS 1706–8, N.S., Vol.VII, Shovell to Prince George, September 10th, pp.411–413; Owen, p.141.
34. House of Lords MSS 1706–8, N.S., Vol.VII, Shovell to Prince George, September 10th, pp.411–415; Owen, p.142.
35. House of Lords MSS 1706–8, N.S., Vol.VII, Shovell to Prince George,

September 10th, pp.411–416.
36. House of Lords MSS 1706–8, N.S., Vol.VII, Hesse Darmstadt to Shovell August 28th, 29th, 30th, September 1st, 2nd, pp.423–426.
37. House of Lords MSS 1706–8, N.S., Vol.VII, Hesse Darmstadt to Shovell, August 29th, pp.423–424, Charles III to Peterborough, August 30th, p.425, Shovell to Prince George, September 10th, pp.411–417.
38. House of Lords MSS 1706–8, N.S., Vol.VII, Hesse Darmstadt to Shovell, August 30th, p.424.
39. Leake, pp.351–352.
40. House of Lords MSS 1706–8, N.S., Vol.VII, Hesse Darmstadt to Shovell, September 1st, p.425; Owen, p.140; D.N.B. Norris; Letters to General Stanhope, p.6.
41. House of Lords MSS 1706–7, N.S., Vol.VII, Shovell to Prince George, September 10th, p.411; Ballard, p.151; Leake, pp.287–288; Owen, p.144; An Account of the Earl of Peterborough's Conduct in Spain, p.7; An Impartial Enquiry into the Management of the War in Spain, p.38.
42. Owen, pp.147–151; Leake, pp.288–290; Ballard, pp.146–151.
43. Ballard, p.151.
44. House of Lords MSS 1706–8, N.S., Vol.VII, pp.412–417; Owen, p.150; Ballard, pp.148–149.
45. Owen, pp.149–151.
46. Stowe MSS 467, 471.
47. ADD MSS 5442 f.2, Orders for Leake from Peterborough and Shovell, October 9th, 1705.
48. House of Lords MSS 1706–8, N.S., Vol.VII, Shovell to Prince George, October 12th, pp.417–422; Burchett, pp.687–688; Owen, pp.151–155; Ballard, pp.153–155; Stephen Martin, pp.83–84; Leake, pp.291–295.
49. An Account of the Earl of Peterborough's Conduct in Spain, pp.7 & 8.
50. RMT MAT 24, 25.

# CHAPTER XXIII
# An Unproductive Year
# 1706

Early in 1706 Parliamentary discussions took place concerning the difficulties in manning the fleet. On January 9th a message was sent to the House of Commons to summon Shovell, George Byng, George Churchill, John Jennings and Stafford Fairborne to the Lords to appear before a select committee on the subject under the chairmanship of Arthur Herbert, Earl of Torrington. Herbert had played a big part in Shovell's earlier naval career, but has been mentioned little in this account since his fall from favour after the Battle of Beachy Head in 1690.[1]

The Commons gave leave for the Admirals to appear before the committee on January 10th and four days later they gave evidence to it. When asked about improving the manning of the fleet they replied:

> We first try bounty money; then we press; but neither will do; the merchants give great wages. The seamen ought to be encouraged. Old men used to man the colliery, but since the last Act, they take our best men and not cripples and boys which used to serve them. They, by that Act, are empowered to take apprentices for three years. They abuse that power given them by taking seamen of thirty years of age, and they lend them to merchants and we cannot meddle with them. The colliery used to breed seamen but now breeds none and is no nursery to the fleet.

In addition, Shovell proposed that the age of boys joining the fleet should be raised from 10 to 12 years.[2]

A bill for the increase of seamen and speedier manning of the fleet was ordered to be prepared by the House of Commons on January 23rd. It reached the House of Lords on March 18th, and received the Royal Assent on the following day. The bill, however, did not solve the problem of manning difficulties that would continue into the next century.[3]

It was fortunate that Shovell was in London at this time, as on the night of January 18th 1706 his father-in-law, John Hill, died. Perhaps Hill's death was hastened by the fact that his wife had died the previous month. Poor Lady Elizabeth Shovell had lost her mother and father within a few weeks. In less than two years, she was to lose much more than that. No doubt the presence of her husband was a comfort at a difficult time. Hill, who lived in the parish of St Olave's, Hart Street, London, was a very wealthy man. Under the terms of his will, dated August 28th 1701, bequests were made to his grandchildren, the Narbroughs and the young Shovell girls, but the bulk of his estate was left to his daughter, Lady Elizabeth Shovell. Luttrell, in his diary, recorded that Hill left Cloudesley Shovell nearly £100,000, which was an enormous sum of money in the early eighteenth century. Although the money had been left to Lady Shovell, under the laws of the period her husband would have had control of it. Shovell, after his long service on the Mediterranean station with its "good voyages", and with his investments, was a wealthy man in his own right. One of the only contemporary criticisms of his character was that "his covetousness goes beyond reason". In any event Hill's death made the Shovell family fabulously rich.[4]

Hill had probably been a merchant navy captain, as he was known as Captain Hill, and his name does not appear in the Pepsyian Register of Sea Officers serving in the Royal Navy between 1660 and 1688. As well as being a successful businessman, John Hill was a commissioner of the navy and an elder brother of Trinity House. His certificate of admission as an elder brother was signed on July 14th 1685 by Samuel Pepys, the then master and his son-in-law of the time, John Narbrough. Perhaps Hill had promoted Shovell's name, as he too was to serve as an elder brother of Trinity House from February 13th 1705.[5]

Trinity House was brought into being in 1512 by a petition of the medieval Guild of Lodesmen (pilots) to Henry VIII, who gave them a charter in 1514. During the Shovell era their headquarters was in Water Lane. The objectives of Trinity House, which have not changed over the centuries, were the advancement and safety of navigation and the welfare of seamen. The first lighthouse built by Trinity House was at Lowestoft in 1609. The elder brothers reported on the construction of ships and the correct complement of sailors, armament and stores. In addition, they examined the boys in navigation from the mathematical school of Christ's Hospital, which had been founded in 1673 by Charles II. Just how active a role Shovell played in this is not certain. No doubt his sea duties abroad restricted the time he was able to devote to the affairs of Trinity House.[6]

During 1706 Shovell paid for renovation work on what was then the Butcher's Market in Rochester, the city he continued to represent in Parliament. A plaque on the building which was built in 1698, states that it was "erected at the sole charge of Sir Cloudesley Shovell Knt in 1706". In fact, Shovell only paid for the market bell, the clock and the brick facade. The building can be seen to this day and is known as the Corn Exchange or Clock House. Shovell had already paid for the magnificent ceiling of the Guildhall, Rochester in 1695 and in 1700 the repair of his local church, St Paulinus, Crayford. The contemporary comment that "his covetousness goes beyond reason" seems a little hard in retrospect.[7]

During the early part of 1706 Louis XIV began preparations to retake Barcelona. Marshal Compte de Mans-Jean-Baptiste-René de Froulay Tessé with 25,000 troops was sent to effect this, supported by the Toulon fleet from the sea under the Comte de Toulouse. Toulouse had the virtual freedom of the Mediterranean as Shovell had taken home the main fleet in the autumn of 1705, leaving John Leake and his squadron to winter at Lisbon. Much of the Earl of Peterborough's army was scattered around Valencia and the Barcelona garrison numbered only 4,000 men. The city was in difficulty, when on March 21st Charles III sent for Leake to come to his assistance. Leake carrying troops in his ships set sail for Barcelona, but before he could get there received contrary orders from Peterborough. Peterborough wished the troops to be landed in Valencia.

Rightly, Leake ignored these orders and pressed on for Barcelona, but before he was able to reach the city, Peterborough joined him from the shore. Peterborough, as senior officer, raised the union flag on the main mast of Leake's flagship and was to claim the credit for breaking the siege of Barcelona. At the first sign that Leake was back in the Mediterranean,

Toulouse took his ships back to Toulon and Tessé, on April 30th, was forced to retreat to the Pyrenees.[8]

Peterborough's behaviour had been deplorable and no wonder Leake wrote to Prince George of Denmark complaining about the matter and indicating that he was expecting Shovell to resume command in the Mediterranean that summer.

> I forgot in my last to acquaint you that my Lord Peterborough came aboard me, when I was within three leagues of this place, and hoisted his flag for that day, by virtue of his former commission, which I was not willing to dispute, though I cannot believe I shall be altogether discharged of my former orders till the arrival of Sir Cloudesley Shovell, and shall take the best care I can, as well of the fleet, as not to have any disputes with his Lordship about that matter, but his business ashore has taken up his time so much that he has been pleased to leave everything to me hitherto.[9]

It is clear from this letter that Leake was expecting Shovell to take the main fleet to the Mediterranean again that summer. On March 10th 1706 both Peterborough and Shovell had had their joint commissions of the previous year renewed, so that the original intention was for Shovell to return to the Mediterranean early in the year. As will be seen shortly, other plans were made in England for Shovell that summer, and it would be early 1707 before he returned to the Mediterranean. In fact, Leake had a let out clause for disobeying Peterborough, under the orders left with him in 1705. Peterborough might have use of the whole or part of Leake's squadron, provided that it had no other commands from Queen Anne and was confirmed at a council of war.[10]

Shovell wrote to Leake from his town house, in Soho Square, congratulating him on saving Barcelona.

> I congratulate you with all my heart on your success in the afaire of Barcelona, and wou'd not slip this opportunity without acquainting you, that you have a great many good friends here who rejoice as well as I in your good fortune, and will not suffer the great fatigues and pains you have taken to pass unregarded, but will improve them to your service: the last winter with the assistance of Mr Churchill who is much your friend, we sett forth your services to the Prince and his highness was mighty well satisfied with your prudence and good management. His highness directed a present as an acknowledgement of your good services, which I dout not but will be a leading card to draw the same honour from her Maj^{tie}; I shall not come abroad, so wish your health and a safe return.[11]

301

Leake was to have a successful summer on the coast of Spain. He was to take Carthagena, Alicante, Ibiza and Majorca during this time. In October 1706 he returned to England leaving George Byng in command. Leake and Shovell were to miss each other by a matter of days, when Shovell eventually sailed for Lisbon, on October 1st. They were not to meet again before Shovell's death. Peterborough's role in Spain gradually declined during the summer of 1706, and in September he sailed for Genoa, ostensibly to organise a combined attack on Toulon with the Duke of Savoy. He borrowed £100,000 from the Jews of Genoa without permission from the court at home, and after a further period in Spain was ordered back to England, in early 1707. After a circuitous tour back through Europe, he reached England in August. The following year Peterborough's conduct was investigated by the House of Lords, who refused to accept the charges against him but gave him no vote of thanks. The taking of Barcelona, in 1705, was the pinnacle of his military career in Spain.[12]

Leake was not the only naval man to be put out by the decision not to send Shovell to the Mediterranean early in 1706. The Dutch Admiral Philip Almonde returned home from Lisbon in July, being unwilling to serve under an inferior flag if Shovell was not to command that year. In fact, Shovell got on well with the Dutch, possibly because of his own Dutch or Flemish ancestry. A contemporary account shows him socialising with the Dutch and demonstrates some of the features of his character.

> Sir Cloudesley Shovell two years ago had always sent the best light frigates of the fleet upon purchase, and frequently all the good sailors; so that if at any time the French had surprised them, they would have been at great loss. His covetousness goes beyond reason, and his courage beyond the bounds of good conduct; he will venture the fleet on any occasion, and it is feared further than Allemonde will sometimes be willing. If we be much superior his forwardness may be of good consequence. He eats and drinks pretty much with the Dutch and is generally beloved amongst the sailors, for his familiar conversation with them, which Sir George Rooke never affected but was very reserved.[13]

Since late in the autumn of 1705 Count Louis de Guiscard, a French refugee in England, had been proposing a landing on the west coast of France, to encourage a rising of the Cevennois. De Guiscard suggested that a number of battalions be raised from the Huguenot refugees and be stiffened with British infantry and dragoons. The landing would take place between Blaye and the mouth of the Charente. Xantes (Saintes) was to be taken and fortified, and French Huguenot officers from there would be used to foment rebellion in this unstable part of France. Marlborough supported the venture, as it would take pressure off the allies in their campaigns in Catalonia and Italy, which were swaying one way and then the other during the summer of 1706.[14]

In May 1706 a small force under Stafford Fairborne was sent on a preliminary mission to the mouth of the Charente, to destroy French shipping there and those fitting out at Rochefort. Fairborne took a few prizes but otherwise achieved little and on his return was sent to take part in the successful siege of Ostend, which fell in June.[15]

During the spring of 1706 five Huguenot regiments and nearly a dozen British battalions were collected at Portsmouth and in the Isle of Wight. The troops were nearly 10,000 strong in number and were to be commanded by Richard Savage, 4th Earl Rivers. Under Rivers were Lieutenant General Thomas Erle and de Guiscard himself. Even the Earl of Peterborough's eldest son was to be a major general. Shovell, who was to command the supporting fleet, may have felt that he had seen more than enough of that particular family the year before. On landing in France Rivers was to publish a manifesto declaring that it was his intention neither to conquer nor to pillage, but to restore the liberties of the French people and the Edict of Nantes.[16]

As was customary, there was difficulty in manning and victualling the fleet which delayed matters until mid summer. The Dutch too were slow in their preparations. In June 700 marines were embarked onto the ships of Shovell's squadron. The troops started to go aboard at Portsmouth in July. While awaiting the arrival of the Dutch, Shovell played with the idea of sailing across to France to alarm their coast. In a letter written to Lieutenant General Thomas Erle on July 24th 1706 from the *Britannia* at Spithead, he discussed the matter.

> Mr Colby brought me yours late last night: I could not be of another opinion but that the troops be immediately embarked, therefore venture to desire your letter might not be delivered to Brigadeer Carpenter; your goodness I hope will excuse me, I intend right for the service, and have sent my Officers and boats to imbarque the food today. As to what has bin said about my standing over to the French shore to allarm the enemy, 'tis with two provisos, first if the winds, keep the Dutch troops back, and next to be sure that it be no hindrance to the intended expedition, which last article lays the design aside, for no body can answer it will be no hindrance, and just now I received advice by express that the Dutch from Ostend are soon from Osale on the back of the Goodwin; so that they are in a days saile of us; if you dine at home today, I will wait on you about noon.[17]

By August 10th preparations were complete and the fleet sailed that day from Portsmouth with the transports and troops. Shovell commanded from the 1st rate, *Britannia*, nineteen large English men of war, ten frigates, 120 transports, twenty-eight Dutch transports and various bomb vessels and fireships. In the *Britannia* with Shovell was a Monsieur Casselope, a French pilot, with local knowledge of the coastline. Several thousand declarations in French had been printed for distribution to the local population after the descent. At last, the fleet had got away after the various delays and all seemed to be going well. However, the weather in the Channel was so poor that on August 14th the fleet and transports were forced to seek shelter in Torbay.[18]

On the day of their arrival at Torbay Shovell wrote from the *Britannia* to Sir Charles Hedges, the Secretary of State, explaining his difficulties.

> Yesterday off the Deadman, we were joined by the Dutch transports. This morning the wind came to S.S.W., blowing hard with thick hazzy weather, which obliged us to put in here; for keeping the sea in such bad weather would not only have been very injurious to the horses, but would have occasioned the disabling or losing company of some of the transports. I cannot forbear being concerned that the Dutch did not send one frigate to keep their transports under some regulation; for their commanders, being all of equal power, not one of them having any superiority over another, it will be a very great difficulty to make them understand our signals and sailing instructions. Our coming in here will enable us to complete the watering of the Dutch transports. It continues to blow fresh at S.S.W., thick, misty weather; but we shall take the first opportunity to proceed.[19]

Shovell was not to have the chance "to take the first opportunity to proceed", for before the weather had improved and he could sail again, he received orders from Queen Anne cancelling the descent on the Charente. Debate had been renewed about the prospects of the local population rising and de Guiscard was searchingly re-examined. Naturally, he could give no guarantees of the outcome of any landing. The Queen and her advisers decided to drop the plan and to send the ships and troops to Spain instead. Marlborough, although accepting this with good grace, was deeply disappointed. De Guiscard was very bitter concerning this about-face and was knocked off balance. His mental derangement seems to have been permanent, as in 1710 he attempted to assassinate the Prime Minister, Robert Harley.[20]

From Windsor, on August 20th, Queen Anne sent new instructions for Shovell to take the fleet and troops to Spain. If the weather in the Channel had not been so poor in mid August, Shovell would not have had to put back into Torbay and in all probability the operation at the mouth of the

Charente would have gone ahead. No wonder de Guiscard was so disappointed, only the elements had prevented his proposals from being attempted. Queen Anne instructed Shovell to take Cadiz, this being considered the most suitable target, with the wider objective of setting Charles III on the throne of Spain. As a preliminary to an assault on Cadiz, Shovell was to sail for the Guadalquivir or River of Seville and discharge Rivers' troops there. It was thought that if Seville could be persuaded to acknowledge Charles as King, Cadiz would be likely to follow. However, Shovell was permitted to modify these orders and attempt Cadiz directly from Cadiz Island or some other suitable place if he thought fit. The Queen instructed Shovell to lose no time in sailing.[21]

Shovell, Rivers and Erle soon got down to detailed planning for the operation. On August 21st Rivers wrote to the Lord Treasurer, Sidney Godolphin, requesting money for his troops. Shovell stated that the money could be collected at Lisbon. John Norris was close at hand to help Shovell. Rivers produced a manifesto that would be distributed to the Spaniards, encouraging them to support Charles III. In order to make this more attractive to them, Rivers put in a section giving them freedom of navigation and trade. Clearly, Shovell was unhappy about this and Rivers sought Lord Treasurer Godolphin's advice. This was not forthcoming and later in the year, once they had reached Lisbon, Rivers accepted Shovell's advice and inserted the following clause.

> And furthermore we declare that all his Catholic Majesty's subjects who shall render their obedience to their lawful King shall be protected in their navigation, to which end the Queen, my mistress, at the request of King Charles has already sent a powerful squadron to the Spanish West Indies to protect and secure the states and effects of those Spaniards who by their loyalty merit this grace and favour, and to convoy and bring back their said Spanish ships to Cadiz or Seville provided the said places are in the obedience of his Catholic Majesty King Charles.[22]

On August 23rd Shovell joined the *Association* from the *Britannia*. The *Association* was a 90 gun 2nd rate and relatively new, having been built at Portsmouth in 1697. With Shovell on his new command were his two stepsons, John and James Narbrough. John was an ordinary seaman and James a captain's servant. The captain of the *Association* was Samuel Whitaker and Shovell's two personal or flag captains were John Norris and Edmund Loades, a nephew of Lady Elizabeth Shovell. A son of Matthew Aylmer, Shovell's colleague in his early days in the Mediterranean, was fifth lieutenant.[23]

Eventually, Shovell sailed with the fleet and Rivers' troops on October 1st. It was very late in the year to be taking ships of the size of the

*Association* to sea. Torbay was to be the last place in England where Shovell would set foot before his death a little over a year later. In the early days of October the *Association* passed not far from her final resting place as they sailed for the fleet's first rendezvous point at Lisbon. On the 10th they had only reached ten leagues to the westward of the Scilly Isles, with contrary winds from the south or south-west. The transports had been forced to separate, and the day before the *Barfleur*, in which Rivers was travelling, sprang a leak. With difficulty, he and some of his servants managed to join Shovell in the *Association*. The *Barfleur* was so leaky that she had to return to England.[24]

The bad weather continued all the way to Lisbon, reached at the end of October. Rivers in a letter to Sir Charles Hedges, the Secretary of State, written from Lisbon on October 29th, stated that the fleet had been dispersed and did not come together until they had reached the Tagus. Two ships had sunk, a further two had been driven to Ireland, nine into St Ubals and the remainder badly damaged in the storms. The soldiers and horses had suffered dreadfully during the voyage out. The English had 1,000 foot soldiers missing and a further 100 dead. Half the horses were also dead. Despite all this, at a council of war on October 27th at which Shovell was present, it was resolved to continue their voyage to Seville and execute Queen Anne's orders.[25]

On arrival at Lisbon, it was clear that considerable time would be needed to repair the ships after the stormy weather on the way out to the peninsula. Shovell discovered that the affairs of the Spanish court of Charles III and the Earl of Galway's army were in disorder. During the summer of 1706 Charles III and Galway had had control of the capital of Spain, Madrid, before being forced to retire to Valencia. Shovell was in a quandary. Should he follow Queen Anne's orders to assault Seville and Cadiz or should he go to Valencia to help Charles and Galway? Shovell sent a Colonel Worsley to Valencia to assess the situation for him. Matters were complicated further during Worsley's absence when the King of Portugal died.[26]

During October word had got back to England of Charles III's difficulties, and Sidney Godolphin, in a letter to Rivers, suggested that the Seville/Cadiz plan might have to be dropped to strengthen the forces already in Spain. In effect, he and Shovell were to take their orders from Charles III and Galway. Shovell was to settle communications between Lisbon and the coast of Spain. Galway, who had lost an arm in the fighting, was keen to return to England, which would leave Rivers as the overall army commander. This was not to be, and in the event Galway remained and Rivers was the one to return to England, being unhappy to serve as second in command.[27]

Don Pedro, King of Portugal, was succeeded by his son, Don John V. Shovell and Rivers were afraid that the new King might not honour the arrangements that had been made with his father. There was a certain amount of relief when he agreed to continue with the war. Further problems with the Portuguese court arose, when one of the young princes of the royal family insulted the seamen as they came ashore from the fleet, and the forts had fired at some of the men of war. Shovell complained to the Portuguese government stating that he maintained the strictest discipline in his fleet while in harbour and would not have his country's flag insulted. The Portuguese King was forced to issue orders so that there was no further difficulty of this nature. Shovell's firm stand against an ally had paid off. As Rivers remarked, "I refer you to Cloudesley Shovell who on this occasion has exerted himself in a manner becoming an English admiral . . ."[28]

The Portuguese were not the only people to be difficult that late autumn. The Barbary states were up to their old tricks. English ships had been seized and men imprisoned in Morocco. The Secretary of State, Sir Charles Hedges, back in England, ordered Shovell to sort the matter out, preferably without a rupture, as a treaty was being concluded. In fact four days before Hedges wrote this letter, Shovell had sent Captain John Baker of the *Monmouth* orders to seize ships and goods belonging to the Emperor of Morocco, in reprisal for English vessels taken off the Barbary Coast.[29]

When Colonel Worsley returned, Shovell was handed letters from Charles III and Galway stating that unless he brought Rivers and the land forces to Valencia to reinforce them, they would be in great difficulty. The ships were still being repaired at Lisbon and Shovell immediately ordered them to be made ready for sea again, as quickly as possible. The Dutch contingent was reluctant to assist in the carriage of troops to Valencia, but Shovell was instructed by the Earl of Sunderland to make them obey his orders.[30]

In these trying times it is interesting to read Earl Rivers' opinion of Shovell. "I cannot help upon this occasion saying that never any man was more zealous for her Majesty's service, nor more kind to her troops in assisting them with everything that is necessary". In connection with leaving three or four frigates on the coast of Spain under Charles III: "I do not say this to offend Sir Cloudesley Shovell, who is very forward and zealous in whatever relates to public service, that this precaution would not be necessary if we were always sure of having him here."[31]

Shovell was on the point of embarking Rivers' troops when he received contrary orders from England. The Portuguese court were behind this, in that they felt that Rivers and his men were better employed locally with their own. Supported by a council of war, Shovell and Rivers decided to ignore their new instructions and to revert to the original plan of sailing to Alicante, to reinforce Charles III. It was the correct action to take, and in late December 1706 the Earl of Sunderland, in a letter to Shovell, told him

307

that Queen Anne entirely approved of his decision. In addition, Shovell was not to come home, as he once desired.[32]

Eventually, on January 7th 1707, Shovell got his fleet with the land forces away from Lisbon and sailed for Alicante, which was reached on the 28th of the same month. Rivers' troops disembarked to reinforce those of Galway. Their number had fallen from 10,000 when they left England to 7,000, mainly through sickness. Finding that he could be of little use in Alicante, Shovell sailed on February 17th for Lisbon, which he reached on March 11th. While he continued with the refitting of his ships, he received orders from England to prepare for an expedition against the major French naval base at Toulon, which was to occupy him over the next few months.[33]

NOTES

1. House of Lords MSS, N.S., Vol.VI, 1704–1706, pp.386–387.
2. House of Lords MSS, N.S., Vol.VI, pp.386–387; Luttrell, Vol.VI, pp.4–5.
3. House of Lords MSS, N.S., Vol.VI, pp.386–387; Commons Journal, XV, p.107; XVIII, pp.159, 162.
4. Duckett, p.83; Dyer, p.207; Luttrell, Vol.VI, p.7; RMT MAT 24, will of John Hill; Portland MSS, Vol.VIII, p.302.
5. Register of Sea Officers serving in the Royal Navy 1660–1688; Duckett, p.83; RMT MAT 25, 26; Trinity House MSS.
6. Grosvenor, Trinity House, pp.23, 75, 95, 96, 98, 99, 108–109.
7. Smith, History of Rochester; A short account of St Paulinus Church.
8. Richmond, pp.319–320; Laird Clowes, pp.408–409.
9. House of Lords, MSS, 1706–8, N.S., Vol.VII, Leake to Prince George May 15th 1706.
10. D.N.B. Mordaunt, Shovell; Luttrell, Vol.VI, p.37; ADD MSS 5442 f.2.
11. ADD MSS 5441 f.185.
12. D.N.B. Leake, Mordaunt.
13. Portland MSS, Vol.VIII, p.302; Luttrell, Vol.VI, p.70.
14. Churchill, pp.80–81; Richmond, pp.322–323; Campbell, Vol.III, p.466.
15. Laird Clowes, pp.509–510.
16. Campbell, Vol.III, p.466; D.N.B. Rivers.
17. Erle 2/57, Shovell to Erle July 24th 1706; D.N.B. Rivers; Churchill, p.162; House of Lords MSS 1706–08, N.S., Vol.VII, p.165; Bath MSS, Vol.I, p.84.
18. Campbell, Vol.III, pp.466–67; Churchill, p.162; Luttrell, Vol.VI, p.70.
19. Portland MSS, Vol.VIII, p.240, Shovell to Hedges August 14th 1706.
20. Churchill, pp.80–81,162; House of Lords MSS, 1706–8, N.S., Vol.VII, p.515, orders to Shovell August 18th.
21. House of Lords MSS, 1706–8, N.S.,Vol.VII, p.515.
22. Bath MSS, Vol.I, pp.91, 98, 104–105, 129–131.
23. Larn, pp.47–53; ADM 33.249; Anderson, Lists of Men of War.
24. Bath MSS, Vol.I, p.108; Campbell, Vol.III, p.167; London Gazette No.4268.
25. Bath MSS, Vol.I, pp.116–118, Rivers to Hedges July 29th 1706.
26. Campbell, Vol.III, pp.467–68.
27. Bath MSS, Vol.I, p.116, Godolphin to Rivers, October 29th 1706, pp.129–131, Rivers to Hedges, December 3rd 1706.
28. Leake, p.165; Campbell, Vol.IV, p.254; Bath MSS, Vol.I, p.144, Rivers to the Earl of Sunderland, December 25th 1706.

29. House of Lords MSS, 1706–8, N.S., Vol.VII, p.516 Hedges to Shovell, November 19th 1706; RMT MAT 27, Shovell to Baker, November 15th 1707.

30. Campbell, Vol.III, pp.468–69; House of Lords MSS, N.S., Vol.VII, p.516, Sunderland to Shovell, December 7th 1706.

31. Bath MSS, Vol.I, p.144, Rivers to Sunderland, December 25th 1706; p.133, Rivers to Hedges, December 6th 1706.

32. Campbell, Vol.IV, pp.254–55; House of Lords MSS, N.S., Vol.VII, pp.516–517, Sunderland to Shovell, December 23rd 1706.

33. Campbell, Vol.IV, p.255.

# CHAPTER XXIV
# The Toulon Campaign 1707

By the end of 1706 the allies were in possession of Flanders. No advance on Paris was to be made, as Marshal Vendome's fortresses and 100,000 men blocked the way. The Duke of Marlborough planned a major offensive in the weaker southern region, rather than batter a way through from the north. If Toulon could be taken and the French fleet destroyed, southern France would be open to invasion. During the summer of 1706 Prince Eugene had broken the siege of Turin and the French had fallen back from Piedmont and Savoy. The campaign in Spain was to be continued vigorously, which would have the effect of holding French troops there and keeping them away from defending Toulon. On the other hand, withdrawal of troops by France from Spain would leave the way open for Charles III to retake Madrid. There would be some dangers in having two major offensives running simultaneously. In the event, Emperor Joseph made it three by insisting on sending troops to take Naples, despite pleas to the contrary from all sides. The Emperor was keen to have Naples for himself prior to any peace negotiations. His selfish action was a key element, as will be seen, in the failure to take Toulon. The capture of Toulon by the allies would have been a devastating blow to France, and might conceivably have brought the war to an end.[1]

There is a certain amount of confusion concerning the originator of the plan to make an assault on Toulon. It is possible that the Duke of Savoy and Prince Eugene proposed to the Earl of Peterborough that an attempt should be made. Peterborough brought it to the attention of the English court. In the meantime, Marlborough had independently come to the same conclusion concerning the advantages of taking Toulon, and also raised the matter in London.[2]

While refitting at Lisbon, Shovell received instructions from Queen

Anne to make an attempt on Toulon. The plan was a better one than that of 1705, in that it had a definite objective. Eugene's lifting of the Siege of Turin in 1706 also allowed the Duke of Savoy to sally forth with his forces into France. Amongst Sir John Norris' papers, now in the British Library, is a copy of the Queen's orders. It runs to some fifteen paragraphs.[3]

1. Queen Anne would supply forty ships of the line and sufficient transports to supply the army in France from Genoa.
2. The Duke of Savoy would give notification of the time and place for the fleet to rendezvous. The fleet would be under his command. ". . . then it shall be absolutely under his orders, and the admirals shall receive positive orders to obey his Royal Highness and shall be entirely at his disposition all the time that he remains with his army in Provence."
3. Ships would be sent to keep the French in their ports and to interfere with their seaborne transport prior to the operation.
4. Savoy was to seek intelligence of "equipments" made at Toulon and was to keep Shovell informed.
5. Shovell would supply cannons for the shore batteries from the fleet and Savoy, their carriages.
6. Savoy was to supply bombs, bullets, cannon balls and carriages for the mortars.
7. The fleet would supply some of the powder.
8. Savoy would supply provisions and mules for their transport both in Dauphiné and Provence.
9. Queen Anne and the States General would continue with 28,000 men in their pay and care was to be taken in their local recruitment. The Court of Vienna would leave all troops used in the last campaign in Piedmont and Lombardy to serve in the expedition, i.e. 13,000 men for the infantry and 4,000 horse for the cavalry. All would be ready to act in April.
10. Savoy would do all in his power to raise his troops to the agreed number.
11. Even the troops paid for by England would be under the command of Savoy.
12. It was desired that the operation should start in May, with the capture of Toulon as the principal aim.
13. £100,000 would be made available to Savoy for extraordinary expenses.
14. The fleet would have no troops on board.
15. The proposed Naples expedition was rejected. Ships taken at Toulon were to be Queen Anne's and stores, Savoy's. Anything unable to be moved was to be destroyed.[4]

Despite the agreement, Emperor Joseph continued with his plan to attack the kingdom of Naples. He said that he had given assurances to his friends in Naples and could not renege on them. Count Daun was told to march there with 12,000 men, who should have been used to attack Toulon. To make matters worse, there were suggestions that the Emperor had ordered Prince Eugene to avoid his troops being exposed to danger during the expedition. Between December 1706 and May 1707 Marlborough had written on a number of occasions to Eugene begging him to take one thing at a time, and that Naples would fall into the allies' hands in due course. This was a crucial decision that undermined the Toulon expedition from the start. At the time, Eugene felt that there were plenty of troops for both tasks.[5]

At Lisbon, Shovell collected together the Anglo/Dutch fleet. He had thirty-one English and fifteen Dutch men of war. In addition, there were twenty frigates and other small vessels. Under Shovell, the Dutch contingent was led by Vice Admiral Philips van der Goes until his death in June 1707, when Captain Johan van Convent replaced him. The subordinate English admirals were Vice Admiral George Byng and Rear Admirals Thomas Dilkes and John Norris. Norris had been promoted to Rear Admiral of the Blue on March 10th, and was discharged from the *Association* on the 18th.

It would take until May before Shovell's main fleet would be ready for sea. On March 30th 1707 Byng and Norris got away from Lisbon with an advance Anglo/Dutch force of twenty-two ships. Hearing of the Earl of Galway's defeat at Almanza in April, Byng diverted to the Spanish coast to support the defeated army. He and Norris spent about a week at Alicante before sailing for Barcelona. On the way to Barcelona, Norris parted company with Byng and sailed for Italy.[6]

Norris had been sent by Shovell to be his emissary at the court of the Duke of Savoy, and was to play a key role in the coming campaign. He had held a similar position with Charles III at Barcelona, two years before. Norris' relationship with Shovell went back a long way. He had been one of Shovell's midshipmen at Bantry Bay in 1689, and his second at Malaga in 1704, after which he had received a knighthood and 1,000 guineas. Norris was married to the eldest daughter of Shovell's contemporary, Matthew Aylmer, and was known in the navy as "Foul Weather Jack". The only blemish on his career had been his arrest in 1702 on the deck of George Rooke's flagship following an altercation with another officer, during which he had drawn his sword. Norris had lived down this episode, and was Shovell's closest lieutenant and friend of the time.[7]

Norris carried a letter from Shovell to the Duke of Savoy. In this Shovell described Norris as, "a man of great fidelity, honour, and experience with whom you may entirely confide". Shovell informed the Duke of Savoy that the fleet would do all in its power to carry out his orders. However, Norris had private instructions from Shovell to see that there were no "improper orders" and that the Duke be acquainted with difficulties or impossibilities of putting them into execution.[8] Norris arrived in Turin on May 5th, and was received in the Duke of Savoy's bedchamber. Prince Eugene, who was away in Milan, was sent for and Norris went to live in the home of John Chetwynd, the British Minister. A few days later Eugene arrived and a council of war was held consisting of Savoy, Eugene, Chetwynd and Norris. They went through the project article by article. The main problem was a lack of cannon balls and powder. Savoy requested more ammunition for the siege than had originally been considered necessary and, notwithstanding the agreement, for Britain to pay the bill. Norris pointed out to him that the fleet had barely enough ammunition for its own needs if they should meet the French Mediterranean fleet. He took it upon himself to write to the Earl of Sunderland, the Secretary of State in England, requesting further supplies. With Chetwynd's support he tried to persuade Savoy to buy shot in Leghorn and Genoa.[9]

Eventually, on May 10th, Shovell and his fleet sailed from Lisbon for the Mediterranean. Near Alicante, Shovell joined Byng and prepared to steer for Italy. While still close to the coast of Spain, Shovell heard from Norris of the ammunition difficulties that faced him. Immediately, Shovell ordered two ships to return to Gibraltar for shot. They were able to return to him with 12,000 cannon balls in time for the crossing of the River Var, at the end of June. Marlborough, who had been kept informed of events, encouraged them to buy what ammunition they could locally, without waiting for clearance from home. Finally, Shovell had to pledge his private credit, and he complained that, "it is with great difficulty that I procure these things, and I do not doubt it might have been done with more ease and dispatch by his Royal Highness's [Duke of Savoy] Ministers and agents". The inadequate supply of shot was one of the reasons that the land attack on Toulon was delayed, with far reaching consequences.[10]

A further worry for Norris was the presence of some six French ships in the Gulf of Genoa. Under article three of the project, French shipping was to be forced to stay in port. Norris had call on Byng's small squadron for this purpose. In the event, Byng, who was trying to support Galway's defeated army on the coast of Spain, could only spare three ships of the line and some frigates. Perhaps it was as well that this small force did not meet the superior French squadron, which returned to Toulon in late May.[11]

About this time Charles III asked both the Emperor Joseph and the Duke of Savoy to send troops from Italy to help him in Spain. Norris, as Shovell's representative, was concerned at any possible diversion of forces away from the Toulon project. He wrote to both Sunderland, the Secretary of State, and Marlborough on the subject. Marlborough made clear his views on the matter in letters to Chetwynd, the Minister at Turin, and to Prince Eugene. He said that the fleet should not be involved with affairs in Spain and that England and Holland would not countenance any further weakening in the forces for Toulon.[12]

Charles III even went to the length of writing to Queen Anne, asking her to see that Shovell transported troops from Italy to Spain, and that he should not leave the Mediterranean until Catalonia was secure. However, no troops could be carried from Italy to Spain unless Byng's squadron or Norris' few ships took them. At Barcelona, Byng and the Dutch Admiral van der Goes pretended to get ships ready for the task while awaiting Shovell's approval or more certain intelligence from Italy. Norris, in Genoa, went through a similar charade to Byng. The "preparations" were misleading not only to Charles III and his court, as was intended, but more importantly to the French.[13]

Shovell arrived with the fleet at Barcelona on May 20th, and he managed to persuade Charles III that a successful assault on Toulon would indirectly help him in Spain. "The most advantageous measures . . . to repair the loss in Spain, and for the good of the common cause and the interest of the Allies and honour of their arms". Shovell suggested to Charles III and his court that they would rather "endure a great deal than that any number of troops be withdrawn from his Royal Highness that might in the least obstruct the vigorous prosecution of this project". Of course, Shovell had the only means of transporting troops, his ships, under his orders. But it was as well that he carried Charles III with him. The humble sailor from Norfolk was capable of making kings change their minds if it was necessary.[14]

The fleet sailed from Barcelona and on June 2nd anchored at Finale about sixty miles to the east of Nice. Shovell had under his command forty-three men of war and fifty-seven transports. Norris informed him on his arrival that the land forces would be ready in a week. Shovell in a graceful reply to Norris, which was clearly for the Duke of Savoy's eyes, wrote:

> You have done me particular satisfaction by letting me know the great esteem and regard his Royal Highness has for her Majesty's friendship and alliance. I am sure her Majesty and the people of England have equal friendship and affection for his Royal Highness . . . and am further sure that his Royal Highness has already so great and just a share of the esteem of the Allies, but in particular of her Majesty's subjects, the vigorous prosecution of this great and acceptable design will for ever make his friendship and alliance memorable and grateful to the English nation. I esteem it the greatest honour of my life that I have the happiness to serve under his Royal Highness's direction for carrying on a service so agreeable to the public.[15]

If the troops were to march in a week, there was still a great deal to be done by the fleet in the supply of provisions and ammunition. Before arriving at Finale, Shovell had sent transport ships, with men of war as escorts, to Livorno and Genoa. After arrival further transports were sent to Savorna. Strong convoys were necessary, as Shovell did not know of the movements of the French Toulon fleet, which might have destroyed them. The work of loading the transport ships was slow, as the local inhabitants did little to help, and the sailors were inclined to make the most of their time ashore by getting drunk. The subordinate admirals, Byng, Norris and Dilkes, all spent time at Genoa trying to speed up the loading. Shovell even showed willingness to give Emperor Joseph's expedition to Naples a helping hand, by sending fast ships to try to intercept a French convoy carrying troops from Marseilles to reinforce Naples. They were unsuccessful.[16]

Shovell was concerned about the delays in getting the expedition under way and urged the Duke of Savoy to start moving without waiting for the transport ships. Savoy intended to take Monaco, Villefranche and Antibes on the road to Toulon. Shovell felt that this should be done immediately without taking the intervening towns. He pointed out to Savoy on June 10th that:

> it is no new thing for us to be sometimes three weeks or a month getting to a place which at other times we may get to in twenty four hours, which will show your Royal Highness that our motions are not so regular nor cannot be so timely adjusted as marches by land.

Movement by sea in the early eighteenth century was a very haphazard affair. A week later, on June 17th, having heard how little protected Toulon was against an assault, Shovell wrote to Norris a letter for Savoy to see.

> If these accounts be true, that there are so few troops about Toulon, I cannot forbear to offer my judgement that we fall first upon that place; for if we secure Toulon, which is a harbour for our ships, and his Royal Highness should think of keeping it, I would venture to leave a squadron of twenty sail of ships there all winter, which should be at his Royal Highness's commands for such services as he should think proper on these coasts. And the taking and keeping of Toulon would be so well liked in England and Holland that, if his Royal Highness should think it practicable from Toulon to penetrate into France next spring, I dare almost venture my reputation and all I am worth in the world that his Royal Highness will neither want men, money, ships, nor other materials to execute his designs.

In a further letter to Norris, Shovell stated:

> I must desire you will positively assure his Royal Highness that,
> though our main design be upon Toulon, even if that was done and
> over, either you or I will myself remain with a squadron there to
> execute all his Royal Highness's other designs.[17]

Shovell was not alone in wishing to take Toulon rapidly, preferably
without damage, so that it could be used as a naval base for an
Anglo/Dutch fleet, and as a springboard into the French interior.
Marlborough kept in close touch with events as Norris sent him copies of
Shovell's letters. He agreed with Shovell that an intact Toulon could be
used as a winter base for the fleet, and also that the land forces should
ignore the intervening towns such as Antibes. Savoy and Prince Eugene
rejected the views of Shovell and Marlborough. On hearing of Shovell's
recommendations they "passed some jest how they should get back again,
if the enemy should prove too strong". Nothing was to be settled until the
army reached the coast.[18]

Instead of the expected seven days after Shovell's arrival at Finale, it
was to be seventeen days before Prince Eugene was ready to march.
Eugene, having feinted at Susa, marched with about 35,000 men from
Turin. Scarcely one sixth of this force was supplied by Emperor Joseph, as
8,000 of his best men were on the way down Italy to take Naples.
However, Eugene had at his side the redoubtable German mercenaries
paid for by England, and the ardent Savoyards who followed their duke.
Until the last moment, Eugene attempted to persuade the Anglo/Dutch
commanders to abandon the attempt on Toulon, and to send 5,000 men for
action in Spain. Eugene raised the matter with Shovell who, supported by
the English and Dutch ministers, flatly refused to drop Toulon from their
plans. As Shovell controlled the ships, men and money, there was little
Eugene could do. Perhaps this gives a clue to his subsequent irresolution
in the attack on Toulon. Shovell had behaved in a characteristically
straightforward manner. His sovereign had given him orders and he
would follow them through, come what may. Besides, he understood the
strategic value of Toulon to the allies.[19]

A day or two after Eugene left Turin, the Duke of Savoy, Norris and the
English Minister Chetwynd followed him. The two Englishmen joined
Eugene and the army some sixty miles south of Turin, on the eastern
slopes of the Alps. The mountains were crossed at a rate of ten to fifteen
miles a day through Tenda, Briel, Sospel and L'Escarere to Nice, which
was reached on June 29th. The journey was a difficult one with men and
animals sliding down the mountainside. The mountain passes had been
slow to clear of snow that year, which was one of the reasons for the
delayed start of the expedition. In a letter to Shovell, Norris gave an

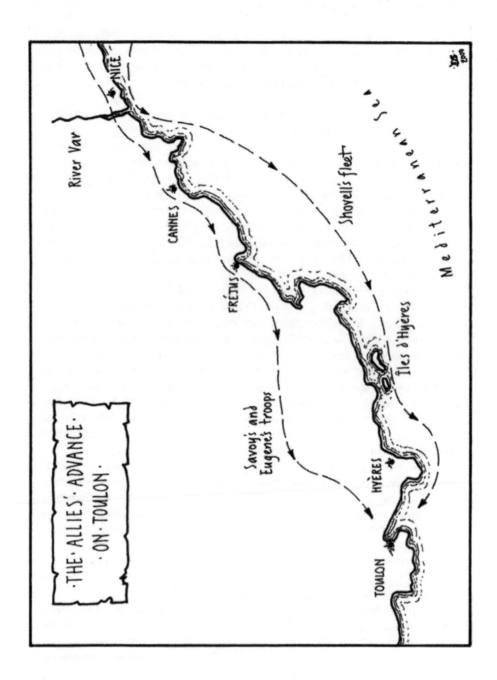

·THE·ALLIES'·ADVANCE· ·ON·TOULON·

River Var

NICE

CANNES

FRÉJUS

Savoy's and Eugene's troops

Shovell's fleet

Mediterranean Sea

Îles d'Hyères

HYÈRES

TOULON

account of the taking of Sospel. The town made a nominal attempt to defend itself before surrendering. Norris had been told that it was lawful to hang the officer on the gate if he stopped a royal army![20]

At the Duke of Savoy's request, Shovell had moved the fleet westwards to a point between Nice and the River Var. On the night of June 29th Shovell entertained to dinner, aboard his ship the *Association*, the Duke of Savoy, Prince Eugene, most of the general officers, and the English and Dutch ministers. By all accounts it was a memorable occasion. Campbell records:

> Sir Cloudesley Shovell, though he was not one of the politest officers we ever had, showed a great deal of prudence and address, in the magnificent entertainment he made upon this occasion. The duke, when he came on board the Association, found a guard of halberdiers, in new liveries, at the great cabin door. At the upper end of the table was set an armed chair, with a crimson velvet canopy. The table consisted of sixty covers, and every thing was so well managed, that his royal highness could not forbear saying to the admiral at dinner. "If your excellency had paid me a visit at Turin, I could scarcely have treated you so well." [21]

After dinner was over, a council of war was held, at which it was resolved to force a passage across the Var.[22]

The Var was a rapidly flowing river just to the west of Nice and seventy miles from Toulon. The French had made entrenchments on the western bank that extended from the mouth of the river to four miles inland. Defending the entrenchments were six battalions of foot soldiers, 800 dragoons, and a further reinforcement of three battalions under Lieutenant General Arthur Dillon was expected daily. Dillon was a very experienced Irish soldier, who in the past had served James II. The Var acted as a barrier to any advance the allies wished to make on Toulon. Shovell pointed out to Savoy that the French lines, on the banks of the river, were close enough to cannonade from the sea. Following bombardment seamen in boats could attack the entrenchments. Savoy consented to this and it was agreed that, while the French were occupied with the boats of the fleet, ten battalions of foot soldiers and 600 horse would cross the river to the north.[23]

John Norris was given command of the squadron that was to attack the French at the mouth of the Var. The ships selected by Shovell were the *Monmouth* 70 guns, *Panther* 54, *Tilbury* 54, *Romney* 54, *Rye* 32, *Landskroon* 36, *Isabella yacht*, two bomb vessels and the armed boats of the fleet. On the morning of June 30th 1707 this small force moved in and anchored at Cagnes, close to the French side of the river. At noon Norris was sent by the Duke of Savoy to tell Shovell that he would like the fleet to start engaging the French in two hours time, when the land forces would try to cross the Var. Norris hoisted his flag on the *Monmouth* and was followed on board by Shovell himself, Byng and Dilkes. All the English admirals in the Mediterranean were now on one ship at the mouth of the Var and were soon to be in range of French fire. No doubt the lure of action after the many delays was too great a temptation for them to resist![24]

Shovell, who had taken over direct command of the enterprise from Norris, ordered fire to be opened. Soon Shovell noticed that the French dragoons posted on the west bank of the River Var were moving away from the water. He thought that an assault by the fleet's boats might, with covering fire from his ships, take the angle of the entrenchments nearest the water. Accordingly, Shovell sent Norris into the shore with 600 men (sailors and marines), to drive the French out of the entrenchments. Norris and his men got ashore from their boats and occupied the French positions with little opposition. While Norris' force dug in, so that they could hold what they had so boldly gained, Shovell sent a message to Savoy and Eugene informing them that he had secured a footing and that the army might cross the river. Meanwhile, Savoy, Eugene and 8,000 men had come under fire while trying to cross higher up the river. Shovell's flank attack, at the mouth of the river, had driven the French out of their positions and allowed the army to cross in relative peace. Some 100 men were swept down the rapidly flowing river, of whom ten were drowned. The remainder of the army crossed the river next day and a camp was made a mile beyond it.[25]

The retreating French met Dillon and his reinforcements eight miles to the west of the Var. Dillon was so astonished to see them that he allowed himself to be persuaded to give up the town of St Paul. All the French forces retreated to Toulon leaving the way open for the allies. It was an auspicious opening to the campaign.[26]

Failure to cross the River Var would have been the end of the expedition for the allies. Shovell with his keen tactical eye had rapidly disadvantaged the French enemy, making the crossing for the Duke of Savoy and his army a relative formality. The only criticism that can be levelled at Shovell is that he sailed in too close to the mouth of the river, in the *Monmouth*, with all his subordinate admirals aboard. It might have been more sensible for him to have stayed behind with the fleet and left the assault of the entrenchments to Norris or one of the other junior admirals. However, Shovell had suggested forcing the passage of the river and had executed it.

Following the successful crossing of the River Var, on July 2nd Shovell entertained to dinner again the Duke of Savoy, Prince Eugene, Chetwynd and Norris. After dinner, consideration was given to the best way to conduct the march on Toulon, a matter that had been discussed before the start of the expedition and a decision delayed. Should they march directly on Toulon without capturing the smaller towns on their route or not? The French had garrisons at Monaco and Antibes, which might not only interfere with their communications, but also stop a retreat by land from Toulon if things did not go well for them there. A rapid advance on Toulon was essential, before the French collected sufficient forces together to defend the place properly. Since Almanza and the overrunning of the Lines of Stollhofen by the Duc de Villars, the French had made available troops from both Spain and Germany. The members of the post-dinner council of war in the *Association* appreciated only too well that speed was all essential. Shovell understood the potential dangers of leaving intact French garrisons behind their line of advance, as he explained in a letter to Marlborough. He reassured Savoy that, if Toulon was not taken, the fleet and its transports could carry the army back by sea. "I hope better things from your Royal Highness's fortune; but, if there should be any appearance of such an event's happening, your highness may rely upon me, I will take care to supply a sufficient number of transports to embark all your troops." The English view was to go straight for Toulon without delay and that view was accepted.[27]

The army set off on July 4th for the march to Toulon. The weather was very hot and the road difficult, particularly the steep hill between Cannes and Fréjus. Two days' rest at Fréjus was required and a considerable number of soldiers fell out from the effects of heat. Several men died on the way and others shot themselves in despair. The road after Fréjus was easier and passed through wine groves and cornfields. At last, on the 15th, they reached La Valette, two miles north-east of Toulon. Much has been made of the time taken by the Duke of Savoy and his army to reach Toulon. Eleven days going there and only seven in retreat. Suggestions have been made that this was the first sign of irresolution in Prince Eugene, or that Shovell, by withholding his subsidies on crossing the Var, angered Savoy. There is no evidence for the latter, and indeed Savoy is unlikely to have marched at all if the money had been withheld.[28]

Shovell had been ordered by Savoy to make a base for the fleet in the Îles d'Hyères, twenty or so miles to the east of Toulon. Once the army reached Toulon he would be summoned before that place. Byng, with some twelve men of war and provision ships, went ahead to keep in contact with the army as they marched along the coast. At Fréjus, Byng took on board 500 sick soldiers. A violent storm on July 13th stopped Shovell from making his base in the Isles of Hyères. Hearing that the town of Hyères, on the mainland, was ready to capitulate, Shovell decided to make his base there. He garrisoned the town with marines under a major. The townspeople proved helpful in providing ovens to bake bread for the army, hospitals for the sick and oxen for transport. At one stage, the marines clashed with their German allies, who wanted to plunder the town, but were not allowed to.[29]

The Duke of Savoy's advance had thrown the French into great confusion. At first they could not be certain of his objective. Was it to be Provence or Dauphiné? It was not until Savoy had crossed the Var that the French started to fortify Toulon and mobilise troops for its defence. By some accounts, the local inhabitants of Toulon did more to defend themselves than their King, Louis XIV, or his generals! They armed themselves and their servants, coined their plate and sold their jewels to pay workmen to raise fortifications. In anguish Louis XIV turned to the disgraced* Marshal Catinat, by reputation the best officer in France, for advice. Catinat, with the aid of female intrigue, recommended Marshal de Tessé to command the defending forces. Tessé was in the Dauphiné and he immediately marched south with twenty-eight battalions of soldiers. He had farther to travel to Toulon than the allies, but arrived there one day before them. It is likely that his troops were better acclimatised and of course better motivated, in that they were defending their homeland. When Tessé arrived at Toulon, he found Dillon and the defenders of the Var there.

At this stage, the total defending French force numbered some 20,000 men. Leaving the Marquis de Goesbriant in command, Tessé went off to rally more men. He returned at the end of July with 10,000 further foot soldiers and 1,000 horse. The allies had begun the march to Toulon with about 35,000 men, of whom a few thousand had dropped out through sickness and desertion. The two sides were to be closely matched in numbers, but if the allies had arrived a little earlier they would have found Toulon relatively undefended. The allies were in no position to completely surround the town.[30]

Not only land forces faced the Duke of Savoy and Shovell. In the harbour of Toulon were forty-six ships of between 50 and 110 guns, plus some fireships and other smaller vessels. In fact, they were no great threat to Shovell's fleet, in that there were insufficient funds to man, repair and victual them for sea duty. However, they provided a significant future threat to Anglo/Dutch shipping.

The main ships were:

| Le Terrible | 110 guns | L'Eclatant | 66 guns |
| Le Foudroyant | 104 guns | L'Henri | 66 guns |
| Le Soleil Royal | 102 guns | L'Ecueil | 64 guns |
| L'Admirable | 100 guns | Le Thoulouse | 62 guns |
| Le Triomphant | 96 guns | L'Eole | 62 guns |
| L'Orgueilleux | 92 guns | Le Sérieux | 60 guns |
| Le Triomphant | 92 guns(sic) | Le Content | 60 guns |

* In 1705 Catinat had been defeated by Prince Eugene and hence his disgrace.

| | | | |
|---|---|---|---|
| Le St Phillippe | 90 guns | Le St Louis | 60 guns |
| Le Magnifique | 90 guns | Le Fendant | 60 guns |
| Le Tonnant | 90 guns | Le Vermandois | 60 guns |
| Le Sceptre | 90 guns | Le Temeraire | 60 guns |
| La Couronne | 86 guns | Le Laurier | 60 guns |
| Le Vainqueur | 86 guns | Le Furieux | 60 guns |
| Le Monarque | 84 guns | La Zelande | 60 guns |
| Le Pompeux | 80 guns | L'Entreprenant | 58 guns |
| L'Intrepide | 80 guns | Le Fleuron | 56 guns |
| Le Neptune | 76 guns | Le Trident | 56 guns |
| Le Parfait | 76 guns | Le Diamant | 56 guns |
| Le St Esprit | 70 guns | Le Sage | 54 guns |
| Le Bizara | 70 guns | Le Ruby | 54 guns |
| L'Invincible | 70 guns | Le Mercure | 52 guns |
| L'Heureux | 68 guns | La Perle | 50 guns |
| Le Constant | 68 guns | La Meduse | 50 guns [31] |

Louis XIV was so concerned that Shovell might set fire to his ships with shells and carcasses that he ordered them to be temporarily sunk. The three deckers would lie with their upper decks out of the water, and the others would be completely submerged. For a short period of time, the ships would be safe, but long term submersion would lead to rot setting in in their timbers. Two of the 90 gun ships, *Le Tonnant* and *Le Saint Phillippe*, were turned into floating batteries. Mantlets of rope and extra planks of wood on their upper decks protected them from bombs, and sunken vessels screened them from fire ships. Seamen from the sunken ships defended the port and manned new batteries of naval cannons.[32]

On arrival at Toulon, the allies' generals climbed Mount Faron to view the place. Norris, still acting as Shovell's representative, went with them. He has left a record of the scene below him.

> The town has ten bastions, a shallow dry ditch, but no palisadoes or outworks to the bastions and curtains. In their two basins lay their ships without mast or anything, I believe, on board them. I endeavoured to count them, but could not distinguish them; but I judge the number of men-of-war to be upwards of forty sail; they seem to lay lashed on board each other, and mostly in the West Basin. The front of the basins to the water is walled as high as a ship and has an entire range of cannon placed upon it; and at each end of the town was placed a three decked ship to help flank any attack that should be against the town. Between the two land gates of the town toward the mountain [Faron], their army lay encamped in two lines; but the tents looked thin, our officers did not judge them above seven thousand men; and they had made entrenchments and were working at them.

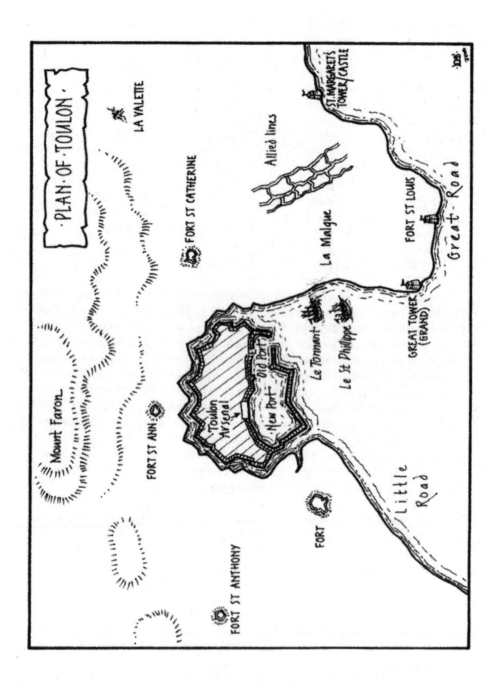

There are many forts and batteries that command the two roads [harbours], and they seemed to be so narrow that a ship cannot any ways ride, but is commanded by one shore or the other.[33]

Of the many forts mentioned by Norris, three were particularly important. Fort St Catherine, in the foothills of Mount Faron, was closest to the allied army. Fort St Ann lay between the north wall of the town and Mount Faron. Fort St Anthony, although playing little part as the assault took place, controlled a potential advance from the west. The defences of the forts were improved in the period between the allies crossing the Var and arriving at La Valette. Trench systems had also been dug mainly in a roughly north/south direction facing La Valette. Although Savoy's army developed their own trench system facing the French, they were lethargic about doing it. Prince Eugene was criticised for making no attempt to hinder French preparations on his reaching Toulon.[34]

Two days after his arrival at La Valette, close to Toulon, on July 17th, the Duke of Savoy sent for Shovell. Shovell came from his base at Hyères and went ashore with Byng, Norris, Chetwynd and the new Dutch Commander, Convent. A private meeting took place between Savoy, Eugene and Shovell, with Norris in attendance. Savoy told Shovell that he was glad to see him at last, as the maritime powers had made him wait a long time. Shovell replied that he had not delayed a moment to wait upon the Duke. Savoy smiled and said: "I did not say you, but the maritime powers had made me wait; for this expedition I concerted so long ago as 1693; and fourteen years is a long time to wait, Sir Cloudesley."[35]

At this meeting, on July 17th, Shovell called for the immediate storming of Toulon before its defences were further strengthened. The Duke of Savoy was inclined to the idea, but he deferred to Prince Eugene who was not. Eugene did not understand amphibious operations, and was more at home in central Europe. He feared being cut off by the French and wanted to retreat. Shovell disagreed. Eugene reported to Emperor Joseph: "In spite of the representations I have made to the Admiral, he absolutely insists upon carrying on with the enterprise of Toulon." Later in another letter. "Although the Admirals do not understand the land service, they refuse to listen to facts, and adhere obstinately to their opinion for good or ill everything must be staked on the siege of Toulon. Yet the pure impossibility of this is clearly before their eyes." Finally a compromise was thrashed out – no grand storming of Toulon but a local assault and bombardment.[36]

Having come to a compromise, Savoy and Eugene wanted to know just what the fleet could do to help them. Shovell agreed to land cannons, ball and powder. There was always a shortage of shot and Shovell, on his own initiative, reduced the lowest reserve of forty shot per cannon in the fleet to thirty-five, without express authority. Such was his desire to help the land forces. Shovell would blockade Toulon by sea. Dilkes was already intermittently venturing into the harbour roads and, on July 19th, Byng with an Anglo/Dutch squadron sailed for Sanary, a few miles to the west of Toulon, to stop shipping getting in or out in that direction. Shovell even agreed to send three ships to carry artillery from Genoa to Naples. Savoy and Eugene asked what the fleet would do if the French army, at Toulon, was too strong for the allies. Shovell replied that he would evacuate the foot soldiers by sea and that the naval cannons that were ashore would have to be abandoned.[37]

Later, Shovell explained to Byng that he had agreed to assist with shipping artillery to Naples purely to keep Prince Eugene in the fold. "In order to engage Prince Eugene to go vigorously on with this affair here, for I believe it stops most on his account." Shovell's assessment of Eugene's frame of mind was a correct one. There were suggestions that Emperor Joseph had given him instructions not to risk his troops. Certainly this was not the bold Eugene who had broken the siege of Turin the previous year.[38]

The following day, the 12th, Prince Eugene did attack Fort St Catherine, the north-east point of the French outworks, in the foothills of Mount Faron. It was a half-hearted attack and the next day it was stormed successfully by a German general with fifty-five men killed and wounded. The French blew up the magazine and spiked their guns before they retired. The allies began setting up batteries and pushed their trench system forward closer to the town of Toulon. The new system extended from the foothills of Mount Faron, at Fort St Catherine, to the hill of La Malgue on the coast. Shovell proposed attacking Fort St Louis and St Margaret's Castle. He said that he would assist with a cannonade by his ships. Norris was sent to investigate, but the engineer who was with him thought that although the fort and castle could be taken easily by land, a cannonade would damage their own camp. Norris took this opportunity to note the possibility of bombarding Toulon over the narrow neck of land.[39]

By July 23rd the shore batteries were ready to be manned and the Duke of Savoy asked Shovell to send gunners ashore. Norris wanted the naval gunners to man the batteries closest to the shore, partly to make supplying them with food and drink easier. The main reason was that, if things did not go well for the army, at least the French fleet could be battered in their protected harbour. At this stage, there was a brief period when Savoy lost faith in Shovell and the sea commanders. This appears to have been precipitated by the fact that galleys had escaped from Toulon to Marseilles and by fears that the fleet might abandon them. Norris, on Shovell's behalf, patiently explained that it was not possible for men of war to stop galleys breaking the blockade. Galleys were also too strong for the ship's boats. He was sure that Shovell and the fleet would stay until at least

September. Undoubtedly Prince Eugene's pessimism had infected the Duke. For a time, Norris' calming words reassured him.[40]

By July 27th Shovell was expressing his doubt about the success of the attack on Toulon in a letter to the Earl of Manchester. Two days later the Duke of Savoy wanted to see Shovell privately again. Forewarned by Norris that what he was to hear might not be to his liking, Shovell went ashore again on the 29th.[41]

In his quarters at La Valette the Duke of Savoy received Shovell. Norris was with him as usual and Chetwynd did the interpreting, as Shovell spoke no French. Savoy was losing heart. He explained that they had now been before Toulon for fifteen days and had not been as successful as he had hoped. There was a general slackness amongst the troops building the trenches. When Prince Eugene came, a final decision could be made on whether to continue the siege or not. Eugene, on arrival, was non-committal and suggested that the opinions of the generals should be taken into account. Finally, with some misgivings, it was agreed to land further cannon to bring the number up to ninety, and to attack Fort St Louis and St Margaret's Castle. The taking of the latter would improve communications between the army on shore and the fleet. Shovell had used all his considerable powers of persuasion to keep the assault on course. No doubt he did this in his usual direct and honest manner. Norris has left an account of Shovell's thoughts at this juncture.

> The Admiral [Shovell] in the discourse used all means possible to persuade the continuance of the siege, alleging, if the town could not be taken, that, as the enemy were daily sinking their ships, we should by degrees so disable them as not suddenly to be in any condition to put to sea.

In a letter to George Byng at about this time, Shovell expanded his views on the situation.

> Everything has almost been at a stand ashore. I find neither officers nor soldiers very forward; these great guns don't well agree with them; but now they seem to design to proceed more vigorously, and resolve to attack Fort Louis and St Margaret's. We continue to land every day ammunition and provisions for them, and we are going to land more guns to make up the whole number between ninety and one hundred, and I believe I shall in a little time be ready to come to you.[42]

The fleet had been much involved with the transport of supplies from Hyères and the blockade. Now they were to become more active. Dilkes, since early July, had been an intermittent presence in the Roads of Toulon.

Shovell sailed from Hyères on August 2nd, and arrived in Toulon Bay during the afternoon of the same day. He brought back Byng with his ships from Sanary on August 3rd and 4th. Byng's flagship broke her cable during a period of forty-eight hours of continuous gales. Cruisers were sent to Marseilles to prevent the return of the galleys. On land, seamen operating from La Malgue bombarded Fort St Louis from batteries. By August 2nd much of the facing of the Fort had been knocked down. Progress against the castle at St Margaret's was slower. The Duke of Savoy asked for Shovell's help. Both fort and castle were in range of the fleet, but the gale that had damaged the *Royal Anne*, Byng's flagship, also precluded a bombardment from the sea.[43]

Life at sea had been made difficult by the weather. On land matters were equally unpropitious, with the Duke of Savoy telling Norris that he had only 18,000 to 20,000 men fit for service. The reasons for this were battle casualties, sickness and, no doubt, desertion. With Tessé's 10,000 reinforcements arriving at the end of July, increasing the total French force to near 30,000 men, the allies were now outnumbered.

At this juncture, early in the morning of August 4th the French sallied forth from their lines. Twelve thousand men, in five columns, attacked the allies' lines from Mount Faron in the north to La Malgue in the south. Fort St Catherine was taken and the Prince of Saxe-Gotha was killed there after being isolated with forty men and two officers. South of the Toulon to Hyères road, the allies did better and repulsed the French from their batteries on La Malgue. The blow was softened a little when St Margaret's Castle surrendered during the afternoon, because of a shortage of water and ammunition. When the main body of the allies' army prepared to go into action, the French returned to their own lines, although they continued to hold part of Mount Faron.

Although the damage done to the allies during August 4th was not catastrophic on the ground, in the minds of Savoy and Eugene it appeared to be. The French sally merely confirmed their belief that Toulon was not to be taken whatever Shovell and his admirals may have felt.[44]

The land commanders may have given up, but at sea Shovell had not. Although he accepted that Toulon could not be taken, he intended the navy to leave its mark in the way of a bombardment from the sea. Shovell wanted to destroy the French fleet and dockyard area by means of bomb ketches hurling bombs across the neck of land between Fort St Louis and the Grand Tower. Before this could be attempted, batteries close to the unmanned Grand Tower and Fort Louis would have to be silenced, or they would sink the bomb ketches. Byng was sent by Shovell to deal with the twenty guns of Fort St Louis, and Dilkes with the smaller batteries to the west.

By August 5th the weather had improved, and following Shovell's orders both Byng and Dilkes led their ships in closer to the coast. Byng's task of neutralising Fort St Louis was the more difficult. Among the ships of Byng's squadron were the *St George* under Shovell's protégé, James Dursley, and the *Swiftsure* with Richard Griffiths as captain. Unfortunately, the wind freshened as they approached the coast so that by midday it had become a gale. The *St George* sprang a topmast and split her sails. Dursley was unable to bombard Fort St Louis and spent an uncomfortable night at sea trying to hold his position. Griffiths in the *Swiftsure* went aboard the *Association* early in the morning to receive instructions directly from Shovell. Accompanying the *St George*, the *Swiftsure* managed to anchor in range of the Fort, and started a vigorous exchange of shot that lasted for three hours. While in front of Fort St Louis, Griffiths had five men killed and about forty wounded. He was forced to withdraw. Fort St Louis had not been silenced.[45]

Dilkes and his squadron attacked a battery of nine guns positioned by the French halfway between the Grand Tower and Fort St Louis, and a small three gun battery farther west. The next day, August 6th, Dilkes intended to send in his boats to assault and destroy the batteries. He was delayed until the 7th, when his men found the batteries deserted by the French and the guns spiked. The guns were dismounted and the carriages burnt before the squadron joined Shovell and the rest of the fleet off St Margaret's Castle.[46]

That same day, August 7th, seamen manning a battery still functioning on shore made a large hole in the wall of Fort St Louis. Troops were sent to take the fort, now that a breach had been made. They found the fort abandoned and they spiked its twenty-two cannons. Norris, who was on shore at the time, hurried to survey the scene. After discussion with the Duke of Savoy and Prince Eugene, Norris reported to Shovell that it was now practicable to bombard Toulon and the ships in its harbour.[47]

Shovell sent for Dilkes and ordered him to take frigates and bomb vessels off Fort St Louis and to bombard Toulon Harbour. Dilkes was unable to comply at once because of poor weather, but on August 9th he was able to go on shore with at least one captain of a bomb vessel and set up markers so that the bombing could be done more accurately. The following day the English bomb ketches *Basilisk*, *Blast*, *Grando* and a further two Dutch ones, anchored in the bight between the Grand Tower and the ruins of Fort St Louis. Dilkes shifted his flag to the *Romney* and covered the bomb ketches with an escort of frigates. The bombardment lasted from the afternoon of August 10th throughout the night until the morning of August 11th. During the night the French set up new batteries that damaged the frigates and bomb ketches, forcing Dilkes to withdraw. He had acted bravely by going on shore with the masters of the ketches, and had signalled directions to his ships on observing where the shells fell. The dispatch of some 500 shells plus incendiary carcasses made a great deal of noise, but the damage done was not that great. *Le*

*Sage* (54 guns) and *Le Fortuné* (52 guns) were destroyed by fire. The partially sunken *Le Diamant* (58 guns) had the upper deck burned, and two frigates *La Salamandre* and *L'Ardromede* were badly damaged. Some of the storehouses around the harbour had also been set on fire. Dilkes reported to Shovell after his withdrawal and a council of war was called. At this, it was agreed that no further bombardment was possible. Shovell told Byng: "I would we had had more time, but they brought guns to the water side and mauled our bomb vessels."[48]

While the fleet was making every effort to do as much damage as was possible to Toulon, plans were being effected to withdraw the army. The Duke of Savoy ordered Norris, on August 5th, to find a suitable beach to embark cannon and stores. The following day Savoy told Shovell to be ready to receive 3,000 sick and wounded soldiers. On the 7th Shovell sent Byng to his base at Hyères to make preparations for the withdrawal from there. Because bread was baked for the troops there, Savoy was keen for the marines to remain at the garrison until the last moment, as he had no alternative supply. Byng had his way, partly by threatening the inhabitants of Hyères with destruction of their town if they did not co-operate, and partly because of the marines' strict discipline, and the good relations that they had enjoyed with the local inhabitants. In the event, the town's people persuaded the French Commander Tessé to let the marines leave peacefully, and there were even exchanges of presents![49]

During August 7th, 8th and 9th the fleet were busy taking men and equipment on board off St Margaret's Castle. The Duke of Savoy, on the 9th, told Shovell that he and Prince Eugene had decided to retreat at once. The next morning the bulk of Savoy's army marched for Fréjus leaving a rearguard of 4,000 men to follow a day later. With all this activity going on, Shovell still found time to write to the Emperor of Fez and Morocco asking him to bring pressure to bear on Vanisha to deliver up British subjects, ships and their goods that had been taken. The fleet sailed from Toulon Bay on August 12th, and accompanied Savoy's army until they had got back across the River Var. On the 20th Shovell was off Nice and two days later he held a council of war. Following this, Shovell proposed that he should transport 5,000 to 6,000 men from Savoy's army to Spain for further action. Both Savoy and Eugene declined, claiming that they had no spare men. The forces dispersed on August 23rd, Savoy to his own country, Eugene to Lombardy and Shovell with the fleet to Gibraltar. Savoy, the following month, took the fortress of Susa. That gave him an open passage into Dauphiné and at the same time shut the French out of his homeland. At Gibraltar, Shovell divided his fleet. He took the main part home under his own command, leaving Dilkes with a smaller squadron on the peninsula. Dilkes, like Shovell himself, had little time to live, dying the following December 12th at Livorno, possibly having been poisoned.[50]

The bid to take Toulon by the allies had failed despite Shovell's best efforts. The sending of troops to Naples by Emperor Joseph, instead of to Toulon, lack of vigour by Prince Eugene, and the various delays may all have been crucial. There was delay in the fleet reaching Italy, delay in the expedition starting and possibly most important of all, the delay in reaching Toulon after the River Var had been successfully crossed. The Duke of Savoy's army took two days on the way back from Toulon to cover a distance that had taken six days in the advance. Marlborough felt that if the army had reached Toulon five days earlier, it would have fallen with ease. It was not to be, and Savoy was lucky to get his army away without its destruction.

Some good had come out of the attempt on Toulon. As Marlborough consoled Shovell: ". . . has been of great use to the King of Spain, and likewise put a stop to the successes of the French in Germany by the detachments they were obliged to make from all parts of Provence".[51] In addition, the French Toulon fleet had scuttled itself.

Shovell had done everything in his power to drive his colleagues forward to Toulon and his support of the army there was exemplary. He had no reason to reproach himself for the failure of the enterprise. As Churchill wrote in the biography of his illustrious ancestor, the Duke of Marlborough: "In our history the Navy has sometimes stood by to watch the Army do the work. Here was a case where a navy tried by its exertion and sacrifice to drive forward an army."[52] Unfortunately it did not succeed.

NOTES

1. Richmond, pp.324–335.
2. Campbell, Vol.III, p.514.
3. Campbell, Vol.IV, pp.255–256; Owen, pp.158–159.
4. Owen, pp.158–161; ADD MSS 28153; House of Lords MSS 2426, pp.372, 517.
5. Campbell, Vol.III, p.515; Owen, p.161; Murray, Marlborough Despatches, Marlborough to Count Noyelles, June 3rd 1707.
6. Campbell, Vol.III, pp.512–513; Owen, p.162; D.N.B. Norris; Larn, p.50; ADM 33.249.
7. Owen, p.162; D.N.B. Norris; Campbell, Vol.V, pp.155–156.
8. Owen, p.162; ADD MSS 28153 f.19, Shovell to Savoy, March 28th 1707.
9. Owen, pp.162–163; ADD MSS 28153 f.23.
10. Campbell, Vol.IV, p.256; Owen, pp.162–163; Murray, Marlborough's Dispatches, Shovell to Marlborough, July 3rd 1707.
11. Owen, pp.163–164.
12. Owen, p.164; ADD MSS 28141, Norris to Shovell, May 22nd, Norris to Sunderland, May 24th, Norris to Marlborough, May 24th 1707; Murray, Marlborough's Dispatches, Marlborough to Chetwynd, May 28th, Marlborough to Eugene, May 31st 1707.
13. Owen, pp.164–165; ADD MSS 2841; House of Lords MSS, 1706–8, N.S., Vol.VII, p.443.

14. Owen, p.165.
15. Owen, pp.165–166; ADD MSS 28141, Shovell to Norris, June 1st & 3rd 1707; Campbell, Vol.III, p.515; London Gazette No.4343.
16. Owen, pp.166–167; Churchill, p.247.
17. Owen, pp.167–168.
18. Owen, p.168; Murray, Marlborough's Dispatches, Norris to Shovell, June 19th 1707; ADD MSS 28141.
19. Churchill, p.248; Owen, p.168.
20. Churchill, p.247; Owen, pp.168–169.
21. Campbell, Vol.III, p.516.
22. Campbell, Vol.III, p.516; Owen, p.169; Charnock, p.27.
23. Campbell, Vol.III, p.516; Vol.IV, pp.256–257; Owen, p.169; Burchett, pp.731–732; Secret Memoirs.
24. Owen, pp.169–170; Campbell, Vol.III, p.516; Vol.IV, p.257.
25. Owen, p.170; Norris' journal; Captains' journals *Monmouth, Blast*; Murray, Marlborough's Dispatches, Shovell to Marlborough, July 3rd 1707; Byng papers I, p.220; London Gazette No.4532; Campbell, Vol.III, p.517; Secret Memoirs.
26. Owen, p.170; Campbell, Vol.IV, p.257.
27. Campbell, Vol.III, pp.517–518; Owen, pp.170–171; Murray, Marlborough's Dispatches, Shovell to Marlborough, July 3rd 1707.
28. Owen, pp.171–172; Campbell, Vol.III, p.518.
29. Owen, p.172; Byng Papers I, pp.199–207, 224–225.
30. Owen, pp.170, 174; ADD MSS 28141; Byng Papers, I, pp.219–220; La Roncière, p.392; Campbell, Vol.III, pp.518–520.
31. London Gazette No.4357.
32. Owen, pp.173–174; Brun, I, pp.119–121; La Roncière, pp.391–394; ADD MSS 28141; Campbell, Vol.III, p.519.
33. ADD MSS 28141.
34. Owen, p.175.
35. Campbell, Vol. IV, p.259; Mercure Historique 1707, Vol.II, p.331.
36. Owen, pp.175–176; Churchill, pp.251–254; Feldzüge Series I IX, Suppt. 179 & 182.
37. Owen, pp.175–162; Churchill, p.247.
38. Owen, pp.175–176; Churchill, pp.246–247, 252; Byng Papers, I, pp.207–208.
39. Owen, p.177.
40. Owen, p.178; ADD MSS 28141.
41. HMC 8th Report, Appendix Part II, p.90; Owen, p.179.
42. Owen, pp.179–181; ADD MSS 28141; Byng Papers, I, pp.209–210.
43. Owen, pp.181–184; Captain's journal, *Royal Anne.*
44. Owen, pp.184–185; Campbell, Vol.III, p.521.
45. Owen, pp.185–186; ADD MSS 28141;Journal of the *Swiftsure.*
46. Owen, pp.186–187; Captains' journals *Tryton, Milford, Falcon*; Masters' journals *Somerset, Lancaster.*
47. Owen, p.188; ADD MSS 28141.
48. Owen, pp.188–189; ADD MSS 28141; Byng Papers, I, pp.213–214.
49. Owen, pp.187–188; Byng Papers, I, pp.210–213.
50. Owen, pp.189–190; Captain's journal *Royal Anne*; Byng Papers, I, pp.215, 243–245; Campbell, Vol.III, pp.523–524; Vol.IV, p.260.
51. Murray, Marlborough Dispatches, Marlborough to Shovell, September 17th 1707.
52. Churchill, p.247.

# CHAPTER XXV
## *The Build Up to Disaster*
## *1707*

Shovell left Gibraltar with the main part of the Mediterranean fleet on September 29th, and sailed for England. The fleet consisted of twenty vessels.

| 1st Rate | Guns | Captain |
|---|---|---|
| *Royal Anne* | 96–100 | James Moneypenny |
| Flagship of Sir George Byng | | |

| 2nd Rate | | |
|---|---|---|
| *Association* | 90 | Edmund Loades (1st Captain) |
| Flagship of Sir Cloudesley Shovell | | Samuel Whitaker (2nd Captain) |
| *St George* | 96 | Lord James Dursley |

| 3rd Rate | | |
|---|---|---|
| *Eagle* | 70 | Robert Hancock. |
| *Lenox* | 70 | Sir William Jumper |
| *Monmouth* | 66 | John Baker |
| *Orford* | 70 | Charles Cornewall |
| *Somerset* | 80 | John Price |
| *Swiftsure* | 70 | Richard Griffiths |
| *Torbay* | 80 | William Faulkner |
| Flagship of Sir John Norris | | |

| 4th Rate | | |
|---|---|---|
| *Romney* | 48 | William Coney |
| *Rye* | 32 | Edward Vernon |

| 6th Rate | | |
|---|---|---|
| *Cruizer* | 24 | John Shales |
| *La Valeur* | 24 | Robert Johnson |

| Fireships | | |
|---|---|---|
| *Firebrand* | 8 | Francis Percy |

| | | |
|---|---|---|
| *Griffin* | 8 | William Holding |
| *Phoenix* | 8 | Michael Sanson |
| *Vulcan* | 8 | William Ockman |

Sloop
| | | |
|---|---|---|
| *Weazle* | 10 | James Gunman |

Yacht
| | | |
|---|---|---|
| *Isabella* | 8 | Finch Reddall [1] |

Off Tangier, Shovell's fleet was increased to twenty-one when they were joined by the 54 gun 4th rate, the *Panther*, under Captain Henry Hobart. Their last sight of land as they sailed north-west into the Atlantic was Cape Spartel, on September 30th.[2]

As might be anticipated in October, Shovell's fleet had poor weather on their journey home. From October 5th until the 10th gales blew from the west, and then the wind went round to the east north-east, before dying down next day. The 12th and 13th were also squally, followed by two days of light winds. Then strong easterly gales blew on the 16th and 17th before dying away on the 18th, although the cloud remained. On October 19th there was a strong north-westerly gale that was renewed on the 21st after a day of north-easterly squalls. The 21st also saw the fleet come into soundings of between ninety and 140 fathoms, which showed that they were on the edge of the continental shelf with land not too far away. Sounding was carried out with a lead weight and a line, so that the depth of the seabed could be measured. In addition, the sounding weights were smeared with tallow so that sand, shells and small stones would come up when the line was drawn in. The seventeenth and early eighteenth century mariner relied to some degree upon the depth of his soundings and the constituents of the seabed to tell him where he was in relation to the entrance of the English Channel.[3]

The following day, October 22nd, Shovell detached the *Lenox*, *La Valeur* and the *Phoenix* to Falmouth for convoy duty. They sailed away to the north of the remainder of the fleet. The exact time of their departure is not known with certainty but was probably about 11.00 a.m. The times given in the various journals of the three ships concerned varied between 7.00 a.m. and 11.00 a.m. Timing at sea was not accurate and was mainly given to the nearest half hour. October 22nd was overcast and no sights could be taken to calculate their latitude that day. However, some of Shovell's fleet had managed sights on the previous day. At about 4.00 p.m. the fleet hove to for about two hours to obtain further soundings, and then at 6.00 p.m., satisfied that they were in the mouth of the Channel and clear of all danger, the ships ran to the eastward before a favourable south-westerly gale. Within two hours, the fleet found themselves amongst the Western Rocks, off the Scilly Isles. The disaster was about to unfold.[4]

The waters between the Bishop Rock and the south-west of the island of St Agnes have claimed more ships, and more lives, than any other part of the coastline of the British Isles. Between the sixteenth and nineteenth centuries, there was almost a wreck a year in this area.[5] Why did Shovell and his fleet find themselves, by accident, in these inhospitable waters?

Criticism has been levelled at Shovell for bringing his fleet home so late in the year. If a suitable port, such as Port Mahon, had been available in the Mediterranean, there would have been no need to bring the fleet home in winter. This was recognised by George Rooke, who in 1702 expressed his hopes that the government "are very well assured of a southern winter port for our great ships or I'm sure I shall dread the consequences of their coming home in that season". After the disaster of October 22nd 1707, even the press of the day recognised this fact. *The Observator* recorded, "had we possessed of a port in the Mediterranean to winter in there had been no need for Sir Cloudesley's return".[6]

Clearly Shovell believed that the opportunity to eclipse French naval power in the Mediterranean, by taking their main base at Toulon, outweighed the risks of a late voyage home. In any event, he had remained inside the Mediterranean until the end of October in 1703 and again in 1705 and had got safely home on both occasions, with a course similar to the one he used in 1707. The one occasion that Shovell had found himself amongst the Western Rocks, off the Scilly Isles, was as master's mate of the *Fairfax* in 1673, and that was in mid May. Clearly avoiding a return in winter was no guarantee of a safe homecoming. According to Horace Walpole: "Sir Cloudisley Shovel said that an admiral would deserve to be broke, who kept great ships out after the end of September, and to be shot if after October." These alleged words were to be used against Shovell.[7]

On the evening of October 22nd 1707 Shovell and his fleet had found themselves farther north and east than they had expected to be. The opening into the safety of the English Channel was a mere 100 miles wide. To the north were the Scilly Isles, consisting of some 150 rocks and islands, twenty-eight miles south-west of Lands End. To the south were the Channel Islands and the French coast. One hundred miles may seem to be a large distance, but with the navigational aids of the early eighteenth century it was easily missed. The fleet's navigation was inaccurate.

Over thirty years ago, Commander W.E.May R.N. made a detailed study of the logbooks of the sixteen surviving ships. As captains, masters and lieutenants were all required to keep records, he calculated that there should be sixty-one log books, in theory, available to study. May traced forty-four of these. Latitude (in this case the distance travelled north) was calculated either from observations taken with the primitive backstaff or by dead reckoning. During Shovell's last voyage, the greatest difference between the most northerly and southerly figures for a single day was forty-one miles, with an average of twenty-five and a half miles when two or more officers made an observation. Latitudes taken by dead reckoning were even worse, with a maximum of 141 miles and with a daily average of seventy-two miles difference. One of the great myths of Shovell's final voyage was that the weather was so poor that the officers of the various ships of the fleet were unable to make observations, and therefore were uncertain of their position. This was not the case at all. In fact, on fifteen of the twenty-two days of the voyage at least one officer was able to make an observation, including the day before the disaster, October 21st. However, most of the observations made were not accurate. An additional error would have occurred if the navigating officers had been using Colson's 1697 edition of his *Seaman's New Kalender*. In this book, the latitude of the Isles of Scilly was given as 50° 12′ north and that of the Lizard as 50° 10′, whereas Bishop Rock is in 49° 52′ and the Lizard 49° 58′. There would have been between twelve and twenty miles less sea room than they anticipated.[8]

During Shovell's era, it was customary to measure longitude (east to west) from the last land seen. In this case, most officers used Cape Spartel, although a few appear to have used a point in the sea that corresponds to Tenerife. Matters were further complicated by the fact that sea charts were not graduated for longitude, and recourse had to be made to navigational manuals. These differed and were not accurate. For example, Colson's error in estimation of the difference of longitude between Cape Spartel and Scilly was 2° 16′. The errors in the standard navigational books of the day must have introduced a danger, just as great as any errors in reckoning longitude. May found that thirty-three officers had a spread of only 2° 20′ in their longitudes and an error of up to 48′ in their latitudes. This was a surprise, as it was said that the old time navigators knew their latitude accurately but not their longitude.[9]

Navigationally, May considered the log of Lieutenant Anthony Lochard of the *Torbay* to have been among the best. Each noon he gave the bearing and distances of Cape Spartel and the departure and difference of longitude from it. Also the direct reckoning latitude, and when he was able to get one, the observed latitude, and the course and distance made good from the previous noon. May's interpretation of the *Torbay*'s course is shown in the accompanying map, as it gives an idea of how Shovell's final voyage progressed.[10]

Sir William Jumper, Captain of the *Lenox*, recorded in his journal: "I am surprized to find my ship so far to the northward . . . and indeed can impute it to nothing but the badness of the compass which was old and full of defects." At an inquiry following the disaster, only four out of 112 compasses from nine of Shovell's ships were found to be working

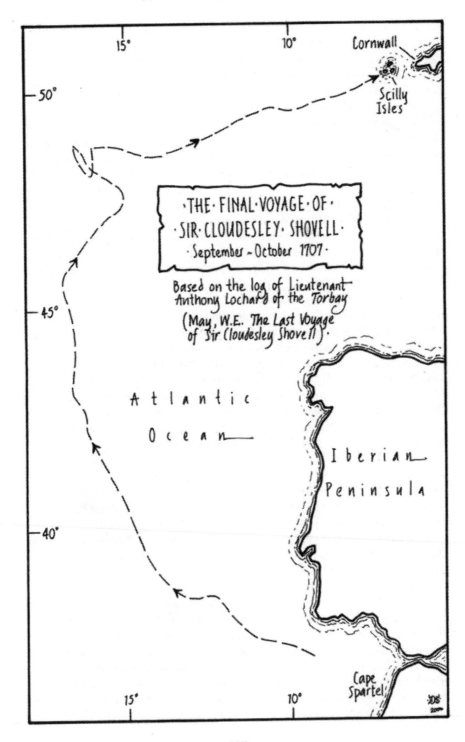

Cornwall

Scilly
Isles

15°

10°

50°

45°

40°

15°

10°

·THE·FINAL·VOYAGE·OF·
·SIR·CLOUDESLEY·SHOVELL·
·September ~ October 1707·

Based on the log of Lieutenant
Anthony Lochard of the Torbay
(May, W.E. The Last Voyage
of Sir Cloudesley Shovell).

A t l a n t i c

O c e a n

I b e r i a n

P e n i n s u l a

Cape
Spartel

335

accurately. Part of the problem was that the compasses were kept in the boatswain's store that was damp and led to their deterioration. Recommendations were made to switch to brass compasses, which would be stored in a seasoned chest fitted with partitions, in the bread room. May considered that the inaccuracy of the compasses was a contributory factor to the disaster but not the sole one.[11]

Early in the eighteenth century little was known about the possible deviation of a compass caused by magnetic material in a ship. In fact, with ships of the type that Shovell had in his fleet, records show that any magnetic deviation with ships steering easterly or westerly would have led them to be southward of their course. As the fleet was northward of its reckoning, magnetic deviation was not a factor.[12]

A final potential influence of the compasses was that no allowance had been made for variation. This would have increased progressively from 4° to 7° west as the voyage progressed, and if not allowed for would have placed the ships one or two degrees to the westward of their reckoning, i.e. away from the rocks.[13]

In spite of taking a sight on October 21st, most of Shovell's ships were too far southward in their estimates of latitude on the 22nd. A commonly held view is that this was due to the "Rennell Current". After exceptionally heavy or prolonged westerly gales, a current runs across the approaches to the English Channel, driving ships northward. This is known as the Rennell Current after the man who first described it in 1815. Mariners in the seventeenth and eighteenth centuries were aware of a current that might sweep them obliquely across the Channel approaches, but it was not until the next century that a name was given to it. The set of the Rennell Current can be at the rate of 1.5 knots, which means that if it were running strongly, the ships might have been twenty-four to thirty-six miles north of their reckoning at noon on October 22nd. However, the preconditions for the Rennell Current to run, of heavy or prolonged westerly gales, did not apply at the time, so its effect would have been much less. Allowing a generous fifteen-mile set in twenty-four hours, only nine of the known log keepers would have considered themselves to be in danger. It is fair to say that the Rennell Current may have been a factor in Shovell's fleet finding themselves to be to the northward of their reckoning, but it was a minor one.[14]

Mention has already been made of the early eighteenth century sailor's reliance on soundings, to indicate from depth and type of seabed where he was in the approaches to the English Channel. Although the crew of Shovell's ship, the *Association*, made soundings at about 4.00 p.m. on October 22nd, we do not know what they found, as their records were lost. The *Monmouth* found sixty fathoms, fine white sand. The *Torbay* fifty-five fathoms, rocky ground. The *Cruizer* found fifty-three fathoms, branny sand with pieces of red masked shells. The *Panther* found forty-seven fathoms, fine white sand. With soundings of fifty-five to sixty fathoms the fleet might equally have been to the west or south of the Scilly Isles, as the depths are not materially different. Undoubtedly the soundings made by the *Association* between 4.00 and 6.00 p.m. on the 22nd were a factor in Shovell's decision to sail on into the night.[15]

Criticism was made at the time of Shovell's decision to sail at night, rather than wait for daylight. Burchett, with his intimate knowledge of the navy at the time, recorded:

> As I cannot undertake to give the true cause of this unhappy miscarriage, I shall leave it with the common observation, that upon approaching land after so long a run, the best looker out is the best sailor, and consequently the lying by in the night time and making of sail in the Day is the most safe which I think this unhappy gentleman did not do and might principally occasion not only the loss of himself and all his ships company; . . .

Certainly Shovell's decision to sail at night was, with hindsight, wrong and proved to be tragically fatal. In mitigation, it can be said that it was not unusual to bring the fleet into the Channel at night. In March 1684 Lord Dartmouth sailed boldly up the Channel at night, with his officers disagreeing about whether they were still to the west of Scilly or not, and with fears of striking the English or French coasts! Dartmouth was lucky, as was John Narbrough, in May 1673, when he found himself amongst the Western Rocks also at night. In any event, should not the lookouts on the *Association* and other ships of the fleet have seen the lighthouse on St Agnes at night?[16]

A coal-burning lighthouse on St Agnes had become operational in 1680. In a sense seventeenth and eighteenth century mariners were fortunate to have a lighthouse at all. The Governor of the Scilly Isles was against the project, on the grounds that it would lead to a loss of profits on wrecks! No wonder a prayer was said at St Mary's Church. "We pray thee, O Lord, not that wrecks should happen, but that if any wrecks should happen, Thou wilte guide them into the Scilly Isles for the benefit of the poor inhabitants."

On St Agnes there is a well named after St Warna, the patron saint of shipwrecks. The light on St Agnes was a fixed one that might have been confused with the admiral's stern lamps. It was not until 1790 that a revolving light was installed. St Agnes' lighthouse had a tower of fifty-two feet, and stood on a hill 100 feet above sea level, at low water. For the 1790 revolving light, it was calculated that an observer at sea level should see it at fifteen and a half miles distance. At twenty feet above sea level (roughly the height of a ship's deck) the distance was increased to twenty-one miles. Undoubtedly, with the 1680 coal-burning light, its visibility would not have been as great. At times, through inefficiency, the light keeper allowed the fire to go out, so that it could not be relied on. In fact, on the evening of October 22nd the light was working and was visible to some of Shovell's ships. However, the vast majority of the fleet did not spot the light until after they were in mortal danger amongst the Western Rocks. Some mistook it to be Shovell's stern lights. Poor weather conditions that evening would have considerably reduced the distance from which the St Agnes light could be seen. Campbell suggested that Shovell set sail again at 6.00 p.m., "believing, as it is presumed, that he saw the light on St Agnes". This is mere supposition and seems unlikely. Undoubtedly the relatively modern lighthouses on Bishop Rock (1887) and Peninnis (1911) would have prevented the disaster.[17]

Often when fleets sailed, the admiral in command would send the smaller men of war and frigates out ahead to warn of potential danger. This Shovell does not appear to have done although it was his customary practice. Certainly he had no 5th rates and only two 6th rates, the *Cruizer* and *La Valeur*, to be used for this purpose. In fact, *La Valeur* was detached, by Shovell's command, with the *Lenox* and the *Phoenix*, on the morning of October 22nd and sent to Falmouth. The suggestion has been made that Shovell normally used these three ahead of the rest of the fleet, and that by detaching them he had increased the risks. This view is not borne out by the facts.[18]

It was customary to send cruisers to the Channel approaches or soundings to meet fleets returning from the Mediterranean. Captain Edward St Lo, of the *Tartar*, had orders:

> to look out for Sir Clo. Shovell and his squadron to give him an account how the land bears from him, and the better to enable him to give a just account thereof, he is to make the land once every day if conveniently he can: to continue till she meets Sir Clo. Shovell, hears he is passed by him, or till further order.

The *Tartar* sailed from Plymouth on October 21st, and returned on the 24th, without seeing anything of the squadron. If the *Tartar* had sailed a little earlier and had been lucky, she might have come across Shovell's fleet and have prevented the disaster.[19]

Two legends have come down through the centuries concerning the faulty navigation of Shovell's fleet. Both appear to have originated from an expedition made to the Scilly Isles in 1709, by a Mr Edmund Herbert, to recover property lost in the disaster. Details of this expedition are in existence in the form of a manuscript belonging to one of Herbert's descendants.[20]

The first legend has it that on October 22nd Shovell held a council of sailing masters of all the ships in the fleet, on board the *Association*, before making his fateful decision to sail on into the night.

Abt. one or two aft. noon on the 23rd (22nd) Oct$^r$ Sir C. call'd a council and examd ye Masters wt lat. they were in; all agreed to be in that of Ushant on ye coast of France, except Sr W. Jumper's Mr of ye Lenox, who believ'd 'em to be nearer Scilly, and yt in 3 hours should be up in sight thereof, (wch unfortunately happen'd) but Sr Clowd listened not to a single person whose opinion was contrary to ye whole fleet.[21]

Pickwell, in an article on Shovell's shipwreck, rightly points out the inconsistencies in this theory. Sir William Jumper (captain of the *Lenox*), according to surviving ships' logs, had been detached from the fleet earlier in the morning of the 22nd and his master could not have taken part in any council. Indeed, Pickwell could find no record in any of the surviving ships' logs of discussions having taken place in the *Association* at any time on the 22nd with officers from the other ships. Yet the various ships' logs do show visits of officers to the *Association* earlier in the voyage. It is known that at 4.00 p.m. on the 22nd the fleet hove to, to take soundings. The taking of soundings involved launching boats, and this may have been misinterpreted as a council of sailing masters having taken place in the *Association* that day.[22]

Before leaving the legend of the council of sailing masters, it is worth recording some hearsay evidence in favour of it having taken place. In the 1880s a Frederick Locker owned a document in the handwriting of his ancestor, Captain Locker, pertaining to Shovell's shipwreck.

> 31st May 1793 – In a conversation with Admiral Forbes who had been Sir John Norris's Lieut: in the Britannia at Lisbon – he told me he had often heard Sir John say, that the evening before the Admiral brought too [to] many of the captains and himself went on board him with their different Reckonings which disagreed from each other very much and that he was determined when they left him to lay too [to] all night, but Sir John Norris supposed he was persuaded by his captain to make sail, which he did, and the unfortunate accident happened before morning – He also told me that Sir George Byng afterwards Lord Torrington saved himself and the ships near him by hauling his wind when close to the surf immediately and crowded his ship off by carrying sail.[23]

Second-hand reports of this type must be treated with caution. However, the man quoted, Sir John Norris, was a longstanding friend and protégé of Shovell's. On August 23rd 1706, the day Shovell was appointed to the *Association*, Norris went with him as captain. He remained in this position until March 18th 1707, when he was made up to a rear admiral and left for the *Torbay*. Promotion may have saved Norris' life for his successor in the *Association*, Edmund Loades, was drowned with Shovell. Anything that

Norris had to say concerning Shovell's death must be taken seriously. The final sentence in the document concerning Sir George Byng is materially correct, which again adds weight to the authenticity of the document.

The second legend regarding the faulty navigation of Shovell's fleet concerns the warning that they were too far to the north, given to him on the 22nd by one of the seamen of the *Association*.

> . . . but a lad on board ye ——— said the light they made was Scilly light, tho' all the ships crew swore at and gave him ill language for it; howbeit he continu'd in his assertion, and that wt they made to be a saile and a ship's lanthorn prov'd to be a rock and ye Light afore-mentioned, wch rock the lad call'd ye Great Smith, of ye truth of wch at day-break they was all convinced.[24]

It seems likely that this story has been embroidered somewhat. A seaman, a native of the Scilly Isles, on the *Association*, is supposed to have warned Shovell that they were too far to the north and, unless their course was changed, they would run on to the Western Rocks. For his insubordination the seaman was, on Shovell's instructions, hanged from the yardarm. Prior to his death, the seaman was supposed to have been given leave to read aloud Psalm 109. Part of this Psalm is as follows:

5. Set thou an ungodly man to be ruler over him: and let Satan stand at his right hand.
6. When the sentence is given upon him, let him be condemned: and let his prayer be turned into sin.
7. Let his days be few: and let another take his office.
8. Let his children be fatherless: and his wife a widow.
9. Let his children be vagabonds, and beg their bread: let them seek it also out of desolate places.
10. Let the extortioner consume all that he hath: and let the stranger spoil his labour.
11. Let there be no man to pity him: nor to have compassion upon his fatherless children.
12. Let his posterity be destroyed: and in the next generation let his name be clean put out.

The seaman had used the Psalm to put a curse on Shovell and his family.
A nineteenth century poem alludes to this legend:

> Dark on the Gilstone's rock shore
> The mist came lowering down,
> And night with all her deepening gloom
> Put on her sable crown.

# THE BUILD UP TO DISASTER 1707

From sea a wailing sound is heard,
And the seamen's shrilly cry,
And booming surge and shrieking birds
Proclaim strange danger nigh.

Wrong you steer, Sir Cloudesley, sure;
The rocks of Scilly shun;
Northern move, or no sailor here
Will see to-morrow's sun.

Hold, wretch! Dare tell your Admiral
What dangers to evade?
I'll hang you up on yon yard-arm
Before your prayers are said.

Oh, Admiral, before I die
Let someone read aloud
That one hundred and ninth dread Psalm
To all this sailor crowd.

Let it be done, cursed marineer;
As if I know not how
To steer my Association clear
Of every danger now.

The Psalm was read, the wretch was hung;
Drear darkness stalked around;
Whilst all aloft the dead man swung,
Three ships had struck the ground.

How sad and awful was the sight,
How black and dark the shore.
Two thousand souls went down that night,
And ne'er saw daylight more.

One man alone of that brave crew
Was saved to tell the tale.
How swift and sure God's vengeance came;
He can alone prevail.
(Robert Maybee)

A romantic story no doubt. However, it does not fit the facts. Shovell, although very much a leader, was kind and merciful to his men. Unlike the more reserved Rooke, Shovell frequently spoke with his men, and was

341

popular with them. Finally, if the story was true it would never have been told as all the officers and crew of the *Association*, without exception, were drowned that night. The story is a romantic myth. So too for the same reason is the story that the crew was drunk in celebrating a safe home-coming.[25]

Before leaving the navigational failures of Shovell's fleet, it is worth noting that one man, the master of the *Panther*, was nearly correct in his estimated position. Was this the reason that the *Panther* remained on the southern flank of the fleet, and was one of the few ships that did not have to alter course to avoid the rocks? It is an intriguing thought.[26]

Without question, Shovell took the final decision to sail on into the darkness on the night of October 22nd 1707. In truth, he did no more than many another commander of that era, but his luck was out. On balance the evidence is against the rest of the fleet advising him of their position that day. No doubt he listened to the two captains, lieutenants and master of his own ship, the *Association*, before making his mind up. It was a disaster that was bound to happen at some time.

In summary it is fair to say that while the Rennell Current and faulty compasses might have contributed to the disaster, much more must be attributed to the lack of accurate knowledge of geographical positions, and the low standard of accuracy of navigational practice.[27]

NOTES

1. Anderson, Lists of Men of War; Larn, pp.14–15; Boyer, Vol.VI, pp.241–245; Log book of the *Isabella yacht* Sept. 30th 1707 in the P.R.O.
2. May, pp.324–325.
3. May, p.324.
4. May, pp.324–325.
5. Holland, Pieces of Land, p.74.
6. Marcus, p.542; Observator Nov. 29th–Dec. 3rd 1707.
7. Marcus, p.542; Anderson, Narbrough's journals; letters of Horace Walpole, Toynbee (1902), IV, p.340.
8. May, pp.325–331.
9. May, pp.326–332.
10. May, pp.328–329.
11. May, pp.331–332; Marcus, p.547; Captain's journal *Lenox*; Larn, p.32; ADM 106.617 Navy Board letters; May, Naval Compasses in 1707, NMM JIN, Vol.VI, No.4, 1953, pp.405–406.
12. May, p.332.
13. May, p.332.
14. May, p.331; Marcus, p.540; Laughton, Physical Geography 1870, p.214; James Rennell, Observations on a Current etc (1815) p.53; Larn, pp.13 & 32.
15. Marcus, pp.544–545; Master's journals *Monmouth, Torbay, Cruizer, Panther*.
16. Burchett, p.733; Marcus, p.541; Tangier Papers of Samuel Pepys, p.248; Anderson, Narbrough journals, pp.286–287.
17. Holland, Pieces of Land, p.73; Mathews G.F., The Isles of Scilly: A Constitutional, Economic and Social Survey of the Development of an Island

People from early times to 1900, 1960; Graeme Spence, A Geographical Description of the Scilly Isles 1793; Journal of Lieutenant Wiscard of the *St George*; Journal of Captain Baker of the *Monmouth*; Journal of Captain Griffiths of the *Swiftsure*.

18. Cooke, Shipwreck of Sir Cloudesley Shovell etc; Extracts from a Complete History of Europe 1707, London 1708, pp.343, 344.
19. Owen, p.192; Board Minutes especially Oct 1707; Captain's journal *Tartar*.
20. Cooke, Shipwreck of Sir Cloudesley Shovell etc.
21. Herbert MSS.
22. Cooke, Shipwreck of Sir Cloudesley Shovell etc; Pickwell, Improbable legends etc; Larn, p.25; Marcus, p.544; Masters' journals *Cruizer, Monmouth, Panther, Swiftsure*.
23. RMT MAT 25 Section 12.
24. Herbert MSS.
25. Cooke, Shipwreck of Sir Cloudesley Shovell etc; Bowley R.L., The Fortunate Islands, pp.75–76.
26. May, pp.330–331.
27. May, p.332.

# CHAPTER XXVI
# *The Disaster of*
# *October 22nd 1707*

Soon after 6.00 p.m. on October 22nd 1707 Shovell gave the signal to wear and the fleet sailed in a north-easterly direction into the darkness. With a favourable south-westerly gale behind them, they believed that the English Channel was open ahead of them and that they would soon be home. In fact, many of the fleet were steering directly onto the Western Rocks, to the south-west of the Scilly Isles.

From just before 7.00 p.m. until 8.00 p.m. most of the ships found themselves amongst some of the most treacherous rocks of the entire English coastline. Cannons were fired as a signal of danger, and it was every man for himself in the desperate struggle for life. Some ships steered to the north and others to the west and south. In the murky darkness, the light of St Agnes was not seen until too late, and it must have been then that the crews realised where they were.

Of Shovell's fleet of twenty-one vessels, six struck the rocks and four sank. The four ships that were lost were the *Association, Eagle, Romney* and *Firebrand*. The *Phoenix* had to be beached and the luckiest of all, the *St George*, escaped with minimal damage.

Shovell's *Association* was, in all probability, a little ahead of the other

343

ships and one of the first into danger. Soon after 7.00 p.m. Lieutenant Joseph Short of the *Griffin fireship* recorded in his journal that Sir Cloudesley was dangerously near the rocks. According to the *London Gazette*, which had spoken to Captain Francis Percy, a survivor from the *Firebrand*, at Plymouth on October 28th, the *Association* hit the rocks and sank at approximately 7.45 p.m.

> Captain Francis Percy reports, that on the 22nd instant sailing with Sir Cloudesley Shovell, and Her Majesty's fleet, about three quarters past 7 at night, he heard the Admiral fire a gun, and immediately lost sight of his lights. He soon after perceived that the Admiral was lost, being then close aboard the Rocks call'd the Bishop and Clarks . . .[1]

Despite the fact that Percy's ship struck the same rocks, it was not the Bishop and Clerks as he reported, but the Gilstone Rock which sank both the *Firebrand* and the *Association*. In some quarters, it would for obvious reasons be known as the Shovell Rock. It was probably Percy's report that led to one contemporary view, which was repeated until at least the nineteenth century, that the *Association* had struck the Bishop and Clerks Rocks. The earliest mention of the Gilstone is in Herbert's 1709 account of the disaster and in Edmund Gosselo's chart of 1707–10. Clearly the local inhabitants knew the correct wreck site at the time.

In the same edition of the *London Gazette* (4380) was a report from on board Sir George Byng's flagship, the *Royal Anne*, dated three days after the disaster.

> We made sail under our courses. Soon after several ships made Signal of Danger, as did Sir Cloudesley himself. The Royal Anne that was not then half a mile to windward of him, saw several Breaches, and soon after the Rocks above water: Upon one of which she saw the Association strike, and in less than two minutes disappear. The Royal Anne was saved by great presence of mind both in Officers and Men, who in a Minutes time set her top sails, one of the rocks not being a Ship's length to leeward of her, and the other on which Sir Cloudesley was lost, as near, and in a Breach of the Sea.

Byng's own brief account is given by the Under Secretary of State, Joseph Addison, in a letter to Lord Manchester, dated October 28th 1707.

> Admiral Byng passed by him within two cables length of him, and heard one of his guns go off as a signal of distress, but the sea ran so very high that it was impossible to send him any succour. Sir George Byng adds that, looking after him about a minute after the firing of the gun, he saw no lights appear and therefore fears he sunk.[2]

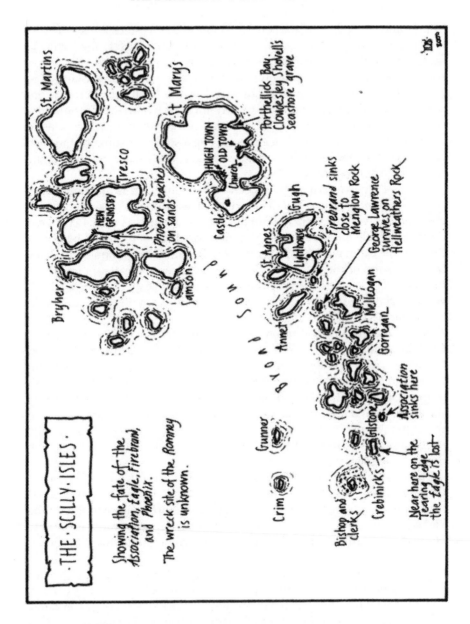

Byng had had a very lucky escape. Within a matter of minutes, the fleet had lost their commander-in-chief and very nearly his second in command.

We have seen already that the *Firebrand* struck the Gilstone and came off with a huge wave. Her hull had been badly damaged and she was taking in water rapidly. Her Captain, Francis Percy, set the men to work the pumps and steered along the southern edge of the Western Rocks. He was heading for the light on St Agnes, but before reaching safety the *Firebrand* sank in ten fathoms of water, not far from the Menglow Rock. Percy and some of his men saved themselves in a boat by rowing to the island of St Agnes. Just how many men were saved in the boat with Percy is not certain. The most likely figure is twenty-three or twenty-four judging by the records of the captain and lieutenant of the *Salisbury*, which was to carry them to Plymouth. Other reports suggested that some of the men had saved themselves on pieces of wreckage, and that Percy had come ashore on a hencoop!

Francis Percy, described by Queen Anne as her handsome lieutenant, was a romantic figure but a survivor if ever there was one. In an engagement with the French, thinking that the action was over, Percy bent down to buckle his shoe, when a cannon was fired at him. The ball went through the cabin wall, but he received only a small laceration on his back from the wind of the projectile. Percy kept the cannon ball as a weight to his kitchen jack, a fitting memorial to his narrow escape! Like Shovell, he was associated with Rochester, Kent, and there is a monument to him in St Margaret's Church there.[3]

Both the *Eagle*, under Captain Robert Hancock, and the *Romney*, under Captain William Coney, were lost that night. According to Edmund Gosselo's 1707–10 chart of the Scilly Isles, the *Eagle* sank on the Crim Rocks and the *Romney* on the Crebinicks. The Crim Rocks lie to the north of the Bishop and Clerks and the Crebinicks to the south. Recent underwater research suggests that Gosselo may be inaccurate with respect to these two ships. A wreck found on the Tearing Ledge close to the Crebinicks is now thought likely to be the *Eagle* and not the *Romney*. The final resting place of the *Romney* is unknown.[4]

There were to be no survivors from the *Eagle*, but George Lawrence, Quarter Master, was the sole survivor from the *Romney*. Lawrence saved himself from drowning by clinging to an oar, before being swept onto the Hellweathers Rock off Annet Island, where he was found next day. Herbert's manuscript gives an account of Lawrence's treatment ashore.

> . . . & but one soul sav'd from off the rock, call'd – who was Quarter Mr of ye Rumney, a north country-man near Hull, a butcher by trade, a lusty fat man but much batter'd with ye rocks. (Most of ye Captains, Lieutenants, Doctors & c of ye Squadron came on shoar and ask'd him many questions in relation to ye wreck, but not one man took pity on him, either to dress or order to be dress'd his bruises & c, wherefore had perish'd had not Mr Ekins, a Gentm of ye Island, charitably taken him in; and a doctor of a merchant ship then in ye road under convoy of Southampton & c, search'd his wounds and applied proper remedies).[5]

Poor Lawrence was thoroughly questioned about the event of the previous night, but he was treated callously in a typically early eighteenth century manner, with his personal comfort and injuries ignored. Lawrence was in fact able to give a little further information, which is quoted by John Ben in his letter to Jonathan Trelawney, Bishop of Winchester, of November 16th 1707.

> They can say nothing in particular concerning Sir Cloudesley's loss, only the man saved out of the Rumney tells that Sir Cloudesley was to windward of all the ships and fired three guns when she struck, and immediately went down, as the Rumney a little after did. Upon hearing the guns, the rest of the fleet, that were directly bearing on the same rocks changed their course and stood to the Southward or else in all probability they had run the same fate, as never enough to be admired . . .[6]

Perhaps the most fortunate ship of all Shovell's fleet was the *St George*, commanded by his young friend, Lord James Dursley, afterwards the third Earl of Berkeley. The *St George* was dashed onto the Gilstone with the *Association* and the same wave which Dursley saw beat out all of Shovell's lights, set his own ship afloat. It was a miraculous escape.[7]

The last ship of Shovell's original fleet to fall foul of the rocks of Scilly was the *Phoenix*. We have seen earlier how, at 11.00 a.m. on October 22nd, Shovell had detached the *Lenox*, *La Valeur* and the *Phoenix* for convoy duty at Falmouth. Sir William Jumper, in command of this small contingent, ordered a course to the north-east until early in the evening, when thinking himself at risk of hitting the coast of Cornwall, changed course to a south-easterly direction. Having been unable to make an observation that day, he was uncertain how far north he was and the course he followed was a logical one. Unfortunately for Jumper and his ships, he was not as far to the east as he had anticipated, and at 3.00 a.m. on the morning of October 23rd he found himself among the rocks to the south-west of Samson Island. This occurred approximately seven hours after the *Association* had struck the Gilstone. Jumper in the *Lenox*, and the *La Valeur* escaped unscathed into Broad Sound that runs between Samson, Tresco and St Martin's Island to the north and Annet, St Agnes and St Mary's to the south. There they anchored for the remaining hours of darkness before proceeding on their way to Falmouth, seemingly unaware of the fate of the *Phoenix*.[8]

Throughout the night of October 22nd/23rd Captain Michael Sanson of the *Phoenix* had intermittent contact with the *Lenox*. At about 4.00 a.m. the *Phoenix* started to draw ahead and shortly afterwards the light of Scilly became visible, about half a mile away to the south-west. At first this light was taken to be that of Shovell's ship, the *Association*. Lieutenant Samuel Percival of the *Phoenix* recorded in his journal.

At 4 in the morning being called up we saw the light of Scilly which they took to be the Flagues light saying they were falen in with the fleet again; it bore SE ½ a mile off, but I being very uneasie ordered all hands to keep the Deck and immediately called up the Captn, who being upon deck the Master whose opinion this was ran forward and called out there's a ship ahead we will go under his stern and know who they are; but we soon found the mistake it being a rock.

A little later in the journal he continued:

... in wareing a second time struck fast on a sunken rock and continued there some minutes but a great sea that almost filled us hove us of into 9 fathm water where we came to an anchor and fireing guns a Pilot came aboard, but we being sore shattered, and the ship ready to founder, the water in the hold gaining much upon us, 'twas concluded to run her ashore between Samson and Bryer Islands.

Captain Sanson then laid the *Phoenix* ashore on sand and sent Lieutenant Percival to see the Governor. "I immediately went ashore by my Captns order to the Governour and got great boates to lighten our Ship we struck yards and topmasts unbent our sails and got them and severall other baggage ashore and got 3 pumps to work . . ."

It was not until October 25th that Sanson was able to get the *Phoenix* off, and move her to the sands at New Grimsby, Tresco Island. Not a single member of the crew of the *Phoenix* lost his life in this incident.[9]

A number of the surviving journals of the officers of Shovell's fleet give graphic accounts of the events of the night of October 22nd/23rd. Before recording some of them, the dating must be explained. In the early eighteenth century navy, the date changed at the preceding noon, and not at midnight. i.e. the day at sea was measured from noon to noon. This meant that at sea Shovell had sounded between 4.00 p.m. and 6.00 p.m. on October 23rd, and the *Association* sank at about 7.45 p.m. the same night. On land the date was October 22nd, which was the correct one. Matters became even more confusing in that some of the officers were not consistent in recording the date.[10]

Lieutenant Arthur Field of Sir John Norris' ship, the *Torbay*, wrote in his journal:

1707 October 23rd. Hard gales with hazey weathr and rain . . . att 6 the Gener.ll made the Sigll to wear: wch we repeated at 7 the Monmouth made the Sigll of Danger: at ½ past 7 on our weather bow we unexpectedly see ye breaks on the Bishop & Clarks we Immediately wore and made the Sigll of Danger, wch was very Emminent, in wch we had infallible Demonstrations of Almighty

348

providence, first our wearing sooner than usuall with main and fore course 2dly when we judg'd our selves inevitably on ye rocks yett preserved from ye mighty danger: at 9 ye light of Scilly bore E b S ½ S, about 3 miles: we then steer'd between ye wt and ye N.W. till 7 this morning: ye wind shifting to ye WNW, we wore, sett small saile, and steer'd S b W. at 9 sound'd and had 60 fathom water, brown sand, then told [counted] 11 Saile who followed us: God preserve the rest.

Considering how close Lord James Dursley's ship, the *St George*, had come to destruction, his 5th Lieutenant Benjamin Wiscard was remarkably circumspect in his journal. "October 23rd . . . at ½ pst 7 we heard severall Gunns fired & at 8 wee discovered ye breakers off from ye Island of Scilly we wore ship and stood to ye Wnd . . ."

Joseph Lyne Master of the *Somerset* recorded in his journal:

Wednesday October 22nd 1707 . . . thick weather with small rain at 8 we saw the Westernmost of ye Islands of Scily bearing N. at ½ an hour after 8 we lost sight of our Admiral's light at once & saw Silly Light bearing NNE 3 miles. Then ye Royal Anne who was ½ a Mile to leeward of us Extinguisht her lights & did not light them again in an hour we heard & saw a great many Guns fired in severall places which we supposed to be from ships in danger.

From this account the *Association* appears to have been lost rather later than other reports suggest. Time was measured to the nearest half hour and was notoriously inaccurate. No doubt Sir George Byng had his lights extinguished in the *Royal Anne*, to avoid leading others into danger.

One of the first ships to see the Western Rocks was Captain John Baker's *Monmouth*. In his journal Baker wrote: "Oct. 22nd . . . Endeavouring to get ye Flaggs light ahead of us, we discovered a Rock to leeward of us we Imediately Wore Shipp and just got clear of it . . ." Baker's 2nd Lieutenant, John Furzer, recorded: "Oct. 23rd . . . at 7 last night saw ye Rocks of Scilly bearing ENE about a Stones throw. Wee fired sevll Guns and showed lights and gave the fleet Notice of being in Danger & afterwards bore away."

The Captain of the *Swiftsure*, Richard Griffiths, saw the end of the *Association*.

Oct. 23rd . . . at ½ past 7 fell in with the Islands of Scilly; the Generall fired one Gun, as we plainly saw, and immediately lost sight of him: then Rear Admll Norrifs fir'd four Guns hoisted severall lights and wore, and put all his lights out, at ye same time made ye Light on St Mary's under our lee bow . . .

A number of the ship's officers, like Griffiths, did not appear to know that Scilly light was on St Agnes Island and not St Mary's.

The *Griffin* fireship was close to the *Association* and was probably one of the last ships to see the *Romney* afloat. Lieutenant Joseph Short of the *Griffin* wrote in his journal:

> Oct. 23rd ... but forst [forced] to edge away from ye Royl Ann & afterwards came up wth a ship we supposd to be the Romney went to leeward of him See 3 or 4 flashes under our lee at 7 saw the light house of Silly & the Rocks just undr our lee and Breakers Close by us the Association had at this Time come Neer us upon our weathr Beam we wore & sett the Topsl we crowded off Leavg Sr Cloudsly Dangerously neer the Rocks that while we Got our tacks on bord & the Topsl sett had lost sight of him.

One of the fullest accounts is in the journal of Captain Finch Reddall of the *Isabella yacht*.

> October 23. This 24 houres hard gails of wind untill 10 at night (of 22nd) then weather somewhat Moderate. at 4 in ye Afternoon (of the 22nd) ye Admiral brought to & Sounded we likewise Sounded & had between 50 & 55 Fathom water a Course Sand intermint wth Shells he lay by till six Foll (following) at which time we heard Several guns fired to ye Soward of us supposing they had Discovered danger at 8 at night saw ye Light of Silly bearing SE by S Dist to Judgt about 4m, we took it to be one of our Admiral's lights we steered after it till we Perceived it to be a fixed light it being very thick dark Rainey weather. we Perceived ye Rocks on both sides of us we being very near to them we immediately wore our yacht & layed our head to ye Westward Crowding all ye Sail we Could to weither ye Rocks under our lea. We filled full & full & by God's Mercy we got Clear of them all for which Deliverance God's holy Name be Blest & Praised which caused a great Separation in ye fleet for happy was he that Could Shift for himself some Steering wth their heads to ye Soward & others to ye Nthward & those that lay wth their heads to ye Soward ware most of the lost.

When Sir William Jumper arrived at Falmouth, he was given a first-hand account by the master's mate of the *Orford*, of two ships actually lying on the rocks on the night of October 22nd. Jumper reported this conversation to the Admiralty.

> I am likewise to acquaint you that a small French prize laden with fish taken some days since by the Orford is arrived here. The Masters

Mate of the Orford who commands the said prize told me this at that ye 22nd instant in the evening lying about 8 o'clock he heard many guns fired as from a ship in distress, and about 9 his company cried out a Rock on which he set his foresail and weather it but a very little, which he says was the body of a great ship wreck and many crying out for God's sake save them which he could nott, but standing on them soon cried out Another Rock which bit he says was a wreck of a ship to butt standing a little further to ye South East about 10'o'clock they see the Bishop and Clerk two great rocks but weathered all almost attaching the bigger rocks . . .[11]

The vessels of Shovell's fleet were not the only ones in the vicinity of the Scilly Isles at this time. The day before the disaster, October 21st, the Welsh fleet from Milford Haven had anchored off St Mary's Island. They consisted of the *Southampton*, *Arundell*, *Lizard* and some sixty coasters bound eastwards. In addition to the Welsh fleet, the *Salisbury*, *Antelope* and the *Charles galley* had come into the Roads of St Mary's during the afternoon of October 22nd, from cruising to the west.[12]

During the hours of darkness, on October 22nd/23rd, the ships in St Mary's Roads heard numerous guns being fired to the south-west. Rightly they conjectured that there were ships in distress, but they were powerless to render assistance in the face of a gale also from the south-west. Next morning, their suspicions were confirmed by the sight of an enormous amount of wreckage and bodies floating in the sea. The Master of the *Salisbury* recorded his experiences in his journal.

> . . . att 6 a clock we moored our ship and struck our yards and Topmasts and att ye same time I standing in ye Starboard Gangway looking towards the SW I see severall flashes of guns and told them to the no of 30 and about halfe an hour after I see one more and heard the Report and this morning before day being little wind Drove by us vast quantity of Ship Rack as beames caridges Drumheads of capstones peices of masts and yards and a crofs peice of the bitts and as soon as Day light came on we sent our boats to see if they could save any of the men which might be wash'd upon the rocks . . .

John Ben in his letter to Sir Jonathan Trelawney, Bishop of Winchester, recorded:

> There is a great quantity of timber all round the islands and abundance of sails and rigging just about the place where the ships sunk, and a mast, one end a little above water which makes them conclude that an entire ship to be foundered there because all the force they can procure is not able to move the mast.

351

Over 1,600 men, at the very least, were lost from the *Association, Eagle, Romney* and *Firebrand*. Their bodies floated around the Western Rocks and were washed on shore. St Agnes had to deal with the largest number, and the likely sites of mass graves near to the old life boat station can be seen to this day.[13]

The boats of the *Southampton, Arundell, Lizard, Salisbury, Antelope* and *Charles galley* went out, early in the morning of October 23rd, to salvage what they could.

> ... whose boats were early out ye next morning in quest of ye flotsham goods, very much whereof were by them taken up; they matter'd not the wines brandys & c. at ye first, but let 'em swim by their boats, and pursued wt they had hopes were richer, so yt most of ye casks stav'd, and ye liquors were lost in ye ocean.[14]

Assistance was rendered to the beached *Phoenix*, which had driven in through a narrow rocky sound. Captain Joseph Soanes, of the *Southampton*, went on board her and was surprised that all her crew were "wonderfully preserved". Soanes confirmed that the *Association* was sunk, by finding a paper in the sea directed to Ral. Fatherinton, who he knew was on board her. Although no Fatherinton appears on the *Association* crew list, Ralph Farrington was a midshipman in her and it is possible that it was his paper that was found. Later the collectors at Scilly gave Captain Soanes "bundles of orders writ to Sr Cloudsley Shovell wth four journells of Capt Loads, all wett". The boats of the *Charles galley* "took up Sr Jno Nolbrough's [Narbrough] Journall by yt we believed it be ye Afsociation which Sr Clowdsly Shovell was on board". There is no record of the Loades and Narbrough journals having survived to the present day. Loades', in particular, might have thrown some light on the fatal decision to sail on, at 6 p.m. on October 22nd.[15]

Later, further papers from the *Association* were found at Topsham in Devon. On October 29th 1707 Joseph Quash wrote to Sir Robert Cotton and Sir Thomas Frankland, Postmaster General in London, describing how Shovell's papers were found and brought into Topsham. The Minister there put them into the custody of the local custom's house official, a Mr Morley. The documents were said to include Shovell's commission and "other papers of concern". Unfortunately, Morley did not appreciate the importance of the papers placed in his care, for he allowed them to be thrown over the quay at Topsham! Following their second immersion, three books were salvaged by one Elias Griggs and sent to London. Fortunately, Shovell's commission was wrongly stated to be amongst the papers thrown into the river, as it was actually in the hands of the Governor of Scilly.

The whereabouts of the three surviving books are not known, but it is unlikely that they would throw any light on the disaster. The first was an account book from June 8th 1706 to October 1st 1707. The second the account of "Biscet Baggs", 1705. The third consisted of forty-six leaves with no description of what was written on them. It is difficult to explain how the documents had reached Topsham in the first place. Although wreckage was thrown ashore at Land's End and up the Bristol Channel, it seems inconceivable that documents could float this far and still be in a legible condition. Perhaps they were dumped in Devonshire, but the time scale is short, as Quash wrote his first letter exactly one week after the disaster.[16]

NOTES

1. London Gazette No. 4380 Oct. 30th – Nov. 3rd 1707.
2. Cooke, Shipwreck of Sir Cloudesley Shovell etc.; Pattison, S.R., Sir Cloudesley Shovell, Journal of Royal Institute of Cornwall, Vol.I., 1864/5.
3. RMT MAT 25, 26; Captain's, Lieutenant's, Master's journals of the *Salisbury*; Captain's journal *Arundell*; Larn, p.19; Biographia Britannia.
4. Gosselo chart 1707–1710, P.R.O.; Larn, pp.20–21, 39–40.
5. Herbert MSS; Cooke, Shipwreck of Sir Cloudesley Shovell etc.
6. Cooke, Shipwreck of Sir Cloudesley Shovell etc; Quiller Couch T., J.R.I.C. Vol. II, p.19, Ben to Bishop of Winchester; Larn, p.21; Post Boy Oct. 30th 1707.
7. Boyer, History of the Reign of Queen Anne 1708.
8. Marcus, Sir Clowdisley Shovel's last voyage, pp.546–547; Larn, pp.19–20; Captain's journal *Lenox, La Valeur*.
9. RMT MAT26; Larn, p.20; Captain Sanson's journal, P.R.O. ADM 51/4290; Lieut Percival's journal.
10. May, Last Voyage of Sir Clowdisley Shovel, p.324.
11. RMT MAT 26; Cooke, Shipwreck of Sir Cloudesley Shovell etc;
    Captains' journals *Monmouth, Swiftsure, Isabella*; Lieutenants' journals *Torbay, St. George, Monmouth, Griffin*; Master's journal Daily Courant Oct. 30th 1707.
12. RMT MAT 26; Captain's journal *Arundell*; Master's journal *Salisbury*.
13. RMT MAT 26; Master's journal of *Salisbury*; Cooke, Shipwreck of Sir Cloudesley Shovell etc; T. Quiller Couch, Sir Cloudesley Shovell, Transaction of the Penzance National History and Antiquarian Society, John Ben to the Bishop of Winchester November 16th 1707; Larn, p.20.
14. Cooke, The Shipwreck of Sir Cloudesley Shovell etc.
15. RMT MAT26; Journal of Capt. Soanes of the *Southampton*; Journal of the Master of the *Salisbury*; Journal of the Lieutenant of the *Antelope*.
16. RMT MAT26; C.S.P., Anne 1707, Bundle 13. No 44, 48, 48I, 49. Letters, Joseph Quash to Sir Robert Cotton & Sir Thomas Frankland Oct. 29th & Nov. 8th 1707.

# CHAPTER XXVII

# The Finding of
# Cloudesley Shovell's Body
# 1707

A number of legends have come down through nearly three centuries since Cloudesley Shovell's body was found in Porthellick Cove, St Mary's. The earliest reports of the discovery of the body appeared in the local press of the day.

### The London Gazette

Plimouth [sic] October 28. Her Majesty's Ship the Salisbury, commanded by Capt. Hosier is come into our Sound, and hath a-board the Body of Sir Cloudesley Shovell, which was taken up under the Rocks of St Mary's.[1]

### The Daily Courant

Plymouth October 28th. Of the Afsociation not a man was saved: Sir Cloudsly Shovel was taken up, stripp'd, and Bury'd in the Sand the 23rd: On inquiry made by the Boats of the Salisbury and Antelope it was discover'd, either on Occasion of a Dispute between those who stripp'd Sir Cloudsly (as some say), or on a Person asking the Man who bury'd him whether he had not taken up a large Corps (as say others), where he was laid: Being taken out of the ground again, and the Earth wash'd off, he appear'd as fresh as if alive, though he had lain Interr'd from the 23d to the 26th, on which Day he was brought on Board the Salisbury and embowell'd; and was to Day brought in hither.[2]

### The Post Boy

London November 4th. The Country-Fellows belonging to the Islands of Scilly, finding Sir Cloudesley Shovel's Corps, took a fine Emerald Ring from off his Finger, and buried him Seven Foot deep in the Sand; but quarrelling about the said Ring, and Mr Paxton, Purser of the Arundel, having some Information of the Matter, order'd him to be dug up, and put on board the Arundel; where Capt. Windall order'd it to be embalm'd, and afterwards put on board the Salisbury, which was then sailing for Plymouth.[3]

None of the log books of the ships at St Mary's gives an account of the discovery of Shovell's body at Porthellick Cove. This is particularly surprising in the case of the *Salisbury*, which transported the corpse to Plymouth.[4]

The Master of the *Salisbury* simply recorded, on Sunday October 26th: "... att 8 made $y^e$ signall to Unmoor and att 10 we unmoored at $y^e$ same time the corps of $S^r$ Cloudsly Shovell came on board ..."[5]

Other early accounts give further information. The Under Secretary of State, Joseph Addison, wrote to a Mr Cole, on October 31st 1707.

> Yesterday we had news that the body of Sir Cloudesley Shovel was found on the Coast of Cornwall. The fishermen, who were searching among the rocks, took a tin box out of the pocket of one of the carcasses that was floating and found in it the commission of an Admiral; upon which, examining the body more closely, they found it was poor Sir Cloudesley.[6]

Gilbert Crockatt's book, *Consolatory Letter to Lady Shovell*, published in 1708, has no details of his death. In *Secret Memoirs of the Life of the Honourable Sir Cloudesley Shovell*, also published in 1708, it is merely recorded that, "the sea cast his body upon the sands of the same island where he suffer'd shipwreck, which was found by his friends and convey'd aboard the Arundel Man of War".

Without doubt, the fullest of the early accounts of Shovell's death is that of Mr Edmund Herbert, who was in charge of the expedition, in 1709, to recover property lost in the wrecks of Shovell's ships.

> Sir C. Shovel cast away 8 br 23, being Wednesday, between 6 and 7 at night, (others say between 4 and 5, bet: night & day,) off Guilstone (south) by west, was found on shoar (at Porthellick Cove) in St Marie's Island, stript of his shirt, wc by confession was known, by 2 women, wch shirt had his name at $y^e$ gusset at his waist; (where by order of Mr Harry Pennick was buried 4 yards off ye sands; which place I myself view'd, & as was by his grave, came by sd woman yt first saw him after he was stript;) His ring was also lost from off his hand, wch however left ye impression on his finger, as also of a second. The Lady Shovel offered a considerable reward to any one [who] should recover it for her, and in order thereto wrote Capt. Benedick, Dep. Governor & Commander in Ch. of Islands of Scilly, (giving him a particular description thereof,) who used his utmost diligence both by fair and foul means, though could not hear of it. Sr

Cloud. had on him a pr of thread stockings and a thread waistcoat. (Others say a flannel waistcoat and a pair of drawers.) Mr Child (Mr Paxton) Purser of ye Arundel caused him to be taken up and knew him to be Sr Cloudesley by a certain black mold under his left ear, as also by the first joynt of one of his forefingers being broken inwards formerly by playing at Tables; the sd joynt of his finger was also small and taper, as well as standing somewhat inwards; (he had likewise a shot in his right arm, another in his left thigh.) Moreover he was well satisfied 'twas him, for he was as fresh when his face was washt as if only asleep; his nose likewise bled as tho' alive, wch Mr Child (Paxton) said was bec. of himself, for Sr C. had preferred him to Purser of Arundel and was his particular friend. They carried him to Mrs Bant's in ye island, & had on shoar sevrll Doctors of ye ships of ye fleet, but none could embalm or embowell him; (neither did any of ye fleet take much notice of him, but as Mr Paxton was carrying him on board ye Arundell, Capt __ (Hosier) Commander of ye Salisbury ordered him on board his ship;) wherefore they put him on board ye Salisbury on a bare table, (the table was Mrs Bants,) and a sheet only to cover him; the table they kept but the sheet was sent on shoar; and on board the Salisb. they carried him to Plimo where he was embalmed, and afterwards conveyed to London by land carriage. (Sir Cloudesley was the first man came on shoar, saving one, of the almost 1800 lost in the wreck. His Commission was brought on shoar by one __, and his chest wch was by him taken up floating.) Many that saw him sd his head was the largest that ever they had seen, and not all swell'd with the waters, neither had he any bruise or fear about him, save only a small scratch above one of his eyes like that of a pin. Was a very lusty, comely man, and very fat.

Capt. Loads, Commander of ye Association, (Sir Cloudesley's Captain as Admiral, but Capt. Whitacre was Captain of ye ship) wch Sr C. was on board of wn cast away, was also taken up on St Marie's island, (in ye same cove near Sir C.) and buried in Old-town Ch. whose burial 'twas reported cost £90, but Mr Withe who was manager of it says ½ that sum.

(This Mr Withe rais'd a report by Mr Pennick buried Sr C. before cold, but had sd gent. liv'd 'twould have cost him dear, but himself had misfortn to be cast away, A.D. 170-.) Mr James Narborough, (others say Sr John Narborough) and the Ld Bishop Trewlawney's son, was likewise buried in sd Church very honourably. Sir C. had a naked small greyhound cast on shoar in ye same cove with, and not far distant, (as about a bowshot,) from him, with a collar of his name &c. round its neck. (There came on shoar in or very near ye same cove the stern of Sir C.'s barge, wch gives ground to believe he had time to get in it with some of his crew, tho' most people are not of that mind;

Captain Loads, Sr John and Mr James Narborough, also the Bishop
Trelawney's son, being all cast on shoar on St Marie's island, give
further matter of credit;)[7]

Although Edmund Herbert's notes were written within two years of the
disaster, they did not appear in the public domain until they were
presented by his descendant, James Cooke, to a meeting of the Society of
Antiquaries in 1883, and subsequently published. Mid eighteenth century
accounts of the finding of Shovell's body, such as John Campbell's *Lives of
the Admirals*, were based on the 1707 account in the *Mercure Historique et
Politique*, and this in turn on the *Post Boy* edition for November 1st–4th
1707, already quoted in full.[8]

None of the early accounts gave any inkling that Shovell had died by
any means other than drowning. John Charnock, late in the eighteenth
century, in his *Biographia Navalis*, suggested for the first time the
possibility that Shovell had reached the shore alive and had then been
murdered. This was repeated by George Cunningham in his nineteenth
century *Lives of Eminent and Illustrious Englishmen*.[9]

In the Romney family, who are the descendants of Shovell's eldest
daughter, Elizabeth, there is a tradition that he was alive when he came
ashore in Porthellick Cove, but was then murdered. Around 1792 Robert,
the second Lord Romney, Shovell's grandson, wrote a letter to a Captain
Locker giving him details of the career of his illustrious grandfather. It is
possible that Locker had a connection with John Charnock, as the letter
appears almost verbatim in his *Biographia Navalis*. Perhaps he was
gathering information for him. Doubt has been expressed recently by J. E.
Pickwell concerning the authenticity of the letter, as it is not among the
existing Romney Papers.[10] However, according to Robert Marsham
Townshend, a draft copy was in the possession of Charles 6th Baron and
4th Earl of Romney in 1860. That same year Marsham Townshend also
saw a further copy of the draft letter, owned by Captain Locker's
descendant, Frederick Locker. The draft letter is given in full in Appendix
4, but the relevant section states that:

There is one circumstance relating to Sᵣ Cloudesly Shovell's death
that is known to very few persons, namely; he was not drowned,
having got to shore, where, by the confession of an ancient woman,
he was put to death. This, many years after, when on her death bed,
she revealed to the minister of the parish, declaring she could not die
in peace 'till she had made this confession, as she was led to commit
this horrid deed for the sake of plunder. She acknowledged having,
among other things, an emerald ring in her possession, which she had
been afraid to sell lest it should lead to a discovery. This ring, which
she delivered to the minister, was by him given to James Earl of

> Berkeley at his particular request, Sʳ Cloudesly Shovell and himself
> having lived on the strictest footing of friendship.[11]

Although there is no corroborative evidence for this story, its author, Robert, second Lord Romney, ought to be taken seriously as he was Shovell's grandson. He was an adult at the time of the deaths of both his grandmother, Elizabeth Shovell, in 1732 and his mother, Elizabeth, Countess of Hyndford, in 1750. If the tradition was known in their lifetimes, presumably it was from them that Robert first heard it.[12]

Based principally on the November 4th 1707 *Post Boy* story, the Herbert manuscript, and the Romney letter to Captain Locker, it is possible to hypothesize about the events surrounding Shovell's death.

The *Association* sinks within a few minutes of running onto the Gilstone Rock, at approximately 7.45 p.m., on the night of October 22nd 1707. Shovell is thrown into the sea with the rest of the crew and drowns. The south-westerly gale and currents carry the body to Porthellick Cove, St Mary's, where it is found either floating amongst the rocks or on the seashore, early next morning, the 23rd. Having removed the valuables from his body, including an emerald ring, the local inhabitants bury it just off the sands, close to where it was found. This seems to be the most likely course of events.

As an alternative, it is possible that Shovell, Captain Loades, his two Narbrough stepsons, and some of the crew get away from the wrecked *Association* in the admiral's barge. The barge breaks up in the heavy seas close to St Mary's Island, and all are drowned. There are a number of factors in favour of this theory. The bodies of Shovell, Loades and one of the two Narbroughs were all found on St Mary's; that of Loades actually in Porthellick Cove close to Shovell's. The drowned greyhound, belonging to Shovell, with its name on the collar, was found within a bowshot of its master. Shovell's chest was found floating in the sea near him. The majority of the drowned sailors were washed ashore on nearby St Agnes, which was much closer to the wreck site. It seems more than a coincidence that Shovell, with two of his relatives by marriage, were washed ashore close together, some eight miles away from the Gilstone, unless they travelled at least part of the way by boat. The injury to Shovell's body, a trivial scratch above an eye, was not consistent with any prolonged battering against the rocks. In addition, the stern of the barge was found near Porthellick, although a more modern theory is that it was the coat of arms from the stern of the *Association*, now to be seen in the Magistrate's Court in Penzance.

Against this supposition is the fact that it would have been extremely difficult to launch the barge in a gale and high seas. If they managed it, why did they not steer for nearby St Agnes like Francis Percy and the men of the *Firebrand*? On balance, it seems unlikely but not impossible that

Shovell and his staff were able to get off the sinking *Association* in a boat.

What of the murder theory? It seems improbable that an obese man in his 57th year could have survived immersion for the eight odd miles from the Gilstone Rock to Porthellick Cove, even if he had clung to wreckage or sailed part of the way in his barge. Possibly, Shovell's corpulence would have allowed him to stay alive longer in the cold October sea. With the exception of one man from the *Romney*, who was swept to a rock close to the wreck site, no man survived from the three major ships that sank that night. Many of the sailors were in their twenties, and much fitter than the middle aged admiral. If Shovell came ashore dead, as seems most likely, then the islanders could not possibly have murdered him.

The legend of Shovell's murder on the seashore is an old one. In Herbert's 1709 document it states, "Mr Pennick buried Sr C. before cold." Almost certainly this Mr Pennick was the Reverend Henry Penneck, who had been a clergyman on St Mary's for only a short time before the disaster of 1707. Larn has suggested that having to deal with burials on such a large scale was too much for him, as he went away the same year, according to the parish register. Some might argue that he had a guilty conscience![13]

According to the legend in the Romney family, Shovell was murdered on the seashore for the sake of plunder, the perpetrator of the crime being an elderly woman who stole an emerald ring from her victim's finger. More will be said of the emerald ring in due course.

In summary, the probable course of events was the drowning of Shovell, the washing up of his body on shore, and subsequent burial, just off the sands of Porthellick. Possibly, he travelled part of the way in his barge. Murder seems most unlikely, if only on the balance of probabilities.

Porthellick Cove means "marshy" or "herring" cove. A stone cairn just off the sands now marks the site of Shovell's first grave, to the north-west of the cove. Tradition has it that grass will not grow on it, because of Shovell's alleged hanging of one of the *Association*'s seamen on October 22nd for telling him that he was in danger of running onto the rocks at Scilly. Both grass and flowers grow in close proximity to the grave, and there is no truth in either part of the story.[14]

Shovell's body lay seven feet deep, just off the sands at Porthellick, from the early morning of October 23rd until the 26th. The boats of the *Salisbury* and *Antelope* were out enquiring about the matter, but it was the purser of the *Arundell*, a Mr Paxton, who was responsible for finding the grave, and having the body dug up. There are conflicting views about what led to its discovery. Either it followed an enquiry about a large corpse or a dispute amongst the strippers of Shovell's body concerning the distribution of their spoils. In particular, the emerald ring was at the centre of it.

In any event, Paxton had the body dug up on October 26th, three days after its burial. Once the face was washed, Paxton, who had had previous contact with Shovell, was able to identify him by a mole below an ear, old limb wounds, and finger deformities from the gaming tables. The impressions left from the rings that had been on the corpse's fingers were noted. From Porthellick Cove, Shovell's remains were carried to the home of a Mrs Bant and were placed on a table. Although a number of sailors from the ships anchored at Scilly were around, little notice was taken of the body. Paxton was carrying him on board his ship, the *Arundell*, when Captain Hosier of the *Salisbury* gave orders that the body should be taken to his own. On the same day that the body came on board the *Salisbury*, October 26th, it was disembowelled. None of the fleet's doctors present were capable of embalming the mortal remains of the unfortunate Shovell.

All three of the most important eighteenth century accounts of Shovell's demise mention the loss of a ring or rings from his fingers on the seashore of Porthellick. The earliest, the *Post Boy* of November 4th 1707, records: "the country-fellows belonging to the Islands of Scilly, finding Sir Cloudesley Shovel's Corps, took a fine emerald off his finger . . .". Herbert, in 1709, records "His ring was also lost from off his hand, wch however left ye impression on his finger, as also a second." No mention of the emerald, but there appears to have been a second ring. Romney, in his draft letter to Captain Locker, written around 1790, stated: "She acknowledged having, among other things, an emerald ring in her possession, which she had been afraid to sell lest it should lead to a discovery."[15]

One of the reasons given for Mr Paxton, purser of the *Arundell*, discovering Shovell's grave, was a dispute among the strippers of his body concerning the emerald ring. Clearly Paxton did not find the ring, for Lady Elizabeth Shovell wrote to Captain Benedick, the Deputy Governor and Commander-in-Chief of the Scilly Isles, offering a reward for its return. Benedick, using both fair means and foul, was unsuccessful. At a later unspecified date, according to the tradition in the Romney family, an elderly woman on her deathbed in St Mary's gave up the ring. Having admitted killing Shovell for plunder, she gave the ring to the minister. "This, ring which she delivered to the minister, was by him given to James Earl of Berkeley at his particular request, Sr Cloudesley Shovell and himself having lived on the strictest footing of friendship."[16]

Pickwell, in his article on Shovell, has cast doubt on the Romney/ Locker draft letter, on the grounds that a minister of the church would not make public a deathbed confession. Perhaps he would not divulge a killing, but he certainly would return a ring to its rightful owner if he had been asked to.[17]

The accepted view is that the emerald ring was given to James, third Earl of Berkeley (James Dursley, Captain of the *St George*), at some time between 1732 and his death in 1736. Lady Elizabeth Shovell died in 1732, and it is felt that, having gone to the lengths of writing to the deputy governor of the Scilly Isles asking for his assistance in its return, she would have had first claim on it. This is not necessarily the case as the ring could have been returned at any stage from the time of the Herbert expedition in 1709 until Berkeley's death in 1736. Lady Shovell could have given the ring to Berkeley "at his particular request", and this is made quite likely by the suggestion that he had given the ring to Shovell in the first place.[18]

The emerald ring, in all probability, descended in the Berkeley family certainly until 1879, when Mrs Caroline Mary Rumley, wife of General Randal Rumley, owned it. Robert Marsham Townshend saw it that year. The ring itself had been altered into the form of a locket by Caroline Rumley, with the emerald surrounded by small diamonds in its original setting, with Shovell's name and date of death added on the back, in characters of the nineteenth century. On the death of General Randal Rumley in 1884, the ring passed back into the direct line of the Earls of Berkeley. Attempts by the author to trace the locket to this day have failed. If it was, as the author suspects, in the hands of the eighth and final Earl of Berkeley, Randal Thomas Mowbray, it would have passed on his death to his second wife, Mary Emlen (Lloyd), who was alive in San Lorenzo, Assisi, Italy in 1956. The eighth Earl and his wife had no children, although she had children by her first marriage, who live in the United States of America. Perhaps they have the locket. Certainly the present owner of Berkeley Castle, Gloucestershire, John Berkeley, does not know of its whereabouts. [19] (See Appendix 3)

Larn has conducted some interesting research into the identity of the women who may have found Shovell's body. When S. R. Pattison visited the Scilly Isles in 1864, he was told that Shovell was washed ashore on a grating, with the body of his Newfoundland dog by his side. (According to Herbert the dog was a greyhound.) They were said to have been found by a woman named Thomas, living at nearby Sallakey Farm. According to this story, she buried the body of Shovell at Porthellick with help from Sallakey. From the burial records of St Mary's, Larn has suggested that of the three women who died between 1732 and 1736 (respectively, the dates of the deaths of Elizabeth Shovell and the third Earl of Berkeley), the most likely one to be involved is Mary Mumford, who died on February 1st 1735. This presupposes that Shovell was murdered and that a deathbed confession was made between these years. Unfortunately no Thomas is to be found in the burial records, which only begin in 1726. Robert Heath gives a slightly different version of this story in that Shovell was said to have been washed up on the shore on a hatch with his dead dog by his side. A soldier from the garrison at St Mary's then buried him in the sand.[20]

Before finally leaving the subject of Shovell's rings, it is worth recording that tradition in the Scilly Isles has it that the second ring from his finger is still there, in the hands of a descendant of the original thief. The islanders believe that if the ring ever leaves the Scilly Isles they will sink![21]

The exact number of men who lost their lives with Shovell on the night of October 22nd 1707 will never be known for certain. Without doubt, the three major ships lost that night carried sick and wounded from the Toulon campaign, who would not have been included on the muster lists. Officially the *Association* was carrying 739 men, the *Eagle* 500 men, the *Romney* 365 men and the *Firebrand* forty-five men. This makes a total of 1,649 of whom some twenty-four or twenty-five were saved. The real loss of life that night must have been at least 1,800, allowing for the wounded.[22]

The disaster was made more tragic by the fact that Shovell had with him in the *Association* more gentlemen volunteers than he had ever had before. Among those who were lost on October 22nd were Captain Edmund Loades, the son of Sir John Narbrough senior's favourite sister, Anne. (He wanted to be buried at Nolson in Kent, if he died in England. As will be seen, he was not to be buried there.); Sir John Narbrough junior, an able seaman in the *Association*, and his younger brother James, a captain's servant, before becoming an ordinary seaman in the same ship. (Both young men were Shovell's stepsons.); Henry Trelawney, the second son of Sir Jonathan Trelawney, newly made Bishop of Winchester. (Henry does not appear on the official lists for the *Association*. However, he was certainly drowned that night, and according to a *Post Boy* report, was on her.); Edward Aylmer (the *Association*'s 5th Lieutenant), son of Sir Matthew Aylmer, Shovell's old friend from the Mediterranean campaigns; Lewis Byllingsley, son of Colonel Byllingsley (the *Association*'s 1st Lieutenant); John Shovell (in the Admiral's retinue, and giving Lady Elizabeth Shovell as his next of kin, must have been a relative); and René Jontin (a Huguenot refugee, who was secretary successively to Edward Russell, George Rooke and finally Shovell in the *Association*).

One man who was thought to have survived from the *Association* was the Chaplain, Edward Roach. It was said that he had gone aboard another ship on the morning of the disaster, to administer the sacrament to some dying seamen. He was not so lucky, as he certainly drowned that night, and his wife, Susanne, eventually received the pay due to him in 1714! Perhaps the luckiest man to survive the sinking of the *Association* was young Will Graham, who was discharged to the *Lenox* on October 7th, just over a fortnight before the disaster.[23]

Edmund Loades was buried in the chancel of Old Town Church, St Mary's. Loades' body had been washed up close to that of Shovell in Porthellick Cove. Herbert has described his funeral. ". . . whose burial 'twas reported cost £90, but Mr Withe who was manager of it says ½ that sum."[24]

Henry Trelawney's body was dug up on the following November 4th from the sands of St Agnes, witnessed by men from the *Phoenix*, and also buried in the chancel of Old Town Church. "November 4. This morning we went to St Agnes Island and heard of a youth that was Bishop Trelawny's son whome we dug up and had interned in the Church."[25]

A fuller account of the digging up of young Trelawney is given in a previously quoted letter, of November 16th 1707, from John Ben to the young man's father, Jonathan Trelawney.

> Your Lordship's commands having been signified to my Brother at Scilly, he immediately made the strictest enquirey that was possible, all the bodies that had been thrown ashore and buried and being told of one buried at Agnes about Mr Trelawney's age, was resolved to have him taken up in order to view him, whether it was he or no. He had seen the young Gentleman at Torbay, but not willing to depend on his own judgement desired the Captain of the Phoenix Fire ship that was stranded there who knew Mr Trelawney intimately well all the voyage to go with him. As soon as they had the body up, they found it actually to be the same, tho somewhat altered having been buried 11 days, and in the water 4, however the Captain presently knew him and my brother took care to have the body brought over to St Mary's and interred it in the chancel of the church there, the 8th instant with all the marks of respect and honour, the Island could show on such an occasion. Some Captains and the best of the inhabitants being present at the funeral, my Brother took of his hair being cut and that so very close that the left [sic] lock was not left to send over, and there is no room to doubt that twas the body of poor Mr Henry Trelawny. It has not been his good luck as yet to meet with any thing belonging to him but whatever of that nature happens to come to his hand or knowledge your Lordship will be sure to have a faithful account of it . . .[26]

James Narbrough and almost certainly his brother, Sir John, were buried in the chancel of the Old Town Church. "Mr James Narbrough, (others say Sir John Narbrough) and the Ld Bishop Trelawney's son was likewise buried in sd Church very honourably."[27] What is known for certain is that the body of Sir John Narbrough junior was found. ". . . where we were told that on Friday last the Body of Sir J. Narbrough, Sir Cloudsly Shovel's Son-in-Law, was taken up after it had been buried 5 weeks in the Sands."[28] Unfortunately the report, from on board the *Salisbury*, did not give any information concerning where the body was then buried.

We left Shovell's body on October 26th, after it had been taken on board the *Salisbury*, and disembowelled probably on Mrs Bant's table. Mrs Bant had the sheet returned which had been covering the body, but she lost the table. The disembowelment complete, the body was placed in a coffin.[29]

That same day the *Salisbury* set sail for Plymouth accompanied by the

*Southampton, Antelope, Charles galley, Lizard* and a fleet of merchantmen. As well as Shovell's corpse, the *Salisbury* carried Francis Percy with his twenty odd survivors from the *Firebrand*, and the quarter master of the *Romney*, Mr George Lawrence. Before reaching Plymouth, the *Salisbury* retook two small English merchantmen from a French privateer.[30]

The *Salisbury* reached Plymouth Sound on October 28th. Between 5.30 and 6.00 p.m. that evening the body of Shovell was taken ashore. "29 Plymouth Sound . . . att 3 yesterday in y^e Afternoon struck y^ds & Topmasts att 6 Fired 30 Guns halfe a Minute a Distance when y^e body of S^r Cloudsly Shovell was Carried on Shore from y^e Salisbury."[31] The Master of the *Salisbury*, Thomas Styles, gave the time as 5.30 p.m. and recorded that his ship fired twenty-four guns at half a minute's interval.[32]

Once ashore, a Doctor James Yonge in the citadel at Plymouth embalmed Shovell's body. Yonge had been born in the town in February 1647 and was apprenticed to a naval surgeon in 1658, when he was just under 11 years old. In 1666 the Dutch took the ship he was in near the Canary Islands, and he remained a prisoner in Holland for about a year. He afterwards lived and practised in his native town of Plymouth, where he was appointed surgeon of the citadel. He died in 1721. Yonge has left a diary of his life from 1657 to 1708 which is now in the Plymouth Museum. In this Yonge recorded dealing with Shovell's remains. "1707 In November this yeare the corps of Sir Cloudesley Shovell was brought into the Citadell. he had been unfortunately drowned 9 days and I embalmed him and had 50£ for it. The Corps was carryed to London and buryed in Westminster Abbey at the Queenes Cost."[33]

Yonge must have made the entry at a later date, as the body came ashore on October 28th. It is not certain who paid the £50. Having been embalmed, Shovell's remains lay in state in the citadel at Plymouth until November 10th.[34]

While the inhabitants of the Scilly Isles were burying the dead and taking stock of the situation, Sir George Byng led most of the survivors of the broken fleet along the English Channel to Spithead, which they reached on October 25th. With Byng, in the *Royal Anne,* were the *Torbay* (Norris), *St George* (Dursley), *Somerset, Orford, Swiftsure, Monmouth, Panther, Rye, Cruizer, Vulcan, Weasel* and *Isabella yacht*. It was not until they went aboard the *Royal Anne* and spoke to Byng that some captains, such as John Price of the *Somerset* and Finch Redall of the *Isabella yacht*, learned for the first time about the death and destruction they had left behind in the Scilly Isles. Later Byng took a few ships into the harbour at Portsmouth, others made for the Downs and then the River Thames, to be laid up for the winter. The campaign season of 1707 had ended disastrously.[35]

NOTES

1. London Gazette No. 4380 Oct 30th – Nov 3rd 1707.
2. London Gazette No. 1783 Nov 1st 1707.
3. London Gazette No. 1945 November 1st – 4th 1707.
4. RMT MAT 26.
5. Master's journal Salisbury.
6. Cooke, Shipwreck of Sir Cloudesley Shovell etc; Court & Society, from Elizabeth to Anne, edited from the Papers at Kimbolton by the Duke of Manchester 2 vols London 1864, Vol II, p.259; Pattison S.R., Journal of the Royal Institution of Cornwall, No.11 1864 pp.61–65.
7. Cooke, Shipwreck of Sir Cloudesley Shovell etc; Herbert MSS.
8. Campbell, 2nd Edition 1750, Vol.IV, p.289; Mercure Historique et Politique, Vol. XLIII, p.669, La Hage 1707; Post Boy No. 1945.
9. Charnock, Vol.II, pp.16–17, 1794–98; Cunningham, Lives of Eminent and Illustrious Englishmen, Vol.IV, pp.46–48, 1835.
10. Pickwell, Improbable Legends, Mariners Mirror 1973.
11. Marsham Townshend, Death of Sir Cloudesley Shovell, Notes and Queries Dec 27th 1884.
12. RMT MAT 64.
13. Larn, p.27.
14. Pattison S.R., J.R.I.C., Vol.I, pp.61–65; Tregellas W.H., Tourist Guide to Cornwall & the Scilly Isles 1878.
15. Post Boy No.1945, 4th Nov. 1707; Herbert MSS; Romney to Locker circa 1790, see Marsham Townshend, Death of Sir Cloudesley Shovell, Notes and Queries Dec 27th 1884.
16. Romney to Locker draft letter.
17. Pickwell, Improbable Legends, Mariners Mirror 1973.
18. Marsham Townshend, Notes and Queries Dec. 27th 1884; RMT MAT 64; Larn, p.26; Charles Knight, Popular History of Eng. 1856–1862.
19. See Appendix 3; Marsham Townshend, Notes and Queries Dec 27th 1884; RMT 64; Research done for the author.
20. Larn, pp.26–27; Pattison S.R., Journal of Royal Institution of Cornwall, 1864 p.63; RMT MAT 48; Heath, 1750.
21. Larn, pp.26–27.
22. Larn, p.18; ADM 8/10; ADM 33/249; Journals of Capt & Lieut. of the Salisbury.
23. Oldmixon 1732; RMT MAT 24 will of Edmund Loades; Post Boy No.1945 Nov 1st–4th 1707; RMT MAT 3 René Jontin; ADM 33/249; RMT MAT 26 Chaplain; Larn, pp.47–53.
24. Herbert MSS.
25. RMT MAT 26; Journal of Sammuell Percivall, Lieutenant in the Phoenix.
26. T. Quiller Couch, Transaction of the Penzance Natural History and Antiquarian Society, John Ben to Sir Jonathan Trelawney, November 16th 1707.
27. Herbert MSS.
28. Daily Courant Dec 9th 1707.
29. Cooke, Shipwreck of Sir Cloudesley Shovell etc; Herbert MSS; Captain Francis Hosier, journal of the Salisbury ADM 51/842.
30. RMT MAT 26; Journal of Thomas Styles, Master of the Salisbury; Journal of Captain Joseph Winder, Captain of the Arundell; Pay books Salisbury, George Lawrence No. 328, entered on Oct 23rd 1707.
31. Journal of Captain Nicholas Smith of the Lizard.

32. Journal of Thomas Styles, Master of the *Salisbury*; RMT MAT 26; London Gazette No.4380, Oct 30th to November 3rd 1707; Daily Courant No.1783 Nov 1st 1707.

33. RMT MAT 8.

34. RMT MAT 8; Daily Courant No.1795, November 15th 1707.

35. Daily Courant No.1779, Oct 28th 1707; London Gazette No.4379, Oct 27th–30th 1707; Journal of Joseph Lyne, Master of the *Somerset*; Journal of Captain Finch Redall of the *Isabella yacht*; RMT MAT 26.

# CHAPTER XXVIII
## *The Funeral*
## *1707*

News of the disaster rapidly came to London, with an express from Sir George Byng reaching the Admiralty on October 26th, telling of his fears that the *Association* had sunk. On the 30th it was confirmed that Shovell's body had been found. Lady Elizabeth Shovell wasted no time, and two days later sent a hearse to Plymouth to collect her husband's body.[1]

The hearse collected the coffin and left Plymouth on November 10th for the long journey to London.

> Plymouth, Nov 11. The Corps of Sir Cloudsly Shovel, after having lain in State in our Citadel, to the View of abundance of Spectators for about a Week; was yesterday carried for London in a plain Herse without Escutcheons, & c drawn by 6 Horses in Company with a Coach and 6: And was attended out of the Town by the Mayor, Magistrates, and Common Council in their Formalities, and also by a Regiment of Soldiers: and near 70 Gentlemen on Horseback rode several Miles with the Corps. At the same time many Minute-Guns were fir'd from the Citadel and St. Nicholas's Island.[2]

The hearse reached Oakhampton on the following day, the 11th, where it spent the night. Next day it was driven into the city of Exeter.

> Exeter, Nov 15th On Tuesday last, our Chamber call'd a Committee, wherein it was agreed, to attend the Corps of the late Sir Cloudesly Shovel, in grat Pomp. The Corps lay that Night at Oakhampton, and the next day entred this City, being met, some Miles out of Town, by several Persons of good Quality, on Horseback. It was thought that

the Corps would have remain'd at the New-Inn, Half-Moon, the Fountain, or some other reputable House in this City, till Thursday morning; but contrary to all Expectation, tho' twas near Night, they drove away, in view of near 20000 People, and lodg'd the Corps at an Ale-house at Honiton Cleft, 4 Miles out of Town.[3]

What Shovell, not noted for his intemperance, would have thought of being lodged in an ale house does not bear contemplation! In this fashion the funeral cortege travelled up the road to London. Shovell's body then lay in state for many days, at Queen Anne's expense, in his town house on the north-east side of Soho Square, near Sutton Street. The misery of his wife, Elizabeth, who had lost her only sons and a nephew, as well as her husband, on the rocks of Scilly can be imagined. Her grown-up daughter, Elizabeth (by Sir John Narbrough) and her husband Thomas D'Aeth, must have been a great support to her. The younger children, Elizabeth and Anne Shovell, were only 15 and 11 years old respectively.[4]

While Shovell's body lay in state in his house in Soho Square, arrangements were being made for his funeral. As Queen Anne had agreed to pay for it, the Treasury and the College of Arms were the principal organisers of it. In the Public Record Office are Treasury Papers relating to the funeral. Since the Restoration of Charles II in 1660, excluding members of the Royal Family, there had been three funerals of distinguished naval officers paid for by the Crown. All three, George Monck (Duke of Albemarle), the Earl of Sandwich and Sir Edward Spragge, had been buried in Westminster Abbey. Sandwich and Spragge had died in battle. Monck had died of asthma and dropsy, "like a Roman general and soldier, standing almost up in his chair, his chamber like a text open, and all his officers about him". Shovell was the first to die by accident. He, too, was to be buried in Westminster Abbey. The Treasury looked into the relative costs of the three earlier funerals. Monck's must have been very grand as the estimate was 8,000 or 10,000 pounds.[5]

On December 6th 1707 a meeting took place at the College of Arms between the Lord Chamberlain and the Lord Marshall, to finalise the arrangements for Shovell's funeral. It was agreed that coaches would be used throughout rather than the River Thames for part of the journey to Westminster Abbey, on grounds of cost. The funeral procession would pass from Shovell's home in Soho Square – Piccadilly – St James's Street – Pall Mall – Charing Cross – King Street – Westminster Abbey.[6]

The Admiralty gave instructions for the available flag officers to attend Shovell's funeral, which was to be held on December 22nd 1707.

Letters are to be written to Admirals Churchill, Aylmer, Fairborne, Leake, Byng, Jennings, Hopsonn, Whetstone, Wishart, and Munden, desiring them as flag officers to be at the house of the Lady Shovell in

Soho Square on Monday night next a 5' o'clock to accompany the corpse of Sir Clow. Shovell to Westminster Abbey.[7]

In the hours of darkness on December 22nd, exactly two months to the day since Shovell had drowned, the procession set off from Soho Square. The hearse bearing Shovell's body led, with six horses covered in black velvet adorned with escutcheons, pendant streamers and feathers. Next came Shovell's own coach that was empty and drawn by six horses in mourning. Lady Shovell in coach and six followed. Lastly came a hundred further coaches with persons of quality and distinction. They included the flag officers of the navy and members of Prince George's council of which Shovell had been a member. George Byng must have thought about his own narrow escape on the rocks and Matthew Aylmer about his son, who had been a lieutenant in the *Association*.[8]

The funeral procession was rather a disappointment. It was imagined that it would be pompous and make a great show. The streets were expected to be lined with a vast crowd, and the houses adorned with tapestries, and full of lights and spectators. None of this happened.[9]

The funeral service took place at around midnight with Queen Anne's drums and trumpets present. Her watermen and those of Prince George were also there in their livery. The Reverend D. Butler, Minister of the Church of England, preached the sermon. He took as his text 2 *Corinthians*, Chapter 10, Verse 17. "But he that glorieth, let him glory in the Lord."

Unfortunately the sermon gave no details of Shovell's origins, shipwreck or death. Butler extolled his moral character, patriotism, bravery, modesty, charity, hospitality and said that he was loved by all under his command. He went on:

> As for his apparel, more those that knew him always observed in his habit such a gravity as beseemed a Christian, and yet such a decency as became a gentleman. His discourse and language was grave and noble, serious and weighty. His whole behaviour and carriage was masculine and noble such as became his heroic spirit and his goodness too absolute to grow of love of itself. When the dismal news of Cloudesley Shovell's shipwreck reached our metropolis what streams of tears gushed from her citizens eyes! for the greatness of their sorrow rented their very hearts assunder.[10]

Sir Cloudesley Shovell was interred in a large vault in the south choir aisle, to the west of the east cloister door of the Abbey. The humble Norfolk boy had found rest amongst his country's great.[11]

On January 20th 1708 the Marquis of Kent, Lord Chamberlain of the Household, wrote to the Earl of Godolphin, Lord High Treasurer, asking for £687 5s. 9d. to be paid to the undertakers and others. William Williams, employed by the Society of Upholsterers, was paid £480 5s. 6d for the coffin and hearse. Robert Trevet received £138 4s. 7d. for painting the escutcheons. Fees due to the church for interment came to £46 5s. 8d. Later in September 1708 Grinling Gibbons received £322 10s. 0d. for executing the carved memorial over the tomb. Godolphin was said to have been so upset by Shovell's loss that he considered tearing out the few locks of hair he had remaining on his head![12]

After the funeral the following verses were laid on the tomb.

> As Lambeth pray'd, so was the dire event
> Else we had wanted here a monument;
> That to our fleet kind heaven would be a rock;
> Nor did kind Heaven the wise Petition mock:
> To what the metropolitan did pen,
> The Bishop & his Clerks reply'd Amen.

In April 1707 Archbishop Tenison had prepared a formulary to be used for imploring the divine blessing on England's fleets and armies. An unguarded expression "the rock of our might" unluckily slipped in, which the wits of the time did not fail to recollect. Hence the above epigram.[13]

Soon after the disaster, Prince George of Denmark made clear in a letter to the Navy Board that it would not be investigated.

Admiralty Office. 10th Nov 1707
Gent[m].
Where as her Maj[ts] Ships y[e] Afsociation Eagle and Romney, were on the 22[d]. of last month unhappily lost on the Rocks near the Island of Scilly, and all their Officers & Companys drown'd, soe that noe Inquiry can be made Into their lofs at a Court Martiall, I doe therefore, in Consideration of the Misfortunes of the Widdows & other Relations of the Officers and Companys who perished as aforesaid, hereby desire and direct you to cause to be paid to such persons as shall be empowered to receive the same, the wages due to them, to the time the said ships were lost, without expecting any accounts from their Officers.

I am
Yours &
Navy Board          George.[14]

The local press of the day were in no doubt about where the responsibility lay. "'Twas strange, that Sir Cloudsly, who was bred to the Sea from his Infancy, should be guilty of such a Neglect and Mistake, upon our own Coast too!"[15]

The relatives of the drowned seamen received their back pay up to

October 22nd. Some, including Lady Elizabeth Shovell and Mary Hancock, wife of the captain of the *Eagle*, Robert Hancock, petitioned Queen Anne for a pension. Thomas, Earl of Pembroke, who had replaced Prince George on his death as Lord High Admiral of Great Britain, informed Queen Anne that, unless an officer died in action or of wounds, his dependants were not entitled to bounty. On another document, Josiah Burchett, Secretary to the Admiralty, made the comment that bounty was not allowed except in the case of the Great Storm of 1703. In fact, there were other exceptions. Dame Anabella Wheeler, wife of Sir Francis, was paid £200 a year after he drowned in 1695, and Lady Mary Dilkes, wife of Sir Thomas, a similar sum in 1707. It is not clear from the records whether any pensions were given to the relatives of those drowned on October 22nd. Their circumstances differed. Lady Elizabeth Shovell was a very wealthy woman through inheritance from her father, John Hill, and both her husbands. Mary Hancock, too, had lost her son in the *Eagle* with his father. She was unlikely to have been wealthy despite her husband's twenty-three years' service in the navy. The plight of the families of some of the lowly seamen defies imagination.[16]

Early in the New Year of 1708, on January 13th, Cloudesley Shovell's will was proved with his wife as sole executor. Under the terms of the will, which had been made on April 29th 1701, his wife and daughters were left his house and lands in Kent. The daughters, Elizabeth and Anne, also received legacies of £6,000 each. Shovell's land at Morston, Norfolk, which he may have inherited from his own father, was left for the use of his mother, Anne Flaxman, and his sister, Anne Shorting, during their lifetimes, before returning to his own daughters. Anne Flaxman received a legacy of £500, Anne Shorting one of £100, as did all her children. There were other smaller legacies to various cousins including the children of his uncle, Cloudesley Jenkenson, with whom he had served in the navy. The poor Norfolk boy had died a very wealthy man.[17]

On the same day, January 13th, that Shovell's will was proved, so too were those of his two stepsons, Sir John and James Narbrough. The principal beneficiary under their wills was to be their sister, Elizabeth D'Aeth. In particular, Elizabeth, who had been living with her husband at North Cray, Kent, received her father's former estate at Knowlton near Deal, Kent. The young Narbroughs also left their half-sisters, Elizabeth and Anne Shovell, £2,000 each. James Narbrough left £500 to his old college, Christ Church, Oxford for the "rebuilding and beautifying of Peckwater Quadrangle". Sir Jonathan Trelawney, whose son Henry was drowned in the *Association* with the Narbroughs, was also a Christ Church man. Possibly Henry was too, and it is interesting to speculate that he owed his place in the *Association* that fateful October day to his friendship with the Narbroughs. The respect that young Sir John Narbrough had for his stepfather is shown by the fact that Cloudesley Shovell was the sole executor of his will (although unable to perform the duty), and it referred to him as "my very much honoured father in law". The reputation that Shovell had of treating his stepchildren in the same manner as his own appears to be borne out.[18]

Cloudesley Shovell had no sons to carry on his line. However, both his daughters, Elizabeth and Anne, married twice and had issue. Elizabeth married for the first time on August 19th 1708, at the Chapel Royal, Whitehall, some ten months after her father's death. She was not yet 16 and her husband was Sir Robert Marsham, a Kent neighbour. Perhaps the family was able to start to forget the loss of so many of their men with this happy event. Sir Robert was created Baron Romney in 1716 and died in 1724. He was buried in the family vault in St Paulinus Church, Crayford. There were three children of the marriage, another Elizabeth born in 1711, and a son, another Robert, born in 1712. A second daughter, Harriet, died young. It would be Robert's son, Charles Marsham, who was made the first Earl of Romney, in 1801. The Romney descendants are today numerous. When her husband, the first Baron Romney, died in 1724, Elizabeth remained a widow until September 1732, when she married her second husband, John, Lord Carmichael, afterwards the third Earl of Hyndford. By him, she had a son who died in infancy. It is interesting to speculate that Elizabeth, Baroness Romney, lived with her mother, Lady Shovell, both being widows, after the death of her first husband. She remarried only five months after her mother's death in 1732. Elizabeth, Lady Carmichael, was to die in The Hague, where her husband was the English Minister, on November 17th 1750, aged 58 years. She was a Lady of the Bedchamber to the Princess of Orange.[19]

Shovell's younger daughter, Anne, married for the first time the Hon. Robert Mansell, a neighbour in Soho Square, on March 6th 1718, at St Anne's, Blackfriars. Although she had three children by Robert Mansell, they all died young. He died on April 29th 1723 and was buried at Crayford. Anne's second marriage was to John Blackwood Esq., a merchant of Charlton, in his home diocese on July 28th 1726. John was the son of Sir Robert Blackwood. Anne and John Blackwood had three children, two of whom (Shovell, a son and Mary, a daughter) had offspring themselves. Shovell Blackwood was to have homes in Crayford and at Pitreavie, Fife. His sister, Mary, married a Major General Thomas Desaguillers of Grace, Essex. Anne Blackwood predeceased her elder sister, Elizabeth, and her husband, John, dying on October 20th 1741. She was buried at Crayford. John Blackwood died on November 12th 1777, and although his family name has died out, there are numerous descendants alive today.[20]

Anne Flaxman, Shovell's mother, was alive at the time of his death. She died three months after receiving her son's legacy, in June 1709, and was buried at Morston on the 17th. In her own will she mentioned her daughter and son-in-law, Anne and Thomas Shorting, but there was no reference to her Shovell daughter-in-law and granddaughters. No doubt she considered that they were well provided for. Thomas Shorting was buried on October 6th 1727 and his wife, Anne, Cloudesley Shovell's half-sister, on September 21st 1734, both at Morston.[21]

Lady Elizabeth Shovell did not remarry. Gossip in 1708 associated her with Thomas, Earl of Pembroke.

> The town saith, Lord Pembroke will now marry and have set him three ladies:- Lady Falkland, Lady Shovell, Lady Arundell. Lady Shovell be[ing] told of it, replied she had lately married a daugh[ter] to Sir Something Marsham and had given her fifteen thousand pounds down, and promised twenty thousand more at her death, therefore was disabled for marrying men, looking chiefly at the fortune.[22]

Nothing came of it, and Elizabeth Shovell spent her time between May Place, Crayford and her town house, firstly in Soho Square itself and then after 1713 in a smaller house between the junction of the square and Frith Street. Worn out with age, pain and sickness, as her memorial tablet states, she died on April 15th 1732 and was buried at Crayford. Under the terms of her will, dated October 12th 1726, the estate was principally divided between her daughters Elizabeth and Anne. Her eldest daughter, Elizabeth D'Aeth (by Sir John Narbrough) had predeceased her on June 24th 1721. Lady Elizabeth Shovell's will is interesting in that it mentions several family portraits which are still in existence, a gold tumbler and the Emperor of Germany's picture set with diamonds, which had been presented to her husband. There is no mention of the famous emerald ring/locket in her will or in that of James, third Earl of Berkeley. Finally, she requested burial either in Westminster Abbey close to her beloved husband or at Crayford. One of the trustees of the estate of Lady Elizabeth Shovell was Sir John Norris. Clearly Sir John had not lost touch with the family after more than twenty years since that disastrous night in October 1707. He had first served under Cloudesley Shovell in the *Edgar*, at Bantry Bay, in 1689.[23]

Let the final words on Sir Cloudesley Shovell be those of his Queen at the time of his death and of his contemporary, Abel Boyer. Queen Anne on appointing Sir John Leake to be Rear Admiral of England said that she knew no man so fit to repair the loss of the ablest seaman in her service. Boyer in 1708 wrote of Shovell's end:

> This was the fatal end of one of the greatest sea commanders of our age, or, indeed, as ever this island produced; of undaunted courage and resolution, of wonderful presence of mind in the hottest

engagements, and of consummate skill and experience: But more than all this, he was a just, frank, generous, honest, good man. He was the artificer of his own fortune, and by his personal merit alone, from the lowest, rais'd himself to almost the highest station in the Navy of Great Britain.[24]

NOTES

1. Pattison S.R., J.R.I.C., Vol.I, pp.61–65, Addison to Lord Manchester, Addison to Cole; The Post Boy No. 1945, Nov 1st–4th 1707.
2. RMT MAT26; Daily Courant No 1795, Nov 15th 1707.
3. RMT MAT26; The Post Boy No 1951, Nov 15th–18th 1707.
4. An impartial History of the Life and Reign of our late most gracious sovereign Queen Anne of Blessed Memory, Paul Chamberlain 1738; Secret Memoirs.
5. RMT MAT26; D.N.B. Monck; Monckton Papers, ed Peacock 1885 p.94.
6. RMT MAT25; Records of the College of Arms.
7. Larn, p.23; Admiralty Minute Dec 17th 1707.
8. RMT MAT25; Records of the College of Arms.
9. RMT MAT25; Records of the College of Arms.
10. The Post Boy No.1966, Dec 20th–23rd 1707; Sermon of D. Butler in British Library; RMT MAT25.
11. Westminster Abbey guide.
12. Treasury Papers, Vol. LV, No.18, Kent to Godolphin Jan 20th 17 07/08; C.S.P. Treasury 1708, Vol. XXII, Part II, p.108; Larn, p.23; History of Great Britain from the Revolution in 1688 to the Accession of George I, Cunningham 1787.
13. RMT MAT26; Biographical History of England from the Revolution to the end of George I's reign, Grainger, Noble 1806.
14. P.R.O., Lords of the Admiralty Letter Book, 21 Oct 1706 – 10 March 17 07/08 No.18, p.481; RMT MAT26.
15. RMT MAT26; Observator, Vol.VI, No.76, Nov 29th–December 3rd 1707.
16. RMT MAT26; P.R.O. Admiralty Records 1706–1707, Bundle No.18, ff.153, 154, 155, 156; P.R.O., Secretary of State, letters 3 Sept 1706 to 30 Jun 1708, No.6.
17. RMT MAT24; Transcript in Book Barrett f.21, Somerset House.
18. RMT MAT24; Barrett f.17, Somerset House.
19. Notes & Queries, Jan 19th 1895, Parentage of Cloudesley Shovell; Cooke, Shipwreck of Sir Cloudesley Shovell, Pedigree of Families descended from Cloudesley Shovell.
20. Notes & Queries, Jan 19th 1895, Parentage of Cloudesley Shovell; Cooke, Shipwreck of Sir Cloudesley Shovell, Pedigree of Families Descended from Cloudesley Shovell.
21. Notes & Queries Jan 19th 1895, Parentage of Cloudesley Shovell; Appendix 6.
22. Lady Marow to her daughter Lady Kay, Aug 26th 1708, HMC 15th Report, Appendix Part I, Dartmouth MSS, Vol.III, pp.146–147.
23. Notes & Queries, Jan 19th 1895, Parentage of Cloudesley Shovell; Will of Lady Shovell, Bedford f.120, Somerset House; RMT MAT24.
24. Campbell, Vol.IV, p.263; Boyer A, History of the Reign of Queen Anne, 1708.

# Portraits, engravings and sculpture of Cloudesley Shovell

## The portraits

At least eleven portraits were painted of Shovell, and almost certainly more. The whereabouts of nine of them are known with certainty. Although Shovell was a contemporary of both Sir Peter Lely and Sir Godfrey Kneller, his portrait does not appear to have been painted by either of them. In the case of Lely this is not surprising, as by the time of his death in 1680, Shovell had not advanced far in the navy and was still a relatively young man. Christopher Myngs, Shovell's first patron, had had his portrait painted by Lely as one of the Flagmen of Lowestoft, before dying of wounds received in the Four Day Battle of 1666. There is no known portrait or indeed engraving of Shovell's other great friend and patron, John Narbrough. Kneller painted many of the leading admirals of the late Stuart period, but Shovell was not among them.

The artist most favoured by Shovell was Michael Dahl, a Catholic Swedish painter who was born about 1659. Dahl, after early training in Stockholm under Hannibal, came to London in 1682. After two years in England, Dahl went to Paris and then Rome, before finally returning to London in about 1688–9, when Shovell was beginning to make a name for himself. During his first period in London between 1682 and 1684 Dahl certainly came into contact with Kneller and may have actually studied under him. Dahl was a fine painter, perhaps not of the first rank, who had a mastery of pigment, a taste in colour, and genuine feeling for design. One of the characteristics of his technique was the fluent thinness of his pigment through which the canvas grain could be seen.

In 1696 Dahl took a house in Leicester Fields near the Swedish legation, and close to where Joshua Reynolds was to have his home some seventy years later. As was the custom of the time, Dahl had his studio on the ground floor, where elegantly draped models posed among his paint boxes and easels. On the first floor, his hall was arranged as an art gallery, in which Dutch artists, including Rembrandt, and the Italians were represented. Dahl also took great pride in his collection of medals. The most interesting of these were the Pope's gold medal, and several portrait medals of himself and his friends, including one of George Rooke,

Shovell's fellow admiral. It is not difficult to imagine Shovell being driven the short distance between his town house in Soho Square and Leicester Fields. Perhaps the two of them discussed their mutual complaint of gout and Shovell admired Dahl's works of art. Dahl was known to visit the country homes of his clients, and he could have gone to May Place, Crayford, to undertake a Shovell portrait.

Although Rooke was a friend of Dahl's and belonged to the same club, it is likely that Shovell was introduced to Dahl by Prince George of Denmark, Queen Anne's husband. Dahl had painted a portrait of Prince George in about 1690 and on the accession of his wife, in 1702, he was made Lord High Admiral. Probably, Prince George asked Dahl to paint his series of seven admirals, which were originally at Hampton Court before, in 1824, they were given to Greenwich Hospital by George IV. They are now in the National Maritime Museum. The seven admirals were Cloudesley Shovell, Thomas Hopsonn, Basil Beaumont, John Munden, William Whetstone, James Wishart and George Rooke. Judging by the wide sleeves on their coats and their high wigs, which went out of fashion after 1710, the series of portraits can be fairly accurately dated to between 1702 and 1708, which was the year of Prince George's death.

Dahl's Greenwich Hospital Cloudesley Shovell portrait has been considered his masterpiece (C. H. Collins Baker*), and many of his other portraits of Shovell may have been based on this one (David Piper**). The only other artist associated with a Shovell portrait is W. de Ryck. However, its whereabouts are unknown. The remaining portraits have been painted by unknown artists.

A number of portraits were painted of Lady Elizabeth Shovell and their two daughters, Elizabeth and Anne. (Recorded in Lady Shovell's will of 1732). The whereabouts of only one portrait of Lady Elizabeth, and one of her daughter of the same name, are known to the author. They are both in the private collection of a descendant. The portrait of Lady Elizabeth is by an unknown artist and that of her daughter has been attributed to Jonathan Richardson.

## Catalogue of the portraits of Cloudesley Shovell

### 1. National Maritime Museum.
The Greenwich Hospital Portrait by Michael Dahl.
BHC 3025.   50" x 40".   Oils.
Half length canvas. Unsigned c.1702–1708.

---

* An authority on Stuart portraiture.
** Cataloguer of seventeenth century paintings in the National Portrait Gallery, London.

Shovell standing; grey wig; blue coat with gold braid; blue waistcoat; white cravat; baton in right hand; sword; seascape background with a ship. The flags flown on the ship may have been repainted, as there is a white at the main with a red ensign which is an incorrect conjunction. The white flag at the main may indicate that Shovell was Admiral of the White at the time the painting was done. He was Admiral of the White from May 6th 1702, which may allow a closer dating of the portrait.

The picture was number 22 in the National Portrait Exhibition, South Kensington, in 1867. It was number 15 in the 1858 Greenwich Hospital catalogue. There are illustrations of the painting in *Lely and the Stuart Portrait Painters*, by C. Collins Baker (1912), and in the Concise Catalogue of Oil Paintings in the National Maritime Museum (1988). This is the most famous of the Shovell portraits and is considered to be Dahl's masterpiece.

## 2. National Maritime Museum.
   Signed by Michael Dahl and dated 1702.
   BHC 3026.   94" x 58½".   Oils.
   Whole length canvas.

Shovell standing; in armour; stockings; shoes; white cravat hanging down his chest; leaning on a cannon; holding a baton in his left hand; drapery held to his hip by his right hand; looking at the spectator; to the left a ship firing; to the right a sail is visible.

The seascape to the left of Shovell has a ship with a blue flag at the main, indicating an Admiral of the Blue, which Shovell was from 1696 until early 1702. If the evidence of the flags is taken into account, this portrait predates the Greenwich Hospital portrait (1) which some authorities (Piper) consider to have been the basis for this portrait (2), and for those in the National Portrait Gallery (3) and Guildhall, Rochester (6). This painting was acquired in 1951 through Christie's sale of November 23rd, lot number 73. The previous owner inherited it from a Shovell descendant. It is illustrated in the Concise Catalogue of Oil Paintings in the National Maritime Museum (1988).

## 3. National Maritime Museum.
   Style of Michael Dahl.
   BHC 3027.   20" x 25".   Oils.

This portrait was presented to the National Maritime Museum in 1973 by K. M. Leake Esq. Judging by the surname of the donor of the picture, it is possible that it has come down through the Leake family from Shovell's friend, Sir John Leake, who died in 1720.

## 4. National Maritime Museum.
Seventeenth century English School.
BHC 3024.   50" x 40".   Oils.

This portrait was acquired by the museum from N. M. Hughes D'Aeth Esq.

In the records of the National Maritime Museum, there is a note that the painting is very likely to be a copy, after a painting by Kneller, of the 1st Duke of Devonshire, which was painted in 1682. Also noted is that the face is similar to Shovell's face, in portraits by Michael Dahl. Again the name D'Aeth may indicate descent from the Shovell family. Cloudesley Shovell's stepdaughter, Elizabeth Narbrough (daughter of Sir John Narbrough), had married into the D'Aeth family and possibly the portrait has come down from her.


## 5. National Portrait Gallery.
Considered to be by Michael Dahl with much studio work. c.1702.
797.   87½" x 56".   Oils on canvas.

Whole length standing; in armour; red stockings; black shoes; flaxen wig; leaning on a cannon; holding a baton in his left hand; a white cravat tucked into the armour at the neck; deep blue drapery held to his hip by his right hand; grey eyes looking at the spectator; to Shovell's left a seascape with a ship with a blue flag at the main and a blue ensign, firing a broadside; to Shovell's right a sail visible above the cannon, lit from the left.

This picture was formerly in the family home of the Earls of Romney, the Mote near Maidstone, Kent. Presumably this is the picture which was left in Lady Shovell's will to her daughter, Elizabeth, who had married into the Romney family, in 1708. "Item I give to my said daughter the Lady Romney the picture of the Sir Cloudesley Shovell drawne at full length . . .". In 1888 the picture was sold by the family at Christies and bought by Agnews, before going to the National Portrait Gallery. Piper believes this portrait to be a variant of the signed Dahl (2) in the National Maritime Museum, that it was developed from the Greenwich Hospital portrait (1), and that there were no further sittings in life. The author has his doubts about portrait (1) pre-dating (2) for reasons given earlier.

In any event, the National Portrait Gallery variant is a poor quality picture, which does not stand comparison with that in the National Maritime Museum or indeed the one in the Guildhall, Rochester.

## 6. The Guildhall, Rochester, Kent.
Unsigned but attributed to Michael Dahl.   Oils.

This painting shows Shovell at full length in armour, and is similar to the Dahls in the National Maritime Museum (2), the National Portrait Gallery (5), and the one formerly at Aynhoe Park (9). The provenance of the portrait is uncertain, but it may well have been presented by Shovell himself or his family. Sir John Leake, Shovell's friend, who succeeded him as M.P. for Rochester, presented his own portrait at the request of the Corporation.

## 7. The Guildhall, Rochester, Kent.
Unsigned miniature.   Oils on copper.

This half length miniature shows a young Cloudesley Shovell standing in armour; looking at the spectator; red drapery over his shoulders and down his back; right elbow flexed; right hand raised; wig.

The rather flabby hand is a younger version of the one portrayed in the Greenwich Hospital Portrait (1). It is known that Shovell suffered from gout and this may explain the look of his hands. The author knows of no other portrait showing the young Cloudesley Shovell still in existence. Judging from his unlined face, Shovell was less than 40 when the miniature was painted. This would make its date no later than 1690 and conceivably as early as 1677, to celebrate the events at Tripoli, the preceding year. However this is conjecture.

The painting was presented to the Corporation of Rochester by John Newington Hughes in 1828. In a letter of September of that year, Mr Hughes stated that, ". . . the picture was in the possession of the late Mr Marsham of Boxley House and I believe its authenticity to be undoubted". There is no reason to disbelieve him and, as Marsham is the family name of the Romneys, the miniature is likely to have come down via Shovell's daughter, Elizabeth.

In the author's estimation this picture rates second only to the Greenwich Hospital Portrait (1) in interest and is not widely known.

## 8.  Private Collection.
By an unknown seventeenth century artist.
Half length.   48" x 36".   Oils on canvas.

Shovell facing to the left; his head turned towards the spectator; grey wig; white cravat; brown coat; right hand on his hip and his left hand pointing ahead.

In the picture Shovell appears to be about 45 years old (c.1695), with a massive head, ruddy cheeks and the first signs of his later corpulence.

The owner of the picture inherited it, by descent from Shovell's elder daughter, Elizabeth, through her second husband, John Carmichael, third

Earl of Hyndford. In addition, he owns a portrait of Shovell's wife, Elizabeth, which is similar in size (48" x 36"), and a smaller one of Shovell's daughter, Elizabeth, which is attributed to Jonathan Richardson.

The author has not personally seen any of these three pictures, but has seen photographs of them.

### 9. Private Collection.
Magnificent portrait by Michael Dahl. (Formerly at Aynhoe Park).
Oils on canvas.

Three quarters length standing; in armour; flaxen wig; leaning on a cannon; his left hand over the cannon's muzzle; a white cravat tucked into the armour at the neck; red drapery held to his hip by his right hand; on Shovell's left a seascape with three ships.

The painting has descended to the present owner through Shovell's younger daughter, Anne, and her second husband, John Blackwood. Their daughter, Mary Blackwood married into the Cartwright family of Aynhoe Park.

The composition of the painting is similar to the Dahls in the National Maritime Museum (2), National Portrait Gallery (5) and that in the Guildhall, Rochester (6):

|  | Quality | Length | Cravat | Pigtail | Baton | Drapery colour | Seascape (left) | Seascape (right) | Left hand |
|---|---|---|---|---|---|---|---|---|---|
| NMM | good | full | on chest | on chest | in hand | blue | 1 ship | 1 sail | on baton |
| NPG | poor | full | inside | on hand | in hand | blue | 1 ship | 1 sail | on baton |
| Rochester | good | full | on chest | on chest | in hand | blue | 1 ship | nil | on baton |
| Aynhoe | good | three quarters | inside | behind back | absent | red | 3 ships | nil | on muzzle |

### 10. Missing Portrait.
Three quarter length by W. de Ryck.

Shovell is shown facing to his right; his head turned to the spectator; in ornate armour; long wig; white decorated cravat; cloth belt; puffed sleeves; right hand resting on a terrestrial globe; left hand grasping a baton and flexed at the elbow.

The whereabouts of this picture are unknown. The details are known only through an engraving made by J. Smith, c. 1692. Smith's engraving shows Shovell's coat of arms which he received in 1692. Perhaps the portrait was painted after his marriage in 1691 or after the Battle of Barfleur in 1692.

The picture appears to be particularly attractive and it is a shame that it has been lost.

## 11. Shovell Portrait formerly owned by Sir John Leake.
29" x 24".   Oils on canvas.
The painting shows the head and shoulders of the Greenwich Hospital portrait (1) with a grey background.

Early last century the painting belonged to Lt Colonel W. Martin Leake of Marshalls, Ware. It originally belonged to Sir John Leake and was kept at Beddington, Surrey. In an inventory of July 2nd 1729, it was valued at £4.00. The author does not know the present whereabouts of this portrait. It differs in size from (3) which is the other Shovell portrait associated with the Leake name.

### Sources
1. *Michael Dahl and the Contemporary Swedish School of Painting* by Wilhelm Nisser, Uppsala, 1927.
2. *Lely and the Stuart Portrait Painters by C.H. Collins Baker*. Warner, 1912, pp. 95–102.
3. Concise Catalogue of Oil Paintings in the National Maritime Museum, Antique Collectors Club, 1988.
4. Catalogue of the 17th Century Portraits in the National Portrait Gallery by David Piper, Cambridge University Press, 1963.
5. Portraits (1), (2), (3), (4). Personal communication with the National Maritime Museum, 1988.
6. Portraits (6), (7). Personal communication with the Guildhall useum, Rochester, 1989. In addition, a brief history by M.I. Moad.
7. Portrait (8). Personal communication with the owner, 1989.
8. Portrait (9). Personal communication with the owner, 1989.
9. *Dictionary of British Portraiture I*. 'The Early Middle Ages to the Early Georgians', compiled by Dr Adriana Davies, 1979, National Portrait Gallery.
10. Will of Lady Elizabeth Shovell, 1732.

### Engravings of Shovell portraits

1. **Engraving by J. Smith** of W. de Ryck's missing portrait (10).
Mezzotint 12¼" x 10".   Circa 1692.

The engraving must have been done in 1692 or later as it shows Shovell's coat of arms, records his position as Rear Admiral of the Red in the late defeat of the French, and that he was Lt Colonel of a marine regiment. The late defeat of the French was at Barfleur in 1692. Shovell was made Lt Colonel of the Second Marine Regiment in the autumn of 1691.

2. **Engraving by J. Faber** at three quarters length, of a Michael Dahl
   portrait, showing Shovell in armour.
   Painting 1702.   Engraving 1723.

Marsham Townshend considered this engraving to be of the full length Dahl now in the National Portrait Gallery (5). This is incorrect, as the portrait shows Shovell's cravat to be inside his armour and in the engraving it is on the outside. There is also a discrepancy between the position of the tip of the barrel of the cannon Shovell is leaning on and a ship in the background. Piper considered the engraving to be of the full length Dahl in the National Maritime Museum (2). Again the relationship between the barrel of the cannon and the background ship is not a perfect match. The Rochester portrait (6) and the Aynhoe portrait (9) do not match the engraving either.

The National Maritime Museum portrait (2) is closest of the known portraits to the engraving. Perhaps there is a further missing Dahl.

3. **Engraving by J.T. Wedgwood** at three quarters length of the Michael
   Dahl portrait in the National Maritime Museum (1). Early nineteenth
   century.

4. **Engravings by B. Lens, J. Simon and T. Blood** all reversed and at half
   length of the Michael Dahl portrait in the National Portrait Gallery
   (5).

**Sources**
1. RMT MSS MAT 63. (Robert Marsham Townshend MSS)
2. Catalogue of the 17th Century Portraits in the National Portrait Gallery
   by David Piper.

**Sculpture of Cloudesley Shovell**

1. **Terracota Bust** of Cloudesley Shovell.
   In the Oak room of the Strangers Hall Museum, Norwich.

The inscription reads: Sir Cloudesley Shovell. Rear Admiral of England. Born near Cley in this county 1650. Presented by Richard Ward Esq.

In a personal communication of May 9th 1989 from the Norfolk Museums Service, it is stated that the bust was given to Norwich Museum in 1842 by Mr Richard Ward, of Pierrepont House, Bath. It is not signed.

Experts from the Victoria and Albert Museum and the Courtauld Institute incline to the view that it might be by John Bushnell, but many other attributions are suggested. There is also doubt that it really is Sir Cloudesley.

2. **Marble Bust** of Cloudesley Shovell.
   In the Museum of Costume, Bath.
   On loan from the Victoria Art Gallery, Bath.

In a personal communication of July 21st 1992 from the Bath Museums Service, it is stated that on December 1st 1896 Mr J. M. Ostler, Secretary to the Royal Victoria Park Committee, had written, offering a marble bust of Sir Cloudesley Shovel (sic) with pedestal, to the Bath City Council. It was accepted and placed in the Victoria Art Gallery. The bust is by Francis Bird (1667–1731) and is mentioned in Rupert Gunnis' *Dictionary of British Sculptors*.

3. **Monument** on the tomb of Cloudesley Shovell.
   Situated in the south choir aisle near the east cloister door,
   Westminster Abbey.

Shovell is shown resting on velvet cushions, on his left side. He is wearing a loosely fitting garment, a long wig and a canopy of state is above him. Shovell's contemporary Joseph Addison complained about the monument, ". . . instead of the brave rough English admiral, which was the distinguishing character of that plain gallant man, he is represented on his tomb by the figure of a beau . . .".

The sculptor of the monument was the celebrated Grinling Gibbons who received £322.10s.0d. for his work on September 4th 1708.


# APPENDIX 2

## *Buildings and sites associated with Cloudesley Shovell*

**Norfolk**

**I The Church of St Andrew and All Saints, Cockthorpe.**
Fourteenth Century.

John Narbrough was baptised here on October 11th 1640. Cloudesley Shovell was baptised here on November 25th 1650. The font is perpendicular in a warm coloured stone and stands on a single step. It is octagonal and is decorated with eight shields.

The tomb of Sir James Calthorpe, who died in 1615, can be seen inside the church. He was a member of the family, whose descendants were the leading landowners in Cockthorpe, at the time of Cloudesley's birth. Outside the church can be seen the eighteenth century graves of Mary and Harvey Shorting, who may well have been relations of Cloudesley's half-brother-in-law, Thomas Shorting. With age, the grave stones have become difficult to read.

The church has been declared redundant by the diocese and is now vested in the Norfolk Churches Trust. (Guide and Baptismal Register, Cockthorpe Church).

## II  The Church of All Saints, Salthouse.
Thirteenth Century.

Christopher Myngs was baptised here on November 22nd 1625.

## III  All Saints Church, Morston.
Twelfth Century.

Shovell's mother, Anne Flaxman (second marriage), née Jenkenson, who died on June 17th 1709, is buried here. No gravestone or memorial plaque is visible.

Shovell's half-sister, Anne Shorting, née Flaxman and her husband, Thomas Shorting, who died on September 19th 1734 and October 4th 1727 respectively, are buried here. A memorial inscription to them can be seen in the floor of the church to the south side.

Near the lectern lies the Revd Thomas Shorting, son of the above, who died after preaching his first sermon here aged 24 years. He was a half-nephew of Shovell. (Guide to Morston Church).

## IV  St Margaret's Church, Cley-next-the-Sea.
Thirteenth Century.

Beneath the south transept window is the table tomb of the Greeve family. The inscription on it reads: "Here lyeth the Body of James Greeve who was an Assistant of S$^r$ Cloudisly Shovel in burning y$^e$ Ships in y$^e$ Port of Tripoly in Barbary Jan$^{ry}$ 14th 16 75/76 and for his good service form'd was made Cap$^t$ of the Ship called the Orange Tree of Algier in 1677 presented w$^{th}$ A Medal of gold by King Charles y 2 he died April 14 1686 Aged 48 years Also Martha his wife died Feb 19 1722 Aged 71 years And James their son

Died Sept 26 1728 Aged 45 years. Also Elizabeth their Daugh$^{tr}$ She died July 8 1748 Aged 57 years."

The inscription on the tomb is of one style and it is possible that it was done in 1748, after the death of the daughter, Elizabeth. Certainly Cloudesley Shovell had not been knighted by 1686 when Greeve died. (Guide to Cley Church).

## V  Cockthorpe Hall near Holt.

Grade II Listed Building.

Dates from the late sixteenth century and is said to be associated with Cloudesley Shovell. (*Eastern Daily Press* October 17th 1986).

## Kent

## I  The Guildhall, Rochester.

The magnificent plaster ceilings in the Court Hall and probably also over the staircase were paid for by Cloudesley Shovell in 1695–6. He first became an M.P. for Rochester in 1695.

The work was probably carried out by the master plasterer, John Grove II after designs by his father. The central design of an oval wreath decorated with flowers and fruit was paralleled exactly in a plaster ceiling by John Grove I, formerly in Coleshill House, Berkshire, which was destroyed by fire in 1952. The Groves carried out a number of commissions in England, and their work was known and admired by Samuel Pepys. Among the motifs on the ceiling of the Court Hall are the arms of Shovell. At the far end of the room over the mayor's chair are the royal arms, those of Sir Joseph Williamson and Shovell himself.

Among the portraits on the walls of the Court Hall are those of Shovell, Williamson, Sir John Leake, Sir Stafford Fairborne and Sir John Jennings, who all represented Rochester in Parliament. Portraits of William III and Queen Anne hang there too.

In a cabinet in the Court Hall can be seen a miniature of Shovell as a young man, a silver plate salvaged from the *Association* with a combined Shovell/Hill crest, and a document signed by Shovell in 1704.

The Guildhall and its museum are open to the public. (A Brief History of the Guildhall, Rochester; plaque on the wall of the Court Hall).

## II  The Corn Exchange/Clock House, Rochester.

The Clock House was built in 1698 to house the Butcher's Market. A plaque on the front of the building states that it was, "erected at the sole charge of Sir Cloudesley Shovell, Knt. in 1706". In fact he paid only for the ornate brick frontage to the building, the clock and the market bell. The clock was described as being of most excellent workmanship. However, two years after its construction, a Mr Windmill was summoned from London to repair it. By 1771 the original dial of Shovell's clock was much decayed, and a Mr Edward Muddle of Chatham was employed to replace it. During this renovation, the original square shaped dial was replaced by a circular one, and a larger bell installed.

In the nineteenth century, the Butcher's Market became the Corn Exchange.

The Clock House which is close to the Guildhall can be seen to this day. (Yesterday's Medway Historic Buildings).

### III May Place, Crayford.

In 1694 Shovell bought the May Place estate after the death of the previous owner, Cresheld Draper. It is possible that Cresheld was related to Roger Draper, a close friend of Sir John Narbrough, and that the estate came Shovell's way through this connection. It is likely that the original May Place was constructed for the Apylton family in the reign of Henry V. By Shovell's time, it was a large Jacobean mansion lying to the north of St Paulinus Church. Sadly, in the Second World War, May Place was largely destroyed by enemy action. The local golf club used what was left of the original building. Beneath it are still older foundations and cellars. An engraving of May Place by J. Greig can be found in *Excursions through Kent*, published by Longman and Co. of Paternoster Row, in 1821.

Lady Elizabeth Shovell, wife of Cloudesley, used May Place until her death in 1732, when her eldest daughter, Elizabeth, Lady Carmichael, inherited it. Shovell also owned the manors of Newberry and Howberry and further land at Crayford, Erith and Bexley. (May Place, Bexley Libraries and Museums, A. Halsall 1977; Will of Sir Cloudesley Shovell April 29th 1701, proved January 13th 1707/8. To be found in book "Barrett" f.21 in the Principal Probate Registry, Somerset House; RMT MAT 24 Section 18).

### IV St Paulinus Church, Crayford.

Twelfth Century.

This was Shovell's parish church from 1694 until his death in 1707. From 1688 until 1708 Gilbert Crockatt was the rector there. After Shovell's death he wrote, *A Consolatory Letter to Lady Shovell* which contains details of his early life and has been quoted already in this account. Crockatt records that Shovell had written on his pew, "I was glad when they said unto me: We will go up into the house of the Lord." (Psalm 122). By the year 1700 the Church was in need of repair, and Shovell paid for this to be done, and presented a new reredos.

To this day, there is a plaque on the church wall which states that near this place an inscription formerly recorded that,

This church and chancel
Being of late much injured and decayed
Were restored and beautified at the proper charge and sole expense
of Sir Cloudesley Shovell Knight
Rear admiral of Great Britain
And Admiral and Commander in chief of the fleet
The present tablet was erected at Easter 1879 by a later generation of
worshipers (sic) to keep in memory the pious munificence of one of
the greatest seamen of his age A.D. 1650–1707. Thou shalt be the
repairer of the breach. The restorer of paths to dwell in.

Although Cloudesley Shovell was buried in Westminster Abbey, his wife,
Lady Elizabeth, was buried at St Paulinus Church, Crayford, on April
22nd 1732, having died in her house in Frith Street, Soho, London. A
monument to Lady Shovell is still to be found in the South Chapel, now
the Lady Chapel. It gives a brief resume of her life.

Here lies intered the body of Dame Elizabeth Shovell. She was first
married to Sir John Narbrough admiral and commander of the
English Navy in the Mediterranean seas; afterwards to Sir Cloudesley
Shovell rear admiral of England and commander in chief of the
British fleet, whose fatal shipwreck, if it was a calamity to his country
in general, how grievous must her private share have been;
aggravated by the loss of her only sons by Sir John Narbrough who
perished with him; both grown up to men's estate of excellent natural
talents joined to the learning of Oxford, and the knowledge of men
and foreign country's under the eye of their brave friend and father
in law. This shock of fortune, terrible and uncommon, joined with the
loss of great wealth that was shipwrecked with her husband, and
sharing with him those honours his queen and grateful country had
prepared for him, she bore with a fortitude superior to her own, and
rarely equalled by the other sex. All her after life shewed how dear his
memory was to her, by a decent and frugal retreat from the gaities of
the world and her care of his surviving daughters to whom at her
death she left the most substantial proofs of her affection and
prudence while living.

She was daughter of John Hill Esq. Commissioner of the Navy and
was born in the year 1659 worn out with age, pain and sickness, she
resigned this life April 15th 1732. By Sir John Narbrough she had one
daughter Elizabeth (who died before herself) who was married to Sir
Thomas D'Aeth bart to whom she left two sons and five daughters; by
Sir Cloudesley Shovell she left two daughters Elizabeth, first married
to the right hon the Lord Romney by whom she has the present Lord
Romney and two daughters; afterwards married to the right hon. the

Lord Carmichael, eldest son to the Earl of Hyndford; Ann first married to the Lord Mansel by whom she has the present Lord Mansel and afterwards married to John Blackwood Esq. to who she has two sons and a daughter.

Close to Lady Shovell's memorial is one to her son-in-law, the Hon. Robert Mansel, who was the first husband of her younger daughter, Anne. He died on April 19th 1723, and was buried at Crayford on the following May 12th.

Other close relatives of Shovell who were buried at Crayford are:

Robert, first Baron Romney, the first husband of Shovell's elder daughter, Elizabeth, who died on November 11th 1724 and was buried on the following December 7th; Anne Blackwood (née Shovell), the younger daughter of Shovell, who died on October 20th 1741 and was buried on the following October 27th; Elizabeth Carmichael (née Shovell), the elder daughter of Shovell, who died at The Hague, on November 17th 1750 and was buried on the following November 30th; John Blackwood, the second husband of Shovell's younger daughter, who died on November 12th 1777.

After the death of Sarah Madox Blackwood in 1853, the Shovell vault was filled with concrete and closed. (Crockatt, *Consolatory Letter*; A short account of St Paulinus Church; Notes and Queries, January 19th 1895; RMT MAT 24 and 25).

## V Knowlton Church, near Deal.

The church is close to Sir John Narbrough's country estate at Knowlton Court. It contains an altar tomb in the chancel, with an inscription commemorating the young John and James Narbrough, both of whom were lost with their stepfather, Cloudesley Shovell, off the Scilly Isles and were buried there. (i.e. St Mary's, Isles of Scilly). The inscription on the tomb reads:

In Memory of S$^r$ John Narbrough Bar$^t$ and James Narbrough Esq.

The only surviving sons of S$^r$ John Narbrough Kn$^t$ Admirall of the Fleet in the Reigns of King Charles the 2$^d$ and King James the 2$^d$ who with their entirely belov'd Father in Law S$^r$ Cloudesley Shovel Kn$^t$ Rear Admirall of Great Britain and Admirall and Commander in Cheife of the Fleet under her Present Majesty Queen Anne were unfortunately shipwreckt in the Night upon the Rocks of Scilly the 22$^d$ of October 1707.

Great was the loss of these two Young Gentlemen whose Obliging Conversation Constant Friendship & Religous Duty were y$^e$ Admiration of all that knew them They were Ingenious, Virtuos, Pious. Happy in their inclinations Happy in their Fortunes Unhappy only in their Fate The Ardency of their Affection had this Peculiar in it That their Mutual Impatience of living long Asunder was the Great Occasion of their dying both Together The Elder in the 23$^d$ The Younger in the 22$^d$ Years of their Age.

Dame Elizabeth Shovel their disconsolate Mother as a Perpetual Memorial of her Inexpresible Greife Hath raised and for ever Consumated this Monument.

On the opposite wall of the chancel is a corresponding altar tomb which bears the following inscription.

Here lies the remains of S$^r$ John Narbrough Knight/who departed this life the 27th of May 1688/ in the 49th Yeare of his Age/Alsoe the body of Ann his daughter by Elizabeth his/second wife, who dyed the 6th of November 1683/Alsoe the body of Isack their son, who died 8th of/March 1686/7.

There is a distinction between the *remains* of Sir John and the *bodies* of his children, who had both died in infancy. Only Sir John's bowels were brought home to Knowlton, the remainder of his body being buried at sea, off Hispaniola, where he had died.

In the superstructure of Sir John's altar tomb is an inscription in memory of his eldest daughter, Dame Elizabeth D'Aeth, who died on June 24th 1721 and was buried at Knowlton. (RMT MAT 16e, 17c, 32, 34; Notes and Queries, December 29th 1888; Larn pp.2 & 3).

## VI Knowlton Court, near Deal.
The country home of Sir John Narbrough. After his marriage, on June 20th 1681, to Elizabeth Hill (later Shovell), he bought the Manors of Knowlton, Northcote, Southcote and Sandowne in Kent. Five thousand pounds of the purchase money for these manors came from his wife's dowry. When Sir John died the Manors passed to his eldest son, also John and in turn on his death, in 1707, to Dame Elizabeth D'Aeth, his sister (i.e. young John's sister). (Dyer p.207; RMT MAT 24; Exton f.128).

## Sussex

## I House in All Saints Street, Hastings.
According to tradition Cloudesley Shovell's mother or nanny lived in a house here. It is actually part of two abutting medieval houses and now belongs to the Sussex Archaeological Society. There is no documentary evidence linking Shovell with Hastings, although the tradition is so strong that there must have been some sort of connection. Perhaps he stayed in the house at some time. (Letter from the Museum Curator, Hastings, May

9th 1979; Brett, *St Leonards and Hastings Gazette,* May 6th and 13th 1893; Cousins, *Hastings of Bygone Days and the Present).*

## II The Shipwreck Heritage Centre, Hastings.
The Centre has various artefacts from Shovell's former ship, the *Anne,* that was burnt on the sands near Hastings in 1690. There are also articles from the *Eagle.*

## Oxfordshire

### Christ Church Cathedral and College, Oxford.
Both young Sir John Narbrough and his brother, James were Christ Church, Oxford men. When James was drowned in 1707 on the *Association,* he left £500 in his will to the Dean and Canons of the College for the rebuilding and beautifying of Peckwater Quadrangle. At the west end of the south aisle of the nave of the Cathedral, to the south-west of the entrance, is a plaque commemorating James Narbrough. (RMT MAT 17C).

## Devonshire

### Wembury Church.
In the church there is a monument to the memory of Dame Elizabeth Narbrough, née Calmady, first wife of Sir John Narbrough. The monument is of black and coloured marble surmounted by a kneeling figure of Dame Elizabeth. The inscription reads:

> Here lyeth the body of Dame Elizab; Narbrough the truly loveing and as Truly beloved wife of Sir John Narbrough Knt One of his majesties flagge Officers at Sea. The said Dame Elizab; was daughter of Josias Calmady Esq and of Elizab; his wife married with the said Sir John of the nineth day of April 1677. She was vertuous Pious Charitable Religous Sweet and lovinge Lady mightyly afflicted with a cough and bigge with child departed this Mortall life the first day of January 167/8 To the great griefe of Sir John her husband and her relatives friends and all that knew her. Aged 20 years Elizabeth Lady Narbrough

Sir John Narbrough commissioned a drawing of the monument on vellum. It is still in existence and can be seen in the National Maritime Museum. On the back of it is written, "Received at London February 2: day 1681 – JN" i.e. February 2nd 1681/82 John Narbrough. Robert Marsham Townshend, who did a great deal of research in the nineteenth century into the life of his ancestor, Cloudesley Shovell, was given the drawing by his father, Charles, second Earl of Romney, about 1843. Clearly it had come down to him via Cloudesley's daughter, Elizabeth. It is surprising that it did not go to Narbrough's daughter ,Elizabeth D'Aeth and her descendants who were the direct line. (RMT MAT 17c & 23).

## Cornwall

### I Penzance Magistrates Court.
Coat of Arms said to have come from the wrecked *Association*. It is displayed on a wall.

### II Maritime Museum, Penzance.
The Museum has a collection of artefacts from the wrecks of the *Association, Eagle, Romney, Firebrand* and *Phoenix.*

## Isles of Scilly

### I St Agnes Island.
The modern lighthouse stands to the west of the island overlooking the fearsome Western Rocks. Below it near the old lifeboat house are said to be mass graves, where some of the drowned sailors of the October 22nd 1707 disaster were buried. The Gilstone Rock, where the *Association* foundered, is too distant to see from the land, but Hellweathers, the rock on which George Lawrence, the sole surviving man clung, is clearly visible.

### II The St Mary's Museum.
Situated in Hugh Town.
The Museum has an excellent collection of artefacts salvaged from the *Association*, and the other wrecked ships. Among them are:-
1. Pewter Chamber Pot.
This was sold at Sotheby's on January 28th 1970 for £270. The catalogue of the sale describes it as a rare pewter chamber pot with bulbous body encircled by a band of multiple reeding and with everted rim at top, the single curved handle bearing the trademark of an unrecorded maker RD within a beaded circle; English C1700 very rare. It was suggested that because of the primitive sanitary arrangements at sea in the early eighteenth century, the pot belonged to an officer, if not Shovell himself. The pot is illustrated in the journal of the Pewter Society for September 1976.
2. Bronze Naval Stern Gun.
Salvaged from the site of the wrecked *Association*. It was made by Thomas Pit for Charles, Earl of Devon, Master of Ordnance in 1604, and bears the emblem and motto of the Prince of Wales.
3. Barrel tops, spigots and earthenware cooking utensils.
4. Part of a ship's bell.
5. Lead shot, cannon balls, sounding lead.

6. Lead sheathing, beam balance weight.
7. Window or lantern glass. Bottle glass.
8. Bronze pulley wheel.
9. Pewter buckles and spoon.
10. Almond.
11. Musket butt and brass sword guard.
12. Brass reamer for cleaning touch holes of cannon.
13. Buttons.
14. Dividers.
15. Coins.
16. Silver spoon, c. 1700.

It bears on the back of the terminal, a crest, an upright mailed fist, similar to that used by Captain Edmund Loades and Captain Samuel Whitaker, Sailing Master of the *Association*. Dognose in type.

17. Wood from the *Association*.
18. Signal gun.
19. Lead bars for making shot.
20. Part of a copper cauldron.

## III Longstone Centre, St Mary's.
Display of artefacts from the *Association* and other ships, including the scupper pipe of the *Firebrand*.

## IV Parish Church, Hugh Town, St Mary's.
A carved wooden lion from the *Association* is displayed on the wall of the church with a plaque giving its origin below.

## V Old Town Church, St Mary's.
This was the old Parish Church of St Mary's until 1837. The fragment of the cross at the east end of the roof is Celtic and a doorway piercing the wall of the church from the porch may be Norman. In the seventeenth and eighteenth centuries the church was larger and cruciform. Later it became derelict and was restored to its present form in 1890. Some important victims of the disaster of October 22nd 1707 are buried in the church. Henry Trelawney, son of the Bishop of Winchester, is buried beneath the chancel. Edmund Loades' and James Narbrough's graves are also in the church. The burial place of the young Sir John Narbrough is unknown, but he too may well be buried here in the church.

The Chaplains to the Isles of Scilly during the relevant period were:

| | |
|---|---|
| John Maurice | 1691–1707 |
| Henry Penneck | 1707 |
| Peter Thomas | 1708–1709 |

(Information available in the Parish Church, Hugh Town [New Town Church]; Old Town Church.)

## VI Porthellick Bay, St Mary's.

Cloudesley Shovell's body was washed ashore in a small bay on the south coast of St Mary's. Nowadays, Porthellick, which means "willow bay", can be approached by a path and an upturned stone marks the spot on the foreshore where Shovell's body was first buried. Tradition has it that nothing will grow on the site. Nearby is the appropriately named Camel Rock.

## London

### I Prescot Street, Goodman's Fields.

This was the location of Shovell's first town house after his marriage. His elder daughter, Elizabeth, was born here. Nothing remains of the original house and the open spaces of Goodman's Fields have long since gone.

### II Soho Square.

At some stage in the mid 1690s Shovell moved here from Prescot Street. He used May Place as his country seat and Soho Square when in town.

Soho only came into existence as a residential centre during the later years of Charles II's reign. In 1681 Gregory King laid out Soho Square, which was originally known as King's Square, and carried his name until well into the eighteenth century. One of the earliest houses was built to the south side of the square by the Duke of Monmouth. It was a magnificent building, and a number of other imposing residences sprang up around the square. In the central garden of the square, which was laid out with considerable care, was a statue by Caius Gabriel Cibber of Charles II in armour.

By the time Shovell came to live in Soho Square, it had become a most fashionable address, with an air of aristocratic dignity. Shovell's house was to the north of Sutton Street on the east side of the square. Although its exact site cannot be pinpointed with absolute certainty, it is likely that it was on the corner of the square and Sutton Street, numbered 21. Next door to the north was Falconberg House, numbered 20. Falconberg House was occupied by the first Earl of Falconberg and his wife, Mary, third daughter of Oliver Cromwell. They took up residence about 1689 with the earl dying in 1700 and his wife living there until her own death in 1712. Shovell was a royalist from birth, but no doubt he found the Falconbergs congenial neighbours as they were more at home under Charles II and his successors than under Cromwell! Rimbault states that the Shovells lived at number 20, but this would have been impossible, as the Falconbergs were alive and living there at the time. The numbering in Soho Square has varied over the centuries and was inconsistent.

As well as the Falconbergs and the Shovells, other distinguished people came to live in the square in the 1690s. Among them were Lords Mansel and Barclay. Mansel's son, Robert, was at a later date to marry Shovell's younger daughter, Anne, in 1718. No doubt, the young couple first became acquainted in the square.

The diarist Evelyn was also a resident for a time, but it is uncertain whether he actually owned a house there.

During the eighteenth century, Shovell's former house became the White House, an infamous haunt of Regency bucks.

Nearly six years after Cloudesley's death, his wife Elizabeth moved to a smaller house at the north-west angle of Frith Street, where it enters Soho Square. On July 2nd 1713 Dame Elizabeth was granted a twenty-one-year lease on the house by the Earl of Portland. In 1884 the building was probably still standing and faced the present Women's Hospital. No doubt the original house on the east side of Soho Square, in which her husband Cloudesley had lain in state before his funeral, had become too large for Elizabeth as her children grew up. She was to die in the leased house in Frith Street on April 22nd 1732 but was buried at Crayford.

Alas little remains of the grandeur of the Soho Square of the early eighteenth century. It is now largely commercial rather than residential. Where Monmouth's grand house stood is now the Women's Hospital, and Sutton Street, through which Shovell would have driven in his carriage, is now a seedy, litter-filled back street. No longer does Charles II's statue survey the Square from the centre of its gardens. (*The Romance of Soho*, E.Beresford Chancellor; *The History of the Squares of London*, E.Beresford Chancellor; "Soho and its Associations", Edited from a MSS on Dr Rimbault by G. Clinch; Notes and Queries, December 27th 1884 p.519).

### III  Westminster Abbey.
Sir Cloudesley Shovell was interred in a large vault in the south choir aisle, to the west of the east cloister door, on December 22nd 1707.

The memorial shows Shovell reclining on his left side on a couch with a canopy above. The carving is by the celebrated Grinling Gibbons. The inscription above it reads:

Sir Cloudesley Shovell Knt
Rear Admirall of Great Britain
And Admirall and Commander in Chief of the Fleet
The juft rewards
Of his long and faithfull Services
He was
Defervedly beloved of his Country
And efteem'd, tho' dreaded by the Enemy
Who had often experienced his Conduct and Courage
Being Shipwreckt
On the Rocks of Scylly
In his voyage from Thoulon
The $22^{nd}$ of October 1707 at Night

In the 57th year of his Age
His fate was lamented by all
But efpecially the
Seafaring part of the nation
To whom he was
A Generous Patron and a worthy Example
His body was flung on the fhoar
And buried with others in the fands
But being foon after taken up
Was placed under this Monument
Which his Royall Miftrefs has cauf'd to be erected
To Commemorate
His Steady Loyalty and Extraordinary Vertues.

Grinling Gibbons was paid £322.10s.0d. for executing the carving, on September 4th 1708.

Joseph Addison writing of the tomb commented that, "instead of the brave rough English admiral, which was the distinguishing character of that plain gallant man, he is represented on his tomb by the figure of a beau, dressed in a long periwig, and reposing on velvet cushions under a canopy of state". Addison continued, "the Dutch show an infinitely greater taste of antiquity and politeness in their buildings and works of this nature, than we meet in those of our own country". It is hard to disagree with Addison. (Larn p.23; C.S.P. Treasury 1708, Vol. XXII, Part II, p.108).

# APPENDIX 3
## Cloudesley Shovell's emerald ring

Descent in the Berkeley Family.
1.   James, 3rd Earl of Berkeley – 1680–1736.
2.   Augustus, 4th Earl of Berkeley (son of 1.) – 1716–1755.
3.   Admiral Sir George Cranfield Berkeley
      (second son of 2.) – 1753–1818.
4.   General Sir George Henry Frederick Berkeley
      (eldest son of 3.) – 1785–1857.
5.   Charles Assheton Fitzhardinge Berkeley (son of 4.).
6.   Caroline Mary Rumley (née Berkeley)
      (sister of 5.) – 1815–1882.
7.   General Randal Rumley (husband of 6.) – 1805–1884.

8. Grenville Charles Lennox Berkeley (uncle of 6.) – 1806–1896.
9. George Rawdon Lennox Berkeley, 7th Earl of Berkeley
   (brother of 6.) – 1827–1888.
10. Randal Thomas Mowbray Berkeley, 8th Earl of Berkeley
    (3rd son of 9.) – 1865–1942.
11. Mary Emlen (Lloyd), Countess of Berkeley (2nd wife of 10.)
    Married 10. – 1924. Alive 1956.
12. Francis Lloyd (child of 11.'s first marriage).

The ring was last recorded as being seen when in the possession of Caroline Mary Rumley, in 1879, by Robert Marsham Townshend (RMT MAT 64). Mrs Rumley had had the ring converted into a locket, but retaining the original setting of an emerald surrounded by small diamonds. On the back was engraved Sir Cloudesley's name and the date of his death, in characters of the nineteenth century (RMT MAT 3 & 64).

In the descent of the ring in the Berkeley family, steps 1. to 6. are fairly certain. Marsham Townshend jumps straight from 4. to 6. However, the will of Caroline Mary Rumley states that she received "the pearl necklace and valuable emerald which came to me from my late brother Charles Assheton Fitzhardinge Berkeley". It seems likely that this is the emerald locket.

Under the terms of Caroline Mary Rumley's will, the emerald passed into the trust of her husband, General Randal Rumley and her uncle, Grenville Charles Lennox Berkeley, to be inherited by the "first son hereafter to be born of the said George Rawdon Lennox Berkeley who shall attain the age of twenty one years absolutely". The word "hereafter" is crucial, as when Mrs Rumley signed her will, in 1861, her brother, George Rawdon Lennox Berkeley already had two sons, Hastings Fitzhardinge George and Ernest James Lennox. As George Rawdon Lennox had only married in 1860, Cecilia, the divorced wife of Admiral Fleetwood Pellew, it can be reasonably assumed that these two other boys were illegitimate.

General Randal Rumley died in 1884, and the emerald locket would have been in the sole charge of Grenville Charles Lennox Berkeley, at least until 1886 when George Rawdon Lennox's legitimate son, Randal Thomas Mowbray, reached 21 years or perhaps until his death in 1896.

George Rawdon Lennox, the 7th Earl of Berkeley had the use of the locket during his lifetime.

Steps 9. to 12. in the descent of the emerald locket are conjectural. Randal Thomas Mowbray, the 8th Earl, died in 1942 without an heir. He was outlived by his second wife, the former Mrs Mary Lloyd, of Boston, U.S.A., a divorced woman, who had had at least one child by her first marriage. Her possessions were left to her son, Francis Lloyd who lives in the U.S.A.. Perhaps his family have the locket, unless it was disposed of at an earlier date.

The present Berkeley family at Berkeley Castle, Gloucestershire have no knowledge of the whereabouts of the ring/locket. (RMT MAT 3 & 64; Wills of Caroline Mary and Randal Rumley, Somerset House; *Debretts Illustrated Peerage* 1935 & 1956; *Walford County Families* 1909; 1881 Census for 19 Eaton Terrace, Randal Rumley & 7 Wilton Crescent for Grenville Berkeley.)

# APPENDIX 4
# *Manuscripts concerning Cloudesley Shovell's death*

### Herbert Manuscript.

Sir C. Shovel cast away 8ᵇ 23, being Wednesday, between 6 and 7 at night (others say between 4 and 6, bet night & day) off Guilstone (south) by west, was found on shoar (at Porthellick Cove) in St Marie's Island, stript of his shirt, wc by confession was known, by 2 women, wch shirt had his name at ye gusset at his waist; (where by order of Mr Harry Pennick was buried 4 yards off ye sand; which place I myself view'd, & as was by his grave, came by sd woman yt first saw him after he was stript;) His ring was also lost from off his hand, wch however left ye impression on his finger, as also of a second. The Lady Shovel offered a considerable reward to any one (who) should recover it for her, & in order thereto wrote Capt. Benedick, Dep. Govenor & Commander in Ch. of Islands of Scilly, (giving him a particular description therefof) who used his utomst diligence both by fair and foul means, though could not hear of it. Sr Cloud. had on him a pr of thread stockings and a thread waistcoat. (Others say a flannel waistcoat and a pair of drawers.) Mr Child [Paxton] Purser of ye Arundel caused him to be taken up and knew him to be Sr Cloudesley by a certain black mold under his left ear, as also by the first joynt of one of his forefingers being broken inwards formerly by playing at Tables; the sd joynt of his finger was also small and taper, as well as standing somewhat inwards; (he had likewise a shot in his right arm, another in his left thigh.) Moreover he was well satisfied 'twas him, for he was as fresh when he face was washt as if only asleep; his nose likewise bled as tho' alive, wch Mr Child [Paxton] said was bec. of himself, for Sr C. had preferred him to Purser of ye Arundel and was his particular friend. They carried him to Mrs Bant's in ye island, & had on shoar sevrll Doctors of ye ships of ye fleet, but none could embalm or embowell him; (neither did any of ye fleet take much notice of him, but as Mr Paxton was carrying him on board ye Arundel, Capt. \_\_\_* [Hosier] Commander of ye Salisbury ordered him on board his ship;) wherefore they put him on board ye Salisbury on a bare table, (the table was Mrs Bant's) and a sheet only to cover him; the table they kept but the sheet was sent on shoar; and on board the Salisb. they carried him to Plimo where he was embalmed, and afterwards conveyed to London by land carriage. (Sir Cloudesley was the first man on shoar, saving one, of the almost 1800 lost in the wreck. His Commission was brought on shoar by one ——, and his chest wch was by him taken up floating.) Many that saw him sd his head was the largest that ever they had seen, and not at all swell'd with the waters, neither had he any bruise or fear about him, save only a small scratch above one of his eyes like that of a pin. Was a very lusty, comely man, and very fat.

Capt. Loads Commander of ye Association, (Sir Cloudesley's Captain as Admiral, but Capt. Whitacre was Captain of ye ship) wch Sr C. was on board of wn cast away, was also taken up on St. Marie's island, (in ye same cove near Sir C.) and buried in Old-town Ch. whose burial 'twas reported cost £90, but Mr Withe who was manager of it says ½ that sum. (This Mr Withe rais'd a report that Mr Pennick buried Sr C. before cold, but had sd gent. liv'd 'twould have cost him dear, but himself had misfortn to cast away, A.D. 170–) Mr James Narborough, (others say Sr John Narborough) and the Ld Bishop Trelawney's son, was likewise buried in sd Church very honourably. Sir C. had a naked small greyhound cast on shoar in ye same cove with, and not far distant, (as about a bowshot,) from him, with a collar of his name & c. round its neck. (There came on shoar in or very near ye same cove the stern of Sr C's barge, wch gives ground to believe he had time to get in it with some of his crew, tho' most people are not of that mind; Captain Loads, Sr John and Mr James Narborough, also Bishop Trelawney's son, being all cast on shoar on St Marie's island, give further matter of credit;) The Association, 2nd rate, the Rumney —— rate and the Eagle —— rate were all cast away on sd rock, & but one soul sav'd from off the rock, call'd \_\_\_ who was Quarter Mr of ye Rumney, a north country-man near Hull, a butcher by trade, a lusty fat man but much batter'd with ye rocks. (Most of ye Captains, Lieutenants, Doctors & c of ye Squadron came on shoar and ask'd him many questions in relation to ye wreck, but not one man took pity of him, either to dress or order to be dress'd his bruises & c, wherefore had perish'd had not Mr Ekins, a Gentm of ye Island, charitably taken him in; and a doctor of a merchant ship then in ye road under convoy of Southampton & c, search'd his wounds and applied proper remedies.) At ye time this horrible accident happen'd there was in

* Gaps appear in the original document.

397

Scilly ye Welsh Fleet with —— men of war, viz the Southampton ——,
——, ——, whose boats were early out ye next morning in quest of ye
flotsam goods, very much whereof were by them taken up; they matter'd
not the wines brandys & c at ye first, but let 'em swim by their boats, and
pursued wt they had hopes were richer, so yt most of ye casks stav'd, and
ye liquors were lost in ye ocean. The squadron consisted of 20 Men of war
and 2 Fire ships, and had with them also one prize. Abt. one or two aft.
noon on the 23rd (22nd) Octr Sir C. call'd a council & examd ye Masters
wt lat. they were in; all agreed to be in that of Ushant on ye coast of
France, except Sr W. Jumper's Mr of ye Lenox,who believ'd 'em to be
nearer Scilly, & yt in 3 hours should be up in sight thereof, (wch
unfortunately happen'd) but Sir Cloud. listened not to a single person
whose opinion was contrary to ye whole fleet. (They then alter'd their
opinion and thought 'emselves on ye coast of France, but a lad on board
ye —— said the light they made was Scilly light, tho' all the ships crew
swore at & gave him ill language for it; howbeit he continu'd in his
assertion, and that wt they made to be a saile and a ship's lanthorn prov'd
to be a rock and ye Light afore-mentioned, wch rock the lad call'd ye
Great Smith of ye truth of wch at day-break they was all convinced).
Whereupon despatch'd ye Lenox & ——, ——, for Falmouth wch ships
were drove in between ye rocks to Broad Sound where they came to an
anchor abt 2 in ye morning of the 24th (23rd) after ye wreck had
happen'd,tho' to those ships as yet unknown; about day-break they
weigh'd and sail'd for Falmo' as ordered, wth news of a wreck on Scilly
rocks, but knew not wt sail were lost. After ye departure of ye ships from
ye Fleet, according as Sr W's Mr had believed they were indeed engag'd
with ye rocks; the weather then being stormy, they could not see ye light
on St Agnes; not knowing where they were they fir'd ——, soon after wch
they struck on ye Ledge ——, and bilg'd; the Rumney also struck
immediately and stav'd on the Guilstone. The Eagle was lost on ye
Gunnar or thereabouts, but wt of ye wreck floated to St Just and other
places at ye Lands End & up ye North Channel.

( ) marginal notes in the original MSS
[ ] James Cooke's corrections
(Herbert MSS; *The Shipwreck of Sir Cloudesley Shovell on the Scilly Islands in
1707* by James Cooke).

**Letter from Joseph Addison, Under Secretary of State, to Lord
Manchester.**

Cock Pit: Oct 28th 1707.
My Lord, – Your Lordship will hear by this post a great deal of melancholy
news relating to our sea affairs. Within about a month we have had the

following disasters: Our Hamburgh fleet, when just entering the mouth of the river, were surprised in a storm that cast several of 'em on the coast of France, and made 'em prize to their privateers that put to sea on that occasion. About a week ago, our Lisbon fleet of 130 merchantmen, under convoy of 5 men-of- war, fell in with a squadron of 14 French, who blew up one of the queen's ships, and, as we suppose, took 3 more. We know not what numbers of the merchant escaped, but hope that most of them got into Ireland or proceeded for Lisbon, our ships having kept the French in play till the evening came on. On Sunday morning, an express came from Admiral Byng, with news that the great fleet, returning from the Straits and being near the Isles of Scilly, Sir Cloudesly Shovel's ship (the Afsociation) struck on a rock. Admiral Byng pafsed by him within two cables length of him, and heard one of his guns go off as a signal of distrefs, but the sea ran so very high that it was impofsible to send him any succour. Sir George Byng adds that, looking after him, about a minute after the firing of the gun, he saw no lights appear, and therefore fears he sunk. Two further great ships are mifsing. Sir Cloudesly had on board with him two of his wife's sons by Sir John Narborough, a son of the Bishop of Winchester, another of Admiral Ailmer, and several other gentlemen. We are still willing to hope that he may have escaped in his long-boat or be thrown on one of the islands, but it is now three days since we had our first intelligence. It was about eight o'clock at night when Sir G. Byng saw him in his distrefs. Your Lordship may beleive so many misfortunes have raised great clamour in the City. Our last W. Indian packet-boat brought heavy complaints against Captain Kerr, a commodore in those parts, whom the Govenor of Jamaica accuses of having refused convoy to their ships, and by that means to have lost the nation above 100,000 lbs. sterling in bullion, which was on board some of our sloops which fell into the hands of the French. I am sorry I must entertain your Lordship with such ill news; but since such accidents have happened, I thought it proper to acquaint you with them. There is that noble spirit in the nation and our new British parliament that, I hope, will surmount all difficulties.

The Venetian merchants are busy upon the enlargement of the articles of which I send your Lordship a draught in order to form them into a treaty.

I am with the greatest respect,
Your Lordship's most obedient servant.
J. Addison.

## Letter from Joseph Addison, Under Secretary of State, to Mr Cole.

Cock Pit: Oct 31, 1707.
Sir – yesterday, we had news that the body of Sir Cloudesly Shovel was

found on the coast of Cornwall. The fishermen who were searching among the wrecks took a tin box out of the pocket of one of the carcasses that was floating, and found in it the commifson of an admiral; upon which, examining the body more closely, they found it was poor Sir Cloudesly. You may guefs the condition of his unhappy wife, who lost, in the same ship with her husband, her only two sons by Sir John Narborough. We begin to despair of the two other men-of-war, and fireship, that engaged among the same rocks, having yet received no news of them.

I am, Sir, your faithful humble servant,
J. Addison.


(Both the Addison letters of October 28th and 31st appear in an "Extract from Court and Society from Elizabeth to Anne", edited from papers at Kimbolton by the Duke of Manchester, 2 Vols., London 1864, Vol.II, Chapter XV, pp.254–261; Pattison S.R., *Journal of the Royal Institution of Cornwall*, Oct. 1864, No.11, pp.61–65; The Cole letter only appears in *Memoirs of Affairs of State* by Christian Cole Esq., some time resident at Venice, London 1733, p.496; Cooke, *The Shipwreck of Sir Cloudesley Shovell*; RMT MAT 26).


## Letter from John Ben to Sir Jonathan Trelawney, Bishop of Winchester.

St Hilary, November 16th, 1707.
My Lord,
Your Lordship's commands having been signified to my brother at Scilly, he immediately made the strictest enquirey that was possible, all the bodies that had been thrown ashore and buried and being told of one buried at Agnes about Mr Trelawney's age was resolved to have him taken up in order to view him, whether it was he or no. He had seen the young Gentleman at Torbay, but not willing to depend on his own judgement desired the Captain of the Phenix Fire ship that was stranded there who knew Mr Trelawney intimately well all the voyage to go with him. As soon as they had the body up, they found it actually to be the same, tho somewhat altered having been buried 11 days, and in the water 4, however the Captain presently knew him and my brother took care to have the body brought over to St Mary's and interred it in the chancel of the church there, the 8th instant with all the marks of respect and honour, the island could show on such an occasion. Some Captains and the best of the inhabitants being present at the funeral, my Brother took of his hair being cut and that so very close that the left lock was not left to send over, and there is no room for doubt that twas the body of poor Mr Henry Trelawny. It has not been his good luck as yet to meet with any thing belonging to him but whatever of that nature happens to come to his hand

or knowledge your Lordship will be sure to have a faithful account of it. They can say nothing in particular touching Sir Cloudesley's loss, only the man saved out of the Rumney tells that Sir Cloudesley was to the windward of all the ships and fired three guns when he struck, and immediately went down, as the Rumney a little after did. Upon hearing the guns, the rest of the Fleet, that were directly bearing on the same rocks changed their course and stood more to the Southward or else in all probability they had run the same fate, as never enough to be admired; how twas possible men of so much experience could be mistaken in their reckoning, after they had the advantage of a great deal of fair weather before hand and no bad weather when they were lost. There is a great quantity of timber all round the islands and abundance of sails and rigging just about the place where the ships sunk, and a mast, one end a little above water which makes them conclude an entire ship to be foundered there because all the force they can procure is not able to move the mast. The Eagle most certainly is lost too and I wish no other of the squadron may be wanting besides those, tho I'm heartily sorry for the loss poor England has sustained of so many men and in a most particular manner for the share your Lordship has in it.

Mr Quish by some means or other may convey this letter to your Lordship's hands before you come to Chelsea for which reason I have inclosed to him and am with all possible duty and my hearty wishes for the happiness of your Honourable Family, my Lord.

Your Lordships most faithful and obedient servant, John Ben.

(T. Quiller Couch, Sir Cloudesley Shovell, *Journal of the Royal Institution of Cornwall*, Vol.II, 1866–67; Cooke, *The Shipwreck of Sir Cloudesley Shovell*).

## Draft of a letter from Robert, 2nd Baron Romney, to Captain Locker. Circa 1790.

Lord Romney & Mr Marsham present their Compliments to Captain Locker, and inform him that on enquiry they find that the family papers relative to Sir Cloudesley Shovell's public transactions have from length of time and other accidents been destroyed. He was recommended exceedingly young (it is imagined about nine years of age) to the patronage of S$^r$ John Narborough who made him one of his boys, which was the foundation of his future rise in the Navy. The coat of arms he bore (namely two crescents and one flower de lis) were given to him by Queen Ann is honor of his well known victories over the Turks and also over the French. He married the widow of S$^r$ John Narborough, by whom he left two daughters, Elizabeth, first married to Robert Lord Romney and secondly to John Earl of Hyndford, Ann, first married to Thomas Mansel, eldest son to Lord Mansel, and secondly to John Blackwood Esq$^r$. An early instance of Shovell's bravery is shewn in a story which, though certainly a fact, is very imperfectly known in the family. Whilst he was the Admiral's boy, hearing him express an earnest wish that some papers of importance might be conveyed to the Captain of a distant ship, young Shovell undertook to swim under the enemy's fire with the dispatches in his mouth, which he performed with success. There was one circumstance relating to S$^r$ Cloudesly Shovell's death that is known to very few persons, namely; he was not drowned, having got to shore, where, by the confession of an ancient woman, he was put to death. This, many years after, when on her death-bed, she revealed to the minister of the parish, declaring she could not die in peace 'till she had made this confession, as she was led to commit this horrid deed for the sake of plunder. She acknowledged having, among other things, an emerald ring in her possession, which she had been afraid to sell lest it should lead to a discovery. This ring,which she delivered to the minister, was by him given to James Earl of Berkeley at his particular request, S$^r$ Cloudesly and himself having lived on the strictest footing of friendship.

(RMT MAT 16e, 32, 34; Notes and Queries 27th Dec. 1884).

# APPENDIX 5
## *Cloudesley Shovell's ships*

| Centurion | '62 | Myngs appointed. |
|---|---|---|
| | '63 | Myngs again in Jamaica. |
| | | (C.S.P. America & W. Indies 31/7/58, 1/6/60, 20/6/60, 25/5/64). |
| | | C.S. known to be in W. Indies with Myngs '63 (FinchMSS). |
| | | ?Narbrough in West Indies for part of the time with Myngs. (D.N.B.). |
| | | C.S. to sea with Myngs circa 13 years. (Crockatt). |
| | | C.S. to sea under Narbrough. (Secret Memoirs). |
| | | C.S. recommended to Narbrough about nine years of age. (RMT, MAT64, Robert 2nd Baron Romney to Capt.Locker). |
| Gloucester | '64 | Myngs. |
| Portland | '64 | Myngs, Narbrough. |

| | | |
|---|---|---|
| *Royal Oak* | '64 | Myngs, Narbrough. Myngs flies flag as V. Ad. in Channel squadron under Rupert. |
| *Triumph* | '65 | Myngs V. Ad. at Lowestoft, Narbrough. |
| *Royal James, Old James* | '65 | Narbrough. |
| *Fairfax* | | Narbrough. |
| *Victory* | '66 | Myngs dies off N. Foreland, Narbrough. |
| *Assurance* | '66 | Narbrough. C.S. in W. Indies with Harman & Narbrough on *Assurance* in '67. (Finch MSS). |
| *Bonaventure* | '67 | Narbrough. |
| *Sweepstakes* | '69–71 | Narbrough. Appointed May '69 & leaves England 26th September '69. Returns June'71. C.S. present Oct '71 – Jan '72. (P.R.O. Ad 33/121) |
| *Royal Prince* | '72 | Narbrough 2nd captain. C.S. entered as Midshipman $22/1/^{71}/_{72}$ (P.R.O. Ad 33/103 ticket 55) |
| *Fairfax* | '72 | Narbrough. C.S. as Master's Mate 17/9/72. (P.R.O. Ad 33/91 ticket 1076) |
| *St Michael* | '73 | Narbrough Captain. C.S. as Master's Mate 1/7/73. (P.R.O. Ad 33/104 ticket 1398) |
| *Henrietta* | '73 | Narbrough. C.S. 2nd Lieutenant 23/9/73. (P.R.O. Ad. 33/98 ticket 68) |
| *Harwich* | '74–76 | Narbrough. C.S. Boat burning Jan '76. |
| *Plymouth* | '77 | Narbrough. |
| *Sapphire* | '77 | C.S. Captain 11/9/77. |
| *Phoenix* | '79 | C.S. Captain 12/4/79. |
| *Sapphire* | '79 | C.S. Captain 3/5/79. |
| *Nonsuch* | '80 | C.S. Captain 14/7/80. |
| *Sapphire* | '80 | C.S. Captain 11/9/80. |
| *James galley* | '81–86 | C.S. Captain 22/4/81. |
| *Anne* | '87 | C.S. Captain 6/5/87 – 20/3/88. |
| *Dover* | '88 | C.S. Captain April '88 – March '89. |
| *Edgar* | '89 | C.S. Captain 27/3/89. |
| *Monk/Monck* | '89–?91 | C.S. Captain October '89. |
| *London* | '90 | 30/12/90. |
| *Royal William* | '92 | C.S. joins April '92. |
| *Kent* | '92 | In May '92 C.S. present during part of the Battle of Barfleur. |
| *? Duke* | '92 | C.S. joins 7/6/92. |
| *Britannia* | '93 | C.S. joins 29/4/93. |
| *Neptune* | '94 | |
| *Cambridge* | '95 | |

| | |
|---|---|
| *Queen* | '96–'97 |
| *Swiftsure* | '99 |
| *Barfleur* | '01 |
| *Queen* | '02 |
| *Triumph* | '03 |
| *Barfleur* | '04 |
| *Britannia* | '05 |
| *Association* | '07 |

(Ref: D.N.B; Commissioned Sea Officers; Le Fevre C.S.early career)

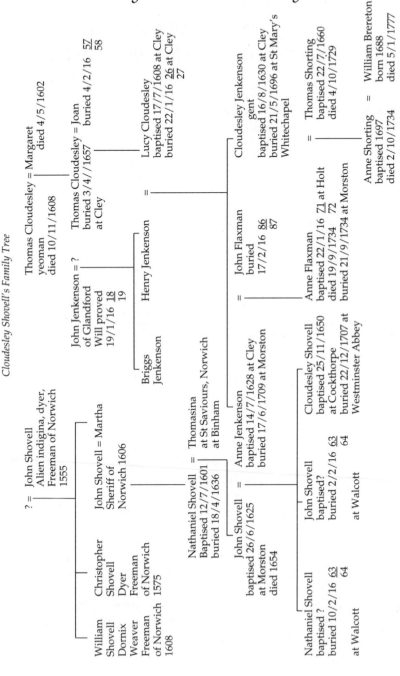

APPENDIX 6
*Cloudesley Shovell's Family Tree*

# APPENDIX 7
## *Descendants of William Brereton*

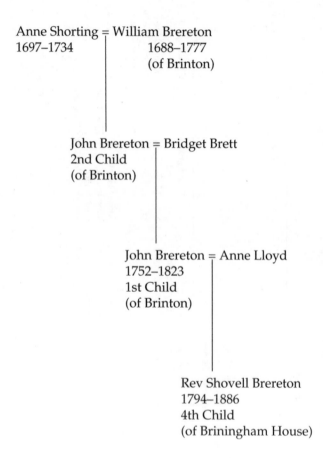

Anne Shorting = William Brereton
1697–1734          1688–1777
                   (of Brinton)

John Brereton = Bridget Brett
2nd Child
(of Brinton)

John Brereton = Anne Lloyd
1752–1823
1st Child
(of Brinton)

Rev Shovell Brereton
1794–1886
4th Child
(of Briningham House)

Descendants of William Brereton of Brinton and his wife Anne Shorting, who was half niece of Cloudesley Shovell. Compiled from *Burke's History of the Landed Gentry*, 1852 and 1871. The monumental subscriptions of the hundred of Holt, collected by Walton N. Dew, edited and indexed by Walter Rye, Norwich 1885. Entries in newspapers and MS notes of the Brereton family. RMT MAT 18.

# BIBLIOGRAPHY
## Manuscript sources

Admiralty Minute Book. Vol. XV. (1699–00).
Admiralty Orders and Instructions. Vol. XXIV. (1699–00).
All Souls, Oxford MSS.
Bodleian Library.
   Bodleian MSS Antogr. C. 19.
   Rawlinson MSS A 144, 181, 190, 195, 214, 215. C353.
British Library/Museum. BL.BM.
   ADD MSS: 816, 978, 5131, 5439, 5440, 5441, 5442, 5724, 5753, 5795, 7077, 9764, 12102, 15903, 15909, 17677, 18986, 19872, 21494, 23904, 28056, 28093, 28103, 28141, 28153, 29591, 35855, 35898, 38146, 38626, 38708, 46412.
   Egerton MSS 2618, 2621. Sloane MSS 978, 2755.
   Stowe MSS 467, 471.
Coventry MSS 99.
Churchill College, Cambridge. Erle MSS 2/57.
House of Lords MSS 2426.
Huntington Library MSS. San Marino, U.S.A.
Kent County Archives, Maidstone.
   Marsham MSS U1515 011–18.
Lay Subsidy Rolls for Norfolk.
London University MSS 859.
Magdalene College, Cambridge. Pepysian Library.
   Pepysian MSS 2555, 2877.
National Maritime Museum. (NMM).
   Marsham Townshend MSS. (RMT MAT)
   SMF 221 (PHB/17).
Northamptonshire Record Office.
   Finch Hatton MSS.
Public Record Office. P.R.O.
   (a) Muster books of ships ADM 33–39.
   (b) Log books of ships ADM 51–55.
   (c) Appointments and Commissions from 1695, some arranged by ships and some by men in ADM 6 & ll.

(d) Officers appointed 1660–88 with services ADM 10/10.
(e) Note. Captains' and masters' logs are in the P.R.O., lieutenants' logs are in the National Maritime Museum.
(f) ADM 1, 8, 106.
(g) Gosselo chart 1707–10.
Trinity House Court Minutes.
Yale University Library.
  MSS in the Beinecke rare books and manuscripts library.
  MSS in the James Marshall and Louise Osborn collection.

## Reports of the Historical Manuscripts Commission

| | | |
|---|---|---|
| Bath MSS | Vol. I – III | 1904–08. |
| Buccleuch MSS | Vol. II Part I | 1903. |
| Cowper MSS | Vol. III | 1888. |
| Dartmouth MSS | Vol. I, III | 1889, 99. |
| Finch MSS | Vol. II, III, IV | 1922–65. |
| Fortescue MSS | Vol. I | 1892. |
| Heathcoate MSS | | 1899. |
| HMC 1st, 2nd, 3rd, 6th, 8th, 12th, 15th Reports | | 1874–96. |
| House of Lords MSS N.S. Vol. I–VII | | 1900–21. |
| Ormonde MSS N.S. | Vol.VIII | 1920. |
| Portland MSS | Vol. III, IV, V, VIII, X | 1894–. |

## Printed sources

| | |
|---|---|
| Administration Act Book at Somerset House. | 1657. |
| Aiken, William. Conduct of the Earl of Nottingham. | 1941. |
| Allyn, Richard. A narrative of the Victory obtained by the English over that of France in the year 1692. | 1744. |
| An Account of the Earl of Peterborough's Conduct in Spain. | 1702. |
| An Account of the late bloody sea fight between part of their majesties fleet commanded by Cloudesley Shovell and that of the French commanded by Sieurs Turville and Ampheville. | 1690. |
| Anderson, R.C. Journals and Narratives of the Third Dutch War. | 1946. |
| Anderson, R.C. Lists of Men of War 1650–1700. | 1939. |
| Ballard, Colin. The Great Earl of Peterborough. | 1929. |
| Beresford Chancellor, E. The History of the Squares of London. | 1907. |
| Beresford Chancellor, E. The Romance of Soho. | 1931. |
| Biographia Britannica. | 1763. |
| Blomefield, Francis, County History of Norfolk Vols. 8 & 9. | 1808. |
| Bowley, R.L. The Fortunate Islands. | 1945. |

Boyer, Abel. History of the Reign of Queen Anne.          1709–14.
Brandt, Gerard. Vie Michel de Ruijter.                    1698.
Brett, Thomas. St Leonards and Hastings Gazette
     May 6th & 13th.                                       1893.
Brown, D. Life and Glorious Actions of
     Sir Cloudesley Shovell.                               1707.
Browning, Oscar.
     The Journal of Sir George Rooke. N.R.S.               1897.
Bryant, Arthur. Samuel Pepys, The Man in the Making.      1933.
Bryant, Arthur. Samuel Pepys, The Years of Peril.         1935.
Burchett, Josiah. A Complete History of the most
     remarkable transactions at sea etc.                  1702.
Burnett, Gilbert. History Of His Own Time.                1823.
Burney, James. Voyage to the South Seas.                  1803–17.
Calender of State Papers (Dom).
          1663–4, 1665–6, 1671, 1673, 1689–90, 1691–92, 1693.
Calender of State Papers (Col) America and West Indies.
                    1574–1660, 1661–68, 1669–74, 1675–76.
Calender of State Papers Car II. No. 157, No.261, No. 380.
Calender of State Papers Anne. No. 44, No.48, No.48I, No.49.
Calender of State Papers Treasury. Vol. LXXXIX.           1702–07.
     Vol. LV, XXII.                                        1708.
Callender, G. Life of Sir John Leake. N.R.S.              1920.
Campbell, John. Lives of the British Admirals.
     Vol. III, IV, V, VI.                                  1817.
Carleton, George. The Memoirs of.                         1743.
Carmarthen, Peregrine. Journal of the Brest Expedition.   1695.
Carter, E.H. The Norwich Subscription Books. 1637–80.     1937.
Charnock, John. Biographia Navalis. Vol. II.              1794–95.
Childs, J. The Army, James II, and the Glorious
     Revolution of 1688.                                  1980.
Churchill, Winston. Marlborough, His Life and Times.      1936.
Clinch, George. Soho and its Associations.
     (Edited from a MSS by Dr E. Rimbault).               1895.
Cobbett, William. Parliamentary History of England.      1811–13.
Cole, Christian. Memoirs of Affairs of State.            1733.
Collins, Grenville. Journal of.
Collins Baker, C.H. Lely and the Stuart Portrait Painters.  1912.
Commissioned Sea Officers 1660–1815. National Maritime Museum.
Concise Catalogue of Paintings in the
     National Maritime Museum.                            1988.
The Complete History of Europe for 1705, 1707.
Cooke, James. The Shipwreck of Sir Cloudesley Shovell
     on the Scilly Islands in 1707.                       1883.

Corbett, Julian. A note on the drawings . . . of the
   battle of Sole Bay and the Texel.                         1908.
Corbett, Julian. England in the Mediterranean 1603–1713.     1904.
Daily Courant. October 28th – December 9th.                  1707.
Crockatt, Gilbert. Consolatory Letter to Lady Shovell.       1708.
Crossley Holland, Kevin. Pieces of Land.                     1972.
Cruickshanks, Eveline (Ed). By Force or Default?
   The Revolution of 1688–89.                                1986.
Crump, G.M. (Ed). Poems on Affairs of State.                 1968.
Cunningham, George. Lives of Eminent and Illustrious
   Englishmen. Vol.IV.                                       1835.
Cunningham, George. History of the Revolution in 1688
   to the Accession of George I.                             1787.
Dan, Pierre. Histoire de Barbarie of ses Corsaires.         1637.
Davies, Adriana. Dictionary of British Portraiture I.
   The Early Middle Ages to the Early Georgians.             1979.
Davies, David. Gentlemen and Tarpaulins.                     1991.
Davies, David. James II, William of Orange and the
   Admirals. (Article in By Force or Default?
   The Revolution of 1688–89 Ed. E. Cruickshanks).           1986.
Debrett's Illustrated Peerage                                1935,1936.
De Jonge, J.C. Geschiedensis van het Nederlansche
   Zeewezen. (6 Vols.).                                      1858–62.
De La Gravière, Adm Jurien. Dernier Jours de la Marine
   a Rames.                                                  1788.
De la Pryne, Abraham. Diary.                                 1870.
The Descendents of Strangers now residing at Norwich.
De Villette, Marquis. Mémoires du.                           1788.
Dictionary of National Biography. (D.N.B.)
   Benbow, Berkeley, Berry, Carter, Grafton, Herbert,
   Monck, Mordaunt, Munden, Myngs, Narbrough, Rivers,
   Rooke, Rupert, Russell, Sandwich, Shovell, Willoughby
   et al. (Mainly written by J.K. Laughton).
Duckett, G.F. Naval Commissioners.                           1889.
Dyer, Florence. Life of John Narbrough.                      1931.
Eastern Daily Press. Oct. 17th 1986. (Article on the
   possible former home of Cloudesley Shovell).              1986.
Edye, Major C. Historical Records of the Royal Marines.      1893.
Ehrmann, John.
   The Navy in the War of William III 1688–97.              1953.
Entick, John. A New Naval History.                           1757.
Eugene, Prince of Savoy. Feldzuge Series I.
   Imperial General Staff, Vienna.                           1876–81.
An Exact Relation of Several Engagements.                    1673.

| | |
|---|---|
| Feiling, Keith. A History of England. | 1950. |
| Folger Lib. Newdigate newsletter lc 2523. | 1695. |
| Free Books, Corporation of Norwich. Vol.II. | |
| Fyers, W.H. Machine Vessels. Mariners Mirror. | 1925. |
| Grainger, A. A Geographical Description of Norfolk. | |
| Grainger, Noble. Biographical History of England | |
|     from the Revolution to the end of George I's reign. | 1806. |
| Grey, Anchitell. | |
|     Debates of the House of Commons. 1667–1694. | 1763. |
| Grosvenor, J. Trinity House. | 1959. |
| Hales, Jane. Blakeney Point and the Glaven Ports. | 1990. |
| Harris, F.R. Life of Edward Montagu. | 1912. |
| The Hastings and St Leonards Pictorial Advertiser and | |
|     Visitors List. Jan. 1st. | 1914. |
| Heath, Robert. An Account of the Islands of Scilly. | 1744. |
| Hist. Milit. Tom (iii). | |
| History of the Parish of Linkinhorne. | 1727. |
| Holmes, Geoffrey. British Politics in the age of Anne. | 1967. |
| Horowitz, Henry. Parliament, Policy and Politics in the | |
|     Reign of William III. | 1977. |
| House of Commons Journal, | 1693, 1706. |
| House of Lords Journal. | 1693. |
| An Impartial Enquiry into the Management | |
|     of the War in Spain. | 1712. |
| International Genealogical Index. I.G.I. | |
| Japikse, N. (Ed). Correspondentie van Willem III en van | |
|     Hans Willem Benfinck. | 1927–37. |
| Jones, Mrs Herbert. Historic Memorials of the Norfolk | |
|     Coast. Frasers Magazine. Sept. | 1881. |
| Klopp, Onno. Der Fall des Hauses Stuart. | 1875–88. |
| Knight, Charles. Popular History of England. | 1856–62. |
| Kunzel, Heinrich. Life of Hesse Darmstadt. | 1859. |
| Laird Clowes, William. The Royal Navy. A History. | 1898. |
| Lane-Poole. The Barbary Corsairs. | 1890. |
| Larn, Richard and McBride, Peter. | |
|     Sir Cloudesley Shovell's Disaster. | 1985. |
| La Roncière, Charles. Histoire de la Marine Francaise. | 1932. |
| Laughton, John. Memoirs relating to Lord Torrington. | 1889. |
| Laughton, John. N.R.S. Vol.40. | 1912. |
| Laughton, John. Physical Geography. | 1870. |
| Lediard, Thomas. Naval History of England 1066–1734. | 1735. |
| Le Fevre, Peter. Sir Cloudesley Shovell's Early Career. | |
|     Mariners Mirror Vol.70. Part I. Feb. | 1984. |
| Le Fevre, Peter. Tangier, the Navy, and its connection | |

with the Glorious Revolution of 1688. Mariners Mirror.    1987.
Le Neve. Pedigrees of Knights.
London Gazette.          1681, 1689, 1690, 1691, 1695, 1696, 1707.
Luttrell, Narcissus. A Brief Historical Relation of
    State Affairs from Sept 1678 to April 1714.           1857.
Macaulay, Lord. The History of England
    from the Accession of James II.                        1914.
Manchester, Duke of. Court and Society from
    Elizabeth to Anne. 2 vols. London.                     1864.
Marcus, G.J. Sir Clowdisley Shovel's Last Passage.
    Journal of the R.U.S.I. Vol. cii.                      1957.
Marsham Townshend, Robert. Death of
    Sir Cloudesley Shovell. Notes and Queries. Dec. 27th.  1884.
Marsham Townshend, Robert. Death of Sir John Narbrough.
    Notes and Queries. Dec. 29th.                          1888.
Marsham Townshend, Robert. Parentage of
    Cloudesley Shovell. Notes and Queries. Jan 19th.       1895.
Martin, Stephen. Life of. (Edited by Clements Markham).
    N.R.S.                                                 1845.
Martin – Leake, Stephen. The Life of Sir John Leake.
    (Ed Geoffrey Callender). N.R.S.                        1920.
Mathews, G.F. The Isles of Scilly: A Constitutional
    Economic and Social Survey of the Development
    of an Island People from Early Times to 1900.          1960.
Maunde Thompson, E. Correspondence of Admiral
    Herbert during the Revolution. English Historical
    Review.                                                1886.
May, Commander W.E. Naval Compasses in 1707. NMM,
    Journal Institution of Navigation Vol.VI, No. 4.       1953.
May, Commander W.E. The Last Voyage of
    Sir Clowdisley Shovel. Journal Institution of
    Navigation, Vol.XIII.                                  1960.
Mercure Historique et Politique Vol.III, XLIII.            1707.
Moad, M.I. The Guildhall Rochester, a Brief History.
Morris, Roland. Island Treasure.                           1969.
Natkiel, Richard and Preston, Anthony.
    Atlas of Maritime History.                             1986.
Nisser, Wilhelm. Michael Dahl and the Contemporary
    Swedish School of Painting.                            1927.
Norwich City Officers.                                     1453–1835.
Observator. Vol.VI, No.76, Nov 29 – Dec 3                  1707.
Ockley. Account of South West Barbary.                     1713.
Oldmixon.                                                  1732.
Owen, J.H. War at Sea under Queen Anne 1702–08.            1938.

Pattison, S.R. Sir Cloudesley Shovell. Journal of the
   Royal Institution of Cornwall. No.11. 1864.
Peacock. Monkton Papers. 1885.
Penn. Memorials of Sir William Penn. 1833.
Pepys, Samuel. Tangier Papers of. Reprint. 1980.
Pickwell. J.E. Improbable Legends Surrounding the
   Shipwreck of Sir Clowdisley Shovell.
   Mariners Mirror, Vol.59, Part 2. 1973.
Piper, David. Catalogue of the 17th Century Portraits
   in the National Portrait Gallery. 1963.
Playfair, Robert. Scourge of Christendom. 1884.
Post Boy. Oct. 30th – Dec. 23rd. 1707.
Principal Probate Registry. Book Alcin.
Quarterley Review. The Battle of Barfleur/La Hougue.
   Vol. CLXXVI.
Quiller Couch, T. Sir Cloudesley Shovell.
   Transaction of the Penzance Natural History and
   Antiquarian Society.
Quiller Couch, T. Shipwreck of Sir Cloudesley Shovell.
   Journal of the Royal Institute of Cornwall. Vol.II. 1866–67.
Rennell, James. Observations on a Current. 1815.
Return of Members of Parliament. 1213–1874.
A Review of the late engagement at sea being a
   collection of Private letters never printed. 1704.
Richmond, Herbert.
   The Navy as an Instrument of Policy. 1558–1727. 1953.
Robinson, M.S. Van de Velde Drawings in the National
   Maritime Museum, Vols. I & II. 1974.
Rye, Walter. Norfolk Families. 1913.
Secret Memoirs of the Life of the honourable
   Sir Cloudesley Shovell. Anon. 1708.
A Short Account of St Paulinus Church, Crayford.
Smith, Frederick. A History of Rochester. 1928.
Smith, Frederick. Rochester in Parliament. 1933.
Spence, Graeme.
   A Geographical Description of the Scilly Isles. 1793.
Stell. Guide Book of Hastings.
Styles, Showell. Admiral of England. 1973.
Tanner, J.R. A Descriptive Catalogue of the Naval
   Manuscripts in the Pepysian Library.Vol. I, II, III, IV. 1903–22.
Teonge, Henry. Diary of 1675–79. 1825.
Thomas, Charles. Three Early Accounts of Scilly. 1979.
Torrington – see J. K. Laughton.
Toynbee, Letters of Horace Walpole. 1902.

Tregellas, W.H.
    Tourist Guide to Cornwall and the Scilly Isles.      1878.
Van Loon, Gerard. Portus Gratiae exustus et eversus
    bombardis Anglo Batavis.      1694.
    Histoire Metallique des Pays Bas, tom iv.
Walford, Edward. County Families.      1909.
Winks, William. Illustrious Shoemakers.      1883.

# INDEX

Ship names are in *italics*

Acquila, Conde de 85, 88
Acton, Edward 278
*Admirable* 153–4, 268–9, 320
Addison, Joseph 344, 355
*Adventure* 78,148
*Advice* 111, 115, 125, 148
Airis, Robert 242–7
Albemarle, Duke of, see Monck,
    George
*Albemarle* 148, 154, 266, 269, 272–3
*Aldborough ketch* 207–8
Aldeburgh 41–2
Alderney 152–3
Algiers 56–7, 64–73, 78, 89, 95, 98,
    220, 239, 245
Alicante 73, 233, 302, 307–8, 311–2
All Saints Church, Hastings 5–6
All Saints Street, Hastings 5
Allen, Lt Col. 290
Allin, Sir Thomas 16, 22, 25
Allyn, Richard 149–50
Almonde, Philip van 146, 149, 157,
    166, 172, 175, 184, 201, 207, 234,
    240–1, 243–4, 280, 282, 302
Altea Bay 69, 242–5, 284
*Ambitieux* 153–4
Amfreville, Vice Ad. D' 118, 126–8,
    146, 150
*Ann of Friesland* 266
*Ann of Utrecht* 266
*Anne* 59, 95–100,104, 124, 212

Anne, Queen 225, 230–1, 236–44,
    276, 279–81, 295–6, 301, 304–7,
    310, 313, 346–7, 370, 372
Anne of Denmark, Princess 133
*Anne and Christopher* 62
Annet Island 346
Anselme, Abraham 177
*Antelope* 111, 290, 294, 351–2, 359,
    364
Antibes 314–5, 319
*Ardent* 109, 268
*Ardromedre, L'* 328
Armiger, Thomas 35
Arundell, Lady 372
*Arundell* 351–2, 359–60
Ashby, John 91, 94, 108, 111, 114,
    130, 136, 141, 143, 146, 148–53
*Association* 104, 122, 135, 229, 237,
    240, 248, 250, 306, 317, 319, 327,
    331, 336–50, 352, 358–9, 362, 366,
    368, 370
*Assurance* 20–9, 257, 265, 275
Augsberg, League of 111
Austen, R. 167
Aylmer, Edward 362
Aylmer, George 111, 113
Aylmer, Matthew 86–7, 91, 111,
    113, 184
Ayscue, Sir George 19
Azores 37, 233

Bacon, Francis 6
Bacton, Norfolk 9

415

Goodwin Sands 132, 145, 251, 303
Gosselo, Edmund 344, 346
Gottenburgh 195, 250
*Gouden Leeuw* 52–3
Goulet, The 187
Gourdon, Sir Robert 96
Grafton, 1st Duke of, see Fitzroy, Henry
*Grafton* 147, 229, 266, 272
Graham, Will 362
Grantham, Caleb 148
Granville 200–1
Gravesend 132, 140, 212
Graydon, John 147, 181
Greenwich 229
Greenwich Hospital 160
*Greenwich* 111, 147, 158
Greeve(s), James 62–3, 66
*Greyhound* 50, 125–6, 158
*Griffin* 148, 158, 332, 344, 350
Griffiths, Richard 327, 331, 349–50
Groix 219
Grove II, John 210
Guadalquivir 305
Guernsey 108, 142, 200–1
*Guiney* 61
Guiscard, Count Louis de 302–5
Gunfleet 20, 40, 44, 50, 53, 97, 101–6, 248–51, 255–6
Gunman, Christopher 41
Gurney, Edward 148

Hacket, Captain 125
Haddock, Sir Richard 97, 130, 136, 144, 164
Haen, Rear Adm. N.A.de 52
Hague, The 51, 202, 228, 371
*Half Moon* 76, 78, 125, 148, 151
Halls, Nicholas 74
Hamburg 16, 19
Hamoaze 124–5, 138
*Hampton Court* 147, 181, 242
Hancock, Mary 370
Hancock, Robert 122, 147, 275, 331,

346, 370
Happisburgh 9
Hardy, Sir Thomas 241, 245, 247
Harley, Robert 304
Harman, Sir John 25–6, 29–30, 44, 159, 177
Harman, Thomas 68
Harteloire, Vice Ad. de 268
Harwich 16, 61, 68, 102
*Harwich* 59–60, 62, 65–6, 120, 138
Hastings, Anthony 74, 76 91, 93, 105– 6, 147, 141
Hastings, Sussex 5, 6
Havre de Grace (Le Havre) 189, 191
Heath, Robert 361
Heath, Thomas 148, 153
Hedges, Sir Charles 239, 255, 262, 304, 306–7
Hellweathers Rock 346
*Henri* 268, 320
*Henrietta* 54, 56, 58–62, 115
Herbert, Arthur, Earl of Torrington 46, 72–83, 88–92, 102–5, 108–9, 111–5, 124, 130, 245–6, 256, 263, 281, 298
Herbert, Edmund 338, 344, 346, 355, 359–62
*Heureux* 267, 321
Hewer, Will 74
Highway, Thomas 36
Hill (née Kingsman), Elizabeth 133–5, 296
Hill, John 66, 95, 133–4, 169, 209, 220–2, 299, 370
Hispaniola 96–7
Hoat 219
Hobart, Henry 332
Hoedic 219
*Hollandia* 52
Hollar, W. 62
Holmes, Sir Robert 25–6, 29–30, 44, 159, 177

240, 256–8, 263, 338, 344, 346,
354–5, 363–4, 366
*Plymouth* 67–9, 73, 111, 138, 147
Pointis, Jean de 221–2, 267–8
Pontchairtrain, M. 143, 145
Popoli, Duchess of 295
Port Louis 182, 255–6
Port St Ubes 240
Porthellick Cove 354–5, 357–62
Portland, Hans Bentinck, 1st Earl
of 156, 185
*Portland* 13, 16, 111
Portsmouth 19, 40, 49, 56, 75,
113–5, 142, 156, 166, 171, 182,
189, 199, 208, 217–8, 220, 233,
254–6, 303–5, 364
*Portsmouth* 59, 61–3, 106, 111, 173
Portugal, King of (Pedro II) 95, 97,
241, 282, 306
Portugal, Queen of 95, 97, 99
Post Boy 354, 357–8, 360, 362
Powis, William Herbert, Duke of
106, 126
Prescot St, Whitechapel 218
Price, John 331, 364
*Prince* 31, 39–45, 52–3, 143
*Prince George* 240, 250–1, 265, 268
Provence 310, 320, 329
Pryne, Abraham de la 4

Quash, Joseph 352–3
*Queen* 218–20, 222–3, 232
Quelern Peninsula 187
Quince Fort 200

Raife, Jonas 77
*Ranelagh* 252, 257, 260, 266, 269,
272
Reddall, Finch 332, 350
Reifi 262
Rennell Current 336, 342
*Resolution* 46, 148
*Restoration* 147, 157, 250
*Revenge* 248–9, 251, 257

Rhé, Island of 219
Richards, Col. John 215, 293
Richmond, Duke of 53
Rivera, Marquis of 294
Rivers, Richard Savage, 4th Earl
303, 305–8
Roach, Susan 362
Rochefort 115, 143, 232, 255–6, 303
Rochelle 230
Rochester, Laurence, 1st Earl of
156, 166, 173
Rochester 106, 210, 221–2, 226,
228–9, 279, 280, 300, 346
*Roebuck* 56, 59, 147, 158, 257
Romney, 2nd Baron, see Marsham,
Robert
Romney, Charles, 6th Baron, see
Marsham, Charles
Romney, Henry Sidney, 1st Earl of
156, 228
*Romney* 317, 327, 331, 343, 350, 352,
359, 362, 364, 369
Ronquillo, Don Pedro 88
Rooke, George 72, 74, 91–2, 94,
111, 114, 132, 139, 148, 154, 164,
166–77, 197, 208, 216–8, 220–3,
228–38, 254–6, 258–60, 262–6,
268–74, 276–9, 284, 302, 311, 333,
341, 362
Rooke, Thomas 149
*Rose of Algier* 69
Rousselet, Louis François, Compte
de Châteaurenault, see
Châteaurenault
*Royal Anne* 326, 331, 344–5, 349, 364
*Royal Charles* 18, 25, 52, 218
*Royal James* 19, 43–4, 217
*Royal Katherine* 147, 266, 268, 270
*Royal Oak* 16, 72, 138, 148, 169,
248–9, 257, 266
*Royal Prince* 39, 143
*Royal Sovereign* 147, 230, 279
*Royal William* 143–4, 147, 149, 152,
157